Autodesk® Inventor® 2027 Introduction to Solid Modeling

Part 2

Learning Guide

Mixed Units - Edition 1.0

ASCENT - Center for Technical Knowledge®
Autodesk® Inventor® 2027
Introduction to Solid Modeling - Part 2
Mixed Units - Edition 1.0

Prepared and produced by:

ASCENT Center for Technical Knowledge
11201 Dolfield Blvd, Suite 112
Owings Mills, MD 21117

866-527-2368
www.ASCENTed.com

Lead Contributor: Jennifer MacMillan

ASCENT - Center for Technical Knowledge (a division of Rand Worldwide Inc.) is a leading developer of professional learning materials and knowledge products for engineering software applications. ASCENT specializes in designing targeted content that facilitates application-based learning with hands-on software experience. For over 25 years, ASCENT has helped users become more productive through tailored custom learning solutions.

We welcome any comments you may have regarding this guide, or any of our products. To contact us please email: feedback@ASCENTed.com.

AS-INV2701-ISM1MU-SG2 // IS-INV2701-ISM1MU-SG2

Contents

Preface ix

In This Guide xi

Practice Files xiii

Chapter 16: Assembly Environment **16-1**

16.1 Assembling Components Using Constraints **16-2**
16.2 Place and Insert **16-18**
16.3 Assemble Mini-Toolbar **16-20**
16.4 Content Center **16-22**
16.5 Assembly Browser **16-24**
16.6 Saving Assembly Files **16-27**
Practice 16a: Assembly Basics I (Constraints) **16-28**
Practice 16b: Assembly Basics II (Place and Insert) **16-48**
Chapter Review Questions **16-52**
Command Summary **16-58**

Chapter 17: Joint Connections **17-1**

17.1 Assembling Components Using Joints **17-2**
Practice 17a: Assembly Basics II (Joints) **17-14**
Practice 17b: Assembly Basics III **17-26**
Chapter Review Questions **17-30**
Command Summary **17-33**

Chapter 18: Manipulating Assembly Display **18-1**

18.1 Moving and Rotating Components **18-2**
Moving Components 18-2
Rotating Components 18-3
Updating the Assembly 18-4
18.2 Suppressing Constraints or Joints **18-5**

18.3 Controlling Assembly Component Display 18-6
Visible Components 18-6
Enabling Components 18-7
Isolating Components 18-7
Transparent Components 18-8

18.4 Sectioning Assembly Models 18-9

18.5 Assembly View Representations 18-12

18.6 Assembly Selection Filters 18-16

Practice 18a: Manipulate Components 18-18

Chapter Review Questions 18-25

Command Summary 18-29

Chapter 19: Model Information 19-1

19.1 Measurement Tools 19-2
Measuring Entities and Points 19-3
Measure the Distance Between Components 19-5
Measuring an Angle 19-6
Measuring Planar Faces 19-7
Measuring Cylindrical Faces 19-7
Restart a Measurement 19-8
Add to Accumulate 19-8
Context Sensitive Measurements 19-10
Using Measure When Entering Required Values 19-10
Region Properties 19-11

19.2 Model Material and Appearance Settings 19-12
Material 19-12
Appearance 19-14

Practice 19a: Properties and Measurements 19-16

Practice 19b: (Optional) Model Measurements 19-22

Chapter Review Questions 19-24

Command Summary 19-26

Chapter 20: Presentation Files 20-1

20.1 Getting Started with Presentation Files 20-2

20.2 Presentation Files – Storyboard Animations 20-5
Creating and Editing Animations 20-7
Actions 20-14
Playing a Storyboard Animation 20-17

20.3 Presentation Files – Snapshot Views 20-18
Creating Snapshot Views 20-18
Editing Snapshot Views 20-20
Creating a Drawing from a Snapshot View 20-21

20.4 Publishing Presentation Files 20-23

Practice 20a: Create an Animation 20-27

Practice 20b: Create Snapshots 20-39

Chapter Review Questions 20-45

Command Summary 20-48

Chapter 21: Assembly Tools 21-1

21.1 Replacing Components 21-2
Replace Components 21-2
Save and Replace Components 21-2

21.2 Duplicating Components 21-3
Mirror 21-3
Copy 21-5
Pattern 21-6

21.3 Restructuring Components 21-7
Promote 21-8
Demote 21-8
Assembly Folders 21-9

21.4 Drive Constraints 21-10

21.5 Contact Solver 21-12

21.6 Interference Detection 21-14

21.7 Error Recovery 21-17

Practice 21a: Use Assembly Tools 21-18

Practice 21b: Replace Components 21-23

Practice 21c: Restructure the Assembly 21-27

Practice 21d: Control Assembly Motion 21-30

Chapter Review Questions 21-36

Command Summary 21-39

Chapter 22: Assembly Parts and Features ... 22-1

22.1 Creating Parts in an Assembly ... 22-2

22.2 Creating Assembly Features ... 22-5

Practice 22a: Create Parts and Features in an Assembly ... 22-8

Chapter Review Questions ... 22-19

Command Summary ... 22-21

Chapter 23: Assembly Bill of Materials ... 23-1

23.1 Create Virtual Components ... 23-2

23.2 Create Bill of Materials ... 23-4
- BOM Structure ... 23-8
- Quantity ... 23-9
- Material ... 23-10
- Column and Row Organization ... 23-10
- BOM Settings ... 23-11
- Item Numbering ... 23-12
- Part Number Merge Settings ... 23-15

23.3 Instance Properties in a BOM ... 23-19

Practice 23a: Bill of Materials ... 23-25

Chapter Review Questions ... 23-36

Command Summary ... 23-39

Chapter 24: Working with Projects ... 24-1

24.1 Project Files ... 24-2
- Activating a Project File ... 24-3
- Loading a Project File ... 24-3
- Creating a New Project File ... 24-4
- Project Tree Customization ... 24-6
- Search Sequence ... 24-8

24.2 Resolving Links ... 24-10

Practice 24a: Create a Project File ... 24-13

Chapter Review Questions ... 24-19

Command Summary ... 24-21

Chapter 25: Drawing Basics ... 25-1

25.1 Creating a New Drawing ... 25-2

25.2 Base Views ... 25-4

25.3 Projected Views ... 25-9

25.4 Raster Views **25-11**
25.5 Auxiliary Views **25-12**
25.6 Section Views **25-13**
25.7 Detail Views **25-16**
25.8 Overlay Views **25-18**
25.9 Draft Views **25-20**
25.10 Break Views **25-21**
25.11 Break Out Views **25-22**
25.12 Slice Views **25-24**
25.13 Crop Views **25-26**
25.14 Manipulating Views **25-28**
Delete Views 25-28
Suppress Views 25-28
Move Views 25-29
View Orientation 25-29
Transparent Components 25-29
View Alignment 25-29
Change View Scale 25-30
Editing View Labels 25-30
Replace Models 25-31
View Properties 25-32
Practice 25a: Create a Drawing I **25-33**
Practice 25b: Create a Drawing II **25-44**
Practice 25c: Create a Drawing III **25-48**
Chapter Review Questions **25-51**
Command Summary **25-55**

Chapter 26: Detailing Drawings **26-1**

26.1 Adding Dimensions to Drawing Views **26-2**
Model Dimensions 26-2
Drawing Dimensions 26-4
Editing Drawing Dimensions 26-11
Dimension Styles 26-13
26.2 Drawing Sheets **26-15**
26.3 Parts List **26-18**
Creating the Parts List 26-18
Editing the Parts List 26-20
26.4 Drawing Balloons **26-25**

26.5 Styles and Standards 26-29
Standards 26-30
Styles 26-31

26.6 Drawing View Hatching 26-33

Practice 26a: Detail a Drawing I 26-35

Practice 26b: Detail a Drawing II 26-48

Practice 26c: (Optional) Create a Drawing 26-55

Chapter Review Questions 26-56

Command Summary 26-60

Chapter 27: Drawing Annotations 27-1

27.1 Drawing Text 27-2

27.2 Symbols 27-6

27.3 Hole and Thread Notes 27-8

27.4 Chamfer Notes 27-12

27.5 Center Marks and Centerlines 27-14
Center Marks 27-14
Centerlines 27-14
Centerline Bisector 27-15
Centered Pattern 27-16

27.6 Hole Tables 27-17

27.7 Revision Tables, Tags, and Clouds 27-20
Revision Tables 27-20
Revision Tags 27-22
Revision Clouds 27-22

Practice 27a: Add Text and Symbols 27-24

Practice 27b: Add Notes, Center Marks, and Centerlines 27-32

Practice 27c: Add a Revision Table and Tags 27-38

Practice 27d: Add Hole Tables 27-43

Chapter Review Questions 27-47

Command Summary 27-49

Chapter 28: Customizing Autodesk Inventor 28-1

28.1 Application Options 28-2

28.2 Document Settings 28-8

28.3 File Properties 28-13

28.4 Changing Part Units 28-15

28.5 Inventor User Interface Customization 28-16
Ribbon Customization 28-16
Custom Panels on the Ribbon 28-17
Keyboard Shortcuts 28-19
Marking Menu Customization 28-21

Practice 28a: Customize File Properties 28-23

Chapter Review Questions 28-26

Command Summary 28-28

Appendix D: Effective Modeling Final Review D-1

D.1 Tips for Capturing Design Intent in Your Models D-2
Considerations for Getting Started D-2
Modeling Strategies D-3

Appendix E: Additional Practices II E-1

Practice E1: Assembling with Joints E-2

Practice E2: Turntable Assembly E-23

Practice E3: Assembly Parts and Features E-28

Practice E4: Drawing Creation I E-34

Practice E5: Drawing Creation II E-35

Practice E6: Drawing Creation III E-37

Index Index-1

Preface

Autodesk® Inventor® 2027: Introduction to Solid Modeling (Part 1 and Part 2) provides you with an understanding of the parametric design philosophy through a hands-on, practice-intensive curriculum. You will learn the key skills and knowledge required to design models using Autodesk Inventor, starting with conceptual sketching, through to solid modeling, assembly design, and drawing production.

Topics Covered in Chapters 1 to 15 (Part 1)

- Understanding the Autodesk Inventor software interface
- Creating, constraining, and dimensioning 2D sketches
- Creating and editing the solid base 3D feature from a sketch
- Creating and editing secondary solid features that are sketched and placed
- Creating equations and working with parameters
- Manipulating the display of the model
- Resolving feature failures
- Duplicating geometry in the model

Topics Covered in Chapters 16 to 28 (Part 2)

- Placing and constraining/connecting parts in assemblies
- Manipulating the display of components in an assembly
- Obtaining model measurements and property information
- Creating presentation files (exploded views)
- Modifying and analyzing the components in an assembly
- Simulating motion in an assembly
- Creating parts and features in assemblies
- Creating and editing an assembly bill of materials
- Working with projects
- Creating and annotating drawings and views
- Customizing the Autodesk Inventor environment

Prerequisites

- Access to the 2027.0 version of the software, to ensure compatibility with this learning content. Future software updates that are released by Autodesk may include changes that are not reflected in this content. The practices and files included are not compatible with prior versions of the software (e.g., 2026).
- *Autodesk Inventor 2027: Introduction to Solid Modeling* is designed as an introductory course that does not require previous experience with 3D modeling or CAD software. However, familiarity with the Windows operating system is required and having a background in drafting of 3D parts is recommended.

Note on Software Setup

This guide assumes a standard installation of the software using the default preferences during installation. Lectures and practices use the standard software templates and default options for the Content Libraries.

Note on Learning Guide Content

ASCENT's learning content is designed to teach the technical skills needed to use the software. The focus is not on engineering design principles or design codes, as codes and standards can be specific to region and organization. Instead, the content aims to help you explore and understand the software's key features and capabilities.

Lead Contributor: Jennifer MacMillan

With a dedication for engineering and education, Jennifer has spent over 25 years at ASCENT managing courseware development for various CAD products. Trained in Instructional Design, Jennifer uses her skills to develop instructor-led and web-based training products as well as knowledge profiling tools.

Jennifer has achieved the Autodesk Certified Professional certification for Inventor and is also recognized as an Autodesk Certified Instructor (ACI). She enjoys teaching the training courses that she authors and is also very skilled in providing technical support to end-users.

Jennifer holds a Bachelor of Engineering Degree as well as a Bachelor of Science in Mathematics from Dalhousie University, Nova Scotia, Canada.

Jennifer MacMillan has been the Lead Contributor for *Autodesk Inventor: Introduction to Solid Modeling* since 2007.

In This Guide

The following highlights the key features of this guide.

<table>
<tr><th>Feature</th><th>Description</th></tr>
<tr><td>Practice Files</td><td>The Practice Files page includes a link to the practice files and instructions on how to download and install them. The practice files are required to complete the practices in this guide.</td></tr>
<tr><td>Chapters</td><td>A chapter consists of the following: Learning Objectives, Instructional Content, Practices, Chapter Review Questions, and Command Summary.<ul><li>Learning Objectives define the skills you can acquire by learning the content provided in the chapter.</li><li>Instructional Content, which begins right after Learning Objectives, refers to the descriptive and procedural information related to various topics. Each main topic introduces a product feature, discusses various aspects of that feature, and provides step-by-step procedures on how to use that feature. Where relevant, examples, figures, helpful hints, and notes are provided.</li><li>Practice for a topic follows the instructional content. Practices enable you to use the software to perform a hands-on review of a topic. It is required that you download the practice files (using the link found on the Practice Files page) prior to starting the first practice.</li><li>Chapter Review Questions, located close to the end of a chapter, enable you to test your knowledge of the key concepts discussed in the chapter.</li><li>Command Summary concludes a chapter. It contains a list of the software commands that are used throughout the chapter and provides information on where the command can be found in the software.</li></ul></td></tr>
<tr><td>Appendices</td><td>Appendices provide additional information to the main course content. It could be in the form of instructional content, practices, tables, projects, or skills assessment.</td></tr>
</table>

Errata Sheets

If there are any updates or corrections to this guide, they will be published in an errata sheet.

Access it here: ***https://resources.ascented.com/errata-sheets-autodesk***

or

visit **ASCENTed.com > RESOURCES > RESOURCE CENTER > Errata Sheets** and select **Autodesk** from the drop-down list.

Practice Files

1. Type the URL *exactly as shown below* into the address bar of your Internet browser to access the Course File Download page.

   Note: If you are using the ebook, you do not have to type the URL. Instead, you can access the page by clicking the URL below.

   https://www.ascented.com/getfile/id/psilochilusPF

2. On the Course File Download page, click the **DOWNLOAD NOW** button, as shown below, to download the .ZIP file that contains the practice files.

3. Once the download is complete, unzip the file and extract its contents.

   The recommended practice files folder location is:
   C:\Autodesk Inventor 2027 Intro Practice Files

   Note: It is recommended that you do not change the location of the practice files folder. Doing so may cause errors when completing the practices.

Stay Informed!

To receive information about upcoming events, promotional offers, and complimentary webcasts, visit:

www.ASCENTed.com/updates

Chapter 16

Assembly Environment

An assembly file in Autodesk® Inventor® enables you to combine the components that have been modeled to create a top-level assembly that communicates how all the components are combined. Both parts and other assemblies, referred to as subassemblies, can be referenced in an assembly.

Learning Objectives

- Create a new assembly file using a standard template.
- Place, constrain, and edit components in an assembly file.
- Place a selected family member from the Content Center into an assembly.
- Use the Model browser to find items, filter information, and switch between the *Modeling* and *Assembly* tabs for an assembly.
- Save new and existing assembly files.

16.1 Assembling Components Using Constraints

You place and constrain components to create an assembly. Constraints are specified to locate components parametrically with respect to other components. Similar to the dependencies between features in a part, relationships also exist in an assembly when components are assembled relative to one another.

Use the following general steps to create an assembly and place components:

1. Create an assembly file.
2. Place components in the assembly file.
3. Drag parts and display degrees of freedom.
4. Select a constraint type.
5. Select references on the components.
6. Assign an offset value, as required.
7. Repeat Steps 4 to 6 until the components are fully constrained.
8. Complete the component placement.
9. Edit the component placement, as required.

Step 1 - Create an assembly file.

The first step in creating an assembly is to start a new file based on an assembly template. This can be done using the default template that is assigned in the software or you can start the assembly by selecting a template. These methods are described:

- To create an assembly using the default template, expand the **New** menu on the *Home* page and select **Assembly**. Alternatively, in the Quick Access Toolbar, expand (New) and select **Assembly**, or in the **File** menu, select **New>Assembly**.
- To access the *Create New File* dialog box to select a specific assembly template, click **New** on the *Home* page. Alternatively, in the Quick Access Toolbar, click (New) or in the **File** menu, click **New**.

Step 2 - Place components in the assembly file.

To add a component to the assembly, in the *Assemble* tab>*Component* panel, click (Place). In the *Place Component* dialog box, select the component to add and click **Open**. It is possible to select multiple components by holding <Ctrl> or <Shift> while selecting.

> ***Note:*** *Components that can be added to an assembly include parts (.IPT), library components, and other assembly models called subassemblies (.IAM). Subassemblies act as single components.*

To locate the first component, you can freely place it in the assembly or ground it to the assembly coordinate system (0,0,0).

- To freely locate the component in the assembly, click in the graphics window with the left mouse button to place it. However, before locating a component in the assembly, you can use **Rotate X 90**, **Rotate Y 90**, or **Rotate Z 90** to reorient the model before placement.
- To ground the component, right-click and select **Place Grounded at Origin** in the marking menu, as shown in Figure 16–1.

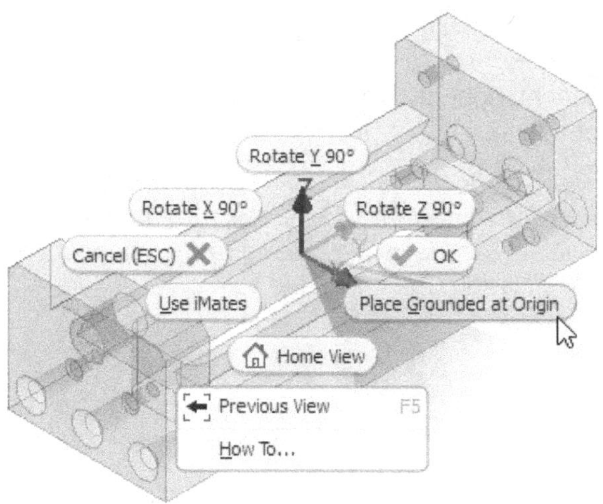

Figure 16–1

Once placed freely or grounded, a second instance of the component is immediately available for further placement. To complete the operation without assembling any additional instances of the same component, right-click and select **Cancel [Esc]** or **OK**. Alternatively, you can press <Esc>.

- Grounded components are indicated by the pushpin symbol in the Model browser, as shown in Figure 16–2.
- The [•] icon indicates that the component is fully constrained.
- The cursor changes from to when you hover over a grounded component in the model.

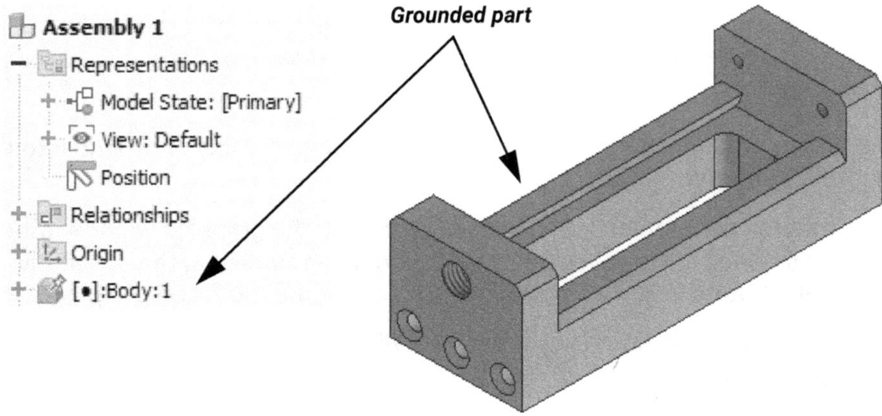

Figure 16–2

- To unground a component, right-click on it in the assembly window or Model browser and clear the **Grounded** option.

  Note: *It is good practice to ground at least one component. This component serves as the base on which the rest of the assembly is built. To automatically ground the first assembled component, set the* ***Place and ground first component at origin*** *option in the Assembly tab in the Application Options dialog box.*

In the *Assemble* tab>*Component* panel, click (Place) to add a second component to the assembly. To freely locate the component in the assembly, click in the graphics window with the left mouse button to place it. The [▫] icon in the Model browser indicates that the component is not fully constrained, as shown in Figure 16–3.

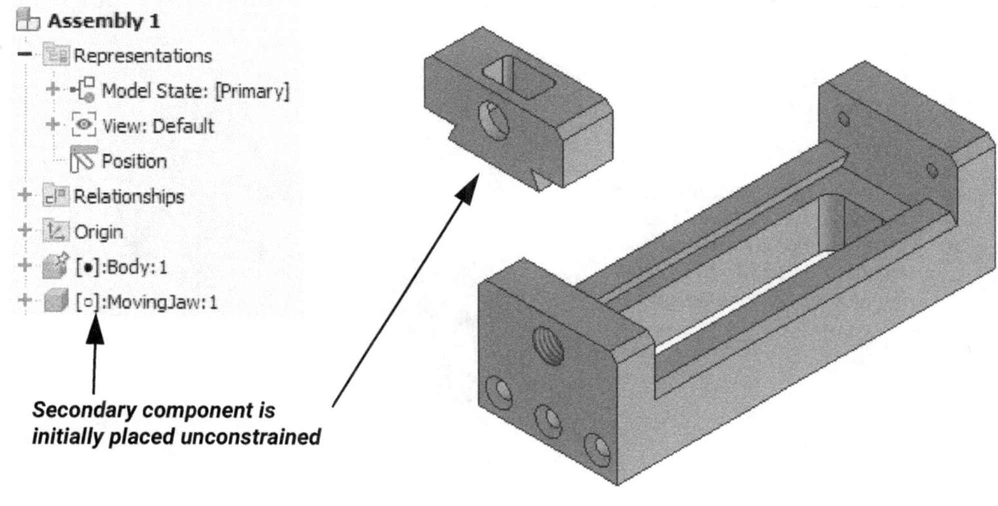

Figure 16–3

Note: *Any secondary component can also be grounded, if required, by right-clicking and selecting* **Place Grounded at Origin** *in the marking menu.*

Step 3 - Drag parts and display degrees of freedom.

Once components are placed in the assembly, you can begin constraining any non-grounded components. To prepare for constraining you might want to move them. This can be done using any of the following methods:

- To drag a part, select it and drag it to a new location in the assembly window (hold the left mouse button while dragging). Alternatively, you can use (Free Move) in the *Assemble* tab>*Position* panel.
- To rotate a single component in the assembly, in the *Assemble* tab>*Position* panel, click (Free Rotate) and select the component. Similar to globally rotating the assembly, hold the left mouse button while dragging to rotate only the selected component.

To display the degrees of freedom for components, in the *View* tab>*Visibility* panel, click (Degrees of Freedom). By default, they are not displayed. A completely unconstrained component (as shown in Figure 16–4) has six degrees of freedom, as indicated by green arrows on the component. It can translate in three directions (X, Y, and Z) and rotate about three axes (X, Y, and Z), as shown in Figure 16–4. Note that degrees of freedom symbols do not display on a grounded part because the part does not have any degrees of freedom.

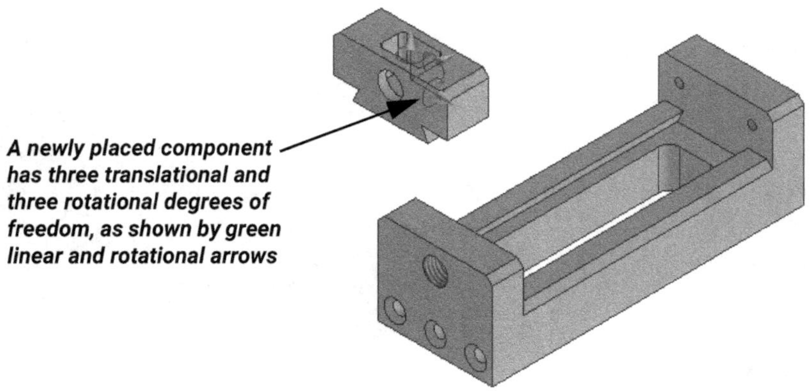

Figure 16–4

Hint: Degree of Freedom Analysis

The **Degree of Freedom Analysis** command provides a summary of the degrees of freedom remaining in all of the components in the assembly. To open the *Degree of Freedom Analysis* dialog box, in the *Assemble* tab>*Productivity* panel, click (Degree of Freedom Analysis). This dialog box lists all assembly components and lists the translational and rotational degrees of freedom remaining for each component.

- To graphically display the remaining degrees of freedom in the graphics window, select a component name in the dialog box.
- To visually animate the degrees of freedom remaining, select **Animate Freedom** in the dialog box and select a component name.

Step 4 - Select a constraint type.

In the *Assemble* tab>*Relationships* panel, click (Constrain) to open the *Place Constraint* dialog box. In this dialog box, you select the constraint type in the *Type* area and define how the components are oriented relative to one another in the *Solution* area. Depending on the type of constraint being created, the dialog box updates appropriately to provide the required options.

The available constraint types are described as follows:

Mate

The Mate constraint (icon) positions two components adjacent to each other. It can be assigned between two planes, edges, center points, or work points. The Plane-Plane Mate constraint removes one translational and two rotational degrees of freedom. When planes or the center point of a circular edge are selected, the Mate orientation solutions are shown in Figure 16–5.

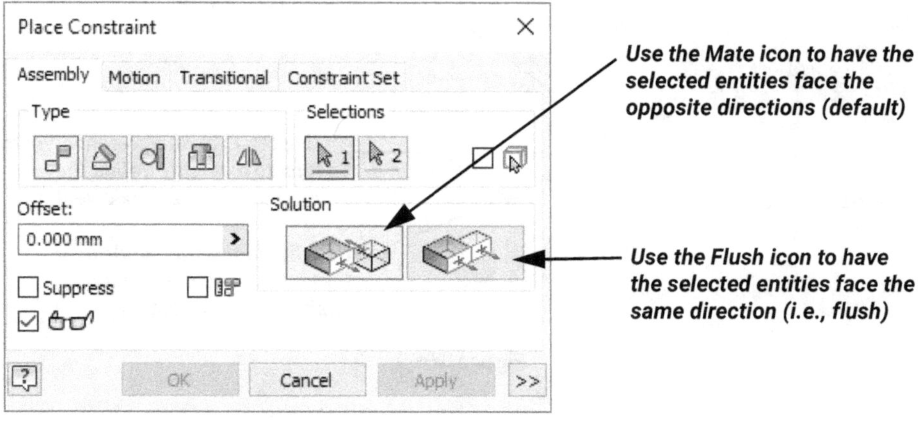

Figure 16–5

When linear edges or axes selected, the Mate orientation solutions are shown in Figure 16–6.

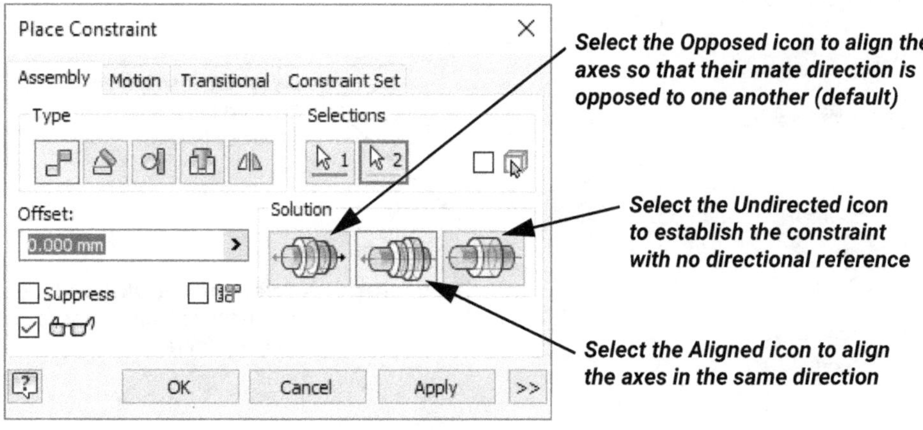

Figure 16–6

Angle

The Angle constraint ( ) specifies the angle between two edges, two planes, or an edge and a plane of the components. This constraint removes only two rotational degrees of freedom. The available Angle orientation solutions are shown in Figure 16–7.

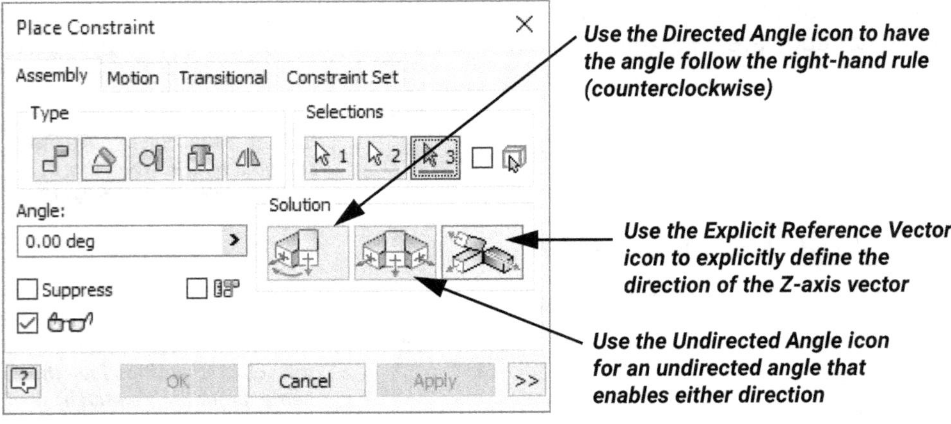

Figure 16–7

Tangent

The Tangent constraint ( ) positions two components tangent to each other. This constraint only removes one translational degree of freedom. The available Tangent orientation solutions are shown in Figure 16–8.

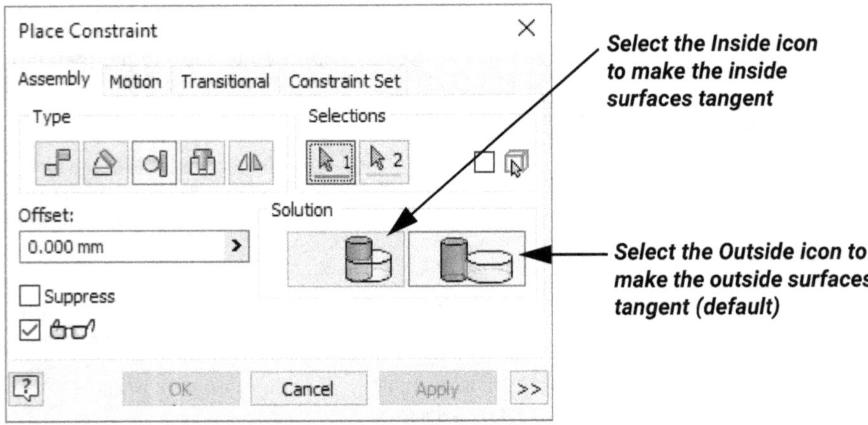

Figure 16–8

Insert

The Insert constraint ( ) enables you to position two components to fit into each other. This constraint removes three translational and two rotational degrees of freedom by mating the axis of two components, as well as applying a Mate constraint between two planar faces. To remove the final rotation degree of freedom, enable (Lock Rotation). The available Insert orientation solutions are shown in Figure 16–9.

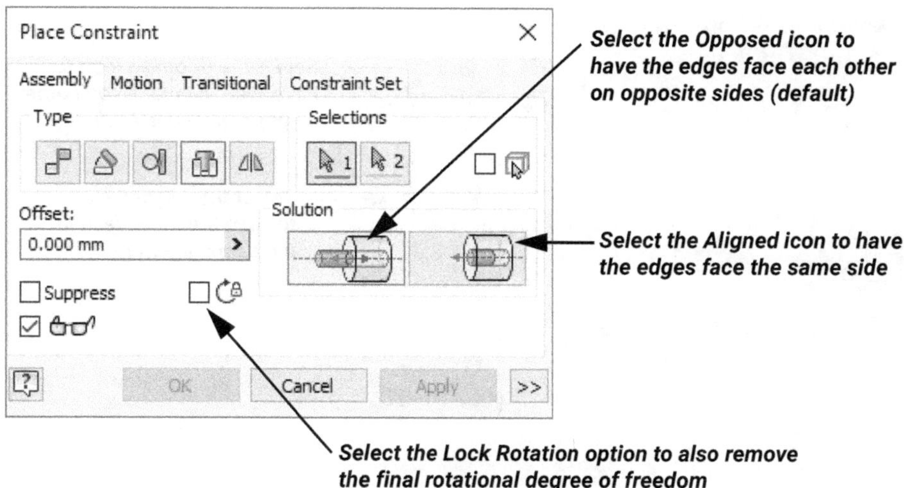

Figure 16–9

Note: *The Model browser icon used to identify an Insert constraint varies depending on whether* ***Lock Rotation*** *has been set. The icon indicates constaints where a rotational degree of freedom is still available and the icon indicates constraints where it has been locked.*

Symmetry

The Symmetry constraint ( ) enables you to position two components symmetrically about a plane or planar face. This constraint removes one translational and two rotational degrees of freedom by creating symmetry between reference planes or edges. When you place a Symmetry constraint, the dialog box opens as shown in Figure 16–10.

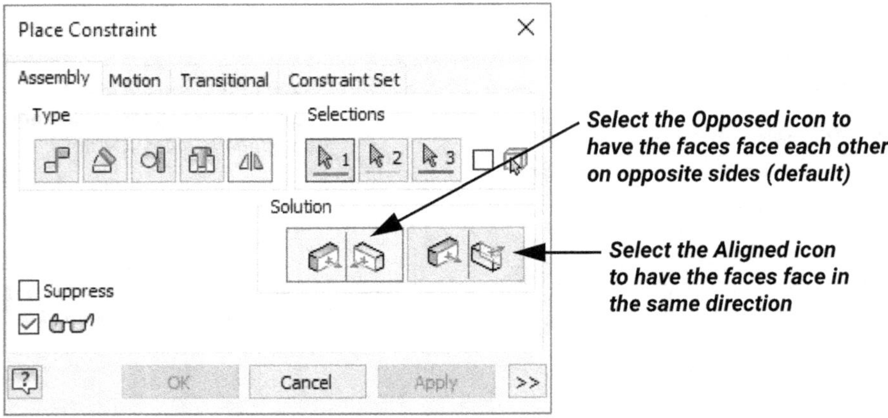

Figure 16–10

UCS

A UCS constraint enables you to position two components so that the UCS in each component is selected to be constrained to the other. This constraint removes three translational and three rotational degrees of freedom. It can be assigned on the *Constraint Set* tab in the *Place Constraint* dialog box, or using the **UCS to UCS** assemble option, as shown in Figure 16–11.

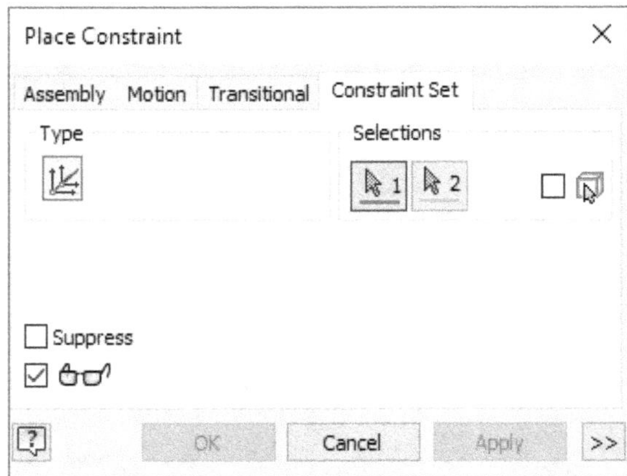

Figure 16–11

Step 5 - Select references on the components.

Reference selection on both components is required to fully define each constraint. Depending on the type of constraint being defined, you can select any of the following geometry types to define the reference:

- Faces
- Planes
- Lines (edges, curves, or axes)
- Points (work points, center points, or vertices)

Note: When selecting references, you can select faces through parts by hovering the cursor over the face and selecting it in the Select Other drop-down list.

How To: Assign References

1. Ensure the (First Selection) field is active.
2. Select the geometry reference on the first component appropriate for the constraint type.
3. Ensure the (Second Selection) field is active.

Hint: Multi Selection for Mate Constraint References

When assigning Mate constraints, the second selection option provides a drop-down list enabling you to select whether the second reference will be a single or multi reference selection. With the **Multiselect** option selected, you can now select references from different components to mate with the first selection, and you can add the same constraint to multiple components at once.

4. Select the geometry reference on the second component that is appropriate for the constraint type.

To preview the effect of the added constraint in the assembly, click (Show Preview).

Hint: Isolating Components During Reference Selection

To isolate a component so that you can only select specific reference geometry on that component, click (Pick part first) in the *Place Constraint* dialog box and then select the component to isolate. This option is valuable during reference selection when components are close to each other or when one component obscures another.

Step 6 - Assign an offset value, as required.

You can assign an offset value between selected references in the *Place Constraint* dialog box.

- If the (Predict Offset and Orientation) option is enabled when you select two component references, the current distance (offset value or angle) between them automatically displays in the *Offset* field in the dialog box. The option is only available for the Mate and Angle constraints.

Step 7 - Repeat Steps 4 to 6 until the components are fully constrained.

Once references and any offset value has been selected, click **Apply** to complete the constraint definition. Continue adding constraints between components until all required degrees of freedom are removed and the [•] icon appears in the Model browser for the component, indicating that the component is fully constrained.

Step 8 - Complete the component placement.

Once the components have been fully constrained, click **Cancel** to close the *Place Constraint* dialog box. Alternatively, right-click in the graphics window and select **Cancel (ESC)**.

- The default naming convention for a constraint includes the constraint type and a sequential numerical number. To rename a constraint, double-click on the constraint name in the Model browser and enter a new name.
- The assembly file stores links to and constraint information for the components used in the assembly. The geometry of the components is still defined in the individual .IPT (part) files.

Hint: Showing Constraints in the Graphics Window

To show glyphs in the model that indicate an assigned constraint, click (Show) in the *Relationships* panel and select a component. Preselecting all of the components and selecting this option displays all of the glyphs. Use (Hide All) to clear them from the display.

Step 9 - Edit the component placement, as required.

Constraints are listed in the Model browser under the component(s) to which they are applied. Expand the component in the Model browser to display all of its constraints. Additionally, all of the constraints are listed in the **Relationships** node at the top of the Model browser. Consider the following:

- To modify an offset value, select the constraint in the Model browser and enter a new offset value in the field that displays at the bottom of the Model browser.
- To edit a constraint, right-click on the constraint in the Model browser and select **Edit**, or you can double-click on the constraint name in the Model browser. The original *Edit Constraint* dialog box opens and you can change any of the elements. Alternatively, you can show the constraint glyphs by selecting (Show) in the *Relationships* panel, selecting a component, and then double-clicking on the required constraint glyph to access its *Edit Constraint* dialog box.
- To review failed (sick) constraints, click (Show Sick) in the *Relationships* panel. Edit the references as required to resolve the issues.
- To delete a constraint or a sick constraint, right-click on its glyph and select **Delete** or delete it in the Model browser.

  Note: *When components are copied and pasted, their constraints are only copied with them if both of the components used in defining the constraint are copied.*

Assembly Examples

The following examples use different combinations of Mate constraint references to create fully constrained assemblies. The components to be placed are shown in Figure 16–12.

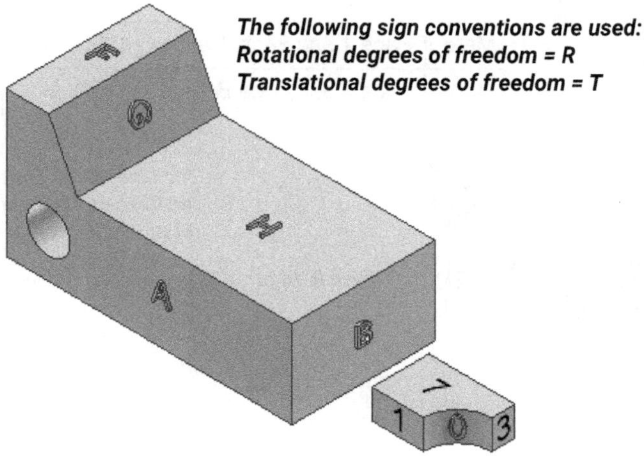

Figure 16–12

Example 1: Mate (Plane - Plane)

The combination of constraints and references shown in Figure 16–13 is used to create the fully constrained assembly.

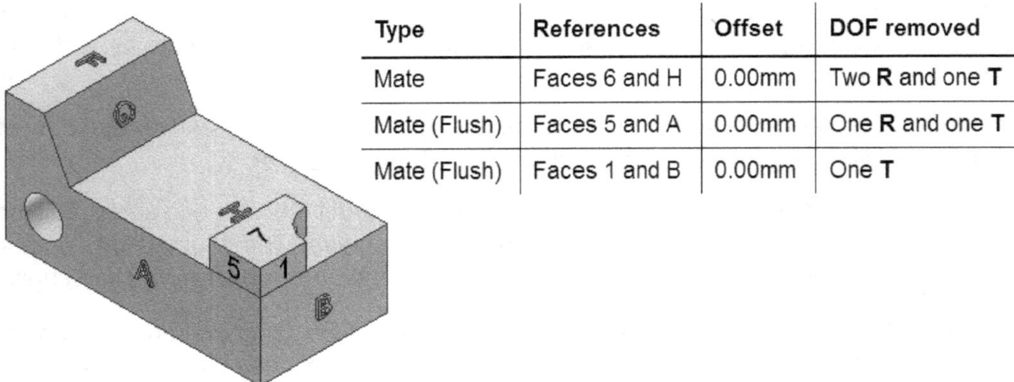

Type	References	Offset	DOF removed
Mate	Faces 6 and H	0.00mm	Two **R** and one **T**
Mate (Flush)	Faces 5 and A	0.00mm	One **R** and one **T**
Mate (Flush)	Faces 1 and B	0.00mm	One **T**

Figure 16–13

> ***Note:*** *Mate constraints orient components so that surface normals are facing one another. This can sometimes make reference selection difficult, as it can hide references. Alternatively, consider using the Mate - Flush constraint until all of the references have been selected and then switch back to the Mate constraint.*

Example 2: Mate (Line - Plane)

The combination of constraints and references shown in Figure 16–14 is used to create the fully constrained assembly.

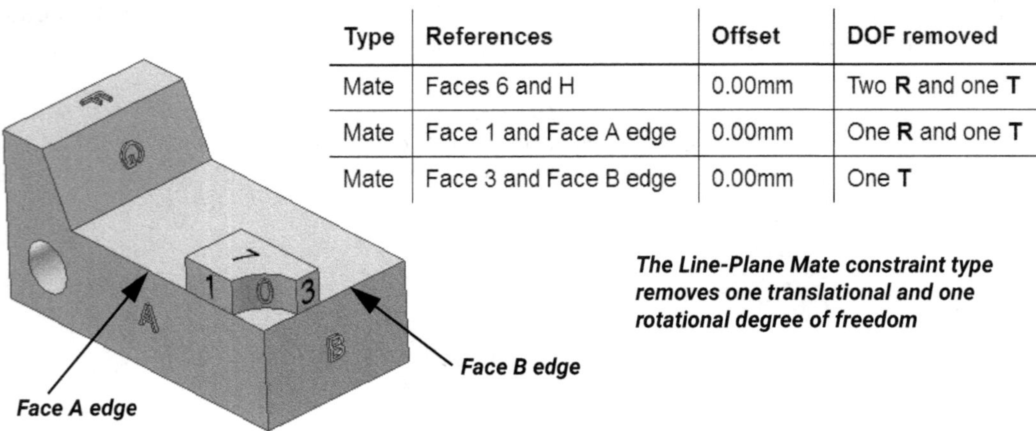

Type	References	Offset	DOF removed
Mate	Faces 6 and H	0.00mm	Two **R** and one **T**
Mate	Face 1 and Face A edge	0.00mm	One **R** and one **T**
Mate	Face 3 and Face B edge	0.00mm	One **T**

Figure 16–14

Example 3: Mate (Line - Line)

The combination of constraints and references shown in Figure 16–15 is used to create the fully constrained assembly.

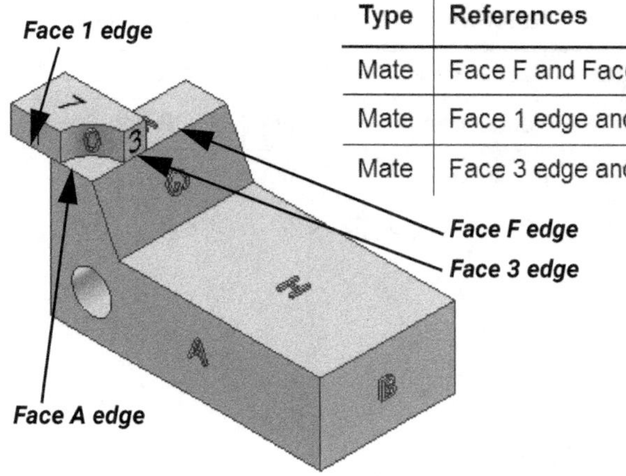

Type	References	Offset	DOF removed
Mate	Face F and Face 6	0.00mm	One **T**
Mate	Face 1 edge and face A edge	0.00mm	Two **R** and two **T**
Mate	Face 3 edge and face F edge	0.00mm	One **R** and one **T**

The Line-Line Mate constraint type removes two translational and two rotational degrees of freedom

Figure 16–15

Example 4: Mate (Work Point - Work Point)

The combination of constraints and references shown in Figure 16–16 is used to create the fully constrained assembly.

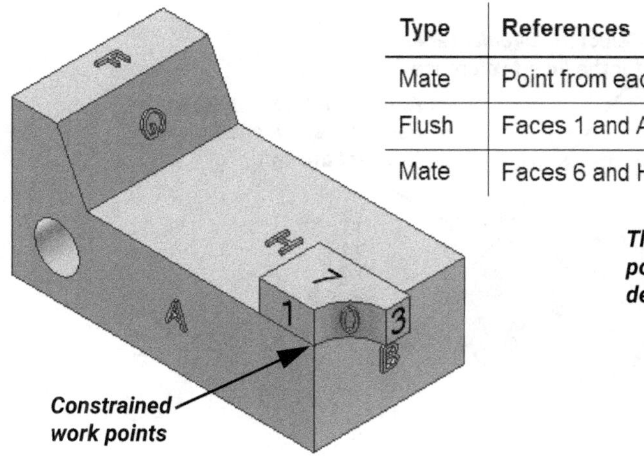

Type	References	Offset	DOF removed
Mate	Point from each part	0.00mm	Three **T**
Flush	Faces 1 and A	0.00mm	Two **R**
Mate	Faces 6 and H	0.00mm	One **R**

The Mate constraint type between work points removes three translational degrees of freedom

Figure 16–16

Example 5: Tangent and Angle

The combination of constraints and references shown in Figure 16–17 is used to create the fully constrained assembly.

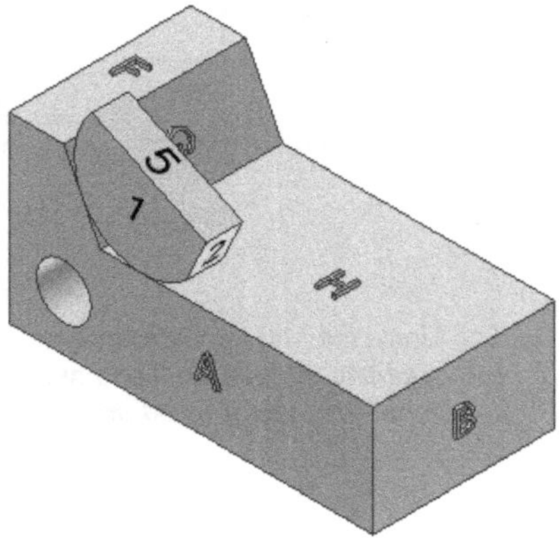

Type	References	Offset	DOF removed
Tangent	Faces H and 4	0.00mm	One **R** and one **T**
Flush	Faces 1 and A	0.00mm	One **R** and one **T**
Tangent	Faces G and 4	0.00mm	One **T**
Angle	Faces F and 5	25deg	One **R**

Figure 16–17

Example 6: Insert and Mate

This example uses different combinations of constraints to create the fully constrained assembly. You can create this assembly with only one constraint (Insert). However, if you want to orient the bolt in a certain direction, add an additional Mate constraint (Flush) or an Angle constraint. The components to be placed are shown in Figure 16–18.

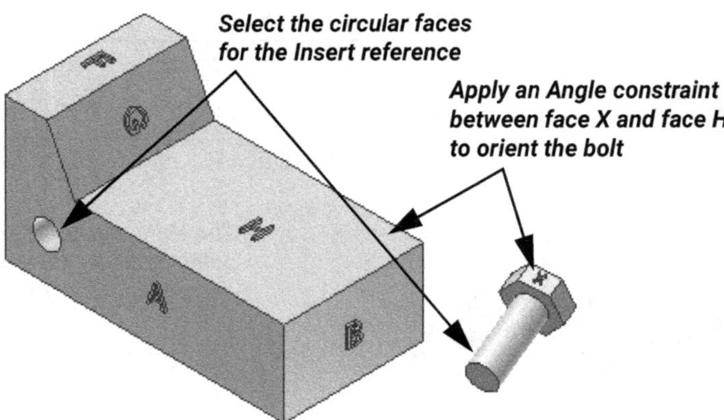

Figure 16–18

The combination of constraints and references shown in Figure 16–19 are used to create the fully constrained assembly.

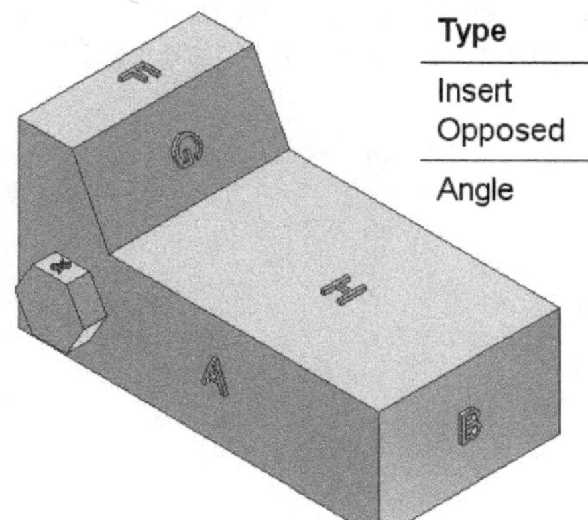

Type	References	Offset	DOF removed
Insert Opposed	The circular faces	0.00mm	Two **R** and Three **T**
Angle	Face H and X	0.00deg	One **R**

The Insert constraint removes three translational and two rotational degrees of freedom

Figure 16–19

16.2 Place and Insert

To simplify the placement of components that are constrained to circular edges you can use the **Place and Insert** command on the expanded Place option, as shown in Figure 16–20.

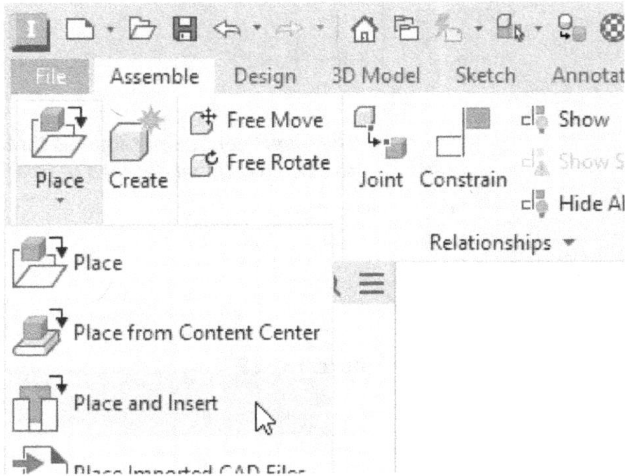

Figure 16–20

Once the option is selected, the *Properties* panel opens, as shown in Figure 16–21.

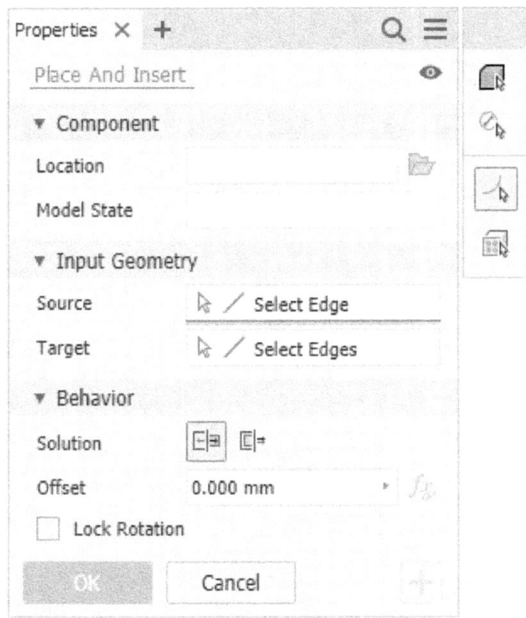

Figure 16–21

How To: Place and Insert a Component

1. In the *Component* area of the panel, select to open the *Place Component* dialog box. Navigate to and select a component for placement, and click **Open**. If the component has a model state associated with it, you can also select the required state.
2. Place the component in the graphics window using your left mouse button.
3. With the *Source* field active in the *Input Geometry* area, select the circular edge on the component being placed.

   Note: *By default, the (Pick Target Component is ON), option is disabled in the Tool panel. This ensures that the Source component reference must be selected on the newly placed component. Enable this option to select the source reference from existing components.*

4. With the *Target* field active, select either the (Select Target Edges) or (Select Target Planar Faces with Edges) options to determine the type of reference that will be selected.
   - With (Select Target Edges) selected, select a single circular edge on the target component.
   - With (Select Target Planar Faces with Edges) selected, select a face and all circular edges on the face will be automatically selected.
5. In the *Behavior* area, use the (Opposed) and (aligned) options to flip the alignment solution to orient the component as required.
6. In the *Behavior* area, enter an offset between the edges, if necessary.
7. (Optional) Select **Lock Rotation** to fully constrain the component and prevent it from leaving the rotational degree of freedom open.
8. Click **OK** to complete the place of the component(s). Alternatively, select to add the component and keep the *Properties* panel open to continue adding new components.

16.3 Assemble Mini-Toolbar

The Assemble mini-toolbar provides an alternative to using the *Place Constraint* dialog box when assigning constraints. This tool eliminates the need to interact with a dialog box and enables you to work directly with the model to assign constraints.

You can access this interface using either of the following methods:

- Once a component is initially placed, and prior to right-clicking and selecting **OK**, select a reference entity on the new component to begin assigning a constraint.
- In the *Assemble* tab>expanded *Relationships* panel, click (Assemble) to activate the mini-toolbar interface.

By default, when the mini-toolbar is activated, the (Automatic) constraint is selected in the mini-toolbar. Based on the selected model references, the software decides which constraint to assign. Alternatively, you can manually select the constraint type in the drop-down list, as shown in Figure 16–22. Each constraint type is listed with multiple orientation options, if available.

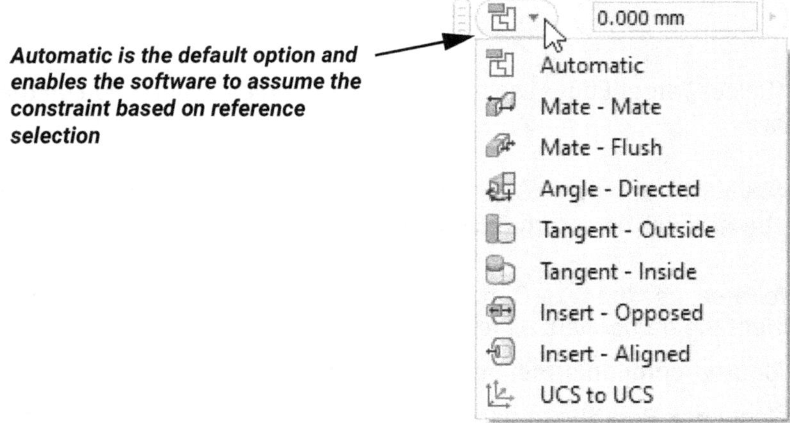

Figure 16–22

As references are selected, the components are immediately previewed in their new position, as shown in Figure 16–23. Click [+] to apply the constraint.

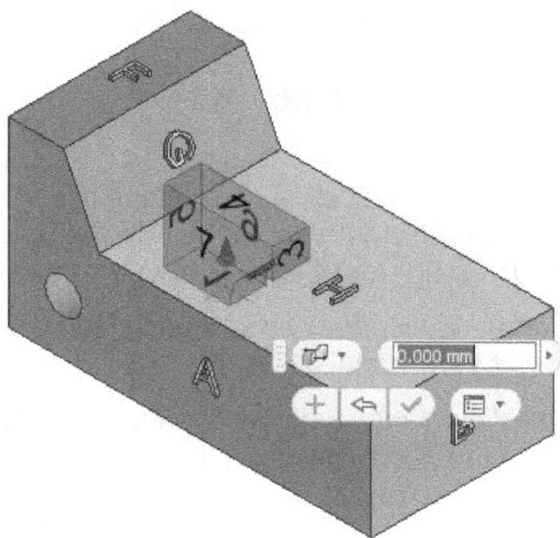

Figure 16–23

- As references are selected, the drop-down list in the mini-toolbar refines the list of possible constraint options. If required, you can switch from (Automatic) to a more specific constraint type or it will automatically change for you depending on the references selected. Continue to select references and assign them until the component is fully located in the assembly.
- Click [✓] to apply the constraint and close the Assemble mini-toolbar.
- If you initiated the Assemble mini-toolbar during component placement, a duplicate of the assembled component will display in the graphics window. You can continue to assemble another copy, or right-click and select **OK** to cancel placement.

Constrain vs. Assemble

The following are some differences between the **Constrain** option and the Assemble mini-toolbar when used to constrain components:

- When using the Assemble mini-toolbar, you can focus on the reference selection first. Once references have been selected, you can refine the constraint type.
- When using the Assemble mini-toolbar, each constraint is added independently and is not compared to existing constraints. This means that conflicting constraints are not recognized until you click [✓] to complete the command. At this point, any conflicting constraints are reported and must be fixed.
- When using the **Constrain** option, you can permit the software to interpret an offset value. This is not possible with the Assemble mini-toolbar.

16.4 Content Center

The Autodesk Inventor software has a standard library (Content Center) that contains a variety of common parts (e.g., nuts, bolts, and screws) that can be used instead of creating a new part.

How To: Add a Library Part to an Assembly

1. In the *Assemble* tab>*Component* panel, click (Place from Content Center) in the expanded *Place* drop-down list. Alternatively, In the **File** menu, select **Open>Open from Content Center**. The *Place from Content Center* dialog box opens.
2. Select the type in the *Category View* panel, as shown in Figure 16–24. All of the families for that type are listed in the *List View* panel.
3. Click on a family in the *List View* panel, as shown in Figure 16–24. All of the parts available from that family are listed in the *Table View* panel.

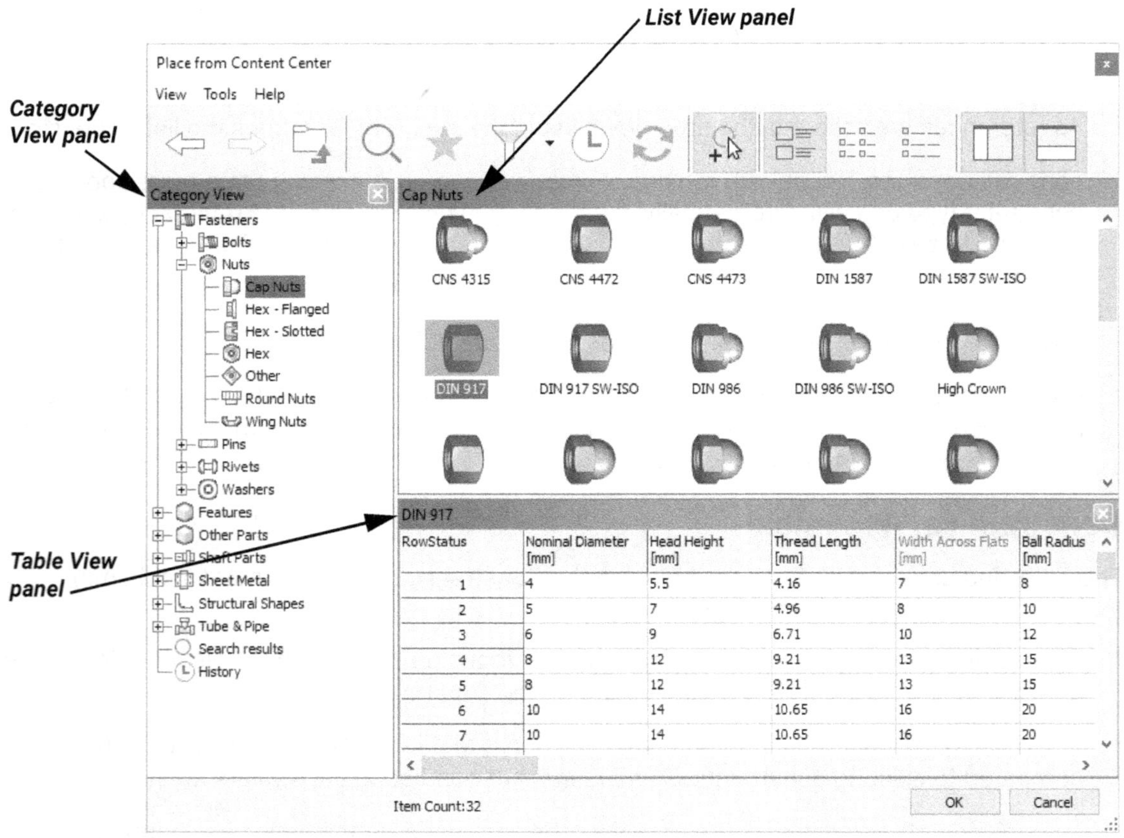

Figure 16–24

4. Use any of the following to add the library part.

   - With (Autodrop) enabled, double-click on the required family type in the *List View* panel. Select references in the assembly to place the new component. Once references are selected, the part is automatically generated to fit the selected references. Use the options in the *AutoDrop* dialog box to change the size (), place the part and add another (), or place a single instance of the part (). Constraints are automatically assigned based on the selected references.

   Note: *The (Autodrop) command is available in the Content Center toolbar. You can also hold <Alt> while double-clicking on the part or feature in the Content Center to toggle the AutoDrop status.*

   - With (Autodrop) disabled, double-click on the required family type in the *List View* panel. Select a size from the sizing dialog box that opens, click **OK**, and then place and constrain the new part.
   - Double-click on the required family member in the *Table View* panel. The part is generated and attaches itself to the cursor to be placed and constrained in the assembly. When selecting directly in the *Table View* panel, the Autodrop setting does not have any impact.

   Note: *As an alternative to using the Place from Content Center dialog box, you can switch to the Favorites browser when a part or assembly is open and use its interface to locate and open content center items. To open this browser, click in the Model browser header and select **Favorites** from the drop-down list.*

Searching the Content Center

A significant number of features are stored in the Content Center. To use the search environment, click (Search) or select **Tools>Search** to open the **Quick Search** tool at the top of the *Place from Content Center* dialog box. If you are using the content center through the Favorites browser you cannot search, however, you can filter the data that is listed.

Hint: Content Center Features

The Content Center not only provides access to a library of part files, it also contains commonly used and sized features that can be added to a model. The Content Center contains both parts and features when working in an assembly model, but only contains features when working in a part model.

16.5 Assembly Browser

The Model browser lists all of the parts, subassemblies, and representations and model states that make up an assembly. The following can be done using the Model browser.

- You can change the Model browser's display style. Select **Modeling** at the top of the Model browser to display component features and select **Assembly** to display the constraints, as shown in Figure 16–25.

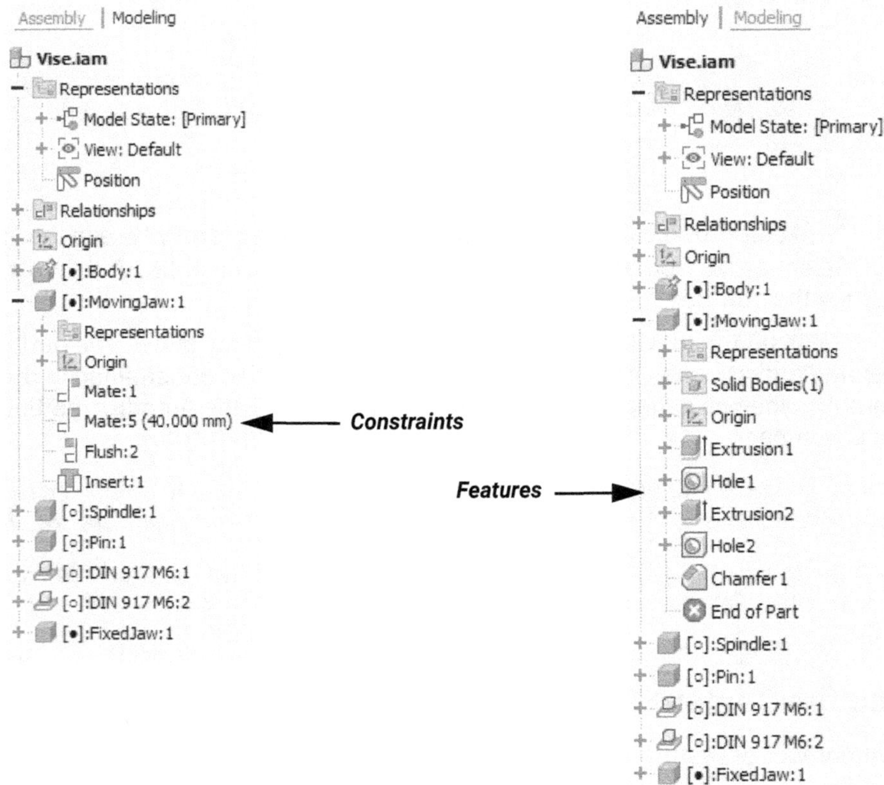

Figure 16–25

- You can find objects using the Model browser options:
  - Use (Find) in the Model browser header to search for objects, such as components, features, constraints, and sketches. If an item is located, the browser display updates to only show the located item(s).
  - Expand (Advanced Settings Menu) and click **Find**. The *Find Assembly Components* dialog box opens, providing advanced search options. This icon opens the same dialog box and options as when you click (Find Component) in the *Tools* tab>*Find* panel.

- You can identify the types of components in the assembly by the component icons adjacent to the names (e.g., parts ( ), subassemblies ( ), or content center items ( )).
- You can identify if components are fully constrained in the Model browser by reviewing the constraint states of components.
    - The (Pushpin) icon adjacent to a component name indicates that it is grounded (fully constrained).
    - The [•] icon adjacent to a component name indicates that the component is fully constrained.
    - The [◦] icon adjacent to a component name indicates that the component is not fully constrained. To review which degrees of freedom remain, you must review the existing constraints.
    - The [-] icon adjacent to a component name indicates that the component constraint status is unknown. To attempt to resolve it, in the *Manage* tab>*Update* panel, click **Rebuild All** or review constraints and assign as needed.

Hint: Enabling the Display of Constraint States

Constraint states were introduced in Inventor 2022, and the current default templates have them set to display by default. If they are not displayed, the assembly may have been created in an older version. To turn on constraint states, expand (Advanced Settings Menu) and select **Display Preferences>Show Constraint State**. Alternatively, you can set the **Show Constraint State in Browser** option from the *Tools* tab>**Document Settings**>*Modeling* tab.

- To open a component from the Model browser, right-click on the component in the Model browser and select **Open**. The part or subassembly opens in a separate window.
- You can open a drawing directly from the Model browser by right-clicking the assembly name and selecting **Component>Open Drawing**. If a drawing with the same name as the assembly exists, it automatically opens. If not, the *Open* dialog box opens for you to select the filename.
- You can create a drawing file directly from the Model browser by right-clicking on the assembly name and selecting **Create Drawing View**. You are immediately prompted to select a template. You can then begin the placement of the base view and any of its dependent projected views. Similarly, you can create a presentation file by right-clicking and selecting **Create Presentation**.

- You can manipulate the display of the Model browser using the **Display Preferences** options shown in Figure 16–26.
  - There are options that enable you to hide work planes, notes, documents, and warnings.
  - Using the **Show Children Only** option, you can list only first-level components in the Model browser (components in subassemblies are not listed).
  - Use **Hide Fully Constrained** to quickly turn off the display of components that are fully constrained in the assembly.
  - Enable **Show Constraint State** to display the icons ([-], [◦], [•]) to help you identify the constraint status of a component. You can disable this option to turn off the display of the icons.

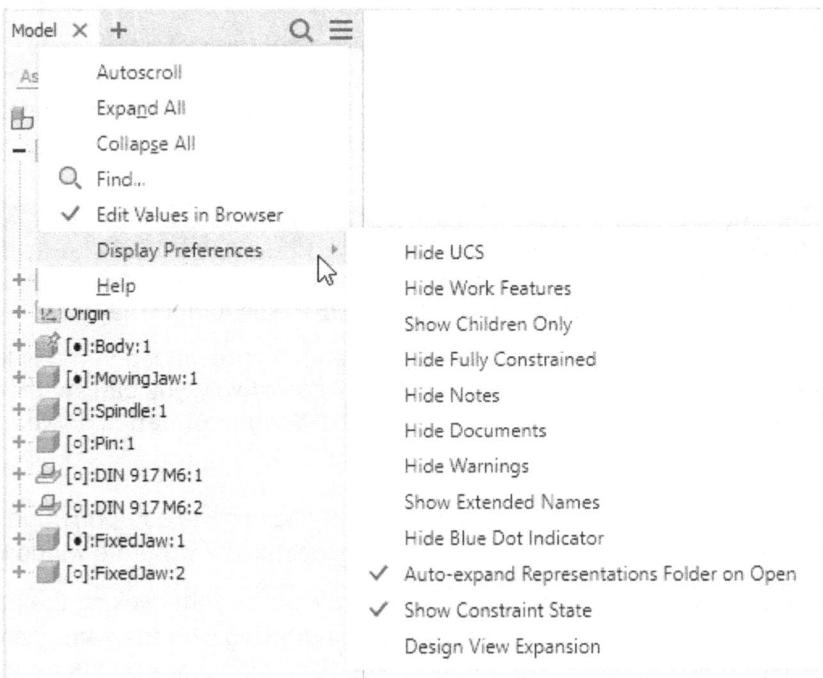

Figure 16–26

16.6 Saving Assembly Files

To save an assembly file, click (Save) in the Quick Access Toolbar or click **Save** in the **File** menu. If the assembly has not been saved before, the *Save As* dialog box opens. Enter a name for the assembly and click **Save**. If the assembly has been saved before, the *Save* dialog box opens as shown in Figure 16–27.

The *Save* dialog box lists the components that require saving and their checkout status (if a Vault project is active), and it enables you to set whether or not to save each file. The *Save State* column provides some information on why the file needs saving. If a row appears in red, it indicates the file is outside the active project folder.

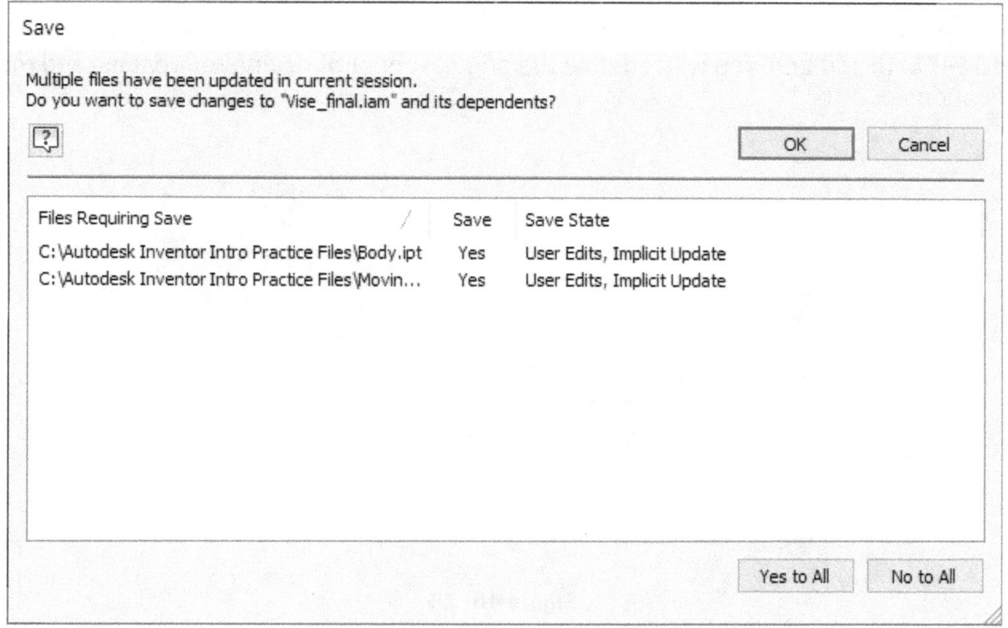

Figure 16–27

Note: *By default, all of the modified files are marked to be saved. Clicking **Yes to All** saves all files regardless if changes were made. Additionally, if you are working with the Autodesk Vault software, all of the saved files receive new versions based on the save date, not based on whether the physical model was actually changed.*

- If you do not want to save a particular file, change the **Yes** to **No** by clicking on it in the *Save* column.
- Files available for checkout (which you have edited without checking out) are marked **Yes** for saving and the file is saved and available for check out. If you click **Yes** to change it to **No**, the file is not saved.

Once you have decided which files to save, click **OK** to save the selected files.

Practice 16a
Assembly Basics I (Constraints)

Practice Objectives

- Place and constrain components in an assembly.
- Place a Content Center component in an assembly.
- Modify assembly dimensions to change the position of components relative to one another.
- Edit existing component placement references.

In this practice, you will create a new assembly and assemble the components, as shown in Figure 16–28. In addition, you will redefine the original constraints and references, and make modifications.

Figure 16–28

Task 1: Create an assembly and assemble the first component.

1. Create a new assembly file using the **Standard (mm).iam** template.
2. In the *Assemble* tab>*Component* panel, click (Place). You might need to expand the *Place* drop-down list to access this option.
3. Select **Body.ipt** in the *Place Component* dialog box and click **Open**. The component is added to the assembly.
4. If the component displays in a 2D orientation, return the model to its default Home view using the ViewCube. If the default orientation is not as shown in Figure 16–29, right-click and select **Rotate X 90**, **Rotate Y 90**, or **Rotate Z 90** to reorient it as shown. Once reoriented, right-click on the model and select **Place Grounded at Origin** to ground the component.

5. Right-click and select **OK** to assemble a single instance of the component into the assembly. If you select again an additional **Body** component is added.
6. Review the Model browser. Note that the base part has been added to the browser with (Pushpin) next to it, as shown in Figure 16–29. This indicates that the component is grounded. A grounded part is fixed to a location in the assembly and is not dependent on other parts. The [•] icon indicates that the component is fully constrained.

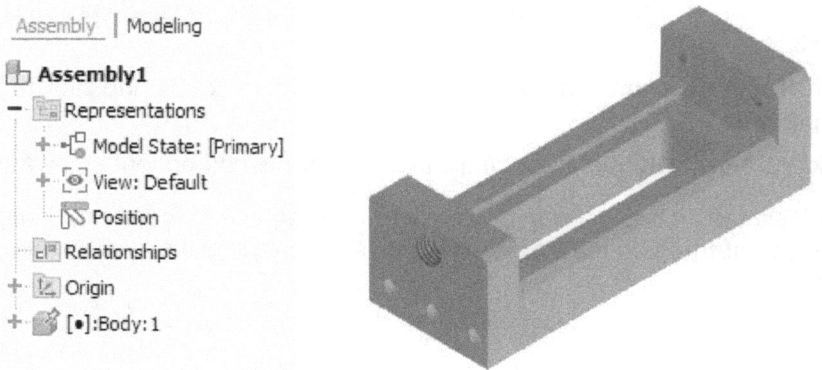

Figure 16–29

7. Hover the cursor over the **Body.ipt** component in the graphics window and note that the cursor symbol has changed to , indicating that it is grounded.

Task 2: Add another part and apply the first constraint.

In this task, you will add and apply the first constraint to place the **MovingJaw** component in the assembly. The final placement of the component in the assembly is shown in Figure 16–30.

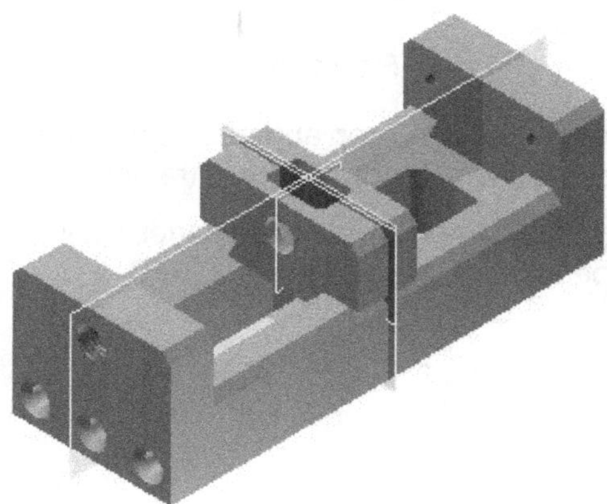

Figure 16–30

When assembling components in this practice, it is important to read the instructions and review the images as you are selecting references during constraint creation. If you receive a Place/Edit Constraint error, it may be because of either reference selection or that an incorrect *Solution* option was selected.

1. In the *Component* panel, click (Place).
2. Select **MovingJaw.ipt** in the *Place Component* dialog box and click **Open**.
3. Right-click on the model and select **Rotate X 90**. Right-click and select **Rotate X 90** again to rotate the component into a more convenient orientation for constraining, as shown in Figure 16–31.
4. Position the **MovingJaw.ipt** component as shown in Figure 16–31 and click the left mouse button to place it.
5. Right-click and select **OK** to place a single instance of the component in the assembly.
6. Select the *View* tab. In the *Visibility* panel, click (Degrees of Freedom). Note that there are six degrees of freedom for **MovingJaw.ipt**, as indicated by the symbol that displays on the model.

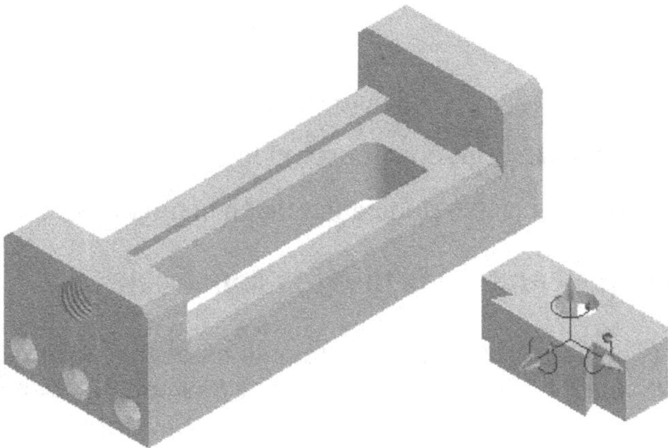

Figure 16–31

7. Note in the Model browser that the icon appears adjacent to the MovingJaw component. This indicates that the component is not fully constrained.
8. Select the *Assemble* tab and in the *Relationships* panel, click (Constrain). The *Place Constraint* dialog box opens.

9. Leave (Mate) selected. Select the face of the **MovingJaw** and the face of the **Body** component, as shown in Figure 16–32. Note how the references remain highlighted once selected.

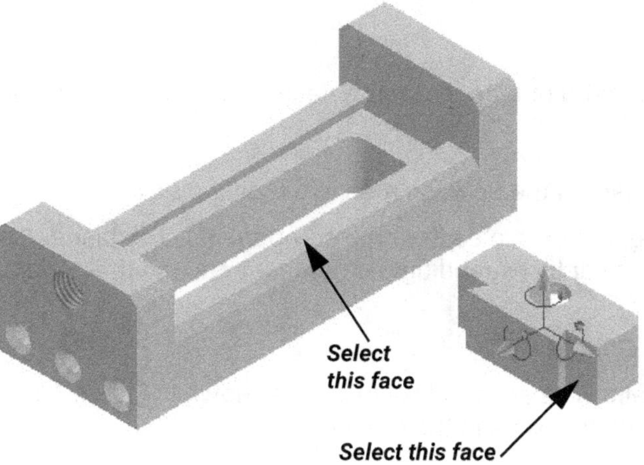

Figure 16–32

Note: *When selecting references, you can select faces through parts by hovering the cursor over the face and selecting it in the Select Other drop-down list.*

10. Click **Apply** to apply the constraint. The assembly displays similar to that shown in Figure 16–33. Once applied, the references are no longer highlighted. Note that the component can still rotate and translate.

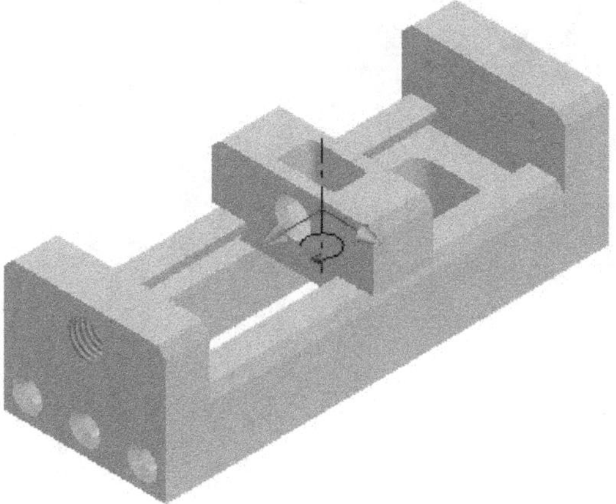

Figure 16–33

Task 3: Apply a second constraint.

The second constraint flushes the XZ origin planes of the two components with a zero offset. Where possible, assembling to origin features is preferable as these features are never deleted or modified.

1. The (Mate) constraint type remains selected by default in the *Place Constraint* dialog box.
2. Click (Flush) in the *Solution* area in the dialog box.
3. Select the XZ origin planes in each of the components. The planes can be selected in the model (if displayed) or by expanding the components and their origin nodes in the Model browser.
4. Enter **0.00** in the *Offset* field.
5. Apply the constraint. The assembly displays as shown in Figure 16–34. Note that one degree of freedom still exists in the model.

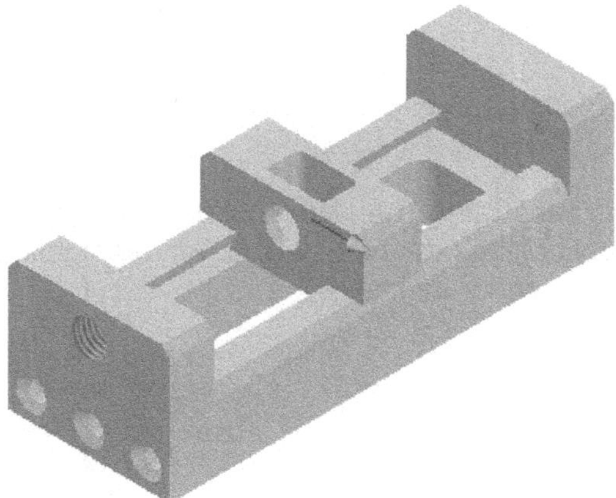

Figure 16–34

Task 4: Apply a third constraint.

The third constraint flushes the YZ origin planes of the two components with a zero offset.

1. Select the YZ origin plane from **Body** and **MovingJaw** ((Mate) and (Flush) are still active) to constrain the final degree of freedom.
2. Enter **0.00** in the *Offset* field.
3. Apply the constraint. The assembly displays as shown in Figure 16–35. Note that the degrees of freedom are completely removed and the icon displays adjacent to the component name in the Model browser, which means that **MovingJaw.ipt** is fully constrained.

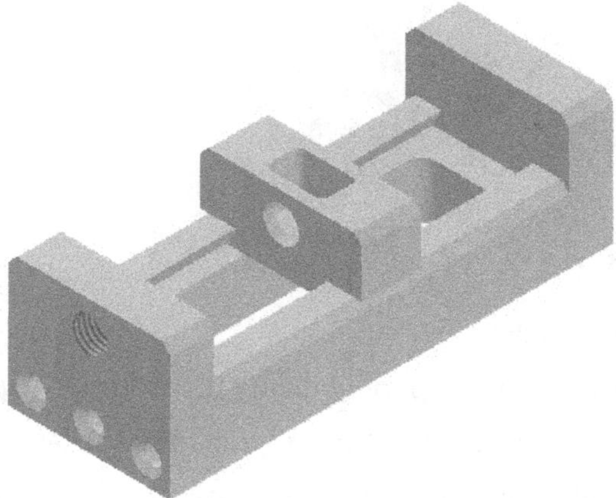

Figure 16–35

4. Click **Cancel** to close the *Place Constraint* dialog box.
5. Expand the two component's nodes in the Model browser and note that the constraints are listed. Expand the **Relationships** node at the top of the Model browser and note that the constraints are also listed in this node.

   Note: *Constraints are only listed in the component nodes if the Model browser's Assembly tab is active. The* ***Relationships*** *node is available if either the Assembly or Modeling tab is active.*

Task 5: Add and constrain the spindle part.

In this task, you will add and constrain **Spindle.ipt** into the assembly. The final placement of the **Spindle** part in the assembly is shown in Figure 16–36.

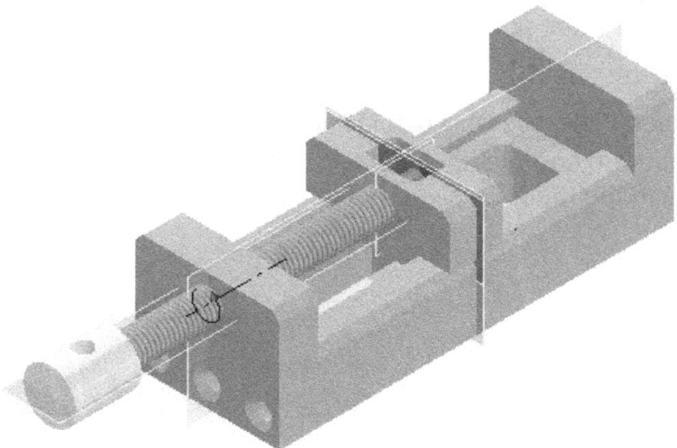

Figure 16–36

1. In the *Component* panel, click (Place).
2. Select **Spindle.ipt** in the *Place Component* dialog box and click **Open**.
3. Position **Spindle.ipt** as shown in Figure 16–37 and click the left mouse button to place it.
4. Right-click and select **OK** to assemble a single instance of the component in the assembly.
5. Toggle on the display of the origin planes shown in Figure 16–37.

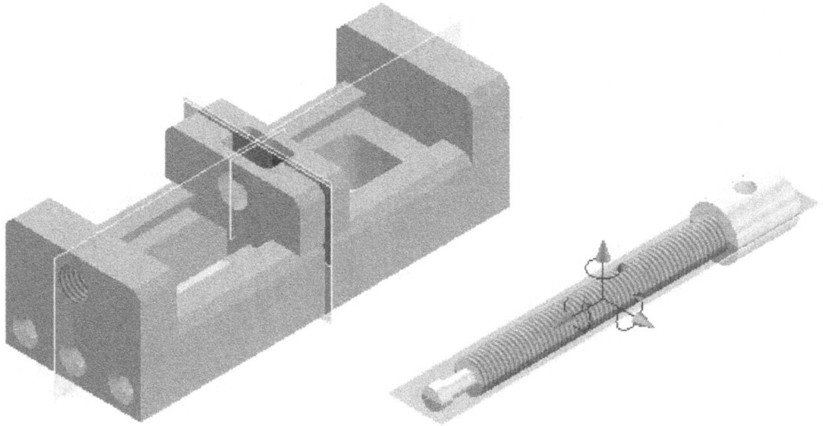

Figure 16–37

6. In the *Relationships* panel, click (Constrain). The *Place Constraint* dialog box opens.

7. Click (Insert) in the *Place Constraint* dialog box.
8. Ensure that (Opposed) is selected in the *Solution* area in the dialog box.
9. Hover the cursor over the hole in the **MovingJaw**, as shown in Figure 16–38. When the edge of the hole and the axis highlight, click to select the edge.

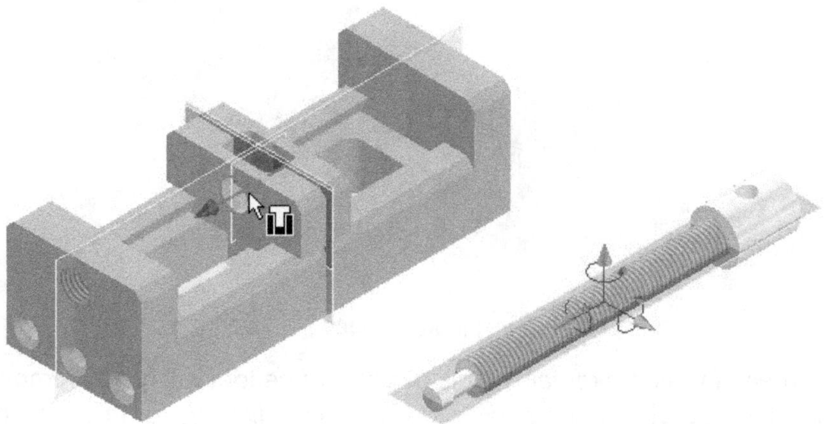

Figure 16–38

10. Hover the cursor over the area shown in Figure 16–39. When the edge and axis highlight, click to select the edge. An Insert constraint is applied between the two highlighted axes.

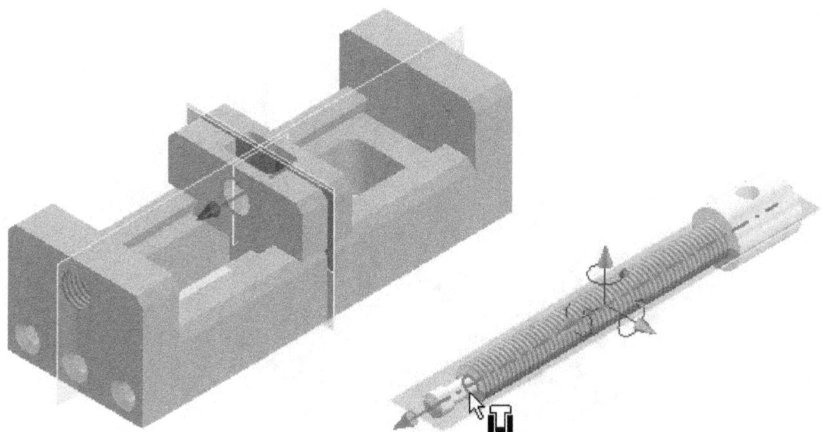

Figure 16–39

Note: *Activating the* ***Free Rotate*** *command to rotate a component independent of another in the assembly cancels the current command. To spin during component placement, use the global* ***Orbit*** *command to rotate the entire assembly.*

11. Click **OK** to apply the constraint and close the dialog box. The assembly displays similar to that shown in Figure 16–40.

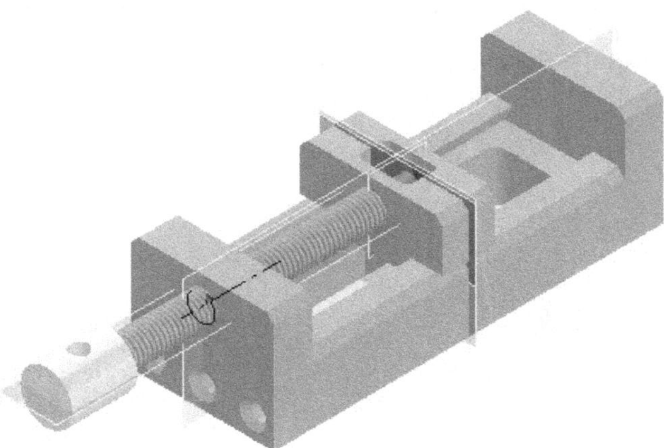

Figure 16–40

A rotational degree of freedom remains. This degree of freedom will not be removed, and the spindle will be allowed to rotate about its axis. The [◦] icon displays for this component in the Model browser, indicating it is unconstrained.

Task 6: Add and constrain the pin part.

In this task, you will add and constrain **Pin.ipt** into the assembly. Its final placement is shown in Figure 16–41.

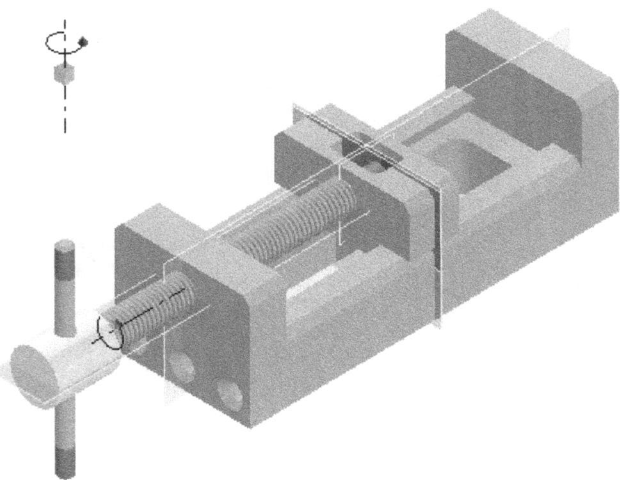

Figure 16–41

1. Place one instance of **Pin.ipt** into the assembly, as shown in Figure 16–42.

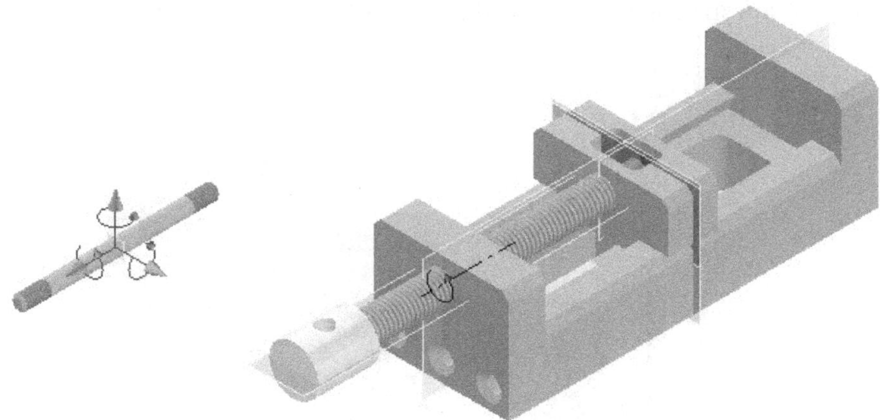

Figure 16–42

2. In the *Relationships* panel, click (Constrain).
3. In the *Place Constraint* dialog box, ensure that (Mate) is selected.
4. Select the axis of the pin and spindle, as shown in Figure 16–43. In the *Solution* area, also ensure that (Undirected) is selected.

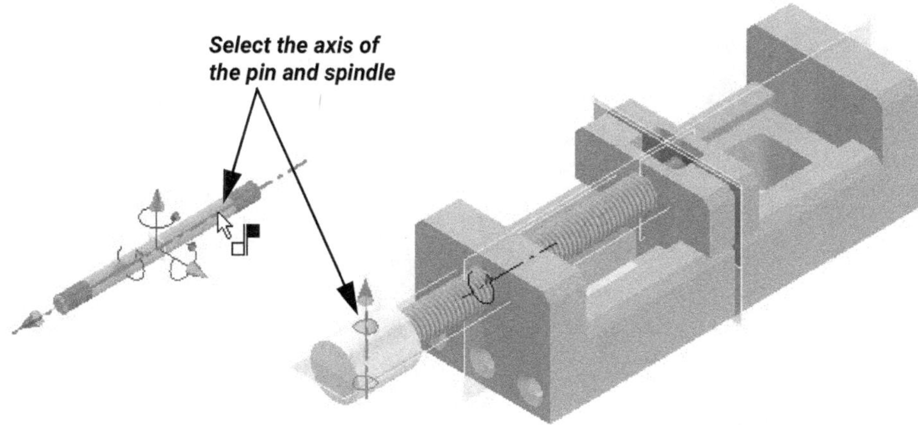

Figure 16–43

5. Click **Apply** to apply the constraint.

6. Select (Mate) and (Flush) in the *Place Constraint* dialog box and select the XZ origin plane of the spindle and the XY origin plane of the pin, as shown in Figure 16–44.

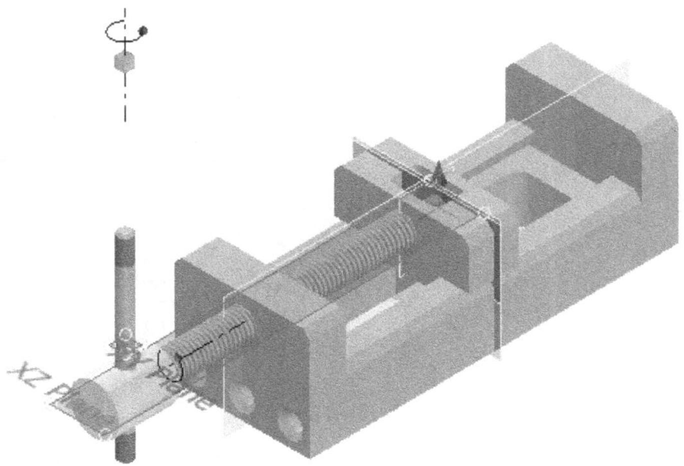

Figure 16–44

7. Click **Apply** to apply the constraint.
8. A rotational degree of freedom remains. This degree of freedom will not be removed, and the pin will be allowed to rotate about its axis. Click **Cancel** to close the *Place Constraint* dialog box.

Task 7: Assemble a cap nut from the Content Center.

1. In the *Component* panel, expand the *Place* drop-down list and click (Place from Content Center). The *Place from Content Center* dialog box opens, as shown in Figure 16–45.

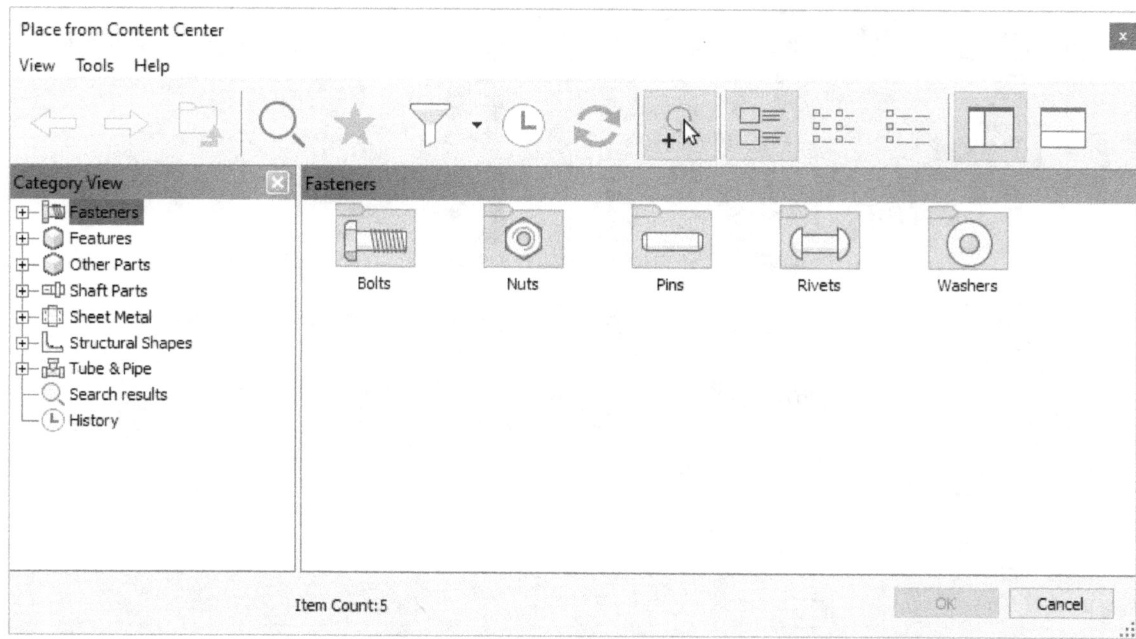

Figure 16–45

Note: The Welcome dialog box might open if your system has not previously logged into the Content Center. If required, click ***Log In****, select the* ***Content Center library read only user*** *option, and click* ***OK****.*

2. Toggle on (Table View) to display the *Table View* panel, if it is not already displayed.
3. Verify that (Autodrop) is toggled on.
4. In the *Category View* panel, click **Fasteners**.
5. In the *List View* panel, double-click on **Nuts** and then double-click on **Cap Nuts**.

6. Select **DIN 917**. The dialog box displays as shown in Figure 16–46. You may have to adjust the size of the window to see the table.

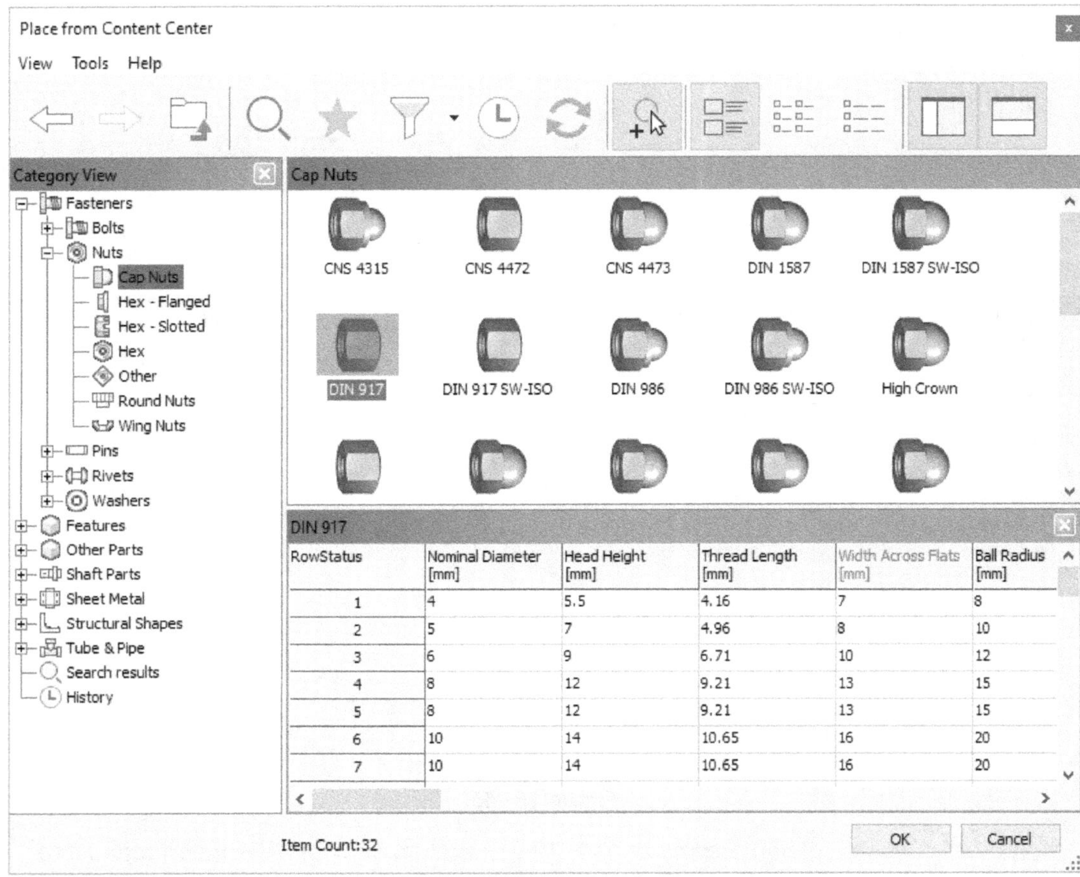

RowStatus	Nominal Diameter [mm]	Head Height [mm]	Thread Length [mm]	Width Across Flats [mm]	Ball Radius [mm]
1	4	5.5	4.16	7	8
2	5	7	4.96	8	10
3	6	9	6.71	10	12
4	8	12	9.21	13	15
5	8	12	9.21	13	15
6	10	14	10.65	16	20
7	10	14	10.65	16	20

Figure 16–46

7. The diameter of the pin is 6mm. Verify that there is a cap nut with a diameter of 6mm by reviewing the *Table View* panel.

8. A nut with the required dimensions does exist in Row 3. To insert the nut, double-click on **DIN 917** in the *List View* panel. Do not left-click yet; hover the cursor over the outer surface of the pin. The nut is automatically resized and snapped in position. Click to place the nut using **AutoDrop** when the outer surface of the pin highlights.

9. Move the mouse. Note that the nut can still move along the pin. A second Mate constraint needs to be applied.

10. Select the edge shown in Figure 16–47. The Autodrop toolbar displays.

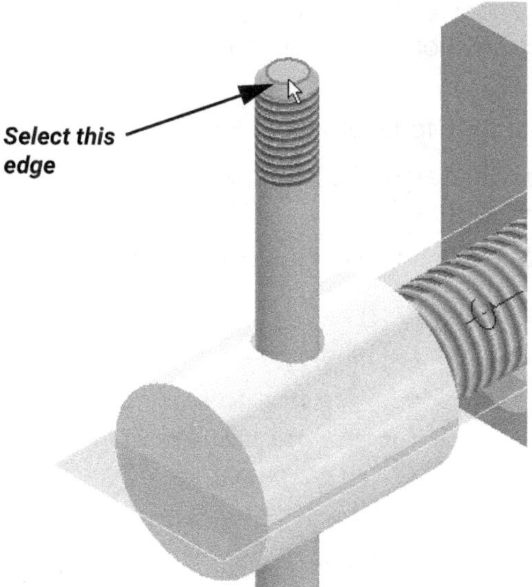

Figure 16–47

Note: *The degree of freedom display has been turned off for the remainder of the images in this practice to improve image quality.*

11. Click (Place) to insert the component and finish the command. The model displays as shown in Figure 16–48. A rotational degree of freedom remains. This degree of freedom will not be removed and the nut can be rotated about its axis.

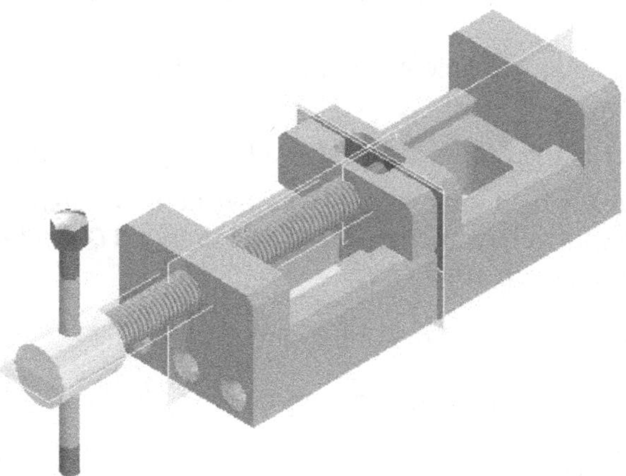

Figure 16–48

Note: *If you had to change the size of the nut, you do not need to place the component. It will be done automatically.*

Task 8: Modify the offset value.

The nut is not in the correct position on the pin. It needs to be offset from the selected pin surface.

1. Expand **DIN 917 M6:1** in the Model browser.
2. Highlight the last Mate constraint. The offset value displays beside it in the Model browser, as shown in Figure 16–49.
3. Change the *Offset* to **-6.5**, as shown in Figure 16–49, and press <Enter>.

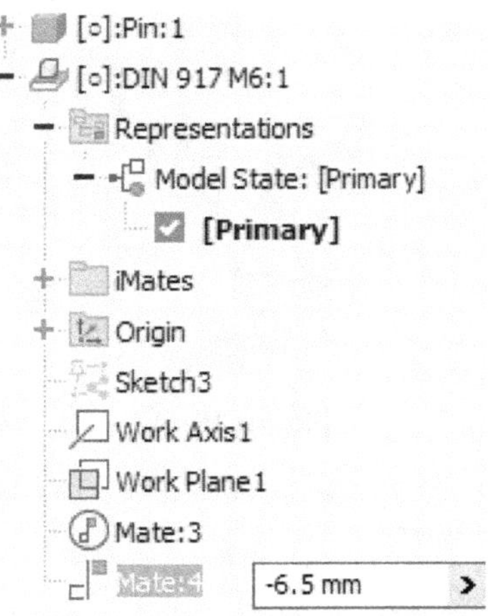

Figure 16–49

Task 9: Assemble an additional instance of the cap nut.

In this task, you will add and assemble a second cap nut by creating a copy of the existing **DIN 917** component.

1. Select **DIN 917 M6:1** in the Model browser, right-click, and select **Copy**.
2. Place the cursor anywhere in the graphics window, right-click, and select **Paste** to create a copy of the nut. Alternatively, you could also have dragged **DIN 917 M6:1** in the Model browser into the model to create a copy.
3. In the *Relationships* panel, click (Constrain).
4. In the *Place Constraint* dialog box that opens, click (Insert).
5. Ensure that (Opposed) is selected in the *Solution* area in the dialog box.

6. Hover the cursor over the hole in the nut, as shown in Figure 16–50. When the edge of the hole and the axis highlights, click to select it.

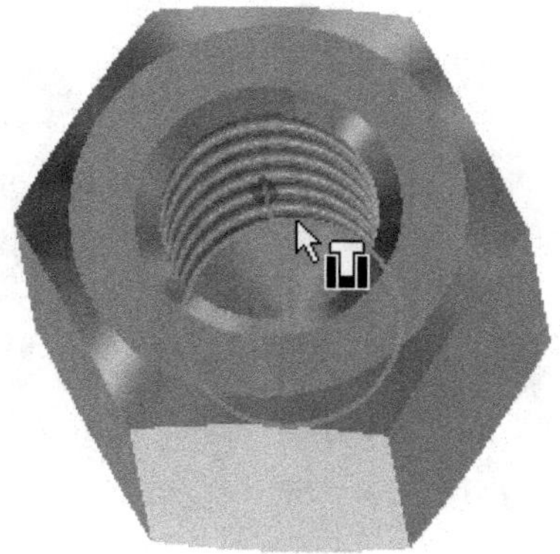

Figure 16–50

7. Hover the cursor over the area shown in Figure 16–51. When the edge and axis highlight, click to select the axis. An Insert constraint is applied between the two highlighted edges.

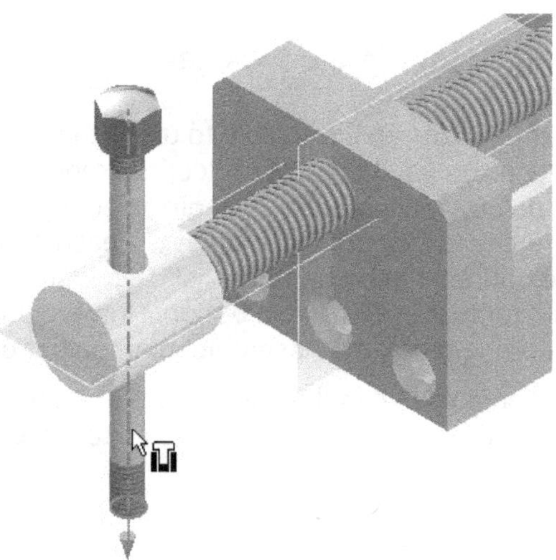

Figure 16–51

8. Apply the constraint and close the *Place Constraint* dialog box. The assembly displays as shown in Figure 16–52.

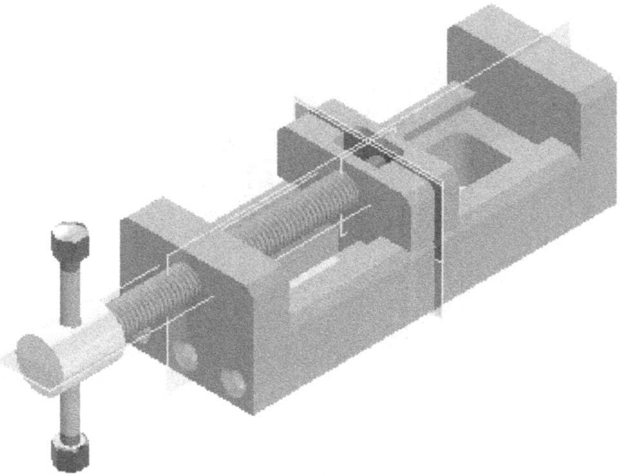

Figure 16–52

Task 10: Assemble and constrain the fixed jaw.

The Assemble mini-toolbar provides an alternative to using the *Place Constraint* dialog box to constrain components. It enables you to quickly select references in components without activating any constraint tool. On placement, you begin selecting references and a constraint is assigned based on the references that are selected. If the assumed constraint is incorrect, you can select the appropriate option in the drop-down list. Depending on the user preference, you can use the Assemble mini-toolbar or **Constrain** option. However, once you become more familiar with assembling components, the Assemble mini-toolbar can be more efficient.

1. Place one instance of **FixedJaw.ipt** in the assembly. Rotate the model as shown in Figure 16–53. A second component remains attached to the cursor. Do not right-click and select **OK**.

2. Only the newly placed component is active for reference selection. Hover the cursor over the first circular edge reference, shown on **FixedJaw.ipt** in Figure 16–53, and select it.The Assemble mini-toolbar opens immediately. Select the second circular edge reference on the **Body.ipt** component, as shown in Figure 16–53. The (Insert - Opposed) constraint is assumed and displays in the Assemble mini-toolbar.

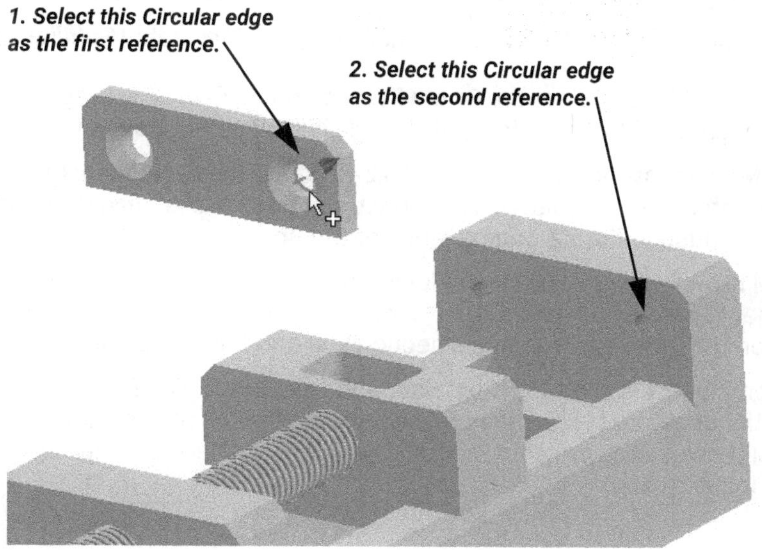

Figure 16–53

3. Click to apply the constraint.
4. Select the equivalent edges on the **FixedJaw** and **Body** parts for the left-hand hole.
5. Click to apply the constraint.
6. Click to apply the constraint and close the Assemble mini-toolbar.
7. The component is now fully located in the assembly. Because the constraints were assigned immediately on component placement, you can continue to place a second instance of **FixedJaw.ipt**. Right-click and select **OK** to end component placement. Activating and using the Assemble mini-toolbar in this way is excellent if repeating the assembly of the same component multiple times or to quickly constrain components without having to interact with the assembly commands in the ribbon.

Task 11: Modify the constraint references.

In this task, you will modify the constraint references between the **MovingJaw** and the **Body** components. The **MovingJaw** will be able to move along the **Body**. In this task, you will modify the references so that a zero offset will place the **MovingJaw** against the front wall of the **Body** component. Entering positive offset values will simulate its motion in the Y-direction.

1. To hide all of the visible work planes if displayed, in the *View* tab>*Visibility* panel, expand (Object Visibility) and clear the **Origin Planes** option. Click (Degrees of Freedom) to remove the degrees of freedom from display. This is done for clarity.
2. Expand the **MovingJaw** branch in the Model browser and select **Flush:1** to verify that this is the constraint that is to be edited. (Your constraint might be labeled differently. Locate the constraint that flushed the XZ origin planes of the **Body** and the **MovingJaw**.)
3. In the Model browser, double-click on **Flush:1** to open the *Edit Dimension* field. To display the components (as shown in Figure 16–54), set the *offset* value to **20** and press <Enter>. Depending on the order of reference selection you might need to enter **-20**.
4. Right-click on **Flush:1** in the Model browser and select **Edit**. The *Edit Constraint* dialog box opens with the constraint references highlighted on the model, as shown in Figure 16–54. The constraint selections are color-coded to indicate the selection numbers that correspond in the model.

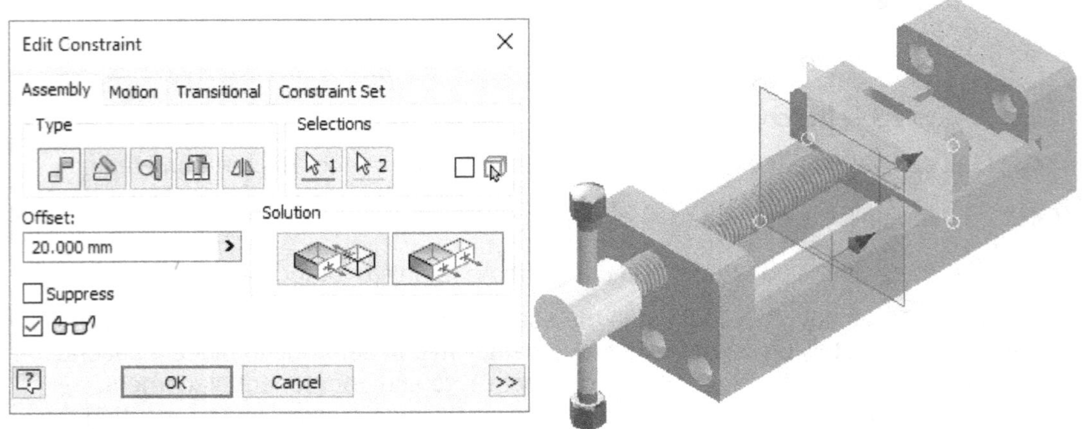

Figure 16–54

5. In the *Solution* area, click (Mate).
6. In the *Selections* area, click both the and the buttons to clear the two reference selections that were previously made for this constraint.

7. Select the [1] button and select the face on the **MovingJaw**, as shown in Figure 16–55.
8. Select the [2] button and select the face on the base as shown in Figure 16–55 to assign the second reference.

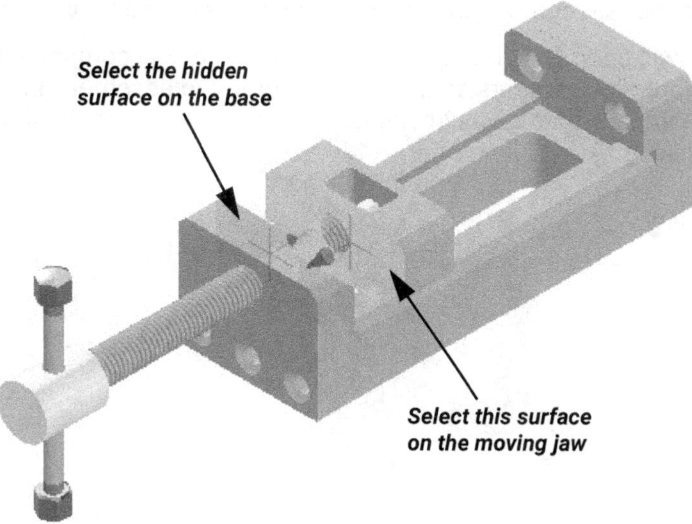

Figure 16–55

9. Click **OK**.
10. Modify the offset value of the new Mate constraint to view the motion of the **MovingJaw** along the **Body**.
11. Save the assembly. Enter **Vise** as the filename.
12. Close the window.

End of practice

Practice 16b
Assembly Basics II (Place and Insert)

Practice Objectives

- Place and fully constrain components in an assembly using the **Place and Insert** command.

In this practice, you will open an existing assembly and place new components, as shown in Figure 16–56. This practice presents an alternative method to assembly and constrain components, like fasteners, that have circular edges using one command that allows for both placing and constraining.

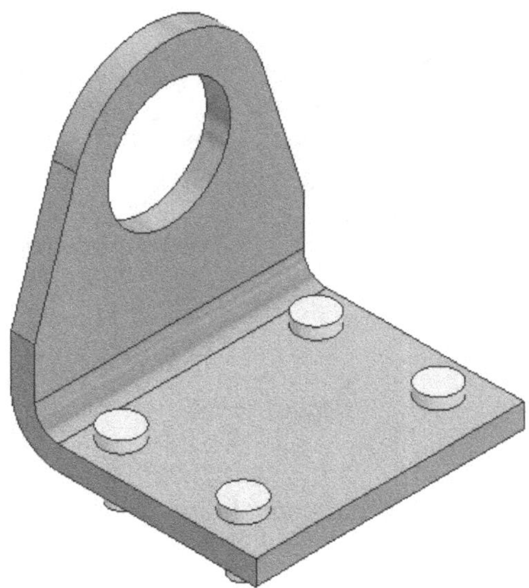

Figure 16–56

Task 1: Place and insert a component on a selected edge.

1. Open **Insert.iam**.
2. In the *Assemble* tab>*Component* panel, expand the **Place** option and select **Place and Insert**. The *Properties* and *Tool* panels open.
3. In the *Component* area of the panel, select .
4. In the *Place Component* dialog box, locate and select **fastener.ipt** and click **Open**.

5. Place the component in the graphics window using the left mouse button. The *Properties* panel and components display as shown in Figure 16–57.

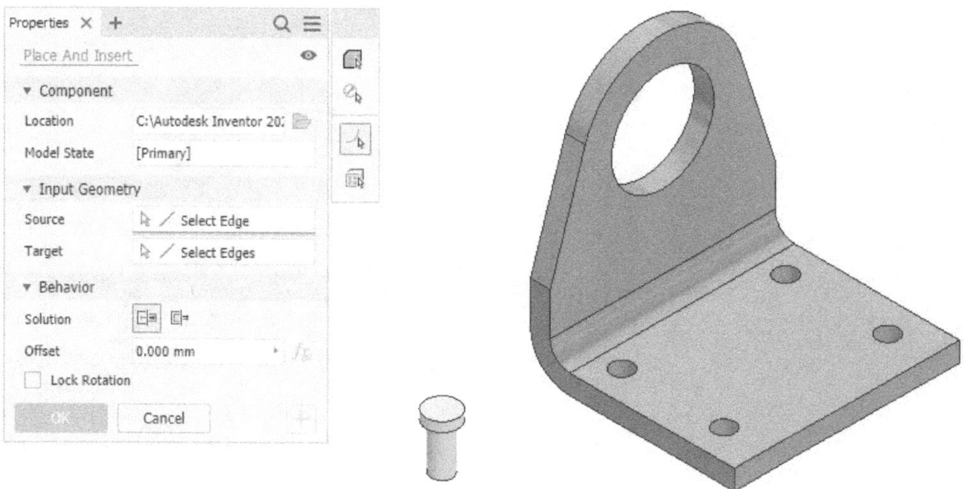

Figure 16–57

6. In the *Tools* panel (right-side of the *Properties* panel), select (Select target edges), if not already active.
7. By default, the *Source* field should be active. If not, select it. In the graphics window, select the hidden circular edge on the fastener component (as shown in Figure 16–58) as the *Source* reference.
8. The *Target* field should activate automatically. Select the circular edge on the mount component, as shown in Figure 16–58, as the *Target* reference to place the component.

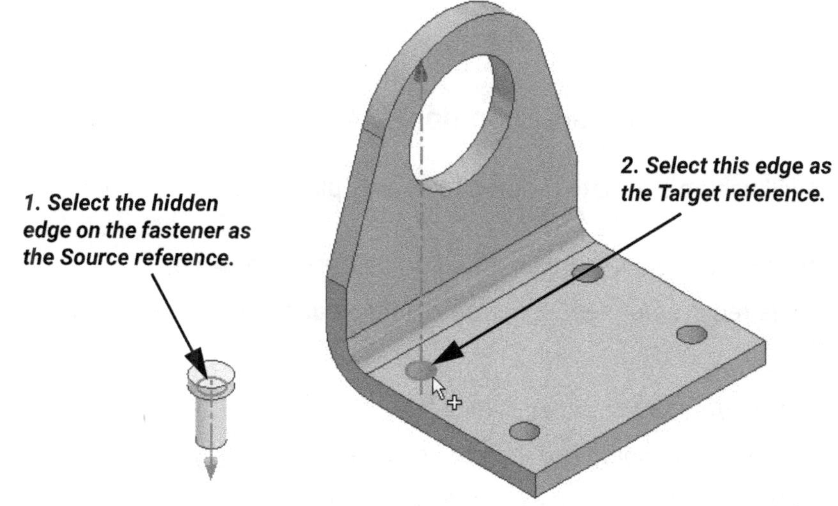

Figure 16–58

9. Ensure that the *Solution* option is set to (Opposed) so that the component is assembled as shown in Figure 16–59.

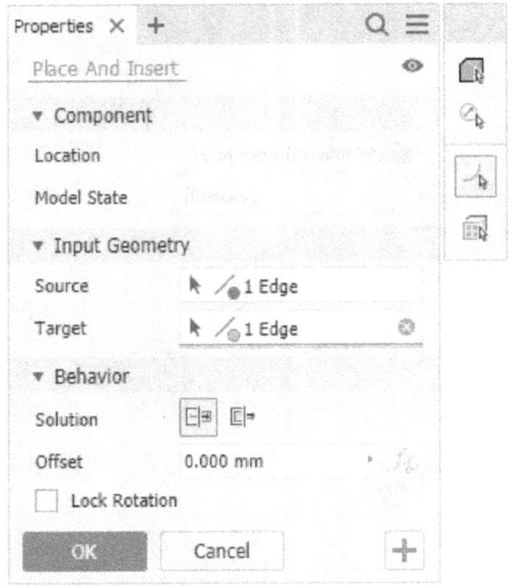

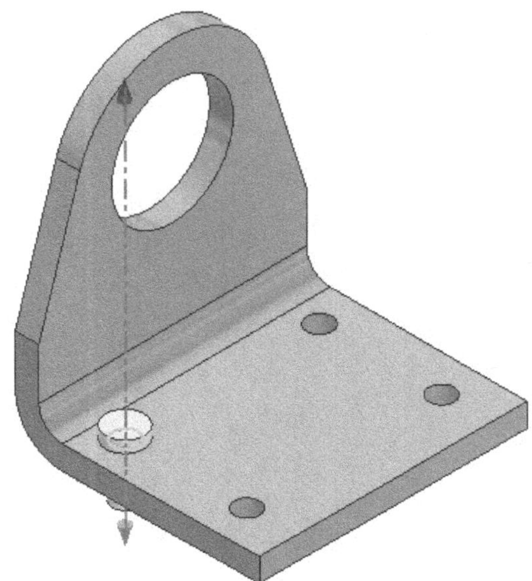

Figure 16–59

10. Select the **Lock Rotation** checkbox to fully constrain the component.
11. Select **OK** in the *Properties* panel to place the component and close it.
12. Notice that the fastener is added to the Model Browser and is fully constrained ([•]).

Note: To continue to place the four remaining fasteners, you could click , select the component again and reassign the references.

Task 2: Place and insert multiple components on a selected face.

In this task, you will use an alternate method to quickly place the four components at the same time.

1. In the Model Browser, select *fastener:1* and press the **<Delete>** key.
2. In the *Assemble* tab>*Component* panel, select **Place and Insert**. The *Properties* and *Tool* panels open.
3. In the *Component* area of the panel, select .
4. In the *Place Component* dialog box, locate and select **fastener.ipt** and click **Open**.
5. Place the component in the graphics window using the left mouse button.

6. In the *Tools* panel, select (Select Target Planar Faces with Edges).
7. By default, the *Source* field should be active. If not, select it. In the graphics window, select the hidden circular edge on the fastener component (as shown in Figure 16–60) as the *Source* reference.
8. The *Target* field should activate automatically. Select the surface that contains the fours holes on the mount component, as shown in Figure 16–60, as the *Target* reference to place the component.

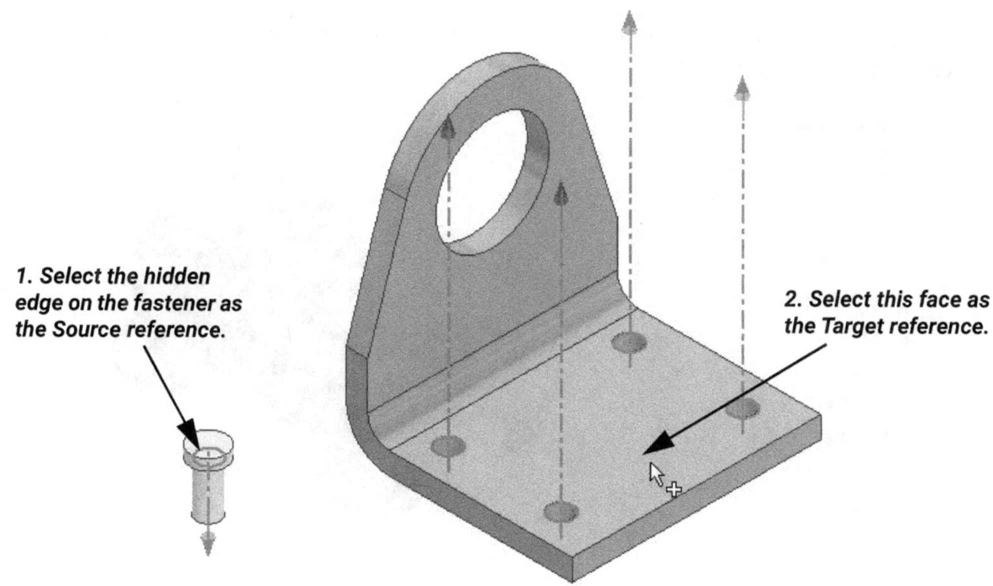

Figure 16–60

9. Ensure that the *Solution* option is still set to (Opposed) and that **Lock Rotation** is selected to remove the rotational degree of freedom.
10. Click **OK**. Four fully constrained fasteners are added to the assembly.

    Note: *To make changes to the Insert constraint assigned to each component, right-click on the* ***Insert*** *constraint listed under the component name and select* ***Edit****. You are unable to re-access the Properties panel to make changes.*

11. Save the assembly.
12. Close the window.

End of practice

Chapter Review Questions

1. You cannot assemble components so that two parts occupy the same space at the same time.
   a. True
   b. False

2. In the Model browser shown in Figure 16–61, what does the pushpin icon next to the **Base_vise** part indicate?

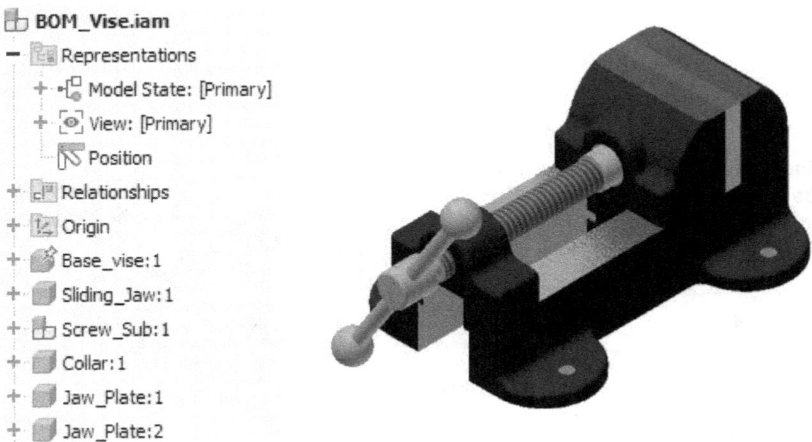

Figure 16–61

   a. The component requires additional constraints.
   b. The component is adaptive (size adjusts to fit constraints).
   c. The component was imported in SAT format (not parametric).
   d. The component is grounded (does not move).

3. How many rotational degrees of freedom (R) and translational degrees of freedom (T) does an unconstrained part or subassembly have?
   a. 1 R and 3 T
   b. 3 R and 3 T
   c. 2 R and 2 T
   d. 3 R and 1 T

4. Which area of the *Place Constraint* dialog box circled in Figure 16–62 enables you to assign a constraint between two parallel surfaces as **Flush**?

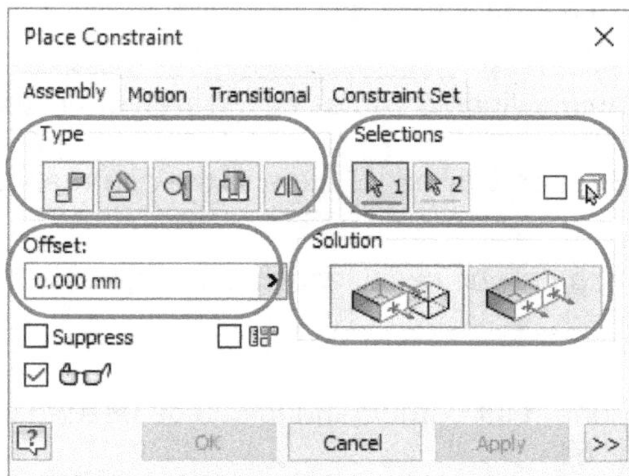

Figure 16–62

a. Type
b. Solution
c. Offset
d. Selections

5. Which of the following constraint types is highlighted in the *Place Constraint* dialog box, as shown in Figure 16–63?

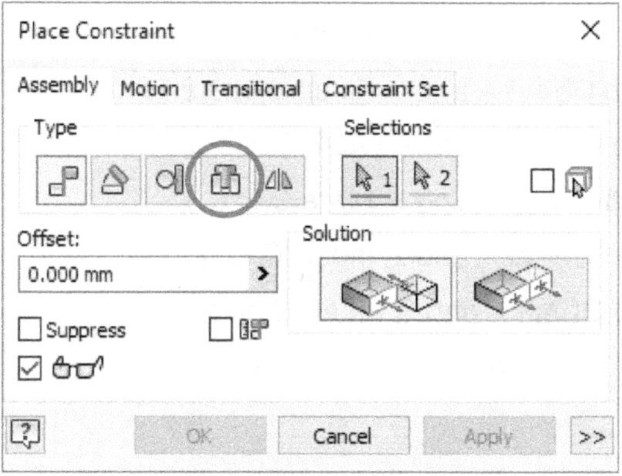

Figure 16–63

a. Pin
b. Flush
c. Insert
d. Mate

6. How would you determine how many degrees of freedom exist on a partially constrained part?
   a. All degrees of freedom are automatically displayed in the model when the *Place Constraint* dialog box is open.
   b. Right-click in the graphics window and select **Degree of Freedom** in the marking menu.
   c. In the *Assemble* tab>*Productivity* panel, expand the commands and click (Degree of Freedom Analysis).
   d. Degrees of freedom can only be reviewed in a sketch, not in an assembly.

7. Which of the following constraint combinations can be used to create the assembly shown on the right in Figure 16–64?

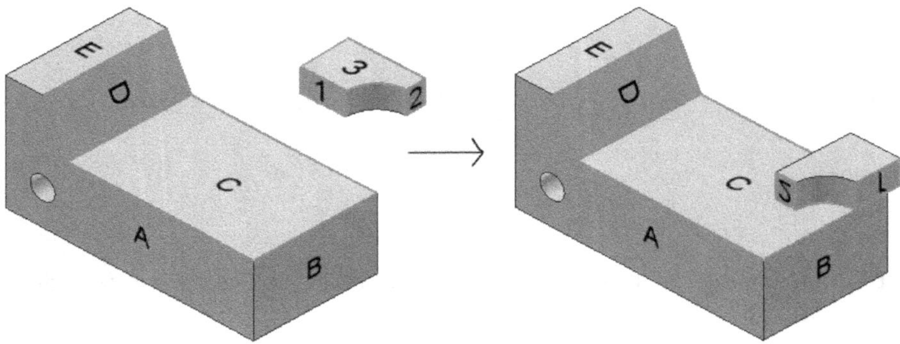

Figure 16–64

   a. Flush 1 and B, Flush Offset A and 2, Flush C and 3
   b. Mate 1 and B, Mate Offset A and 2, Flush C and 3
   c. Flush 1 and B, Flush Offset A and 2, Mate C and 3
   d. Flush 1 and B, Flush Offset A and 2, Insert C and 3
   e. Mate 1 and B, Mate Offset A and 2, Insert C and 3
   f. Mate 1 and B, Mate Offset A and 2, Mate C and 3

8. The pin is constrained in the holes on the part, as shown in Figure 16–65. How would you precisely control the distance between the pin heads and the sides of the part?

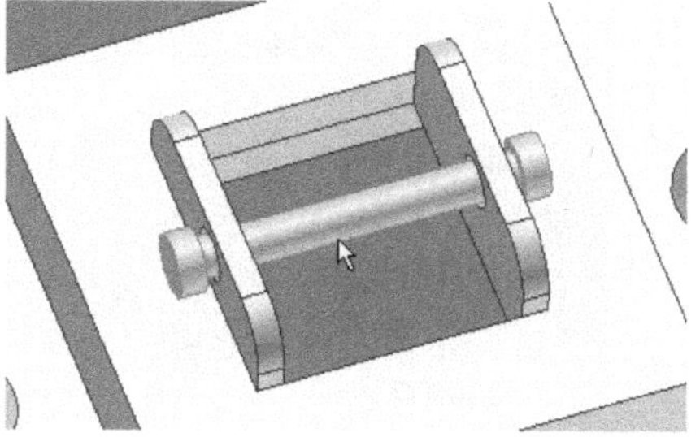

Figure 16–65

   a. Set the offset value for the constraint.
   b. Use **Move Component**.
   c. Use **Tweak Component**.
   d. Apply a model dimension in the assembly.

9. Which of the following statements are true of subassemblies? (Select all that apply.)
   a. They are always grounded in the assembly.
   b. They can contain other subassemblies.
   c. They are always stored as .IAM files.
   d. They act like a single component in the assembly.

10. What happens when you use the **Place** command to place an assembly file?
   a. It becomes a subassembly in the assembly.
   b. The parts of the assembly are placed as individual components at the top level of the assembly.
   c. It becomes a grounded component in the assembly no matter how many components have been assembled before it.
   d. The parts of the assembly are placed but are not enabled.

11. Which constraint type creates a Flush constraint, as shown in Figure 16–66?

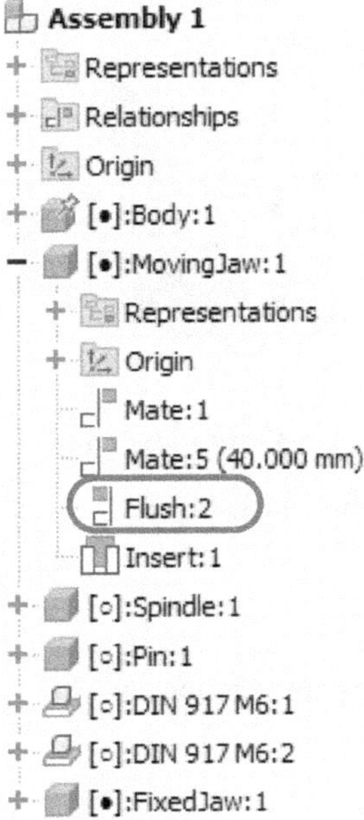

Figure 16–66

a. Insert
b. Tangent
c. Mate
d. Angle

12. What type of entities can be constrained with the Insert constraint?

a. Cylindrical entities
b. Linear entities
c. Flat entities
d. Points

13. When the Model browser's *Assembly* tab is active, which of the following are listed in the Model browser display? (Select all that apply.)
    a. Origin features
    b. Assembly constraints
    c. Assembly features
    d. Part features

14. For the software to automatically set the size of a Content Center model, the **AutoDrop** option must be toggled off.
    a. True
    b. False

Command Summary

Button	Command	Location
	Assemble	• **Ribbon:** *Assemble* tab>*Relationships* panel
	Constrain	• **Ribbon:** *Assemble* tab>*Relationships* panel
	Degrees of Freedom	• **Ribbon:** *View* tab>*Visibility* panel
	Degrees of Freedom Analysis	• **Ribbon:** *Assemble* tab>*Productivity* panel
	Free Move	• **Ribbon:** *Assemble* tab>*Position* panel
	Free Rotate	• **Ribbon:** *Assemble* tab>*Position* panel
	Hide All	• **Ribbon:** *Assemble* tab>*Relationships* panel
	Place	• **Ribbon:** *Assemble* tab>*Component* panel
	**Place from Content Center**	• **Ribbon:** *Assemble* tab>*Component* panel • **File Menu:** Open>Open from Content Center • **Favorites Browser** (*with Part or Assembly open*)
	Show	• **Ribbon:** *Assemble* tab>*Relationships* panel
	Show Sick	• **Ribbon:** *Assemble* tab>*Relationships* panel

Chapter 17

Joint Connections

The use of Joint connections to join components in an assembly is an alternative technique to assigning constraints. Depending on the Joint type selected, the assigned connections remove multiple degrees of freedom at once and enable you to test the movement between components based on the references you select.

Learning Objectives

- Use the **Joint** command to connect components in an assembly while maintaining the defined degree of freedom.
- Edit a joint connection so that the type, its references, or its values can be changed.

17.1 Assembling Components Using Joints

The **Joint** command offers an alternative to using the **Constrain** and **Assemble** commands. Joints enable you to define the allowable movement of a component by selecting a joint connection type. Based on the allowable movement for the selected type, all of the required degrees of freedom are removed at the same time.

Use the following general steps to join components:

1. Launch the **Joint** command.
2. Select a joint type.
3. Select references on the components.
4. Assign a gap value, as required.
5. Assign limits, as required.
6. Complete the joint.
7. Edit the joint, as required.

Step 1 - Launch the Joint command.

To join components using the **Joint** command, in the *Assemble* tab>*Relationships* panel, click (Joint), or press <J>. The *Place Joint* dialog box and the mini-toolbar interface open, as shown in Figure 17–1.

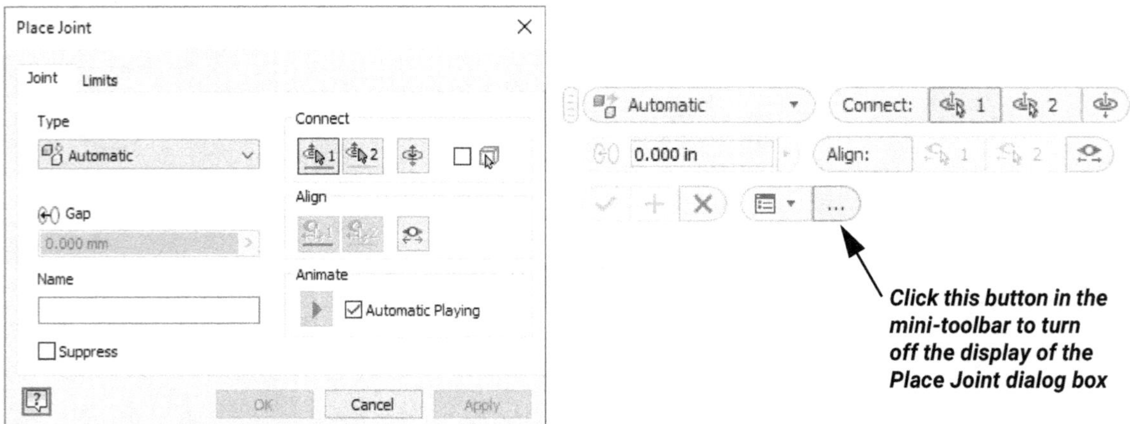

Figure 17–1

The *Place Joint* dialog box contains the same options as the mini-toolbar as well as the following options that can't be accomplished in the mini-toolbar:

- You can toggle the visual animation when components are joined (**Automatic Playing**).
- You can assign a name to a Joint.
- The *Limits* tab enables you to specify a limit on the range of motion for a specific connection.

Step 2 - Select a joint type.

The (Automatic) joint type is used by default. Alternatively, you can manually select a joint type in the drop-down lists, as shown in Figure 17–2.

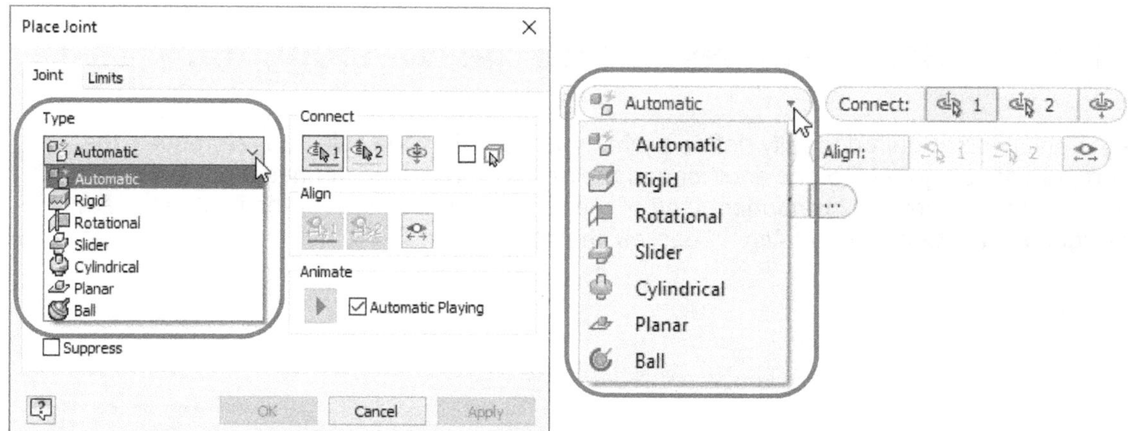

Figure 17–2

Each joint type connection removes various Degrees of Freedom (DOF). The degrees of freedom that remain permit the type of movement indicated by the joint type. The (Automatic) joint type enables the software to assume the joint type based on the selected references. Once assumed, the type can be changed if the software's assumption is incorrect.

The available joint types are as follows:

Joint Type	Icon	Remaining DOF
Rigid		0 Translational, 0 Rotational
Rotational		0 Translational, 1 Rotational
Slider		1 Translational, 0 Rotational
Cylindrical		1 Translational, 1 Rotational
Planar		2 Translational, 1 Rotational
Ball		0 Translational, 3 Rotational

Step 3 - Select references on the components.

References are required to fully define a joint type. Based on the selected references, the components are joined to one another and the selected joint type defines the allowable movement between the components. All of the references required for the joint types are assigned in the *Connect* and *Align* areas, as shown in Figure 17–3.

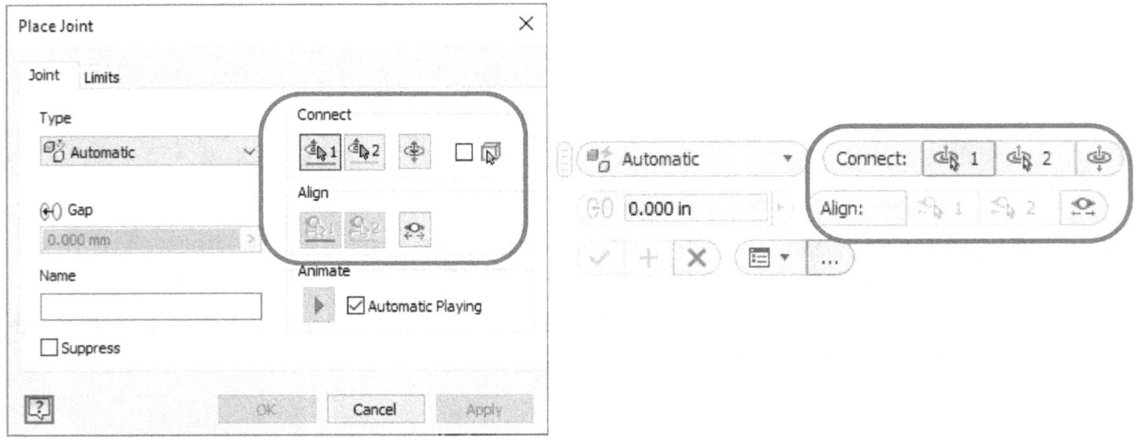

Figure 17–3

By default, once a joint type is selected, the reference selection fields are automatically active.

The first reference selected is assigned to the (*First Origin)* field and the second to the (*Second Origin)* field.

Before selecting a reference, it is important to note the active green dot on the highlighted entity. This point represents the Joint origin and is the point to which the joint is assigned. The location of the cursor on the entity controls which point is active. If the required point is not active, move the cursor closer to the required point to activate it. The entity on which it resides plays a secondary role in defining the orientation or alignment.

> ***Note:*** *When selecting references, you can select faces through parts by hovering the cursor over the face and selecting it in the Select Other drop-down list.*

The selectable entity types are as follows:

Entity Type	Description
Face	For a rectangular face, the active point can be on: • A corner, • The midpoint of an edge (as shown on the right), or • At the center point of the face (as shown on the left). The location of the cursor when selecting defines which point is assigned. 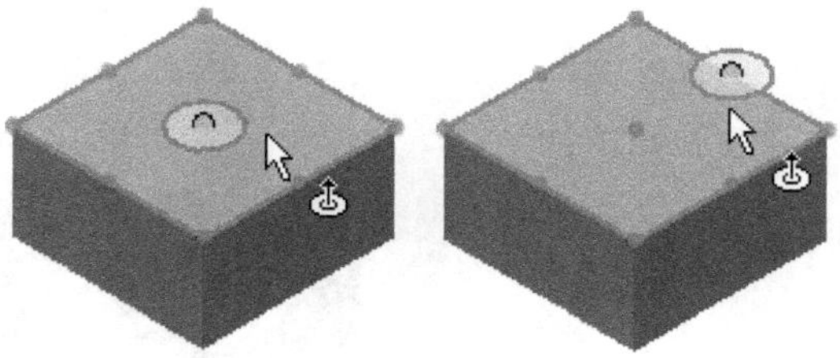
Edge (linear)	For a straight edge, the active point can be: • At either end (as shown on the right), or • At the center point of the edge (as shown on the left). The location of the cursor when selecting defines which point is assigned. 

Entity Type	Description
Edge (circular)	For a circular edge or face, the active point is always at the center of the edge. 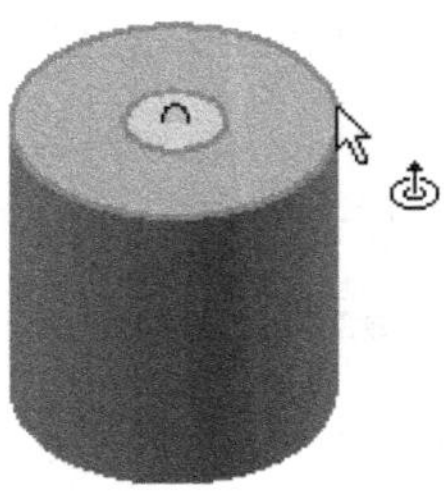
Spherical	For spherical geometry, the active point can be: • At the center of the geometry (as shown on the left), or • At points where geometry intersects with the surface of the sphere (as shown right). The location of the cursor when selecting defines which point is assigned. 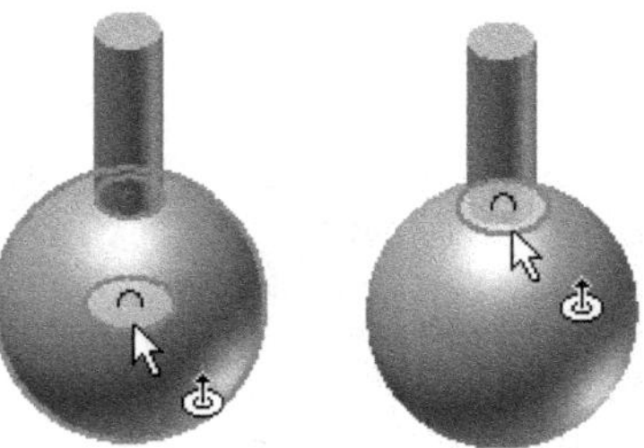

Hint: Working with Joint Origins

A new joint origin can be created by right-clicking and selecting **Between Two Faces**. Once active, select two faces to create the joint origin between them. Alternatively, you can right-click and select **Offset Origin** and then enter offset values to locate a joint origin. These two options are only available as you hover over the reference and right-click, as shown in Figure 17–4. By default, the **Infer Origin** option infers the origin based on the existing geometry.

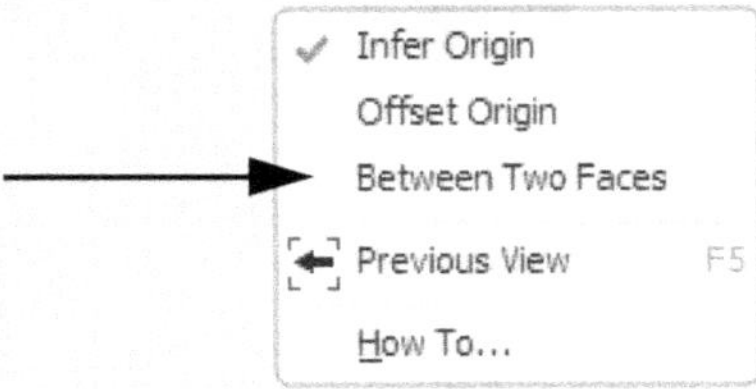

Figure 17–4

- Use (Pick part first) in the *Place Joint* dialog box to isolate a selected component so that you can ensure that the correct references on the isolated component are selected. Alternatively, you can use the **Isolate** option to isolate specific components for constraining. This is valuable when components are close to each other, or when one component obscures another.
- When selecting references, the first component you select is the component that is going to move. If it is a grounded component, you are prompted that a grounded component has been selected to be moved. You can accept this and the component remains grounded, but doing so changes the orientation of the grounded component.

Once the *First Origin* and *Second Origin* references have been defined, the alignment is automatically assumed based on the selected references, and the components automatically move into position. A short animation is played indicating the type of motion that remains between the components.

> ***Note:*** *To toggle off the animation preview when references are selected, clear the* ***Automatic Playing*** *option in the Animate area in the Place Joint dialog box. Click to play the animation at any time.*

If the component is assembled in the wrong direction, consider the following:

- Click (Flip Component) in the *Connect* area to flip the component's orientation.
- Click (Invert Alignment) in the *Align* area to try inverting the alignment.
- In the *Align* area, select (First Alignment) or (Second Alignment) and select new references (e.g., faces, edges, or work geometry), similar to that shown in Figure 17–5.

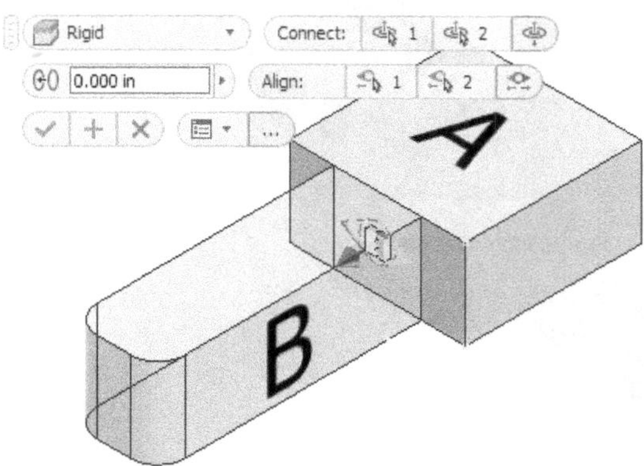

Once the center points on the two faces were selected as references, a Rigid joint was added and the components were automatically aligned

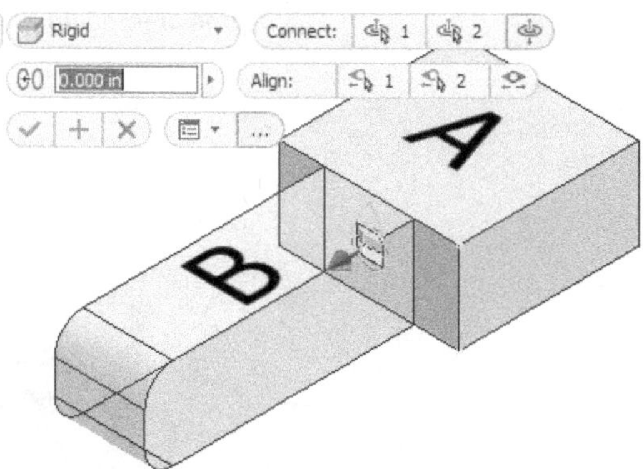

To reorient component B relative to A, the alignment references were edited and both the A and B faces were selected

Figure 17–5

The following examples explain how components were joined using the various joint types.

Rigid

The (Rigid) joint type removes all of the degrees of freedom, eliminating any relative motion between it and its referenced component. Welded or bolted connections are examples of the **Rigid** joint type, similar to that shown in Figure 17–6.

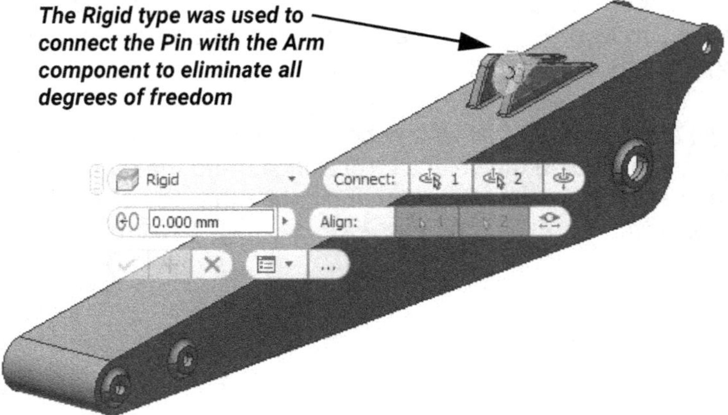

Figure 17–6

Rotational

The (Rotational) joint type allows for rotation about an axis, similar to that shown in Figure 17–7. This joint type removes five degrees of freedom.

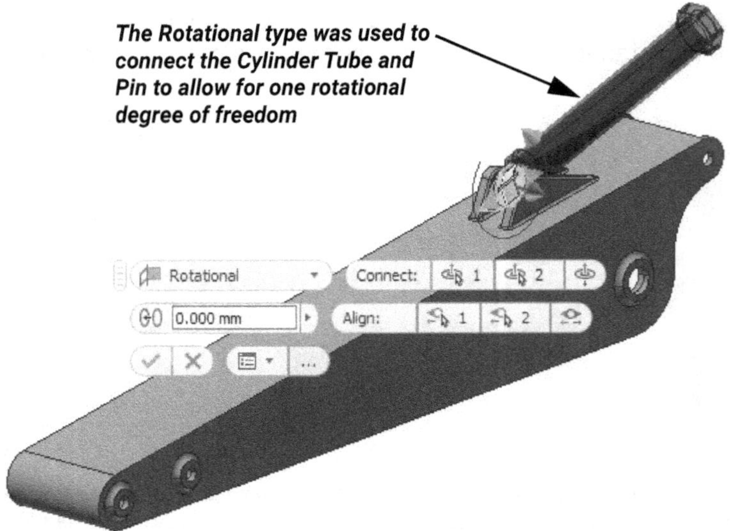

Figure 17–7

Slider

The (Slider) joint type allows for translational movement along an axis, as shown in Figure 17–8. This joint type removes five degrees of freedom.

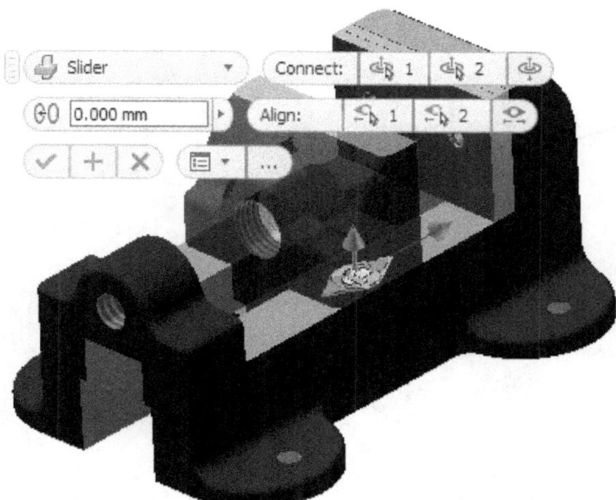

Figure 17–8

Cylindrical

The (Cylindrical) joint type enables a component to translate and rotate about a specific axis leaving two degrees of freedom available, as shown in Figure 17–9.

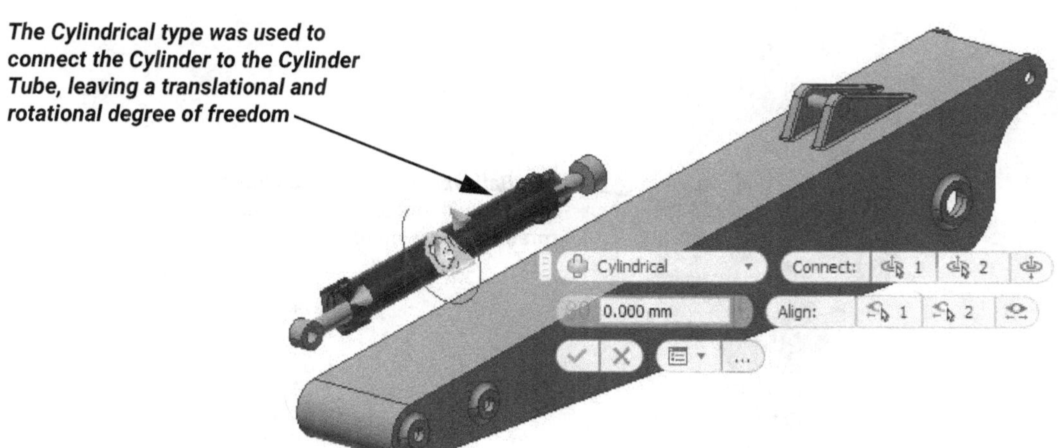

Figure 17–9

Note: *The preview for a new joint type does not maintain previous connections. Once assigned, the relationships between all of the joint connections display.*

Planar

The (Planar) joint type enables a component to move in a plane, as shown in Figure 17–10. Two translational and one rotational degree of freedom remain with the component.

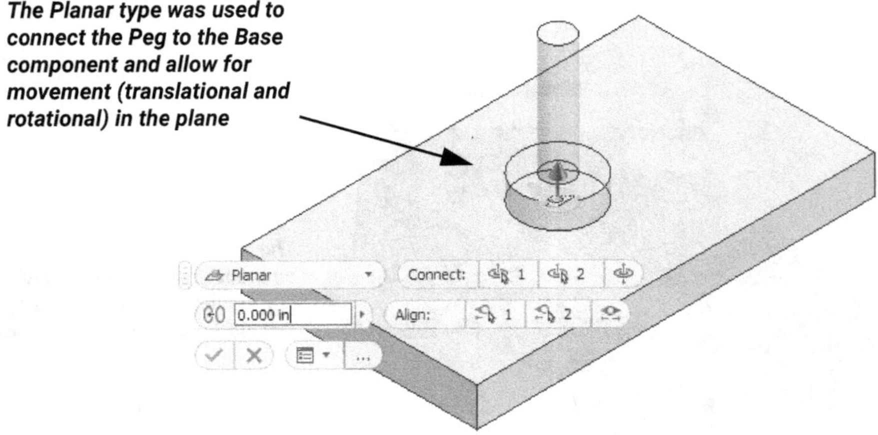

Figure 17–10

Ball

The (Ball) joint type enables a component to rotate in any direction about the origin joint, as shown in Figure 17–11. All translational degrees for freedom are removed.

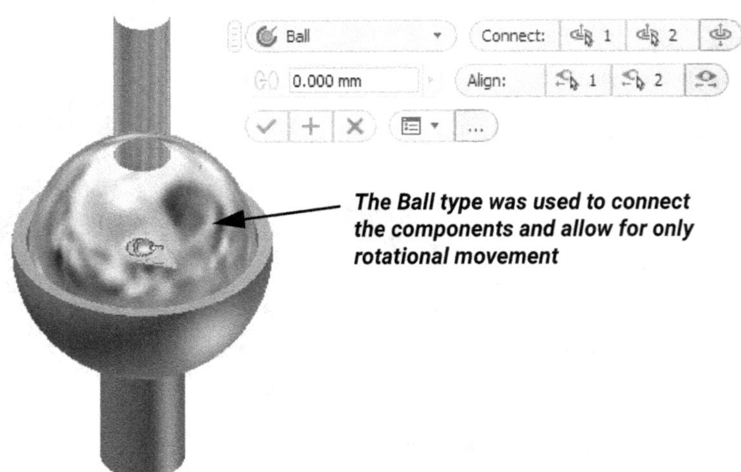

Figure 17–11

Note: *Once a joint has been assigned, you can use (Degrees of Freedom) to graphically display the remaining degrees of freedom to help with visualization.*

Step 4 - Assign a gap value, as required.

You can assign an gap value between selected references in the *Place Joint* dialog box or in the mini-toolbar. Entering a *Gap* value provides you with the flexibility of joining Origins that are at locations other than the end and center points.

Step 5 - Assign limits, as required.

To further control the motion that is permitted by a joint, you can define a specific range of motion. This is done by selecting the *Limits* tab in the *Place Joint* dialog box and entering values in the *Angular* and *Linear* areas, as shown in Figure 17–12. Limits can only be assigned in the *Place Joint* dialog box. You cannot set limits in the mini-toolbar.

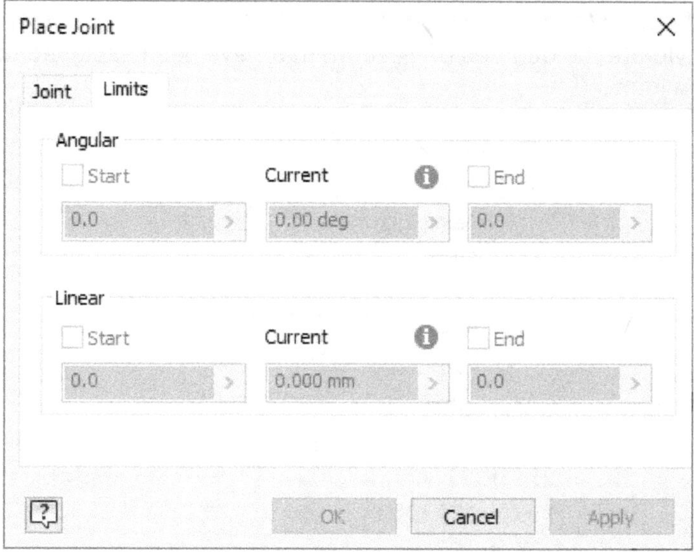

Figure 17–12

> ***Note:*** *Limits cannot be specified for any option that is disabled, because the degree of freedom does not exist in the model.*

To specify a range, select **Start** or **End** and enter values to define a limit on the range of motion. For example, the angular range for a **Rotational** joint type can be controlled and a linear range can be specified for a **Slider** joint type. The *Current* value listed in each area defines the current position of the component in the assembly.

Step 6 - Complete the joint.

Click **OK** in the *Place Joint* dialog box or click in the mini-toolbar to complete the joint. Alternatively, you can right-click in the graphics window and select **OK (Enter)** or press <Enter> to complete the joint.

- The default name for a joint is its type, followed by a number that indicates the number of joints of that type that have been assigned. Double-click on a joint's name in the Model browser to rename it. Alternatively, it can be renamed in the *Name* field of the dialog box.
- Use the **Lock** option (shown in Figure 17–13) to maintain the current position of the component without disabling the degrees of freedom that have been set in the component. A locked component cannot be selected to be moved. However, it updates if the connected components are moved, as opposed to grounding a component, which would lock the component in place regardless of any changes made.
- Use the **Protect** option (shown in Figure 17–13) to enable whether you should be prompted if relationships violate the degrees of freedom that have been assigned to the component with the use of a joint.

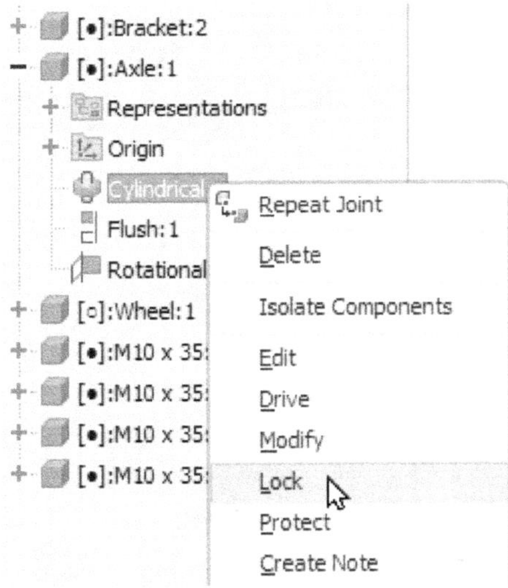

Figure 17–13

Note: *The* ***Lock*** *and* ***Protect*** *options are only available for joints, not for constraints.*

Hint: Combine Joints with Constraints

You can use the **Constrain** or **Assemble** commands to add additional constraints between components to further constrain any open degrees of freedom.

Step 7 - Edit the joint, as required.

Joints are listed in the Model browser under the component(s) to which they have been applied, as well as in the **Relationships** node at the top of the Model browser. Consider the following to edit a joint:

- To modify any value associated with a joint, double-click on the joint's name in the Model browser or right-click and select **Modify**. A mini-toolbar displays that enables you to enter the new values for linear or gap values.
- To change references used for a joint, right-click on the joint name in the Model browser and select **Edit**. The *Edit Joint* dialog box opens and you can change any of original references.
- To delete a joint, right-click the joint name in the Model browser and select **Delete**.
- To review the relationships between components, click (Free Move) and drag a component. The connections are indicated by connecting lines, and glyphs indicate the type of joints that were used, as shown in Figure 17–14.

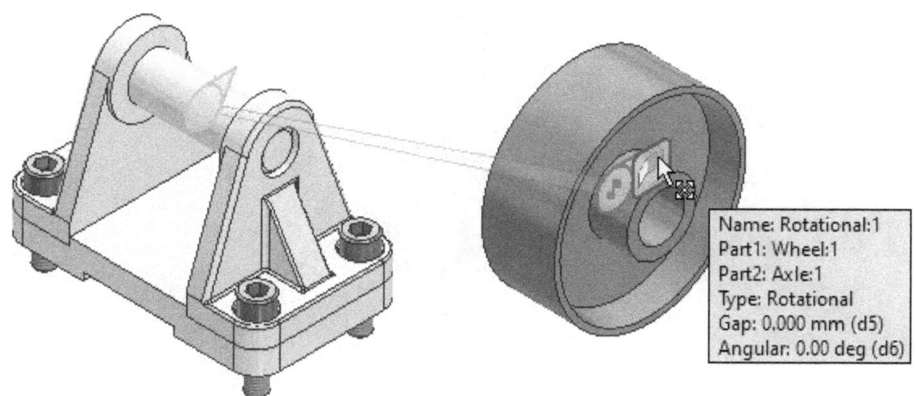

Figure 17–14

- Use (Show) in the *Relationships* panel to display the glyphs for any selected components. Preselecting all of the components and selecting this option displays all of the glyphs. Use (Hide All) to clear them from the display.
- You can right-click on the icons to suppress or delete a joint type. You can also select **Suppress** in the *Place Joint* or *Edit Joint* dialog box to suppress a joint during creation or editing.
- If any of the joints are failing you can use (Show Sick) in the *Relationships* panel to review them. This command is only available if there are sick joints in the assembly. Edit the references as required to resolve the issues or delete the joint.

Practice 17a
Assembly Basics II (Joints)

Practice Objectives

- Use the **Joint** command to fully connect components in an assembly.
- Drag components to verify the movement in the assembly.

In this practice, you will create a new assembly and assemble the components as shown in Figure 17–15. To assemble the components, you will use the **Joint** command, which will connect components relative to one another so that the assembly can easily be tested for movement.

Figure 17–15

Note: *Refer to* ***Appendix E Additional Practices II*** *for additional practice creating joints.*

Task 1: Create a new assembly and assemble the first component.

1. Create a new assembly file using the **Standard (mm).iam** template file.
2. In the *Component* panel, click (Place).
3. Select **Plate.ipt** in the *Place Component* dialog box and click **Open**. The component is added to the assembly.
4. If the component displays in a 2D orientation, return the model to its default Home view using the ViewCube.

5. If the default orientation isn't as shown in Figure 17–16, right-click and select the **Rotate X 90**, **Rotate Y 90**, or **Rotate Z 90** to reorient it as shown. Once reoriented, right-click on the model and select **Place Grounded at Origin** to ground the component. The model displays as shown in Figure 17–16.

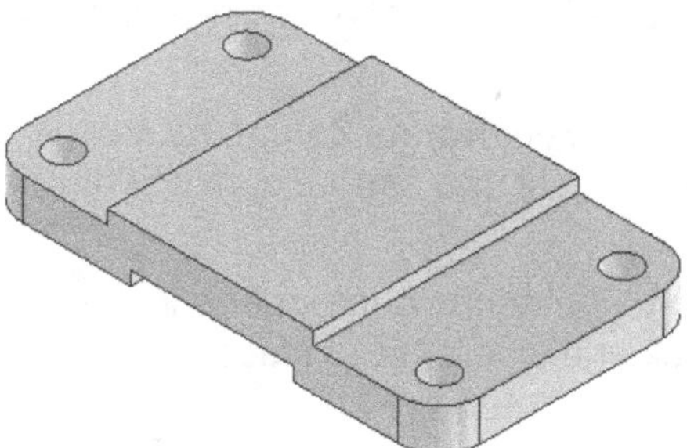

Figure 17–16

*Note: The assembly's visibility style has been set to **Shaded with Edges** for clarity in the images.*

6. Right-click and select **OK** to assemble a single instance of the component into the assembly.

7. Review the Model browser and note the pushpin ( ) symbol next to the **Plate**, as shown in Figure 17–17. This indicates that the component is grounded. The [•] icon indicates that the component is fully constrained. Hover the cursor over the **Plate.ipt** component in the graphics window. The cursor symbol also indicates that it is grounded.

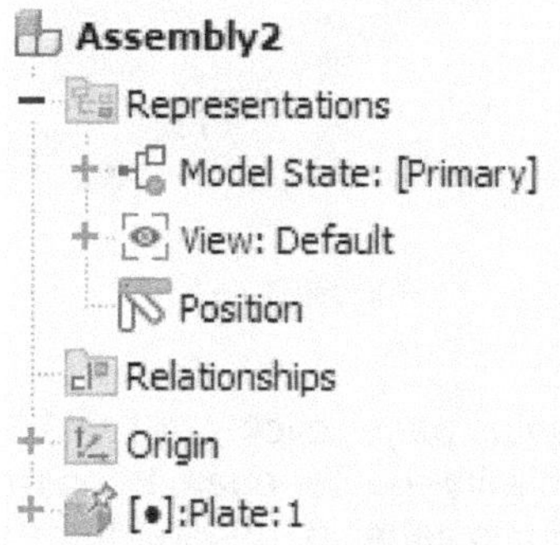

Figure 17–17

Task 2: Assemble the Bracket component.

1. Select the *Assemble* tab, and in the *Component* panel, click (Place).
2. Select **Bracket.ipt** in the *Place Component* dialog box and click **Open**. The component is added to the assembly.
3. Right-click on the model and select **Rotate Z 90** to rotate the component, right-click again and select **Rotate Y 90** to rotate is into a more convenient orientation for reference selection.
4. Use the left mouse button to locate the component next to the **Plate** component, as shown in Figure 17–18. Right-click and select **OK** to place a single instance.

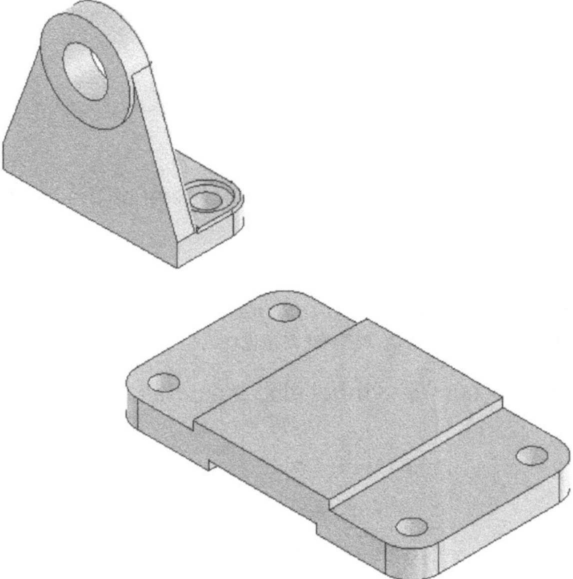

Figure 17–18

5. In the *Assemble* tab>*Relationships* panel, click (Joint). Alternatively, you can press <J>. The *Place Joint* dialog box and mini-toolbar open. If the mini-toolbar is not displayed, enable it in the *View* tab>*Windows* panel in the User Interface list.
6. In the mini-toolbar, click to toggle off the display of the *Place Joint* dialog box. You will use the mini-toolbar to join components.

   Note: *Once the Place Joint dialog box is toggled off, it must be enabled again to open it.*

7. In the *Type* drop-down list in the mini-toolbar, select **Rigid**.

8. Rotate the assembly as shown in Figure 17–19.
9. On the **Bracket** component (first reference), hover the cursor over the edge shown in Figure 17–19. It will display in red with a green dot at the midpoint of the edge. Use the left mouse button to select the reference.
10. On the **Plate** component (second reference), hover the cursor over the edge shown in Figure 17–19. It will display in red with a green dot at the midpoint of the edge. Use the left mouse button to select the reference.

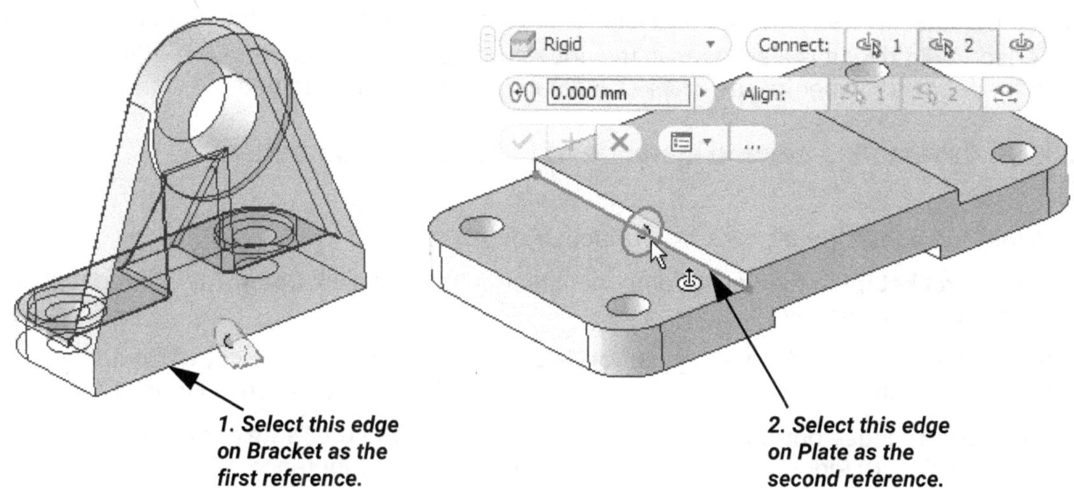

Figure 17–19

Note: Figure 17–19 shows the reference on ***Bracket*** *already selected and the reference on* ***Plate*** *highlighted. The images displaying the reference selection in this practice will be shown in this way for the remainder of the practice. The images may also be reoriented for clarity. You can spin the model, as required, to select the required references.*

The **Bracket** component (reference 1) moves into position and displays animated movement indicating its allowable degrees of freedom. In this case, it is a rigid joint, and because no movement is permitted, the animated movement is very small.

Note that you did not have to activate any of the fields in the mini-toolbar. The first reference field is immediately active and the second is activated once the first reference has been selected. Selecting the reference fields in the *Connect* field is only required when redefining a reference.

11. The components assemble in the wrong orientation. In the *Connect* area in the mini-toolbar, click (Flip component) to flip the component.

12. Note that while the **Bracket** component has been flipped, the alignment must also be inverted to correct the orientation. In the *Align* area in the mini-toolbar, click (Invert alignment) to invert the component.
13. Click (Flip component) again to locate the component, if required.
14. Click in the mini-toolbar to complete the joint.
15. In the Model browser, expand the **Relationships** node and note that the **Rigid** joint has been added. A **Rigid** joint is also listed in the nodes for the two components. The [•] icon is added to the Model browser for the Bracket, indicating it is fully constrained.

Task 3: Assemble a second instance of the Bracket component.

1. In the *Component* panel, click (Place).
2. Select **Bracket.ipt** in the *Place Component* dialog box and click **Open**. The component is added to the assembly.
3. Right-click on the model and select **Rotate Z 90** and **Rotate Y 90** (twice) to rotate the component into a more convenient orientation, similar to that shown in Figure 17–20.
4. Use the left mouse button to locate the component next to the **Plate** component, as shown in Figure 17–20. Right-click and select **OK** to place a single instance.

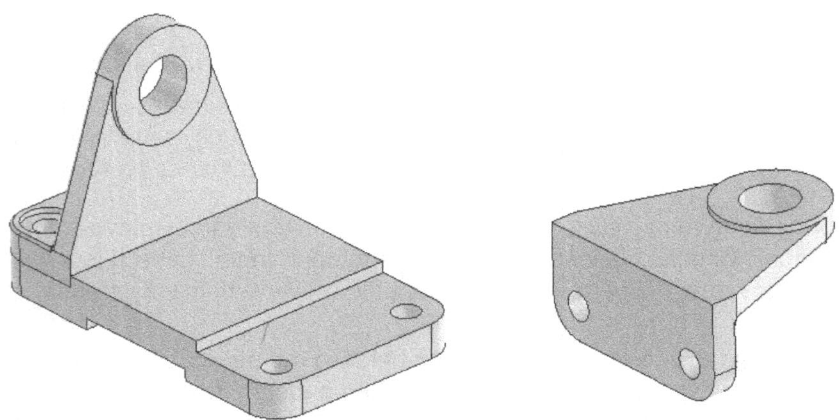

Figure 17–20

5. In the *Assemble* tab>*Relationships* panel, click (Joint), or press <J>.
6. In the *Type* drop-down list in the mini-toolbar, select **Rigid**.

Previously, the two components were joined using reference edges, but for this component, faces will be used. Faces are generally the more stable selection reference.

7. On the **Bracket** component (first reference), hover the cursor over the surface shown in Figure 17–21. It will display in red. Continue to move the cursor so that the green dot displays at the midpoint of the top edge. Use the left mouse button to select the reference.
8. On the **Plate** component (second reference), hover over the face shown in Figure 17–21. It will display in red. Continue to move the cursor so that the green dot displays at the midpoint of the long edge. Use the left mouse button to select the reference.

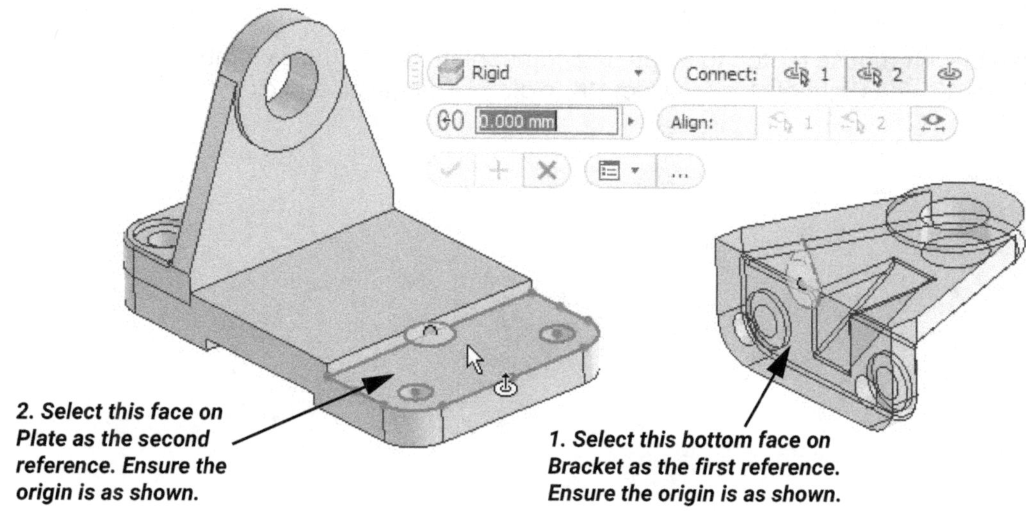

Figure 17–21

9. The **Bracket** component (reference 1) moves into position. If the components assemble in the wrong orientation, use the (Flip component) and (Invert alignment) options to reposition the component, as required.
10. Click in the mini-toolbar to complete the joint.

Task 4: Assemble the Axle component.

1. In the *Component* panel, click (Place).
2. Select **Axle.ipt** in the *Place Component* dialog box and click **Open**. The component is added to the assembly.
3. Use the shortcut menu options to rotate the component into a more convenient orientation.
4. Use the left mouse button to locate the component next to the assembly, as shown in Figure 17–22. Right-click and select **OK** to place a single instance.

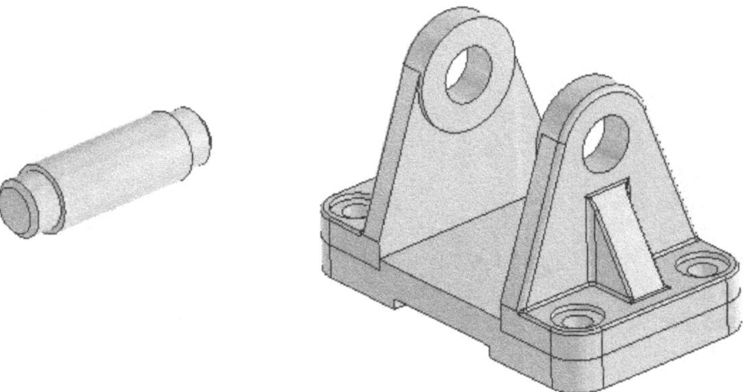

Figure 17–22

5. In the *Assemble* tab>*Relationships* panel, click (Joint).

Ideally, the **Axle** component should join the midpoint of its central axis to a point midway between the two **Bracket** components. Joint references must be selected in a single component. To join the **Axle** you will be required to use both a **Joint** and **Constraint** option.

6. In the *Type* drop-down list in the mini-toolbar, select **Cylindrical**. This type allows for 1 translational and 1 rotational degree of freedom. The translational degree of freedom will be removed in a later step using a Mate constraint.
7. On the **Axle** component (first reference), hover the cursor over the midpoint of the cylindrical surface, shown in Figure 17–23. It will display in red with a green dot at the center point of the central axis. Use the left mouse button to select the reference.
8. On the **Bracket** component (second reference), hover over the edge shown in Figure 17–23. It will display in red with a green dot at the midpoint of the edge. Use the left mouse button to select the reference.

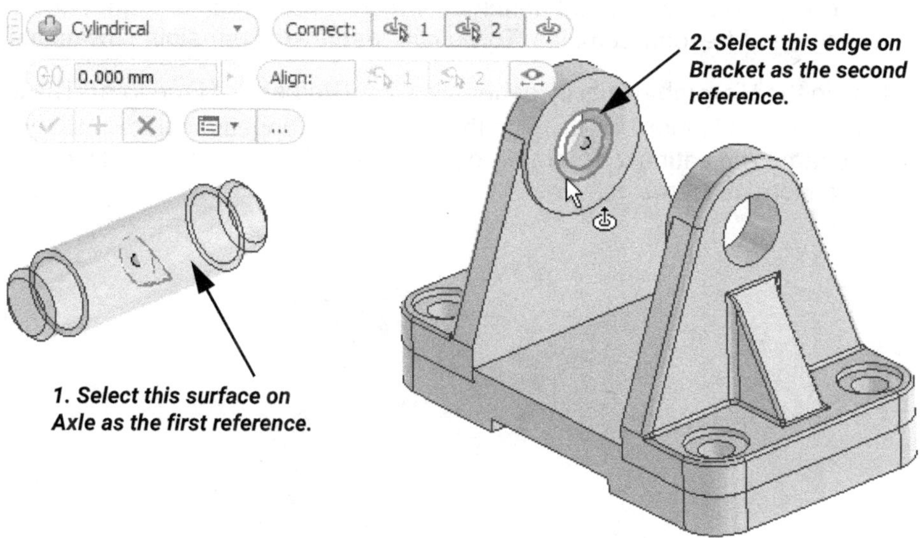

Figure 17–23

9. Click [check icon] in the mini-toolbar to complete the joint. The assembly displays as shown in Figure 17–24.

Figure 17–24

10. Drag the **Axle** and note how it moves. It can rotate in the hole and translate along the axis of the hole.
11. In the *Assemble* tab>*Relationships* panel, click [icon] (Constrain). Constraints can be used to remove any unwanted degrees of freedom that result from a joint connection. In this case, you will remove the translational degree of freedom in the **Axle** component.
12. Assign a Mate (Flush) constraint that aligns the XY Plane in the **Axle** with the YZ Plane of the assembly.

13. Click **OK** to complete the constraint definition. Drag the **Axle** and note that only one rotational degree of freedom remains. To visually identify the remaining rotational degree of freedom, in the *View* tab>*Visibility* panel, click (Degrees of Freedom). The assembly displays as shown in Figure 17–25. Note that the [◦] icon appears adjacent to the component name, indicating it is not fully constrained. This is as expected as the rotational degree of freedom still remains.

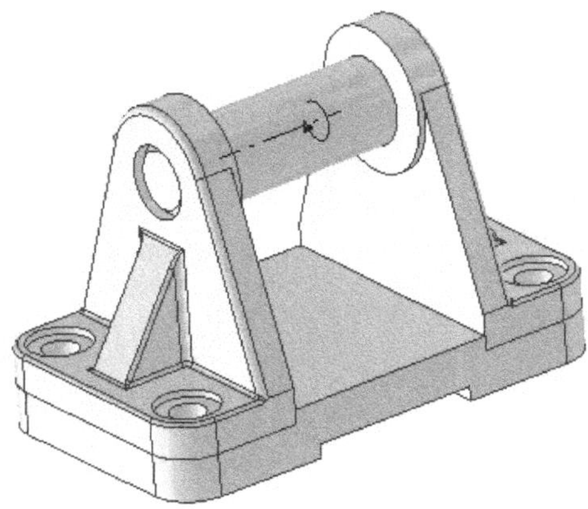

Figure 17–25

14. To further remove any degrees of freedom from the assembly, you can lock joint connections. Right-click on the Cylindrical joint connection and select **Lock**. This removes the remaining rotational degree of freedom and the [•] icon now displays.
15. Expand the **Relationships** node and note that the Cylindrical joint and Flush constraint have been added.

Alternatively, you can use a **Rigid** joint and set the correct offset value to locate the Axle.

Task 5: Assemble the Wheel component.

1. Place one instance of the **Wheel** component, similar to the orientation shown in Figure 17–26.

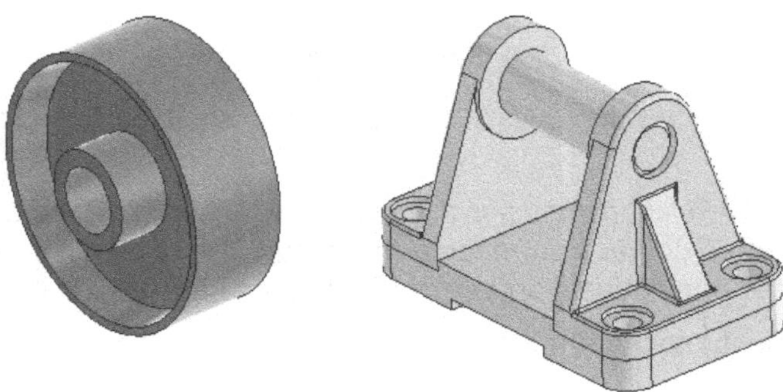

Figure 17–26

2. In the *Assemble* tab>*Relationships* panel, click (Joint).
3. In the *Type* drop-down list in the mini-toolbar, leave **Automatic** as the joint type.
4. On the **Wheel** component (first reference), select the midpoint of the inner cylindrical surface, shown in Figure 17–27, as the origin reference. To ensure that you are snapping to the proper reference, once you hover over the required surface (inner cylindrical face), press and hold <Ctrl> to maintain surface selection. You are now able to move between the origin references while remaining on the original surface.
5. On the **Axle** component (second reference), select the midpoint of the cylindrical surface shown in Figure 17–27, as the origin reference.

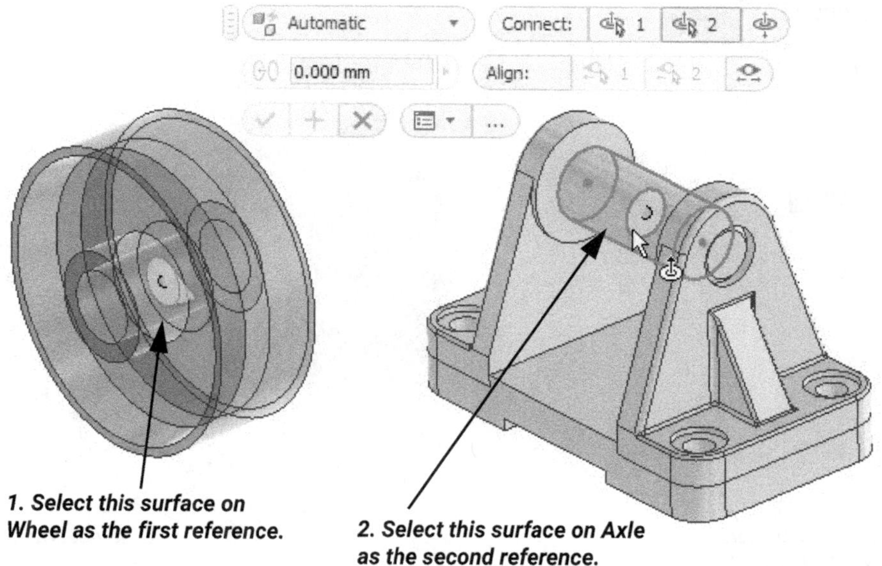

Figure 17–27

The **Wheel** component (reference 1) moves into position and displays animated movement indicating its allowable degrees of freedom. Note that the system assumed a Cylindrical joint type. A Rotational joint is required.

6. In the *Type* drop-down list in the mini-toolbar, select **Rotational**.
7. Click in the mini-toolbar to complete the joint.

Task 6: Assemble the Bolt components.

1. Place one instance of the **M10 x35** component.
2. Begin the creation of a new joint. In the *Type* drop-down list in the mini-toolbar, select **Rotational**.
3. On the **M10 x35** component (first reference), hover the cursor over the bottom face of the bolt head so that the origin reference is shown as in Figure 17–28. Select to assign the reference.
4. On the **Bracket** component (second reference), hover the cursor over the bottom face of the counterbore hole so that the origin reference is shown as in Figure 17–28. Select to assign the reference.

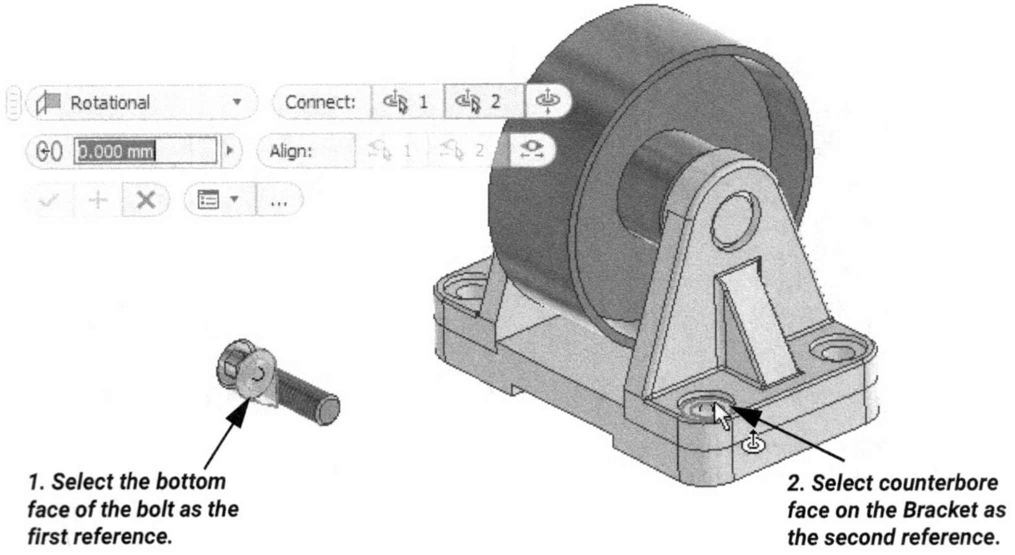

Figure 17–28

5. The component moves into position and displays its remaining rotational degree of freedom. Complete the joint.
6. Right-click on the **Rotational** joint (for the **M10 x35** component) in the Model browser and select **Lock** to remove its rotational degree of freedom.

   Note: *In general, it is recommended to remove degrees of freedom to eliminate the possibility to unexpected changes and so that Inventor is not forced to calculate the open movement after each update.*

7. Place a second instance of the **M10 x35** component. Instead of using a **Rotational** joint, assign a **Rigid** joint connection to remove all degrees of freedom with a single constraint.

8. Add and join the remaining bolt components, as shown in Figure 17–29. Ensure all degrees of freedom are removed from the bolts using either of the two methods. Review the Model browser icons to verify that the Wheel is the only component that is not fully constrained.

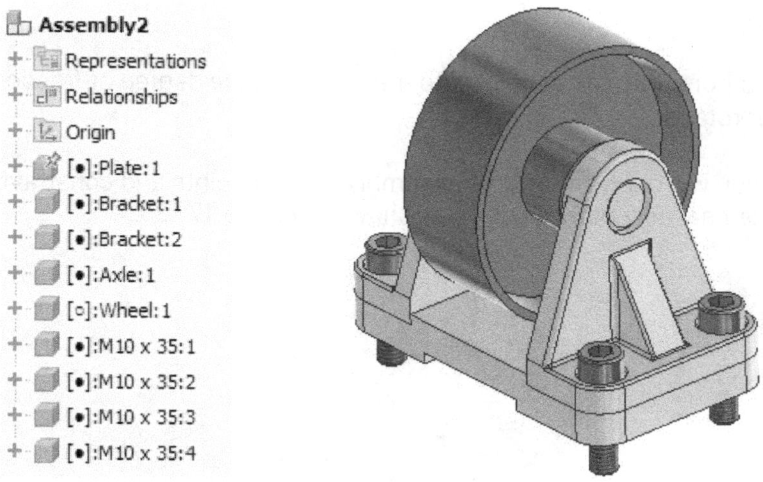

Figure 17–29

9. Save the assembly as **Assembly_Joints.iam.**

End of practice

Practice 17b
Assembly Basics III

Practice Objective

- Constrain components in an assembly to maintain a single degree of freedom for translation or rotation.

In this practice, you will open an existing assembly and add joints and constraints to components. The final assembly displays as shown in Figure 17–30.

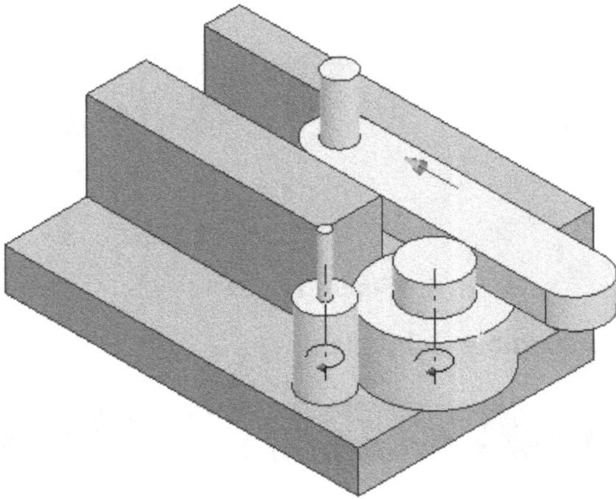

Figure 17–30

Task 1: Open an assembly file.

1. Open **constraints.iam**. The **base** component is grounded and the other three components are not constrained, as indicated by the [▫] icons in the Model browser.
2. Display the symbols for the degrees of freedom on the parts to help you identify the remaining degrees of freedom for the components as they are constrained.

8. Add and join the remaining bolt components, as shown in Figure 17–29. Ensure all degrees of freedom are removed from the bolts using either of the two methods. Review the Model browser icons to verify that the Wheel is the only component that is not fully constrained.

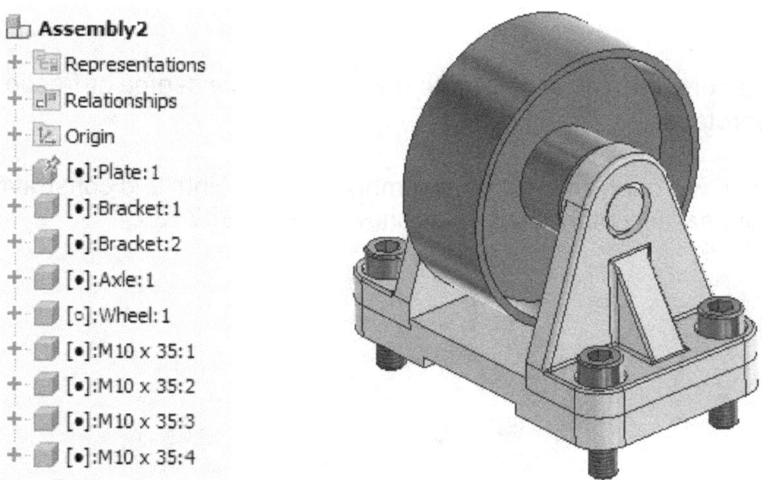

Figure 17–29

9. Save the assembly as **Assembly_Joints.iam.**

End of practice

Practice 17b
Assembly Basics III

Practice Objective

- Constrain components in an assembly to maintain a single degree of freedom for translation or rotation.

In this practice, you will open an existing assembly and add joints and constraints to components. The final assembly displays as shown in Figure 17–30.

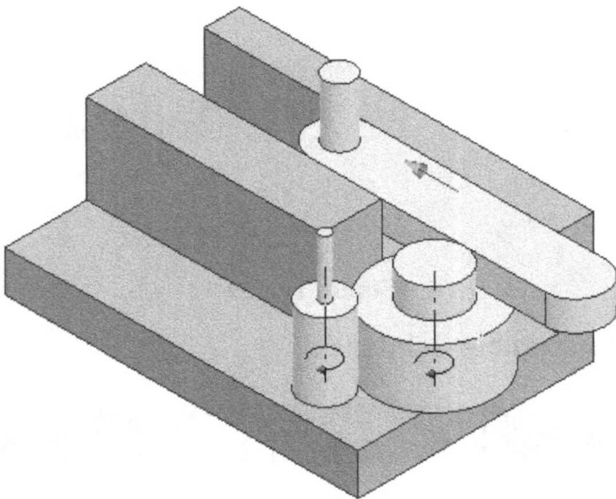

Figure 17–30

Task 1: Open an assembly file.

1. Open **constraints.iam**. The **base** component is grounded and the other three components are not constrained, as indicated by the [▫] icons in the Model browser.
2. Display the symbols for the degrees of freedom on the parts to help you identify the remaining degrees of freedom for the components as they are constrained.

Task 2: Apply Rotational joint connections to the rotating components.

1. Apply a **Rotational** joint connection between **Roll1** and **Base**. Place the shorter end of **Roll1** into the hole closest to the corner of the base, as shown in Figure 17–31. Only a single rotational degree of freedom remains for this component.

   Note: The assembly's visibility style has been set to ***Shaded with Edges*** *for clarity in the images.*

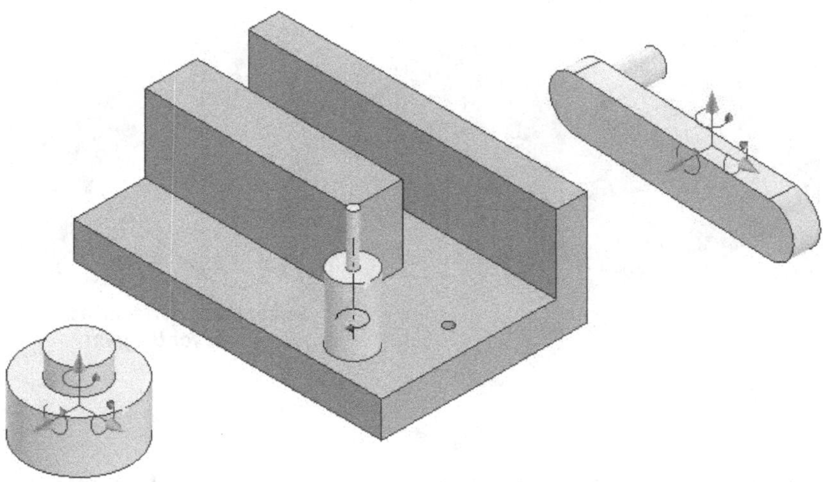

Figure 17–31

2. Apply a **Rotational** joint connection between **Roll2** and **Base**, as shown in Figure 17–32. Only a single rotational degree of freedom remains for this component.

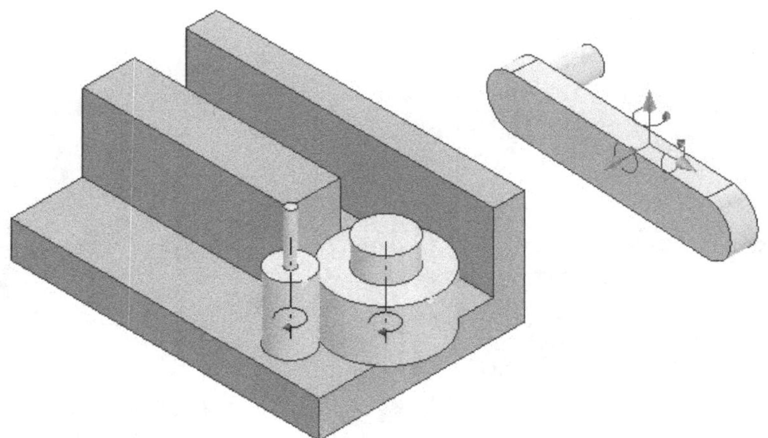

Figure 17–32

Task 3: Apply a joint and constraint to the Sliderarm to allow for sliding movement.

1. Apply a **Planar** joint between the large flat face of the **Sliderarm** and the large circular face of **Roll2**, as shown in Figure 17–33.

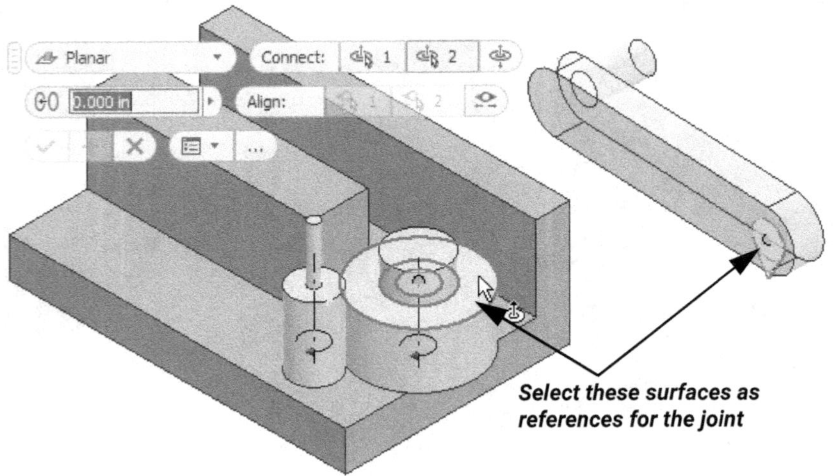

Figure 17–33

2. Apply a **Tangent** constraint between the rectangular side of the **Sliderarm** and the cylindrical surface on **Roll2**, as shown in Figure 17–34.

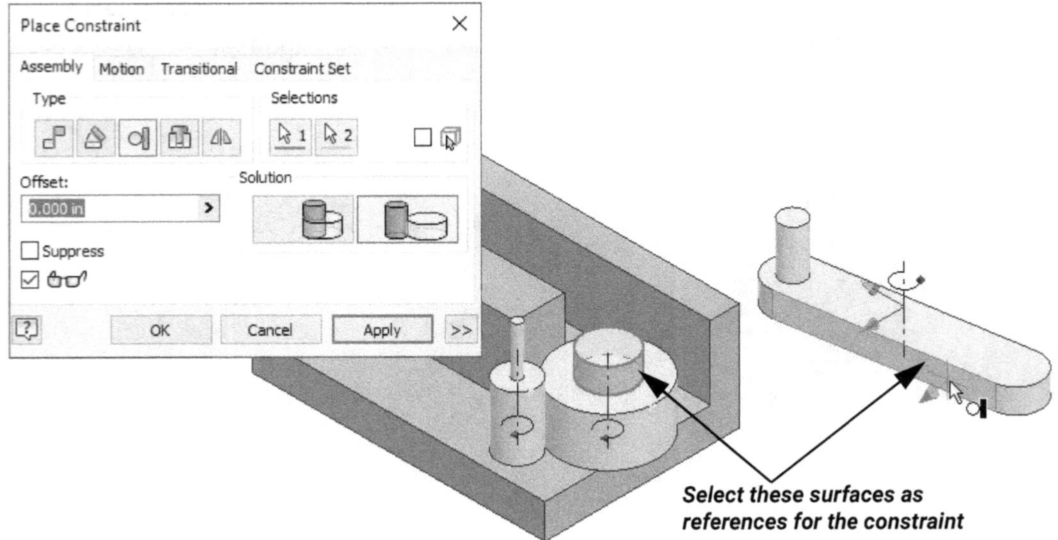

Figure 17–34

3. Apply a **Mate** constraint between the rectangular side of the **Sliderarm** and the rectangular side of the **Base**, as shown in Figure 17–35.

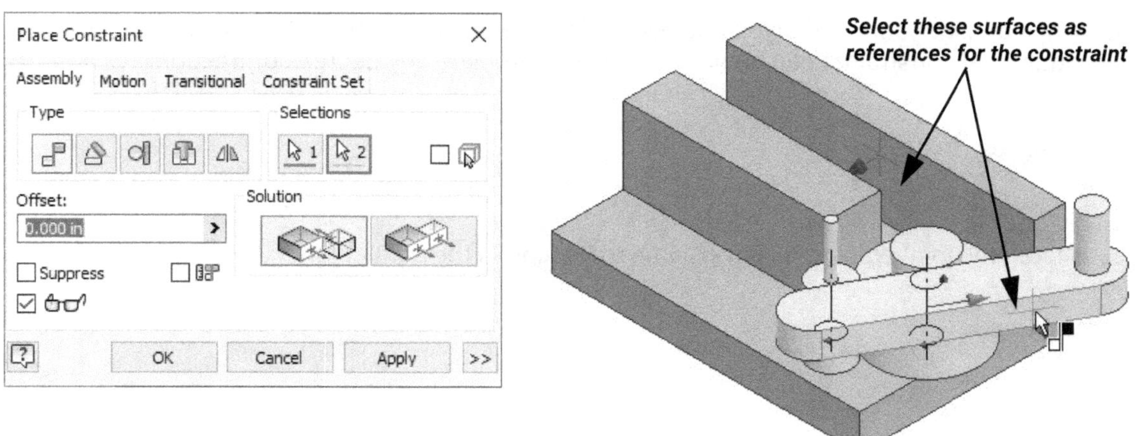

Figure 17–35

4. Select the **Sliderarm** and drag it. Note that it only moves as permitted by its one remaining degree of freedom, as shown in Figure 17–36. You can also rotate the two cylindrical parts. Work Points are provided on the edges of the cylinders to help visualize the movement.

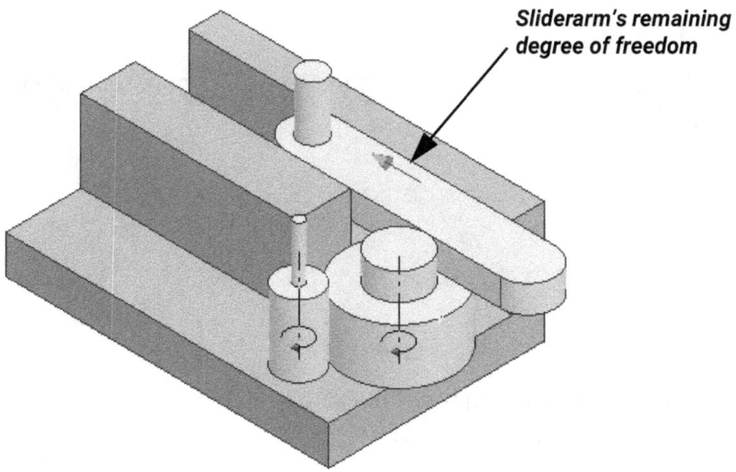

Figure 17–36

5. Save the assembly and close the window.

End of practice

Chapter Review Questions

1. Once a Joint connection type has been added between components in an assembly, additional constraints can be used to further eliminate any degrees of freedom.
   a. True
   b. False

2. Match the joint type in the left column to its icon in the right column.

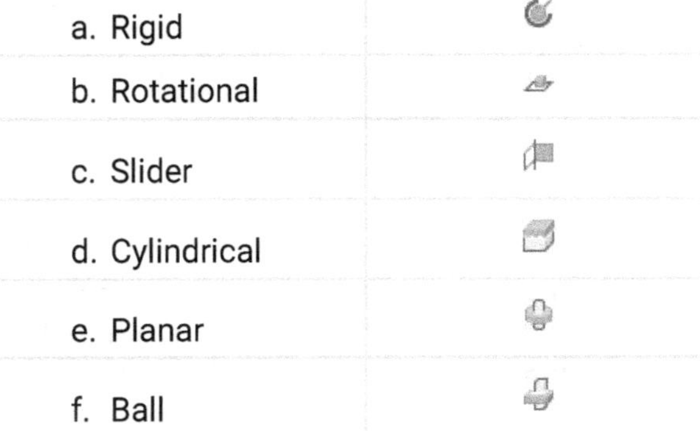

a. Rigid	
b. Rotational	
c. Slider	
d. Cylindrical	
e. Planar	
f. Ball	

3. Which of the following cannot be accomplished using the mini-toolbar shown in Figure 17–37? (Select all that apply.)

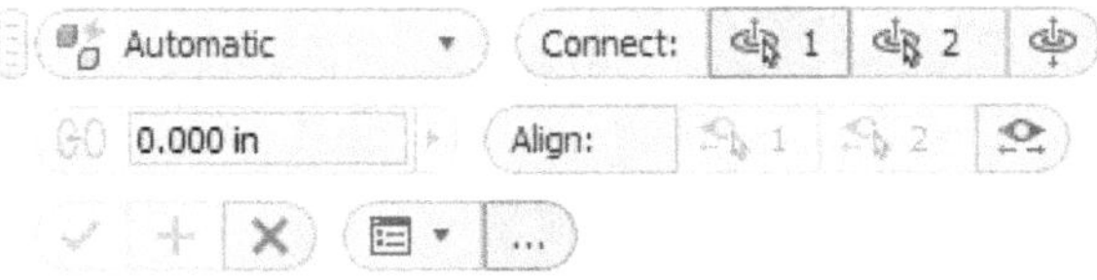

Figure 17–37

   a. Define a gap value for offsetting references.
   b. Define a limit value for range of motion.
   c. Flip components.
   d. Control whether an animation displays when components are joined.
   e. Assign a name for the joint.

Command Summary

Button	Command	Location
	Degrees of Freedom	• **Ribbon:** *View* tab>*Visibility* panel
	Joint	• **Ribbon:** *Assemble* tab>*Relationships* panel • **Keyboard:** <J>
	Place	• **Ribbon:** *Assemble* tab>*Component* panel • **Keyboard:** <P>

Chapter 18

Manipulating Assembly Display

You have learned that components are constrained to one another to form assemblies. The constraints that you use result in feature relationships between the components. You now learn how to use a number of other tools in Assembly mode to evaluate and review an entire assembly.

Learning Objectives

- Temporarily relocate a constrained component to a new location in an assembly by moving or rotating it.
- Suppress constraints or joints in an assembly.
- Control component display in an assembly using the **Visibility**, **Enabled**, **Isolate**, and **Transparent** commands.
- Create section views in an assembly that display portions of an overall assembly based on selected planes.
- Create view representations that store assembly display configurations.
- Use appropriate selection priority options to efficiently make selections in an assembly.

18.1 Moving and Rotating Components

Viewing or selecting references in components of a large assemblies can be challenging. Moving and rotating components is a simple way of temporarily relocating assembly components.

Moving Components

To move components in an assembly, click (Free Move) in the *Assemble* tab>*Position* panel, and select the component to move in the graphics window. Alternatively, you can select the component in the graphics window, right-click and select **Free Move**. Hold the left mouse button, and drag the component to a new location. Once you have moved the component, release the mouse button to drop the component. When moving components, you can only select one component to move at a time and grounded components cannot be moved.

- If the component being moved is constrained, the **Free Move** command displays relationships as elastic bands between the constraint references. Icons indicate the original constraint type, as shown in Figure 18–1. Relationships are not displayed between unconstrained components.

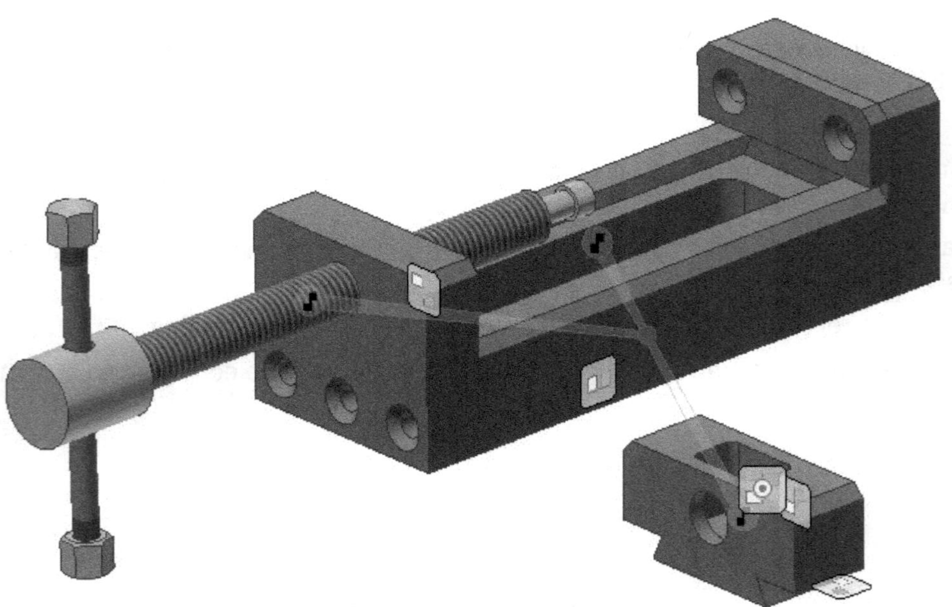

Figure 18–1

- Select any of the constraint icons once a moved component has been placed and right-click to display the marking menu, as shown in Figure 18–2. The commands in the marking menu enable you to **Edit**, **Suppress**, **Delete**, or **Modify** (offset value) the selected constraint.

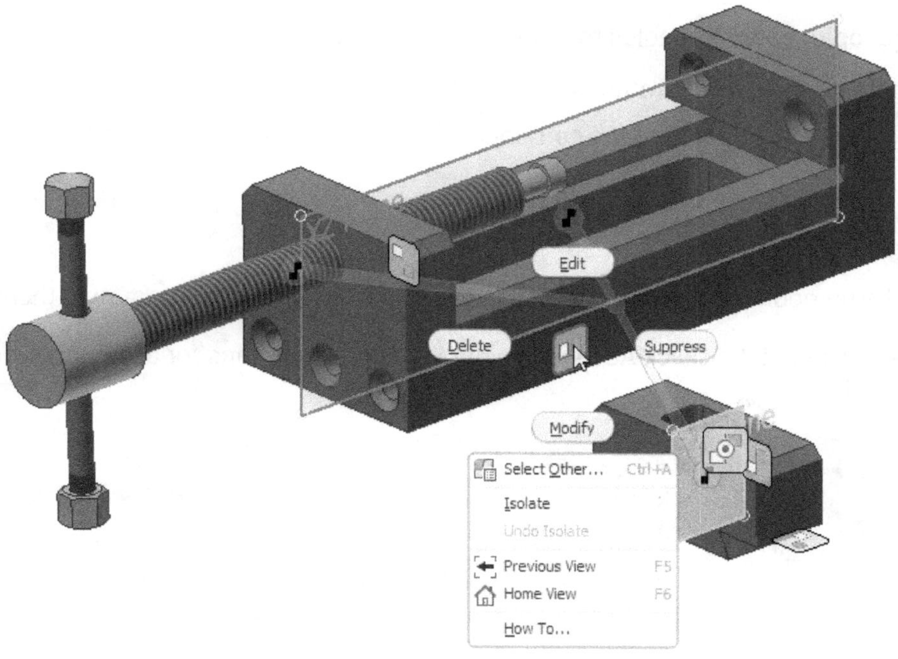

Figure 18–2

- To clear the relationship display from the model, press <Esc>, or right-click and select **OK**.

Rotating Components

Rotating components enables you to manipulate the orientation of selected assembly components independent of the overall assembly and can help with constraint selection. Unlike the **Free Move** command, the **Free Rotate** command does not function differently for constrained and unconstrained components. Grounded components cannot be rotated.

To rotate assembly components, click (Free Rotate) in the *Assemble* tab>*Position* panel and select the component to rotate in the graphics window. Alternatively, you can select the component in the graphics window, right-click and select **Free Rotate**. A rotation circle displays in the assembly window, as it does when using the **Orbit** command.

Use the following methods to rotate (hold the left mouse button while dragging the mouse):

- Click inside the circle to rotate freely.
- Use the left or right handles to rotate about the Y-axis.
- Use the top or bottom handles to rotate about the X-axis.
- Click outside the circle to rotate about the Z-axis.

When you have finished rotating the component(s), press <Esc> or right-click and select **OK**.

Updating the Assembly

To return the components to their constrained positions after moving or rotating them, click (Local Update) in the Quick Access Toolbar. The update options for assemblies are shown in Figure 18–3.

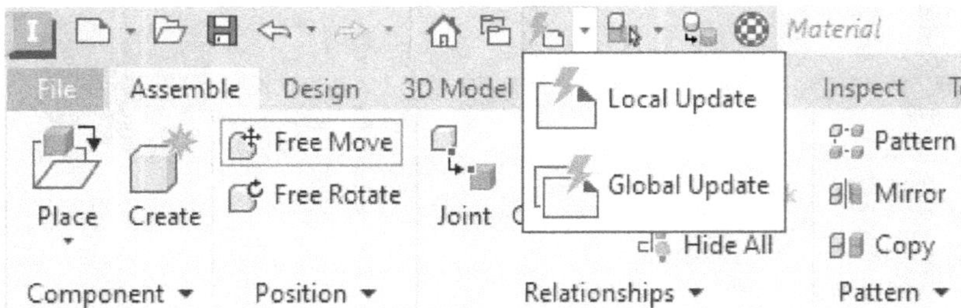

Figure 18–3

- Select (Local Update) to update an individual part or subassembly. This option is useful for large assemblies with long update times.
- Select (Global Update) to update the entire assembly. All subassemblies including the top-level assembly are updated.

18.2 Suppressing Constraints or Joints

In complex assemblies, suppressing constraints or joints is useful to help ease the assembly of other components. Once suppressed, a component can be easily moved to allow for selecting references or to test an alternate constraint. A suppressed constraint or joint displays in the Model browser as a grayed symbol. To suppress a constraint (shown in Figure 18–4):

- Right-click on the constraint (or joint) in the Model browser and select **Suppress**.
- With constraint (or joint) symbols shown in the model, right-click on the symbol and select **Suppress**.
- In the *Edit Constraint* (or *Edit Joint*) dialog box, select **Suppress**.

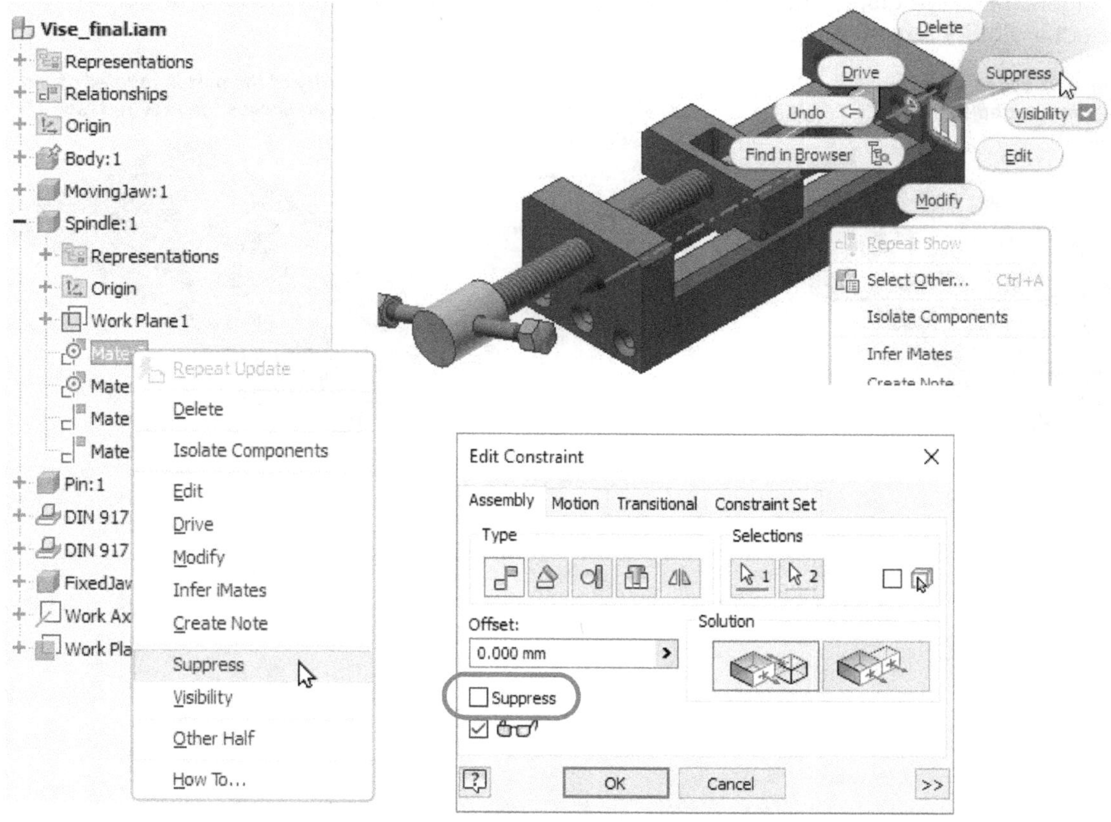

Figure 18–4

- If you have suppressed any constraints or joints, you must reactivate them if you want them to update. To resume them, right-click on the constraint or joint in the Model browser and clear the **Suppress** option or clear the **Suppress** option in the *Edit Constraint* or *Edit Joint* dialog box.

18.3 Controlling Assembly Component Display

When you add components to an assembly, they are visible and enabled by default. The following tools are available to simplify the display of assembly components:

Visible Components

You can toggle off the visibility of a component to more easily modify components, as shown in Figure 18–5. To toggle off the visibility of a component, right-click on a component in the Model browser and select **Visibility** so that it is toggled off. Alternatively, you can right-click on the component in the graphics window and select **Visibility**. The component symbol in the Model browser displays in gray and the model is no longer displayed in the graphics window, as shown in Figure 18–5. To display the component again, right-click on it in the Model browser and select **Visibility** so that it is toggled on.

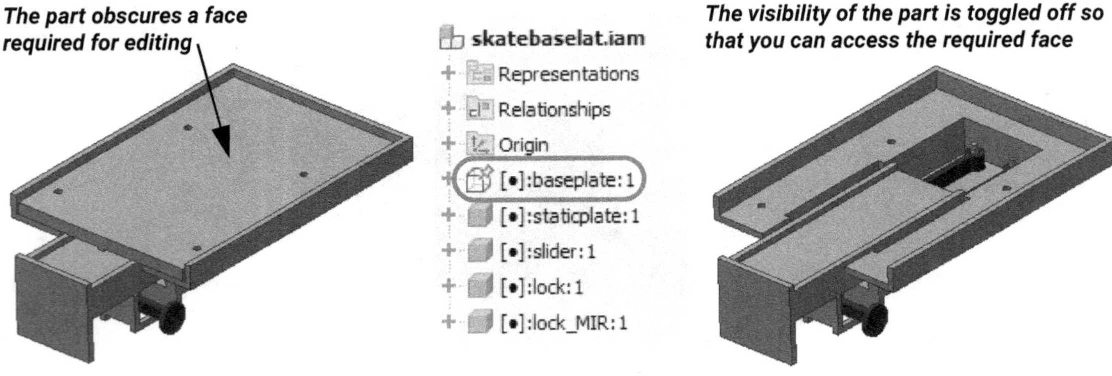

Figure 18–5

Enabling Components

You can restrict a component from being selected by disabling it, as shown in Figure 18–6. To disable a component, right-click on the component in the Model browser or in the graphics window and select **Enabled** so that it is toggled off. The component symbol in the Model browser displays in green and the model displays in a lighter shading, as shown in Figure 18–6. To re-enable the component, right-click on the component in the Model browser and select **Enabled** so that it is toggled on.

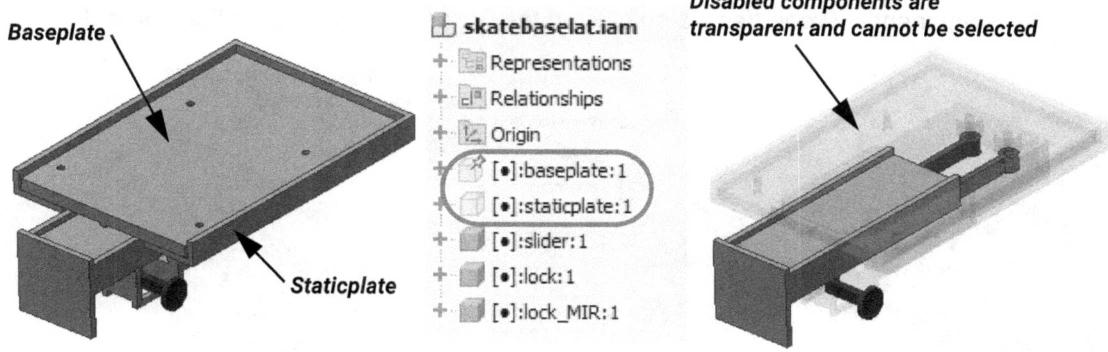

Figure 18–6

Hint: Advantages of the Visibility and Enabling Options

- Helps easily edit components inside or behind others.
- Helps in selecting geometry that might be obscured.
- Simplifies the display of the assembly.
- Enables faster opening and updating of assembly files, because components that are not required until later in the design process are toggled off.
- Enables you to make non-solid geometry (e.g., planes or axes) visible for constraining or referencing.

Isolating Components

The **Isolate** command enables you to toggle off the visibility of all of the components except the ones you need. To use the **Isolate** command, select the components in the Model browser or in the graphics window, right-click and select **Isolate**. This is useful in a large assembly to easily select references to create constraints.

To undo the **Isolate** command, right-click anywhere in the window and select **Undo Isolate**.

> ***Note:*** *Consider using a Design View if you isolate the same components routinely to create a working view.*

Transparent Components

The **Transparent** command enables you to set the visibility of an assembly component as transparent in an assembly view. Once set, the component can be selected and remains visible in a transparent display style, as shown in Figure 18–7. To set a component to transparent, use one of the following methods:

- Right-click on the component name in the Model browser or in the graphics window and select **Transparent**.
- In the component's *iProperties* dialog box, on the *Occurrence* tab, select **Transparent**.

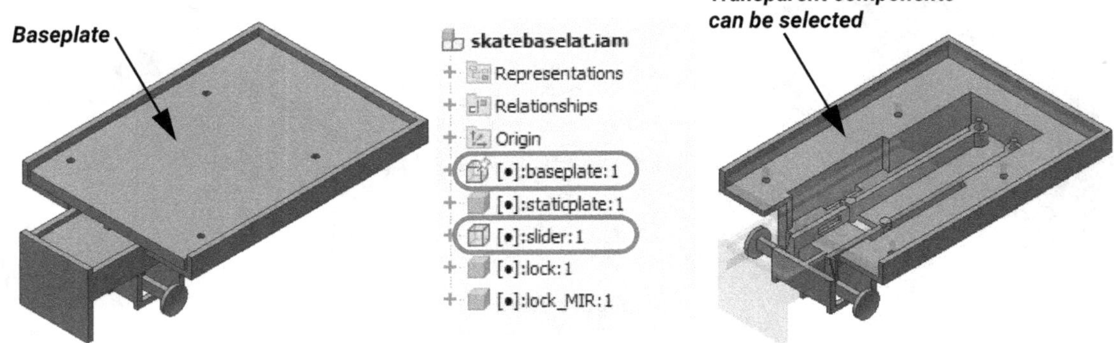

Figure 18–7

- To undo the **Transparent** command, reselect the component and clear the option.

18.4 Sectioning Assembly Models

Creating a section view enables you to work inside assemblies (or components) while still keeping the required components visible and enabled. Section views display portions of the assembly that lie on one side or between reference planes. The three section views shown in Figure 18–8 can be created.

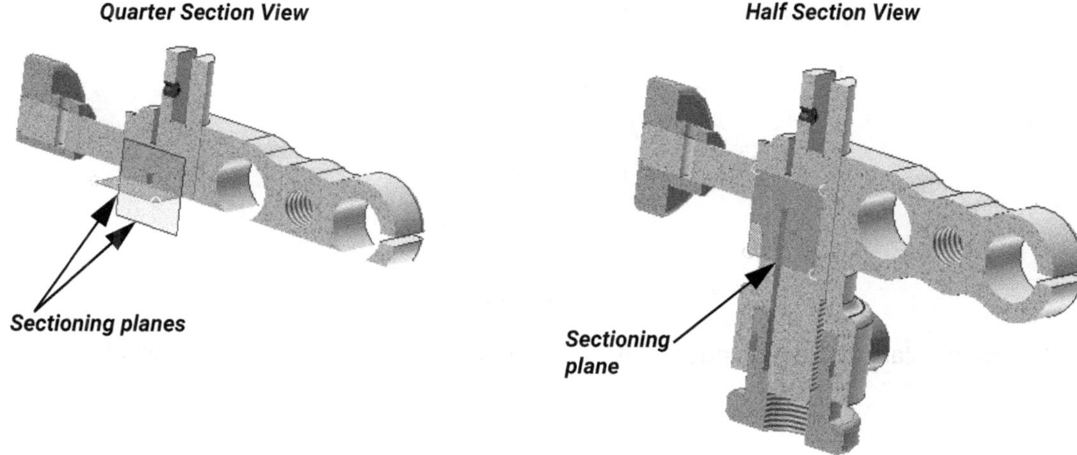

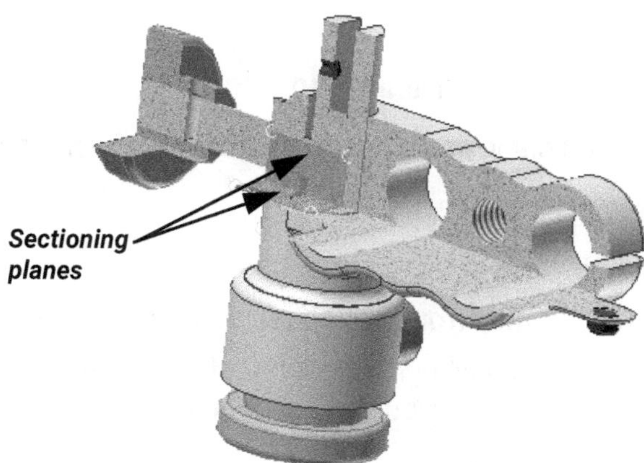

Figure 18–8

How To: Section an Assembly Model

1. In the *View* tab>*Visibility* panel, select the type of section view in the *Section View* drop-down list, as shown in Figure 18–9.

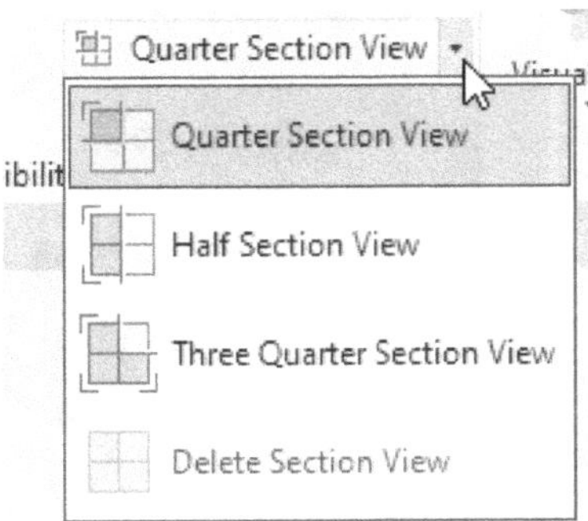

Figure 18–9

2. Select the plane to section about. The mini-toolbar appears in the graphics window as shown in Figure 18–10.

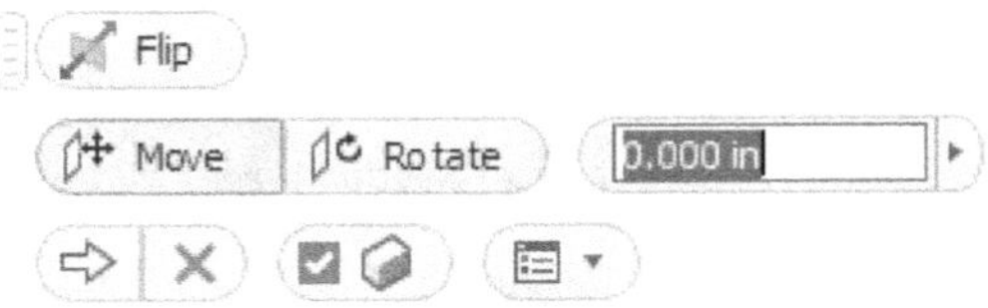

Figure 18–10

3. If required, move the selected plane using one of the following techniques with the (Move) option selected.
   - In the mini-toolbar, enter a value in the *Offset* field.
   - In the graphics window, drag the arrow that appears on the section plane.
   - In the mini-toolbar, use the scroll wheel in the *Offset* field to offset incrementally. To change the scroll increments when modifying section plane placement, right-click in the graphics window and select **Scroll Step Size**, enter an increment value, and click (✓).

   Note: *To rotate the plane, select* (Rotate) *and enter or drag the rotation handle as needed.*

4. If required, flip the section about the plane by selecting (Flip).

5. If creating a quarter or three quarter section view, click (⇨) to continue or click (✓) to combine the section.

6. Select an additional plane to section about. If required, enter an offset value or flip the direction of the new plane using the same techniques as mentioned above. The mini-toolbar appears as shown in Figure 18–11 when a quarter or three quarter section view is being created.

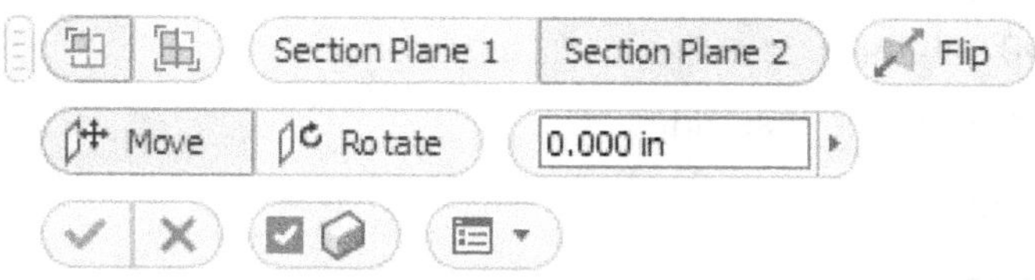

Figure 18–11

7. To further modify the offset from a selected plane, the correct plane must be active. In the mini-toolbar, select Section Plane 1 or Section Plane 2, as needed, to switch the active plane and then modify as required.

   ***Note:** If creating a Quarter Section or a Three Quarter Section View, you can toggle between the two. This can be done in the mini-toolbar by selecting (Three Quarter Section View) or (Quarter Section View), as needed.*

8. Right-click and select **OK (Enter)** or click to complete the view.
9. To return to a view of the entire part, select **Delete Section View** in the *Section View* drop-down list.

Note the following:

- Once in a section view, you can select references on cut components. Note that edges that are generated by the cut are not selectable as they are not physical edges in the model.
- Once created, a section view cannot be redefined, you would have to recreate it to make changes. However, if the section view is used in a design view, it can be modified or suppressed).

18.5 Assembly View Representations

A view representation enables you to save a configuration of an assembly (or part) view for future use. It can store the following:

- Visibility/Isolation settings
- Enabled/disabled component settings
- Color override of components
- Assembly orientation

Saving view representations has the following advantages:

- Saves a configuration where components are toggled on and off for ease of viewing or to ease selection.
- Creates different displays of your assembly for various purposes or different users.
- Reduces the loading or updating time of assemblies by displaying only the required components.

Figure 18–12 shows two saved view representations of an assembly.

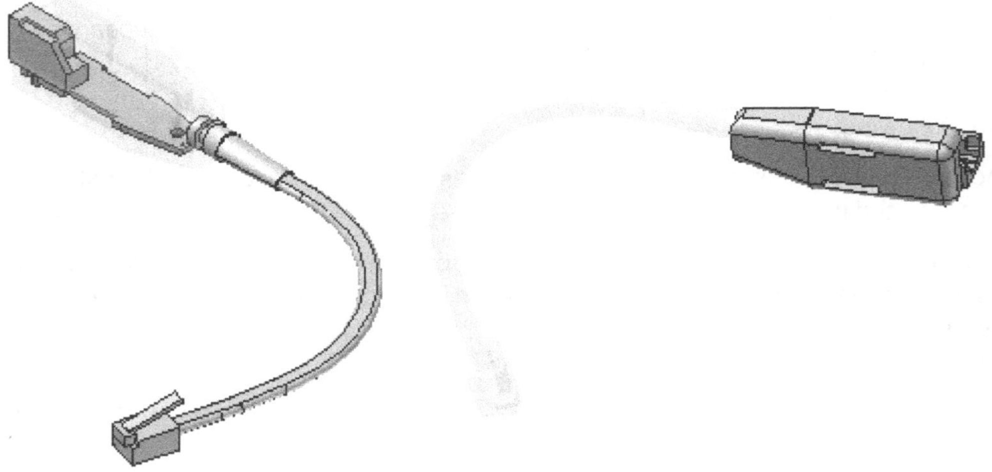

Figure 18–12

How To: Save a View Representation

1. Expand the *Representations* folder in the Model browser, right-click on the **View** node, and select **New**, as shown in Figure 18–13.

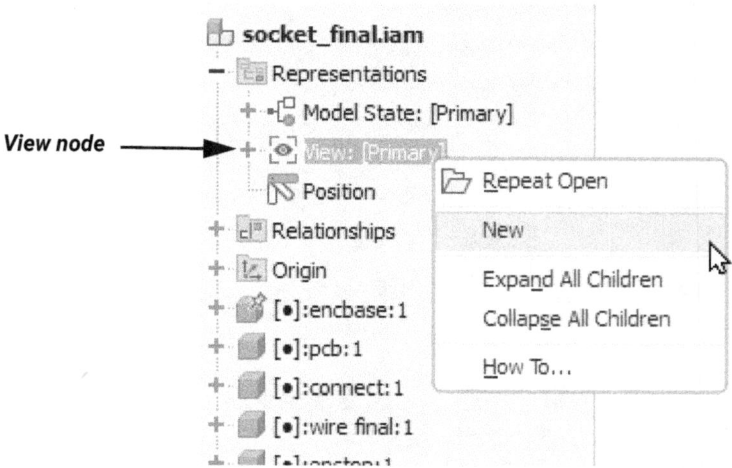

Figure 18–13

2. Enter a name for the new view or press <Enter> to accept the default name.

   Note: *Once a view is created, it can be renamed by slowly selecting the view name twice (do not double-click), entering a new name, and pressing <Enter>.*

3. Configure the view display for the assembly.
4. To lock the view, right-click on the view in the Model browser and select **Lock**. This restricts you or others from making changes to the view at a later time and prevent newly assembled components from being included in the view representation.

The newly created view representation is automatically made active. To switch to a different view, either double-click on that view name or right-click on the view name in the Model browser and select **Activate**, as shown in Figure 18–14.

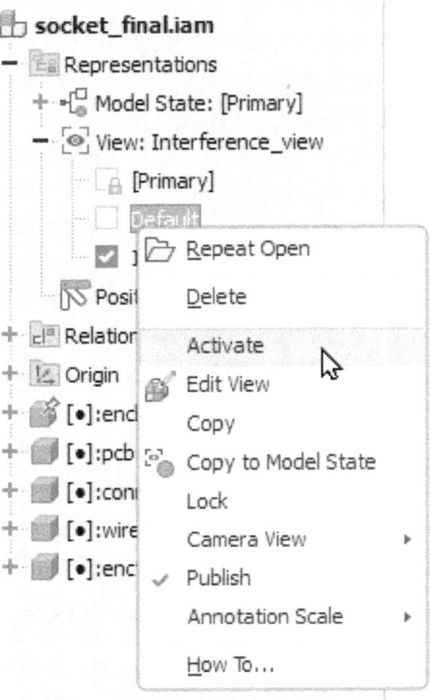

Figure 18–14

Modifying View Representations

> ***Note:** A View representation in a model can be modified only if it is unlocked.*

To unlock a view, right-click on its name in the Model browser and select **Unlock**. Once it is unlocked, you can modify it as follows:

- Change the visibility of the components in the view.
- If a view representation has a section view, you can modify the section view or suppress it.
- Use the **Undo Isolate** command if the components were previously isolated in the view.
- Change which components are disabled or enabled.
- Override the appearance color of components.
- Change the assembly orientation.

As an alternative to using the **Visibility**, **Enable**, and **Undo Isolate** commands to return components to the display in a view, you can also edit the included components by right-clicking on the view name in the Model browser and selecting **Edit View**. Once selected, the mini-toolbar opens, as shown in Figure 18–15.

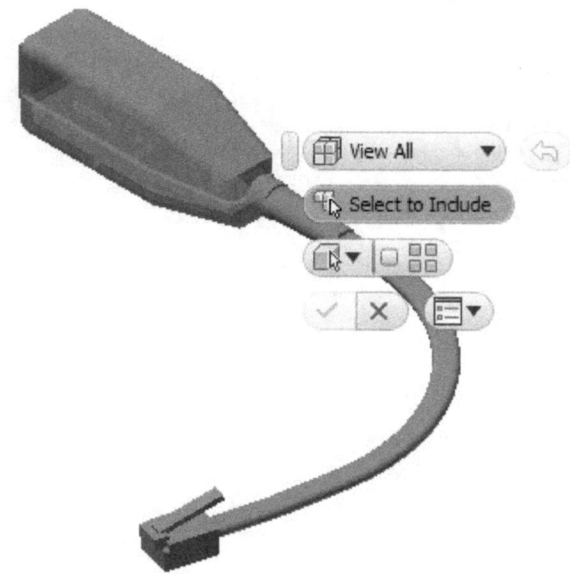

Figure 18–15

- To add additional components to the view representation, ensure **View All** and **Select to Include** are active. The components highlighted in blue indicate the current components that display in the view. Select additional components, as required, to add components to the view.
- To remove previously included components to the view representation, ensure that **View Included** and **Select to Exclude** are active. Select components in the assembly to clear them from the view.
- Click ✓ to complete the modification.

Note: Click View Excluded *in the drop-down list to filter the display so that only those previously excluded display.*

Hint: Camera Views

Right-click and use **Camera View** for the new view to control how a custom orientation is saved with the view. The options enable you to automatically save the view orientation when the view representation is active (**Autosave Camera**). You can also clear this option and save the required orientations for the view. By default, the **Autosave Camera** option is enabled.

18.6 Assembly Selection Filters

Assembly selection priority options are located in the Quick Access Toolbar ( ), as shown in Figure 18–16. The assembly selection options can also be accessed by pressing and holding <Shift> as you right-click in an assembly.

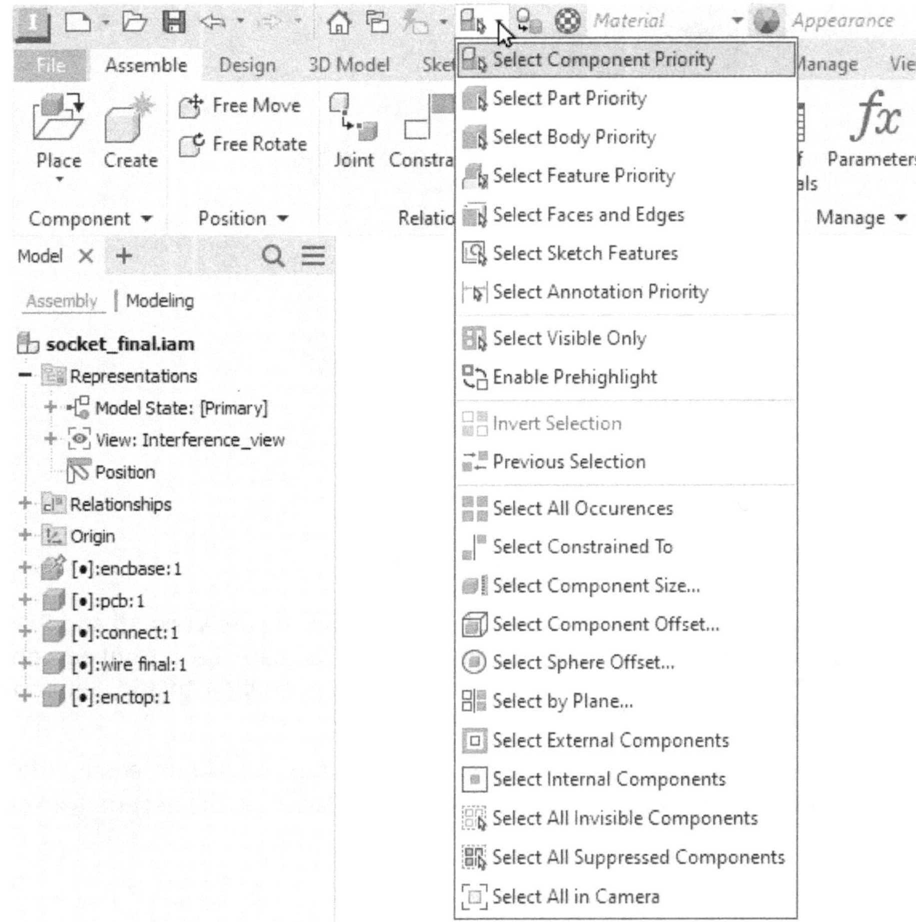

Figure 18–16

When making selections in an assembly consider enabling any one of these options to ease selection. The available options are as follows:

Option	Description
Select Component Priority	Selects an entire component, a part, or a subassembly.
Select Part Priority	Selects a part (the *leaves* in the Model browser).
Select Body Priority	Selects a Body.

Option	Description
Select Feature Priority	Selects a feature.
Select Faces and Edges	Selects a face or part edge.
Select Sketch Features	Selects lines, arcs, circles, splines, or other features in a sketch.
Select Annotation Priority	Selects 3D annotations.
Select Visible Only	Excludes invisible parts from the selection set.
Enable Prehighlight	Enables prehighlighting when you hover the cursor over an object. The option is activated by default. Toggle this off in large assemblies to improve performance.
Invert Selection	Selects all currently deselected components.
Previous Selection	Restores the previous selection set.
Select All Occurrences	Enables you to select a component and have all of its occurrences automatically selected.
Select Constrained To	Selects components constrained to the selected component.
Select Component Size	Selects components that are larger or smaller than a selected component or a specified size.
Select Component Offset	Selects components in a bounding box, based on their distance from a selected component.
Select Sphere Offset	Selects components in a sphere, based on their distance from a selected component.
Select by Plane	Selects components based on one side of a work plane or a planar face.
Select External Components	Selects external assembly components based on a set tolerance value. 100% returns all visible components and 0% returns only the most visible component.
Select Internal Components	Selects internal assembly components based on a set tolerance value. 100% returns all components that are not visible and 1% returns all the components except for the most visible.
Select All Invisible Components	Selects all components that have had their visibility cleared. This provides an easy method to select all invisible components at once to enable their visibility again.
Select All Suppressed Components	Selects all components that are suppressed. This provides an easy method to select all suppressed components at once to unsuppress them.
Select All in Camera	Selects the components in the camera view.

Practice 18a
Manipulate Components

Practice Objectives

- Create a Half Section view to display geometry through a selected work plane.
- Add a new view representation to an assembly such that it does not include any additional components that are added to the model.
- Use the **Visibility**, **Enabled**, and **Isolate** tools to control whether components are displayed and available for selection in an assembly.

In this practice, you will open a previously created vise assembly (shown in Figure 18–17) and use the tools available in Inventor to control component visibility, create a section view, and store the manipulated view in a design view.

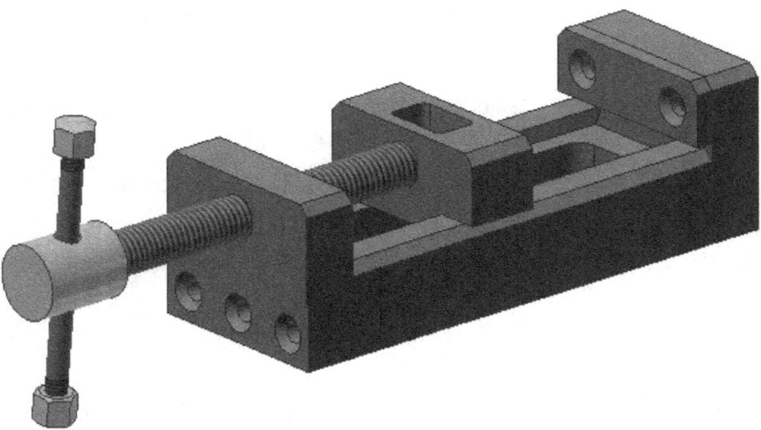

Figure 18–17

Task 1: Create a new assembly and section it through the spindle component.

1. Open **Vise_final.iam**.
2. Select the *View* tab. In the *Visibility* panel, click (Half Section View). You might need to expand the *Section View* drop-down list to access this command.

3. Expand the **Spindle** component and its **Origin** node in the Model browser. Select **XZ Plane**. The assembly displays similarly to that shown in Figure 18–18. Note how the section is not parallel to the top or bottom of the vise. This is because the spindle rotates. A better reference plane for the section would be one that is stationary in the assembly.

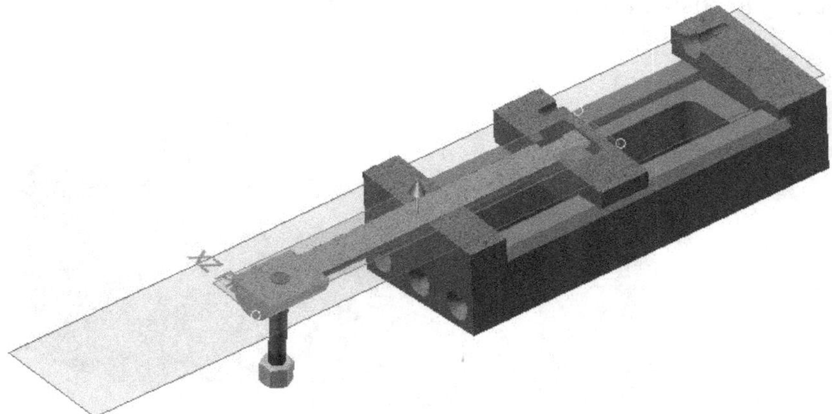

Figure 18–18

4. Click ✕ to cancel section creation.
5. Right-click on **Body** in the Model browser and select **Isolate**. This displays only the Body component, which enables you to create a new work plane by selecting references only in the Body component.
6. Select the *Assemble* tab. In the *Work Feature* panel, click (Axis) and select the circular hole that the Spindle inserts into. Work Axis 1 is created, as shown in Figure 18–19.

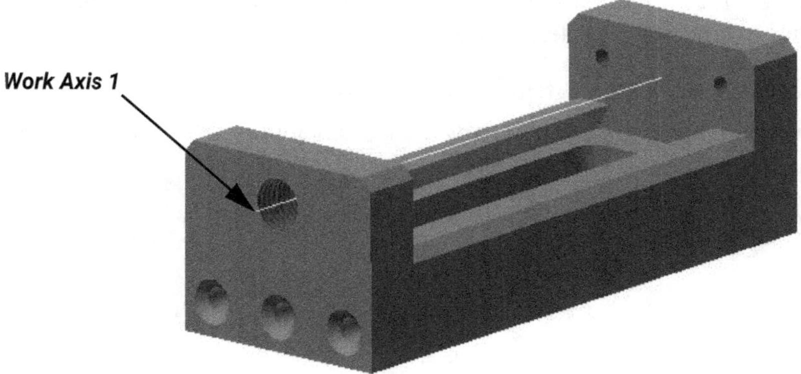

Figure 18–19

7. In the *Work Features* panel, click (Work Plane) and select the newly created **Work Axis 1**. As a second reference, select the top planar face of the component, as shown in Figure 18–20.
8. Enter **0.00 deg** to ensure that the new work plane is parallel with the top of the component. Click .

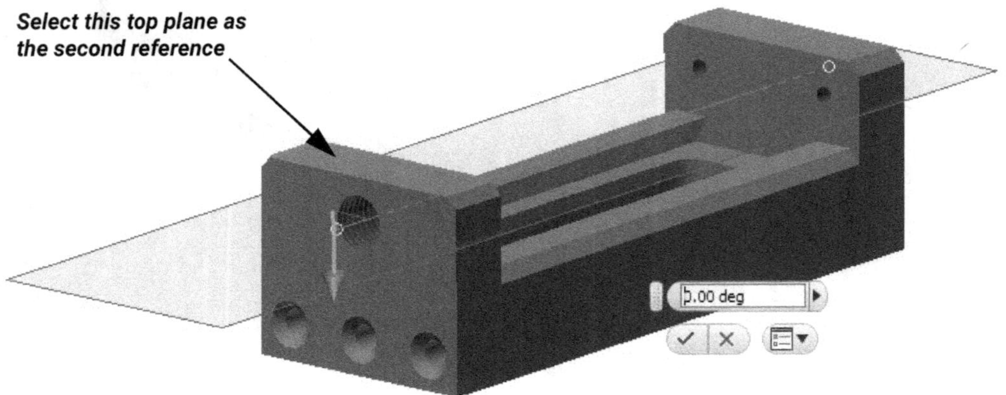

Figure 18–20

9. Right-click on **Body** in the Model browser and select **Undo Isolate** to return all components to the display.
10. Press and hold <Ctrl> and select **Work Axis 1** and **Work Plane 1**. Right-click and select **Visibility** to clear them both from the display.
11. Select the *View* tab. Change the *Visual Style* setting to **Shaded with Edges**. This helps with visualizing the edges of a sectioned view.
12. In the *Visibility* panel, click (Half Section View).
13. In the Model browser, select **Work Plane 1** that was just created. Click in the mini-toolbar to create the section view.

14. Reorient the model to the **Front** view using the ViewCube. The assembly displays similar to that shown in Figure 18–21. Note how the Spindle edge and Moving Jaw edge are connected. Clear the visibility of any remaining work planes if any are displayed.

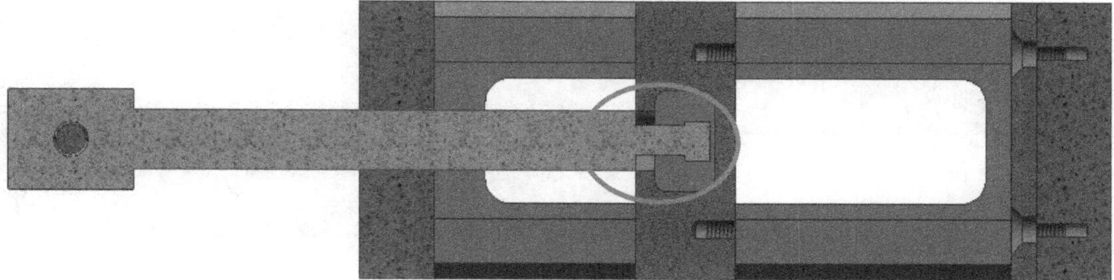

Figure 18–21

15. Expand the **MovingJaw** component in the Model browser and select the **Insert:4** constraint, as shown in Figure 18–22. The Insert constraint connects the two edges such that they align with one another.

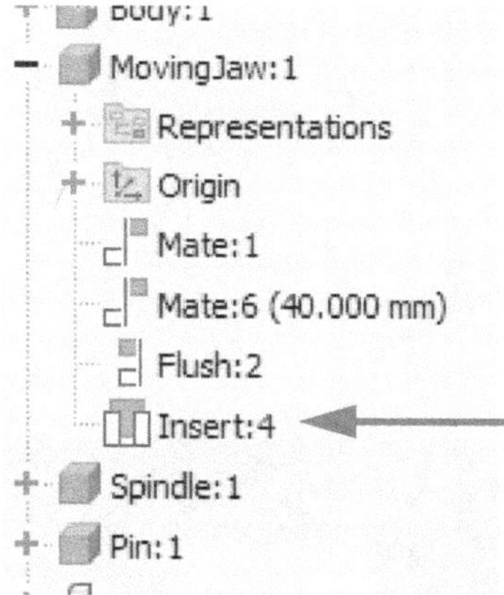

Figure 18–22

16. Right-click the **Insert:4** constraint and select **Edit**.

17. In the *Edit Constraint* dialog box, select (Mate) to change the constraint type. The references do not have to be modified. Click **OK**.

18. Select the **Spindle** and drag it away from the MovingJaw component, as shown in Figure 18–23. Another constraint must be added to fully constrain the component.

Figure 18–23

19. Add an additional **Mate** constraint that mates the end of the Spindle with the inside face of the MovingJaw component. The assembly and Model browser should appear as shown in Figure 18–24.

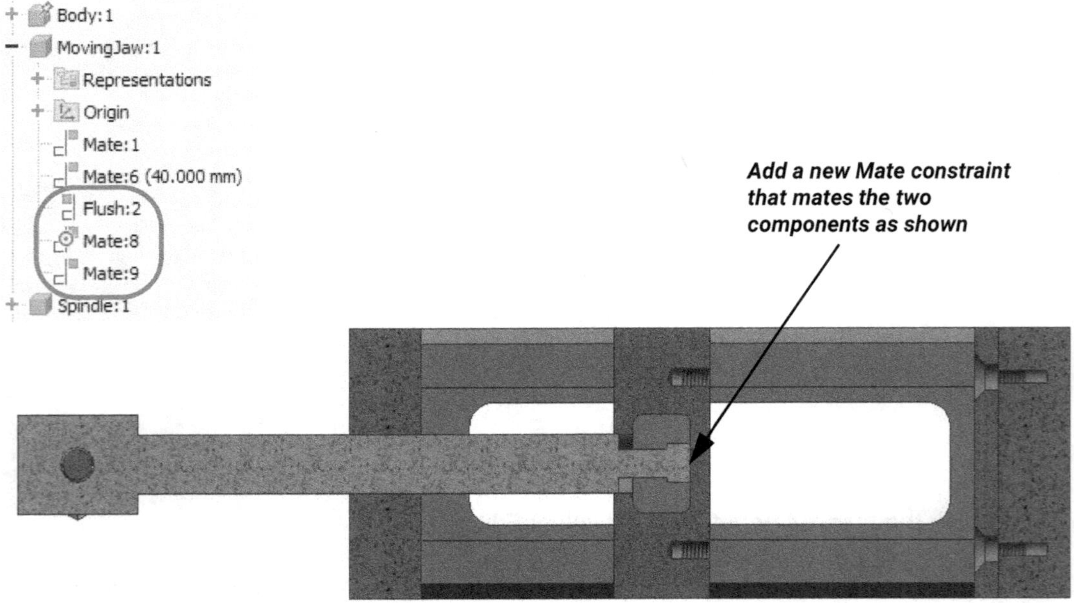

Figure 18–24

20. Select the *View* tab. In the *Visibility* panel, click (Delete Section View) to display the entire assembly. Note that the section view was created to help review placement and could be left displayed while defining new constraints.

21. Reorient the model to its isometric Home view.

Task 2: Create a design view representation.

1. Expand the **Representations** and **View** nodes in the Model browser. The Model browser displays as shown in Figure 18–25.

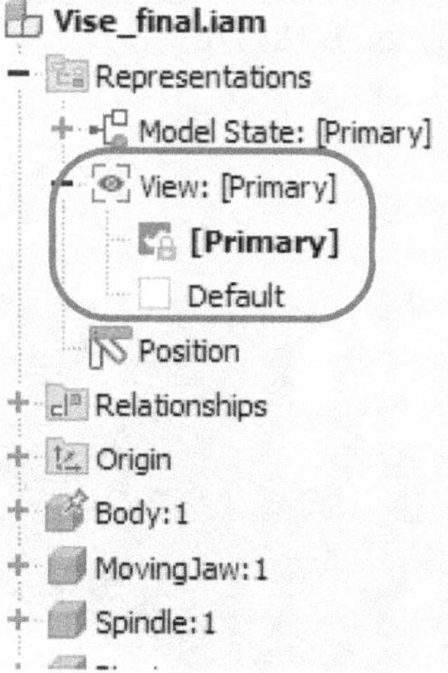

Figure 18–25

2. Right-click on **View: Primary** in the Model browser and select **New** to create a new design view.
3. Enter **Sectioned_View** as the name for the view and press <Enter>. If the view name is not active for editing, select the **View1** node in the Model browser and then select it again (do not double-click) to activate the cell name for editing.
4. Recreate the Half Section view that went through Work Plane 1. Without the design view being used to save the section view, it would have to be recreated anytime it needed to be reviewed.
5. In the Model browser, double-click on the **Default** view name to make it the active design view. The assembly returns to its full display.

   Note: *To lock a design view, right-click on the view name in the Model browser and select **Lock**. This restricts you from adding components to the design view. Any new components in the assembly will not be included in this view.*

Task 3: Modify the existing design view.

1. In the Model browser, double-click on the **Sectioned_View** view name to activate it. The section view is displayed without having to recreate it.
2. Right-click on **Sectioned_View** in the Model browser and select **Edit View**. The mini-toolbar and model display as shown in Figure 18–26.

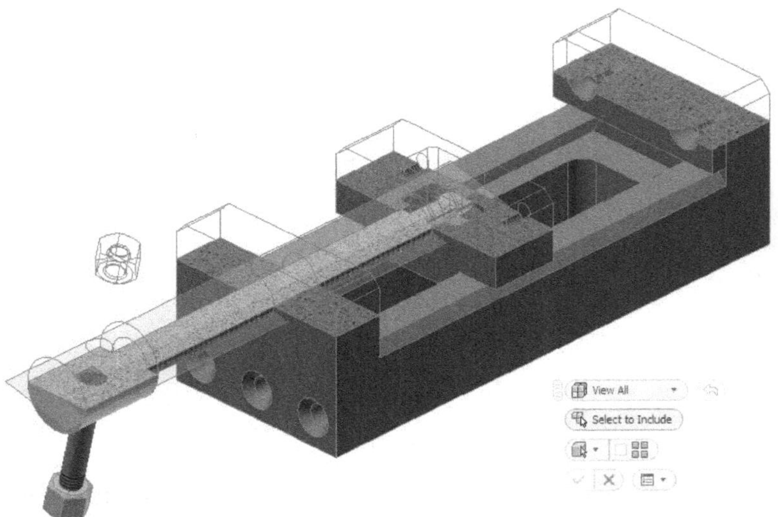

Figure 18–26

3. Ensure that **View All** is selected in the drop-down list, if it is not already active. Note that the components that are currently included are highlighted in blue.
4. Click **View Included** in the drop-down list. Note that **Select to Exclude** is now active.
5. Select **Pin** and the two **DIN 917 M6** components in the Model browser or directly in the graphics window to remove them from the design view. Note how their icon in the Model browser changes.
6. Click (✓) to complete the modification.
7. Activate the **Default** design view. Note that all of the components are still visible.
8. Activate the **Sectioned_View** design view to verify that the components are removed and the section view is displayed.
9. Activate the **Default** design view prior to saving the assembly.
10. Save the assembly. Close the model.

End of practice

Chapter Review Questions

1. Which of the following statements are true about moving components in an assembly? (Select all that apply.)
   a. Components that are partially constrained can be moved by selecting and dragging them.
   b. Components that are fully constrained can be moved using the **Free Move** command.
   c. Components that are partially constrained can be moved using the **Free Move** command.
   d. Components that are fully constrained can be moved by selecting and dragging them.

2. If you move constrained components apart (as shown in Figure 18–27), how can you display them in their constrained positions again?

Figure 18–27

   a. Use **Update**.
   b. Use **Degrees of Freedom** in the *View* tab.
   c. Use **Zoom All**.
   d. Reapply the constraints.

3. Which of the following statements about (Free Rotate) is true?
    a. You can rotate multiple components at the same time.
    b. Only unconstrained components can be rotated.
    c. Grounded components cannot be rotated.
    d. When you rotate a component that is constrained, the constraints change based on a new component position.

4. Which of the following statements is true regarding suppressing constraints?
    a. Suppressing a constraint removes both components referenced in the constraint from the display.
    b. Suppressing a constraint locks the constraint references such that they cannot be edited.
    c. Suppressing a constraint removes its associated component from the display.
    d. Suppressing a constraint enables you to ignore the constraint restrictions and drag the component as required in the assembly.

5. What is the purpose of a section view?
    a. To simplify the display of an assembly.
    b. To update an assembly more quickly.
    c. To create an exploded view of an assembly.
    d. To work inside an assembly while keeping the required components visible.

6. What is the purpose of a view representation? (Select all that apply.)
    a. To simplify the display of an assembly.
    b. To update an assembly more quickly.
    c. To return to a specific view of an assembly.
    d. To rotate assembly components.

7. Which of the following filter options is used in the Edit View mini-toolbar to remove components from an existing view representation?
   a. View All
   b. View Included
   c. View Excluded

8. When a section view is active (as shown in the Three Quarter Section View in Figure 18–28), you cannot select components or reference entities.

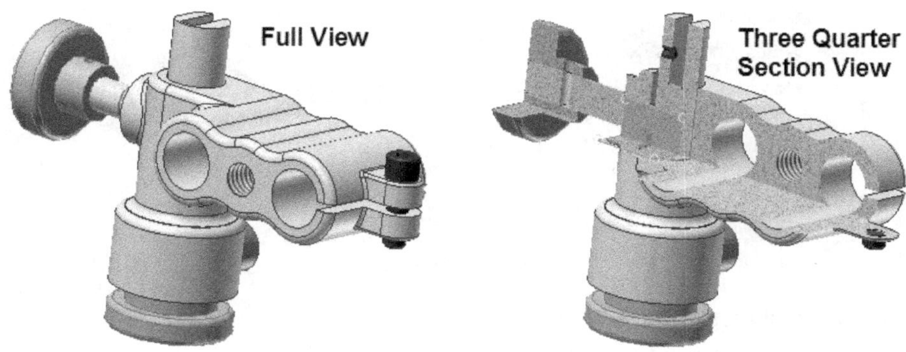

Figure 18–28

   a. True
   b. False

9. What is the difference between toggling off the visibility of a component and isolating that same component?
   a. When the visibility of a component is off, it is not displayed. However, when isolated, the visibility of all of the other components is toggled off and only the selected component is visible.
   b. No difference. Either option can be used to remove the component from the display.
   c. When the visibility of a component is off, it is not displayed; however, when isolated, the component is activated for editing.

10. Which of the following statements are true for the Model browser and assembly shown in Figure 18–29? (Select all that apply.)

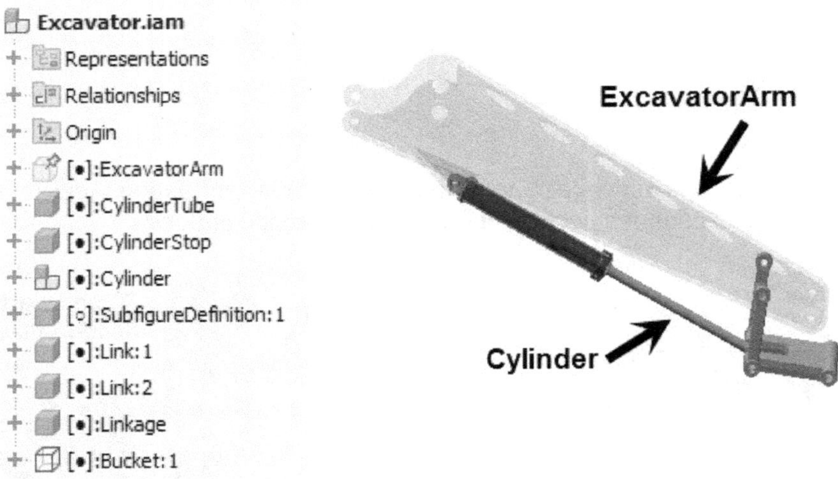

Figure 18–29

a. Bucket's visibility has been cleared.
b. Excavator Arm and Cylinder have been enabled.
c. Excavator Arm is a grounded component.
d. Excavator Arm has been isolated.

11. Which of the following statements is true of a part that is disabled (i.e., the **Enabled** option is cleared) in an assembly?
    a. It is completely invisible.
    b. It is completely visible but not editable.
    c. It is displayed as transparent and is not selectable.
    d. It is not subjected to constraints.

Command Summary

Button	Command	Location
N/A	**Edit View**	• **Context Menu:** In Model browser with a design view selected
N/A	**Enable (component visibility control)**	• **Context Menu:** In Model browser with a component selected • **Context Menu:** In the graphics window with a component selected
	Free Move (component)	• **Ribbon:** *Assemble* tab>*Position* panel • **Context Menu:** In Model browser with a component selected • **Context Menu:** In the graphics window with a component selected
	Free Rotate (component)	• **Ribbon:** *Assemble* tab>*Position* panel • **Context Menu:** In Model browser with a component selected • **Context Menu:** In the graphics window with a component selected
	Global Update (individual part or subassembly)	• **Quick Access Toolbar**
N/A	**Isolate (component visibility control)**	• **Context Menu:** In Model browser with a component selected • **Context Menu:** In the graphics window with a component selected
	Local Update (individual part or subassembly)	• **Quick Access Toolbar**
	Object Visibility (work features)	• **Ribbon:** *View* tab>*Visibility* panel
N/A	**Suppress (constraint)**	• **Context Menu:** In Model browser with a component selected • **Context Menu:** In the graphics window with a component selected
N/A	**Undo Isolate (component visibility control)**	• **Context Menu:** In Model browser with a component selected • **Context Menu:** In the graphics window with a component selected
N/A	**Visibility (component)**	• **Context Menu:** In Model browser with a component selected • **Context Menu:** In the graphics window with a component selected

Chapter 19

Model Information

Obtaining measurements on your model is often required for entities to which explicit dimensions have not been assigned. To accomplish this, the Autodesk® Inventor® software provides a measure tool. In addition, tools are available to assign and work with model properties to capture additional information in your model.

Learning Objectives

- Use the **Measure** command to conduct measurements in part and assembly models.
- Calculate the area of a selected closed sketch.
- Set the physical properties for a model.
- Set material appearances and overrides.

19.1 Measurement Tools

The Autodesk Inventor software enables you to measure the distance, angle, perimeter, or area for entities in part and assembly models. To conduct a measurement, use the **Measure** command using any of the following methods.

- In the *Inspect* tab>*Measure* panel, click (Measure).
- In the *Tools* tab>*Measure* panel, click (Measure).
- Right-click in the graphics window and select **Measure** in the Marking menu.

Once the command is selected, the *Measure* panel and the tool palette (assembly models only) open, as shown in Figure 19–1.

> **Note:** *The Measure panel can be merged with the Model browser by dragging it into the Model browser area so that it is docked.*

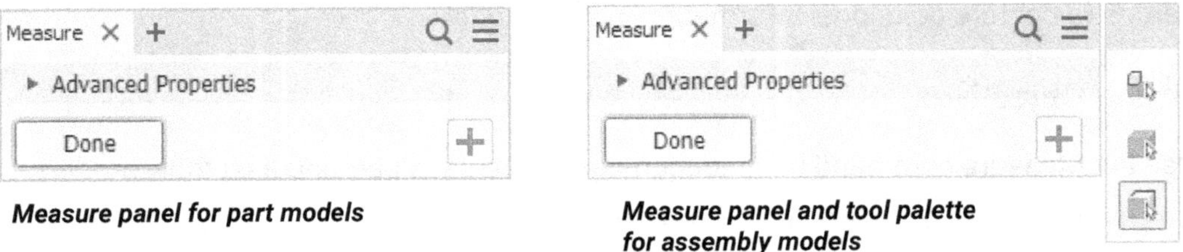

Measure panel for part models

Measure panel and tool palette for assembly models

Figure 19–1

- The *Measure* panel displays the measurement results as geometry is selected.
- The tool palette is only available when measuring assembly models and provides the selection priority buttons that enable you to set whether components, parts, or faces and edges are to be selected. By default, faces and edges are set.
- The expandable *Advanced Properties* area enables you to define the precision for the results and whether to display the result in multiple unit formats when the measurement displays.

Measuring Entities and Points

To measure linear and circular entities and points, the (Select Faces and Edges) option must be active for assembly models. Depending on the type or number of entities selected, the displayed results vary as follows:

- Select an edge to measure length and two edges to measure the distance between them, as shown in Figure 19–2.

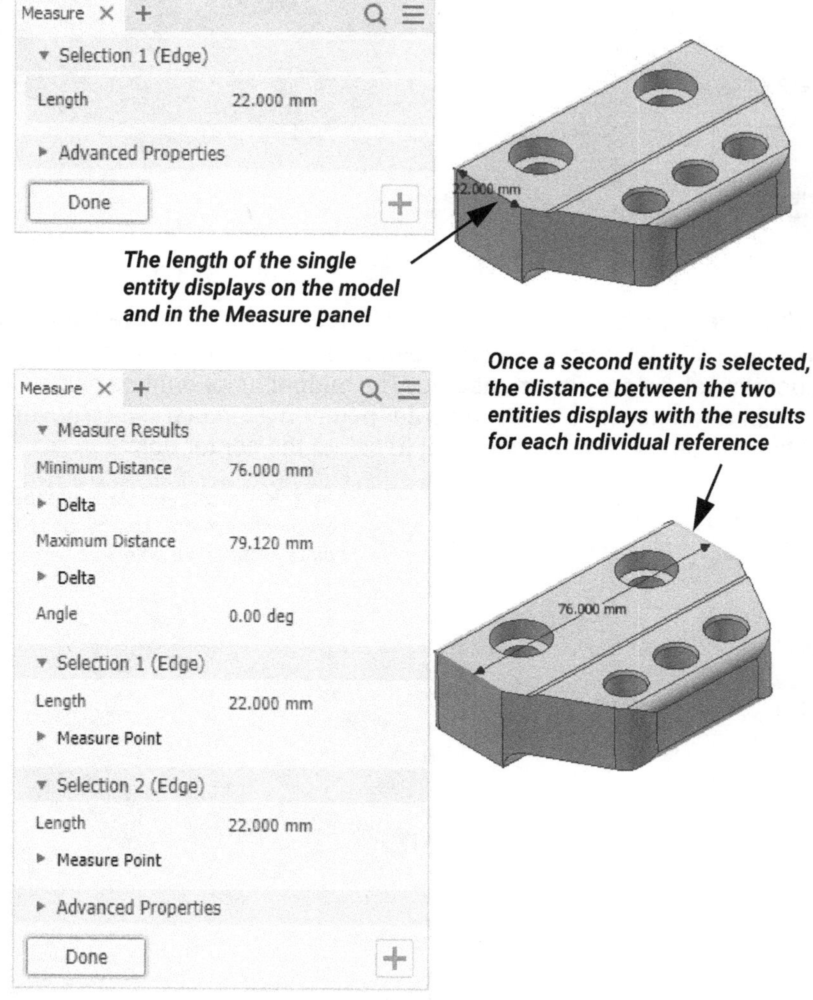

Figure 19–2

Note: *In some cases, you might need to hover the cursor until the* ***Select Other*** *tool displays to select the correct reference, or right-click on the reference and select* ***Select Other****. The references that are selected for measuring are assigned colors for easy identification. The first selection is blue and the second is green.*

- Select a circular edge to measure its diameter, radius, length, and angle, as shown in Figure 19–3.

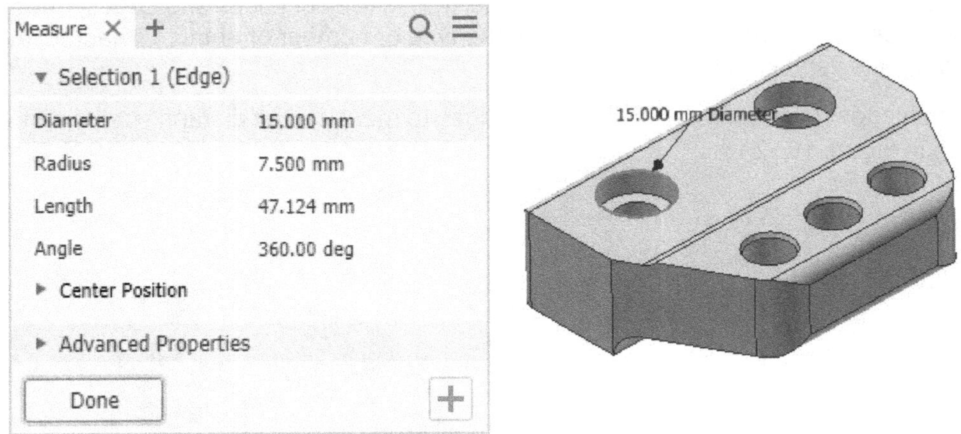

Figure 19–3

- Select a point to measure its location (X, Y, and Z) relative to the active coordinate system, as shown in Figure 19–4. Select a second point to measure the distance between them. Individual position values are also measured. The midpoints of entities can also be selected as measurement references. To select a center point on a circular entity, hover the cursor over the entity and use the **Select Other** tool to select the center point.

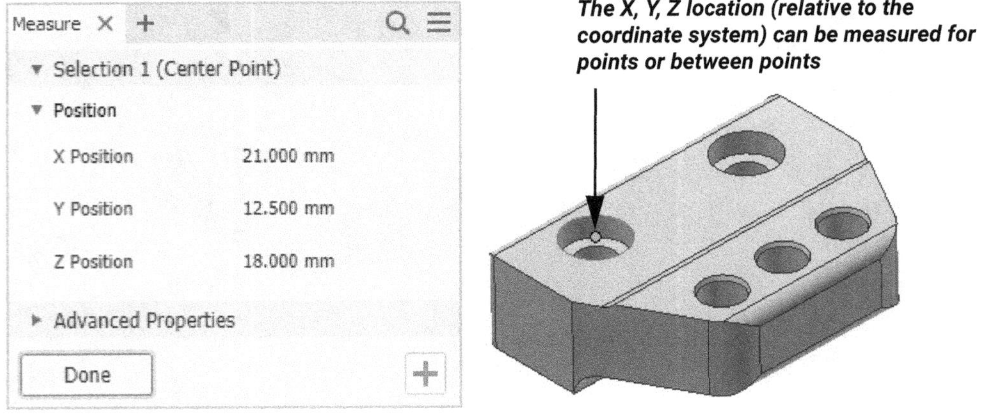

Figure 19–4

Note: *To copy a result or all results to the clipboard, right-click on the value and select* ***Copy*** *or* ***Copy All****.*

Measure the Distance Between Components

To measure the minimum distance between components, change the filter option to (Part Priority) or (Component Priority) and then select two components in the model. The *Measure* panel displays similar to that shown in Figure 19–5.

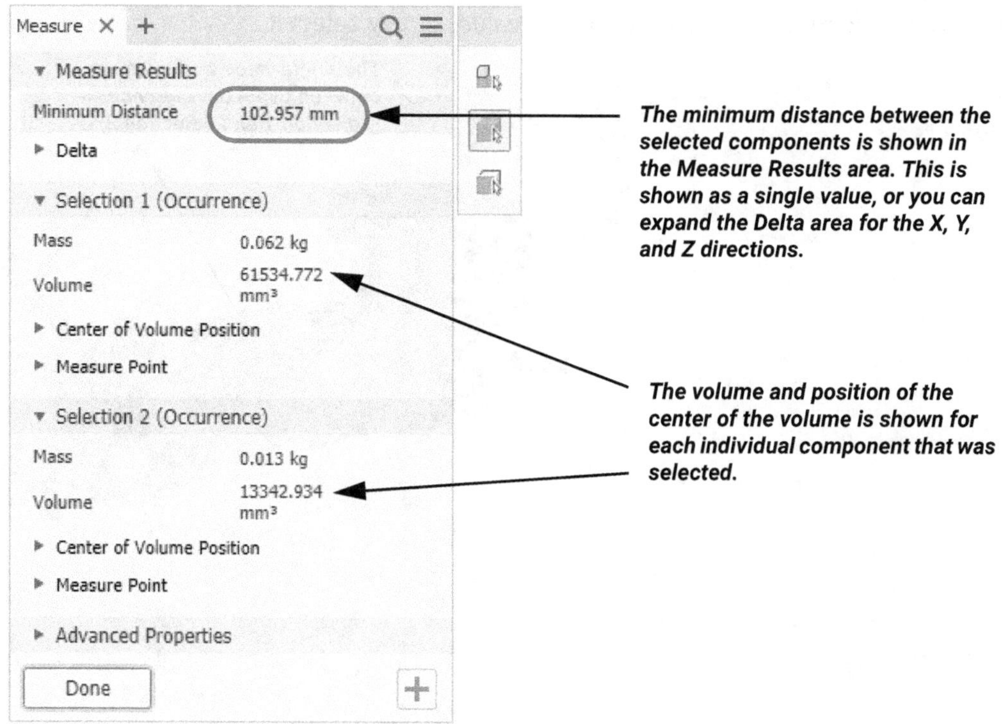

Figure 19–5

Measuring an Angle

To measure an angular value, the (Select Faces and Edges) option must be active in an assembly.

- To measure the angle between two lines or faces, select the two lines or faces. Axes can also be selected. Angular measurements are shown in Figure 19–6.
- The measurement value that is highlighted in blue in the *Measure* panel is the value that displays on the model. To display another value, simply select it.

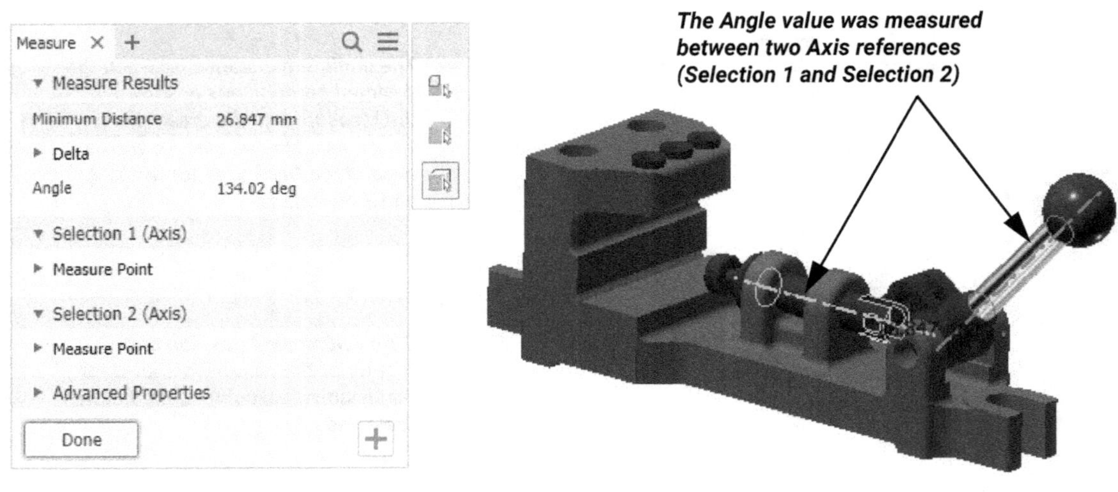

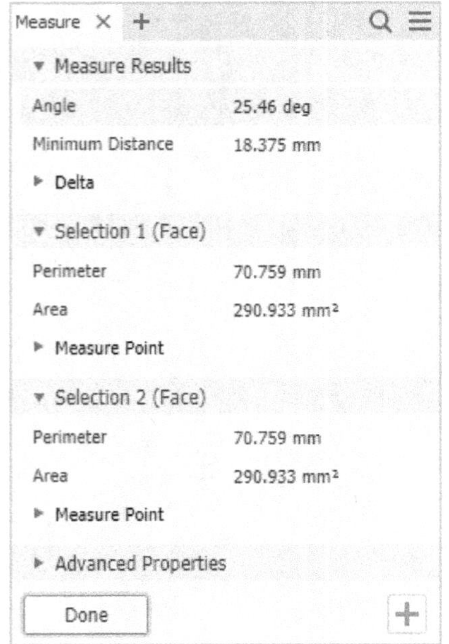

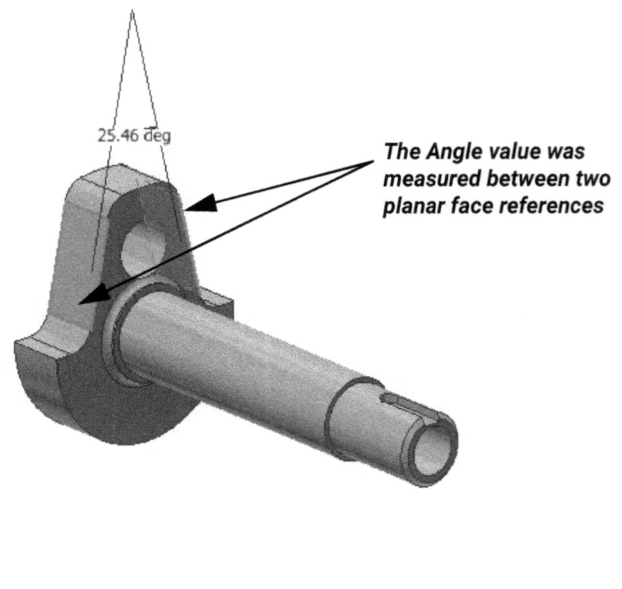

Figure 19–6

- To measure the angle created by three points, select the first two points that define a line, then hold <Shift> and select the third point that defines the angle.
- To measure the angular extent of a circular edge or arc, select it.

Measuring Planar Faces

To select a planar face for measurement, the (Select Faces and Edges) option must be active in an assembly. Once the reference is selected, the outside perimeter, the total loop perimeter (all edges that lie on the face), and the area of the face display as shown in Figure 19–7.

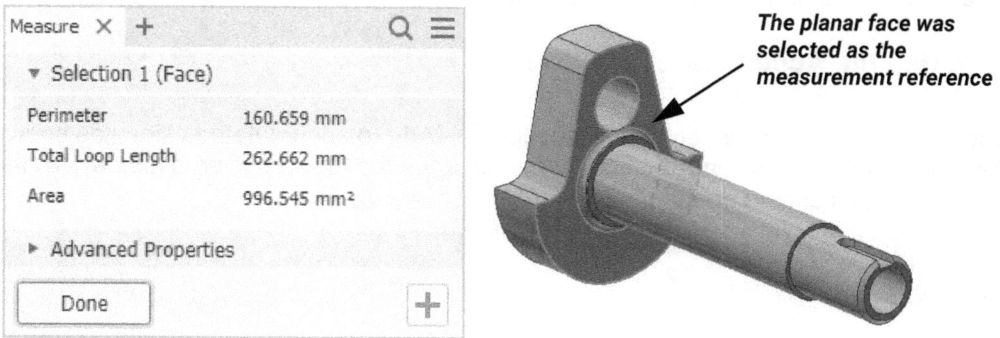

Figure 19–7

Measuring Cylindrical Faces

To select a cylindrical face for measurement, the (Select Faces and Edges) option must be active in an assembly. Once the reference is selected, the radius, diameter, total loop perimeter (all edges that lie on the face), and the area of the face are reported, as shown in Figure 19–8.

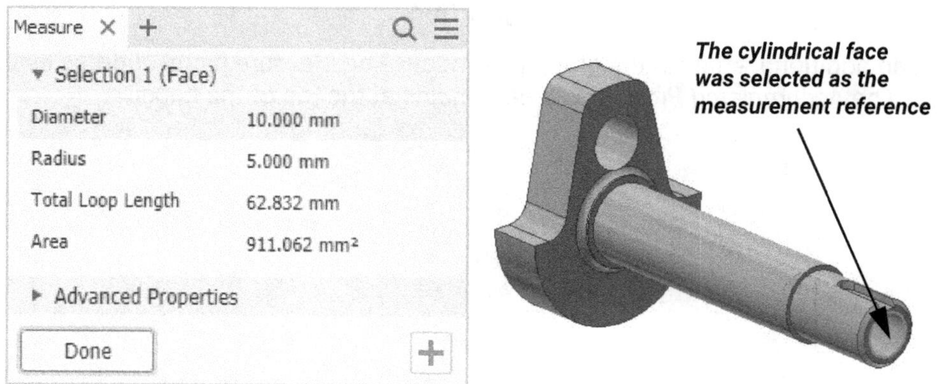

Figure 19–8

Note: *The Measure panel will also report thread data. Thread data is available for any part and assembly files that have a thread assigned to the selected cylindrical face.*

Restart a Measurement

To take a new measurement, left-click in the graphics window to clear the reference selection.

Alternatively, you can right-click and select **Restart** from the drop-down list or click + (Restart Measure) at the bottom of the *Measure* panel.

Add to Accumulate

The sum of multiple linear measurements, as well as area, volume, and angular measurements can be determined using the **Add to Accumulate** option in the *Measure* panel.

How To: Use the Accumulate Function

1. Once the initial measurement is made, click + (Add to accumulated value), as shown on the left in Figure 19–9. Once selected, the *Accumulated Properties* area displays at the top of the panel, as shown on the right.

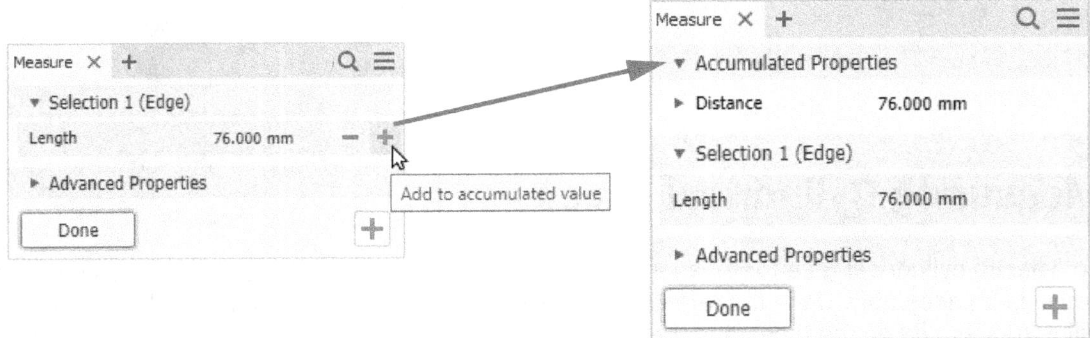

Figure 19–9

2. Select an additional entity in the graphics window. The *Measure* panel updates listing its values. The *Accumulated Properties* area remains at the top of the panel.

3. In the *Selection 2* area, click (Add to accumulated value), as shown on the left in Figure 19–10, to add the new value to the previous one. The value updates in the *Accumulated Properties* area, as shown on the right.

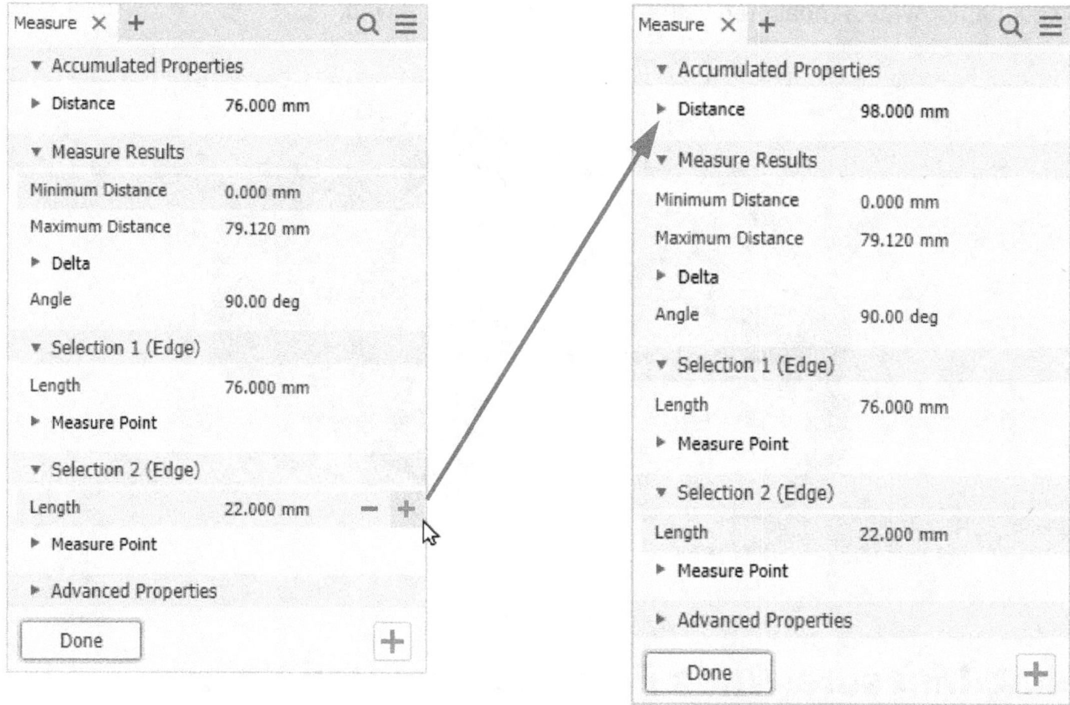

Figure 19–10

4. (Optional) To subtract a single value in the accumulate total, select (Subtract from accumulated value).
5. Continue to measure and add values as required.

Consider the following when working with accumulate values:

- To display the full list of the accumulated values, expand the *Distance* node.
- To clear a single value in the accumulate *Distance* node, hover over it and select (Delete) to remove it from the total.
- To clear a total accumulated *Distance* value, hover over it and select (Delete) to clear it.

Context Sensitive Measurements

If an object is preselected, you can right-click and select **Measure** in the marking menu, or in the expanded **Measure** options in the shortcut menu, as shown in Figure 19–11. If the preselected objects can provide a measured value, the results are displayed.

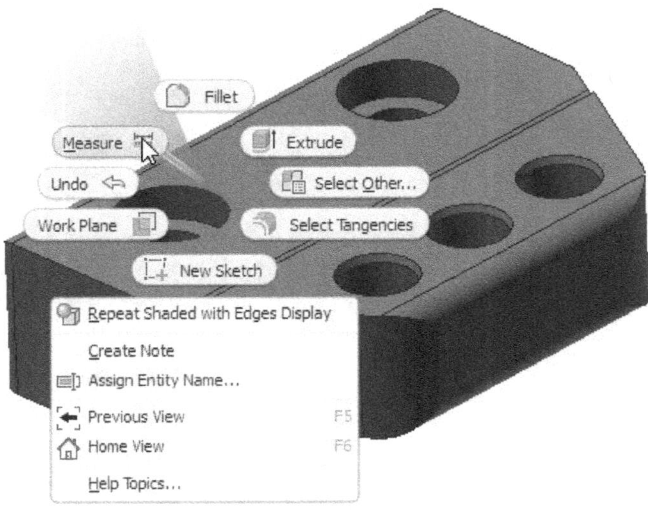

Figure 19–11

Using Measure When Entering Required Values

In most cases, if you are required to enter a value, you can use the **Measure** option (shown in Figure 19–12). This accesses the measuring tool to conduct a measurement on the model that is automatically populated into the value field. The **Measure** option is also available in *Edit Dimension* dialog boxes.

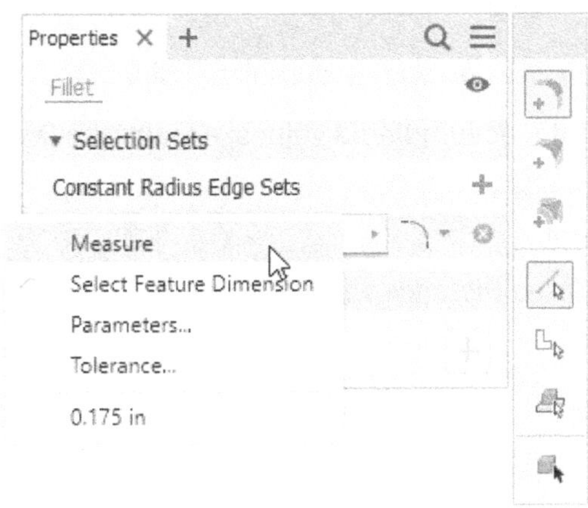

Figure 19–12

Region Properties

The **Region Properties** option calculates properties for a closed sketched area. You must be in the Sketch environment to use this command. To activate the tool, select the *Inspect* tab>*Measure* panel and click (Region Properties). Alternatively, the option can also be accessed in the *Tools* tab>expanded *Measure* panel. In the *Region Properties* dialog box, select **Click to Add** in the *Selections* area, select a section and click **Calculate**. The calculations are completed based on the sketch coordinate system. In Figure 19–13, the results for the sketched oblong section are shown on the right.

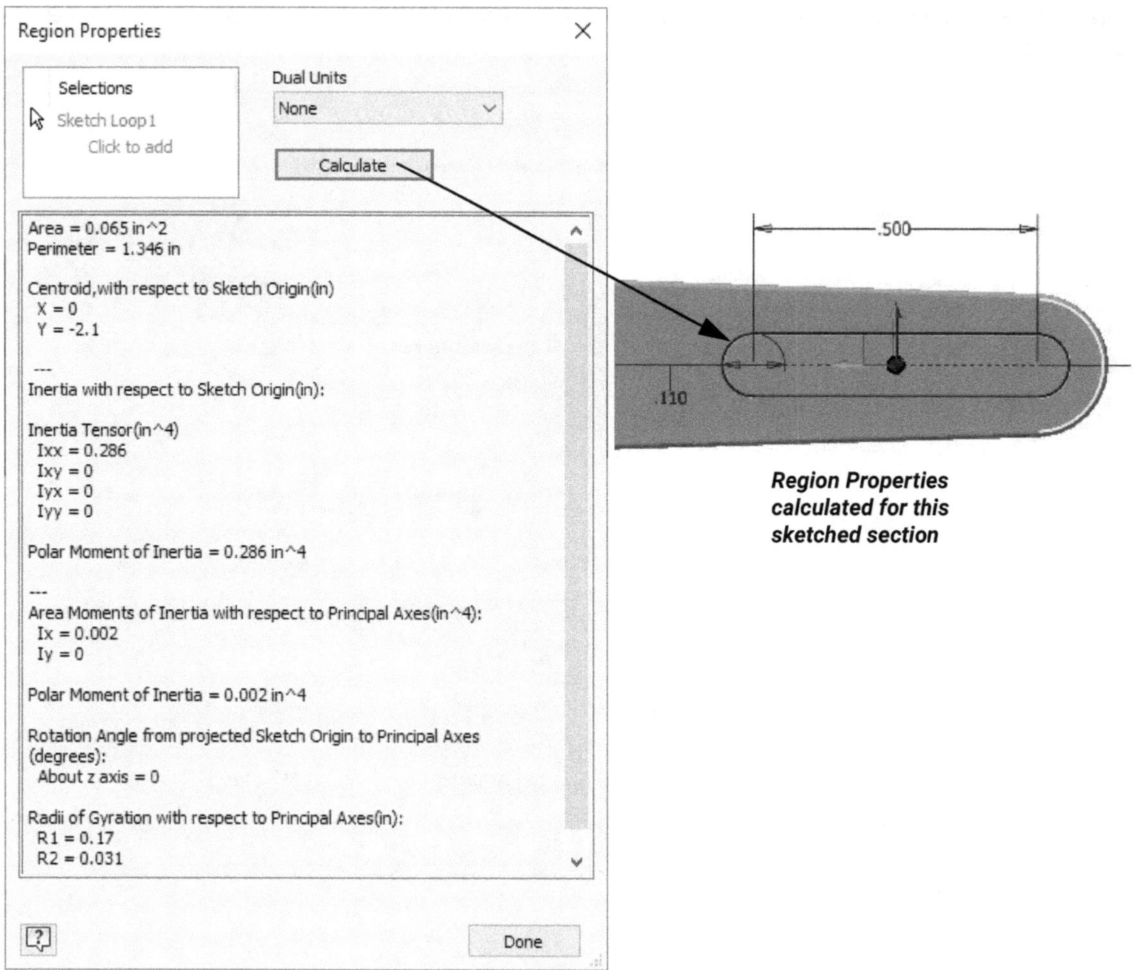

Figure 19–13

19.2 Model Material and Appearance Settings

Material

By assigning a specific material to a model, you can calculate the physical properties (e.g., volume, mass, center of gravity, etc.) of the model based on that material. The physical properties of a model are listed in the model's *iProperties* dialog box. To access this, right-click on the model name in the Model browser, select **iProperties**, and select the *Physical* tab. Alternatively, you can expand the **File** menu and select **iProperties** to open the *iProperties* dialog box. To assign material, select a type in the *Material* drop-down list, as shown in Figure 19–14. The values in the dialog box are automatically calculated based on the material selected.

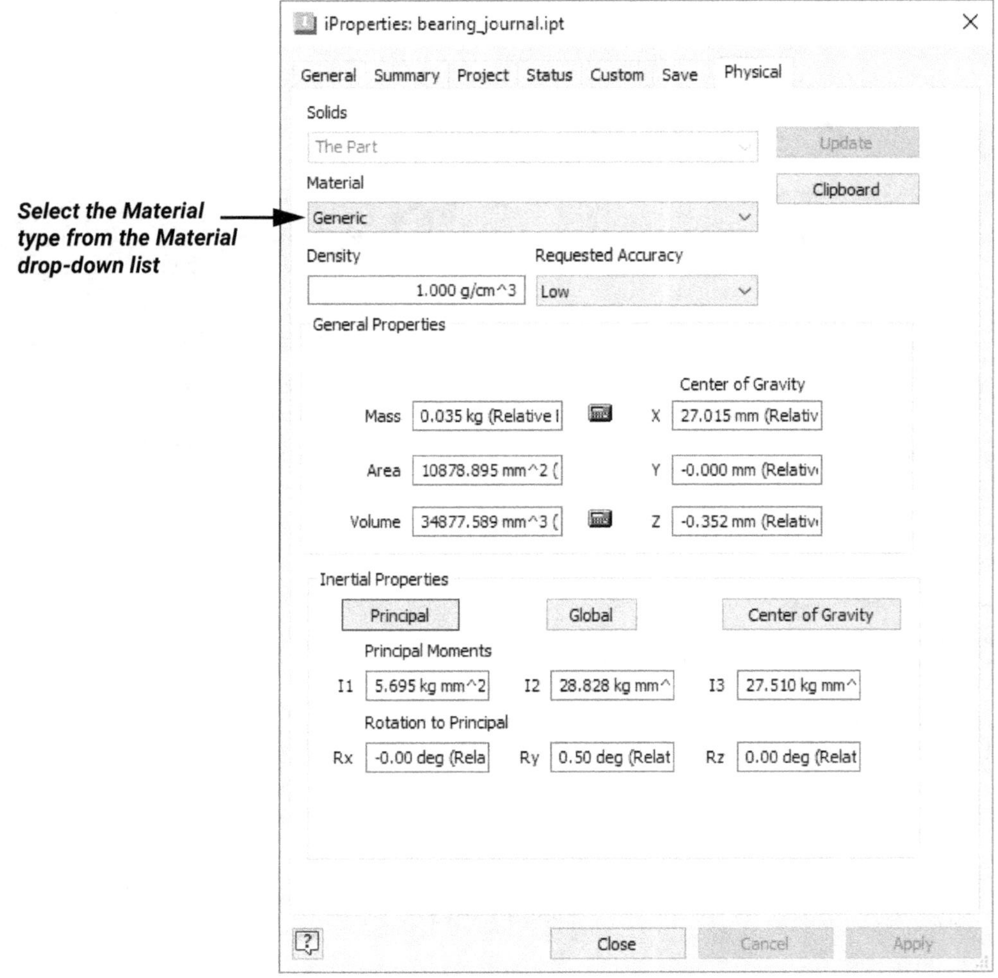

Figure 19–14

- The *Requested Accuracy* field sets the degree of accuracy for calculations. Low accuracy takes less time to calculate but is less accurate.
- Click **Update** to recalculate the physical properties of changes to part features, or to recalculate the physical properties of an assembly after changes are made to it.
- Click **Clipboard** to copy the physical property information to the Windows clipboard for pasting into a text editor.
- Mass and volume properties can be overridden by entering new values directly in their fields and clicking **Apply**. If the mass or volume properties are overridden, the other properties in the dialog box do not update to reflect the new value(s). Once overridden, they are shown with the hand symbol, as shown in Figure 19–15. To remove the override, delete the contents of the field(s) and click **Apply**.

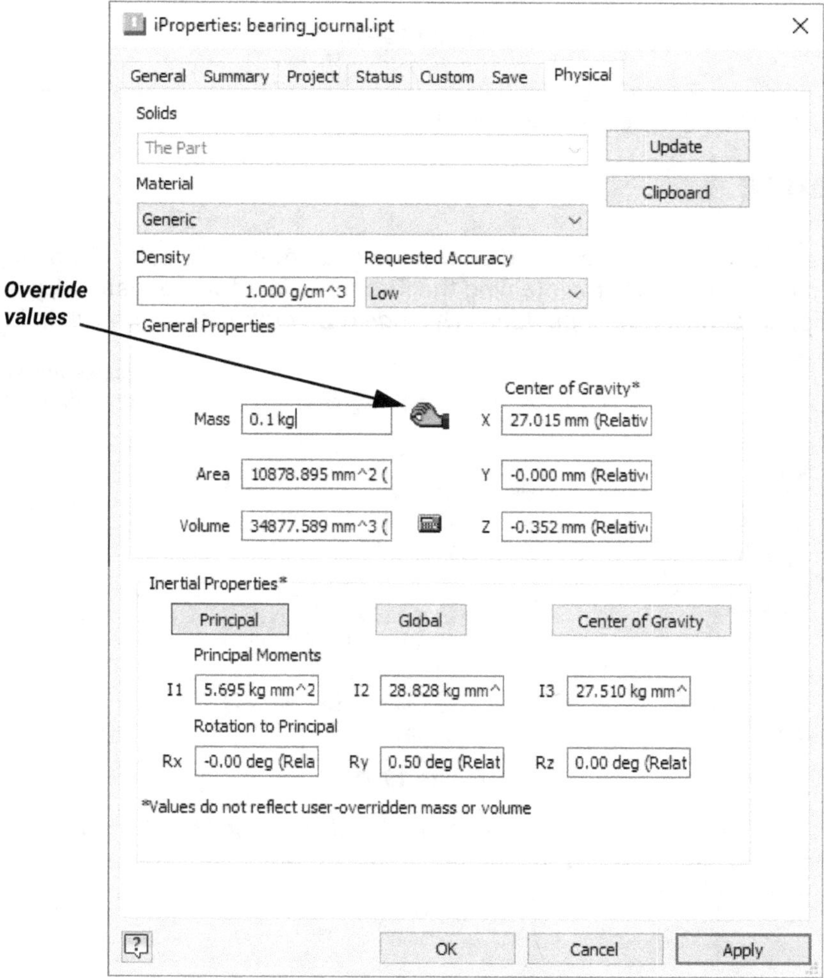

Figure 19–15

- If the material has been changed in the *iProperties* dialog box, the *Materials* drop-down list in the Quick Access Toolbar updates to reflect the change, as shown in Figure 19–16. You can use the *Materials* drop-down list as an alternative to changing the material in the *iProperties* dialog box.

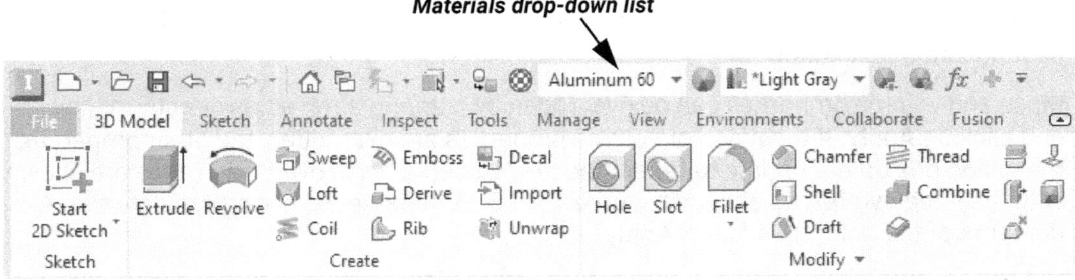

Figure 19–16

Note: *The physical properties are not available in iFeature, presentation, or drawing files. In an assembly file, the material cannot be changed.*

Appearance

By default, the color of a model is based on the assigned material's color. To assign a different appearance to the model while maintaining the iProperty data for the material, you can select an alternate appearance in the *Appearance Override* drop-down list, as shown in Figure 19–17.

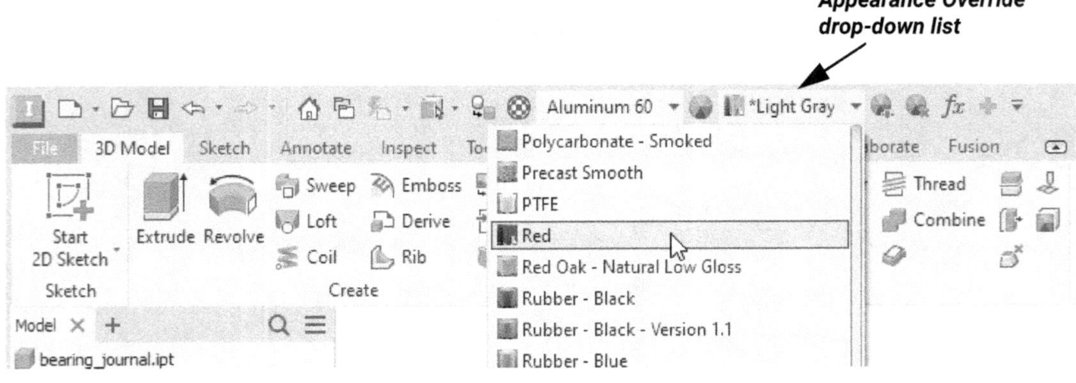

Figure 19–17

Note: *By default, the materials listed in the Materials drop-down list are those from the Inventor Material Library. To switch to the Autodesk Material Library, select it at the bottom of the Materials drop-down list.*

To assign an override color on specific features in the model, select the features, right-click, and select **Properties**. In the *Feature Properties* dialog box, select a feature appearance from the *Feature Appearance* drop-down list.

- Any overriden feature appearances are maintained regardless of a change to the appearance override.
- To clear a feature or model appearance override, in the *Tools* tab>*Material and Appearance* panel, click (Clear) and select the features to clear. This option is also available in the Quick Access Toolbar.

Practice 19a
Properties and Measurements

Practice Objectives

- Use the *iProperties* dialog box to change the material that is assigned to a component in an assembly.
- Use the **Measure** command to conduct measurements in a model

In this practice, you will apply material to components in the Bore Device assembly. You will then practice taking measurements of elements in the assembly.

Task 1: Open an assembly file.

1. Open **BoreDevice_3.iam**. The assembly displays as shown in Figure 19–18.

Figure 19–18

Task 2: Obtain and assign model properties.

1. Double-click on the **Ball Lever** component in the Model browser to activate it. This makes the part model active while remaining in the context of the assembly so that you have access to the part level commands.

2. Right-click on **Ball Lever** in the Model browser and select **iProperties**. Select the *Physical* tab to display the physical properties of the part, as shown in Figure 19–19. Click **Update** to update the values, if required.

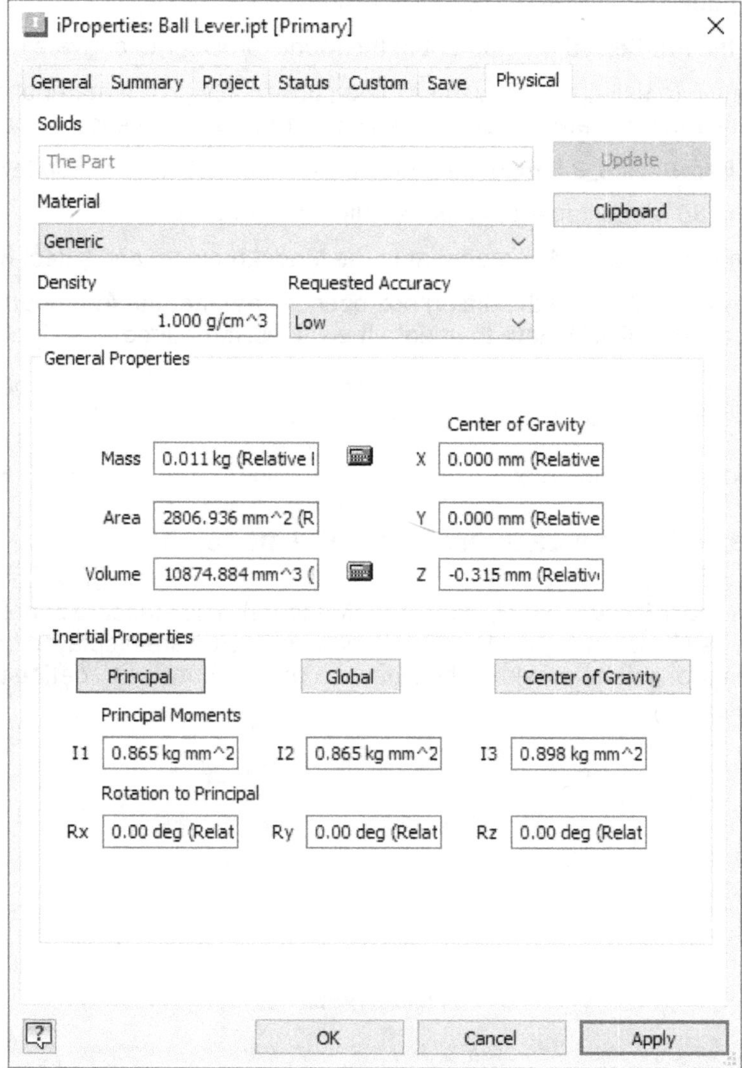

Figure 19–19

Note: *Alternatively, you can expand the* ***File*** *menu and select* ***iProperties*** *to open the iProperties dialog box.*

3. Select **ABS Plastic** in the *Material* drop-down list. The values in the dialog box update.
4. Click **Apply** and click **Close**.

5. In the Quick Access Toolbar, note that the *Material* is set to **ABS Plastic** and the *Appearance Override* is set to **Smooth-White**.
6. In the *Appearance Override* drop-down list in the Quick Access Toolbar, select **Red**. The color of the model updates in the graphics window.
7. Double-click the **Pin Seized** component in the Model browser to activate it.
8. As an alternative to using the *iProperties* dialog box to assign the material, select **Aluminum-6061** in the *Materials* drop-down list in the Quick Access Toolbar.
9. Double-click **BoreDevice_3.iam** in the Model browser to activate the top-level assembly again, or in the *3D Model* tab>*Return* panel, click (Return).
10. Right-click on the **Pin Seized** component in the Model browser and select **iProperties**.
11. Select the *Physical* tab when the dialog box opens. Note that the **Aluminum-6061** material has been assigned. Click **Update** to update the values, if required.

    Note: *While in the context of the top-level assembly, you cannot use the iProperties dialog box to change the material. This is why the Material field is unavailable.*

12. Close the *iProperties* dialog box.

Task 3: Take a series of measurements in the model.

1. In the *Inspect* tab>*Measure* panel, click (Measure). The *Measure* panel and the tool palette open, as shown in Figure 19–20. All measurements are displayed in the *Measure* panel, and the tool palette provides the selection priority buttons to define the type of entities to select.

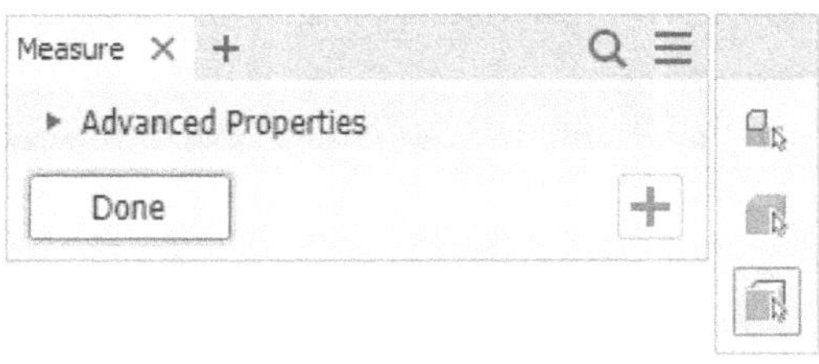

Figure 19–20

Note: *The Advanced Properties area of the Measure panel enables you to define the precision and dual unit settings for the measurement.*

2. Rotate the model as shown in Figure 19–21. Ensure that (Select faces and edges) is selected in the tool palette, and select the cylindrical surface shown in Figure 19–21. The *Measure* panel displays the measurement values for the *Radius*, *Diameter*, *Perimeter*, and *Area* of the selected surface.

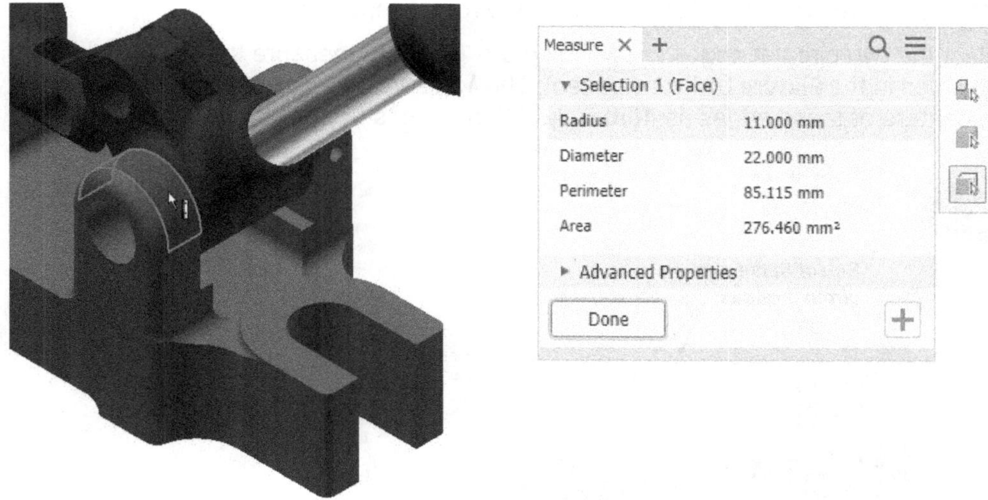

Figure 19–21

3. Left-click in the graphics window to clear the measurements. Alternatively, you can right-click in the graphics window and select **Restart** to clear the *Measure* panel.
4. Select the top edge of the model shown in Figure 19–22. The length displays in the *Measure* panel for *Selection 1*.
5. Select the bottom edge of the model shown in Figure 19–22. The distance between the two edges displays in the *Measure Results* area of the *Measure* panel. The lengths of the individual edges also display.

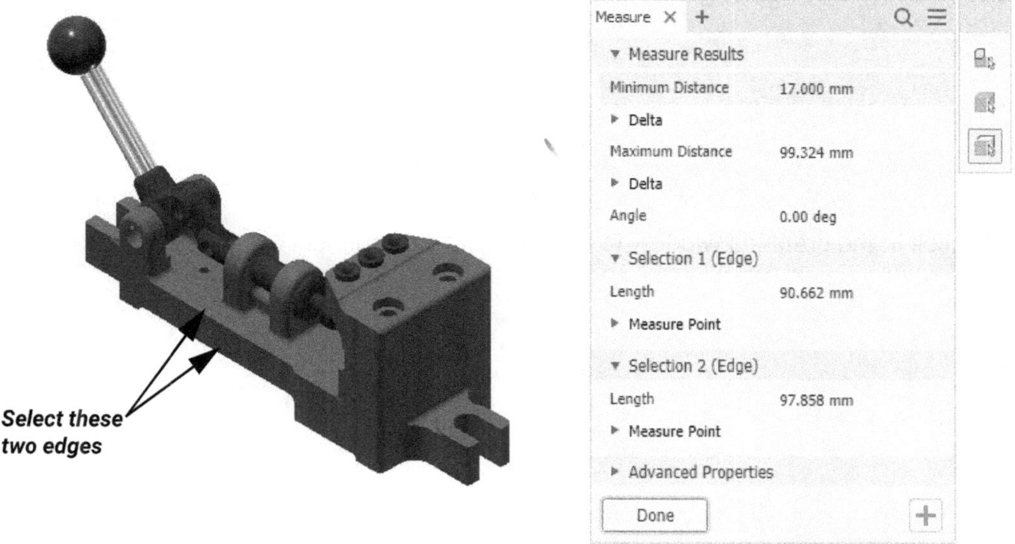

Figure 19–22

6. Left-click in the graphics window to clear the measurements.
7. Select the two circular edges shown in Figure 19–23 to measure the distance between the two holes in the **Fixture Drill** component. The *Measure* panel displays the distance between the centers of these edges as **40mm**. Additional measurements are also shown.

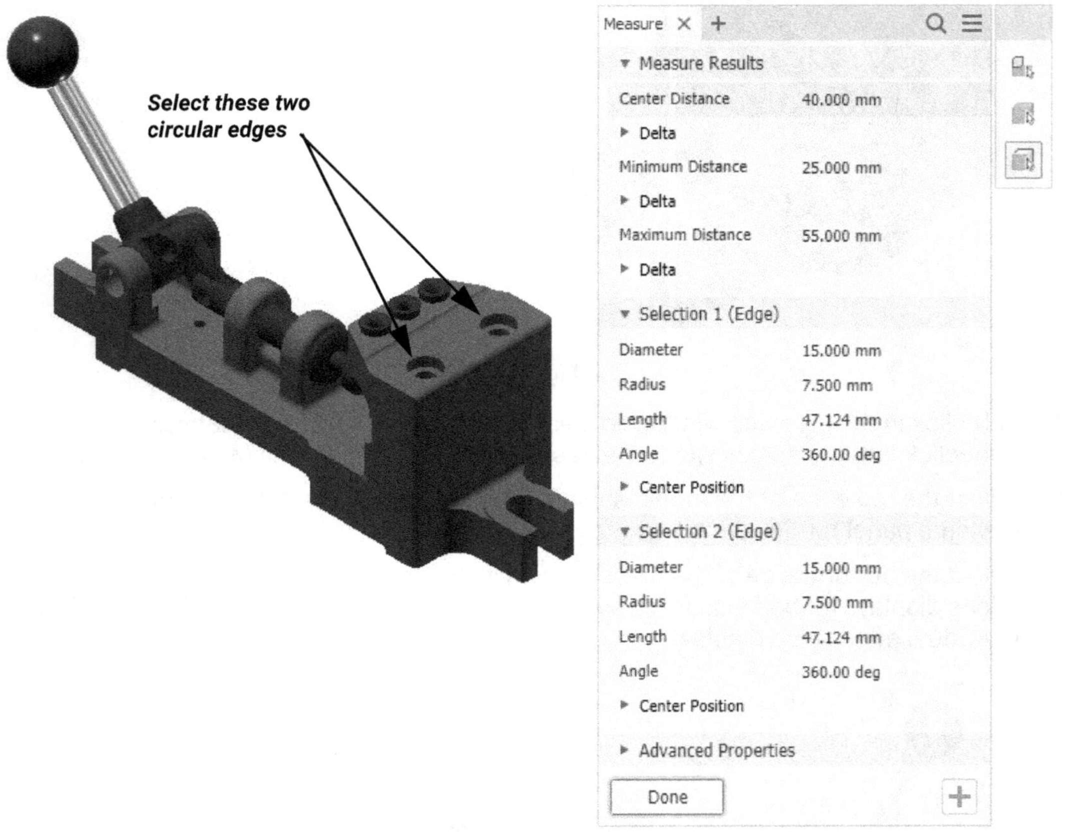

Figure 19–23

8. Left-click in the graphics window to clear the measurements.

9. Measure the distance between the surface and hole of the components shown in Figure 19–24 by first selecting the face and then selecting the circular edge. Note that the reported *Minimum Distance* is the minimum distance to the hole. Clear the measurement.

10. Select the face first and then hover the cursor over the edge of the hole. Right-click and select **Select Other** (or hover the cursor over the edge of the hole until the *Select Other* drop-down list displays). In the *Select Other* drop-down list, select the axis of the hole. The *Measure* panel should display a distance of **119.562mm**. As an alternative, you could have selected the surface of the hole and it would measure to the axis.

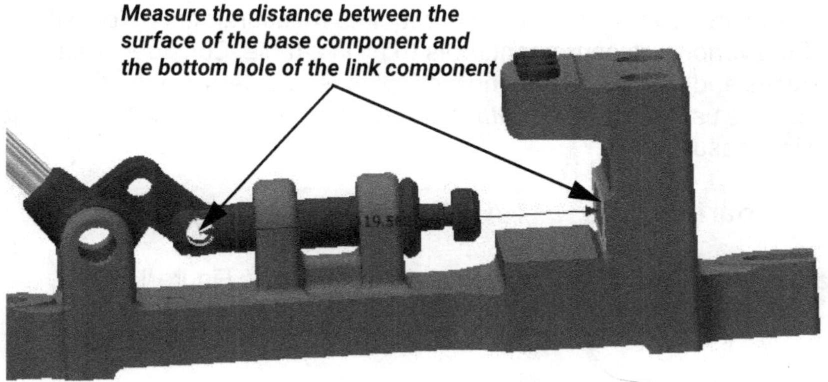

Figure 19–24

11. Practice taking additional measurements.

12. Save and close the model.

End of practice

Practice 19b
(Optional) Model Measurements

Practice Objective

- Select and use the correct measurement tools to obtain values for a list of required measurements.

In this practice, you are provided with a list of required measurements. You will need to select and use any of the various measurement tools to fill in a table. Consider creating work planes tangent to surfaces and parallel to existing work planes to determine the distances between curved surfaces. The use of the *Select Other* drop-down list can help with selecting the correct references while measuring.

Task 1: Open a part file.

1. Open **bearing_journal.ipt**. The model displays as shown in Figure 19–25.

Figure 19–25

Task 2: Take a variety of measurements.

1. Use the measuring options on the *Inspect* or *Tools* tabs to take the measurements shown in Figure 19–26. Compare your results to those listed in the table to ensure that the measurement has been taken correctly.

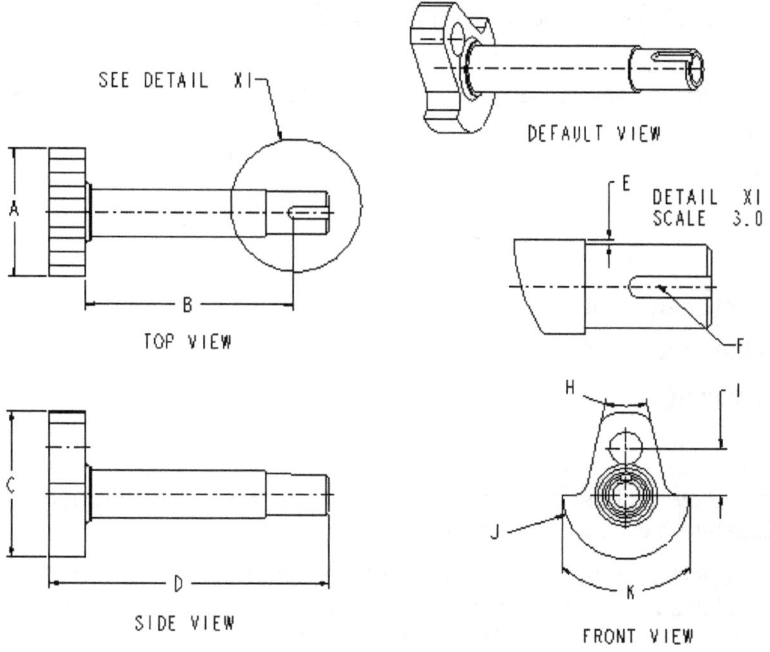

Figure 19–26

Dimension	Description	Value
A	Overall width of model	46.00
B	From face to center of arc on slot	75.00
C	Overall height of model	53.00
D	Overall length of model	101.00
E	Height of step	1.00
F	Surface area of slot	58.28
H	Angle	25.46
I	Center to center between shaft and hole	17.00
J	Diameter	46.00
K	Arc length	72.26

End of practice

Chapter Review Questions

1. Which of the following measurements can be generated using the **Measure** option? (Select all that apply.)
   a. Edge Length
   b. Diameter
   c. Angle
   d. Distance between points
   e. Distance between edges
   f. Area of a sketch

2. Which of the following best describes how to use the **Measure** command to enter a required value when creating a feature?
   a. With the *Properties* panel, dialog box, or mini-toolbar open, in the *Inspect* tab>*Measure* panel, select **Measure**. Select the geometrical references to perform the required measure. This value is automatically used in the value field.
   b. In the *Properties* panel, dialog box, or mini-toolbar, click the arrow next to the value field you want to change and select **Measure** in the drop-down list. Select the geometrical references to perform the required measure. This value is automatically used in the value field.
   c. In the *Inspect* tab>*Measure* panel, select **Measure**. Select the geometrical references to perform the required measure. Create the feature and in the expanded menu for the required dimension value, select the value that was just measured.

3. The *iProperties* dialog box provides you with information about which physical properties of a part? (Select all that apply.)
   a. Mass
   b. Center of Gravity
   c. Area
   d. Volume

4. In an assembly file, the material cannot be changed using the *iProperties* dialog box.
   a. True
   b. False

5. Where do you find information such as the mass and volume of a part, as shown in Figure 19–27?

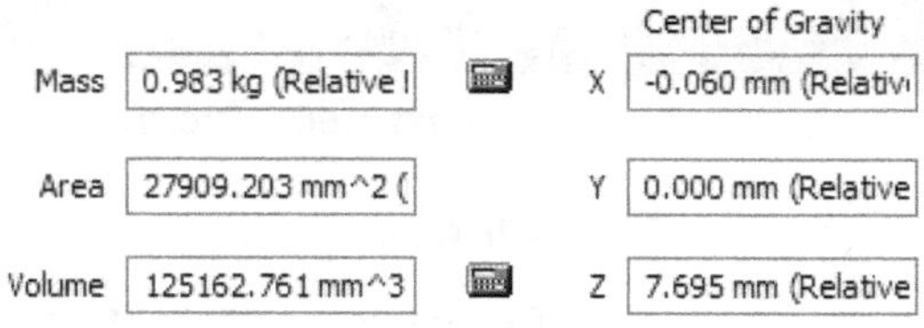

Figure 19–27

a. Analysis Tools (*Inspect* tab>*Measure* panel)

b. *iProperties* dialog box (**File** menu>**iProperties**)

c. *Parameters* dialog box (*Manage* tab>**Parameters**)

d. *Document Settings* dialog box (*Tools* tab>**Document Settings**)

6. Which of the following best describes how to change the color of a specific feature in the model?

a. Select the feature and select a material that uses the appropriate color in the *Materials* drop-down list.

b. Select the feature and select a material that uses the appropriate color in the *Physical* tab in the *iProperties* dialog box.

c. Select the feature and select a color in the *Appearance Override* drop-down list.

d. Select the feature and select a color in the *Feature Properties* dialog box.

Command Summary

Button	Command	Location
N/A	**iProperties**	• **Context Menu:** (*from Model browser with Component name selected*) • **File Menu**
	Measure	• **Ribbon:** *Inspect* tab>*Measure* panel • **Ribbon:** *Tools* tab>*Measure* panel • **Context Menu:** In the graphics window with an entity selected>Measure
	Region Properties	• **Ribbon:** *Inspect* tab>*Measure* panel • **Ribbon:** *Tools* tab>expanded *Measure* panel

Chapter 20

Presentation Files

The presentation tools available in the Autodesk® Inventor® software enable you to create snapshot views and animations to help document an assembly. A presentation file can be used to indicate how parts relate to each other and create an exploded view for a drawing. Animating the exploded view of the assembly enables you to further show how components fit together in the assembly.

Learning Objectives

- Understand how presentation files can be used to document an assembly model.
- Create a presentation file with an animation of how an assembly is to be assembled.
- Create a presentation file with snapshot views that can be used in drawing views.
- Publish a presentation file to create images and videos.

20.1 Getting Started with Presentation Files

To create an exploded view of an assembly, you must use a presentation file. In a presentation file, you can move or rotate the components relative to one another and add trails to indicate how they relate in the assembly. This can be stored as an animation or as static images. An exploded view of an assembly is shown in Figure 20–1. If a component dimension is modified or if a component is removed or added in the assembly, the presentation file updates to incorporate the changes.

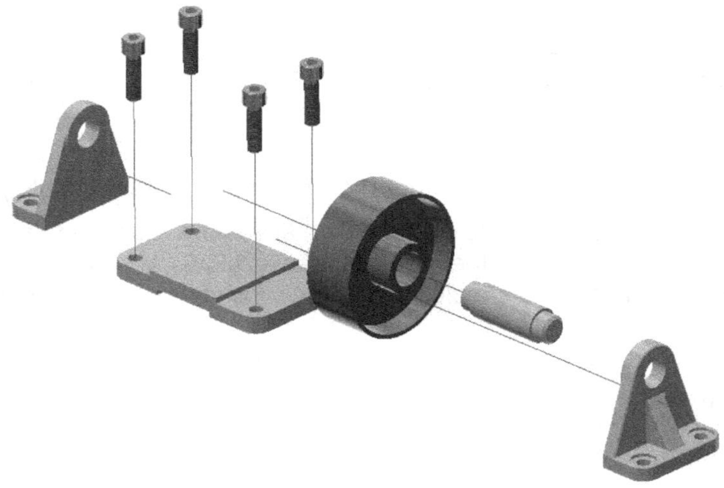

Figure 20–1

The first step in creating a presentation file is to start a new file based on a Presentation template (.IPN). To access the presentation templates, you can use any of the following:

- Click **New** on the *Home* page, or click (New) in the Quick Access Toolbar or in the **File** menu. Select an *.IPN template in the *Create New File* dialog box and click **Create**. You might need to scroll down in the list to locate this template.
- In an open assembly model, right-click on the assembly name at the top of the Model browser and select **Create Presentation**. Once selected, you will be prompted for the template to be used.

  Note: *To verify the default presentation template that is assigned, use the Application Options. In the Tools tab, click (Application Options), select the File tab and click* ***Configure Default Template*** *to review the settings in the Configure Default Template dialog box.*

Once the presentation file is created, the Presentation environment displays and you are immediately prompted to select a model for the first scene. Using the *Insert* dialog box, you can navigate to and open the model that will be used in the presentation. The *Presentation* tab becomes the active tab and the interface includes a Model browser, *Snapshot Views* browser, and the *Storyboards Panel*, as shown in Figure 20–2.

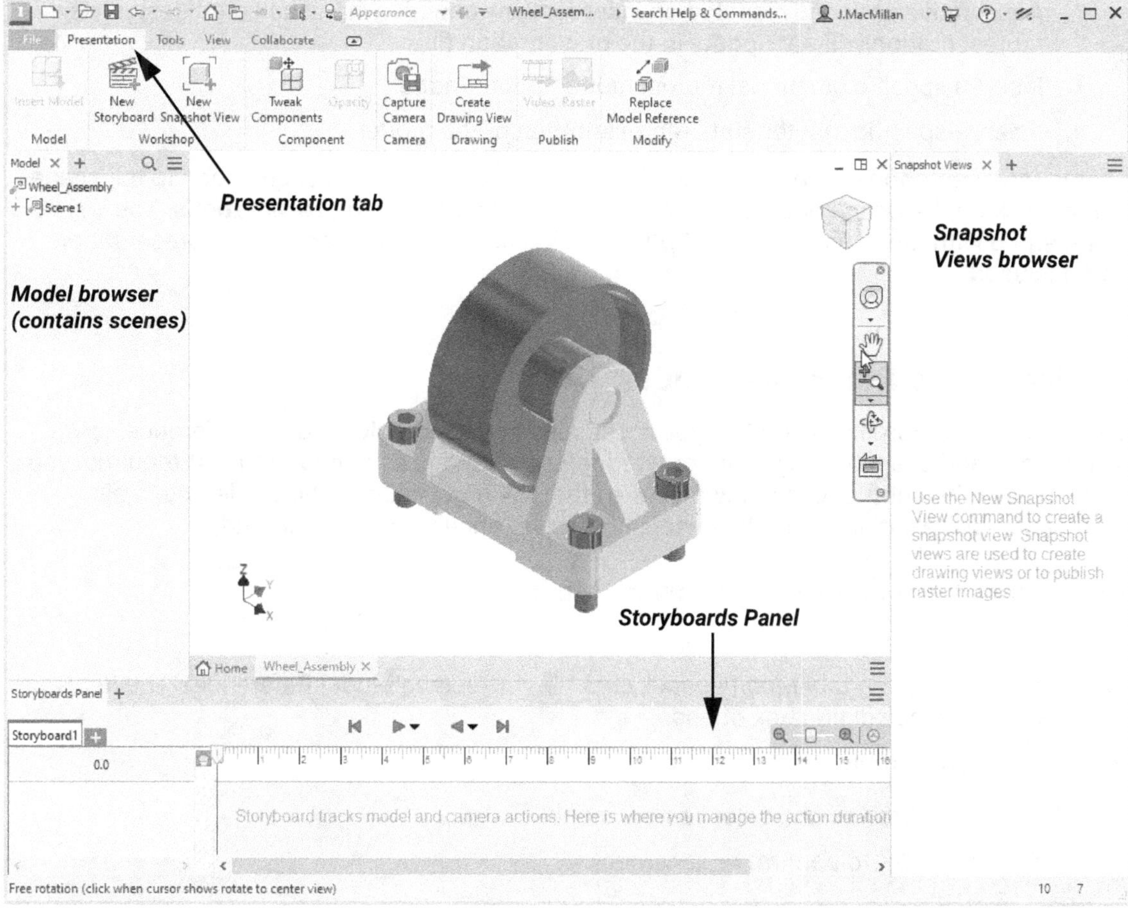

Figure 20–2

A presentation file is automatically created with an initial scene called **Scene1**.

- A file can consist of multiple scenes, all of which are independent and can reference different source models. To create additional scenes, right-click at the top of the Model browser and select **Create Scene**.
- The model inserted in the last scene is listed at the top of the Model browser; however, each scene contains the model that was initially assigned to it.
- Each scene can contain snapshot views and storyboards.

 **Hint: Inserting Models**

When selecting the model to be inserted into a scene, you can click **Options** to open the *File Open Options* dialog box, which enables you to:

- Insert an associative or non-associative version of a design view representation. If the **Associative** option is disabled on insertion, any changes in the selected design view representation will not update in the presentation file.
- Insert a specific positional representation of the model.
- Insert a specific master state representation of the model.

If the representation of the model needs to be changed after it has been added to the scene, right-click on the **Scene** node in the Model browser and select **Representations**. You will be presented with the same *File Open Options* dialog box and can change the representation that is used.

Replacing the Reference Model

When a presentation file is created, you must select an assembly model to reference. Animations and snapshot views are created referencing this assigned model. If required, you can replace with another assembly model so that the new model is then reflected in all animations and existing dependent snapshot views (once views are updated).

How To: Replace an Existing Drawing Model

1. In the *Presentation* tab>*Modify* panel, click (Replace Model Reference). The *Replace Model Reference* dialog box opens.
2. Select the assembly model to be replaced.
3. Click and browse and select a new model.
4. Click **Yes** and **OK** to confirm replacement.

   Note: *Inventor attempts to maintain the animation tweaks made to components in the model; however, depending on how significantly different the replacing assembly model is, Inventor's interpretation may not be as required. It is recommended to verify the animations and snapshot views once you have replaced the model and make edits as necessary.*

20.2 Presentation Files – Storyboard Animations

The *Storyboards Panel* at the bottom of the graphics window contains the list of storyboards that exist in a presentation file. Each storyboard is included on its own tab. A storyboard can be used for the following:

- Creating an animation of the model that records component movements (i.e., assembly/disassembly).
- Creating actions to represent changes in component visibility and opacity at specific times in an animation.
- Capturing changes in camera position at specific times in an animation.

Figure 20–3 shows the components of the *Storyboards Panel* used to create and play animations.

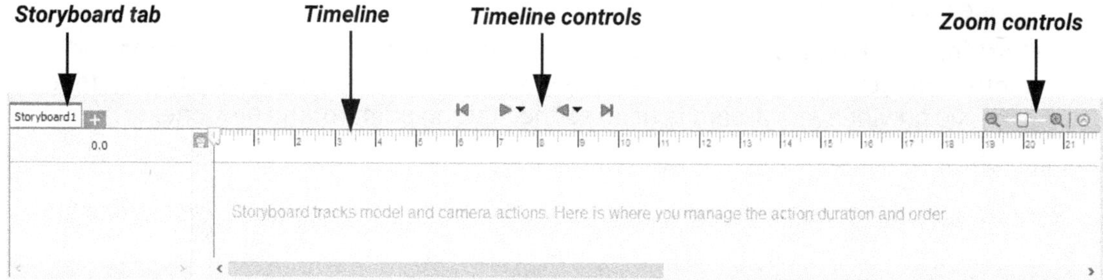

Figure 20–3

When a presentation file is created, a single storyboard is included. Additional storyboards can be included, as required. Storyboards can be independent of one another or they can work in combination with one another.

> ***Note:*** *Snapshot views can be created at specific points along the timeline. This is discussed further in the next section.*

How To: Create a Storyboard

1. Activate the scene to which the storyboard will be added by double-clicking the scene name in the Model browser.
2. In the *Presentation* tab>*Workshop* panel, click (New Storyboard). Alternatively, in the *Storyboards Panel* at the bottom of the graphics window, click adjacent to the storyboard tabs.

3. In the *New Storyboard* dialog box, select the *Storyboard Type* (as shown in Figure 20–4) and enter the *Storyboard Name*. The *Storyboard Type* options are described below.

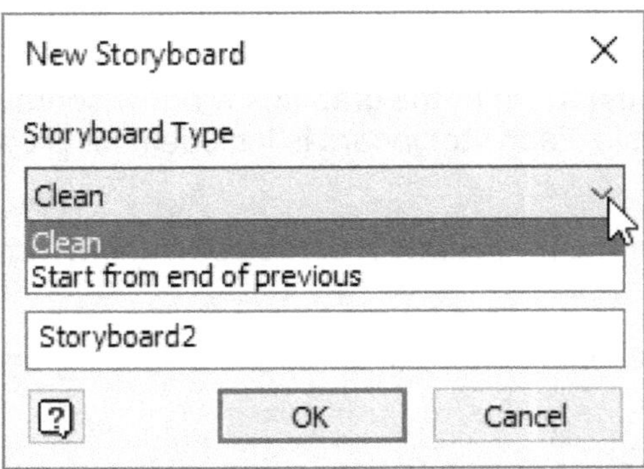

Figure 20–4

- **Clean:** Creates a new storyboard that uses the default appearance and camera settings for the active scene.
- **Start from end of previous:** Creates a new storyboard that is started from the end of another storyboard. The component positions, visibility, opacity, and camera settings from the previous storyboard is used as the starting point for the new one.

4. Click **OK**.

Note: To rename an existing storyboard, right-click on its tab name and select ***Rename****.*

Hint: Storyboards Panel Customization

The *Storyboards Panel* can be customized as follows:

- Click or in the panel to expand or compress it.
- Click and drag the panel titlebar to undock it. To redock it, drag its titlebar back into position at the bottom of the graphics window.
- Use to zoom in or out on the timeline's scale.

Creating and Editing Animations

An animation consists of movements that are applied to selected components in the assembly. The movements are called *tweaks* and can be linear and rotational and are set to run over a timed period (duration).

How To: Add a Tweak

1. Drag the playhead ( ) for the timeline to the required location.
2. In the *Presentation* tab>*Component* panel, click (Tweak Components). Alternatively, right-click and select **Tweak Components**. The mini-toolbar opens.
3. In the *Model Type* drop-down list (shown in Figure 20–5), select whether a **Part** or **Component** will be tweaked. Use **Components** to select subassemblies. Note that some commands will not be available until after a component is selected in the next step.

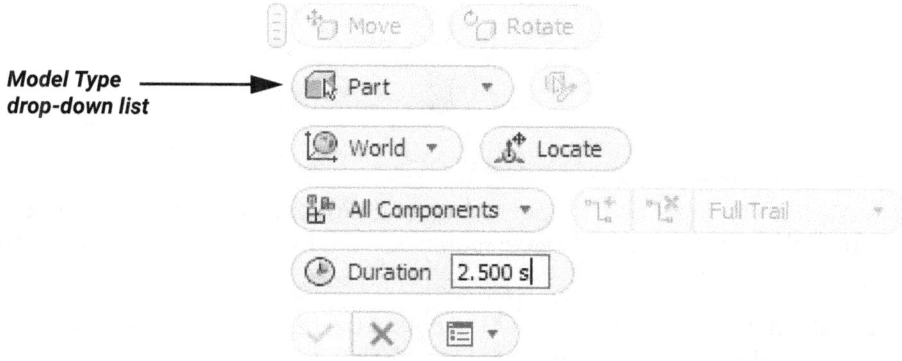

Figure 20–5

4. Select a component or multiple components to be tweaked.
   - Press and hold <Ctrl> and select components in the graphics window or from the expanded model list in the **Scene** node of the Model browser to select multiple components.
   - Press and hold <Shift> to select a range of components in the Model browser.
   - Select individual components or use a window selection technique to select components in the graphics window.
   - To clear a selected component, press and hold <Ctrl> and select it a second time.
   - All selected components are highlighted in blue.

5. Select the type of tweak. A triad will display on a face of the first selected component, similar to that shown in Figure 20–6 for a Move tweak.
    - Click **Move** in the mini-toolbar to move the selected component linearly in the X, Y, or Z directions.
    - Click **Rotate** in the mini-toolbar to rotate the selected components in the XY, YZ, or XZ Planes.

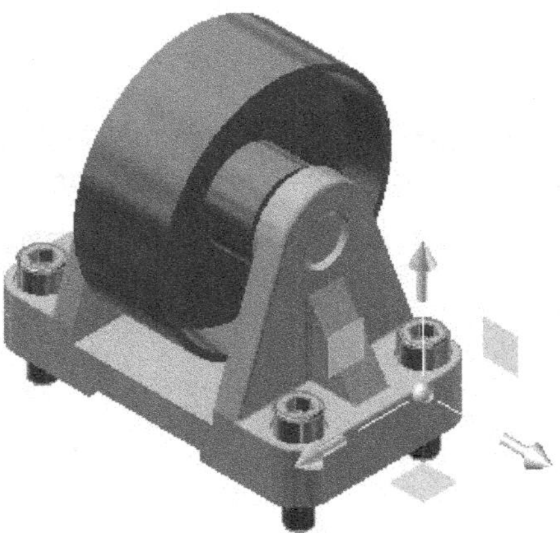

Figure 20–6

6. (Optional) Reposition the triad if it does not meet the orientation requirements for the tweak. If multiple components have been selected for a tweak, the triad displays on the first object that was selected.
    - Click **Locate** in the mini-toolbar. Hover the cursor over a new face reference and once the required control point on the face highlights, click to relocate the triad.
    - Use **Local** or **World** in the mini-toolbar to orient the triad relative to the component's coordinate system or the assembly coordinate system, respectively.
7. Select the control handle on a triad and drag it to define the tweak, as shown in Figure 20–7. The selected direction on the triad is displayed in gold. Alternatively, enter a specific value tweak's entry field.
    - Select an X, Y, or Z arrowhead to move linearly.
    - Select a XY, YZ, or XZ Plane to move in a plane.
    - Select a rotation handle to rotate about the X, Y, or Z.

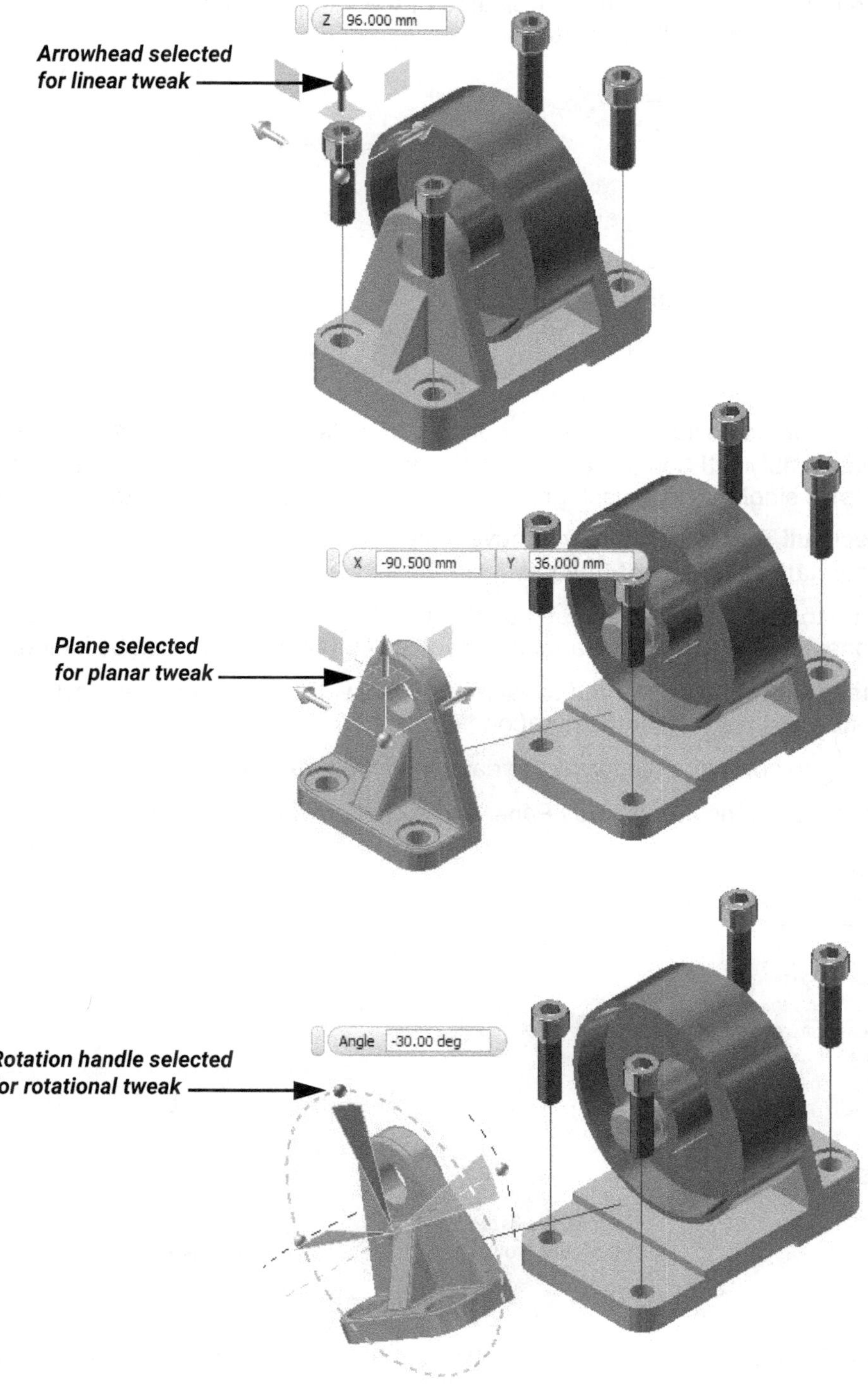

Z 96.000 mm
Arrowhead selected for linear tweak
X -90.500 mm
Y 36.000 mm
Plane selected for planar tweak
Angle -30.00 deg
Rotation handle selected for rotational tweak

Figure 20–7

8. (Optional) Use the options in the *Trail* area of the mini-toolbar (shown in Figure 20–8) to control how the trail will be created.

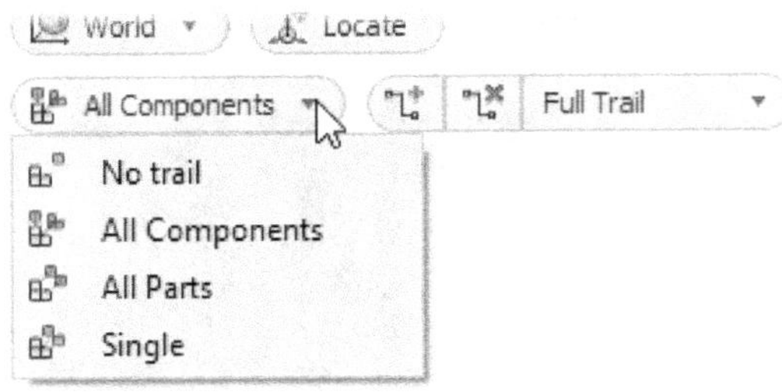

Figure 20–8

- In the drop-down list, select an option to add trails to all components in an assembly or subassembly (**All Components**) and all parts and a single trail for subassemblies (**All Parts**), a single trail for each group of components (**Single**), or no trail at all (**No Trails**).
- Select **Full Trail** to selectively remove or keep an entire trial or select **Trail Segment** to manipulate segments of the trail.

9. Continue to select additional triad handles to fully define the tweak or select additional components. Multiple combinations of handles and tweak types can be included.
10. Enter the **Duration** value for the tweak. The tweak will begin where the playhead was positioned and will run for the duration.
11. Click ✓ to complete the tweak. To cancel the operation, click ✕.

Tweaks are listed in the *Storyboards Panel* and Model browser, as shown in Figure 20–9.

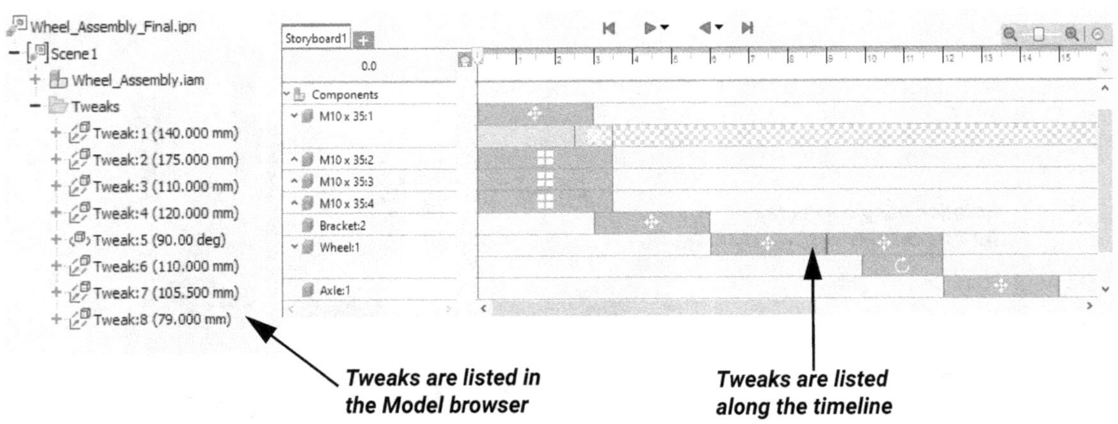

Figure 20–9

- In the Model browser, the icons show whether the tweak is linear ( ) or rotational ( ).
- In the *Storyboards Panel*, the symbols used to identify the duration of the tweak indicates if it is linear or planar ( ), rotational ( ),or a combination of both ( ).

Repositioning/Moving Tweaks

A tweak's timeline entry can be dragged to reposition it on the timeline. To move multiple tweaks at once, press and hold <Ctrl> to select them prior to moving. The *Duration* of the tweaks can be changed by dragging its endline to the appropriate time.

Editing Tweaks

An existing tweak can be modified in any of the following ways:

- Change the translational or rotational values initially assigned to the tweak.
- Change the duration of the tweak.
- Control the visibility of the trail lines for a tweak.

Note: *New translational or rotational movements cannot be added to an existing tweak. A new tweak must be added.*

How To: Edit a Tweak's Values

1. Activate the **Edit Tweak** command.
   - In the timeline, right-click on a tweak's symbol and select **Edit Tweak**.
   - In the graphics window, right-click on a trail line that belongs to the tweak and select **Edit Tweak**.
   - In the Model browser, expand the *Tweaks* folder, right-click on a tweak, and select **Edit Tweak**.
   - In the Model browser, expand the *Tweaks* folder, select a tweak, and enter a new tweak value in the entry field.
   - Alternatively, double-click on the tweak name or trail line to edit it.

   Note: *The tweaks listed in the Model browser are context sensitive. When you are in an animation storyboard, only the tweaks for the storyboard display. When editing a snapshot view, only its tweaks display.*

2. Use the Tweak mini-toolbar to change the properties of the tweak.
   - Enter new values for the defined movements.
   - Press and hold <Ctrl> to add or remove components participating in the tweak.
   - Use the **Trail Line** options on the mini-toolbar to edit them.
   - Note that the duration cannot be edited using **Edit Tweak**.

3. Click ✓ to complete the edit. To cancel the operation, click ✕.

How To: Edit the Duration of a Tweak

1. In the timeline, right-click on a tweak's symbol and select **Edit Time** to open the Tweak mini-toolbar. Alternatively, double-click on the tweak symbol in the timeline.

   Note: *You can select multiple tweaks and edit their duration at the same time.*

2. Enter a new *Start*, *End* time, or *Duration* for the tweak, as shown in Figure 20–10.

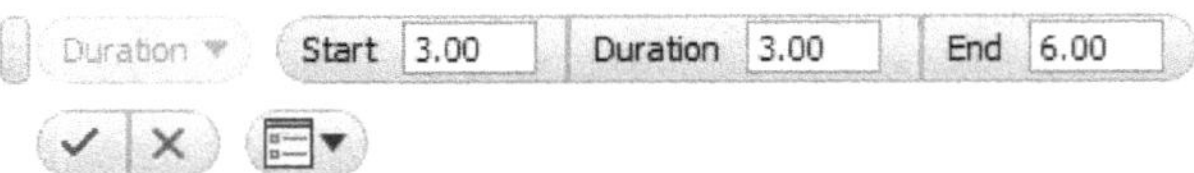

Figure 20–10

3. Click ✓ to complete the edit. To cancel the operation, click ✕.

Trail Visibility

Tweaks that contain trail lines can be manipulated once they are created to clear their visibility. It is a recommended best practice to add trail lines during tweak creation and hide them, as required, after the fact.

- In the graphics window, right-click on a trail line and select **Hide Trail Segment**, as shown in Figure 20–11. Using this method you can clear the trail segment for the individually selected trail line using the **Current** option or clear all trail lines in the group using the **Group** option.

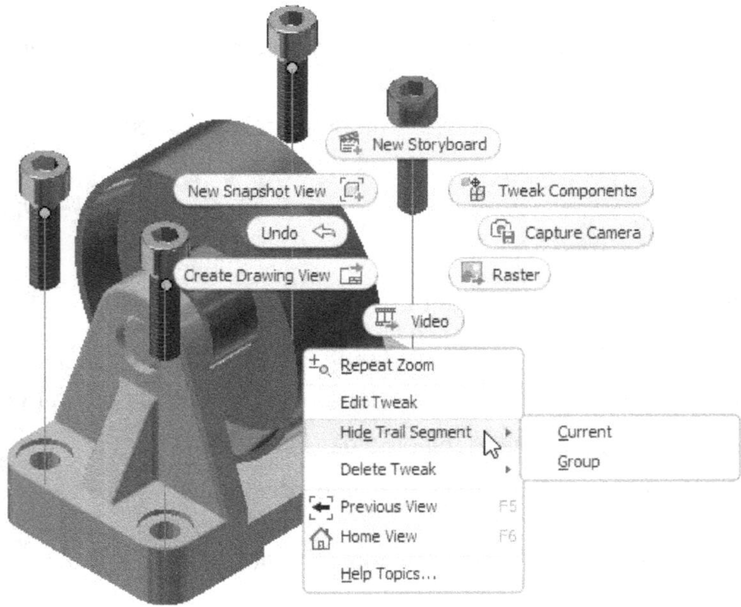

Figure 20–11

- In the Model browser, expand the *Tweaks* folder, right-click on a tweak or its component and select **Hide Trails** or **Hide Trail Segment**, as shown in Figure 20–12. By accessing the command at the tweak level, you control all trails in the group. By accessing it at the component level you can specify it the trail for the current component (**Current**) or all components in the group are to be cleared (**Group**).

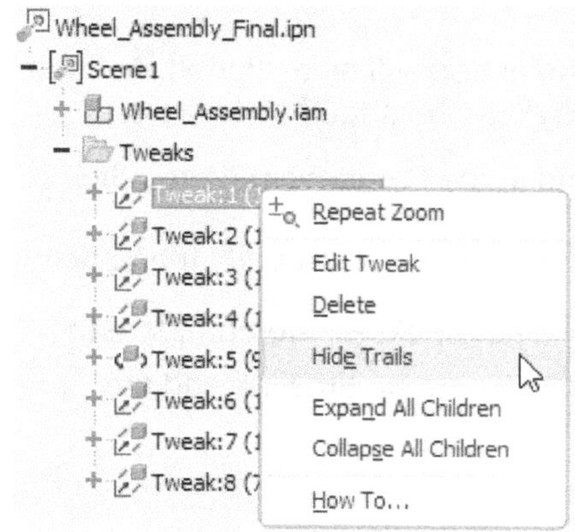

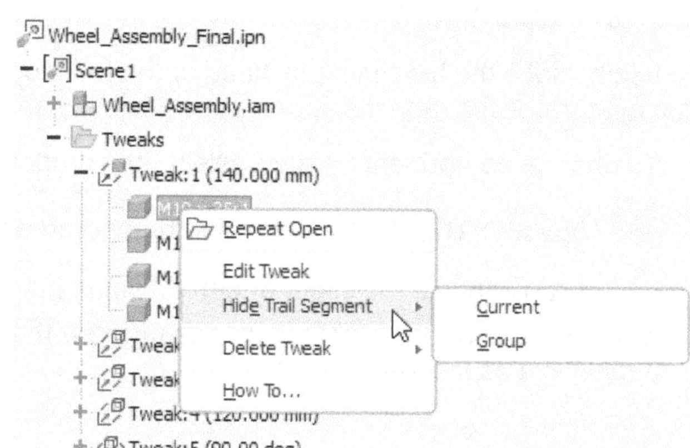

Figure 20–12

- Repeat the process using the Model browser and use **Show Trail Segment** to return the display of trail lines to the model.

Deleting Tweaks

Similar to controlling the visibility of the trail lines in a tweak, you have multiple methods that can be used to delete individual and groups of tweaks from a presentation.

- In the graphics window, right-click on a trail line and select **Delete Tweak**. Using this method, you can delete the tweak for the selected trail line using the **Current** option or delete all tweaks in the group using the **Group** option.
- In the Model browser, expand the *Tweaks* folder, right-click on a tweak and select **Delete**. All tweaks in the group are deleted.
- In the Model browser, expand the *Tweaks* folder and **Tweak** node, right-click on a component and select **Delete Tweak**.
- In the timeline, right-click on the tweak symbol and select **Delete**. You can specify if the tweak for the current component (**Current**) or all components in the group are to be deleted (**Group**).

Hint: Aligning Start/End Time

To quickly align two tweaks to either start or end at the same time, select them using <Ctrl>, right-click, and select **Align Start Time** or **Align End Time**.

Actions

Actions can be added to the timeline of a storyboard to control the appearance of components throughout an animation, or a camera position.

Model Appearance

To begin, place the timeliner playhead at the location that the action will be assigned. Actions that customize the model's appearance (visibility and opacity) can be added as follows:

- To change component opacity, select the component, and in the *Component* panel, click (Opacity). Use the Opacity mini-toolbar (shown in Figure 20–13) to specify the opacity value. You can use the slider or enter a value in the entry field. Click to complete the modification. Opacity actions are identified with the symbol in the timeline and are initially set as instant actions.

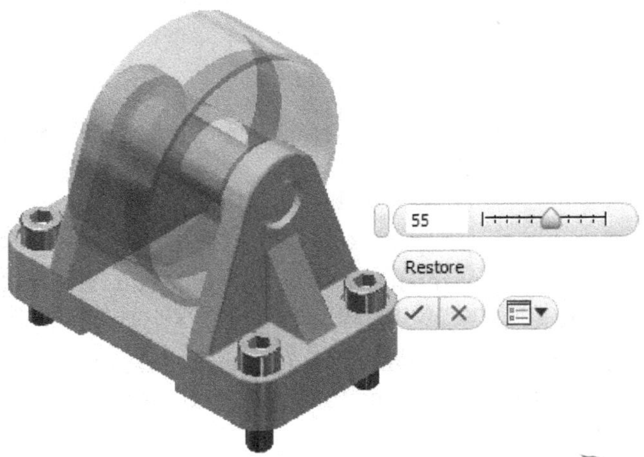

Figure 20–13

- To clear the visibility of a component, select the component in the graphics window or Model browser, right-click and select **Visibility**. This removes the component from display in the animation at the point where the playhead was located. Visibility actions are identified with the symbol in the timeline and can only be instantaneous.
- To modify a Visibility or Opacity action, move the playhead to its location on the timeline, select the component, and use the **Opacity** and **Visibility** options a second time.
- By default, an Opacity action is set to be instantaneous (as shown on the left in Figure 20–14); however, it can be modified to run over a specified duration. To edit the action, right-click the symbol in the timeline and select **Edit Time**. In the drop-down list, change the action type to **Duration**, as shown on the right in Figure 20–14.

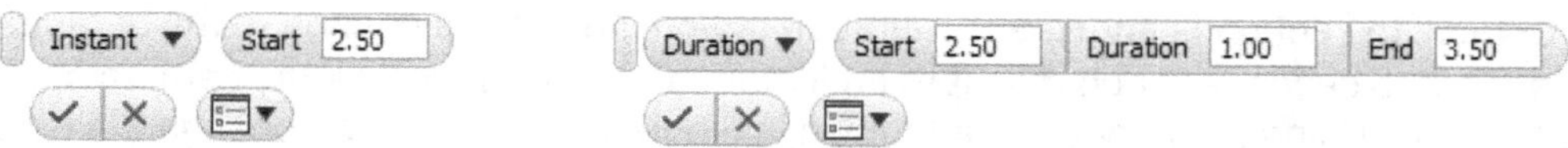

Figure 20–14

*Note: Multiple Opacity settings can be modified at once by preselecting them prior to selecting **Edit Opacity**. The **Edit Time** option for a Visibility action only enables you to change the time to an exact value. You cannot set a Visibility action for a duration. If the visibility is to be returned, move the playhead to the time, and toggle on the component's visibility.*

- Select and drag a Visibility or Opacity action along the timeline to relocate them.
- To delete a Visibility or Opacity action, select it in the timeline, right-click, and select **Delete**.

*Note: If a component was set as **Transparent** in the source assembly, that setting is visible if used in a presentation.*

Camera Position

An action that changes the camera position can be set to run over a specified duration. To begin, place the timeliner playhead at the location that the action will be assigned. The Camera Position action may look compressed at the top of the timeline if the timeline is not large enough and is showing the scroll bar.

How To: Customize the Model's Camera Position

1. To change position of the camera, use the ViewCube or other navigation tools to change the model orientation (camera).
2. In the *Camera* panel, click (Capture Camera). The action is added to the top of the timeline at the point where the playhead was positioned, as shown in Figure 20–15. It is created to run for 3 seconds.

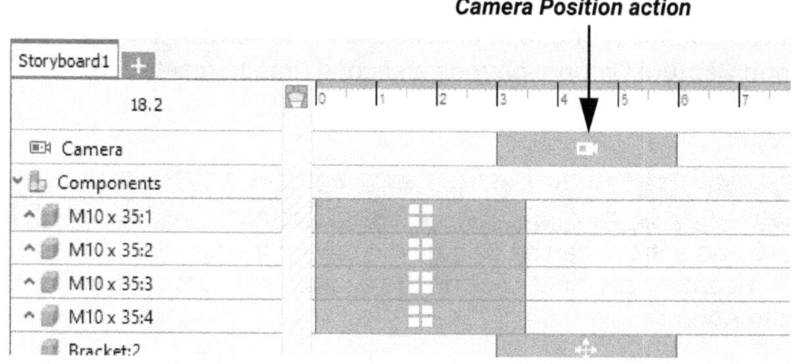

Figure 20–15

- By default, the action is added as a Duration action. To make a change to the default duration (2.5 seconds) or change it to an Instant action, double-click the camera action on the timeline. Using the mini-toolbar (shown in Figure 20–16), you can change the type of action and its *Start*, *End*, or *Duration* times. Alternatively, you can right-click on a Camera Position action in the timeline and select **Edit Time** to open the mini-toolbar.

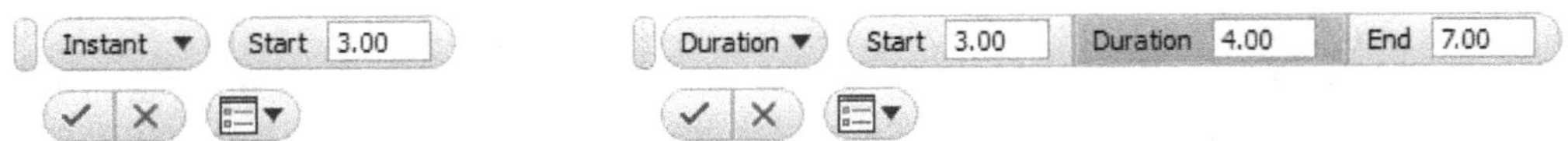

Figure 20–16

- Select and drag a Camera Position action to move it along the timeline.
- To delete a Camera Position action, select it in the timeline, right-click, and select **Delete**.

Hint: Scratch Zone

The area on the timeline that displays prior to the start of the timeline is called the *Scratch Zone*. It is identified with the symbol, as shown in Figure 20–17. The *Scratch Zone* enables you to set the initial view settings, visibility, opacity, and camera position for the assembly. When the settings are made in the *Scratch Zone*, they are not included in the animation. It simply defines how the assembly displays at time 0 on the timeline.

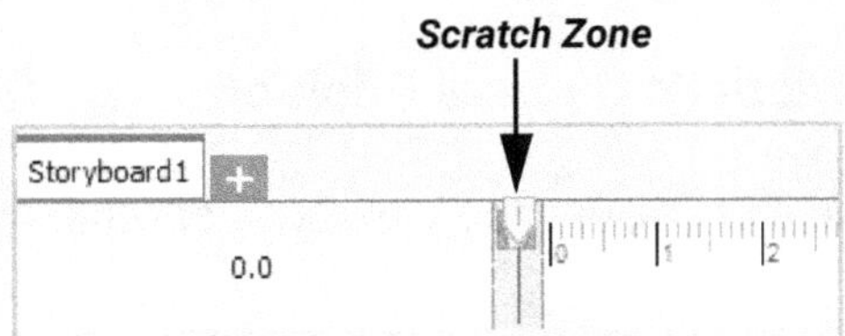

Figure 20–17

- To set the options, position the playhead of the timeliner in this area, and use the **Visibility**, **Opacity**, and **Capture Camera** options, as required.
- Modifications cannot be made to the actions in the *Scratch Zone*. Use the **Visibility**, **Opacity**, and **Capture Camera** options a second time to reset them.

Hint: Deleting All Actions for a Component

Individual tweaks and actions can be deleted directly on the timeline. To delete all actions associated with a component, right-click on the component name in the *Storyboards Panel* and select **Delete Actions**.

If the current storyboard was created using **Start from end of Previous**, the **Delete Actions** option will delete all current and inherited actions from the previous storyboard.

Playing a Storyboard Animation

Once you have created an animation and have added actions, you can use the timeline controls to playback the entire storyboard. The timeline controls are located at the top of the *Storyboards Panel*. The options in this panel are consistent with standard playback controls (rewind to beginning, play, pause, play in reverse, and fast forward to end).

Hint: Tweak and Action Selection

To quickly select all or multiple timeline entries for editing before or after a specific entry, right-click on the entry and select **Select>All Before** or **Select>All After**. When working with groups, right-click on one entry and select **Select>Group** to select all entries in the group.

20.3 Presentation Files – Snapshot Views

Snapshot views store a combination of component display settings and positions in one view to communicate specific information in the model. The snapshot view can be used to create image files for presentations or views in an Inventor drawing file. To create an exploded assembly view in a drawing you must create an exploded snapshot view and reference it in a drawing.

The component display settings that can be assigned in a snapshot view are similar to those used to create animations. They include:

- Component positions using tweaks
- Component visibility settings
- Component opacity settings
- Camera positions defined by the model's orientation
- View settings using the *View* tab.

Creating Snapshot Views

A snapshot view can be created using a previously created storyboard or they can be created independently.

How To: Create a Snapshot View from a Storyboard

1. Activate the scene to which the snapshot view will be added. To activate it, double-click on the scene name in the Model browser.
2. In the timeline, position the playhead at the point at which the snapshot view is required.
3. In the *Workshop* panel, click (New Snapshot View).

A new view is added in the *Snapshot Views* browser. The component display settings that exist in the storyboard at the location of the playhead are used in the snapshot view.

- The marker displays on the snapshot view's thumbnail image, indicating that it is associated with the storyboard animation, as shown in Figure 20–18.
- The marker also displays on the timeline, indicating that a snapshot view was created, as shown in Figure 20–18. The symbol can be dragged to change the snapshot location on the timeline, if required.
- If the snapshot view marker is moved on the timeline or changes are made to any of the actions at that time, the symbol displays on the view in the *Snapshot Views* browser, indicating that it is out of date. Select the symbol to update it.

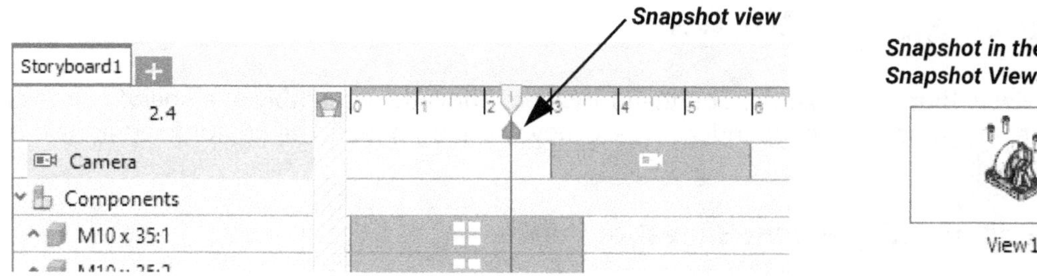

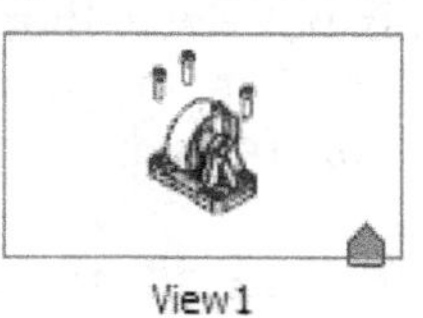

Figure 20–18

> **Hint: Snapshot Views at the Beginning of an Animation**
>
> Snapshot views that are created when the playhead is at the beginning of the animation timeline (0 seconds) will not create a dependent snapshot view.

How To: Create an Independent Snapshot View

1. Activate the scene to which the snapshot view will be added. To activate it, double-click on the scene name in the Model browser.
2. Position the storyboard playhead in the *Scratch Zone*, as shown in Figure 20–19.
   - If an animation or actions exist in the storyboard, position the playhead in the *Scratch Zone*.
   - If no animation or actions exist, independent snapshot views will be created regardless of being in the *Scratch Zone*.

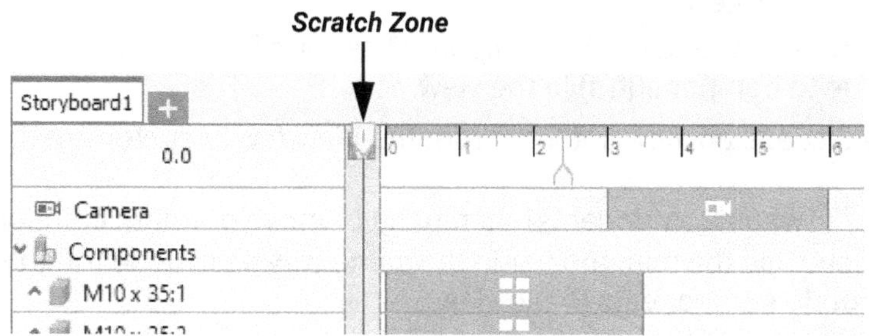

Figure 20–19

3. In the *Workshop* panel, click (New Snapshot View). The view is added to the *Snapshot Views* browser. The marker does not display on the view's thumbnail image as it does for dependent views.

   Note: *To rename a snapshot view, right-click on its thumbnail image and select* ***Rename****. Enter a new descriptive name for the image and press* <Enter>.

Editing Snapshot Views

Snapshot views that are dependent on the storyboard show the assembly at a specific time on the timeline. In the case of independent views, they will likely need to be customized once the view is created.

How To: Edit an Independent Snapshot View

1. Activate the scene to which the snapshot view exists. To activate it, double-click on the scene name in the Model browser.
2. In the *Snapshot Views* browser, right-click the view that is to be edited and select **Edit**. Alternatively, double-click on the view to edit it. The *Edit View* tab becomes the active tab (shown in Figure 20–20) and the *Storyboards Panel* is removed from the display.

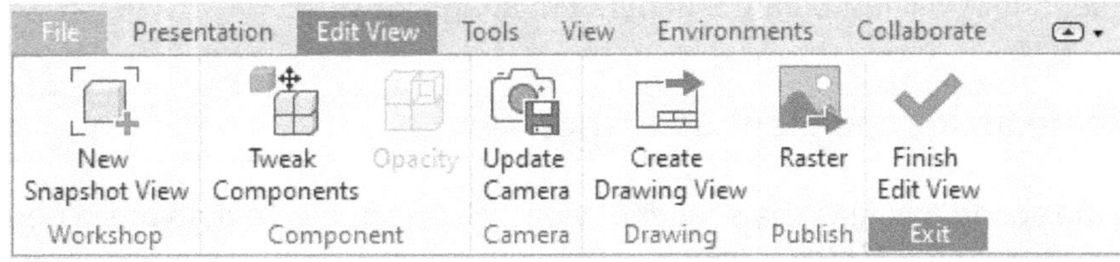

Figure 20–20

3. Set the component's view display using any of the following tools:
   - Use the ViewCube and Navigation Bar to set the model orientation. Click (Update Camera) to update the view.
   - Select components, right-click, and clear the **Visibility** option for components that are not required in the view.
   - Select component(s) and on the *Component* panel, click (Opacity) to assign an Opacity value to component(s) in the view.
   - In the *View* tab, assign view settings from the *View* tab to customize the view.
   - Use the (Tweak Components) command to move or rotate components in the snapshot view. Use the mini-toolbar in the same way as is done for an animation to move and rotate components in the view.
4. Click (Finish Edit View) to complete the edit.

Note: *As you edit an existing view, you can click (New Snapshot View) in the Workshop to create an additional view.*

 **Hint: Making a Dependent Snapshot View Independent**

The marker on a snapshot view's thumbnail image indicates that it is associated (linked) with the storyboard animation. If you edit this type of view, you will be prompted that you cannot make changes to a view that is linked to the timeline (as shown in Figure 20–21). To permanently break the link, click **Break Link**.

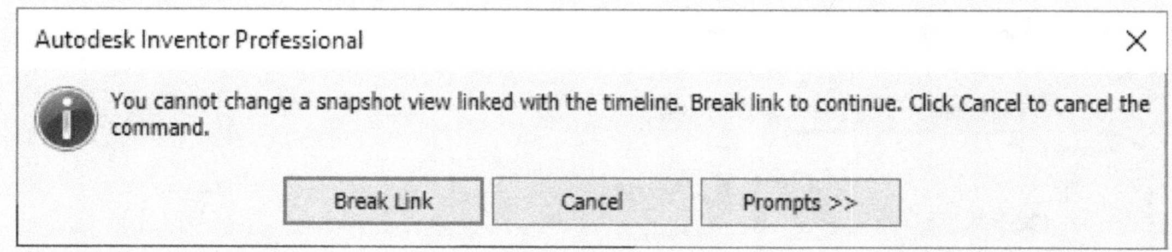

Figure 20–21

The marker is removed from the snapshot view's thumbnail image. Only the addition of a tweak or the change of Opacity and Visibility for a component require you to break the link. Changes to the camera position/orientation are permitted without breaking the link.

Creating a Drawing from a Snapshot View

Any of the snapshot views listed in the Snapshot Views browser can be used as views in a drawing, as long as the presentation file is one of the drawing models. A new drawing can be created directly from the presentation file using the any of the following methods:

- In the *Snapshot Views* browser, right-click on the thumbnail image and select **Create Drawing View**.
- While editing a snapshot view, in the *Edit View* tab>*Drawing* panel, click (Create Drawing View).
- In the *Presentation* tab>*Drawing* panel, click (Create Drawing View).

Once one of these options is selected, you will be prompted to select the drawing template that should be used to create the new drawing. The *Drawing View* dialog box opens and you can place views. If the drawing was created from an active snapshot, the *Presentation* area of the dialog box displays the name of the snapshot view that was active in the presentation, as shown in Figure 20–22. Creating drawings will be discussed in more detail later in the guide.

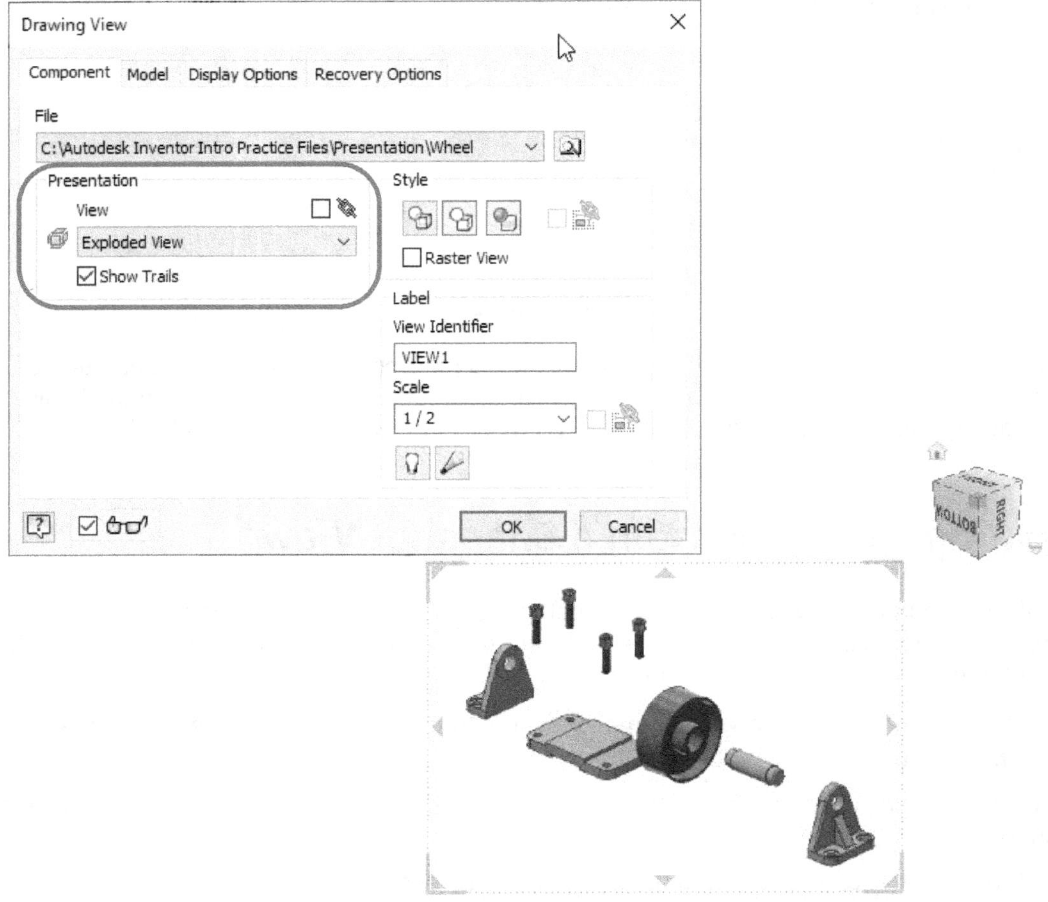

Figure 20–22

Consider the following:

- Select an alternate snapshot view in the *Views* drop-down list.
- Show or clear the trails in the view using **Show Trails**. Trails can only be controlled if they exist in the snapshot view.
- Select to set the new view as associative. This ensures that if a change is made to the snapshot view in the presentation file, it will update the drawing view.
- In an existing drawing, you can add new Base views that reference other snapshots using the *Drawing View* dialog box in the same way.

20.4 Publishing Presentation Files

Both snapshot views and storyboards can be published to various formats. Snapshot views can be published as raster images and storyboards can be published as animations.

How To: Publish Snapshot Views

1. Activate the scene in which the snapshot will be published.
2. Select the view(s) to publish in the *Snapshot Views* browser.
   - To publish multiple snapshot views, press and hold <Ctrl> during selection.
3. Use one of the following methods to open the *Publish to Raster Images* dialog box, as shown in Figure 20–23 to publish a snapshot.
   - In the *Presentation* tab>*Publish* panel, click (Raster).
   - Right-click on a view in the *Snapshot Views* browser and select **Publish to Raster**.
   - During editing, select (Raster) in the *Edit View* tab.

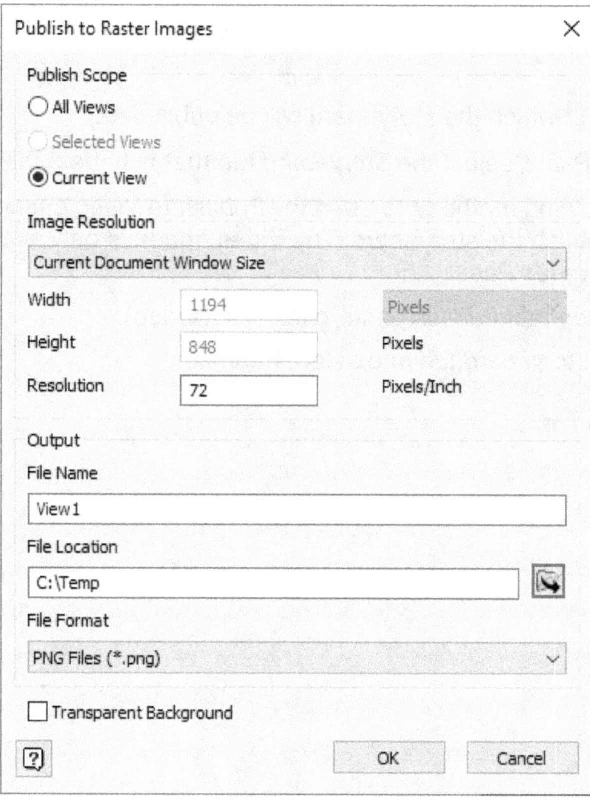

Figure 20–23

4. In the *Publish Scope* area, define the scope of publishing.
   - Click **All Views** to publish all snapshots in the scene.
   - Use **Selected Views** to publish previously selected views.
5. In the *Image Resolution* area, define the image size.
   - Use **Current Document Window Size** in the drop-down list to publish the view as it is currently displayed.
   - Select a predefined image size in the drop-down list.
   - Select **Custom** in the drop-down list and enter a custom *Width*, *Height*, and *Resolution* value by pixel or unit size.
6. In the *Output* area, specify a folder to save the file. The snapshot view name will be used as the published filename.
7. In the *File Format* drop-down list, select a publishing format. The supported image file formats include BMP, GIF, JPEG, PNG, or TIFF.
8. Enable **Transparent Background**, if required.
9. Click **OK** to publish the image.

How To: Publish a Storyboard

1. Activate the scene in which the storyboard will be published.
2. In the *Storyboards Panel*, select the *Storyboard* tab that is to be published.
3. Use one of the following methods to open the *Publish to Video* dialog box, as shown in Figure 20–24 to publish the storyboard. The **Video** option is only available if an animation exists in the *Storyboards Panel*.
   - In the *Presentation* tab>*Publish* panel, click (Video).
   - Right-click on a *Storyboard* tab and select **Publish**.

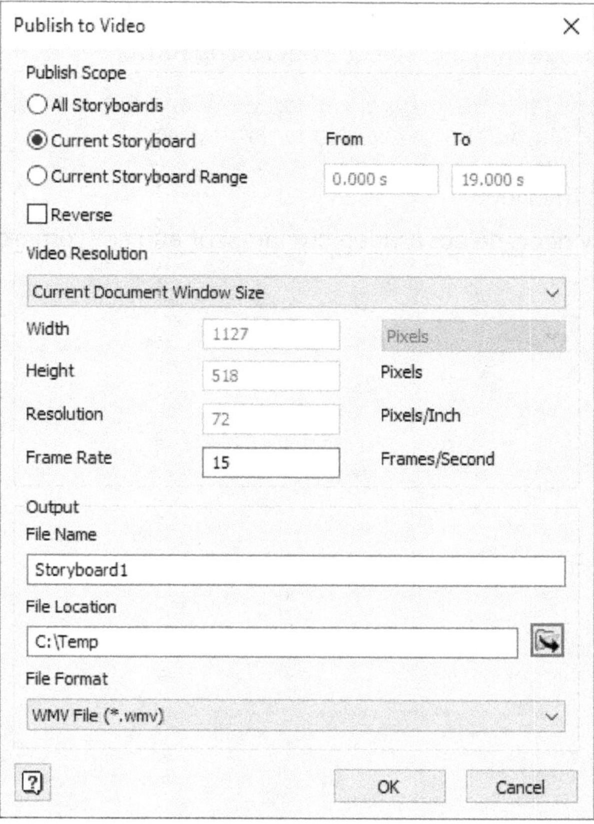

Figure 20–24

4. In the *Publish Scope* area, define the scope of publishing.
   - Use **All Storyboards** to publish all storyboards available in active scene.
   - Use **Current Storyboard** to publish the active storyboard.
   - Use **Current Storyboard Range** to publish a time range in the active storyboard. Enter values in the *From* and *To* fields.
   - Click **Reverse** to publish the video in a reverse order (end to start).
5. In the *Video Resolution* area, define the video size.
   - Use **Current Document Window Size** in the drop-down list to publish the video as it is currently displayed.
   - Select a predefined video size in the drop-down list.
   - Select **Custom** in the drop-down list and enter a custom *Width, Height, Resolution* by pixel or unit size, and *Frame Rate*.

6. In the *Output* area, specify a name for the video and a folder to save the file.
7. In the *File Format* drop-down list, select a publishing format.

   Note: *The supported video file formats include WMV and AVI. A WMV video player must be installed on your computer to publish to WMV format.*

8. Click **OK** to publish the video.
9. For AVI formatted videos, select a video compressor and set compression quality, if available. Click **OK**.

Practice 20a
Create an Animation

Practice Objectives

- Create a new presentation file using a standard template.
- Create an animation that explodes the components of an assembly using translational and rotational movements.
- Control the visual display and orientation of components in an animation.
- Play an animation and then publish it.

In this practice, you will create a presentation file using a wheel assembly. The assembly file that will be used is shown in Figure 20–25. Using the tools in the presentation file, you will create an animation that explodes the components of the assembly to show how it is assembled. A video called **video2.wmv** has been provided in the practice files *Presentation* folder for you to review the animation that will be created in this practice.

Figure 20–25

Task 1: Create a presentation file.

1. On the *Home* page, click **New**.
2. In the *Create New File* dialog box, select the *Metric* folder, select **Standard (mm).ipn**, and click **Create** to create a new presentation file. You might need to scroll down in the list to locate this template.
3. In the *Insert* dialog box, navigate to the *Presentation* folder and select **Wheel_Assembly.iam**. Click **Open**.
    - The presentation environment displays and the *Presentation* tab is the active tab. By default, there is a single scene created using the wheel assembly and **Storyboard1** is active. No snapshots are initially created.

Task 2: Define the initial model display for the animation.

1. The playhead ( ) starts at time 0 seconds. Drag the playhead to the left into the (*Scratch Zone*) area of the panel, as shown in Figure 20–26.

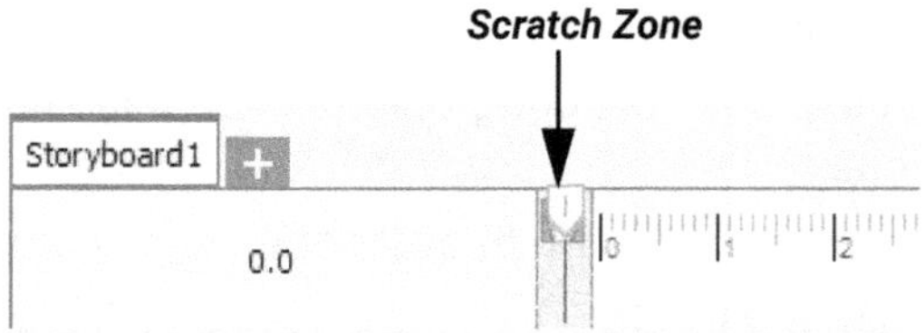

Figure 20–26

Note: *The Scratch Zone is where you can set the initial visibility, opacity, and camera position for the model.*

2. Rotate the model into a custom orientation using the ViewCube. Select the corner shown in Figure 20–27. This positions the model for the start of the animation.

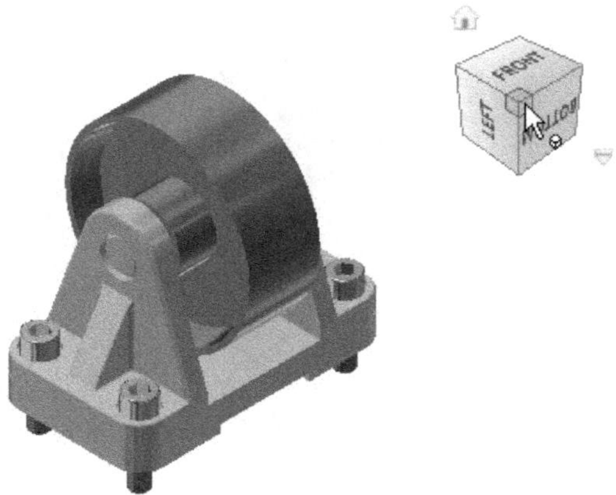

Figure 20–27

3. In the *Camera* panel, click (Capture Camera). This stores the orientation for the start position of the animation.

Task 3: Create an exploded animation of the assembly.

1. Expand the **Scene1** node in the Model browser and the **Wheel_Assembly.iam** node. All of the assembly component's names display. This provides a convenient way to select components.
2. To move components, in the *Presentation* tab>*Component* panel, click (Tweak Components). The Tweak Component mini-toolbar opens.
3. Ensure that **Part** is selected in the *Model Type* drop-down list, as shown in Figure 20–28.
4. Press and hold <Ctrl> and select the four **M10 x 35** components in the Model browser. All four components should be highlighted in the model and the tweak triad should be displayed.

   Note: *Alternatively, you can use the **Select Other** tool in the graphics window to select any hidden components to avoid rotating the model and changing its orientation in the animation.*

5. Ensure that **Move** is selected in the top row of the mini-toolbar, as shown in Figure 20–28, to move components in either the X, Y, or Z direction.

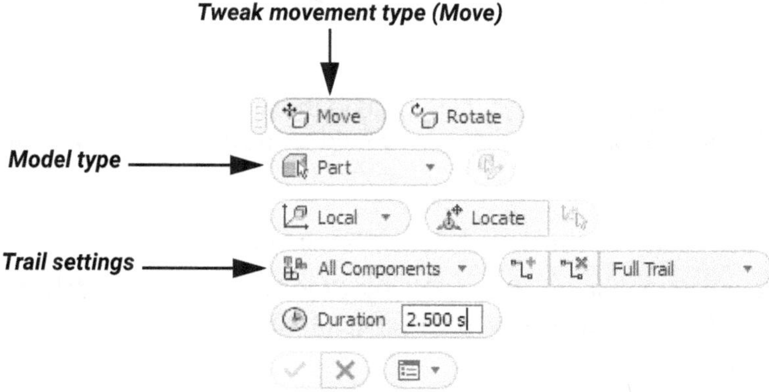

Figure 20–28

6. Expand the *Trail Settings* drop-down list in the mini-toolbar. The options in this field enable you to customize if trails are created. In this practice, they will be created and you will later learn how to quickly toggle them on and off. Ensure that **All Components** is selected.
7. The triad orientation displays the local coordinate system for one of the four parts. Expand the **Local** option and select **World** to change the orientation of the triad to be consistent with the assembly coordinate system.

8. Select the arrow that points in the Z direction relative to the assembly's origin, as shown in Figure 20–29. Depending on the order in which the components are selected, the triad may display in a different location or orientation.

   Note: *If the model origin is not displayed, consider toggling it on in the Application Options dialog box by selecting* ***Show Origin 3D indicator*** *on the Display tab.*

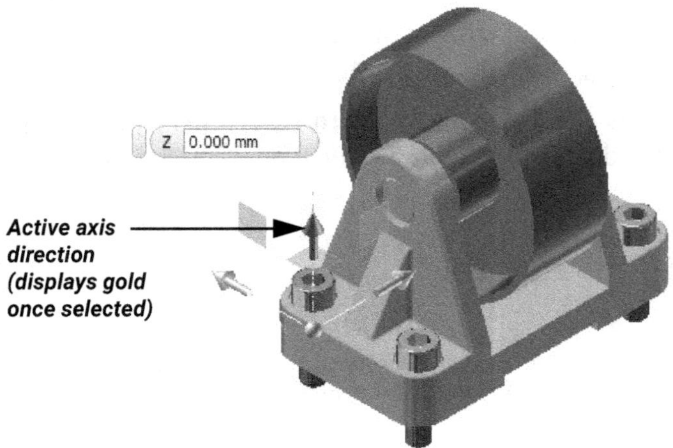

Figure 20–29

9. The active Z axis direction displays in gold. Drag the arrowhead upwards to move the four components. Enter **75** (or **-75**) in the *Z* entry field to move the components a specific distance.
10. Click ✓ to complete the tweak and close the mini-toolbar.
11. Note that the four components are listed in the *Storyboards Panel* and the tweak actions are scheduled to last 2.5 seconds, as shown in Figure 20–30.

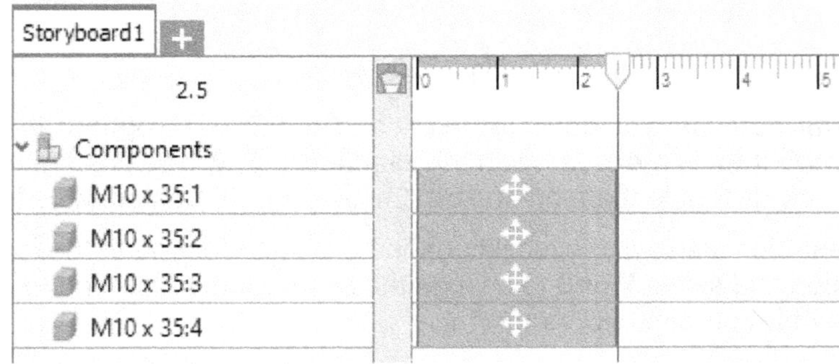

Figure 20–30

Note: *Tweak actions are set at 2.5 seconds by default. This can be modified in the Tweak mini-toolbar prior to closing it or it can be modified after it is created.*

12. Hover the cursor over the tweak action () for the first component in the list, right-click, and select **Edit Time**.
13. In the mini-toolbar, set the *Duration* value to **3.00**. Click .
14. The first component is now set to get into its exploded position slower than the others. Click in the playback controls to rewind the timeline to the beginning and click . Note the differences in the timing.
15. Hover the cursor over the tweak action () for the second component in the list and double-click to edit it. This is an alternative method to edit the timing.
16. Set the *Duration* value to **3.00**. Click .
17. Hold <Ctrl> and select the third and fourth component's tweak actions (), hover the cursor over the right-hand edge of the action bar. Drag to the right to manually extend its duration. Ensure that it snaps to 3 seconds. The *Storyboards Panel* should display as shown in Figure 20–31.

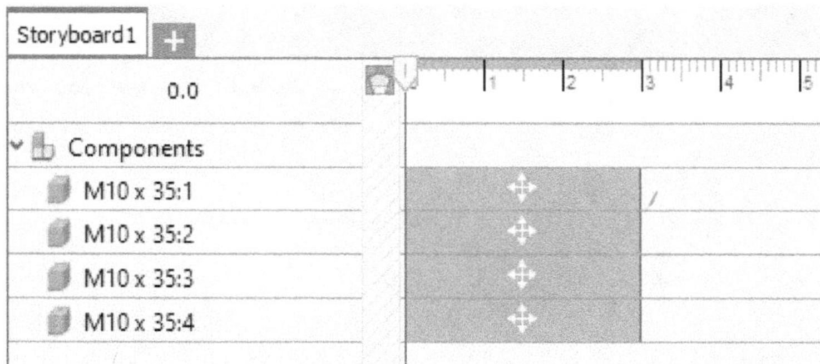

Figure 20–31

18. The fasteners have not been moved high enough. Right-click on any of the actions () and select **Edit Tweak**.
19. In the *Distance* field, enter **140mm** as the new value. Click . Because they are a group, they all are edited together.

Task 4: Add additional tweaks to components.

1. Click to move the playhead to the end of the current actions. This ensures that the next tweak is added immediately at the end of the last tweak.

2. In the *Component* panel, click (Tweak Components). Using the following table, move and rotate the Bracket and Wheel components. The storyboard timeline and component should display as shown in Figure 20–32 after the two components are tweaked. Use the World coordinate system when tweaking. You might need to enter positive or negative tweak values to translate and rotate as shown. Ensure that the playhead is at the correct position on the timeline when defining each tweak.

Component	Tweaks
Bracket:2	• Translate 175mm along the X-axis. • Define the tweak as 3.00 seconds.
Wheel	• Translate 110mm along the X-axis. • Translate 120mm along the Z-axis. • Rotate 90 degrees in the XZ Plane. • Modify each tweak to 3.00 seconds, if not already set.

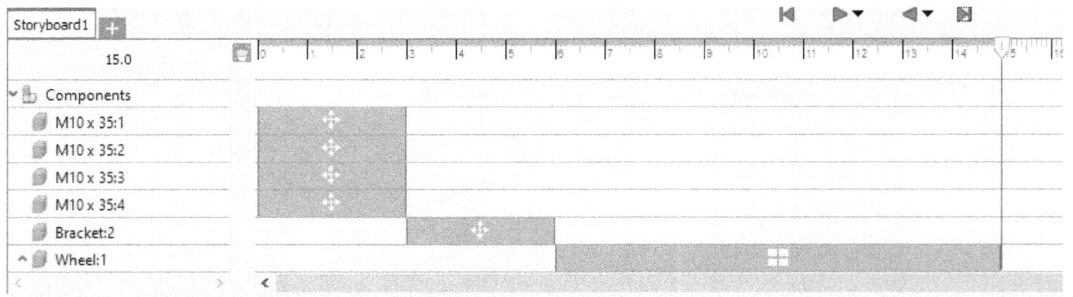

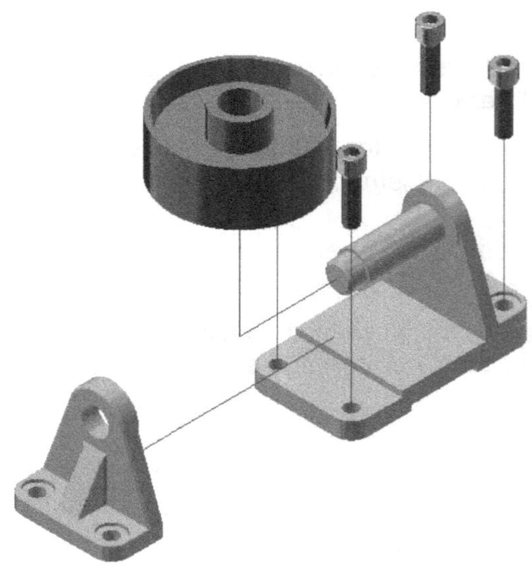

Figure 20–32

3. Play the animation from the beginning and note how the wheel is unassembled with three actions that occur consecutively. After playing, note that the model displays reassembled. This is only because the playhead returns to where it starts on the timeline. The animation will end fully disassembled at 15 seconds once published.

4. The three actions for the Wheel are grouped. In the storyboard, expand the **Wheel** component in the component list to show the individual actions. To manipulate them, it must be expanded.

5. Manipulate the duration of the rotation action ( ) and relocate it on the timeline such that it occurs while the component is moving in the *Z*-direction, similar to that shown in Figure 20–33.

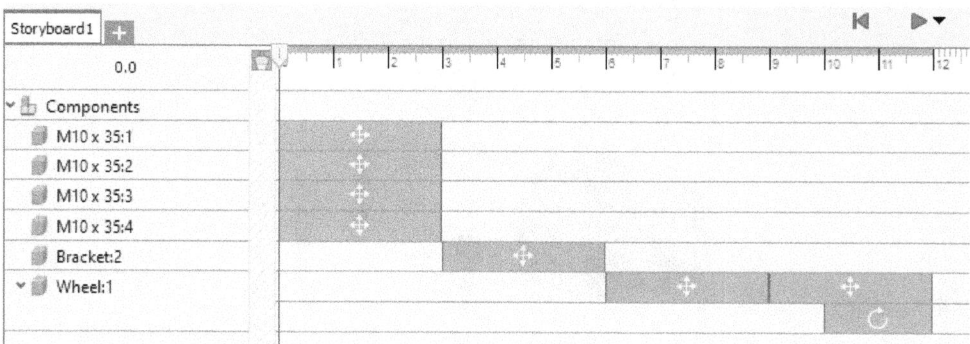

Figure 20–33

6. Use the following table to apply tweaks to the remaining components. The components should display as shown in Figure 20–34 after the remaining three components are tweaked. Use the World coordinate system when tweaking the components. You might need to enter positive or negative tweak values to translate and rotate as shown. Ensure that the playhead is at the correct position on the timeline when defining each tweak.

Component	Tweaks
Axle	• Translate 110mm along the X-axis. • Define the tweak as 3.00 seconds.
Bracket:1	• Translate 110mm along the X-axis. • Define the tweak as 2.50 seconds.
Plate	• Translate 80mm along the Z-axis. • Define the tweak as 2.50 seconds.

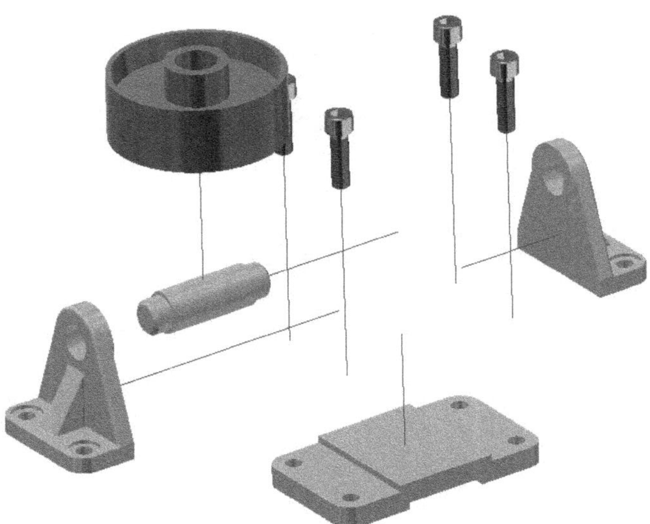

Figure 20–34

7. Manipulate the timeline such that the last two components assemble at the same time and run for 2.00 seconds.
8. Play the animation and verify that it functions as expected. A video called **video1.wmv** has been provided in the practice files *Presentation* folder for you to compare with.
9. Save the presentation file using its default name into the *Presentation* folder.

Task 5: Incorporate visual changes in the animation.

1. In the Model browser, right-click on the *Tweaks* folder and select **Hide All Trails**, as shown in Figure 20–35. If **Hide All Trails** is not available, move your playhead past the start of the timeline and try again.

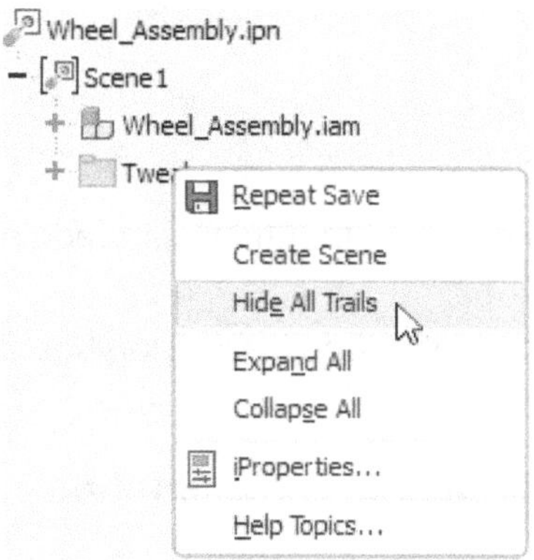

Figure 20–35

Note: If you were to expand the Tweaks folder, it lists all tweaks that were created and you can individually edit them or hide their trail lines.

2. Return the playhead to the beginning of the timeline and play the animation. Note that the trail lines are all removed from the display.
3. Once the fasteners are exploded, they can fade from the display. Place the playhead at **3s** and select all four fasteners.
4. In the *Component* panel, click (Opacity).
5. On the mini-toolbar, drag the *Opacity* slider to **0**. Click .
6. Note how the new component opacity action is grouped with the other actions for these components. Expand the first component, as shown in Figure 20–36.

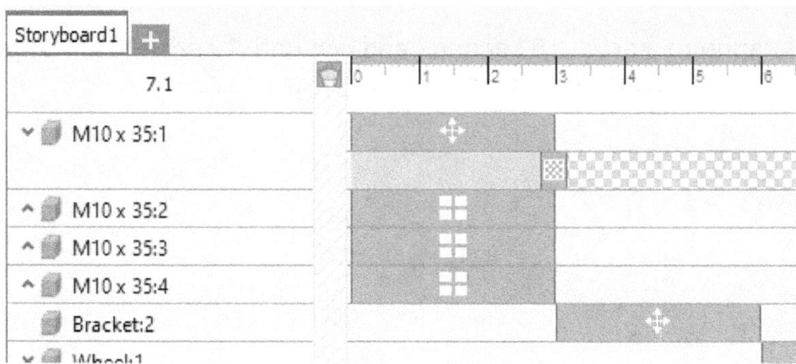

Figure 20–36

7. Right-click on the action for the first fastener and select **Edit Time**. By default, the action is created as an Instant action.
8. Select **Duration** in the drop-down list in the mini-toolbar.
9. Set the *Start* value to **2.50** and the *End* value to **3.50**. Click .
10. Play the animation and note the difference between the first fastener's visibility changes and the other fasteners.

    Note: *As an alternative to using opacity, you could have also cleared the visibility of the components at a specific time. The Visibility action is only instantaneous.*

11. Modify the other three fasteners such that they also fade out over a duration of 2.50 to 3.50 seconds.
12. Collapse the **M10 x 35** component nodes in the Storyboards Panel once your edits are complete.

Task 6: Spin the model at the end of the animation.

1. Click to move the playhead to the end of the animation.
2. Reorient the model to the orientation shown on the ViewCube in Figure 20–37 and zoom in on the model.

Figure 20–37

3. In the *Camera* panel, click (Capture Camera). A camera action is added to the top of the timeline.
4. Modify the length of the camera action by right-clicking on the symbol and selecting **Edit Time**.
5. Modify the duration to start at 16 seconds and last until 19 seconds. Alternatively, you can drag the action and extend its action on the timeline.

6. Move the playhead to the beginning of the animation. The entire timeline should display similar to that shown in Figure 20–38.

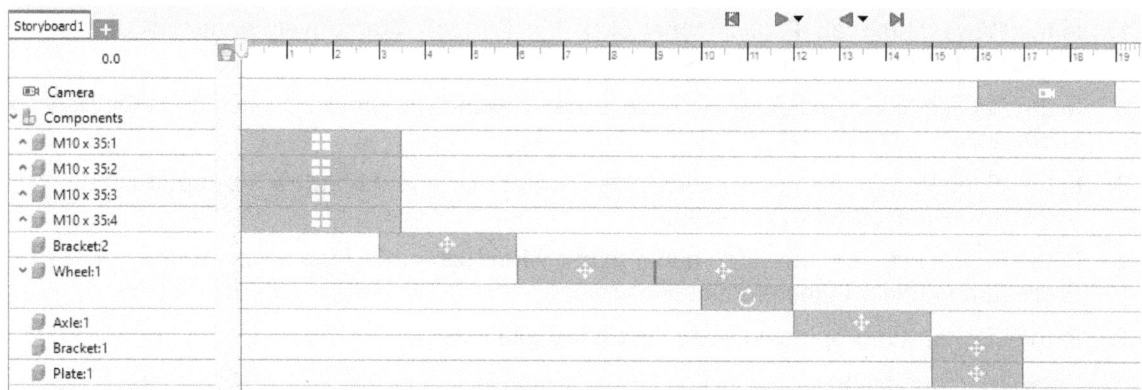

Figure 20–38

7. Play the animation to see how this new Camera action affects the animation.
   - A video called **video2.wmv** has been provided in the practice files *Presentation* folder for you to compare with.

Task 7: Modify the view settings in the model.

1. Return the playhead into the *Scratch Zone* once again.

   Note: *The settings that are defined in the View tab are temporary and are not saved with the presentation file.*

2. On the ribbon, select the *View* tab. Use the tools in the *Appearance* panel to set the following:
   - In the *Shadows* drop-down list, enable **Ambient Shadows**.
   - In the *Visual Style* drop-down list, select **Technical Illustration** or an alternate style. Note that threads do not display in a technical illustration.
3. Play the animation.

Task 8: Publish the storyboard.

1. In the *Presentation* tab>*Publish* panel, click (Video). Alternatively, right-click on the *Storyboard1* tab and select **Publish to Video**.
2. In the *Publish to Video* dialog box, ensure that **Current Storyboard** is selected in the *Publish Scope* area.
3. In the *Video Resolution* area, maintain the **Current Document Window Size** option to publish the video as it is currently displayed.
4. In the *Output* area, set the video name to **my_wheel_assembly** and save it to the *Presentation* folder in the practice files folder.
5. In the *File Format* drop-down list, select **WMV File (*.wmv)**.
6. Click **OK** to publish the video.
7. Navigate to the *Presentation* folder in the practice files and play the video once it has published.
8. Save the presentation file and close the window.

End of practice

Practice 20b
Create Snapshots

Practice Objectives

- Create snapshots that are dependent on a storyboard animation.
- Create snapshots that are independent from a storyboard animation.
- Edit snapshots to manipulate component position and component display.
- Update snapshots that are dependent on a storyboard animation.

In this practice, you will create snapshot views that are both dependent on an animation as well as independent of it. You will also learn how to edit both types of snapshot views using the tools available in the Presentation environment. The independent exploded snapshot view is shown in Figure 20–39.

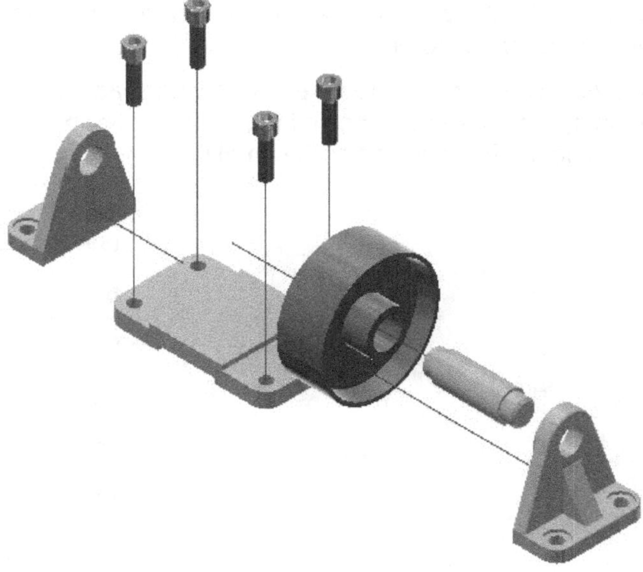

Figure 20–39

Task 1: Create snapshot views that are dependent on a storyboard animation.

In this task, you will create multiple snapshot views all based on the storyboard animation that already exists in the presentation file.

1. Continue working with the presentation file from the previous practice or open **Wheel_Assembly_Final.ipn** from the *Presentation* folder.

2. Note that there is currently one scene in the file (**Scene1**) and that this scene does not currently have any snapshot views in the *Snapshot Views* browser.
3. In the timeline, move the playhead to the beginning of the animation (0 seconds). You can select ⏮ or simply drag the playhead to the beginning of the animation.
4. In the *Workshop* panel, click (New Snapshot View).
5. **View1** is added to the *Snapshot Views* browser. Right-click on the **View1** thumbnail image and select **Rename**. Set the new name to **Fully Assembled**.
6. Move the playhead to approximately 2.5 seconds. This should show the fasteners exploded, but not yet set to an Opacity value of 0.
7. In the *Workshop* panel, click (New Snapshot View).
8. **View2** is added to the *Snapshot Views* browser. The marker displays on the snapshot view's thumbnail image, indicating that it is associated with the storyboard animation. Snapshot views created at 0 seconds are not associative to the storyboard.
9. Select the view label for the **View2** thumbnail image. Set the new name to **Step1**. This is an alternative to using the **Rename** command.
10. Using the steps previously described, create the following snapshots. The *Snapshots Views* browser should display similar to that shown Figure 20–40. Snapshot views can also be created by right-clicking on the playhead in the timeline.

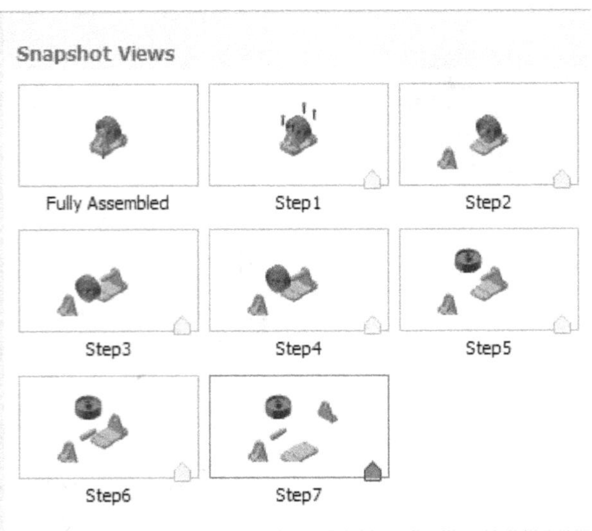

Figure 20–40

Time (seconds)	Snapshot View Name
6	Step2
9	Step3
10	Step4
12	Step5
15	Step6
16	Step7

11. Refer to the *Snapshot Views* browser and the storyboard timeline and note the following:
    - The marker that displays on the last view (**Step7**) is blue and the outline of the view is also blue, indicating that the view is active.
    - The markers displays along the timeline, showing the locations where the snapshots were taken.

Task 2: Modify a dependent snapshot view.

Between 15s and 16s, both the second **Bracket** and the **Plate** are moved apart. For static images, only the **Bracket** needs to be moved. The animation is to stay as it is; however, you will edit the Step 7 view to make the change.

1. Right-click on the **Step7** thumbnail image and select **Edit**. The *Edit View* tab is activated, as shown in Figure 20–41.

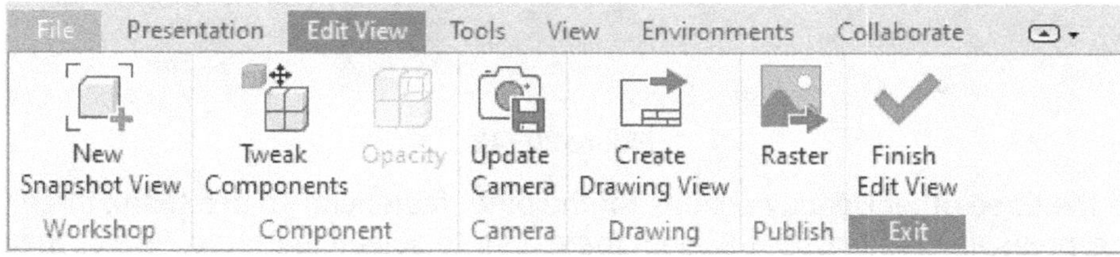

Figure 20–41

2. Select the **Plate** component in the graphics window. Right-click and select **Delete Tweak> Last**.
3. When prompted that you cannot make changes to a view that is linked to the timeline, click **Break Link** to permanently break the link. The **Plate** component returns to its original position. No other changes are required in this view.
4. In the *Exit* panel, click (Finish Edit View).
5. Note that the **Step7** view no longer has the marker. This indicates that it is now an independent view.

Task 3: Modify actions on the timeline.

1. In the timeline, expand the four **M10 x 35** components.

2. Right-click on the symbol for the first component, right-click and select **Delete**, as shown in Figure 20–42. The first fastener is returned to the model display.

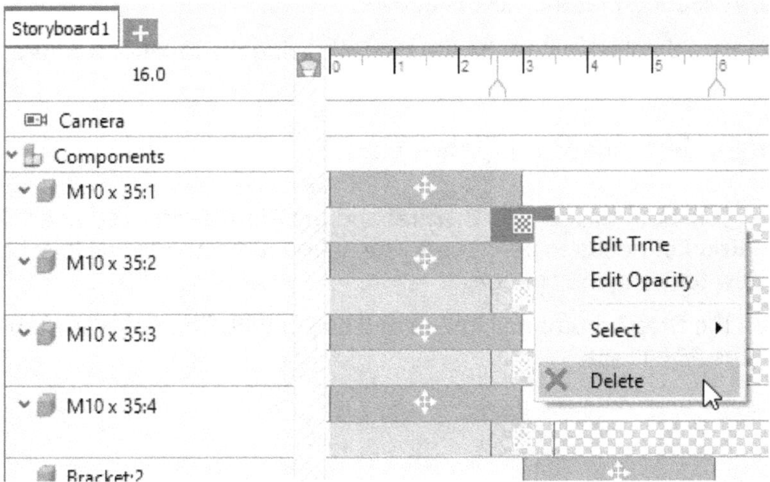

Figure 20–42

3. Delete the three other Opacity actions for the other fasteners. To delete the three fasteners at once, press and hold <Ctrl> to select them prior to selecting **Delete**. Five of the snapshot views that are dependent on the timeline now show the symbol on their thumbnail image, as shown in Figure 20–43.

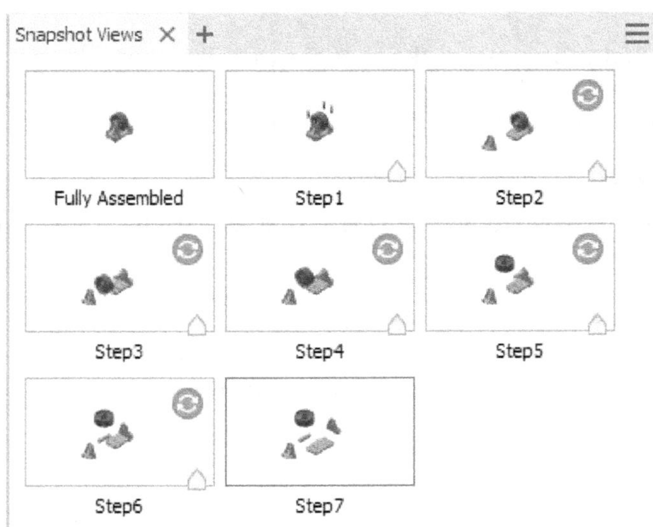

Figure 20–43

4. Select the symbol on each thumbnail image to update them to reflect the change in the animation.

Task 4: Modify the orientation of a model in a snapshot view.

1. Double-click on the **Step6** thumbnail image in the *Snapshot Views* browser to edit it.
2. Using the ViewCube, rotate the model into an alternate position so that you can see all of the fasteners. In the *Camera* panel, click (Update Camera). Note that the view changes in the thumbnail image and you were not prompted that the change would require you to break the link to the animation. Camera position changes do not affect the associativity with the animation.
3. In the *Exit* panel, click (Finish Edit View).

Task 5: Create an independent view.

In this task, you will create a new snapshot view that is independent of the timeline. You will then explode the assembly to create an alternate explode view that can be used in a drawing.

1. In the timeline, move the playhead to the beginning of the animation (0 seconds).
2. Create a new snapshot view and rename it to **Exploded View**.
3. Edit the new Exploded View.
4. Rotate the model and use the (Tweak Components) command to explode the components similar to that shown in Figure 20–44.
   - When creating the exploded view, create it with visible trail lines.

   Note: *For more detail on tweaking components, refer to* ***Practice 20a: Create an Animation****.*

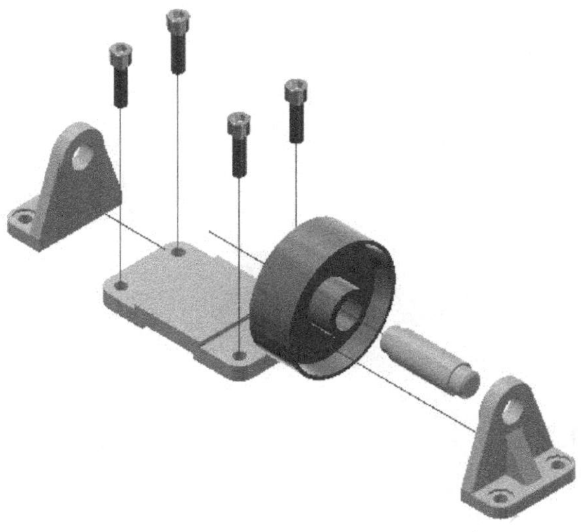

Figure 20–44

5. In the *Camera* panel, click  (Update Camera).
6. Finish the edit to return to the *Presentation* tab.
7. Save the presentation file and close the window.

Hint: Creating a Drawing View from a Snapshot View

A drawing view can be created directly from a snapshot in a presentation file by right-clicking on the snapshot in the *Snapshot Views* browser and selecting **Create Drawing View** option. Drawing views are discussed further in a later chapter.

End of practice

Chapter Review Questions

1. Which of the following file formats is used to create an exploded assembly model in a drawing view?
   a. .IAM
   b. .IPT
   c. .IPN
   d. .DWG

2. What is the purpose of a presentation file? (Select all that apply.)
   a. To simplify the display of an assembly.
   b. To create an exploded view of an assembly.
   c. To update an assembly more quickly.
   d. To create an animation of an assembly.
   e. To help document and visualize the assembly.

3. Which of the following statements are true regarding a presentation file? (Select all that apply.)
   a. Once the Presentation template is selected for use, you are immediately prompted to open the model that will be used in Scene1 of the presentation.
   b. A snapshot view that is oriented in the model's Home view is automatically added to a new presentation file.
   c. Multiple storyboards can be created in a presentation file to document an assembly.
   d. Storyboard animations can be used in a drawing view.

4. It is not possible to edit a snapshot view that was created dependent on a specific time in an animation.
   a. True
   b. False

5. Which command enables you to save a specific view orientation at a set time in an animation?
    a. New Storyboard
    b. New Snapshot View
    c. Tweak Components
    d. Capture Camera

6. What is the purpose of adding a trail?
    a. To define a path for an animation.
    b. To move the position of a component.
    c. To change the color of a component.
    d. To help define the relationships between the components in terms of how they are assembled.

7. To create an animated assembly of a model's assembly process, you must create an animation that uses the _____ command.
    a. New Storyboard
    b. Tweak Components
    c. Opacity
    d. Capture Camera

8. Which of the following are valid methods to change the duration of an action in a storyboard animation? (Select all that apply.)
    a. Enter a *Duration* value in the mini-toolbar during tweak creation.
    b. Use the **Edit Tweak** command and enter a new *Duration* value.
    c. Use the **Edit Time** command and enter a new *Duration* value.
    d. Drag the action's duration directly in the timeline.

9. **Move** and **Rotate** tweaks can be assigned to the same component at one time.
    a. True
    b. False

10. Which type of view setting can only be instantaneous when assigned to an animation?

a. Opacity

b. Visibility

Command Summary

Button	Command	Location
	Capture Camera	• **Ribbon:** *Presentation* tab>*Camera* panel • **Ribbon:** *Edit View* tab>*Camera* panel • **Context Menu**
	Create Drawing View	• **Ribbon:** *Presentation* tab>*Drawing* panel • **Ribbon:** *Edit View* tab>*Drawing* panel • **Snapshot Views browser:** right-click on a view • **Context Menu**
N/A	**Delete** (Tweak)	• **Timeline:** *right-click on a tweak symbol* • **Model browser: right-click on a Tweak** • Graphics Window: right-click on a component
N/A	**Edit Time**	• **Timeline:** *right-click on a tweak symbol* • **Model browser: right-click on a Tweak** • Graphics Window: right-click on a component
N/A	**Edit Tweak**	• **Timeline:** *right-click on a tweak symbol* • **Model browser: right-click on a Tweak**
N/A	**Hide Trails /Hide Trail Segments**	• **Model browser: right-click on a Tweak** • Graphics Window: right-click on a component
	New Snapshot View	• **Ribbon:** *Presentation* tab>*Workshop* panel • **Ribbon:** *Edit View* tab>*Workshop* panel • **Context Menu** • **Storyboards Panel** (right-click on the playhead)
	New Storyboard	• **Ribbon:** *Presentation* tab>*Workshop* panel • **Context Menu** • **Storyboards Panel** (click)
	Opacity	• **Ribbon:** *Presentation* tab>*Component* panel with a component selected • **Ribbon:** *Edit View* tab>*Component* panel with a component selected • **Context Menu** with a component selected
	Raster	• **Ribbon:** *Presentation* tab>*Publish* panel • **Ribbon:** *Edit View* tab>*Publish* panel • **Context Menu**

Button	Command	Location
	Tweak Components	• **Ribbon:** *Presentation* tab>*Component* panel • **Ribbon:** *Edit View* tab>*Component* panel • **Context Menu**
	Video	• **Ribbon:** *Presentation* tab>*Publish* panel • **Ribbon:** *Edit View* tab>*Publish* panel • **Context Menu** • **Storyboards Panel** (right-click on the tab)
N/A	**Visibility**	• **Context Menu** with a component selected • **Model browser** with a component selected

Chapter 21

Assembly Tools

The Autodesk® Inventor® software provides a number of different tools in the assembly environment that enable you to more efficiently modify and analyze your assemblies. For example, there are tools that enable you to replace models and restructure them in the assembly, and other tools that enable you to simulate motion in an assembly. The knowledge and efficient use of these tools can help you to analyze and change a design as required.

Learning Objectives

- Replace single or multiple instances of components in an assembly.
- Duplicate components in an assembly using **Copy**, **Mirror**, and **Pattern** tools.
- Restructure components from a lower-level subassembly to a higher level in the assembly structure.
- Restructure components from a higher level in the assembly structure to a subassembly.
- Create an assembly folder to organize and simplify the display of the Model browser.
- Drive an assembly constraint to simulate a required range of motion for an assembly.
- Limit the range of motion between selected components by defining contact sets.
- Determine interference between components in an assembly.
- Resolve constraint conflicts that arise due to changes made in the assembly.

21.1 Replacing Components

The **Replace/Replace All** and **Save and Replace Component** commands enable you to replace components when design specifications for an assembly change, if you need to know whether new parts are going to fit with other assembly components, or to test alternate design scenarios.

Replace Components

You can replace a single instance of a part or all instances of a part at the same level of the assembly. To replace a part, expand (Replace) in the *Assemble* tab>expanded *Component* panel and select one of the following options:

- **(Replace):** Replaces a single instance of a part. When the *Place Component* dialog box opens, browse to the part to replace the selected part in the assembly.
- **(Replace All):** Replaces all instances of a part at the same level of the assembly.

  Note: *You can also right-click on the component in the Model browser or in the window and select* ***Component>Replace****.*

You can remove the constraints of the old part when the new part is placed, especially if the two parts are different shapes. Once relocated, constrain the new component as required.

Save and Replace Components

The **Save and Replace** command enables you to replace a selected component in an assembly with a copy of itself. The newly created copy maintains the same constraints as the original component.

How To: Replace a Component with a Saved Copy

1. Select the component to be replaced.
2. In the *Assemble* tab>*Productivity* panel, click (Save and Replace). Alternatively, you can click (Save and Replace All) to create a single copy and replace all instances of the same component in the assembly at once.
3. In the *Create Part* dialog box, give the newly copied component an appropriate name and click **Save**. The selected component is replaced with the copy.

21.2 Duplicating Components

Mirroring, copying, and patterning can all be used as an alternative to individually placing components in an assembly. Each of these commands are located on the *Assemble* tab in the *Pattern* panel, as shown in Figure 21–1. Each of these duplication techniques are further described below.

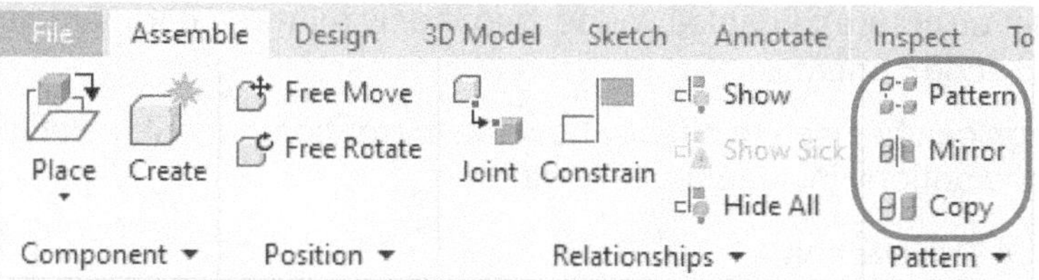

Figure 21–1

Mirror

The **Mirror** command enables you to duplicate a single or multiple components in an assembly based on a mirror plane. For example, the two assembled screws shown in Figure 21–2 were mirrored to place two additional screws in the assembly. The relationships that were established between multiple mirrored components are copied when mirrored. The mirrored instances are created as derived models. Any changes made to the source model(s) will reflect in the mirrored versions.

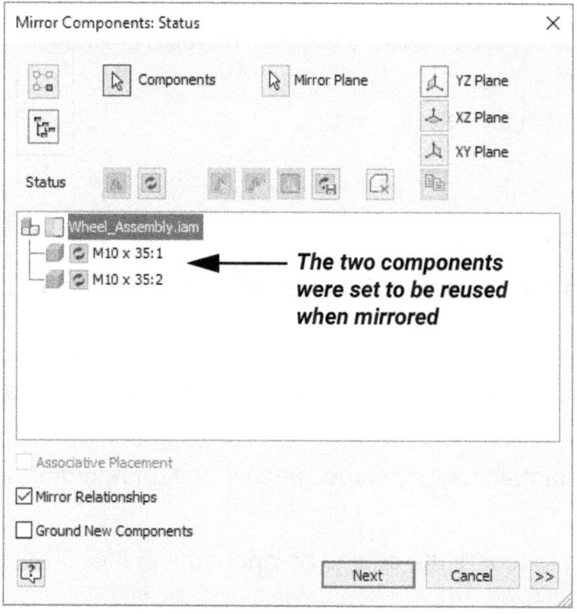

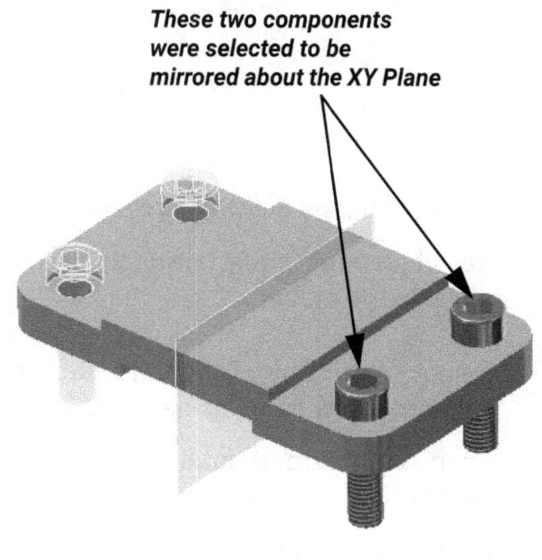

Figure 21–2

When mirroring components, you can determine how the mirrored components will be listed in the Model browser. The two options are as follows:

- **(Create mirror pattern):** Enables you to create a mirror component pattern and place the source and target components under the pattern as elements and keeps their associativity between them.

- **(Create flat structure):** Enables you to create only mirrored components and has no link with the source components.

The status settings can be used to specify how the mirror component (selected object) will be created. The status options include the following:

Icon	Description
	Creates a mirrored copy of the selected object. You will be prompted to define the new name for it.
	Reuses the original object for mirroring.
	Creates a mirrored copy of the selected part and breaks the associative link to the source.
	Creates a mirrored copy of the selected part and suppresses the associative link to the source. The associativity can be restored, as needed, in the future.
	Saves a copy of the selected object, adds a mirror feature, and removes the original geometry in the mirrored part.
	Saves a copy of the selected object and rotates it to create a mirrored orientation, without reusing the original file.
	Removes the selected object from the selection set.

Additional options in the *Mirror* dialog box enable you to:

- Select an origin plane button to use it as the mirror plane, as an alternative to selecting a plane in the model.

- Select to copy a list of unsuitable reuse components to the clipboard. You can paste the list and review them, as needed.

- Enable the **Mirror Relationships** option to maintain relationships between the components being copied, if they exist.

- Enable the **Ground New Components** option to locate the copied components in the assembly by grounding them.

Copy

The **Copy** command enables you to create a duplicate of an existing component(s) in an assembly. Similar to the **Mirror** command, you are required to select the components to be copied and set their status, using the options in the *Copy Components* dialog box shown in Figure 21–3.

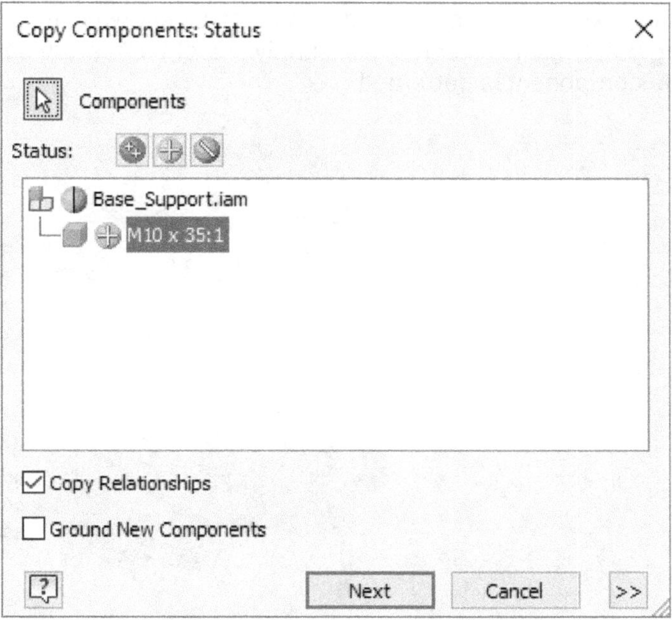

Figure 21–3

The status settings can include the following:

- **(Copy Component):** Enables you to create a duplicate version of the original component. The new instance can be opened and modified independently of the parent component.
- **(Reuse Component):** Enables you to reuse the original component for mirroring.
- **(Exclude Component):** Enables you to remove a component from the selection set.

Similar to the **Mirror** option, the **Copy Relationships** and **Ground New Components** options can be set to copy relationships between copied models or ground the copied instances. Relationships between copied components are retained after a Copy operation.

Pattern

Components can be patterned in any one of three ways using the *Pattern* dialog box. Constraints used to place the original components are not copied to the patterned components. Each tab provides an alternative patterning technique.

- (*Associative*) tab: Enables you to pattern a selected component based on a feature pattern that already exists in an assembly component, as shown in Figure 21–4. Once the component being patterned is selected, you simply select the feature pattern that it should reference and the component is patterned.

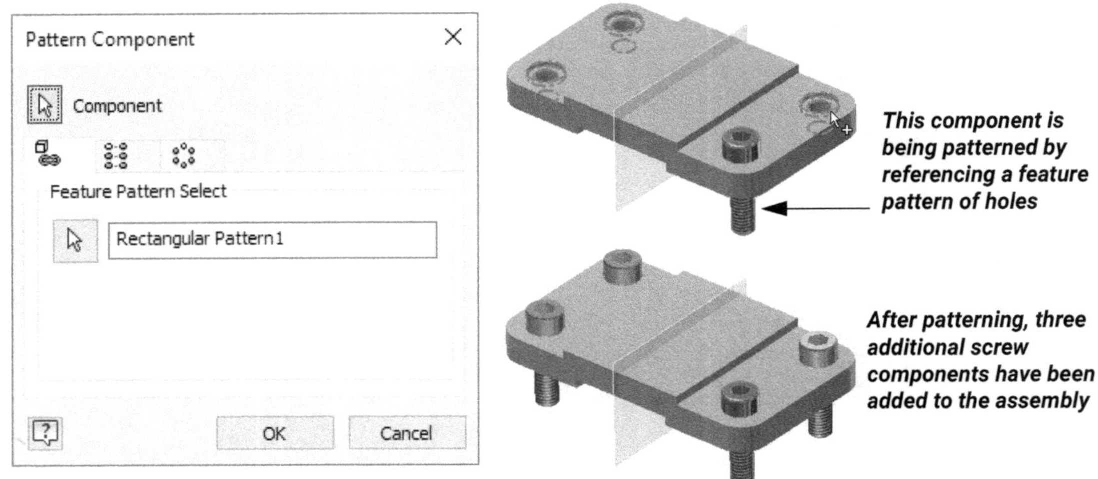

Figure 21–4

- (*Rectangular*) and (*Circular*) tabs: Enable you to pattern components similarly to rectangular and circular feature patterns. You can select direction references and enter the number of occurrences and pattern dimensions to create the pattern of components.

21.3 Restructuring Components

As you design an assembly, you might want to move parts in and out of subassemblies, or up and down in the Model browser hierarchy. You can use the Model browser to restructure assembly components, as shown in Figure 21–5, without changing their physical position.

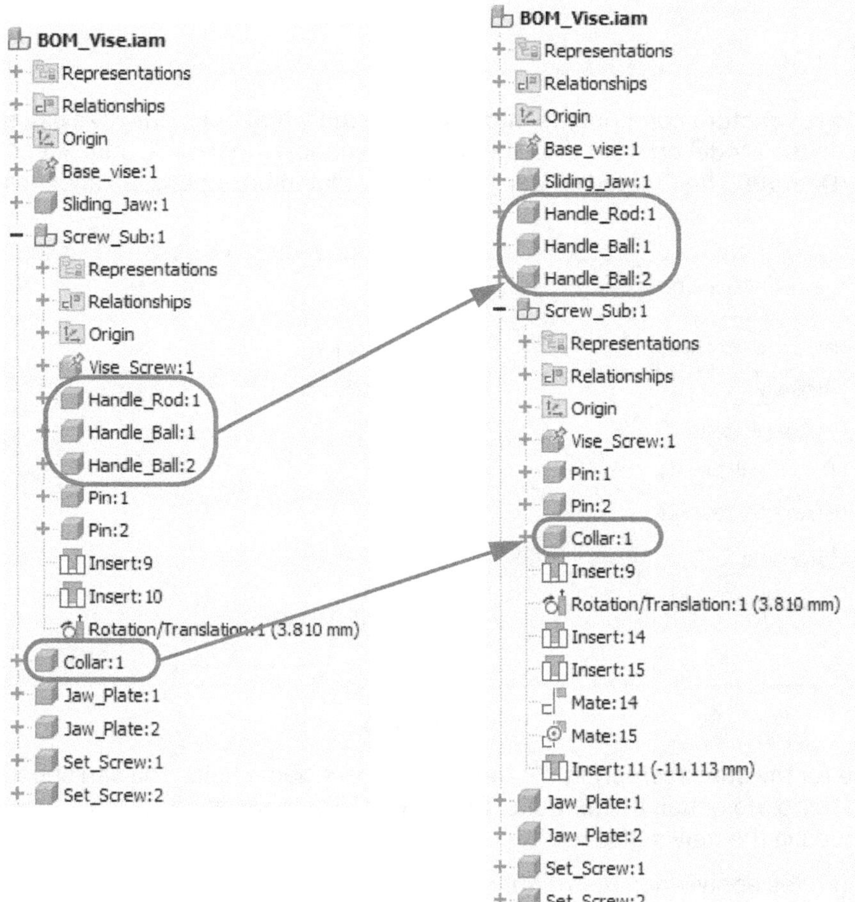

Figure 21–5

- To move an assembly component, drag and drop it in the Model browser. If a circle with a slash symbol (⊘) displays, you cannot place the component in that area.
- A component moved from a different assembly is placed at the bottom of the Model browser list, by default.
- Component patterns cannot be restructured by dragging, but can be repositioned by promoting or demoting.

You can also restructure components using the **Promote** and **Demote** options.

Promote

Use **Promote** to move components out of a subassembly and up one level in the Model browser. To accomplish this, select the component in the Model browser or in the graphics window, right-click, and select **Component>Promote**. The **Promote** option is not available if the selected component is a child of the top-level assembly.

Demote

If you need to restructure components into a subassembly that does not yet exist, select components in the Model browser or in the graphics window, right-click, and select **Component>Demote**. The *Create In-Place Component* dialog box opens, as shown in Figure 21–6.

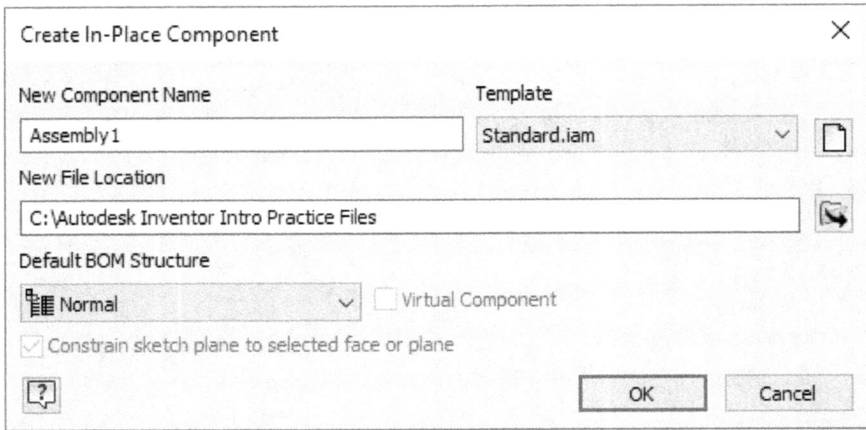

Figure 21–6

Enter a name for the subassembly in the *New Component Name* field. You can specify a new file location and template or use the defaults. Click **OK** to create the subassembly. The demoted parts are placed in the new subassembly.

The following rules apply when restructuring an assembly:

- Moving components in or out of subassemblies might impact assembly constraints. A warning dialog box opens indicating that assembly references might be lost during restructuring.
- Components are removed from existing design view representations and relocated to design view representations in the new assembly.
- The enabled, visibility, and color status of the moved component is preserved in the new assembly.

Assembly Folders

Assembly folders help organize assemblies by grouping components together and can be used to simplify the Model browser. Unlike subassemblies, folders do not create another physical component.

To create a folder, right-click on the component(s) that you want to add to the folder and select **Add to New Folder**, as shown in Figure 21–7. To rename the folder, click on the folder in the Model browser (do not double-click), then click on the folder again and enter a new name.

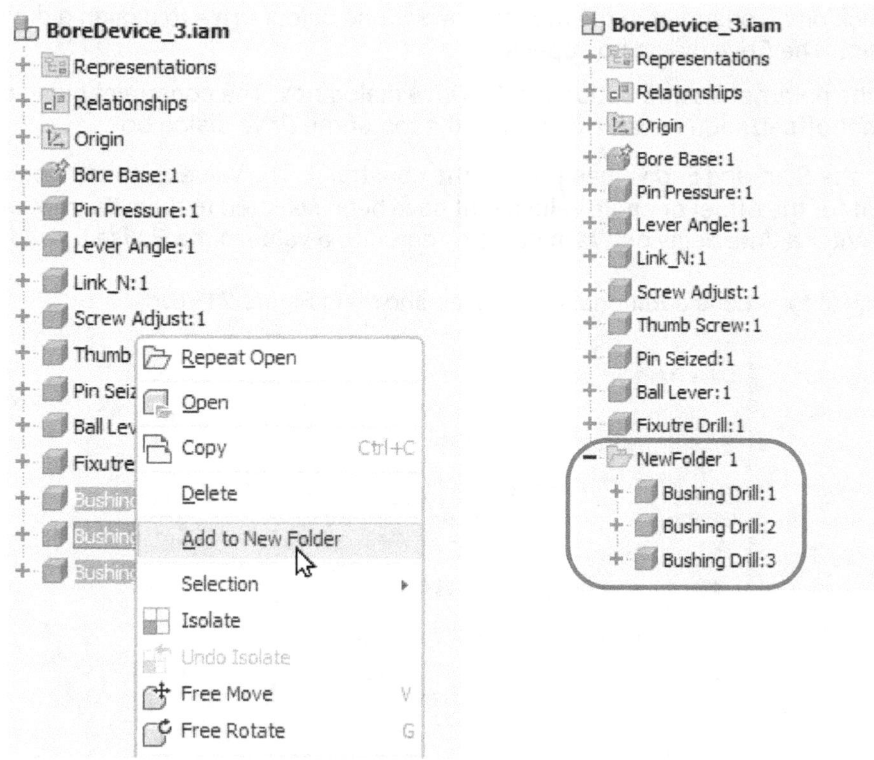

Figure 21–7

21.4 Drive Constraints

Assembly constraints are static. If parts in the assembly are intended to move, you might want to see the assembly in motion. One way to do this is to use a Drive constraint. This enables you to assign motion between constrained components by setting an offset or angle value in a constraint so that it changes incrementally.

How To: Create a Drive Constraint

1. Right-click on a constraint in the Model browser and select **Drive** to assign a driving constraint. The *Drive* dialog box opens.
2. Define the parameters and options in the *Drive* dialog box. The constraint being driven and its current offset/angular value display at the top of the *Drive* dialog box.
   - Enter the *Start* and *End* values to drive the constraint. The values depend on the required extent for the offset or angle values that have been selected to drive the motion. You can also enter a time delay between steps by entering a value in the *Pause Delay* field.
   - Click >> to access additional options, as shown in Figure 21–8.

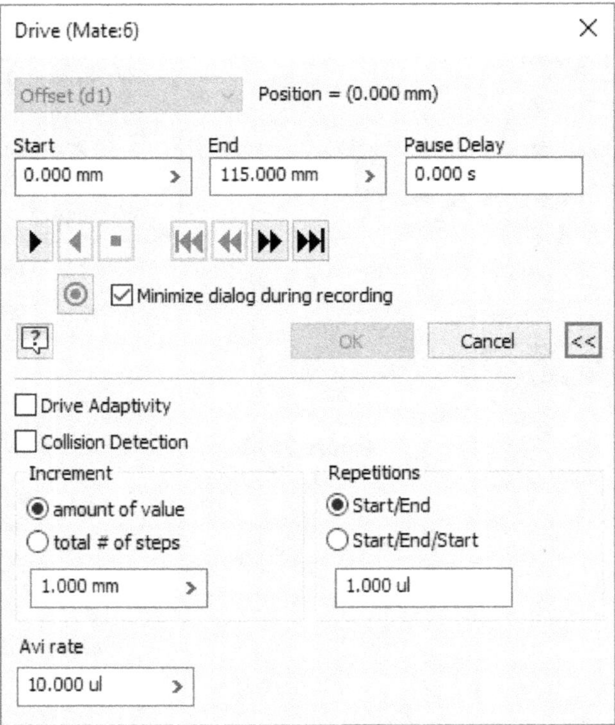

Figure 21–8

- The additional options are as follows:

Option	Description
Drive Adaptivity	Enables you to adapt the components while maintaining the constraints.
Collision Detection	Moves the assembly until interference is detected.
Increment	Sets how to move the assembly. **Amount of value** sets the percentage of the total move to make in each step. For example, if set to 0.1, the total move is completed in ten steps. **Total # of steps** sets the number of steps to move the entire range.
Repetitions	Sets the number of times to complete the movement and how the movement proceeds. **Start/End** progresses from start to end and then begins again at start. **Start/End/Start** progresses from start to end and then returns from end to start.
Avi rate	Specifies the increment for frames in the animation file.

3. Select the standard control buttons in the *Drive* dialog box to play/drive the constraint.
4. Click to record the motion as an .AVI or .MWV file. To stop recording, click again.
   - Before starting, you are prompted for the filename and export properties of the recording.
   - The default export properties provide the optimal quality for both .AVI and .WMV formats. If changes are made to these properties, the new values apply for only the current session.

21.5 Contact Solver

The **Contact Solver** is used to limit the range of motion between components by stopping movement when they come into contact with each other. This tool can be used to help analyze motion in an assembly. For example, in the assembly shown in Figure 21–9 there are two components. The puck is constrained on the tray so that there is two degrees of transitional freedom and one degree of rotational freedom. Contact Solver can be used to limit the motion of the puck so that it can move around the tray, but stops when it comes in contact with its edges.

You can use the Contact Solver to limit the motion of the puck so that it can move along the tray, but stops when it comes in contact with its edges.

Figure 21–9

How To: Create a Contact Set

1. Constrain the assembly, as required. Leave the motion that is to be tested unconstrained.

   Note: *Use* ***Suppress*** *to suppress constraints that may have been previously assigned.*

2. In the Model browser, select the components to be analyzed, right-click, and select **Contact Set**. The Model browser displays the **Contact Set** symbol next to the selected components, as shown in Figure 21–10.

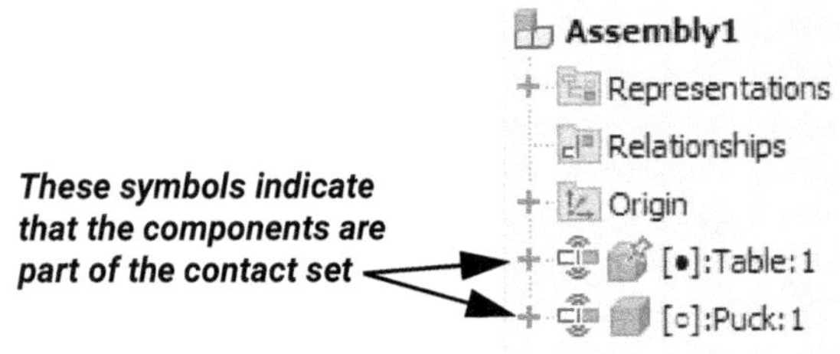

Figure 21–10

3. In the *Inspect* tab>*Interference* panel, click (Activate Contact Solver).
4. Move the components as required. The motion stops once a component comes in contact with one of the other components in the contact set.
5. To toggle off the Contact Solver, click (Activate Contact Solver) again.

You can control how the Contact Solver behaves in the *Interactive Contact* area in the *Document Settings* dialog box (*Tools* tab>*Options* panel, click (Document Settings), and select the *Modeling* tab). When (Activate Contact Solver) is active, contact is only detected between the components specified in the Contact Set (**Contact Set only**). When **All Components** is selected, you do not need to specify a Contact Set. Any contact between any components in the assembly stops the motion.

21.6 Interference Detection

In an assembly, components can be assembled so that two parts occupy the same space at the same time. To identify if components overlap, you should analyze the model. For example, you can check for interference between the parts shown in Figure 21–11.

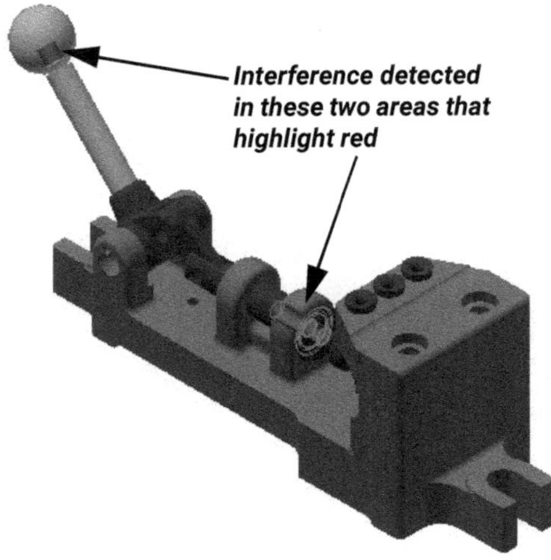

Figure 21–11

How To: Check for Interference

1. In the *Inspect* tab>*Interference* panel, click (Analyze Interference). The *Interference Analysis* dialog box opens, as shown in Figure 21–12.

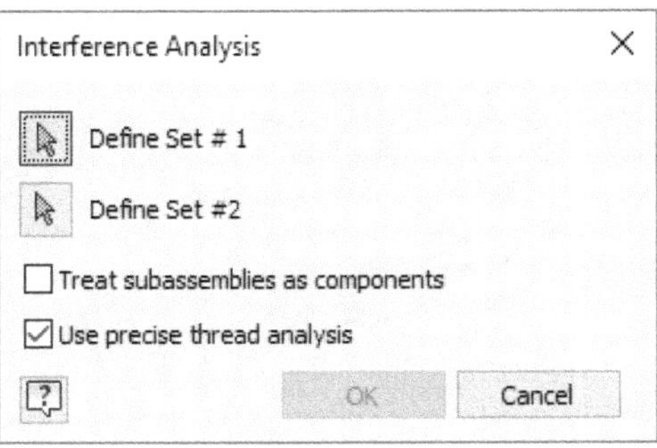

Figure 21–12

2. Click (Define Set # 1) and select the first set of components to include. Alternatively, you can drag a selection box around multiple components when defining the first set and click OK to analyze multiple components at once.

3. Click (Define Set # 2) and select the second set.
4. (Optional) Enable the **Treat subassemblies as components** option, if required, to analyze interference between all of the components in a subassembly. Clear this option to treat the subassembly as one component, ignoring any interferences between its components.
5. (Optional) Disable the **Use precise thread analysis** option, if required. This option is enabled by default and can be disabled to exclude the precise analysis of threads.
6. Click **OK**.

   Note: *Interference analysis can take a long time in large assemblies. As the analysis is proceeding, the percentage completed displays in a dialog box.*

If no interference is detected between the selected sets, a dialog box opens to notify you that no interference was found. If there is interference, the *Interference Detected* dialog box opens similar to that shown in Figure 21–13.

- The dialog box describes the number of interferences and the total interfering volume. The interference volume is also highlighted in the assembly window.
- Click **>>** to display the details of each interference, as shown in Figure 21–13.

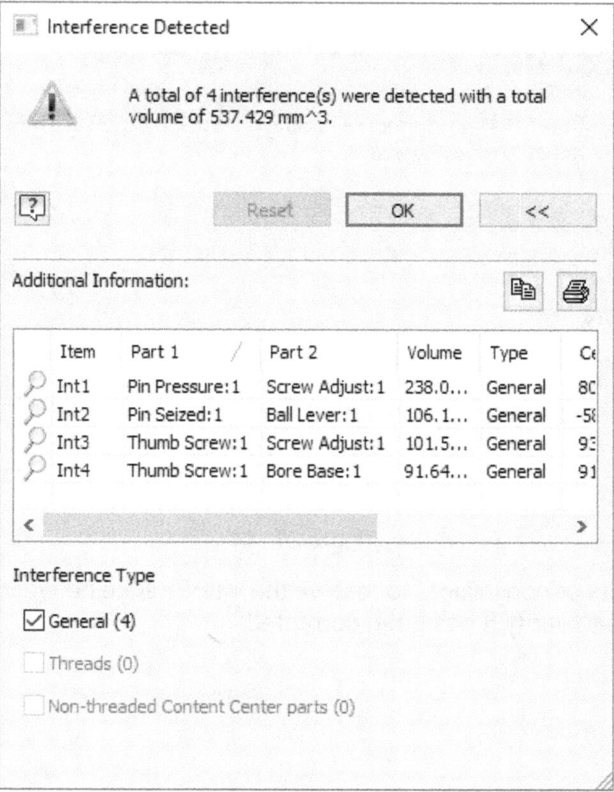

Figure 21–13

- Double-click or click in the first column of any of the interference listings to zoom to them in the model. Click **Reset** to return to a zoomed out view.
- Use the options in the *Interference Type* area to filter which interferences are listed in the dialog box.
- Right-click on an interference and use the **Ignore** options (shown in Figure 21–14) to ignore specific interferences or interferences that are less than the volume that was calculated.

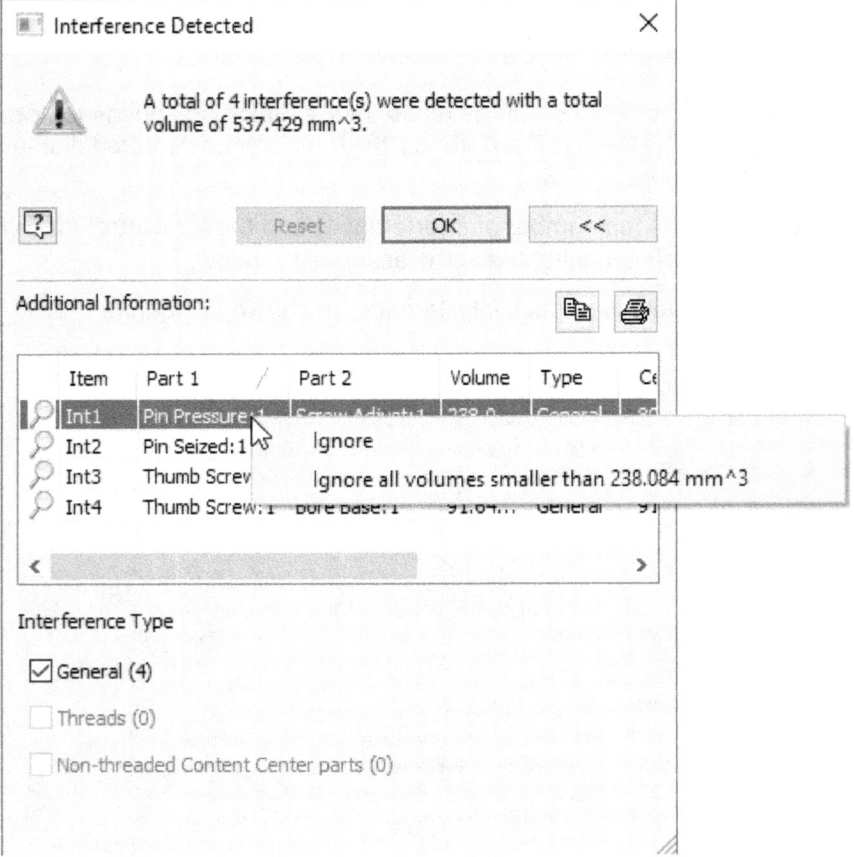

Figure 21–14

Modify the components or constraints to resolve the interference between parts in an assembly and rerun the analysis to verify it has been corrected.

21.7 Error Recovery

When working in an assembly, existing constraints can fail due to conflicts with other constraints or when changes are made to the model. When a constraint fails, a dialog box similar to that shown in Figure 21–15 opens indicating there is a problem.

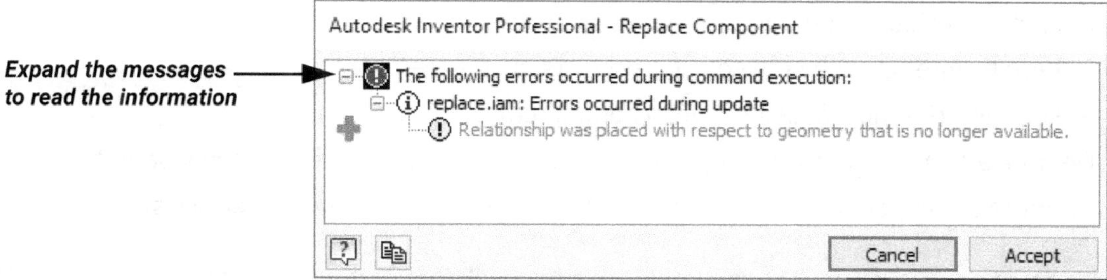

Figure 21–15

Note: Assembly components are not affected when constraints conflict. Only their defined position in the model fails.

- To fix the error, click [+] to start recovering. The *Design Doctor* dialog box opens, as shown in Figure 21–16. The recovery process is similar to that used to correct sketch and feature errors, where you step through the process by clicking **Next**. The components involved are highlighted in the graphics window. You do not have to immediately fix constraint errors. At the **Treat** step, select the **Edit** option in the *Select a treatment* area and click **Finish** to open the *Edit Constraint* dialog box to redefine the missing constraint reference.

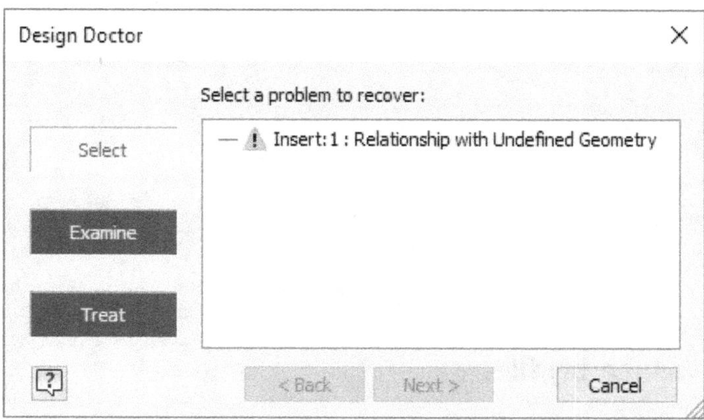

Figure 21–16

- Failed constraints are marked with ⚠ in the Model browser.
- To resolve constraint conflicts that were skipped when initially identified, right-click on the failed constraint (⚠) in the Model browser and select **Recover** to launch the Design Doctor and step you through the recovery process.

Practice 21a
Use Assembly Tools

Practice Objectives

- Replace an existing component in an assembly.
- Determine interference between components in an assembly.
- Resolve interference issues between components.
- Demote a component from a top-level assembly into a newly created subassembly.
- Promote a component from a subassembly to the top level of the assembly structure.

In this practice, you will use the assembly tools to check for interference between two assembly components. You will make changes to the assembly components, and restructure the assembly components in the Model browser. The completed assembly is shown in Figure 21–17.

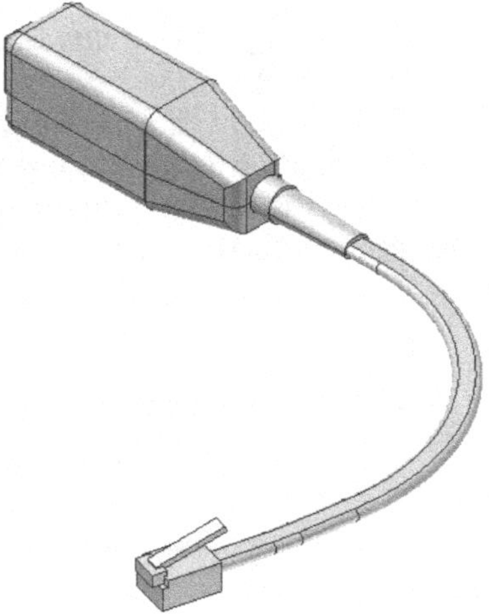

Figure 21–17

Task 1: Open an assembly file.

1. Open **socket_final.iam**.
2. Expand the *Representations>View* nodes in the Model browser. Double-click on **Interference_view** to set it as the active view representation.

Task 2: Replace a component.

1. Toggle off the display of the **encbase**, **wire final**, and **enctop** components. The assembly displays as shown in Figure 21–18.

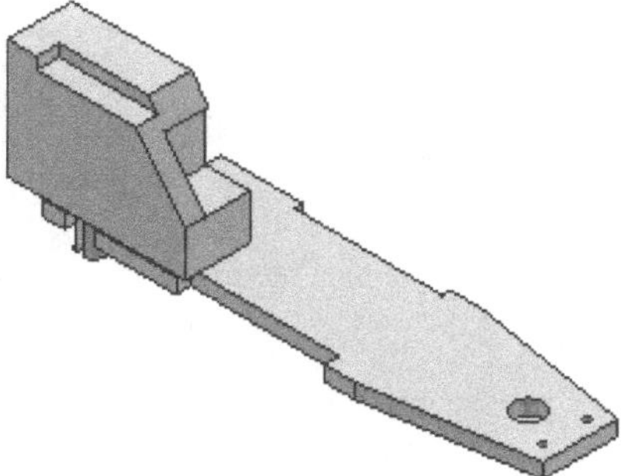

Figure 21–18

2. Right-click on **connect:1** in the Model browser and select **Component>Replace**.
3. Select and open the **connect_mirror** part in the *Place Component* dialog box.
4. If prompted with the warning message about relationships, click **OK**. In this situation, the constraint references are recognized in the new model and it remains fully constrained, as shown in Figure 21–19.

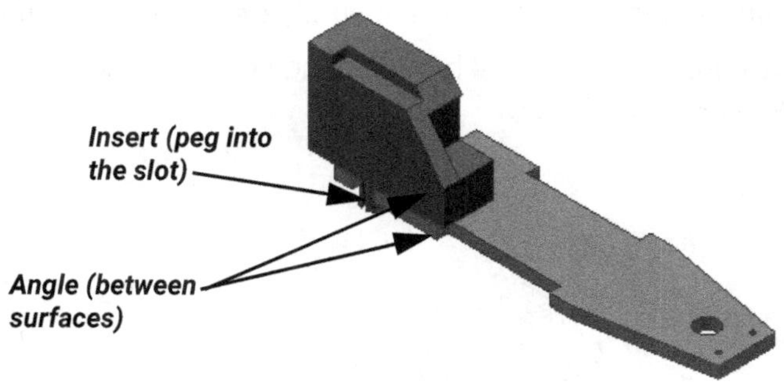

Figure 21–19

Task 3: Conduct an interference analysis.

1. Toggle on the display of the **encbase** part and toggle off the display of the **connect_mirror** part.
2. Select the *Inspect* tab>*Interference* panel, click (Analyze Interference). The *Interference Analysis* dialog box opens.
3. With (Define Set # 1) selected, select the **pcb** part.

4. Click (Define Set # 2) and select the **encbase** part.
5. Click **OK**. The *Interference Detected* dialog box opens, as shown in Figure 21–20, describing the number of interferences and the total volume. The interference volume is highlighted in the assembly window, as shown in Figure 21–20.

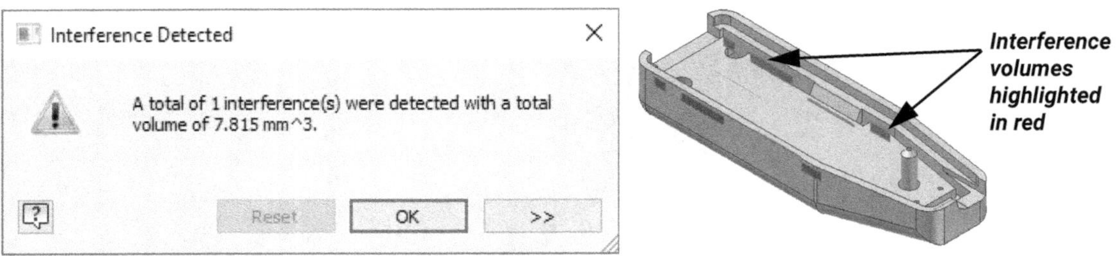

Figure 21–20

Note: Interference analysis can take a long time in large assemblies. As the analysis is processing, the percentage completed displays in a dialog box.

6. Click **OK** to close the *Interference Detected* dialog box.

Task 4: Modify the pcb part.

1. Double-click on **pcb:1**. All assembly components are grayed out except **pcb:1**. This means **pcb:1** is the only active component in the assembly that can be modified.
2. Right-click on **Extrusion1** in the Model browser and select **Show Dimensions**. The model displays as shown in Figure 21–21.

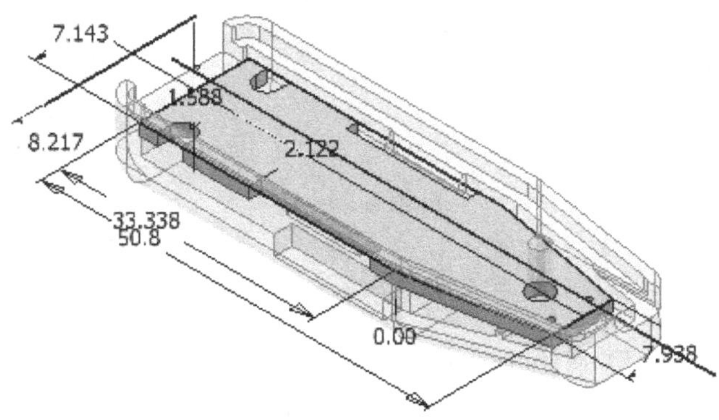

Figure 21–21

3. Modify the **7.143** dimension to **6.80**.
4. In the Quick Access Toolbar, click (Local Update) to update the **pcb** part.

5. Double-click on **socket_final.iam** in the Model browser to activate the assembly.
6. Run an interference check on the two assembly components a second time. The interference has been reduced.
7. Modify the **pcb** part to the following to completely remove the interference:
    - Modify the dimension of **Work Plane5** to **-6.8mm**.
    - Modify the **50.8** dimension of **Extrusion1** to **50mm**.

    Note: *The components were originally built in imperial and the units were changed. When modifying the original imperial unit will display. Ensure that you enter the units of measure when entering the metric value.*
8. Update the model.
9. Activate the top-level assembly.
10. Run an interference check again on the **pcb** and **encbase** parts. No interference was detected.

Task 5: Restructure the assembly components.

In this task, you will create a subassembly and place the **connect_mirror** component in it.

1. Display all of the assembly components.
2. Right-click on **connect_mirror** in the Model browser and select **Component>Demote**. The *Create In-Place Component* dialog box opens, as shown in Figure 21–22.

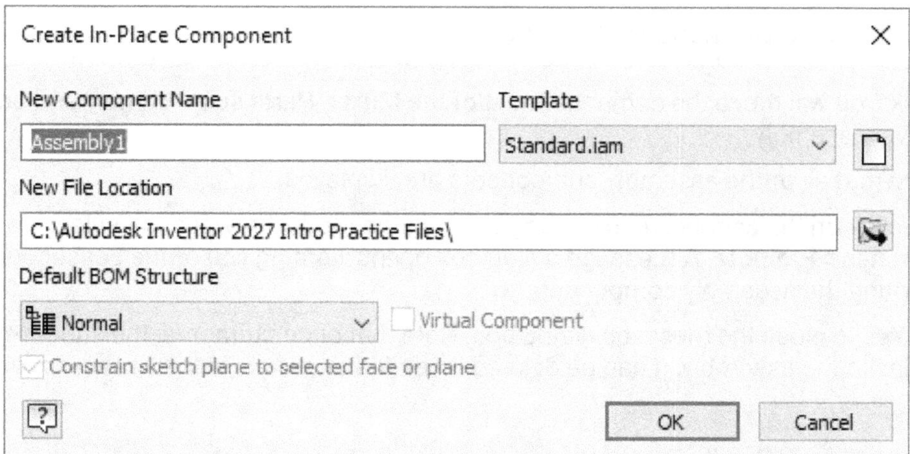

Figure 21–22

3. Enter **Mirror_Parts** in the *New Component Name* field.

4. Click **OK**. The subassembly **Mirror_Parts** displays in the Model browser with the demoted part in the subassembly list, as shown in Figure 21–23.

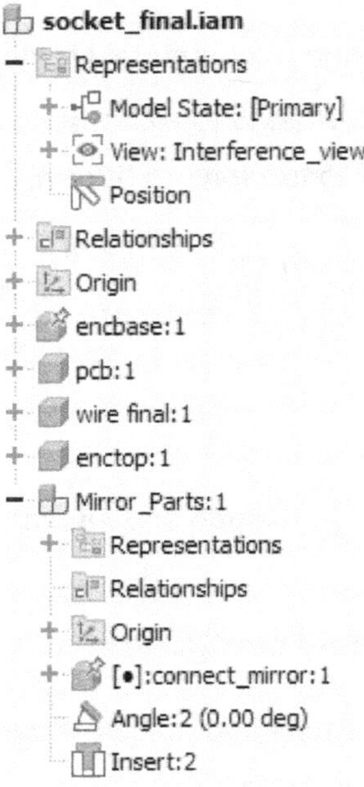

Figure 21–23

5. Save the assembly.

Task 6: Promote the assembly components.

In this task, you will move the component out of the **Mirror_Parts** subassembly and back into the top-level assembly.

1. Ensure that all of the assembly components are displayed.
2. Right-click on the **connect_mirror** component in the Model browser and select **Component>Promote**. A message dialog box opens warning you of the consequences of promoting the assembly components.
3. Click **Yes** to close the message dialog box. Note that once promoted, the subassembly still remains in the assembly. It can be deleted if needed or remain in the assembly for future changes.

   Note: *Moving components in or out of subassemblies might impact patterns and assembly constraints. This means you might need to redefine assembly references that are lost due to restructuring.*

4. Save and close the assembly.

End of practice

Practice 21b
Replace Components

Practice Objectives

- Replace existing components in an assembly with alternate models.
- Redefine constraint references for those that are lost when components are replaced.

In this practice, you will replace similar components in an assembly, as shown in Figure 21–24.

Figure 21–24

Task 1: Replace a single component instance.

1. Open **replace.iam**. There are four instances of a component named **round** in the assembly. They are constrained in the assembly using Insert constraints to the cylindrical pegs.
2. Expand the *Component* panel, click (Replace), and select one of the components named **round** as the component to replace.
3. Right-click in the graphics window and select **Continue**.

4. In the *Place Component* dialog box, select **spacer.ipt** as the replacement component and click **Open**. Only the selected component is replaced, similar to that shown in Figure 21–25.

Figure 21–25

Task 2: Replace multiple component instances.

1. In the expanded *Component* panel, in the *Replace* drop-down list, click (Replace All) and select one of the remaining **round** components as the component to replace.
2. Right-click in the graphics window and select **Continue**.

   Note: *If you preselected the component in the Model browser, you would not be required to select* ***Continue****. The Place Component dialog box would open immediately. Alternatively, you can right-click on the component in the Model browser or graphics window and select* ***Component>Replace****.*

3. Select **spacer.ipt** as the replacement component and click **Open**. This time, the remaining three components are all replaced at the same time, as shown in Figure 21–26.

Figure 21–26

4. Expand one of the **spacer** components in the Model browser and note that it has retained the Insert constraint that was used to originally place the **round** component.

Task 3: Replace with a dissimilar component.

1. Right-click on one of the **spacer** components in the Model browser or graphics window and select **Component>Replace**.
2. Select **square.ipt** as the replacement component and click **Open**. Note that you are prompted about possible constraint loss, as shown in Figure 21–27.

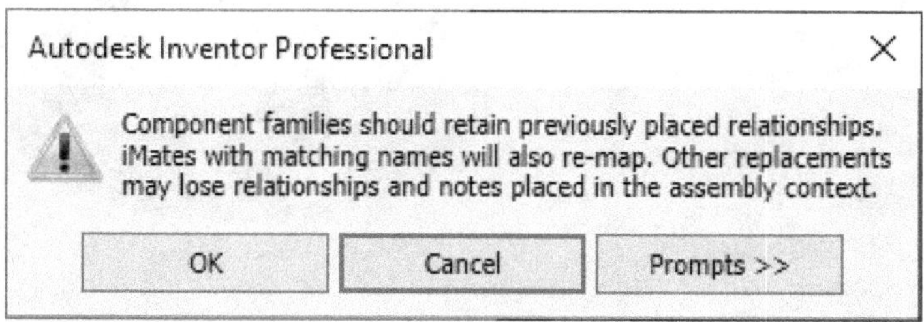

Figure 21–27

3. Click **OK** to the warning message.
4. The **square** component can be placed, but it is not constrained or correctly located because its origin and shape are different from the part that was being replaced. Expand the errors in the dialog box that appears, as shown in Figure 21–28. The message states that an error occurred during command execution and a constraint reference (relationship) no longer exists because the geometry is no longer available.

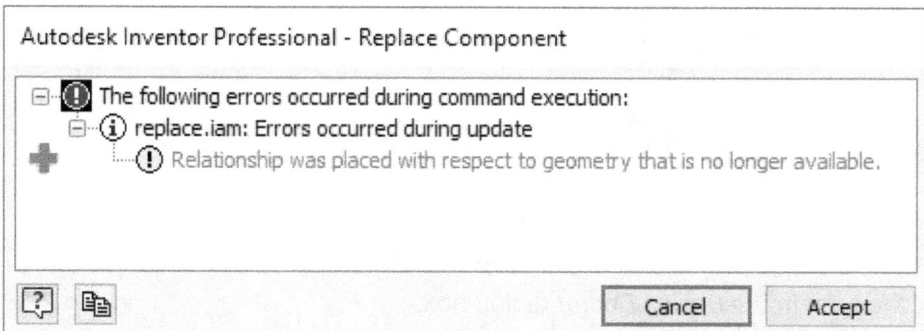

Figure 21–28

5. Click **Accept**. The Model browser displays as shown in Figure 21–29. The selected **round** component is replaced, and the Insert constraint is missing its references.

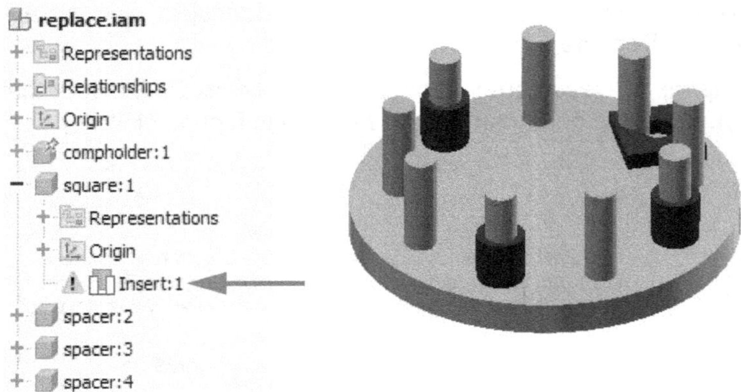

Figure 21–29

6. Select the failed **Insert** constraint in the **square** component in the Model browser, right-click, and select **Recover**. The *Design Doctor* dialog box opens, as shown in Figure 21–30.

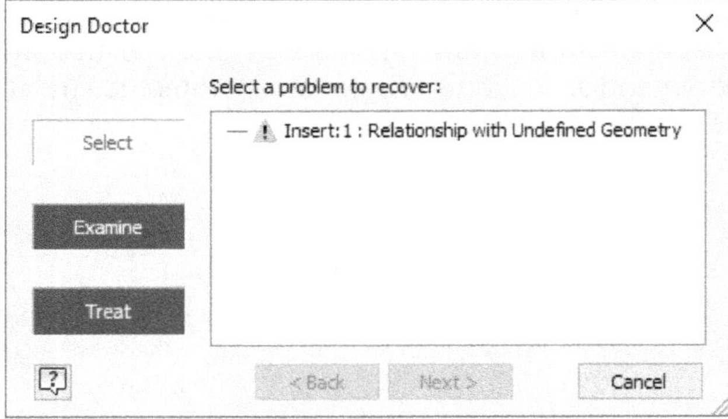

Figure 21–30

7. Select the error in the *Design Doctor* dialog box.
8. Click **Next** to toggle through the steps in the *Design Doctor* dialog box.
9. At the **Treat** step, select **Edit** in the *Select a treatment* area and click **Finish**. The *Edit Constraint* dialog box opens.
10. The reference on the **square** component has been lost. Reapply the lost reference for the Insert constraint.
11. Click **OK** to close the *Edit Constraint* dialog box.
12. Save and close the file.

End of practice

Practice 21c
Restructure the Assembly

Practice Objective

- Restructure components of an assembly by demoting them into a newly created subassembly.

In this practice, you will use the restructuring functionality to restructure components in an assembly. The assembly is shown in Figure 21–31. Note that constraints have not been assigned to these components to avoid errors while restructuring. Keep in mind that you will need to consider constraints as well when restructuring.

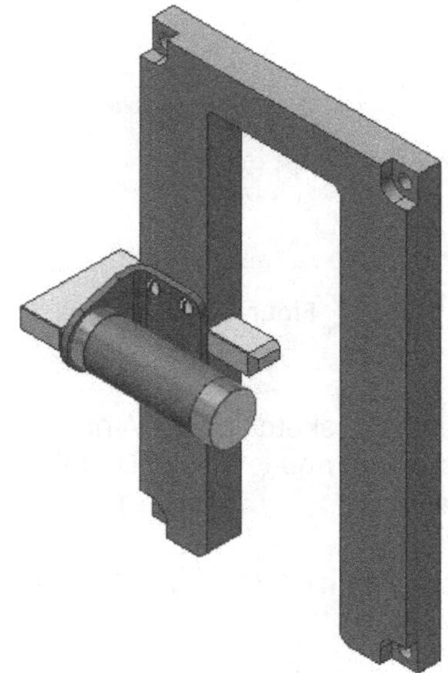

Figure 21–31

Task 1: Open and review an assembly in the Model browser.

1. Open **indexassy.iam**.
2. In the Model browser, double-click on **cylinder.iam** to make the subassembly active. Note that there are four components in this subassembly.
3. Double-click on **indexassy.iam** to make the top-level assembly active again.

Task 2: Create a new component in the assembly.

1. In the *Component* panel, click (Create). In the *Template* area, select **Standard.iam**. In the *New Component Name* area, enter **Finger** and ensure that the file location is set to your working folder. The dialog box should display as shown in Figure 21–32.

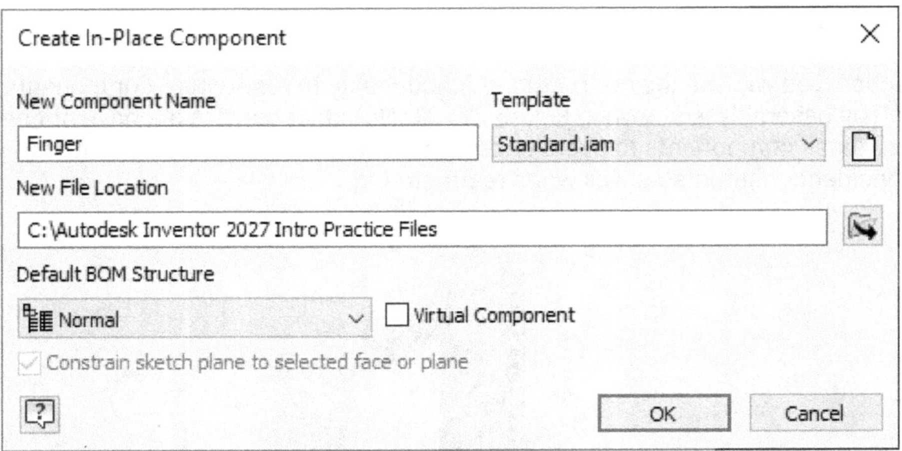

Figure 21–32

2. Click **OK**.
3. Select a point in space to create the sketch plane. A new subassembly is created. It is listed at the bottom of the Model browser and is active. Double-click on **indexassy.iam** to make the top-level assembly active again.

Task 3: Restructure components into the Finger subassembly.

1. Expand the **cylinder** subassembly component in the Model browser. Using the drag and drop technique, restructure **cyl body** under the **Finger** assembly. Click **Yes** in the warning dialog box.
2. Make the **cylinder** subassembly active, and note that the body of the cylinder (**cyl body**) is grayed out because it is not part of the active subassembly.
3. Double-click on **indexassy.iam** to make the top-level assembly active again.
4. Restructure the subassembly **cylinder** and the part **index finger** under the **Finger** subassembly.
5. Make **Finger** subassembly active, and note which parts are grayed. Double-click on **indexassy.iam** to make the top-level assembly active again.
6. Restructure **cyl body** under **cylinder** again.

7. Restructure **cyl mount** under **Finger**. The Model browser displays similar to that shown in Figure 21–33, depending on the order in which the files were dropped during restructuring.

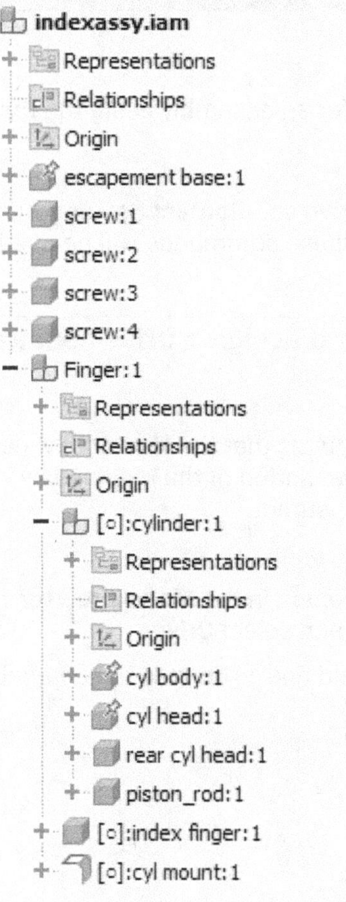

Figure 21–33

8. Save and close the file.
9. (Optional) As additional constraint practice, use constraints or joints to fully constrain the components in the assembly.

End of practice

Practice 21d
Control Assembly Motion

Practice Objective

- Simulate the range of motion for an assembly using the Drive and Contact Solver commands.

In this practice, you will use the **Drive** and **Contact Solver** commands to control the range of motion for an assembly. Each of these commands will be used independently as well as together.

Task 1: Open an assembly and assign a Drive constraint to an existing constraint.

The design intent of the model requires that the **MovingJaw** can move between two parallel faces. In this task, you will limit the motion of the **MovingJaw** component by adding a Drive constraint to the existing Mate constraint.

1. Open **Vise_final.iam**.
2. Expand the **MovingJaw** component in the Model browser, right-click on the **Mate:6(40.00mm)** constraint and select **Drive**.
3. Enter **0.000mm** in the *Start* field and **115mm** in the *End* field.
4. Click >> in the *Drive* dialog box.

5. Enable **Collision Detection**, as shown in Figure 21–34.

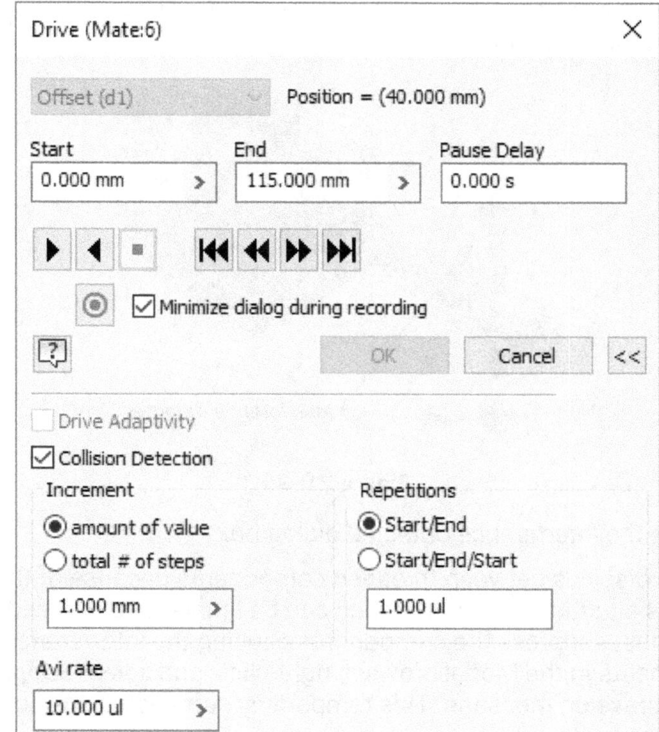

Figure 21–34

6. Click . A dialog box opens indicating that a collision has been detected. Click **OK** and close the *Drive* dialog box.The **Drive** command cannot be used if interferences exist in the model.

   Note: *Disabling* ***Collision Detection*** *enables the animation to play, regardless of collision. Doing so might help you identify where the collision occurred.*

7. Select the *Inspect* tab. In the *Interference* panel, click (Analyze Interference).
8. Click (Define Set # 1) and select the **Pin** component to include.
9. Click (Define Set # 2) and select two **DIN 917** components.
10. Click **OK** to run the interference analysis.

    Note: *Interference analysis can take a long time in large assemblies. As the analysis is proceeding, the percentage completed displays in a dialog box.*

11. There are two interferences found in the model ($104.202mm^3$).

12. To identify the interference, click [>>] to expand the dialog box. Select the **Threads** and **Matching Threads** options in the *Interference Type* area. The interference is highlighted in red, as shown in Figure 21–35.

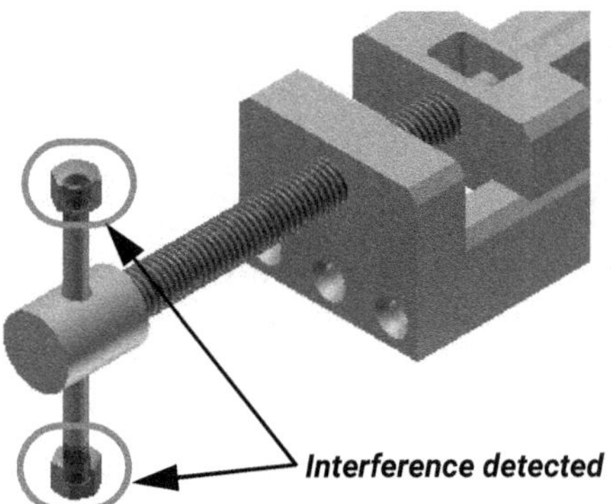

Figure 21–35

13. Click **OK** to close the *Interference Detected* dialog box.
14. The interference displays between threaded components because of the way threads were generated. In this situation, the interference can be ignored. To proceed with the **Drive** command you must suppress the components causing the interference. Select the two **DIN 917** components in the Model browser, right-click, and select **Suppress**. Click **OK** to confirm the Suppression message. This temporarily suppresses the components to work with the **Drive** command.

    Note: *Ignoring interferences in the Interference Analysis dialog box does not ignore interferences experienced when the* ***Drive*** *option is used. Components must be suppressed to ignore them.*

15. Right-click on the **Mate:6(40.00mm)** constraint again and select **Drive**. Ensure that the *Start* and *End* values are still set and that **Collision Detection** is still enabled.
16. Click [▶] in the *Drive* dialog box to view the motion. Another collision is detected. Click **OK**.

    Note that the **Body** and **Spindle** components are highlighted, indicating that they are the components that are in conflict. The **Spindle** is not long enough to permit the full range of motion.

17. Click [◀] to reverse the motion.
18. Disable the **Collision Detection** option in the *Drive* dialog box.
19. Click [▶] in the *Drive* dialog box to continue the motion. Visually you can see that there is also going to be a collision between **MovingJaw** and **FixedJaw**.
20. Click [◀] to reverse the motion.

The Start and End values that were provided did not take into account the thickness of the **MovingJaw** component. This is required because the offset surface that was used to create the constraint is not the face that will initially come in contact with the **Body** component. The actual end value should only be 95mm.

21. Enter **95mm** as the new *End* field and enable **Collision Detection**.

22. Click ▶ in the *Drive* dialog box to view the motion again. As expected the collision is identified between the **Body** and **Spindle** components. Click **OK**.

The appropriate next step in your design would be to modify the length of the **Spindle** component and retest for collision. You are going to leave the size of the **Spindle** model as it is for the next Task so that you can learn an alternate option for testing range of motion.

23. Click **OK** to close the *Drive* dialog box.

Task 2: Use the Contact Solver.

In this task, you will use the Contact Solver as an alternate tool for simulating the required range of motion.

1. In the Model browser, select **Mate:6** and enter **40mm** as a new offset value. Press <Enter>. This ensures that initially there is no collision in the model before getting started.

2. In the Model browser, right-click on the **Mate:6(40.00mm)** constraint and select **Suppress**. The Contact Solver cannot be used with constraints that prevent the required degree of freedom.

3. Select the *Inspect* tab, if not already active. In the *Interference* panel, click (Activate Contact Solver) if not already active.

4. Right-click on **Spindle** in the Model browser and select **Contact Set**. Return to the model and drag the spindle. No other components have been included in the contact set so you are able to drag through other components.

   Note: *If any interference exists between components in the Contact Set, you will not be able to drag the components.*

5. Right-click on **Body** in the Model browser and select **Contact Set**. Return to the model and drag the spindle. Note that this time as soon as the **Spindle** comes in contact with the **Body**, movement stops because a collision is detected. This was also the collision that was found using the **Drive** command.

6. Modify the length of the **Spindle**. Double-click on the **Splindle:1** component in the Model browser to activate it. Edit the sketch associated with the **Revolution1** feature. Change the overall length of the sketch from *140mm* to **160mm**, as shown in Figure 21–36.

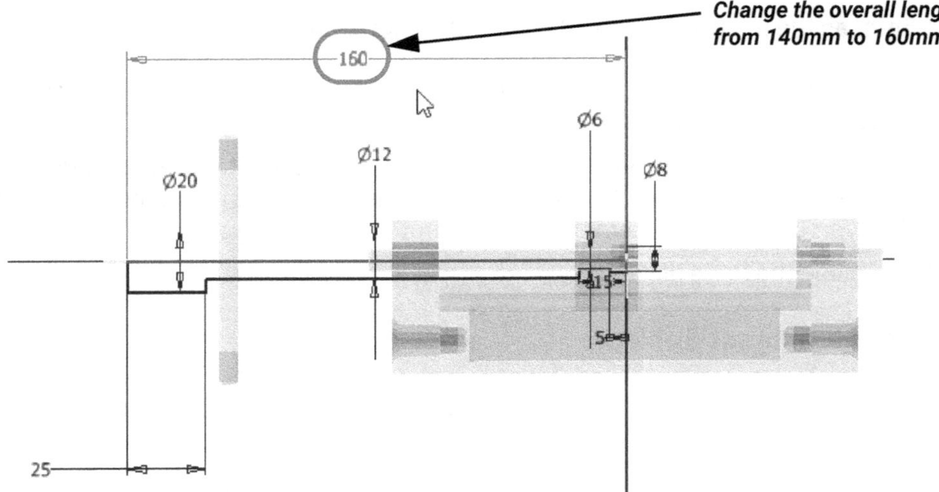

Figure 21–36

7. In the *Exit* panel, click (Finish Sketch) and in the *3D Model* tab>*Return* panel, click (Return) to return to the assembly.
8. Return to the model and drag the spindle. Note that once the **Spindle** and **Body** come in contact there is collision between **MovingJaw** and **FixedJaw**.
9. Right-click on **MovingJaw** in the Model browser and select **Contact Set**.
10. Right-click on **FixedJaw** in the Model browser and select **Contact Set**.

 Note: *The number of components in a Contact Set can affect system performance. It is recommended that only the required components be added.*

11. Return to the model and drag the spindle. The movement is now limited to all of the correct points of contact and there are no interferences for this range of motion.

Task 3: Use the Contact Solver with the Drive command.

In this task, you will learn how to use a combination of the **Contact Solver** and **Drive** commands to simulate motion.

1. Right-click on the **Mate:6(40.000mm)** constraint in the Model browser and clear the **Suppress** option.
2. Right-click on the **Mate:6(40.000mm)** constraint in the Model browser and select **Drive**. All of the contact sets should remain set.

3. Expand the dialog box and clear the **Collision Detection** option.
4. Enter **0.000mm** in the *Start* field, **115.000mm** in the *End* field, and click ▶. Originally, when you entered 115mm as the extent of the offset there was a collision. Note that the motion stops when the offset is 95.000mm, as shown at the top of the dialog box. The Contact Solver can also be used to help determine where components will come into contact with each other when you are using the **Drive** command.
5. Close the *Drive* dialog box.
6. Resume the two suppressed components and save the assembly.

End of practice

Chapter Review Questions

1. When replacing a part in the assembly, you can replace all instances of the part at the same level of the assembly.
   a. True
   b. False

2. What is the effect of promoting a component (as shown in Figure 21–37) in an assembly?

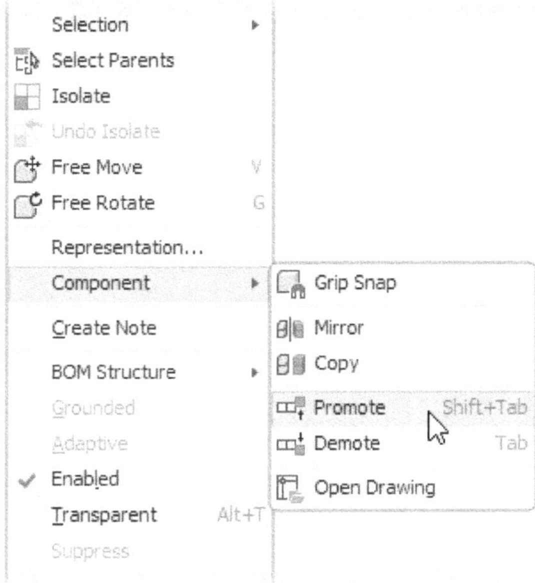

Figure 21–37

   a. It makes that component active for editing.
   b. It moves it from a subassembly into the next higher level assembly.
   c. It makes it a separate part file.
   d. It makes it the grounded component.

3. You can use the **Demote** option to move components into an existing subassembly.
   a. True
   b. False

4. Which of the following best describes the purpose of a Drive constraint?

   a. A Drive constraint is a dimension type that is created in a sketch of an assembly feature so that the value can be easily changed to update the assembly.

   b. A Drive constraint is the terminology used for the full set of constraints to fully locate a component in an assembly.

   c. A Drive constraint enables you to assign motion between the constrained components by setting the offset or angle value in a constraint so that it changes incrementally.

   d. A Drive constraint is a type of constraint that is assigned in the *Place Constraint* dialog box.

5. Which of the following components have been specified as members in a contact set, as shown in Figure 21–38? (Select all that apply.)

Figure 21–38

   a. Body

   b. Moving Jaw

   c. Spindle

   d. Pin

   e. DIN 917 M6:3

   f. DIN 917 M6:4

   g. Fixed Jaw

6. You cannot assemble components so that two parts occupy the same space at the same time.
    a. True
    b. False

7. Which of the following options can be used to determine where two selected assembly components overlap?
    a. In the *Assemble* tab>*Productivity* panel, expand the commands and click .
    b. In the *Inspect* tab>*Interference* panel, click .
    c. *Inspect* tab>*Measure* panel, click 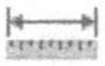 .
    d. All of the above

8. What information can you find in the *Interference Detected* dialog box? (Select all that apply.)
    a. Number of interferences
    b. Total Volume of interference
    c. Part names
    d. Subassembly names

9. Which of the following statements regarding the **Design Doctor** tool is true?
    a. It toggles the visibility of the component.
    b. It displays options to resolve a constraint issue.
    c. It enables a component so that it can be selected.
    d. It moves a component out of the subassembly.

Command Summary

Button	Command	Location
	Activate Contact Solver	• **Ribbon:** *Inspect* tab>*Interference* panel
	Analyze Interference	• **Ribbon:** *Inspect* tab>*Interference* panel
N/A	**Contact Set**	• **Context Menu:** In Model browser with multiple components selected
	Copy	• **Ribbon:** *Assemble* tab>Pattern panel • **Context Menu:** In Model browser with a component selected>Component • **Context Menu:** In the graphics window with a component selected>Component
N/A	**Demote**	• **Context Menu:** In Model browser with a component selected>Component • **Context Menu:** In the graphics window with a component selected>Component
N/A	**Drive**	• **Context Menu:** (*select a constraint in the Model browser to access command*)
	Mirror	• **Ribbon:** *Assemble* tab>Pattern panel • **Context Menu:** In Model browser with a component selected>Component • **Context Menu:** In the graphics window with a component selected>Component
	Pattern	• **Ribbon:** *Assemble* tab>Pattern panel • **Context Menu:** In Model browser with a component selected>Component • **Context Menu:** In the graphics window with a component selected>Component
N/A	**Promote**	• **Context Menu:** In Model browser with a component selected>Component • **Context Menu:** In the graphics window with a component selected>Component
	Replace (components)	• **Ribbon:** *Assemble* tab>*Component* panel • **Context Menu:** In Model browser with a component selected>Component • **Context Menu:** In the graphics window with a component selected>Component

Button	Command	Location
	Replace All (components)	• **Ribbon:** *Assemble* tab>*Component* panel • **Context Menu:** In Model browser with a component selected>Component • **Context Menu:** In the graphics window with a component selected>Component
	Save and Replace	• **Ribbon:** *Assemble* tab>*Productivity* panel

Chapter 22

Assembly Parts and Features

Understanding the process of creating parts and features in an assembly enables you to build parts in relation to other parts, helping you to build the required design intent into your assembly.

Learning Objectives

- Create a new component (part or assembly) in the context of an assembly model.
- Create assembly features in the context of an assembly model.

22.1 Creating Parts in an Assembly

As an alternative to creating components (parts and assemblies) and assembling them, you can create components directly in the assembly. Creating parts in an assembly has the following advantages:

- You can use faces and edges from other assembly components to locate the first sketch in the model.
- You can use geometry (e.g., points, edges) from other assembly components to create entities in the sketch.
- If you use geometry from other components in the sketch, the part automatically references the other components and any changes made in them reflect in the new component.
- If you use geometry from other components, the part is already constrained in the assembly.

How To: Create a New Component in an Assembly

1. In the *Assemble* tab>*Component* panel, click (Create). The *Create In-Place Component* dialog box opens as shown in Figure 22–1.

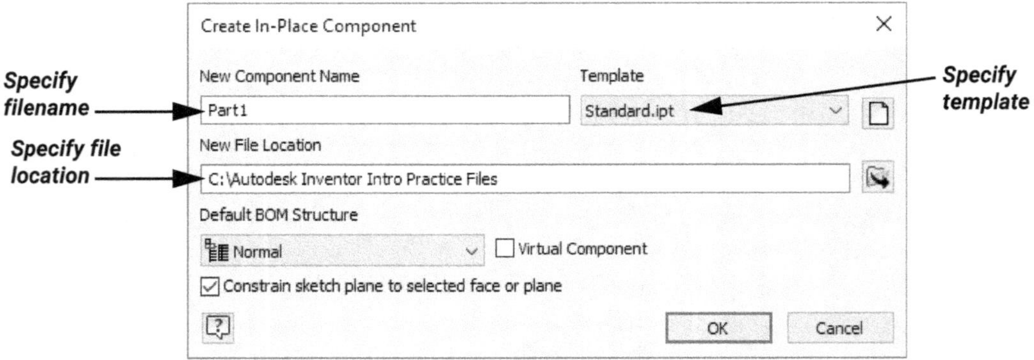

Figure 22–1

2. Define the options in *Create In-Place Component* dialog box, as follows:
   - Enter the name of the new component in the *New Component Name* field.
   - Select the part or assembly template in the *Template* field that should be used for the new file.
   - Define the default bill of materials structure for the new component.
   - Select **Virtual Component** to create a new component that does not have a file (and therefore no geometry). Its information is stored in the assembly file. Select **Constrain sketch plane to selected face or plane** to automatically assign a Mate constraint between the selected part face and sketch plane when the component is created.

3. Click **OK** to create the new component.
4. Select a work plane or face on another component as the sketch plane for the new component. The sketch plane locates the first feature of the component in the assembly. The component is then added to the Model browser and it becomes the active component.

Hint: Creating Subassemblies in the Context of an Assembly

To create a subassembly, select an assembly template when creating the new file. You do not need to select a sketching plane, select anywhere on the display window to activate the subassembly. Avoid creating a subassembly in an assembly unless you are restructuring existing components to prevent any unwanted references.

5. Sketch the base feature for the new component using the standard sketching procedure. Consider incorporating any of following to build relationships between the new component and existing components in the assembly:
   - Project geometry and sketch entities referencing other assembly components to build relationships between components in the assembly.
   - Sketch new geometry and dimension it independently.
   - Sketch new geometry and dimension to the edges or faces of other components.
   - Use a combination of sketched and projected geometry.
   - Consider using the **Project Cut Edges** option to project the edges defined by the intersection of a sketch plane and existing solid geometry.

Hint: Controlling if Projected Geometry Is Associative

To control whether projected geometry or sketched entities are associative with their parent, use **Cross part geometry projection** in the *Assembly* tab of the *Application Options* dialog box. As an alternative, you can also hold <Ctrl> while selecting entities to project so that they lose their associative reference to the selected entities.

6. To complete the sketch, click (Finish Sketch) in the *Exit* panel or right-click and select **Finish 2D Sketch**.
7. Use the sketch to create the first feature of the part (e.g, **Extrude**, **Revolve**, **Loft**, etc.). Create additional features on your part as required.
8. Once you have finished working on the part, click (Return) in the *Return* panel or right-click and select **Finish Edit** to activate the assembly.

   Note: *To open a created part or subassembly in a separate window, right-click on the file and select* ***Open****.*

If you create the new part using references to existing components in the assembly, you are establishing parent-child relationships between the components. When a relationship is established, the adaptive icon ( ) displays next to the part and any of its adaptive features, as shown in Figure 22–2. This icon indicates that references were established with other components when the part was created. Any changes to the source geometry reflect in the new part.

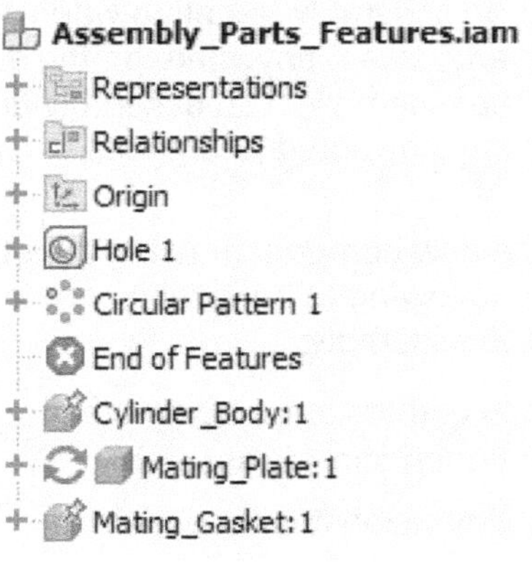

Figure 22–2

To remove adaptivity from a part, right-click on the feature and clear the **Adaptive** option, or right-click on the model name and clear the option. If adaptivity is cleared from the model name, all adaptivity is cleared. If cleared at the feature level, it enables other features to remain adaptive.

22.2 Creating Assembly Features

You can create cuts (extruded, revolved, and swept features), holes, chamfers, fillets, threads, and work features in an assembly using the *3D Model* tab. Assembly features have the following advantages:

- You can define a feature (e.g., hole or cut) to affect multiple components in an assembly.
- You can use geometry from other components for sketching.
- You can constrain assembly components to these features.

Assembly features are useful after you have placed and constrained components, and might need to add features to facilitate manufacturing of the assembly. For example, you might need to create cuts or holes in the assembly so that you can insert pins or screws.

Participant Parts

When you create assembly holes and cut features, you can control which part(s) they affect. Parts affected by assembly features are called participant parts and are identified in the feature's node, as shown in Figure 22–3. Components are added as participants rather than new features being added in each component.

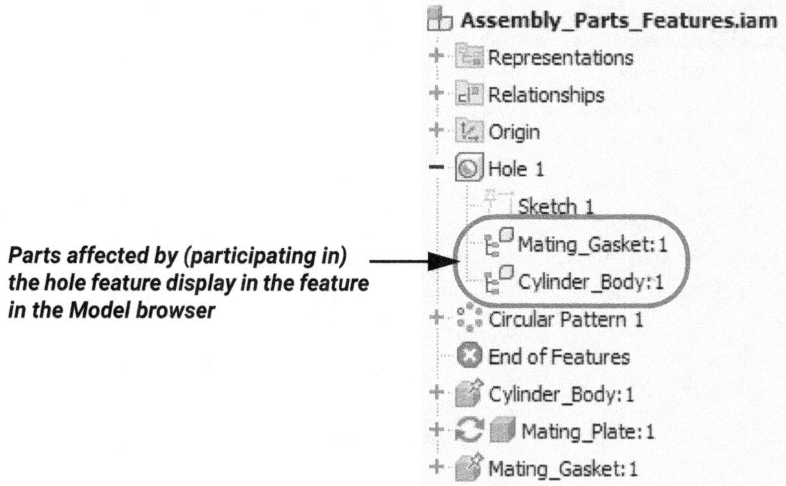

Figure 22–3

By default, components are added as participants. However, you can add or remove participants:

- To add a participant component, right-click on the feature in the Model browser, select **Add Participants** (as shown on the left in Figure 22–4), and select new part(s).
- To remove a participant part, right-click on the participating part(s) in the Model browser and select **Remove Participant**, as shown on the right in Figure 22–4.

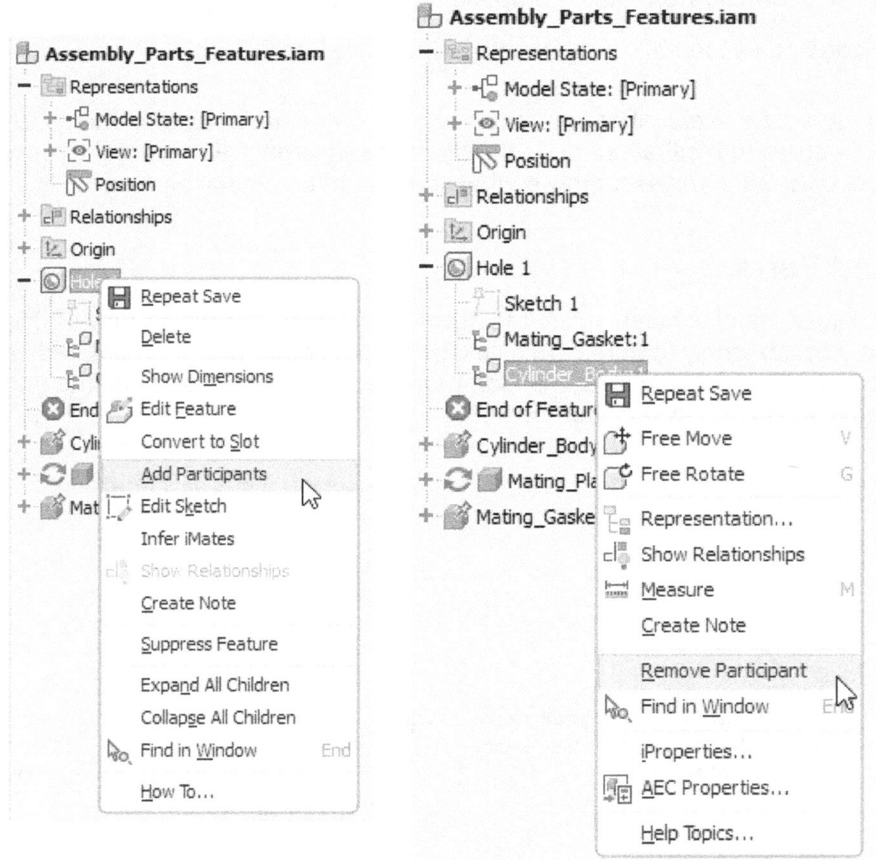

Figure 22–4

Hint: Finish Features

Finish features enable you to assign specific parameters in a model (part or assembly) that define an appearance, a material coating, a heat treatment, a surface texture, or detail on paint that will be applied to a face. This parametric information can be used in drawing notes. To assign a **Finish** feature, complete the following:

1. In the *3D Model* tab>*Modify* or *Modify Assembly* panel, click (Finish).
2. In the tool palette, select whether a face ( ) or body ( ) should be selected and select the geometry in the model to apply the finish to. The entity is added to the *Include* area. To exclude a face, activate the *Exclude* area and select the face in the model.
3. Select the *Type* of finish. The options are an appearance ( ), a material coating ( ), a heat treatment ( ), a surface texture ( ), or paint ( ).
4. Define the finish parameters, as required.

Figure 22–5 shows the *Properties* panel for the Finish feature. The panel on the left shows the options for a heat treatment and the panel on the right shows the options for assigning paint.

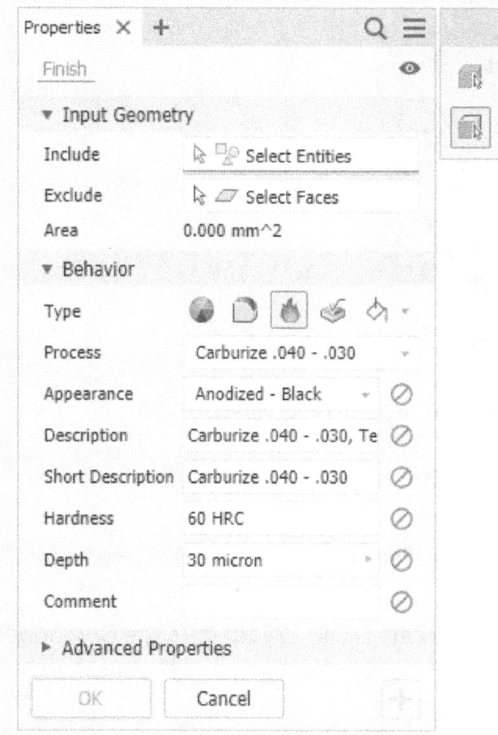

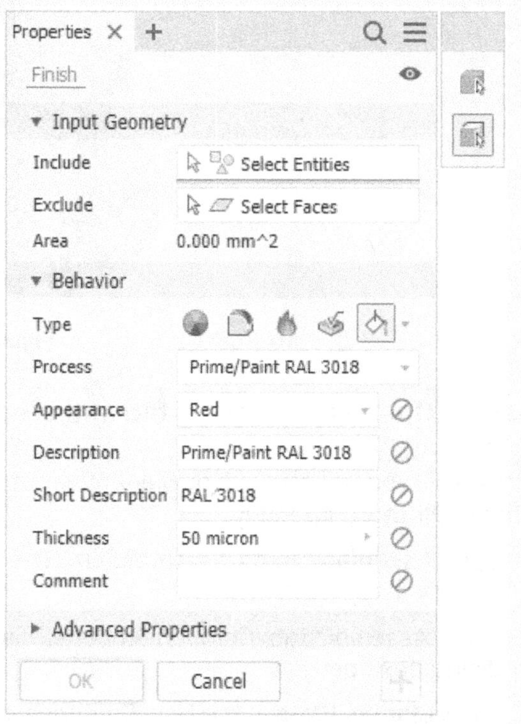

Figure 22–5

Practice 22a
Create Parts and Features in an Assembly

Practice Objectives

- Create a part in an assembly and add solid geometry to it by establishing adaptive references with other components.
- Create a part in an assembly and add solid geometry to it by using, but not establishing a permanent reference with other components.
- Create assembly hole features and ensure that the participant components are correctly assigned.

In this practice, you will work in the assembly environment to create two new components. In both components, you will use entities from another model to create solid geometry. In one of them, you will maintain the reference and in the other, you will not maintain the reference. Additionally, you will create assembly level holes and add/remove the participating parts. The final model created is shown in Figure 22–6.

Figure 22–6

Task 1: Open an assembly file and create a new adaptive component.

In this task, you will create a new adaptive component that references geometry from the **Cylinder_Body** component.

1. Open **Assembly_Parts_Features.iam**. The assembly displays with a single component already assembled.
2. In the *Assemble* tab>*Component* panel, click (Create). The *Create In-Place Component* dialog box opens.
3. Enter **Mating_Plate** in the *New Component Name* field.
4. Browse and select the metric standard part template, **Standard (mm).ipt**. Click **OK**.

5. In the *Create In-Place Component* dialog box, verify that **Constrain sketch plane to selected face or plane** is selected and accept the defaults in the other fields, as shown in Figure 22–7.

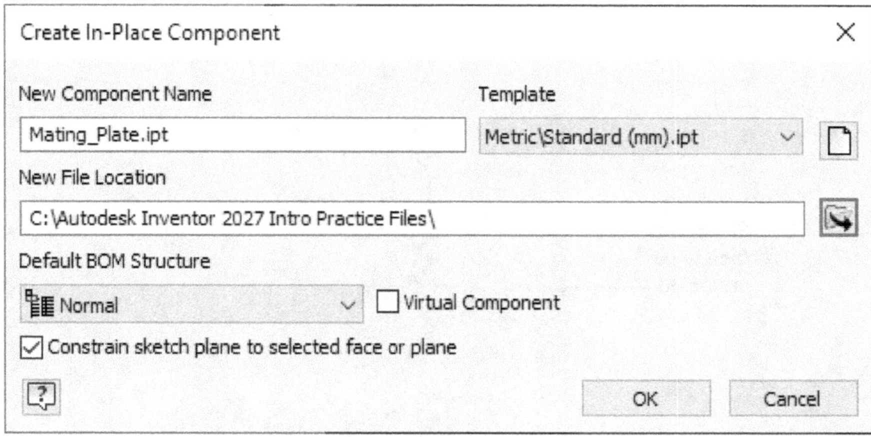

Figure 22–7

6. Click **OK** to create the part.
7. Select the face shown in Figure 22–8 as the sketch plane. All of the assembly components, except **Mating_Plate** are grayed out in the Model browser. This means that only **Mating_Plate** is active and you can add features to it.

Figure 22–8

8. In the *3D Model* tab>*Sketch* panel, click (Start 2D Sketch). Select the XY Plane in the new **Mating_Plate** component as the sketch plane.

9. In the Sketch environment, project the edges of the face shown in Figure 22–9. Rotate the model into a 3D orientation to select the face. The projected edges display in yellow, indicating that they are referencing other geometry. In this case, they are referencing geometry in another model.

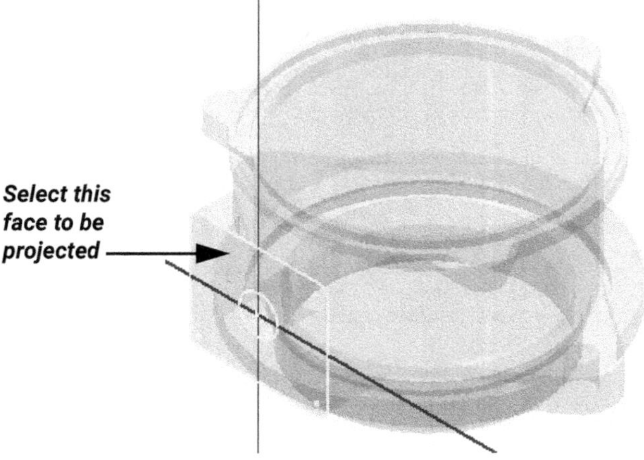

Figure 22–9

10. Sketch a circle and add a **2** dimension value to dimension it relative to the projected circle, as shown in Figure 22–10.

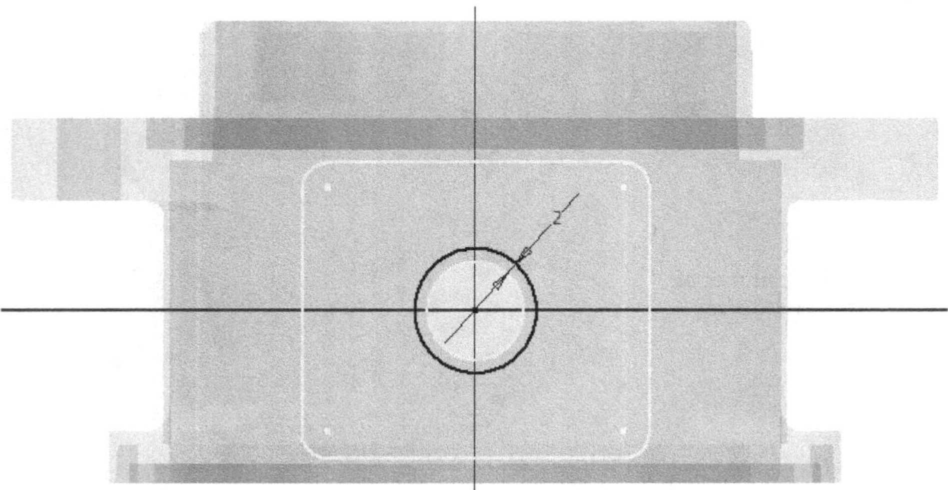

Figure 22–10

11. In the *Exit* panel, click (Finish Sketch). Do not return to the top-level assembly or you will have to reactivate **Mating_Plate**.

12. Extrude the sketch by **10mm** (as shown in Figure 22–11) and complete the feature.

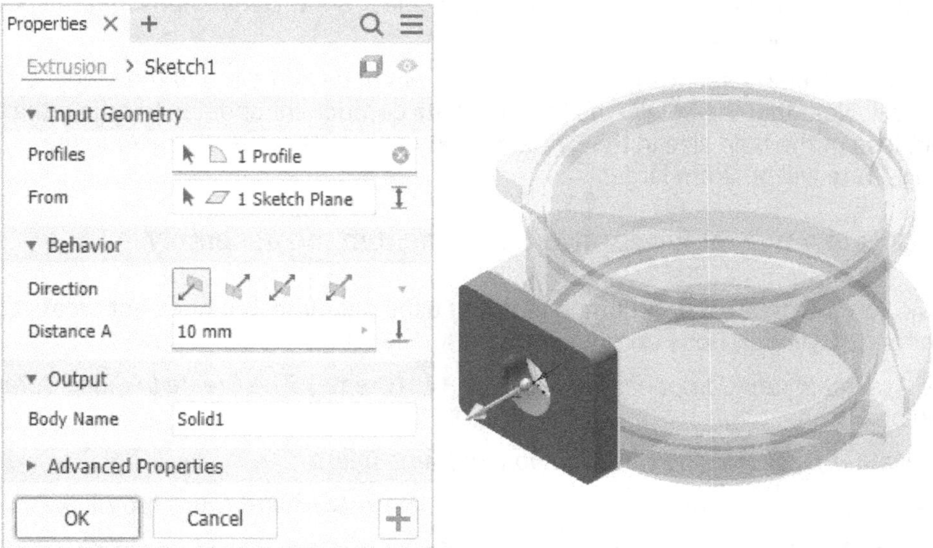

Figure 22–11

13. Double-click on the **Assembly_Parts_Features.iam** node at the top of the Model browser to activate it. The model displays as shown in Figure 22–12. Note that a Flush constraint has been created in the Model browser. This is because you selected **Constrain sketch plane to selected face or plane** when you created the new component. It automatically created the constraint between the selected part face and sketch plane.

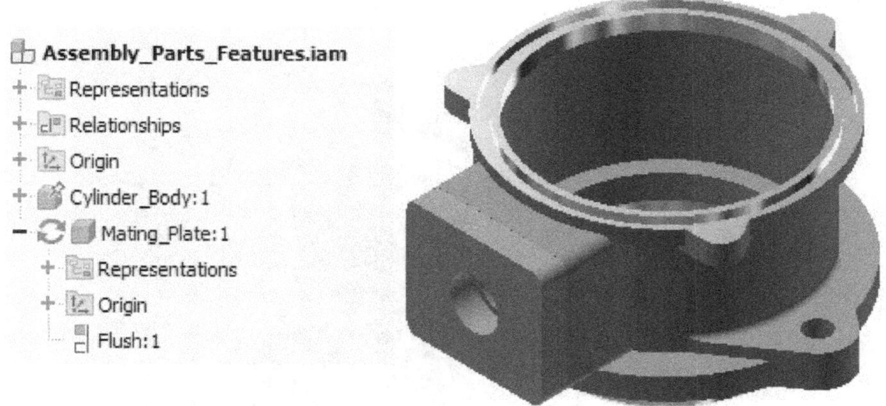

Figure 22–12

14. Note that the (Adaptive) icon displays next to the **Mating_Plate** part indicating that it is adaptive. In the Model browser's header, select **Modeling**. Note that the (Adaptive) icon displays next to the **Extrusion1** feature, indicating that it is an adaptive feature.

15. Double-click on the **Cylinder_Body** component in the Model browser to activate it.
16. Right-click on **Hole9** in the Model browser and select **Show Dimensions**. Set the new diameter for the hole to **20**.
17. Double-click on the **Assembly_Parts_Features.iam** node at the top of the Model browser to activate it. Note that the hole in the **Mating_Plate** component updates to reflect the change. Regardless of the hole size in the **Cylinder_Body** component the diameter in the **Mating_Plate** will be 2mm larger.

Task 2: Create a new non-adaptive component in the assembly.

In this task, you will create a new component that uses geometry but does not create a lasting reference to the **Cylinder_Body** component.

1. In the *Assemble* tab>*Component* panel, click (Create). The *Create In-Place Component* dialog box opens.
2. Enter **Mating_Gasket** in the *New Component Name* field.
3. Browse and select the metric standard part template, **Standard (mm).ipt**. Click **OK**.
4. Verify that **Constrain sketch plane to selected face or plane** is selected and accept the defaults in the other fields.
5. Click **OK** to create the part.
6. Select the face shown in Figure 22–13 as the sketch plane. The selected face is the lower circular face parallel to the top face. A Flush constraint is automatically established between the new component and this face on **Cylinder_Body**. All of the assembly components are grayed out in the Model browser, except **Mating_Gasket**. This means that only **Mating_Gasket** is active and you can add features to it.

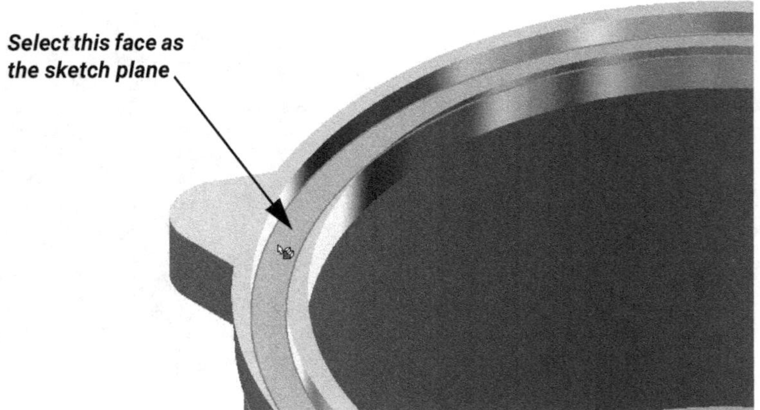

Figure 22–13

7. In the *3D Model* tab>*Sketch* panel, click (Start 2D Sketch). Select the XY Plane in the new **Mating_Gasket** component as the sketch plane.

8. In the Sketch environment, press and hold <Ctrl> and project the two circular edges that lie on the selected sketch plane, as shown in Figure 22–14.
   - Rotate the model into a 3D orientation to select the edges.
   - The new entities display fully constrained as indicated in the Status Bar and the Sketch icon in the Model browser. This is because fixed and reference constraints were automatically added.
   - By using <Ctrl> as you are selecting the entities, you are projecting them without establishing a relationship. The projected entities should display in blue (not yellow). At any point, you can return to the sketch and delete the fixed and reference constraints that were automatically added and explicitly add a dimension scheme.

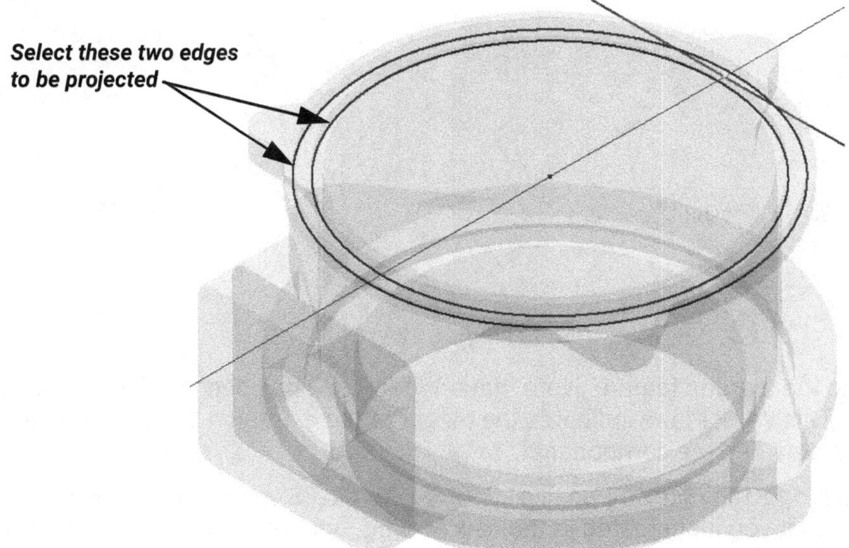

Figure 22–14

9. In the *Exit* panel, click (Finish Sketch). Do not return to the top-level assembly or you will have to reactivate **Mating_Gasket**.

10. Extrude the sketch using the **To** ( ) option and select the face shown in Figure 22–15.

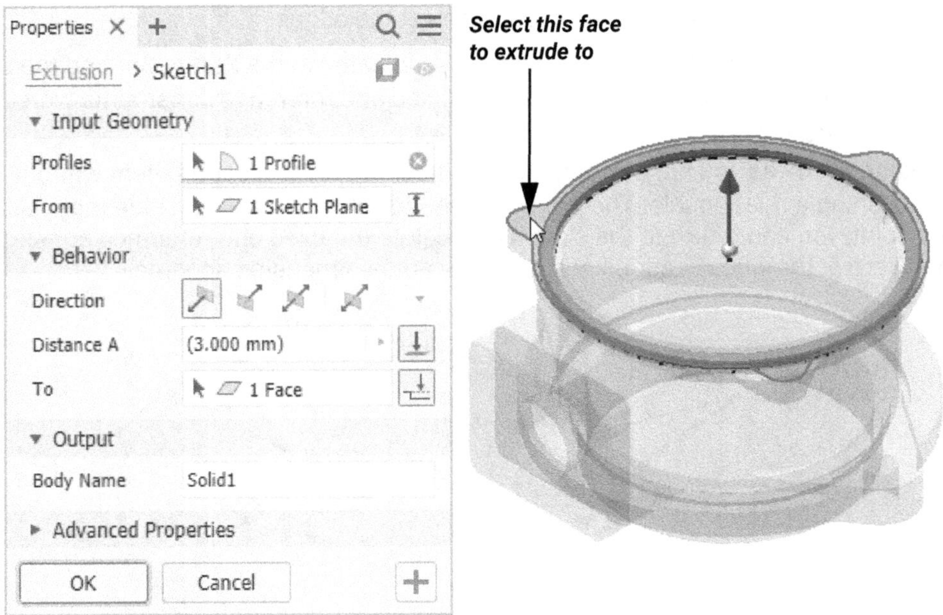

Figure 22–15

11. Complete the extrude feature. Note that a Work Plane has been added to the Model browser. This Work Plane indicates the extent of the extrusion but does not create a reference between the components.
12. In the *3D Model* tab>*Sketch* panel, click (Start 2D Sketch). Select the top of the extrusion that you just created in the new **Mating_Gasket** component as the sketch plane.
13. In the Sketch environment, press and hold <Ctrl> and project all of the edges around the outer edge of the **Cylinder_Body** component and the circular inner edge, as shown in Figure 22–16. Remember to rotate the model into a 3D orientation to select the edges. You will need to select these entities individually. The sketch is also fully constrained with fixed and reference constraints.

 Note: *At any point you can return to the sketch and delete the fixed and reference constraints that were automatically added and explicitly add a dimension scheme.*

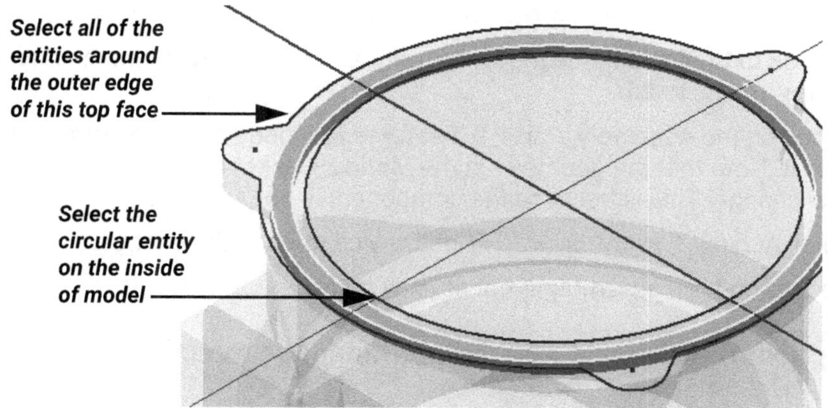

Figure 22–16

14. In the *Exit* panel, click (Finish Sketch). Do not return to the top-level assembly or you will have to reactivate **Mating_Gasket**.
15. Extrude the sketch by selecting the closed sections so that the preview displays as shown in Figure 22–17. Extrude the feature by **10mm**.

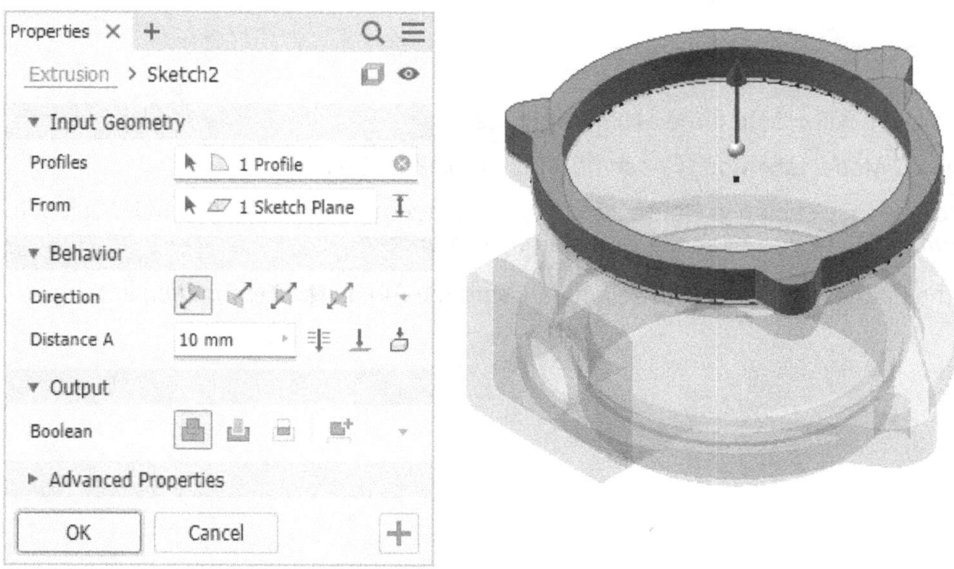

Figure 22–17

16. Complete the extrude feature. Note that there is no adaptive icon ( ) displayed next to the **Mating_Gasket** part, indicating that it is not adaptive. This is because you used <Ctrl> when projecting the references from the **Cylinder_Body** component.

    Note: *In this practice, the adaptivity was cleared to show you how this is done. In this scenario, adaptivity is important to maintain components that fit together.*

17. Double-click on the **Cylinder_Body** component in the Model browser to activate it.
18. Right-click on **Extrusion 5** in the Model browser and select **Show Dimensions**. Set the new diameter for the arc to **20**.
19. Double-click on the **Assembly_Parts_&_Features.iam** node at the top of the Model browser to activate it. Note that the geometry in the **Mating_Gasket** component does not update to reflect the change. This is because the component is not adaptive.
20. In the Quick Access Toolbar, click (Undo) twice to undo the change.
21. Return to the top-level assembly, if not already active.

Task 3: (Optional) Fully constrain the non-adaptive model.

In this task, you will display the Degrees of Freedom that remain in the assembly and ground the **Mating_Gasket** component so that it is fully located.

1. In the *View* tab>*Visibility* panel, click (Degrees of Freedom) to display any degrees of freedom in the assembly. Note that the non-adaptive model, **Mating_Gasket** is missing constraints to fully locate it in the assembly.
2. Right-click the **Mating_Gasket** component in the Model browser and select **Grounded** to fully constrain the components in the assembly.

Task 4: Create assembly holes.

In this task, you will create three assembly holes.

1. In the *3D Model* tab>*Modify Assembly* panel, click (Hole).
2. Select the face shown in Figure 22–18 as the placement plane for this hole. Select the edge shown in Figure 22–18 as the Concentric Reference.
3. Set the diameter to **7mm** and select (Through All) as the *Termination* setting.

4. Complete the feature. The model displays as shown in Figure 22–18.

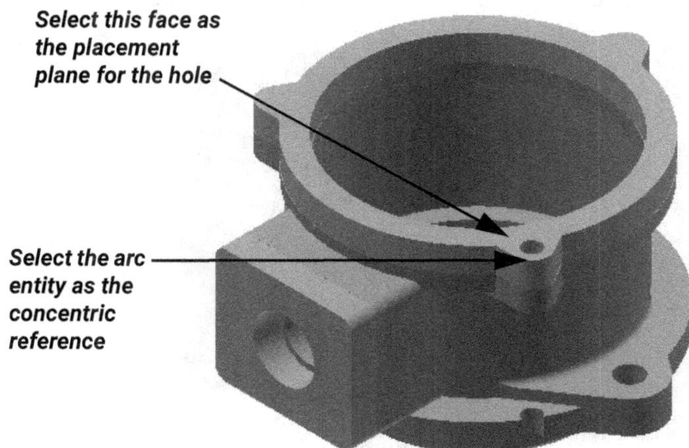

Figure 22–18

5. Note that the hole intersects the bottom of the model as well. In the Model browser, expand the **Hole 1** node, right-click on the **Cylinder_Body** component, and select **Remove Participant** to remove it entirely from cutting through the **Cylinder_Body**.
6. You want the hole to cut through the top portion of the component but not the bottom. In the Model browser, right-click on **Hole 1** and select **Add Participants**. Select **Cylinder_Body** in the graphics window to add it back as a participant in the hole feature.
7. Edit **Hole 1**. Change the *Termination* setting from (Through All) to (To) and select the face shown in Figure 22–19.

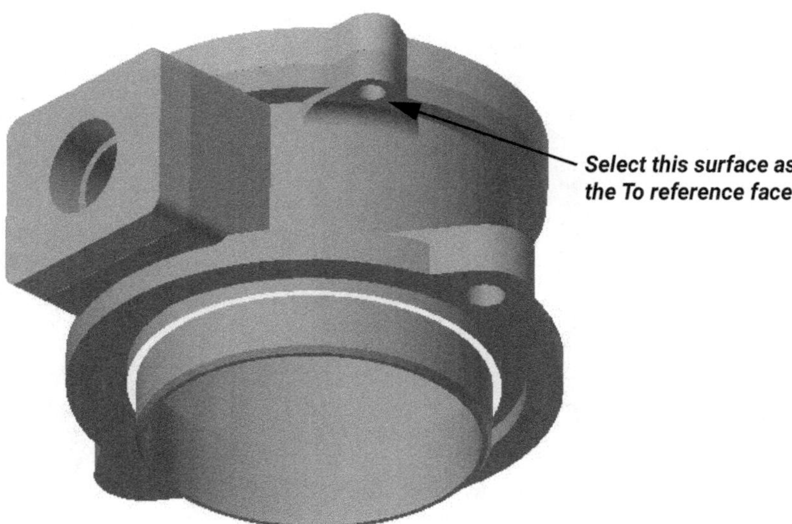

Figure 22–19

8. Create the remaining holes using a circular pattern. Ensure that you are using a feature pattern option on the *3D Model* tab. The model should display as shown in Figure 22–20.

Figure 22–20

9. Save the assembly and its components.

End of practice

Chapter Review Questions

1. Which command sequence is used to create a new part model while in the context of an assembly model?
   a. *3D Model* tab>*Sketch* panel, click .
   b. *Assemble* tab>*Component* panel, click .
   c. *Assemble* tab>*Component* panel, and click .
   d. All of the above.

2. When creating a sketch for an assembly part, why is it advantageous to reference edges or faces on other components? (Select all that apply.)
   a. Creates a parent child relationship to help align components accurately with one another.
   b. If you use geometry from other components, the part is already constrained in the assembly.
   c. Changes made in the referenced component automatically reflect in the new component.
   d. Other than the ease of creating the sketch geometry, there is no significant benefit.

3. When creating a new part model, while in the context of an assembly model, you must use the same template as the last component that was placed into the assembly.
   a. True
   b. False

4. Which of the following types of files can be created in the context of an assembly? (Select all that apply.)
   a. Part (.IPT)
   b. Sheet Metal (.IPT)
   c. Presentation (.IPN)
   d. Assembly (.IAM)
   e. Weldment (.IAM)
   f. Drawing (.IDW)

5. What types of features can be added to an assembly? (Select all that apply.)
    a. Extrude
    b. Revolve
    c. Sweep
    d. Loft
    e. Hole
    f. Fillet
    g. Chamfer
    h. Shell

6. What command would you use after you placed a hole through three part models in an assembly and then wanted to remove that hole from one of the parts?
    a. Extrude
    b. Add Participant
    c. Remove Participant
    d. Visibility

Command Summary

Button	Command	Location
	Create	• **Ribbon:** *Assemble* tab>*Component* panel • **Context Menu**: In the graphics window

Chapter 23

Assembly Bill of Materials

The Bill of Materials (BOM) functionality is used to communicate the parts that are used in an assembly. In addition, you are able to add parts to the BOM that do not have any physical geometry, but are critical to the model (e.g., grease).

Learning Objectives

- Create virtual components that represent non-geometrical parts that are required in the BOM.
- Generate an assembly BOM that lists the components of an assembly.
- Customize and edit the properties that display in the BOM.
- Export a BOM for use in the Engineer's Notebook, an external database, a text file, or a .CSV file.
- Synchronize the assembly BOM and the parts list that documents the BOM in a drawing.
- Assign instance properties to assembly components and show them in the BOM.

23.1 Create Virtual Components

A virtual component is created to represent a non-geometrical part that is required in the bill of materials (e.g., paint, grease, etc.). They can also be used to represent parts you do not want to model, such as fasteners. Like real components, the properties of a virtual component can be fully defined.

How To: Create a Virtual Component

1. In the *Assemble* tab>*Component* panel, click (Create) to open the *Create In-Place Component* dialog box.
2. To create a virtual component, select **Virtual Component** in the *Create In-Place Component* dialog box, as shown in Figure 23–1. The *Template* and *New File Location* areas become gray because information about a virtual component is stored with the assembly.

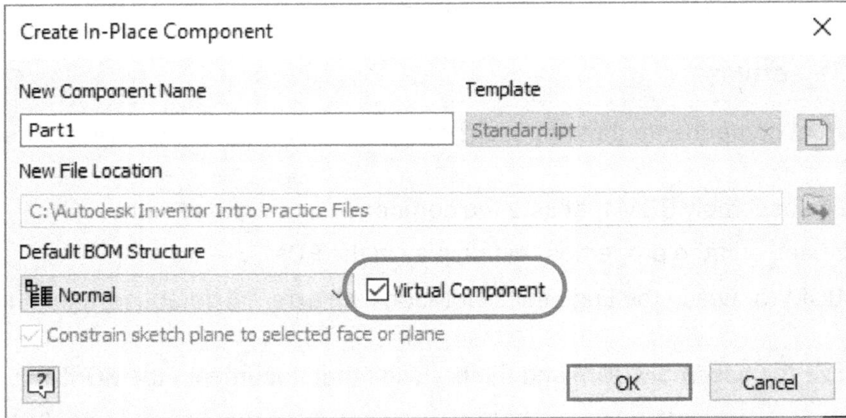

Figure 23–1

3. Enter a name for the virtual component in the *New Component Name* field and click **OK**. The Model browser displays the virtual component, as shown in Figure 23–2.

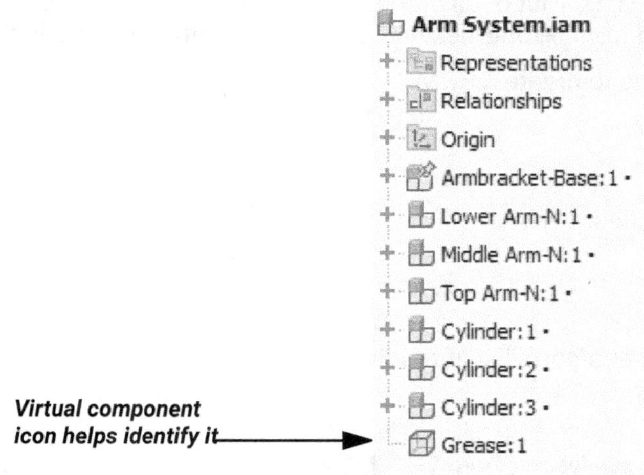

Figure 23–2

Like real components, the properties of the virtual component can be defined in the same manner as other components, either through the *iProperties* dialog box or the BOM Editor.

- Using the *iProperties* dialog box (right-click on the component and select **iProperties**), you can set the default material for virtual components as well as manually enter a value for its mass in the *Physical* tab. Alternatively, you can assign a material by selecting the virtual component in the Model browser and selecting a material in the *Materials* drop-down list in the Quick Access Toolbar.
- The component name, BOM structure properties, and the base quantities can be defined by right-clicking on the virtual component and selecting **Component Settings**.

As an alternative to creating a virtual component in the *Create In-Place Component* dialog box, you can also click (Create Virtual Component) in the *Bill of Materials* dialog box to create a new virtual component. Using this alternative method, you are simply prompted for the component's name and you can define its BOM Structure directly in the dialog box. To make modifications to its base quantities, you must still define its Component Settings.

23.2 Create Bill of Materials

A bill of materials (BOM) is a list of all of the components in an assembly. The information used in a BOM is generated from iProperties and used to generate the parts list in a drawing.

Use the following steps to create a BOM:

1. Generate the BOM.
2. Add properties.
3. Modify the properties.
4. Organize the BOM.
5. Export the BOM.
6. Synchronize BOM and parts list, if required.

Step 1 - Generate the BOM.

In the *Assemble* tab>*Manage* panel and click (Bill of Materials) to create a BOM. Three views can be displayed:

- Model Data
- Structured
- Parts Only

Model Data View

The *Model Data* tab displays BOM data similar to the Model browser, as shown in Figure 23–3. You can use the *Model Data* tab to modify the BOM Structure or component properties. This view is not used for display in a parts list.

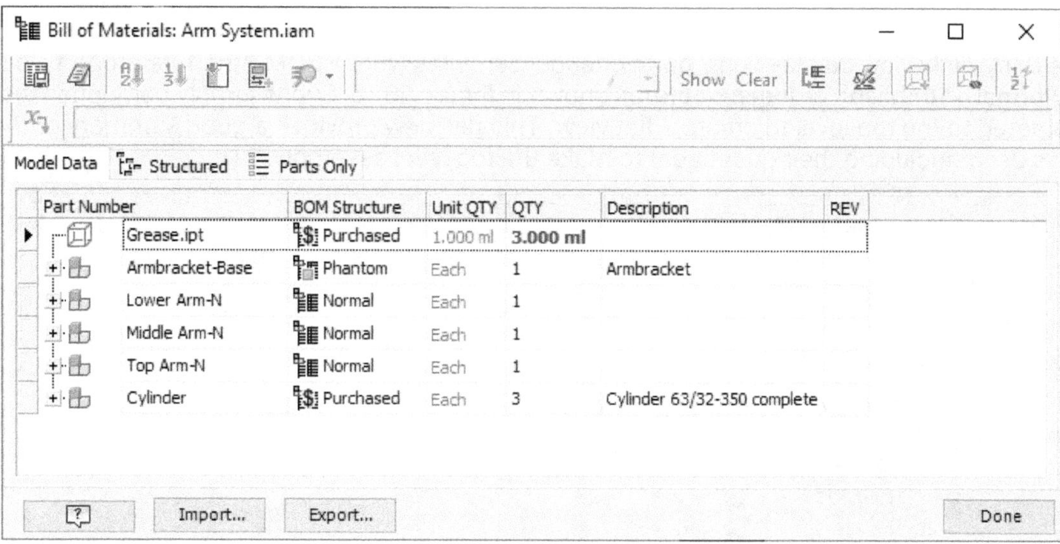

Figure 23–3

Structured View

In the *Structured* tab, components are listed based on the BOM Structure property, as shown in Figure 23–4. This enables you to manipulate how components display in the BOM, enabling you to hide part and subassemblies from display in a parts list.

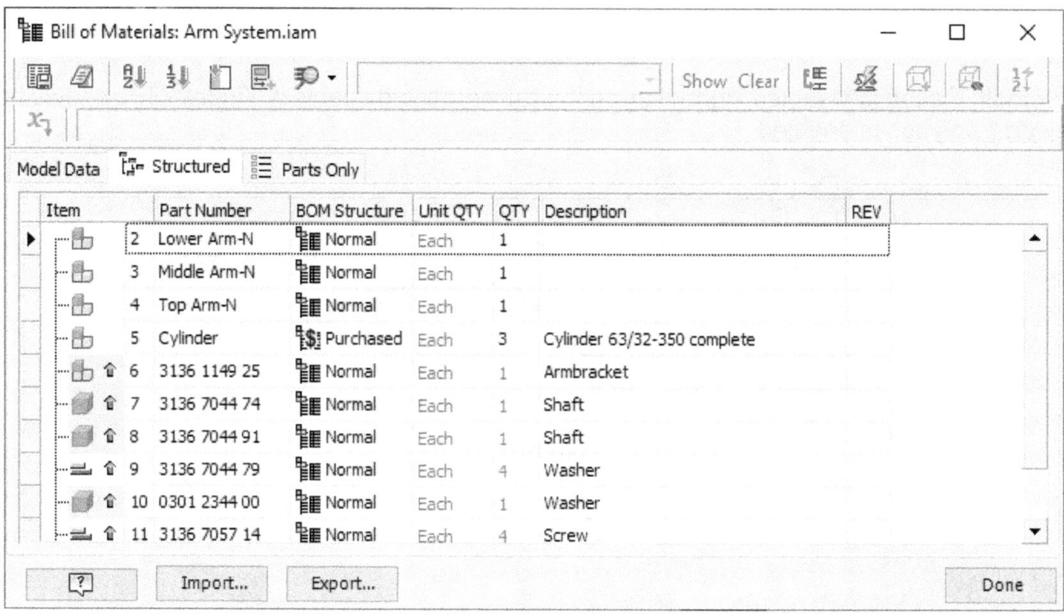

Figure 23–4

Parts Only View

The Parts Only view displays only parts or subassemblies whose BOM Structure property is set to **Normal**, **Purchased** or **Inseparable**, as shown in Figure 23–5. Subassembly components are promoted to the top level to create a flat view. This flat view provides a good summary of the parts used (including their quantities) to make the top-level assembly.

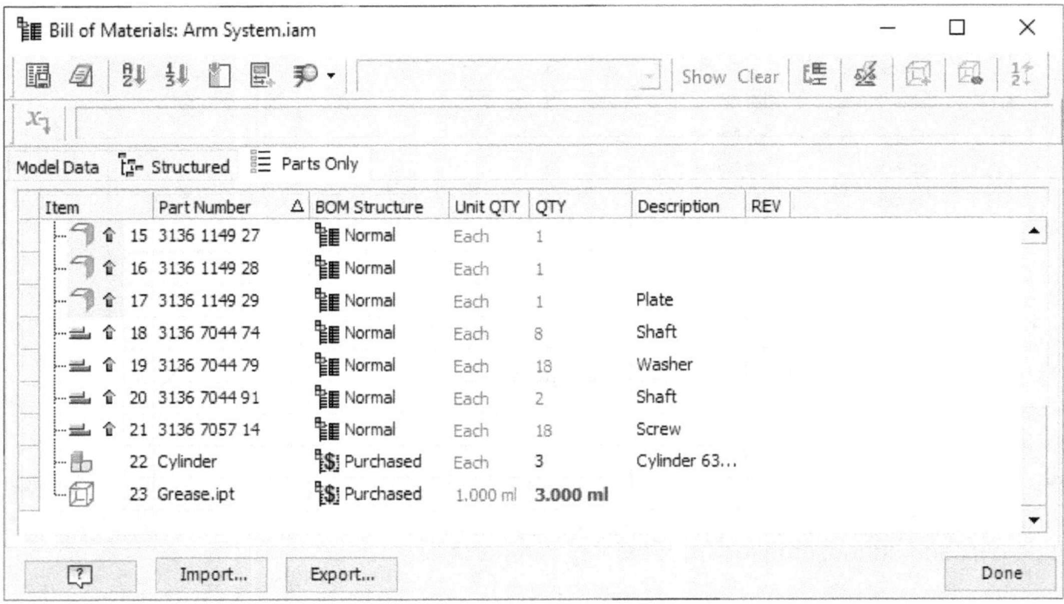

Figure 23–5

By default, if a tab is disabled, right-click on the tab name and enable it. Figure 23–6 shows how the *Parts Only* tab is enabled.

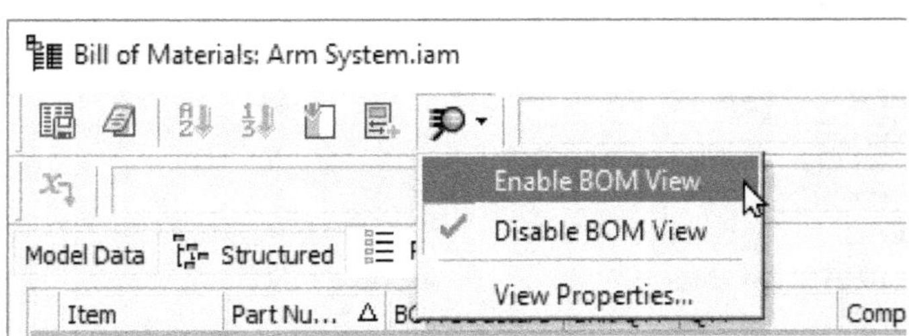

Figure 23–6

Step 2 - Add properties.

Any component iProperty can be displayed in the BOM. The *Part Number, BOM Structure, Quantity, Stock Number, Description*, and *Revision* columns display by default.

System-Defined iProperties

To add a system-defined component iProperty column, click (Choose Columns) in the toolbar to open the *Customization* dialog box, as shown in Figure 23–7. Customized column headings are unique for each of the tabs in the *Bill of Materials* dialog box. To add a column to the table, select the property in the *Customization* dialog box and drag it into position in the column header bar in the BOM table. To remove a column, select the column title and drag it to the *Customization* dialog box.

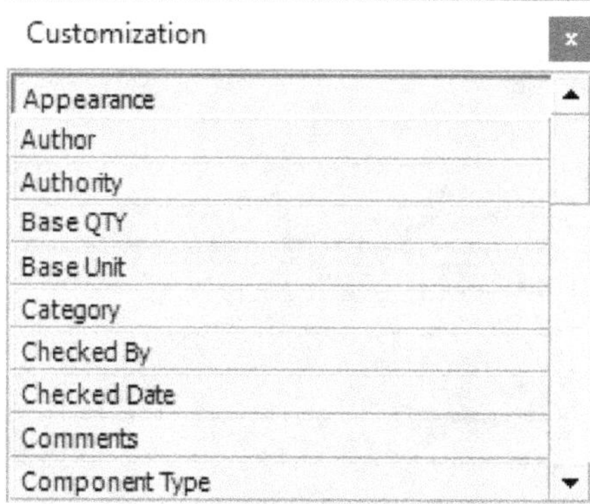

Figure 23–7

Custom iProperties

To add Custom iProperties to the BOM table, use the following steps.

How To: Add a Custom iProperty to the Table

1. Click (Add Custom iProperty Columns) in the top toolbar.
2. Select the *<Click to add iProperty column>* field and enter the name of the property.
3. Define the data type (**Text**, **Date**, **Number**, or **Yes/No**) using the drop-down list.
4. Click **OK** to close the dialog box.

   Note: *You can remove custom iProperty columns using the same drag and drop technique as when removing non-custom columns.*

5. The custom iProperty column is added to the table. If the iProperty name already exists in the component its value automatically updates; otherwise, you can enter the values.

Step 3 - Modify the properties.

Component iProperties can be modified using the *iProperties* dialog box or using the *Bill of Materials* dialog box. Changes made in one location update in the other. To change a property, select the appropriate cell and edit the value.

BOM Structure

The BOM Structure options can be used to provide a more accurate BOM. The BOM Structure is used to filter out components in the assembly that are used in its construction but are not actually part of the assembly design. It can be defined in the *Occurrence* tab in the *iProperties* dialog box or from inside the *Bill of Materials* dialog box, as shown in Figure 23–8.

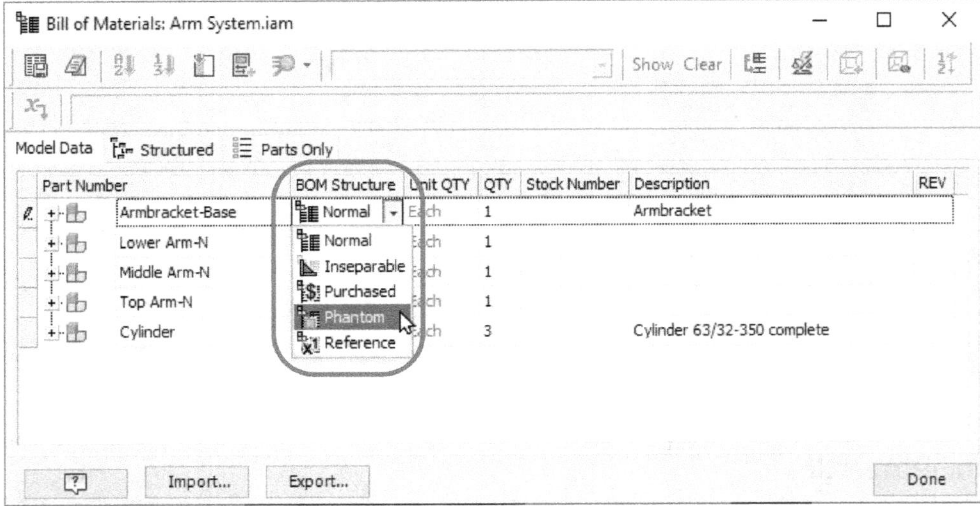

Figure 23–8

The five available BOM Structure options are **Normal**, **Phantom**, **Reference**, **Inseparable**, and **Purchased**.

Normal

A normal component is the default status for a component. Normal components are placed in the BOM based on their parent assembly. They are included in the quantity calculations and have no direct influence on their children's inclusion in the BOM.

Phantom

A phantom component is used to simplify the design. Although they exist in the model, they are not included in the BOM and are not included in the quantity calculations. Children of phantom components are listed in the BOM at the same level as their phantom parent. Phantom components are often used to ease placement of components.

Reference

A reference component is used in the construction of the assembly but is not part of the actual design, such as a skeleton model. Neither the Reference component nor its children are included in mass, volume, BOM, or quantity calculations. If a subassembly is referenced, the entire subassembly's physical properties are excluded. If a single component in the subassembly is referenced, it is the only one that is excluded.

Purchased

Purchased components are purchased instead of fabricated. In the *Structured* tab in the BOM, purchased components display like normal components. In the parts-only view, components with the **Purchased** status are listed as a single item, even if they are an assembly. Children of an assembly with a **Purchase** status are not displayed in the Parts-only view and are excluded in quantity calculations.

Inseparable

Inseparable components are assemblies that must be physically damaged to be taken apart. Inseparable components behave in the BOM like purchased components. However, if a child of an inseparable assembly's status is set to **Purchased**, it is listed in the parts-only BOM.

Quantity

Quantity in the BOM is based on three properties: item quantity, unit quantity, and total quantity.

- Item quantity is the number of instances of a component in the assembly.
- Unit quantity is a multiplier.
- Total quantity (QTY) is the item quantity multiplied by the unit quantity.

For most components, unit quantity equals one and displays in the BOM table as **Each**. However, it can also equal a parameter (i.e., for lengths of wires). To override the quantity value in the BOM, select the ***QTY*** cell and enter a new value. The value displays in blue, indicating that it is a static quantity value. To restore the calculated quantity, right-click on the quantity cell and select **Calculated Quantity**.

Equivalent Components

If two or more components in an assembly have the same part number property, they are considered equivalent components. Equivalent components that are at the same level in the BOM are added together and placed on the same line. If the properties of these components do not match, the BOM reports the line as **varies**. To match the varied properties, select the ***varies*** cell and enter the required value. The value updates in all of the equivalent components.

Material

The material for each item can be modified from the BOM Editor by adding the *Material* column, selecting the *Material* cell for a specific item, expanding the *Material* drop-down list, and selecting a new material. For example, a list of materials is shown in Figure 23–9. Changing the material using this method is equivalent to changing the material properties using the *Physical* tab in the *iProperties* dialog box or activating the model in the Model browser and using the *Appearance* drop-down list in the Quick Access Toolbar.

> ***Note:*** *Use <Shift> or <Ctrl> to select multiple items at the same time and then assign the same material to all of those selected.*

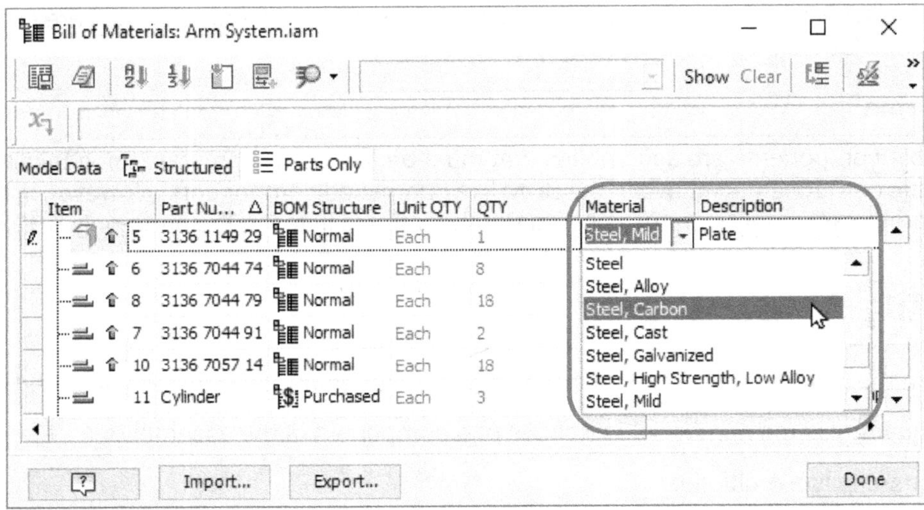

Figure 23–9

Step 4 - Organize the BOM.

Column and Row Organization

You can organize the columns and rows in a BOM table.

- The order of the table columns can be changed by selecting a column header and dragging it to a new location.
- Columns can be resized by selecting and dragging the divider between the column headings. Alternatively, you can right-click on a column heading and select **Best Fit** or **Best Fit (all columns)**. Columns are resized to fit the cell contents.
- Items in the BOM can be reordered by selecting the row and dragging it to a new location.

- Columns can be sorted by right-clicking on the column to be used to sort and selecting **Sort Ascending** or **Sort Descending**. Alternatively, click to combine multiple columns in the sort order or to set whether to sort numerically or by string.

BOM Settings

The (Hide/Show rows with zero quantity) option enables you to customize whether suppressed components are shown in the BOM or not. This option is available in the top-right corner of the *BOM* dialog box, as shown in Figure 23–10. This is a valuable tool when using model states.

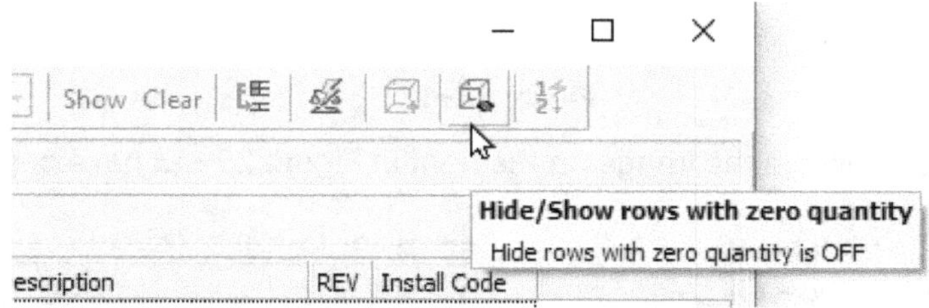

Figure 23–10

- Components that are suppressed in the model are displayed in the BOM in gray if **Hide/ Show rows with zero quantity** is disabled (shown on the left in Figure 23–11). Once enabled, the suppressed component is removed from the BOM list, as shown on the right.

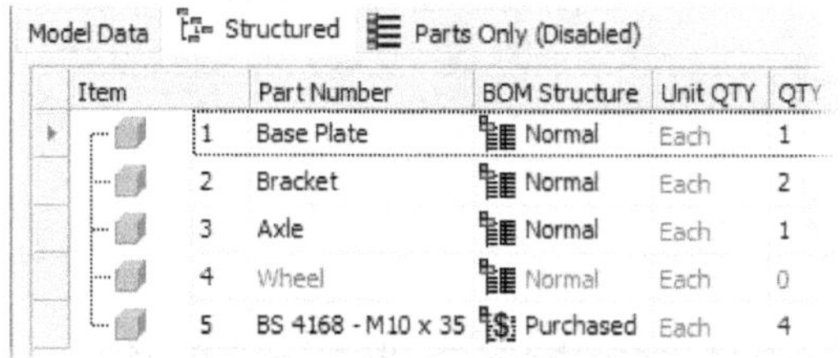

Wheel is suppressed (displays gray) and the Hide/ Show rows with zero quantity option is disabled.

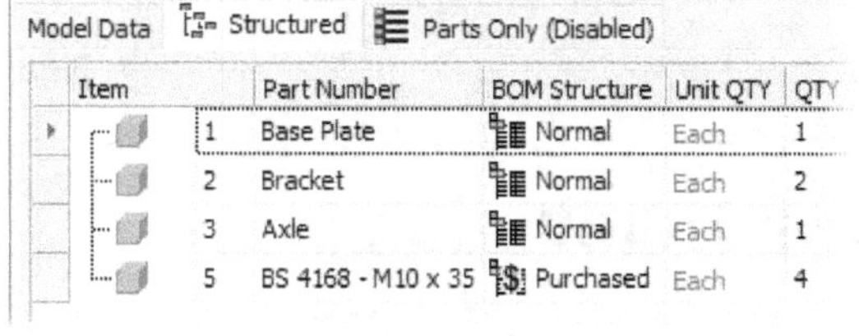

Wheel is suppressed and the Hide/Show rows with zero quantity option is enabled.

Figure 23–11

- To renumber the list of items sequentially to account for suppressed components, select (Automatic re-numbering sequentially) in the top-right corner of the *BOM* dialog box, as shown in Figure 23–12, to turn it on.

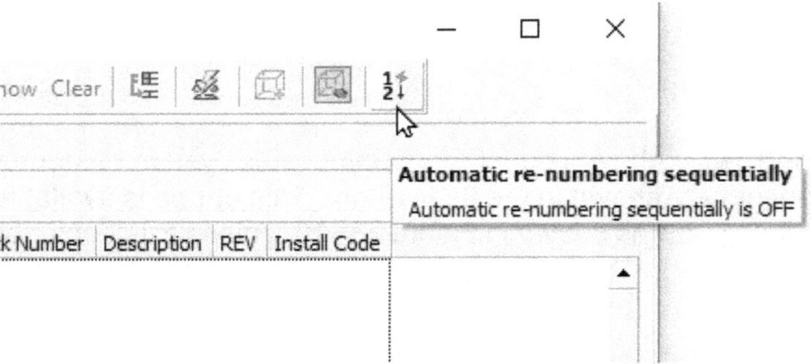

Figure 23–12

The components shown in the image on the right in Figure 23–13 have been renumbered.

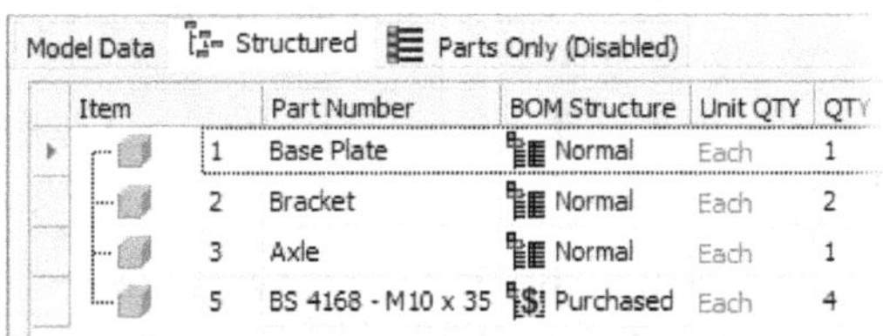

A suppressed component (4) was cleared from the display; however, item numbers were not renumbered.

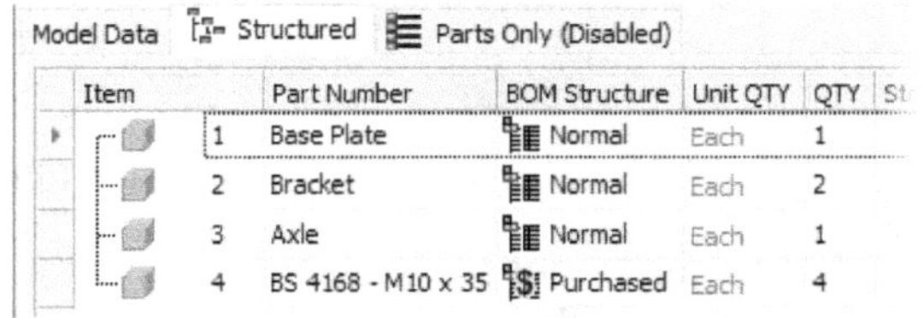

Item numbers were renumbered sequentially to account for the suppressed component.

Figure 23–13

Item Numbering

Once rows are reordered they are generally renumbered to match the customized view.

How To: Renumber

1. Click (Renumber Items) to open the *Item Renumber* dialog box, as shown in Figure 23–14.

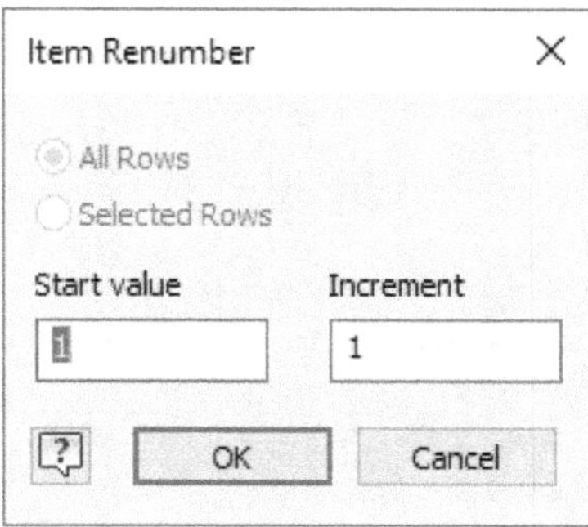

Figure 23–14

2. Enter a value that the first item should begin with in the *Start value* field.
3. Enter the value by which each consecutive item should increment in the *Increment* field.
4. Click **OK**.

   Note: *The number of digits in an item number can be set in the View Properties.*

- To renumber specific items, select the items using <Ctrl> before clicking (Renumber Items).

View Properties

View properties set the options that affect item numbering. To display the view properties for the active tab, click (View Options) and select **View Properties**.

For the *Structured* tab, the *Structured Properties* dialog box opens as shown in Figure 23–15. Select the required options and click **OK** to change the properties.

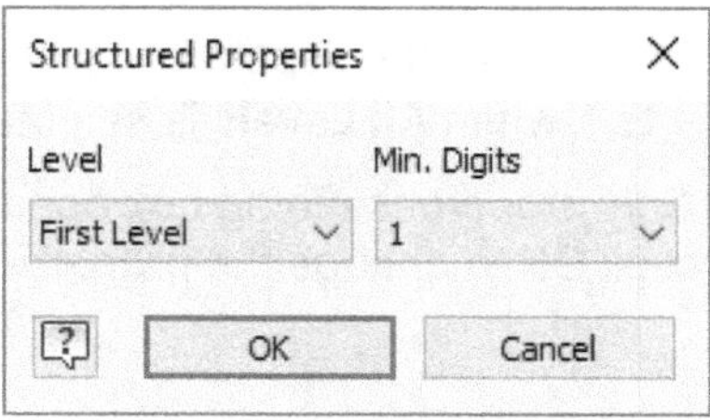

Figure 23–15

Note: *To set minimum digits and display all subassembly models, set the Min. Digits field first, click* ***OK****, re-enter the View Properties dialog box, select* ***All Levels****, and click .*

- The *Level* drop-down list contains two options: **First Level** and **All Levels**. Use **First Level** to assign integers to direct children of the assembly and prevent the components of subassemblies from displaying in the BOM view. Selecting **All Levels** in the *Level* drop-down list includes all of the subassembly components in the BOM view. All subassembly components also have item numbers, as shown in Figure 23–16.

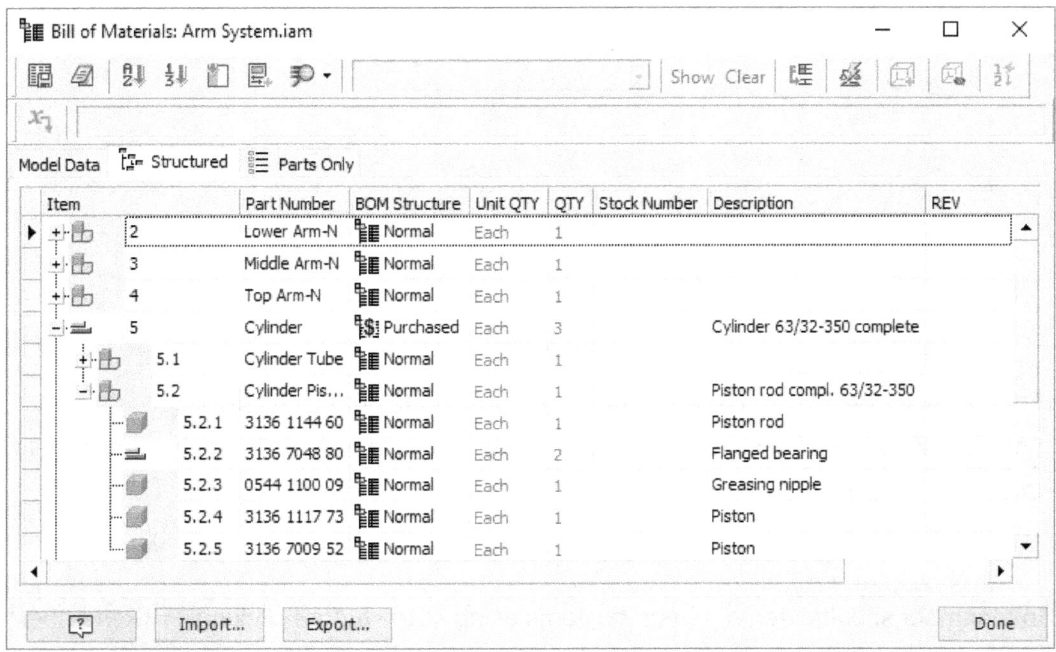

Figure 23–16

- The *Min. Digits* field is available to select the number of digits to include when **First Level** is selected. For example, a *Min. Digits* field to **0001** assigns the first item number at 0001 and the second at 0002.

  Note: *After changing the Min. Digits field and accepting the change, the item numbers do not update until you use* (Renumber Items).

- The *Delimiter* field enables you to select the separator symbol to use for subassembly components (comma, colon, etc.), when **All Levels** is selected.

For the *Parts Only* tab, the *Parts Only properties* dialog box opens, as shown in Figure 23–17. Select the required options and click **OK** to change the properties.

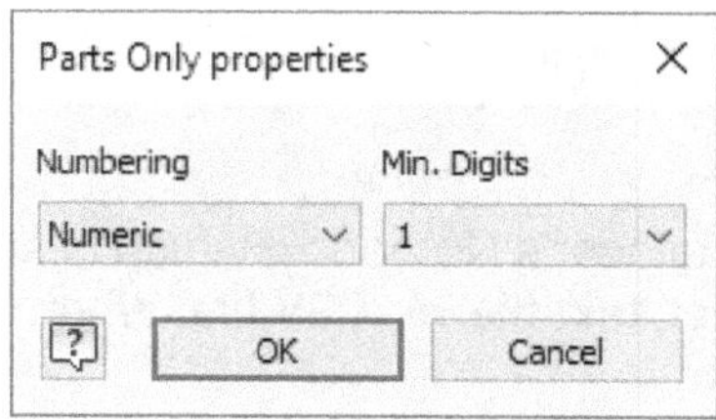

Figure 23–17

- The *Numbering* drop-down list contains two options: **Numeric** and **Alpha**. Use **Numeric** to assign a numerical index for item numbers and use **Alpha** to use a character-based index.
- The *Min. Digits* field assigns the number of digits to include when **Numeric** is selected.
- The *Case* field enables you to set the case as upper or lower when **Alpha** is selected.

Part Number Merge Settings

The **Part Number Row Merge Settings** option enables you to control how different components with identical part numbers are handled. Click (Part Number Row Merge Settings) to open the *Part Number Row Merge Settings* dialog box, as shown in Figure 23–18.

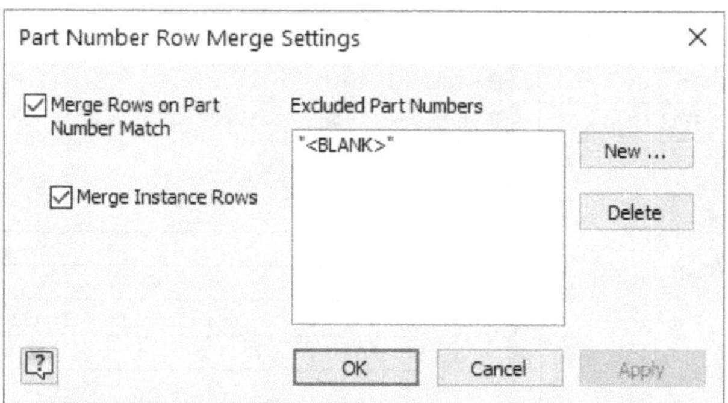

Figure 23–18

> ***Note:*** *Exclusions can be copied and pasted into another BOM list, by selecting the ones to be copied, right-clicking, and selecting* ***Copy****. Right-click and select* ***Paste*** *to paste them.*

By default, components with the same part numbers are merged into one row. To disable this, clear the **Merge Rows on Part Number Match** option. If merging is enabled, you can further specify whether to merge rows with the same instances. When merging, you can exclude specific part numbers from being merged by clicking **New** and entering the part name to add to the *Excluded Part Numbers* list.

> ***Note:*** *If you have customized settings in the Bill of Materials dialog box, you can click* ***Export*** *to create an .XML file with the customizations so that they can be imported again in another assembly.*

Step 5 - Export the BOM.

A BOM can be exported to the Engineer's Notebook, which is stored in the assembly file, or to an external database, spreadsheet, text file, or .CSV file. When exporting you can export using the Structured or Parts Only views.

- To export to an external file, click (Export Bill of Materials).
- To export to the Engineer's Notebook, click (Engineer's Notebook).

Step 6 - Synchronize BOM and parts list, if required.

Item numbers in a BOM and the parts list are fully associative. A change to an item number in the Assembly BOM updates in the parts list, as shown in Figure 23–19.

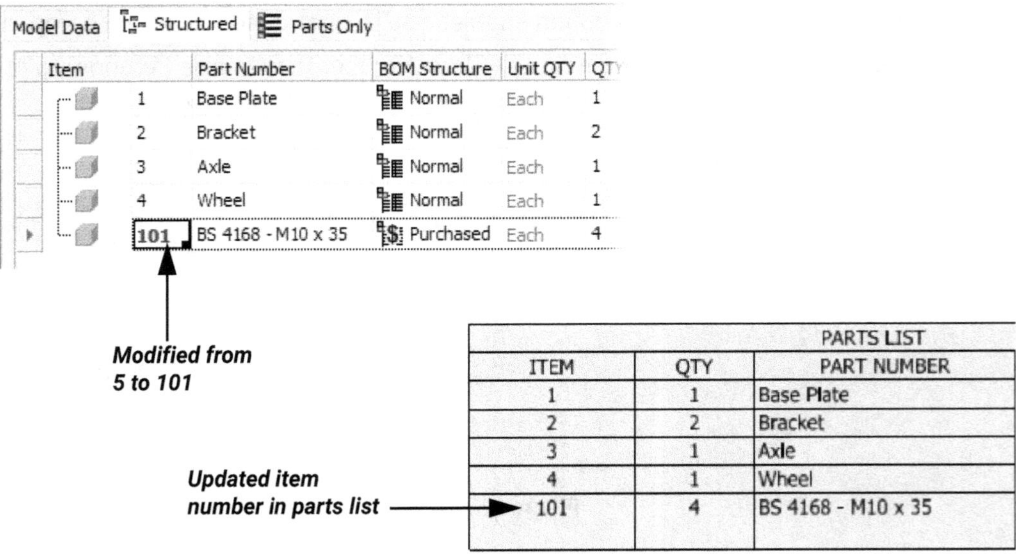

Figure 23–19

- Use the **Static Value** option (shown in Figure 23–20) in the parts list to set an override that prevents item numbers from updating if the Assembly BOM is changed. Static values in the *Edit Parts List* dialog box appear bolded and in blue. The same is true of overwritten values in the BOM.

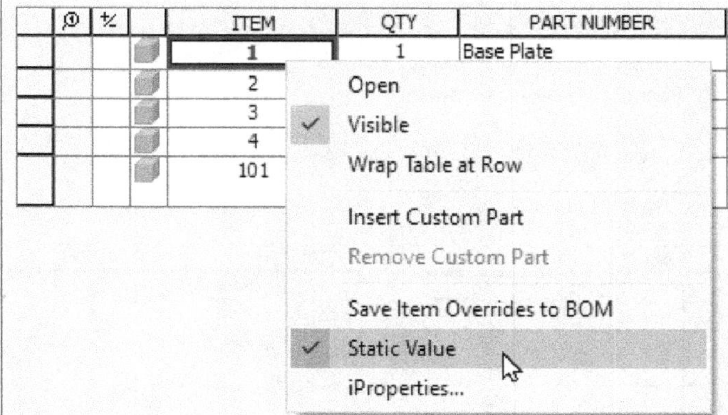

Figure 23–20

- Use the **Lock Items** option (shown in Figure 23–21) in the Assembly BOM to lock an item number to prevent it from being modified in the parts list and updating in the BOM. A locked item number in the Assembly BOM is displayed in orange and is italicized and underlined (*2*). If the number is also overridden, it displays in blue and is bolded, italicized, and underlined (***25***).

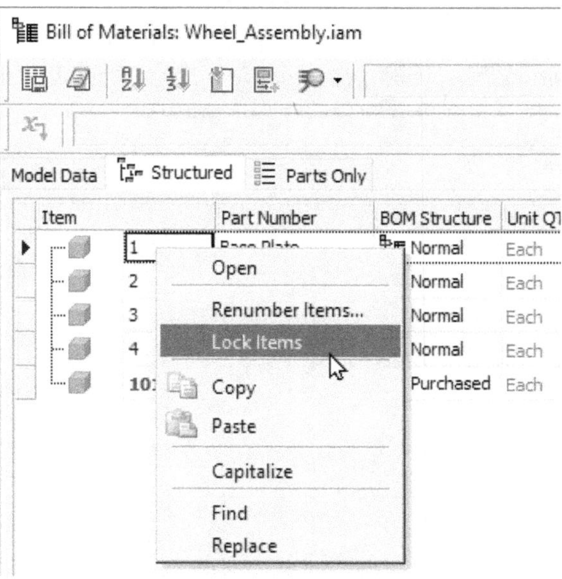

Figure 23–21

- Modifications made to values in the Parts List are immediately set as static and are identified in blue highlight. To apply a static override from the parts list to the BOM, in the parts list, right-click on the item number, and select **Save Item Overrides to BOM**, as shown in Figure 23–22. If the item number is not locked in the BOM, it updates and the parts list item number is no longer static. If the item number is locked in the BOM, you are prompted to unlock it or not.

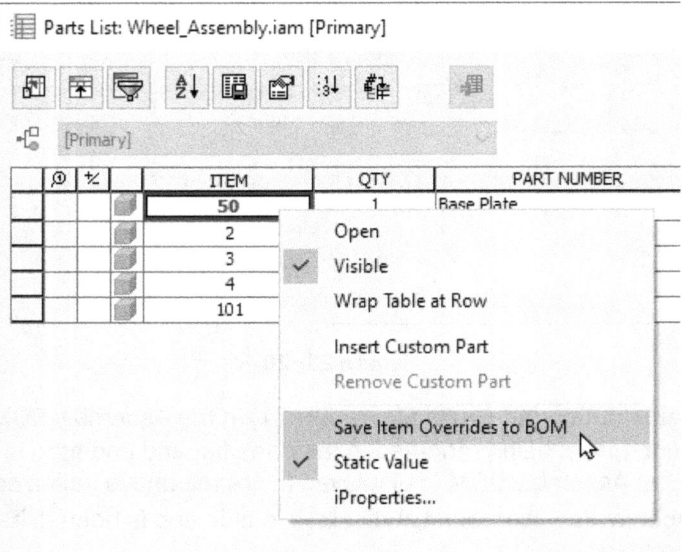

Figure 23–22

Note: *If a modification is made to an item number where two values are the same, the item number fields highlight in yellow to easily identify the duplicates. The highlighting is available in both the BOM and the Parts List dialog boxes.*

23.3 Instance Properties in a BOM

Model data that is generated or explicitly created using the model's *iProperties* dialog box can be used to populate many of the columns that are available for display in a BOM table, as shown in Figure 23–23. In cases where the same component is used multiple times in an assembly or where instance-specific assembly properties are needed, you can incorporate the use of **Instance Properties**. This enables you to assign unique property data to each component for display in the BOM or use in a parts list, balloons, leadered text, or sketched symbols.

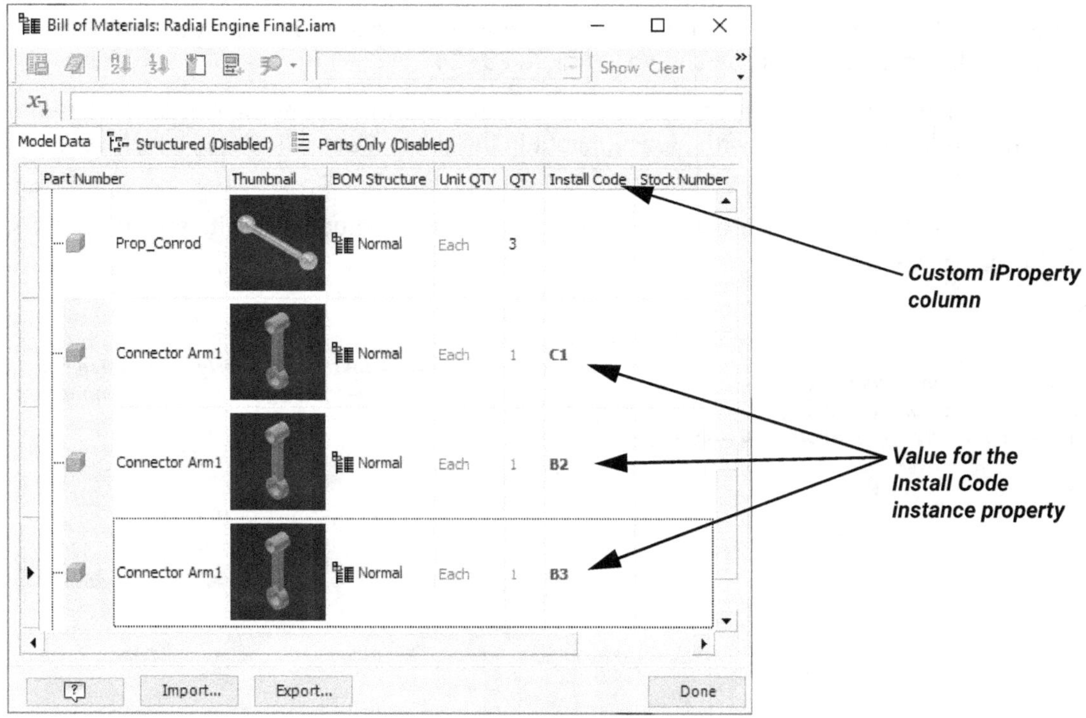

Figure 23–23

Creating Instance Properties

Instance properties are assigned and are subsequently stored in the assembly file.

How To: Add Instance Properties to Components

1. With the assembly active, right-click on a component name in the Model browser and click **Instance Properties**. The *Instance Properties* dialog box opens.
2. Enter a name for the new instance property.

3. Select a type from the *Type* drop-down list. The options include **Text**, **Date**, **Number**, and **Yes or No**.
4. Enter a value for the new instance property.
    - For text properties, you can enter a text string (alphanumeric).
    - For date properties, you can enable the current date or select from a calendar.
    - For number properties, you can only enter numbers.
    - For yes or no properties, you can select an option from the drop-down list to assign the yes or no value.
5. Click **Add** to add the instance property to the model. You can hover over the component icon and display the value, as shown in Figure 23–24.
    - Models that have instance properties are identified with a dot at the end of their name in the Model browser and with blue highlight in the *Bill of Materials* dialog box, as shown in Figure 23–24.
    - You can use the Model browser search (🔍) to locate components with specific instance property values.

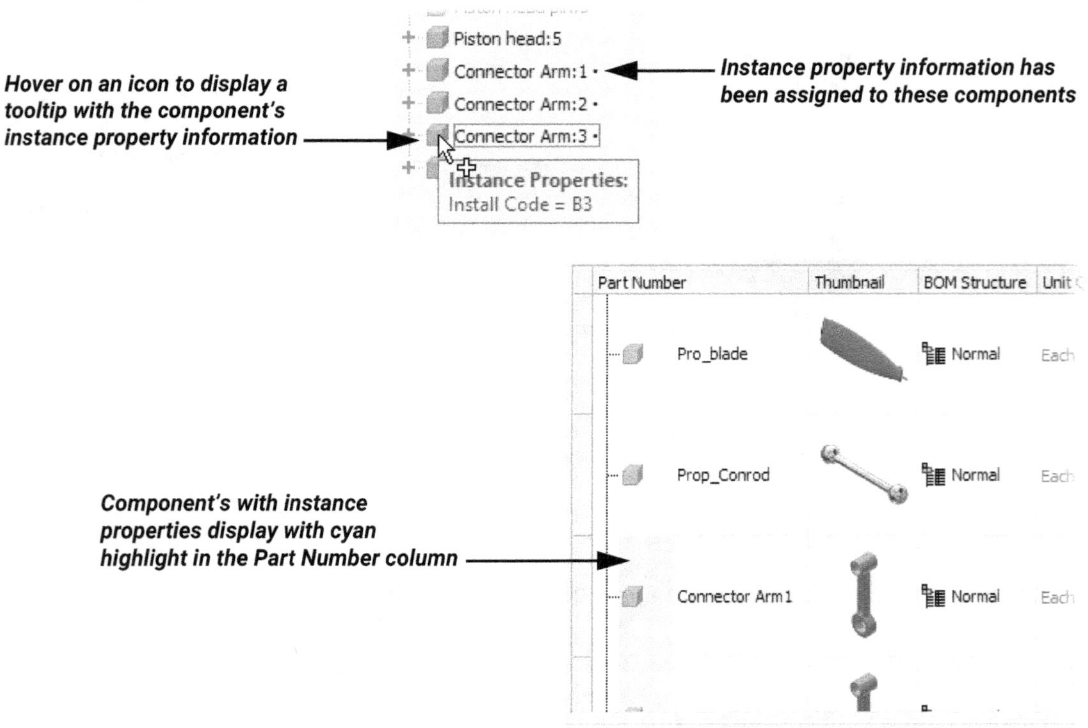

Figure 23–24

Note: *Instance properties can be used to override iProperty data in read-only library components (e.g., Content Center files).*

Displaying Instance Properties in a BOM

Instance property data can be displayed in columns of the BOM by creating a custom iProperty column. Once displayed, the property is populated for any components that have an instance property assigned with the same name.

How To: Display Instance Properties in a BOM

1. In the *Bill of Materials* dialog box, click (Add custom iProperty columns). The *Add Custom iProperty Columns* dialog box opens.
2. In the <click to add iProperty column> row, select the data type in the drop-down list.
   - Similar to creating the instance property, you can select **Text**, **Date**, **Number**, and **Yes or No** as the Property name data types.
3. Select <click to add iProperty column> for the same row and enter a name for the property.
4. Click **OK** to create the column name. The instance properties populate for each component that has an instance property value with this same name.
   - Instance property values appear in bolded blue font in the *Bill of Materials* dialog box, as shown in Figure 23–25.

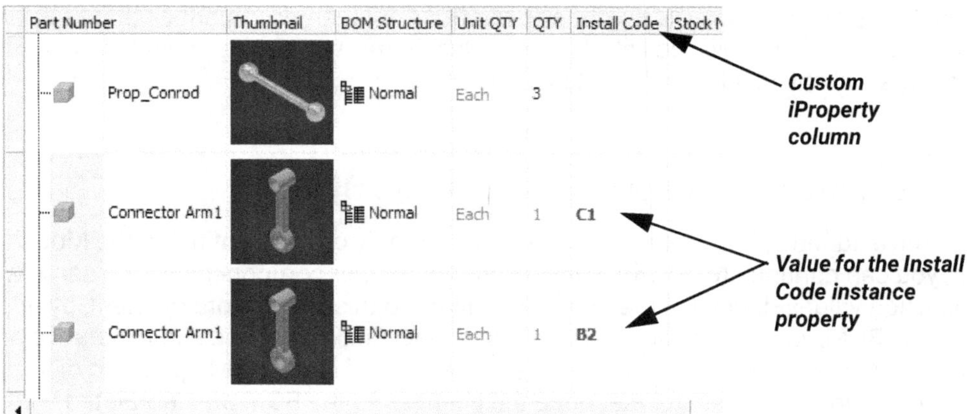

Figure 23–25

Hint: Adding the Instance Property Column to the Structured and Parts Only Views

By default, the Structured and Parts Only views of the BOM merge rows of the same component. If unique instance properties are assigned to the merged components, the cell will read as ***Varies***, as shown in Figure 23–26.

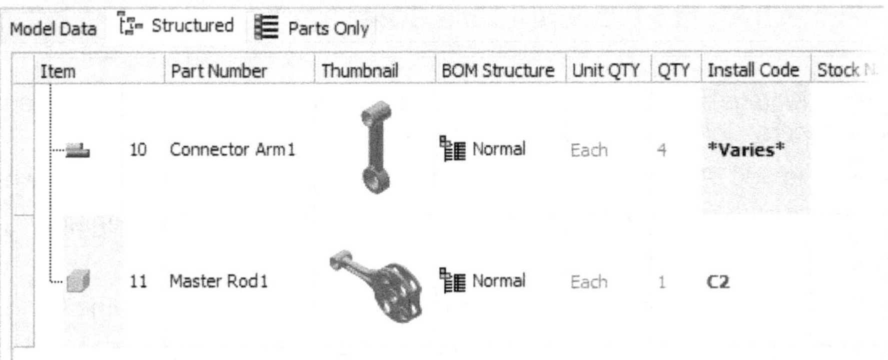

Figure 23–26

To display all the values for each component, you must disable the merging of rows in each view. Click (Part Number Row Merge Settings) and in the dialog box, clear the **Merge Instance Rows** option. Click **OK** to return to the BOM. All merged instances that have unique instance property values will be listed as individual items, while other multi-instance components will still display with multiple quantities.

Assigning Instance Property Values in the BOM

Once you have added an instance property to an assembly component using the Model browser, you can continue to add the same property to other components in the same way, or you can assign values directly in the BOM. In addition to this being more efficient, by adding directly in the BOM, you can ensure that no error is made in creating the same instance property name. Components that have instance properties assigned in the BOM update to display a dot after their name in the Model browser once the changes to the BOM are completed.

Consider the following to assign values in the BOM:

- To add an instance property to a component in the BOM, right-click on the cell and enable **Instance Property**, as shown in Figure 23–27. Once it is enabled, you can enter a value and the instance property is created in the component. Once the instance property is created, the row is identified with cyan highlight and the value is displayed in bolded blue font. If the cell is not changed to an instance property, the value is created as a custom iProperty in the part file.

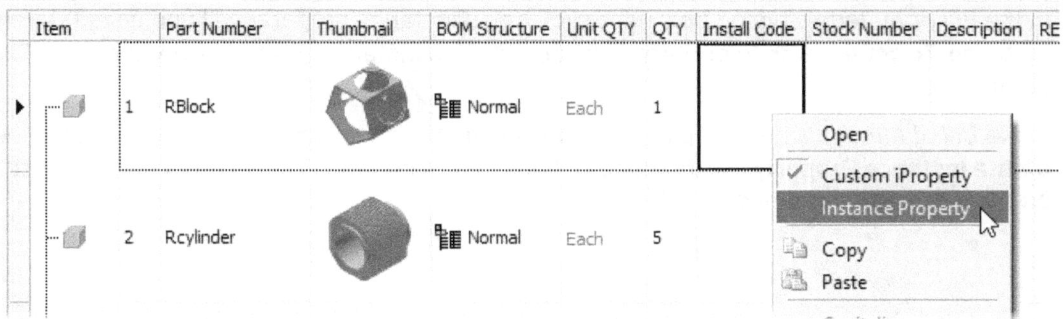

Figure 23–27

- To add an instance property to all components in the BOM, right-click on the column header and enable **Create Instance Property (all instances)**, as shown in Figure 23–28.

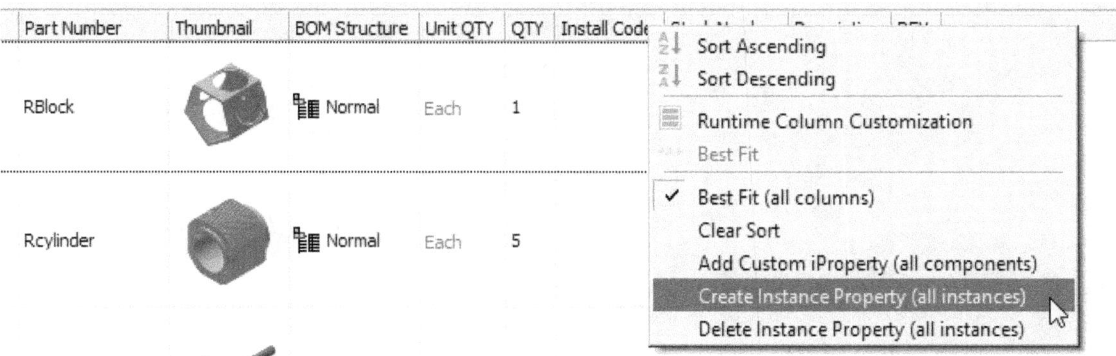

Figure 23–28

Modifying Instance Properties

Instance properties can be modified using any one of the following methods:

- In the Model browser, right-click on the component name and select **Instance Properties**. In the *Instance Properties* dialog box, select the property, then at the top of the dialog box, enter a new value and click **Modify**.
- In the *Bill of Materials* dialog box, double-click on the instance property cell and enter a new value.

Deleting Instance Properties

Instance properties can be deleted using any one of the following methods:

- In the Model browser, right-click on the component name and select **Delete Instance Properties**. Click **Yes** to confirm. All instance properties are removed from the component.
- In the Model browser, right-click on the component name and select **Instance Properties**. In the *Instance Properties* dialog box, select the property and click **Delete**.
- In the *Bill of Materials* dialog box, right-click on an instance property cell and select **Delete Instance Row**. Click **Yes** to confirm. This deletes this instance property from the component.
- In the *Bill of Materials* dialog box, right-click on an instance property cell header and select **Delete Instance Property (all instances)**. Click **Yes** to confirm. This deletes this instance property from all components.

Practice 23a
Bill of Materials

Practice Objectives

- Generate a bill of materials (BOM) for an assembly file.
- Change the BOM structure for purchased and phantom components in an assembly.
- Create a virtual component in an assembly to represent a purchased component.
- Customize the columns and components that are listed in the BOM.
- Display instance properties in the BOM.
- Output a BOM file as a unicode text file.

In this practice, you will create and customize a BOM for a mechanical arm system model. You will define a BOM structure to accurately display the list of parts for the model and output the BOM to a unicode text file.

Task 1: Open an assembly file and generate a BOM.

1. Open **Arm System.iam** from the *BOM* folder.

2. In the *Assemble* tab>*Manage* panel, click (Bill of Materials). The *Bill of Materials* dialog box opens, as shown in Figure 23–29.

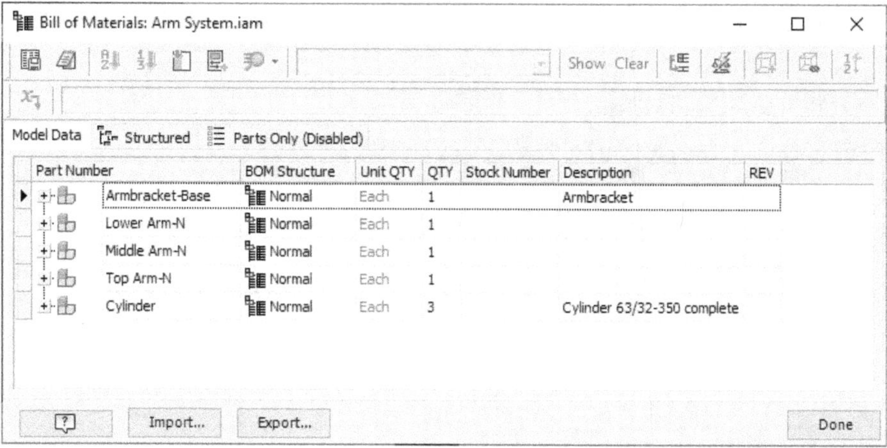

Figure 23–29

3. Review the BOM for the model. This assembly consists of several subassemblies.

   Note: *Your columns and their order may vary from the images shown in this practice depending on settings for your installation. To rearrange, drag and drop the headings, as needed.*

Task 2: View the Parts Only view.

By default, the Parts Only view is disabled. You must first enable the Parts Only view to display the parts list for the assembly. In general, this view is used for weldments and bolt connections. and is being shown with this assembly to show you how to enable it.

1. Select the *Parts Only (Disabled)* tab.
2. Click (View Options) and select **Enable BOM View** in the drop-down list. Alternatively, you can right-click on the *Parts Only (Disabled)* tab name and access the same option.
3. Review the list of parts in the *Parts Only* tab.

Task 3: Change the BOM structure.

The **Armbracket-Base** subassembly was only created to ease in its placement, it should not be listed in the BOM as an assembly. In addition, the **cylinder** assembly is going to be purchased and not manufactured.

1. Select the *Structured* tab and review the listed components.
2. Select the *Model Data* tab.
3. Double-click on the *BOM Structure* cell for the **Armbracket-Base** component to edit its BOM structure.
4. Select **Phantom** in the *BOM Structure* drop-down list, as shown in Figure 23–30.

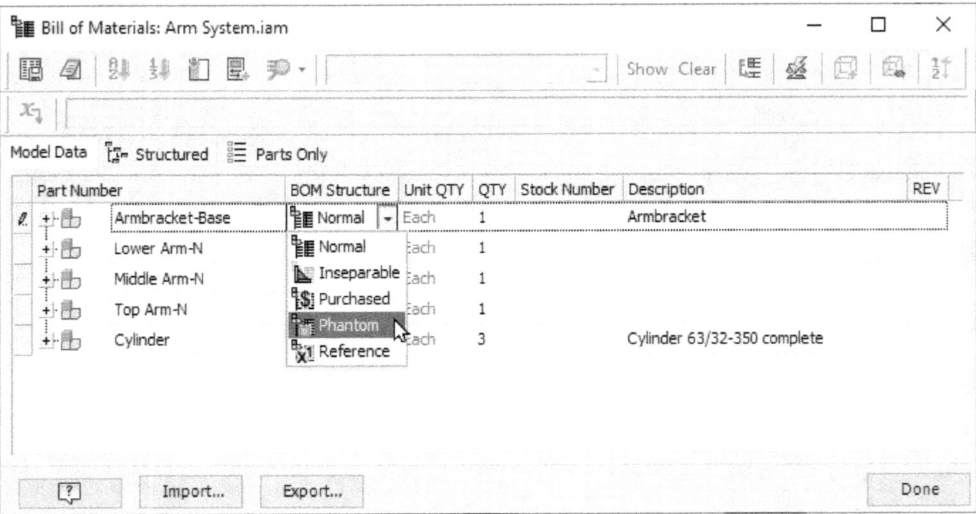

Figure 23–30

Changing the BOM structure of the **Armbracket-base** component to **Phantom** means that all components in this assembly will be promoted to the top-level assembly, and the **Armbracket-base** subassembly will not display in the BOM.

5. Change to the *Structured* tab. Note that the components that have been promoted in the BOM have an upward arrow next to them, as shown in Figure 23–31.

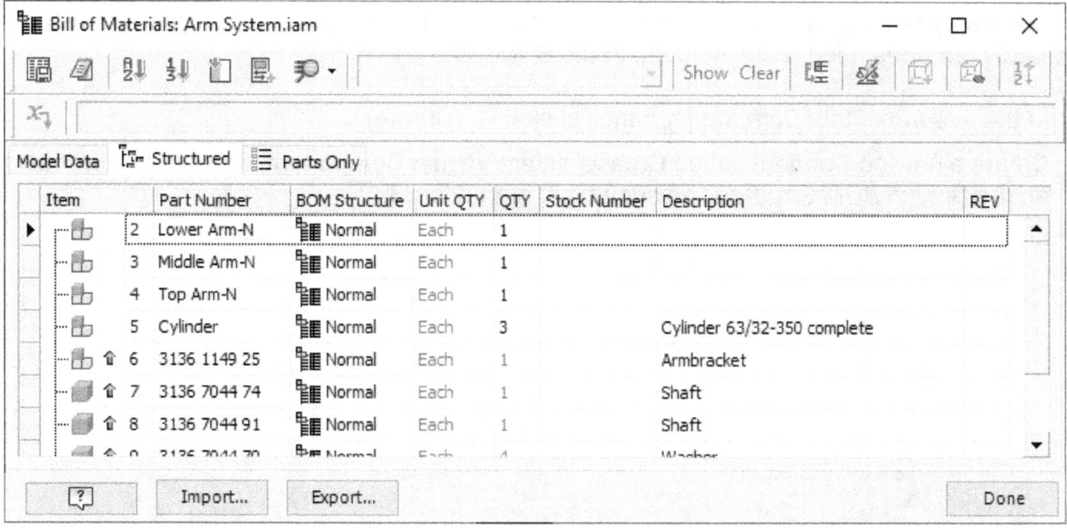

Figure 23–31

6. Select **Purchased** in the *BOM Structure* drop-down list for the **Cylinder**. In the structured view, the Purchased components do not change. However, in the Parts Only view, the individual parts of the **Cylinder** assembly no longer display; only the **Cylinder** assembly displays, as shown in Figure 23–32.

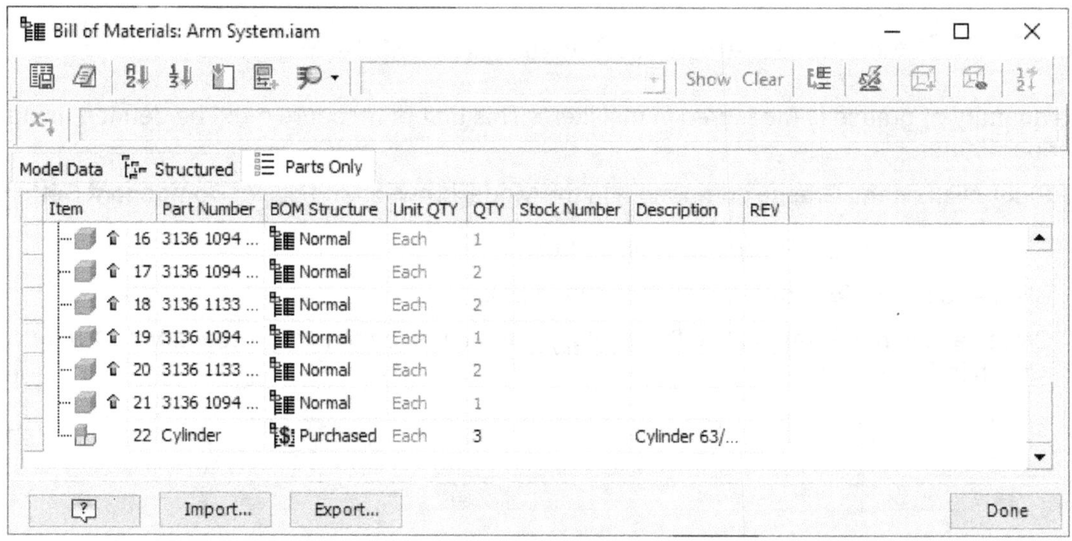

Figure 23–32

7. Click **Done** to close the dialog box.

Task 4: Add a virtual component.

The assembly requires a certain amount of grease. This is not a physical component in the assembly but does need to be included in the BOM.

1. In the *Assemble* tab>*Component* panel, click (Create).
2. Create a new component called **Grease**, select **Virtual Component**, and select **Purchased** as the *Default BOM Structure*, as shown in Figure 23–33.

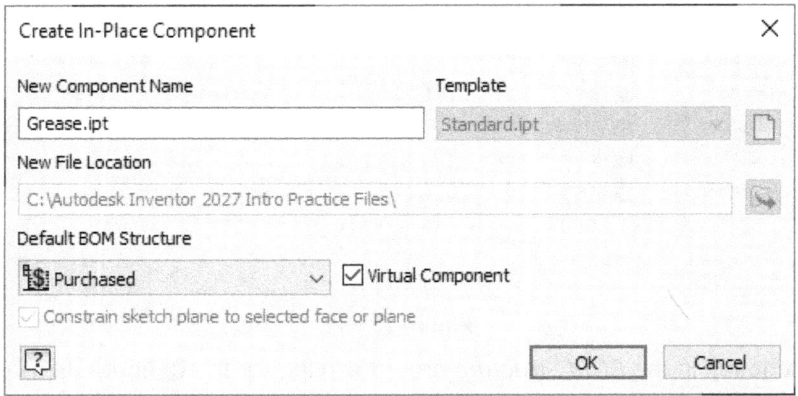

Figure 23–33

3. Click **OK**.

Task 5: Define a Base Quantity for the virtual component.

The quantity of grease is measured in milliliters. This unit of measure must be defined using a user parameter.

1. Right-click on the **Grease** component in the Model browser and select **Component Settings**.
2. Click to open the *Parameters* dialog box.
3. Click **Add Numeric** in the *Parameters* dialog box.
4. Create a new parameter called **Base_Qty**, set the *units* to *ml* and the *equation* to *1.0 ml*, as shown in Figure 23–34.

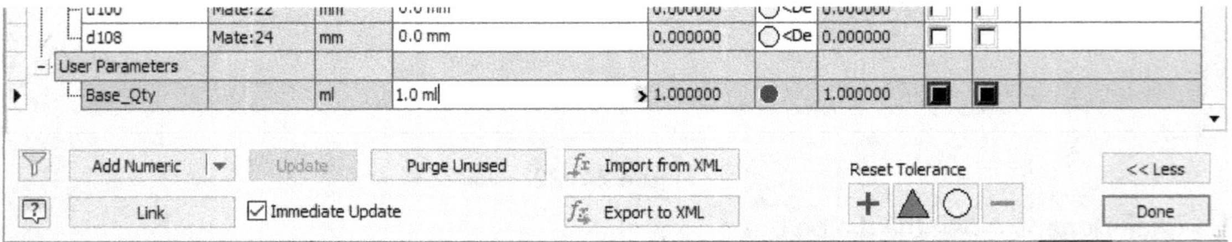

Figure 23–34

5. Click **Done** to close the *Parameters* dialog box.
6. In the *Grease Component Settings* dialog box, select **Base_Qty (1.0 ml)** in the *Base Quantity* drop-down list and click **OK** to close the drop-down list. Set the *BOM Structure* to **Purchased**. The dialog box should appear as shown in Figure 23–35.

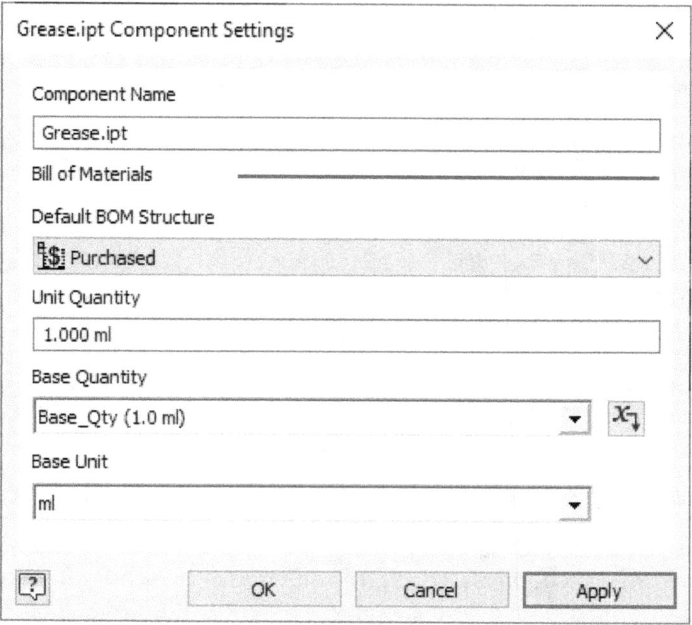

Figure 23–35

7. Click **OK** to close the *Grease Component Settings* dialog box.
8. In the *Assemble* tab>*Manage* panel, click (Bill of Materials).
9. Review the new **Grease** component.

10. Set the *QTY* for the *Grease* component to **3 ml**, as shown in Figure 23–36.

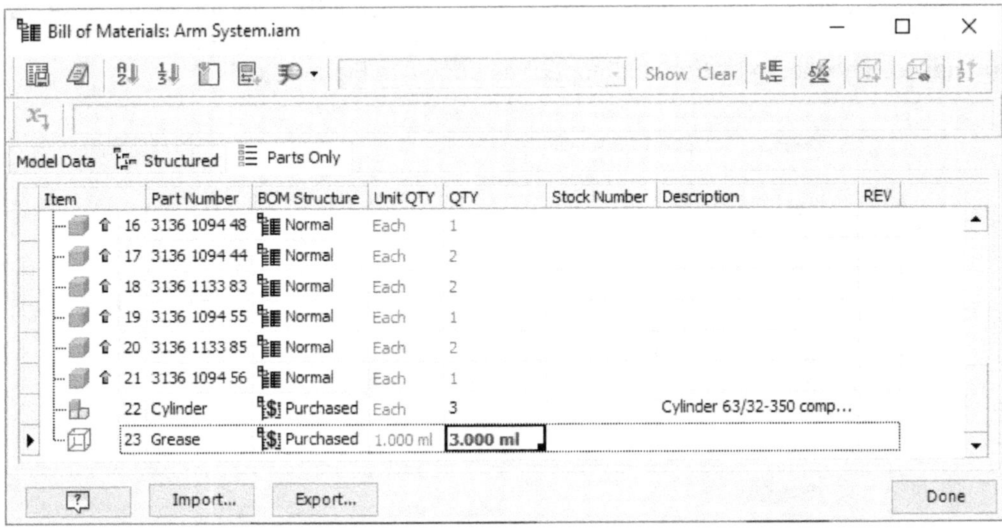

Figure 23–36

Note: *As an alternative to creating a virtual component in the Create Component dialog box, you can also click (Create Virtual Component) in the Bill of Materials dialog box to create a new virtual component. Using this alternative method, you are simply prompted for the component's name and you can define its BOM Structure directly in the dialog box. To make modifications to its Unit QTY, you must still define its Component Settings.*

Task 6: Customize the BOM.

Columns can be customized to display the required information. Columns can be added or removed. Components listed in the BOM can be sorted by any of the columns.

1. Select the *Parts Only* tab, if it is not already active.
2. Click (Choose Columns) to open the *Customization* dialog box.

   Note: *The Customization dialog box does not need to be open to remove columns.*

3. Press and hold the left mouse button over the *Stock Number* column heading and drag the mouse away from the column headings to remove the column from the table, as shown in Figure 23–37.

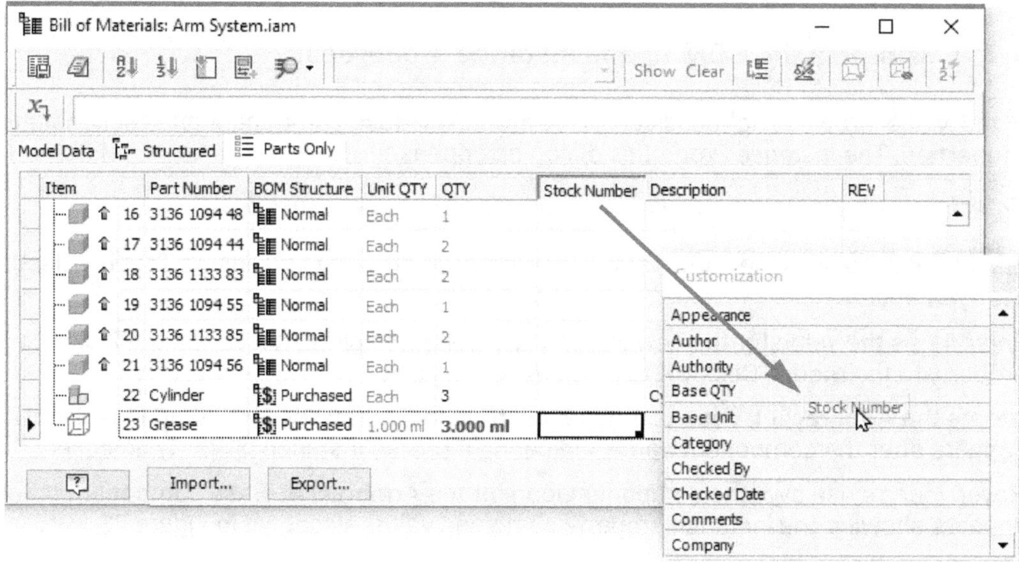

Figure 23–37

4. In the *Customization* dialog box, press and hold the left mouse button on *Company* and drag and drop it over the headings in the table (between *QTY* and *Description*). Close the *Customization* dialog box.

5. Enter the company names for the purchased components, as shown in Figure 23–38.

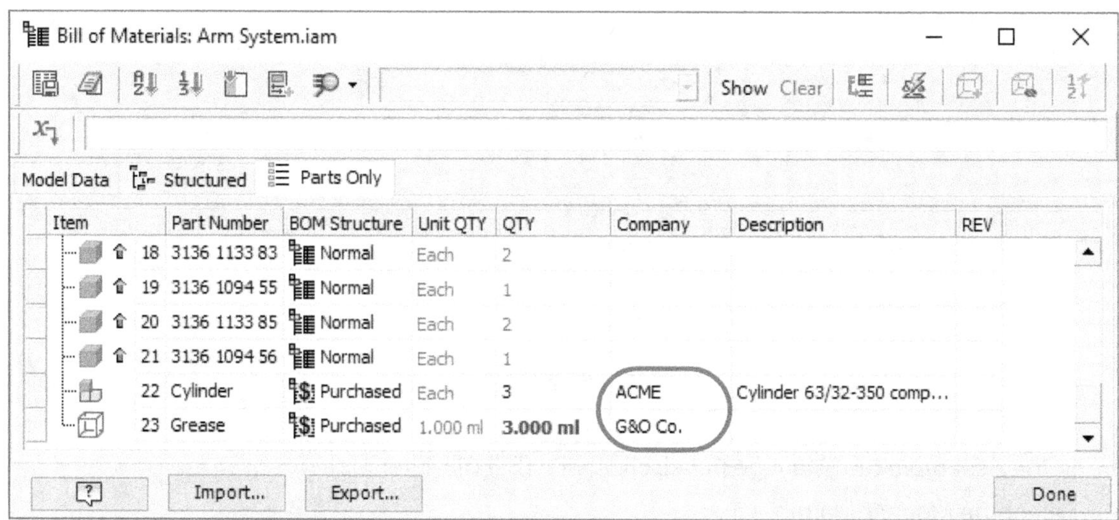

Figure 23–38

6. Select the *Part Number* heading cell to sort the BOM data by this column.
7. Click (Renumber Items). Maintain the defaults and click **OK**.
8. Click **Done** to close the *Bill of Materials* dialog box.

Task 7: Customize the BOM to add instance properties.

1. In the Model browser, right-click on the **Armbracket-Base** component and click **Instance Properties**. The *Instance Properties* dialog box opens.

   Note: *Instance properties can also be assigned to part components.*

2. Enter **Install Code** as the name for the new instance property and ensure **Text** is selected as the *Type* option.
3. Enter **A1** as the value for the new instance property and click **Add** to add the instance property to the model. Click **OK** to close the dialog box.
4. Locate the **Armbracket-Base** component in the Model browser. Note that a black dot appears after the component name, indicating it has an instance property assigned.
5. Hover your mouse over the component icon for the **Armbracket-Base** component. A tooltip appears showing the instance property name and value, as shown in Figure 23–39.

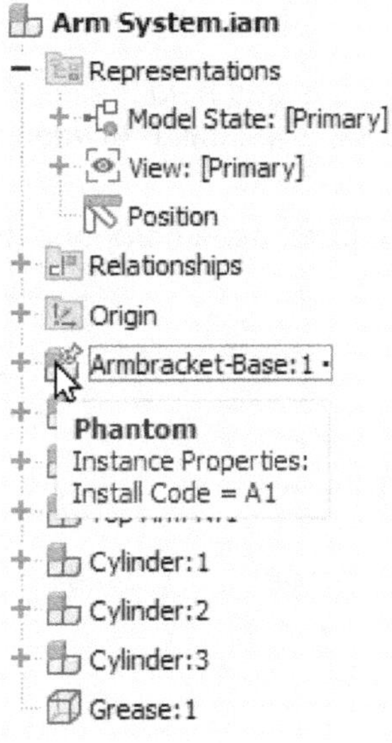

Figure 23–39

6. In the *Assemble* tab>*Manage* panel, click (Bill of Materials).
7. Select the *Model Data* tab.

8. In the *Bill of Materials* dialog box, click (Add custom iProperty columns). The *Add Custom iProperty Columns* dialog box opens. Once a custom iProperty column is added, you can assign it as an instance property to components without having to use the Model browser to create them.

9. In the **<click to add iProperty column>** row, select **Text** as the data type in the drop-down list.

10. Select **<click to add iProperty column>** for the same row and enter **Install Code**. This is the name of the instance property that you just created. Ensure that the spelling is consistent with what was used to create the instance property.

11. Click **OK** to create the column name. The instance property for **Armbracket-Base** now appears in the BOM, as shown in Figure 23–40. Note how in the *Model Data* view tab, the customization of the column header that was done previously on the *Parts Only* tab is not maintained; however, for custom iProperty columns, they are included in all views.

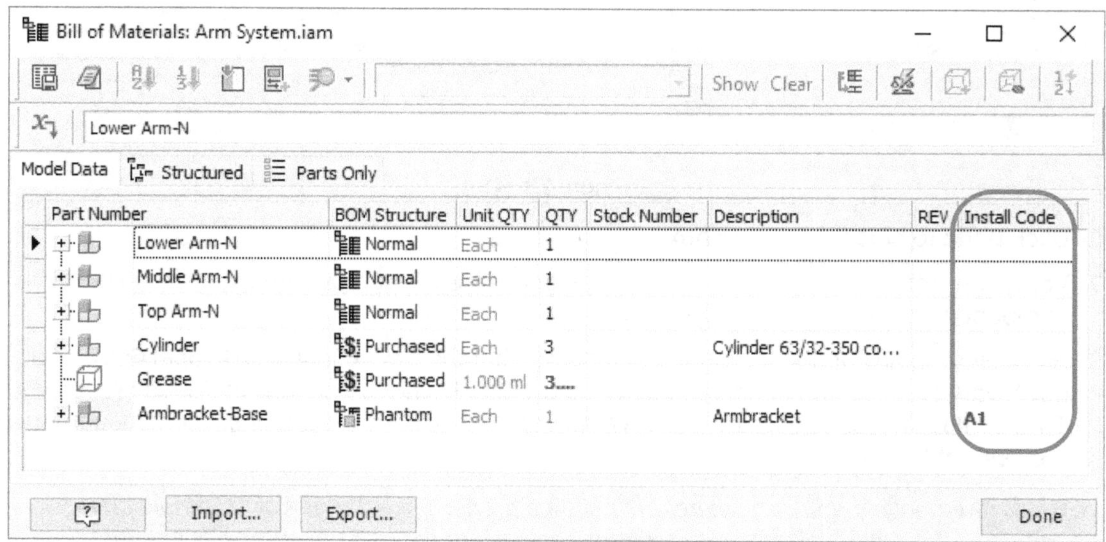

Figure 23–40

12. To assign this same instance property to all of the other components in the BOM, right-click on the *Install Code* column header and enable **Create Instance Property (all instances)**. All but the Grease virtual component now display with cyan highlight, indicating they have instance properties.

13. Note how the BOM now shows each Cylinder component as separate items instead of QTY = 3. This is because you can now assign unique instance properties to each item. Without instance properties, this would not be possible simply by using a custom iProperty.

14. Hover over the component icons in the Model browser and note that the components now have the Install Code instance property assigned but they do not have values assigned.

15. In the *Bill of Materials* dialog box, enter *Install Code* values for the remaining subassemblies, similar to that shown in Figure 23–41.

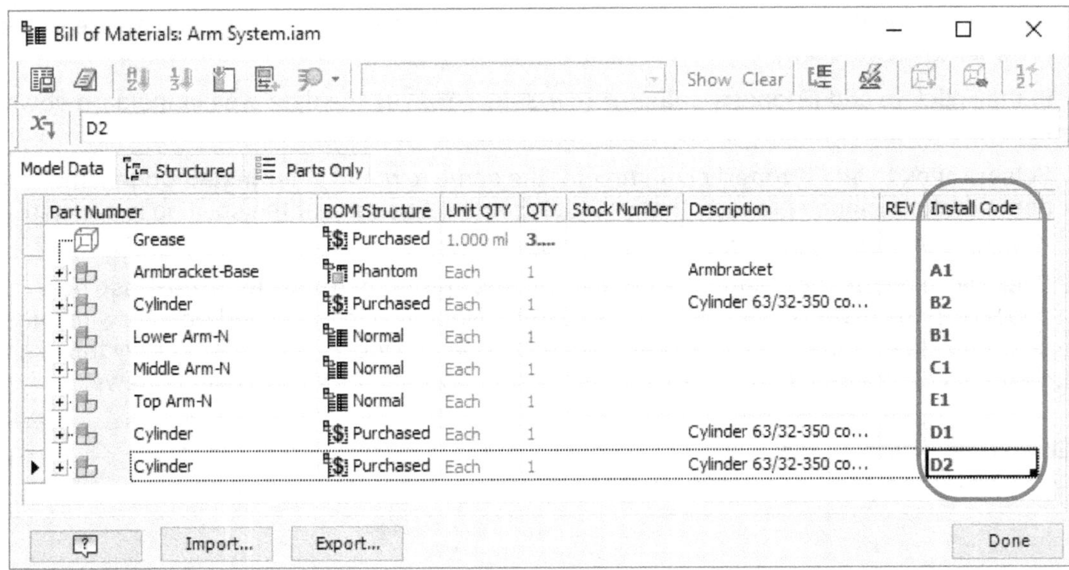

Figure 23–41

16. Click **Done** to close the dialog box.
17. Verify the instance property values are assigned to each component by hovering over their component icons in the Model browser.
18. Right-click on any of the components and note that the **Delete Instance Properties** option is now available. You can use this to delete the value. Do not delete any instance properties. These values could be listed in the drawing parts list or used in balloons when documenting the assembly in a drawing.

    Note: *Alternatively, you can delete the instance properties in the Bill of Materials dialog box using the right-click menu options for each cell or the instance property column header.*

Task 8: Output the BOM.

1. Open the *Bill of Materials* dialog box.
2. Click (Export Bill of Materials) to open the *Export Bill of Materials* dialog box.
3. Select **Parts Only** in the *View to Export* drop-down list. Click **OK** to export the BOM.
4. Select **Text (Tab delimited) (*.txt)** as the file format to which to export. Enter **Arm System BOM** as the name for the exported BOM, ensure it is being saved to the BOM folder, and save the file.
5. Click **Done** to close the *Bill of Materials* dialog box.

6. Right-click on **Arm System.iam** at the top of the Model browser and select **Open File Location**. This opens the *BOM* folder in a File Explorer window. Open the text file. The file displays as shown in Figure 23–42. Note that in the Parts Only view, only a single purchased cylinder is added and the *Install Code* shows as ***Varies***. Exporting the Structured view would show the codes for the normal components.

   Note: *The exported BOM will generate with the same columns that are displayed in the Bill of Materials dialog box.*

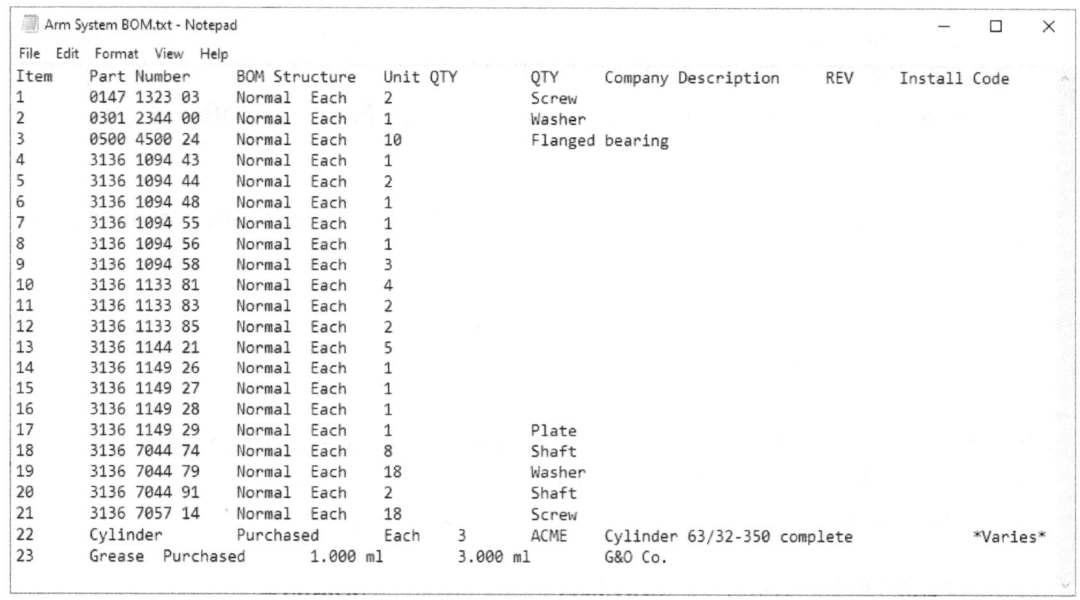

Arm System BOM.txt - Notepad

File Edit Format View Help

```
Item    Part Number     BOM Structure   Unit QTY        QTY     Company Description     REV     Install Code
1       0147 1323 03    Normal  Each    2               Screw
2       0301 2344 00    Normal  Each    1               Washer
3       0500 4500 24    Normal  Each    10              Flanged bearing
4       3136 1094 43    Normal  Each    1
5       3136 1094 44    Normal  Each    2
6       3136 1094 48    Normal  Each    1
7       3136 1094 55    Normal  Each    1
8       3136 1094 56    Normal  Each    1
9       3136 1094 58    Normal  Each    3
10      3136 1133 81    Normal  Each    4
11      3136 1133 83    Normal  Each    2
12      3136 1133 85    Normal  Each    2
13      3136 1144 21    Normal  Each    5
14      3136 1149 26    Normal  Each    1
15      3136 1149 27    Normal  Each    1
16      3136 1149 28    Normal  Each    1
17      3136 1149 29    Normal  Each    1               Plate
18      3136 7044 74    Normal  Each    8               Shaft
19      3136 7044 79    Normal  Each    18              Washer
20      3136 7044 91    Normal  Each    2               Shaft
21      3136 7057 14    Normal  Each    18              Screw
22      Cylinder        Purchased       Each    3       ACME    Cylinder 63/32-350 complete             *Varies*
23      Grease  Purchased       1.000 ml        3.000 ml        G&O Co.
```

Figure 23–42

7. Save and close all of the open models.

End of practice

Chapter Review Questions

1. Which of the following best describe the purpose of virtual components? (Select all that apply.)
   a. Virtual components are models that have been generated using part model geometry.
   b. Virtual components are created to represent non-geometrical parts required in the bill of materials.
   c. Virtual components can be used to represent parts you do not want to model, such as fasteners that are not available in the Content Center.
   d. Virtual components are models that have been placed from the Content Center.

2. The properties of a virtual component cannot be defined like a standard component is defined in a model.
   a. True
   b. False

3. Which command sequence is used to create a new virtual component while in the context of an assembly model? (Select all that apply.)
   a. In the **File** menu, click **New**.
   b. In the *Assemble* tab>*Component* panel, click .
   c. In the *Assemble* tab>*Component* panel, click .
   d. In the *Bill of Materials* dialog box, click .

4. Fill in the *Bill of Materials* dialog box tab, *Model Data*, *Structured*, or *Parts Only*, with the best description of its purpose.
   a. The _____ tab displays only parts or subassemblies whose BOM Structure property has been set to Normal, Purchased, or Inseparable.
   b. The _____ tab displays BOM data in a tree view similar to the Model browser.
   c. The _____ tab displays components based on their BOM Structure property.

5. Which of the following views can be used to display data in the parts list? (Select all that apply.)

    a. Model Data view

    b. Structured view

    c. Parts Only view

6. The numbering format (e.g., from 1, 2, 3, etc., to A, B, C, etc.) cannot be changed in the bill of materials and can only be changed when placed as a parts list in a drawing.

    a. True

    b. False

7. Fill in the BOM Structure type, **Normal**, **Inseparable**, **Purchased**, **Phantom**, or **Reference**, with the best description of its purpose.

    a. A ______ component is an assembly that must be physically damaged to be taken apart.

    b. A ______ component is used to simplify the design. They are often used to ease in placement of components.

    c. A ______ component is used in the construction of the assembly but is not part of the actual design.

    d. A ______ component is used if the component is acquired instead of fabricated.

    e. A ______ component is the default status for a component.

8. Which of the following statements are true regarding synchronizing the bill of materials (BOM) and parts list? (Select all that apply.)

    a. Item numbers in a BOM and the parts list are fully associative. A change to an item number in the Assembly BOM through the BOM Editor results in an automatic update in the parts list.

    b. Item numbers in a BOM are not fully associative with the balloons that are displayed in a drawing. Delete and recreate if the numbers have changed.

    c. Static overrides can be set for individual item numbers in the parts list to prevent them from updating if changes are made in the Assembly BOM.

9. Once an instance property is assigned to an assembly component in the Model browser, you can use the (Choose Columns) option in the *Bill of Materials* dialog box to show its column in the BOM table.
   a. True
   b. False

10. Which of the following statements are true about instance properties and BOM data? (Select all that apply.)
    a. Models that have instance properties cannot be identified simply by reviewing the Model browser.
    b. Models that have instance properties are identified with blue highlight in the *Bill of Materials* dialog box.
    c. Once an instance property column is added to the BOM table, you can assign instance properties to individual or all components using right-click options in this column.
    d. If the same component is used multiple times in an assembly, the same instance property value is used for all instances.

Command Summary

Button	Command	Location
	Bill of Materials	• **Ribbon:** *Assemble* tab>*Manage* panel • **Ribbon:** *Manage* tab>*Manage* panel
	Create Component	• **Ribbon:** *Assemble* tab>*Component* panel • **Context Menu:** In Model graphics window
n/a	**Instance Property**	• **Context Menu:** In Model browser • In *Bill of Materials* dialog box, right-click on the instance property cell or column header

Chapter 24

Working with Projects

When working with assemblies in the Autodesk® Inventor® software, you need to access and manage multiple part, drawing, subassembly, and presentation files. If you work as part of a design team, managing access to the shared data becomes crucial. Project files enable you to organize and access these files.

Learning Objectives

- Activate a project file in an Autodesk Inventor session.
- Create new project files for use with your current working environment.
- Use the *Resolve Link* dialog box to locate, substitute, or ignore missing files.

24.1 Project Files

A **project file** is used to organize and provide access to all files associated with a specific design project. You can create multiple project files as required to manage all of your work.

The project file (.IPJ) is a text file. It assigns a default project location for the files in the project and maintains all of the required links between files. Among other options, a project file also specifies who can access the files, and which libraries to access. When you open a model, the paths specified in the active project are searched to find all of the referenced files.

Project files are managed in the *Projects* dialog box. Use one of the following methods to open the *Project* dialog box:

- On the *Home* page, select ⋮ (Projects and Settings)>**Settings**.
- In the **File** menu, select **Manage>Projects**.
- Click **Projects** in the *Create New File* dialog box.
- Select (Projects Settings) in the *Open* dialog box.

All previously loaded project files are listed at the top of the The *Projects* dialog box. The active project is identified with a checkmark adjacent to its name. When you select a project, its details display in the Project Tree in the lower area of the dialog box, as shown in Figure 24–1.

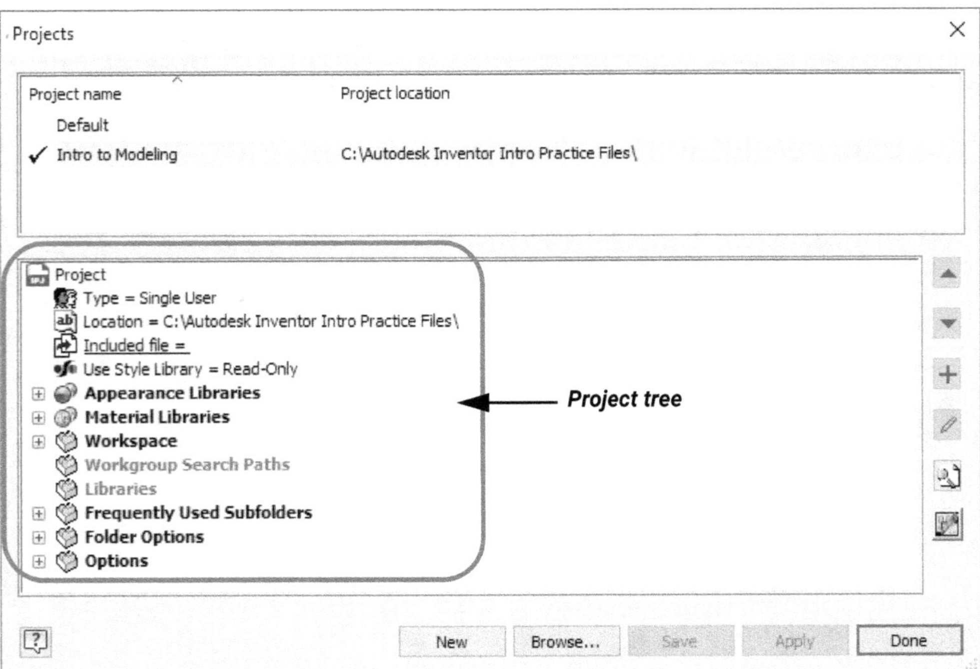

Figure 24–1

3. Enter the project name and home folder (workspace), as shown in Figure 24–4. The project file (.IPJ) is stored in the assigned home folder. The project filename and path are automatically determined based on the name and folder specified. Click **Next**.

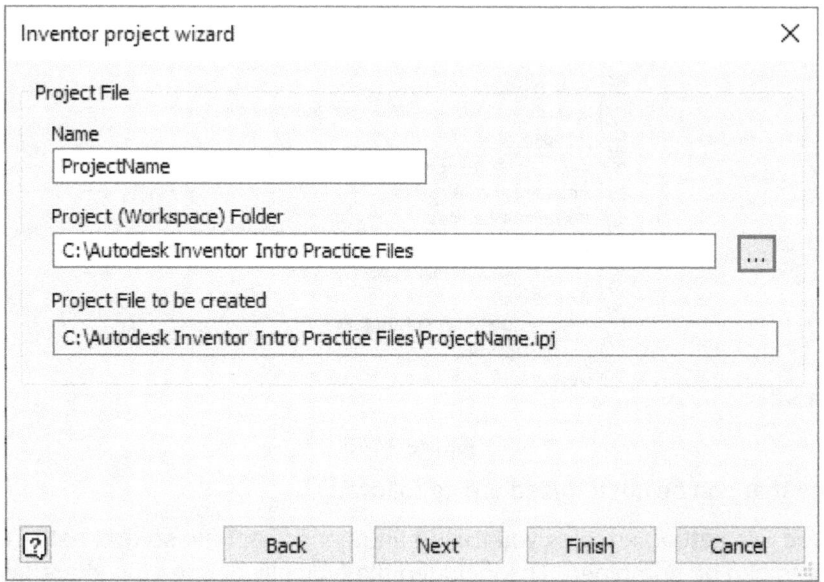

Figure 24–4

Note: *The Inventor project wizard will vary depending on the type of project you are creating.*

4. Define the library paths using the *Inventor project wizard* dialog box.
   - Library paths in existing projects are listed in the *All Projects* area on the left. Library paths that are added to the new file are listed in the *New Project* area on the right. Use the **Arrow** icons to add or remove libraries from the new project. The *Library Location* field displays the path for the selected library.
5. Click **Finish** to create the project and return to the *Projects* dialog box.
6. Modify the Project Tree options to customize the project file, as required. These options will be described in the next section.
7. Click **Done** to close the *Projects* dialog box. The new project becomes the active project.

Project Tree Customization

The project tree enables you to customize specifics on the project using the categories shown in Figure 24–5.

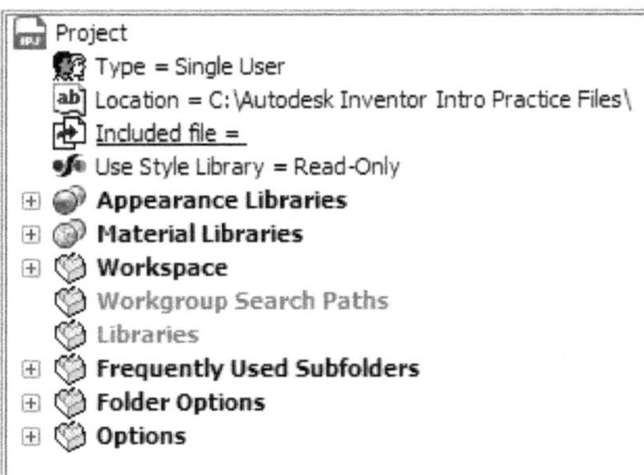

Figure 24–5

The categories that can be customized are as follows:

- The *Included File* setting enables you to add another project file so that path information in both projects can be combined. The included file typically defines the shared workgroup or library paths. To add a file, right-click on the node and select **Edit** or click and browse to and select a file.
- The *Use Style Library* setting defines whether the style library is **Read-Only** or **Read-Write**, controlling whether a designer can make changes to the library. To set this option, right-click on its node and select the required permission setting.
- The *Appearance Libraries* and *Material Libraries* settings (shown in Figure 24–6) enable you to specify the default Appearance and Material Libraries that are initially opened. Additional libraries can be explicitly opened later. To set the default library, expand its node, right-click on the library and select **Active Library**. To load a new library, right-click on the parent node and select **Add Library** or click +. The Inventor Material Library is set as default.

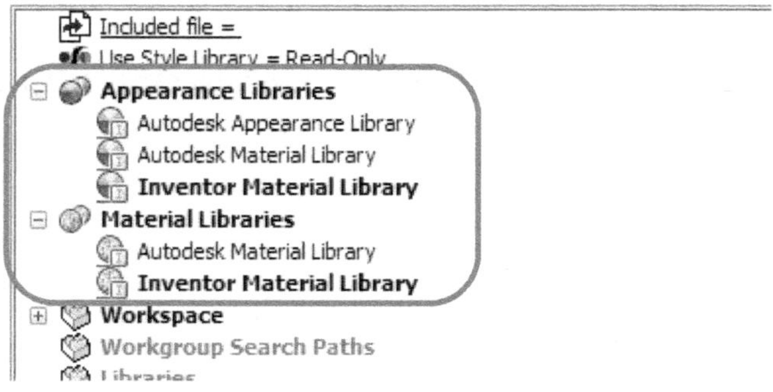

Figure 24–6

- The *Workspace*, *Workgroup Search Paths*, and *Libraries* categories specify locations for new files, files on a server/network drive, or the location of typically non-edited standard and custom parts, respectively. Additionally the *Frequently Used Subfolders* category can be used to add shortcuts to commonly used folders. To add libraries, right-click on the node and select **Add Path** or click +. Note the following when setting library paths:
  - Library paths are searched first. Use the ▲ and ▼ arrows to reorder the paths.
  - Parts placed from a library have a special tag. When searching, the software reads the tag to obtain the path. If no tag exists, the library is not searched.
  - Libraries can be added to a new project from other projects.
  - Libraries should not be renamed, to maintain existing references.
  - Since standard parts are not intended to change, parts in libraries cannot be edited.
  - Any part created or placed in a library folder is considered a library part and cannot be edited in the project.
  - Click to configure the Content Center Libraries.

  Note: *Only one workspace can be set in a project file. Additional options for adding paths are available on the shortcut menu when selecting any of the path categories.*

- The *Folder Options* category enables you to assign locations for design data, templates, and content center files that might be required when working in a project.
- Additional customization for a project can be made using the *Options* category in the project tree, as shown in Figure 24–7. These options enable you to control such things as the number of previous versions stored in the *OldVersions* folder, whether or not files in a project have unique names, identifies the project owner, etc.

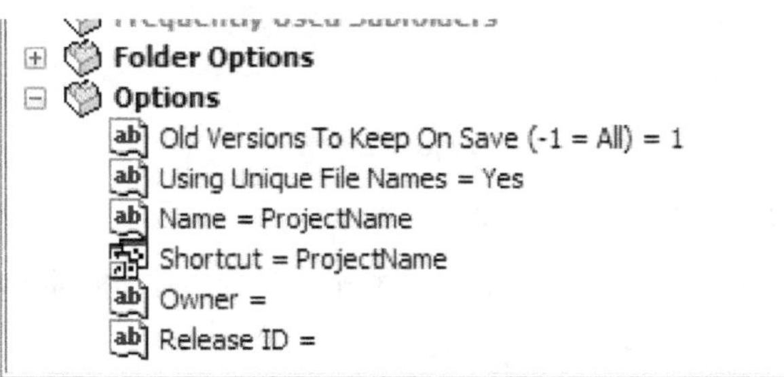

Figure 24–7

Note: *For more information on the Options, refer to the Help documentation.*

Search Sequence

When you open a file, the system searches through the project's Search Paths for referenced components in the following order: Library Paths (1), Workspace (2), Workgroup Search Paths (3), and the folder containing the file to be opened (4).

The search sequence flow chart is shown in Figure 24–8.

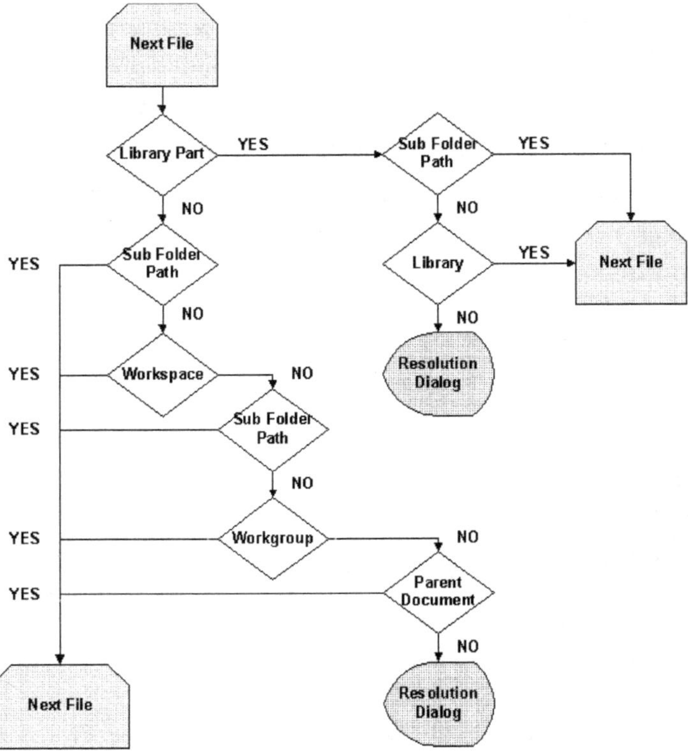

Figure 24–8

Note the following about the search sequence:

- When multiple paths are in a category, the order of listing determines the search order. Use the ▲ and ▼ arrows to reorder the paths.
- If files are found with the same name in multiple paths, the first file found is used.
- Paths can be added after a project has been started, but starting with the appropriate list helps avoid unresolved links.
- In general, the fewer search paths the better. For optimal performance, use a single workspace or workgroup location (plus libraries) per project, with relative paths (subfolders). This speeds file resolution and makes moving data easier.

Hint: Working with Subfolders

Note the following about subfolders:

- Do not define the subfolders of a project location as separate locations in the project. This causes file resolution problems that display red in the project's dialog box.
- When placing assembly components from a subfolder, the subfolder path (relative path) is saved as part of the assembly. When opening the assembly, the system combines the project's search location with this relative path to find components.
- Components moved into subfolders cannot be located because a relative subfolder path was not stored with the assembly. Use the *Resolve Link* dialog box to fix the failure.
- A flat directory structure (few subfolders) increases loading speed.

24.2 Resolving Links

If a referenced file cannot be found in the search paths of the active project, the *Resolve Link* dialog box opens, as shown in Figure 24–9. Use this dialog box to find the referenced file, to substitute another file, or to ignore the missing file.

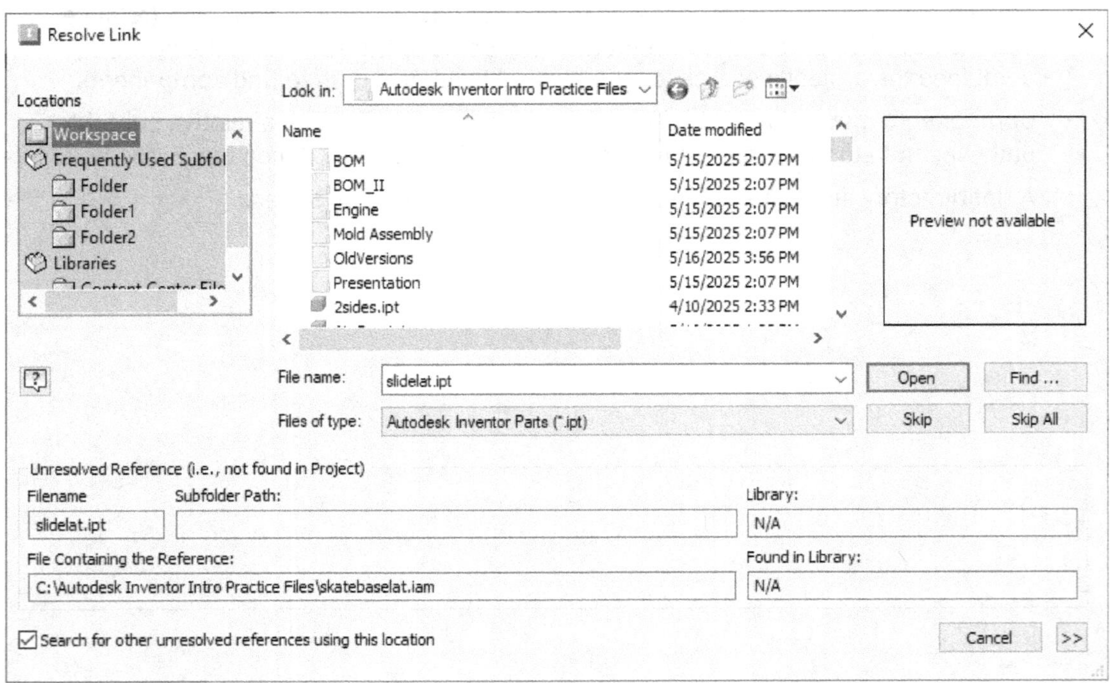

Figure 24–9

The *Resolve Link* dialog box displays the file location, folder, and file format. The operations on the right side of the dialog box are as follows:

Open

Opens a selected file that will resolve the failure. You can also double-click on the name of the file to open it.

Find...

Opens the *Find* dialog box, which enables you to search for a file based on selected criteria.

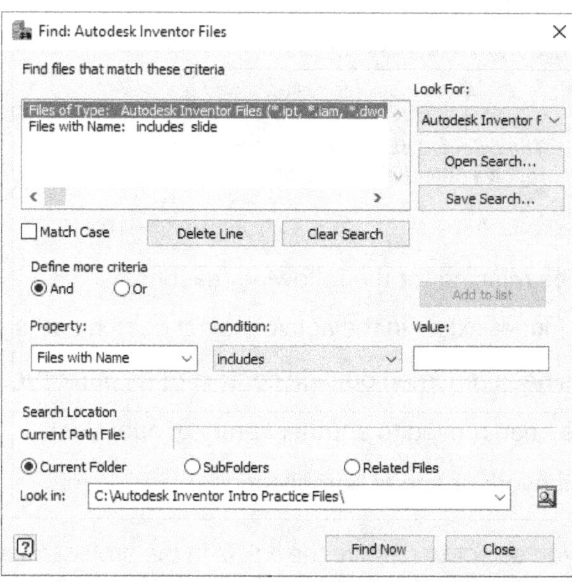

Skip

Skips the unresolved file and goes to the next file. The skipped file does not display in the assembly and any updates that depend on the unresolved component do not solve until the missing link is resolved. You can later replace the component in the assembly or resolve the link by right-clicking on the assembly name at the top of the Model browser and selecting **Resolve File**.

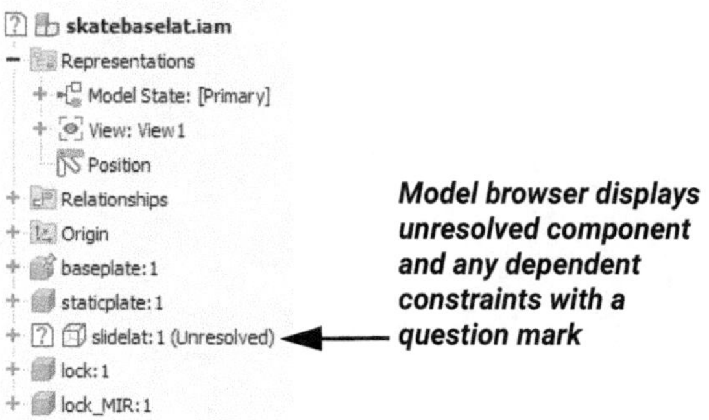

Skip All

Skips all unresolved files. All failed files display in the Model browser with a question mark icon and each should be individually resolved as described for individually skipped files.

The *Unresolved Reference* area in the *Resolve Link* dialog box displays information about the component that is not resolved (e.g., filename, path, etc.), as shown in Figure 24–10.

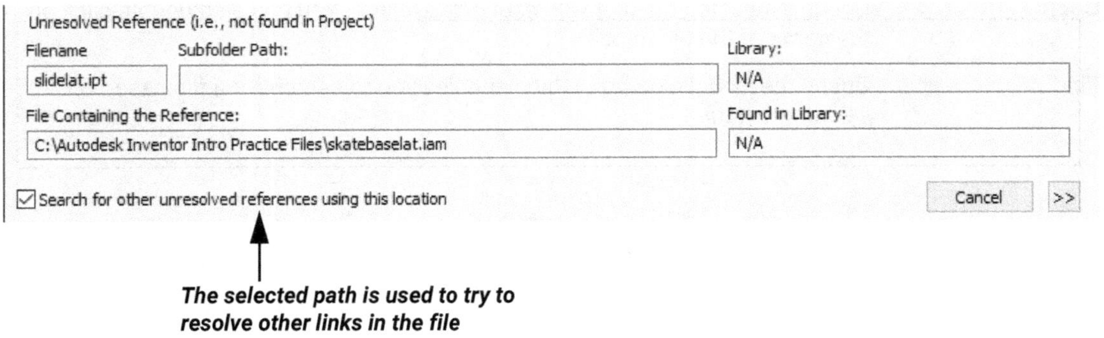

Unresolved Reference (i.e., not found in Project)
Filename: slidelat.ipt
Subfolder Path:
Library: N/A
File Containing the Reference: C:\Autodesk Inventor Intro Practice Files\skatebaselat.iam
Found in Library: N/A
Search for other unresolved references using this location
Cancel
>>

The selected path is used to try to resolve other links in the file

Figure 24–10

The file might be missing for the following reasons:

- The file no longer exists in the active project search paths.
- The file has been renamed outside context of its parent model.
- The file has been moved to another library or subfolder.
- There are network or server complications.

If the file that you select to resolve the link is in the project locations or their subfolders and you save the host file, the link is automatically resolved the next time you open the host file. If the file you select is not in the defined project location, you need to resolve the link each time you open the host file. To avoid this, the unresolved file(s) should be moved to one of the project search locations, or the project should be modified to include the file location.

Practice 24a
Create a Project File

Practice Objectives

- Create a new project that assigns and modifies various categories in the project file.
- Resolve a link for a file that was renamed outside the assembly and is therefore missing when the assembly is opened.

In this practice, you will create a new project file and resolve a link in the project.

Task 1: Create a project file.

1. Ensure that all files are closed in the current session prior to starting this practice. Projects cannot be set with files open.
2. Use one of the following methods to open the *Projects* dialog box. Once open, the active project (Intro to Modeling) displays with a checkmark to the left of its name.
   - On the *Home* page, click ⋮ (Projects and Settings)>**Settings**.
   - Click (Projects) in the Quick Access Toolbar at the top of the interface.
   - In the **File** menu, select **Manage>Projects**.
3. Right-click in the top section of the dialog box and select **New** or click **New** at the bottom of the dialog box. The *Inventor project wizard* dialog box opens.
4. Select **New Single User Project** and click **Next**.
5. Enter **Your_Name** in the *Name* field.
6. Click ... next to the *Project (Workspace) Folder* field. In the *Browse For Folder* dialog box, browse to the directory in which your training files are located.
7. Click **OK** to close the *Browse For Folder* dialog box.
8. Click **Finish** to create the project. The **<Your_Name>** project displays in the *Projects* dialog box and is set as the active project (as indicated by the adjacent checkmark).

Task 2: Assign workspace and libraries to the project file.

1. If a checkmark is not displaying next to the active project name. Double-click on **<Your_Name>** in the upper area of the dialog box to activate it. The lower area of the dialog box displays, as shown in Figure 24–11.
2. Expand the *Workspace* category in the project tree area.

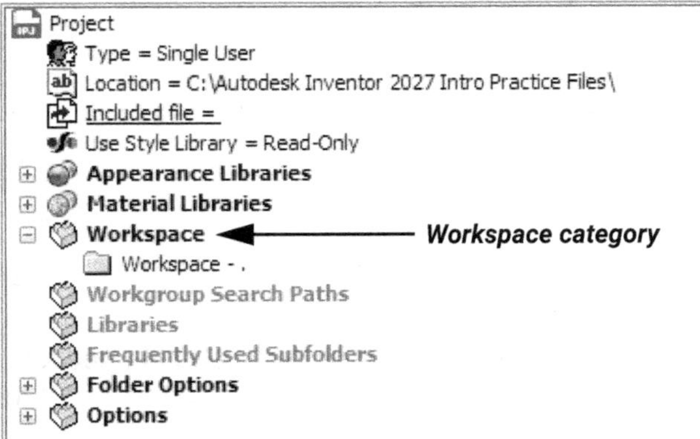

Figure 24–11

3. Select the **Workspace** node in the *Workspace* category, right-click, and select **Edit**.Click and browse to the *C:\Temp* directory, or click **Make New Folder** to create the directory if it does not already exist. Click **OK** to close the *Browse For Folder* dialog box.

   ***Note:** The temp directory is only assigned for this practice. Normally, project files would use a well-defined folder structure.*

4. Press <Enter> to apply the changes.
5. Select **Workgroup Search Paths** in the project tree area, right-click, and select **Add Path**.
6. Click . Browse to your practice files directory. Delete the **Workgroup** node name in the path, if displayed.
7. Click **OK** to close the *Browse For Folder* dialog box.
8. Press <Enter> to apply the changes.
9. Select **Libraries** in the project tree area, right-click, and select **Add Path**.
10. Click . Navigate to and select the following folder:
    - *C:\Users\Public\PublicDocuments\Autodesk\Inventor 2027\Catalog*
11. Select the software's *Catalog* folder in the *Browse For Folder* dialog box.
12. Click **OK** in the *Browse For Folder* dialog box.

13. Press <Enter> to apply the changes. The project tree should display similar to that shown in Figure 24–12.

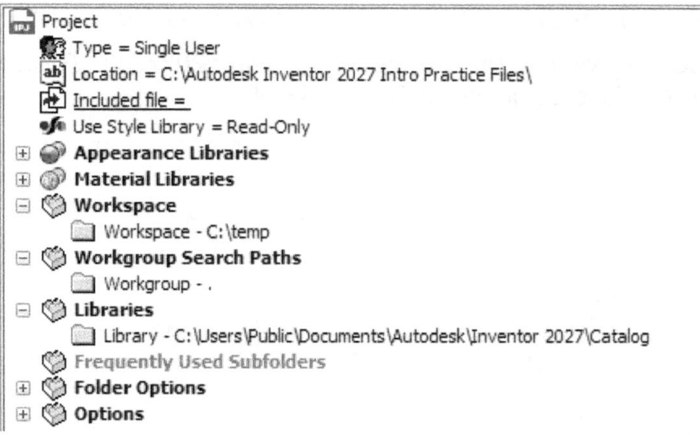

Figure 24–12

14. Expand the *Options* folder and select **Old Version To Keep On Save**.
15. Click on the right side of the project tree. You can also select the option a second time to edit its value.
16. Enter **2** in the field that displays and press <Enter>. This option controls the number of previous versions of the file to keep after a save operation. The default is one.
17. Click **Save** at the bottom of the dialog box to save your changes to the project.
18. Click **Done** to close the *Projects* dialog box.
19. On the *Home* page, expand the projects list, as shown in Figure 24–13. Scroll through the list of projects. Note that the **<Your_Name>** project is listed on the *Home* page and has a check mark adjacent to it on the drop-down list, both indicating that this is the active project.

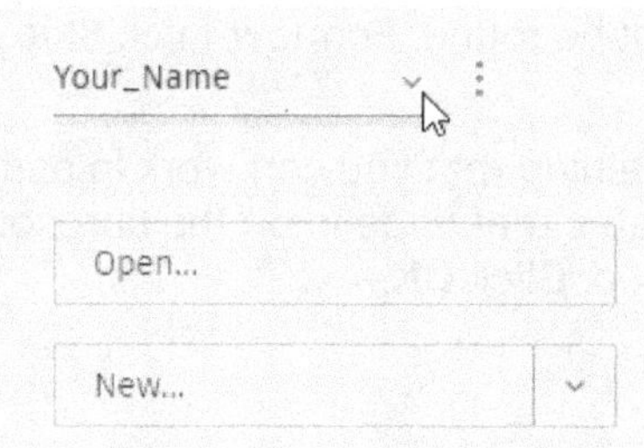

Figure 24–13

Task 3: Open an assembly and resolve the link.

1. Select **Open** on the *Home* page, **File** menu, or Quick Access Toolbar.
2. Select **Workgroup** to switch to the *C:\Autodesk Inventor 2027 Intro Practice Files* path. The *Open* dialog box displays, as shown in Figure 24–14.

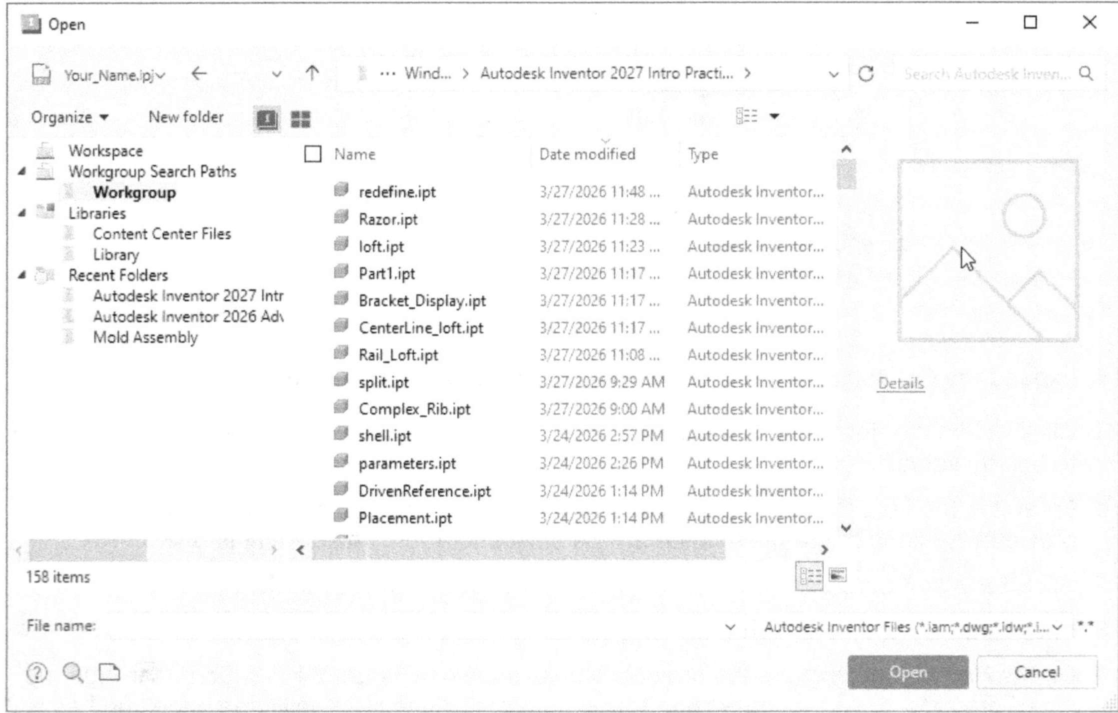

Figure 24–14

3. Select and open **skatebaselat.iam**. The *Resolve Link* dialog box opens and indicates that the **slidelat.ipt** part could not be found. For now, click **Skip** and continue opening the assembly.
4. A warning box displays explaining that you can work in assemblies with unresolved components. However, updates that depend on the unresolved component will not solve until components are resolved. Click **OK**.

5. The assembly displays in the graphics window. Note the missing part (**slidelat**) displays the icon, as shown in Figure 24–15, indicating that the part definition is missing.

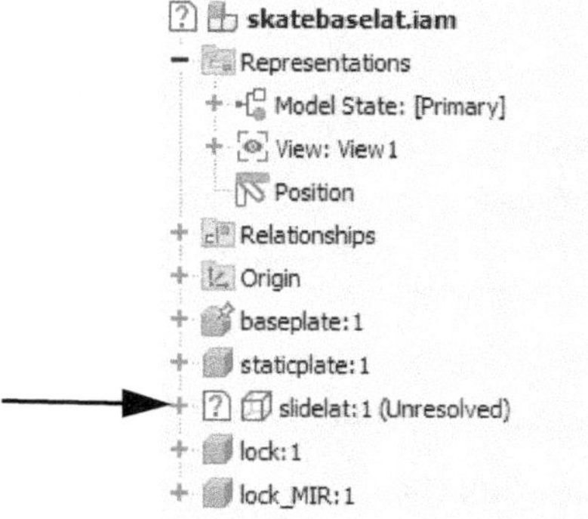

Figure 24–15

6. Right-click on **skatebaselat.iam** in the Model browser and select **Resolve File**.
7. The *Resolve Link* dialog box opens. Click **Find**. The *Find* dialog box opens.
8. Select **Files with Name** in the *Property* drop-down list. Select **includes** in the *Condition* drop-down list. Enter **slide** in the *Value* field. Click **Add to List**.
9. Set the *Look in* folder to your course directory if not already set. The *Find* dialog box should appear as shown in Figure 24–16.

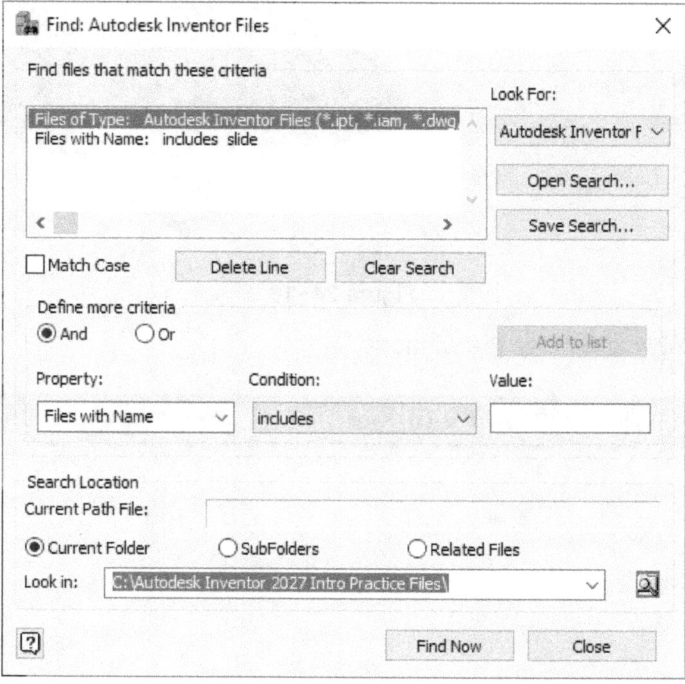

Figure 24–16

10. Click **Find Now** to perform the search. The *Autodesk Inventor Files Found* dialog box opens, as shown in Figure 24–17, indicating that files were found.

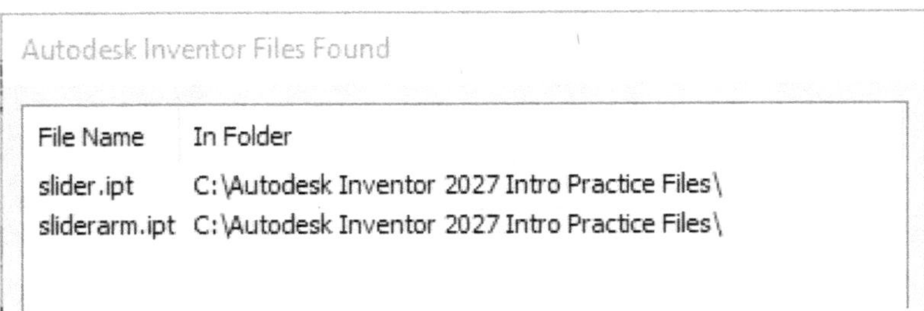

Figure 24–17

11. Select **slider.ipt** in the list and click **OK**.
12. Close the *Find* dialog box. The assembly displays in the graphics window, as shown in Figure 24–18. Note that the filename in the Model browser is now displayed correctly.

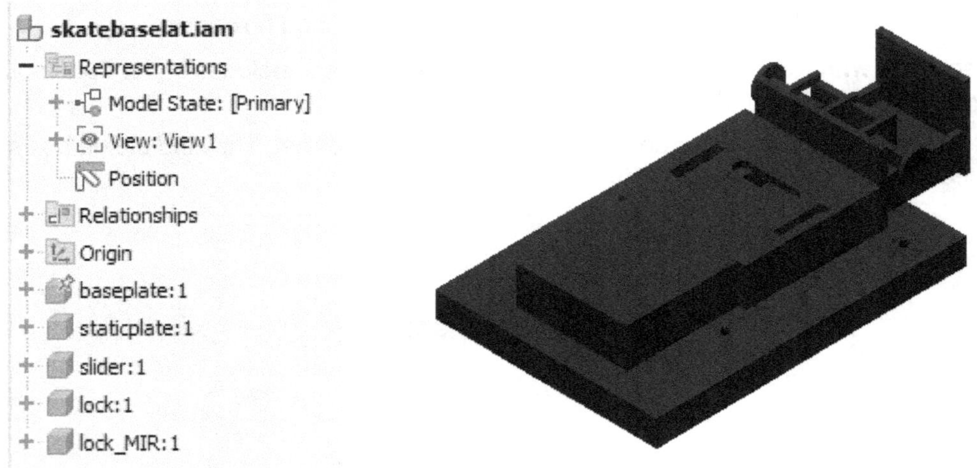

Figure 24–18

13. Save the assembly and close the window.

End of practice

Chapter Review Questions

1. What is the primary purpose of projects in the Autodesk Inventor software? (Select all that apply.)
   a. To set default templates for new files.
   b. To manage file locations and links between related files.
   c. To control default text styles, dimension format, etc.
   d. To define a search sequence for the projects folders.

2. You can change the active project while an Autodesk Inventor file is open.
   a. True
   b. False

3. Which file extension is used to store the information in a project file?
   a. .IPT
   b. .IPN
   c. .IPJ
   d. .IPK

4. Which command sequence is used to open the *Projects* dialog box? (Select all that apply.)

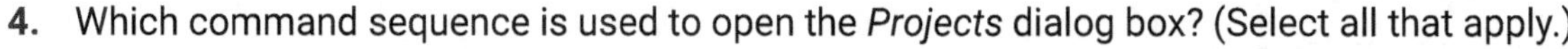

   a. On the *Home* page, click (Projects and Settings)>**Settings**.
   b. In the *Create New File* dialog box, select **Projects**.
   c. In the *Open* dialog box, select click (Projects Settings).
   d. In the **File** menu, select **Manage** and click .
   e. In the *Tools* tab>*Options* panel, click .

5. Which of the following can be customized in the Project tree to create an Autodesk Inventor project file? (Select all that apply.)
    a. Project's directory location
    b. Model names that reference the project file
    c. Library locations
    d. Active Material library
    e. Default Material setting
    f. Template folder location
    g. Number of versions to keep when saving
    h. Content Center folder location

6. All of the missing links must be resolved to open and edit an assembly.
    a. True
    b. False

7. When a component in an assembly is missing during retrieval, what actions can be done to resolve the failure? (Select all that apply.)
    a. Open an alternate file to replace the failed file.
    b. Skip the failed file.
    c. Delete the failed file.
    d. Find the failed file.

Command Summary

Button	Command	Location
	Projects	• **Quick Access Toolbar** • **Home Page:** Projects and Settings • **Dialog Box:** *Open* • **Dialog Box:** *New* • **File Menu:** Manage

Chapter

25

Drawing Basics

A drawing file is used to document the 3D geometry that is created in either part or assembly models in a 2D format. To begin creating a drawing, you must select and add drawing views that best communicate how the 3D geometry is to be created. Learning how to create and select the view types (e.g., base, projected, or section) enables you to efficiently create accurate drawings of your models.

Learning Objectives

- Create a new drawing based on a drawing template.
- Identify and add the available view types to a drawing file to appropriately document model geometry.
- Delete and suppress drawing views.
- Edit existing drawing views to change the properties that were defined during view creation.
- Replace a current drawing model with an alternate model.

25.1 Creating a New Drawing

Once your part or assembly has been designed, the next step is to create a 2D drawing. The shape, dimensions, and orientation of the parts or assemblies have already been defined in Part or Assembly mode. A drawing file is where this information is taken to create the required views. The components are not actually contained in a drawing file. There is a link between the drawing file and the source model (e.g., part, assembly, or presentation file). If a change is made to the source model, all drawing views that reference it automatically update.

The Autodesk® Inventor® software supports the .IDW and .DWG drawing file extensions. Files with an .IDW extension are native files and are typically used for documenting files. Files with a .DWG extension are typically used if the drawing is going be viewed by downstream users (shop personnel, managers, customers, etc.) using the AutoCAD® software. You can save an .IDW file as .DWG or save a .DWG as .IDW, if required.

The first step in creating a drawing is to start a new file based on a drawing template and optional sheet format. Sheet formats are available for the default Autodesk standard drawing templates (as shown in Figure 25–1) and can be included in any custom drawing templates your company has defined.

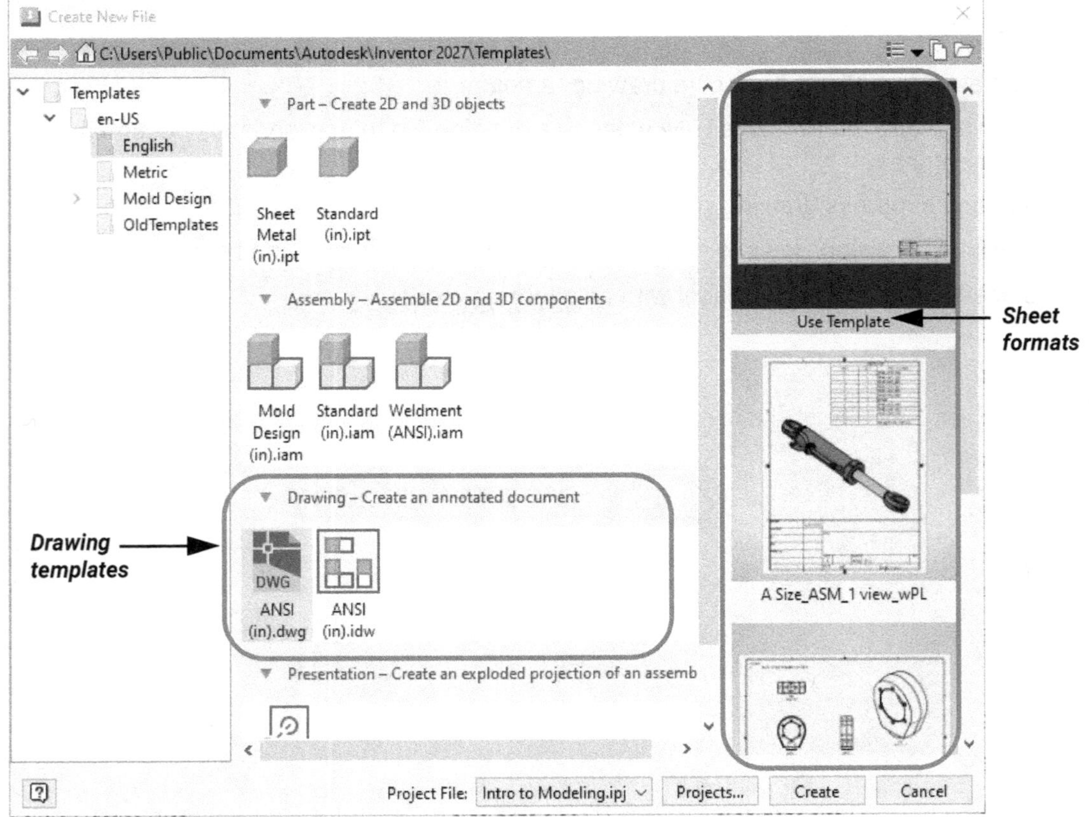

Figure 25–1

You can create a drawing using any of the following methods:

- On the *Home* page, click **New**. In the *Create New File* dialog box, select a .DWG or .IDW template from the *Drawing* area and click **Create**. If the selected template has any sheet formats assigned to it, they will be listed vertically along the right-hand side of the dialog box. Select a sheet format or simply leave the **Use Template** option selected at the top of the list to create the drawing with an empty sheet.
- In the **File** menu, expand **New**. In the expanded list, you can choose to create a drawing using the default template with the empty sheet format, or click **New** to access the *Create New File* dialog box to select a template and sheet format.
- Click (New) in the Quick Access Toolbar to open the *Create New File* dialog box and select the required template and sheet format.
- Expand (New) in the Quick Access Toolbar and expand the **Drawing** option. In the expanded list, you can select the sheet format that is required.

Once a new drawing is created the drawing environment displays with the following:

- The *Place Views* tab is active. It contains tools to create views, sheets, and drafting views.
- The Model browser contains a *Drawing Resources* folder that contains sheet formats, borders, title blocks, sketched symbols, and AutoCAD blocks.

The five drawing resources are as follows:

Sheet Formats	Displays the default formats in the selected drawing template file. These formats can contain title blocks, borders, and views.
Borders	Displays the default border and any user-defined borders.
Title Blocks	Displays the default and user-defined title blocks.
Sketched Symbols	Displays 2D symbols that can be added to a drawing file.
AutoCAD Blocks	Only available for DWG files. Lists any blocks added to the DWG file in the AutoCAD software. AutoCAD blocks cannot be created in the Autodesk Inventor software, but can be inserted into the current sheet.

25.2 Base Views

The first view that is added to a new drawing must be a Base view. It is used as the reference view when placing any additional views that are used to document the drawing model.

How To: Create the Base View

1. In the *Create* panel, click (Base). The *Drawing View* dialog box opens, as shown in Figure 25–2.

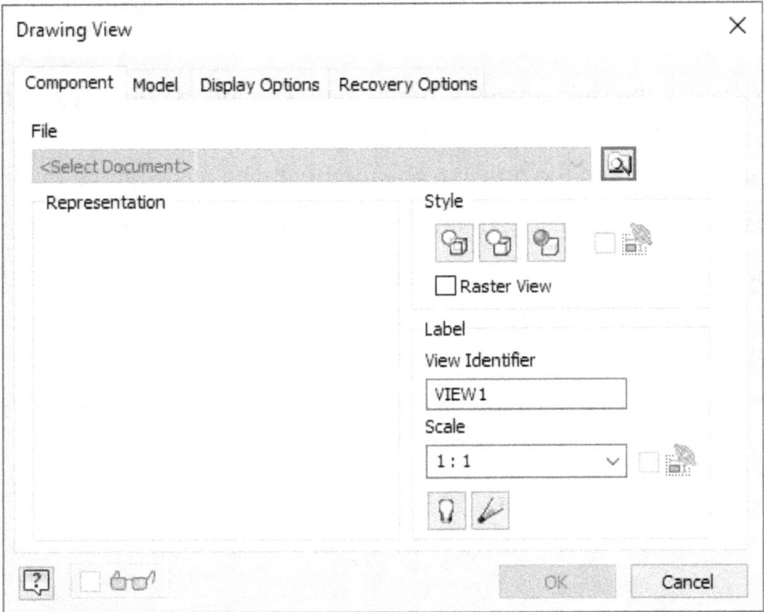

Figure 25–2

2. If a model was active when the drawing was created, it is automatically set as the drawing model in the *File* area. If no model is listed in the *File* area, or if you want to change it, click browse () and select a model to use in the drawing.
3. As soon as a model is assigned in the *Drawing View* dialog box, a base view is placed in a temporary position on the drawing sheet. You may need to move the *Drawing View* dialog box so that it doesn't interfere with the drawing sheet. You can select on the view and drag it to locate on the sheet; however, in a subsequent step (once the scale is set) you will learn how to reorient the model.

4. Select representation(s) of the file to be used in the view, as required.
   - For part and assembly models, you can select a *Model State*, *Design View*, or *Position View* representation that can be used in the drawing view, as shown in Figure 25–3. The representations must pre-exist in the model.
   - Maintain the default as **Primary** if no representation is required.
   - Enable the (Design View) option to update the design view if changes are made in the referenced model or assembly (i.e., sets the view as associative).

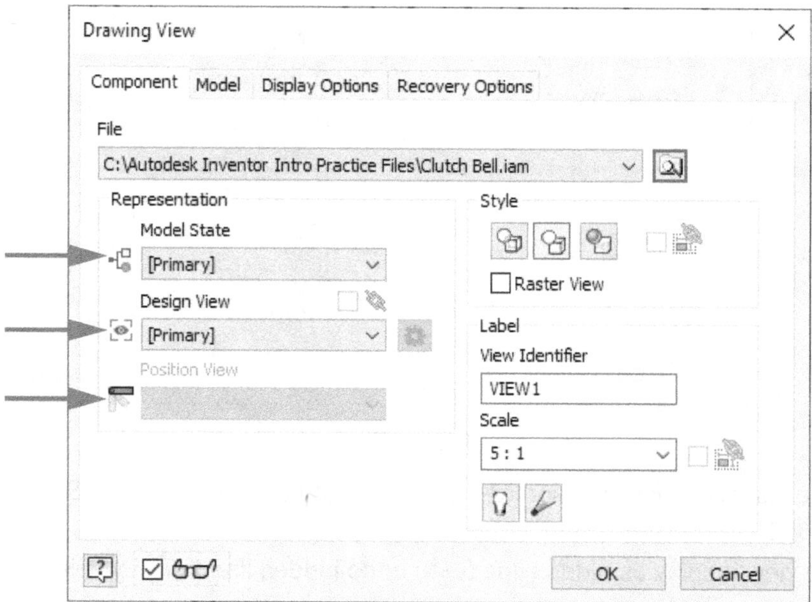

Figure 25–3

Hint: Representation View Types

Consider the following:

- The settings ( ) associated with design views can be used further customize how a selected design view appears in the new view. You can enable the **Camera View** option to disables the ability to set the view orientation and uses the saved view that was stored in the model's design view. The **Include 3D Annotations** option can be enabled so that any 3D annotations that exist in the model's design view will be shown in the view.
- Model states and position views are not discussed in this guide. They enable you to create custom views of components in an assembly to showcase varying manufacturing states or varied positions of components in a mechanism.

- For a presentation file, you can select a snapshot view and whether to display the component's trails, as shown in Figure 25–4.

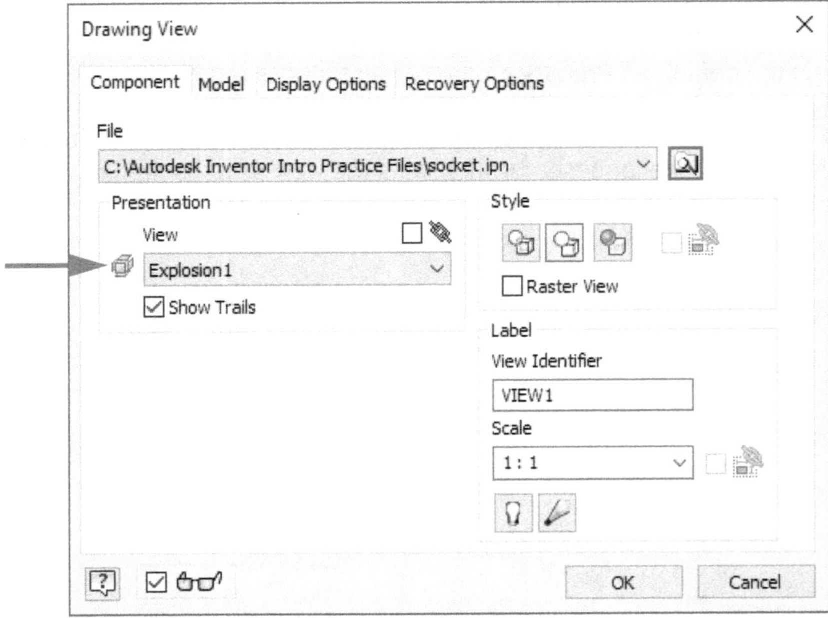

Figure 25–4

5. Assign the visual display style for the new view using the options in the *Style* area. Consider the following:
   - Set the view display as hidden line ( ) or no hidden line ( ) by selecting the required option.
   - Set the view as shaded by toggling the (Shaded) option. Shaded views use the model's lighting style.
   - Select **Raster View** to create the base view so that it remains a raster view once placed.
6. Set the scale of the view in the *Scale* area.
7. (Optional) Select (Toggle Label Visibility) in the *Label* area to display the view name and its scale value below the drawing view.

   Note: *Select (Edit View Label) to edit the format of the label.*

8. (Optional) Use the *Model* and *Display Options* tabs to further customize the view.
9. Modify the initial orientation of the view using either the view or ViewCube manipulators. The manipulations are shown in Figure 25–5 and are described below. By default, the base view is displayed with a FRONT view orientation.

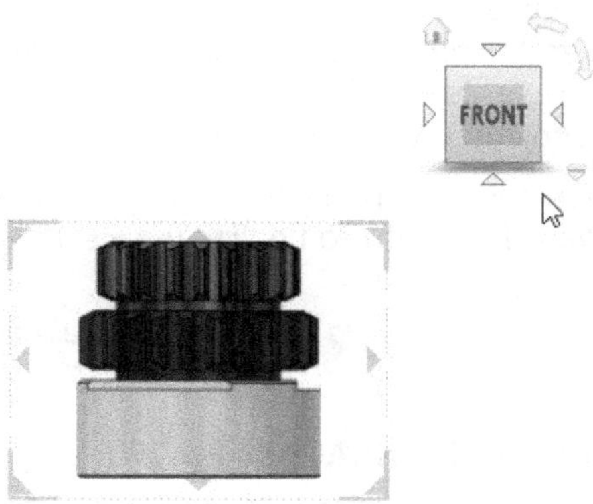

Figure 25–5

- Select alternate faces, edges, or corners on the ViewCube to reorient the model.
- Select the arrows in the right-hand corner of the ViewCube to rotate the view.
- Select (home icon) on the ViewCube to reorient the model to its default isometric view. The expanded ViewCube options also provide access to setting either Orthographic or Perspective views.
- Select inside the view's frame and drag the view to reposition it on the sheet.
- Select any of the four arrow manipulators on the sides of the view to reorient to a perpendicular orientation.
- Select and drag any of the four corner arrow manipulators to scale the view.

Hint: User-Defined Orientation Views

To create a user-defined orientation, click (menu icon) on the ViewCube and select **Custom View Orientation**. A *Custom View* tab opens, as shown in Figure 25–6. You can use this to zoom, pan, and rotate the component to create the view you want to display in the drawing view. You can also change the view to a perspective view. The majority of the icons in this toolbar are the same as those used when modeling. Consider using the **Rotate at Angle** command to obtain more precise orientations. Once the view orientation has been defined, click (Finish Custom View) in the *Exit* panel. The view updates to the custom orientation that was set.

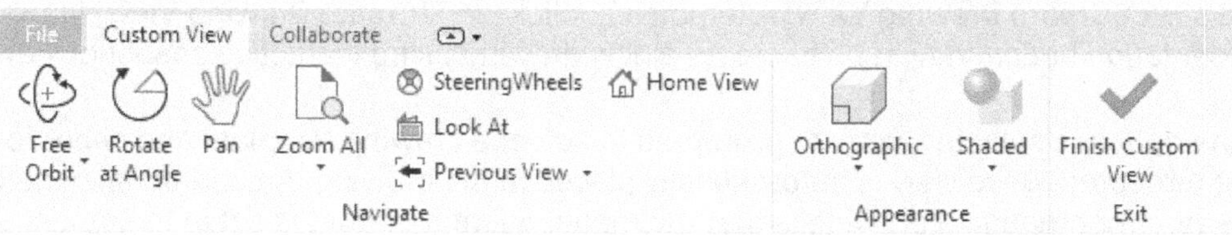

Figure 25–6

10. (Optional) Once you have placed a Base view, you can continue placing projected views by selecting above/below or to the right/left of the Base view. Alternatively, you can drag an orthographic view off the Base view and locate it anywhere on the sheet. These procedures are also explained in the Projected Views section.
11. After locating the base view (and any projected views), right-click and select **OK (Enter)** or click **OK** in the *Drawing View* dialog box to finalize the view(s).

Note: Click in the Drawing View dialog box to obtain Help on the options in the Drawing View dialog box.

Creating Drawings Directly from Models

As an alternative to creating a new drawing and then adding model views you can also create a drawing directly from a part, assembly, or presentation file.

- For a part or assembly model, right-click on the model name node in the Model browser and select **Create Drawing View**, as shown in Figure 25–7.

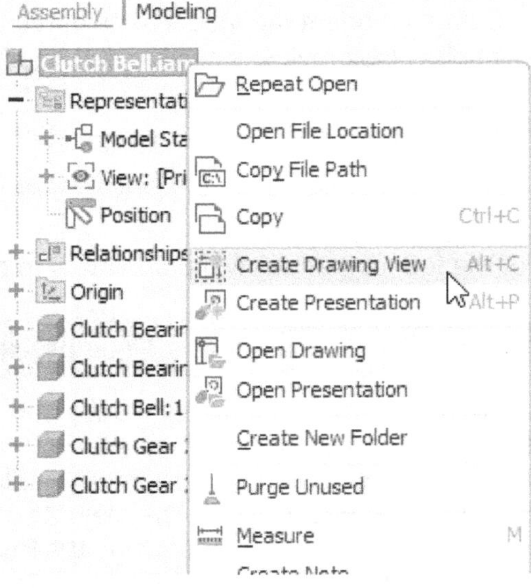

Figure 25–7

- For a presentation file, in the Snapshot Views browser, right-click on the thumbnail image and select **Create Drawing View**. Alternatively, click (Create Drawing View) in the *Presentation* or *Edit View* tabs to create a new drawing using the active snapshot view.

Once the option is selected, you are prompted to select a drawing template and sheet format, and the temporary Base view is automatically placed in the drawing. An additional benefit of this method for creating a drawing is that the model orientation that is set in the model at the time of drawing creation is the default orientation used in the Base view.

25.3 Projected Views

A projected view is a view that is created by projecting from a parent view. The parent view must already exist. You can create eight possible views from one view: four orthographic and four isometric.

- The orthographic views are the top, bottom, and side views, as shown in Figure 25–8. These views align with the parent Base view and are dependent on that view.
- The isometric views are the diagonal views, as shown in Figure 25–8. These views are not dependent on the location of the parent Base view and can be relocated anywhere on the sheet.

Figure 25–8

Once a base view is located, you can continue immediately with projected view placement without having to explicitly create Projected views. With the *Drawing View* dialog box still open during Base view creation, create Projected views using any of the following techniques:

- Drag off of the Base view in any of the eight directions shown in Figure 25–9. Select with the left mouse button to place the new Projected view.
- Select the arrows around the Base view outline to create Projected views, as shown in Figure 25–9.

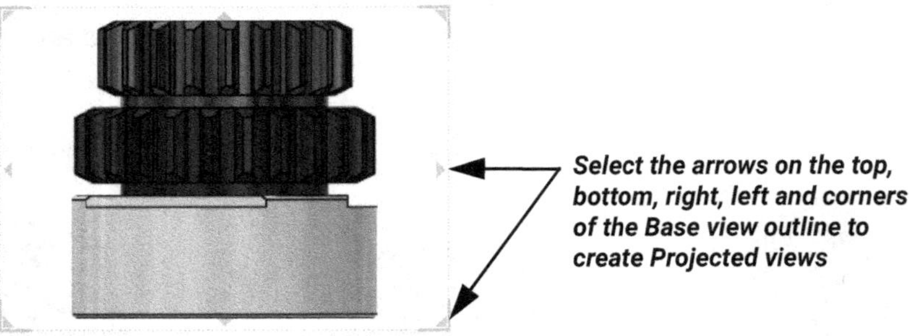

Figure 25–9

How To: Create a Projected View

1. Click (Projected) in the *Create* panel.
2. Select the base view to be referenced. Alternatively, select the base view, right-click and select **Projected View**.
3. Move the cursor in the direction of the new view. Note the preview of the view.
4. Select the placement location of the view using the left mouse button. A rectangle is placed to mark the position of the view.
5. Continue moving the crosshairs to new locations and selecting points for each view you want to create. A rectangle is placed on the screen to indicate each additional view.
6. Right-click and select **Create** to generate the views.

Hint: Creating Projected Views During Base View Creation

When creating a Projected view using the (Projected) option, you will not be provided with the *Drawing View* dialog box. Therefore, the scale of all projected views is the same as the parent view. To modify the projected view's scale, right-click on the view and select **Edit View**. In the *Drawing View* dialog box, clear the (Scale from Base) option in the *Label* area to allow you to set an independent scale value.

25.4 Raster Views

Before a precise view is generated it displays as a raster view until finalized. Views can also be created so that they remain raster views, or you can set an existing view to be a raster view. The purpose of a raster view is to help improve drawing view calculation times when working on complex drawing models. This is done by temporarily breaking the associativity with the drawing model. Consider the following:

- You can continue to annotate and work in a drawing with raster views present. Note that some features of the drawing are not available or work differently for raster views.
- Changes made to the model will not update in raster views unless the view is set as **Precise**.

A raster view can be easily identified in a drawing by its highlighted green corners of the view outline, as shown in Figure 25–10.

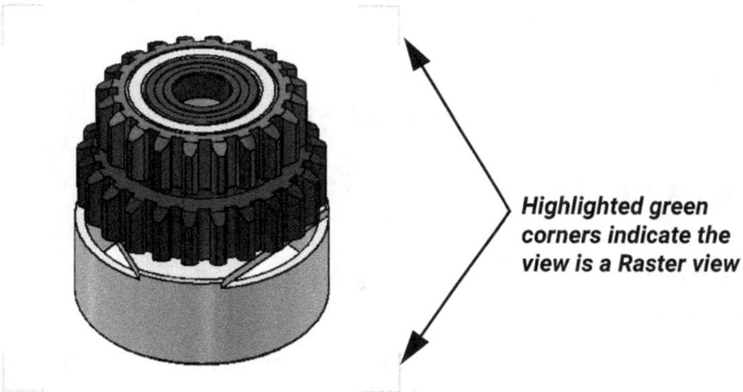

Figure 25–10

To create a new view as a raster view:

- Select **Raster View** in the *Drawing View* dialog box so that the new view is generated and maintained as a raster view.

There are multiple ways to convert views to raster views:

- Right-click on the drawing sheet and select **Make All Views Raster**.
- Hover over a view on the drawing sheet to activate its view outline, and then right-click and select **Make View Raster**.
- Right-click on a view name in the Model browser and select **Make View Raster**.

A raster view displays with a red line through it in the Model browser ( ) and with green corners in the graphics window. To make a raster view precise, use the same techniques listed above for converting existing views and select **Make View Precise** or **Make All Views Precise**.

> ***Note:*** *Raster views can be disabled by clearing the* ***Enable background updates*** *option in the Drawing tab of the Application Options dialog box.*

25.5 Auxiliary Views

Auxiliary views are similar to orthographic views. Orthographic views are created to the left, right, above, or below a parent view. Auxiliary views are created diagonally from a parent view based on a selected edge, as shown in Figure 25–11.

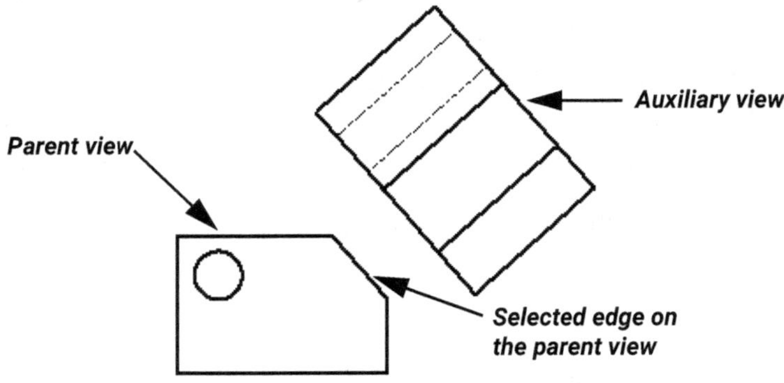

Figure 25–11

How To: Create an Auxiliary View

1. In the *Create* panel, click (Auxiliary). Alternatively, right-click on the parent view and select **Auxiliary View**.
2. Select the parent view that the auxiliary view is going to reference. The *Auxiliary View* dialog box opens as shown in Figure 25–12. Alternatively, select the parent view, right-click and select **Auxiliary View**. The cursor displays as a cursor with a line symbol ( ).

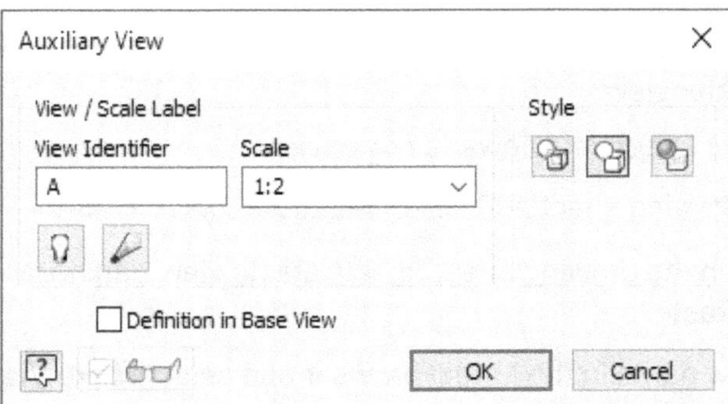

Figure 25–12

3. Set the options in the dialog box as required.
4. Select a line in the reference view as the basis for the view.
5. Move the cursor and select the placement location of the view using the left mouse button.

25.6 Section Views

A section view displays the component with a cutaway, as shown in Figure 25–13. A projection view line, also known as a section line, is drawn on the parent view to locate the cut. Both the resulting section line and section view will display with labels that describe the section number and sheet zone. In the case of the section line, the sheet zone identifies where the section view is located, and in the case of the section view, the sheet zone identifies the zone of the section line.

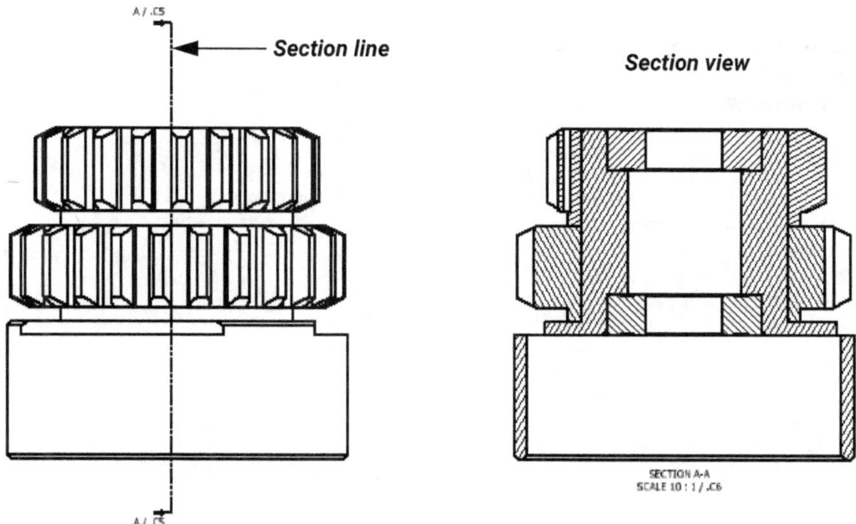

Figure 25–13

How To: Create a Section View

1. In the *Create* panel, click (Section). Alternatively, select a view, right-click and select **Section View** to start the command.
2. Select the view that the section view is going to reference.
3. Select points on the reference view to draw the section line.

4. Right-click and select **Continue**. The *Section View* dialog box opens, as shown in Figure 25–14.

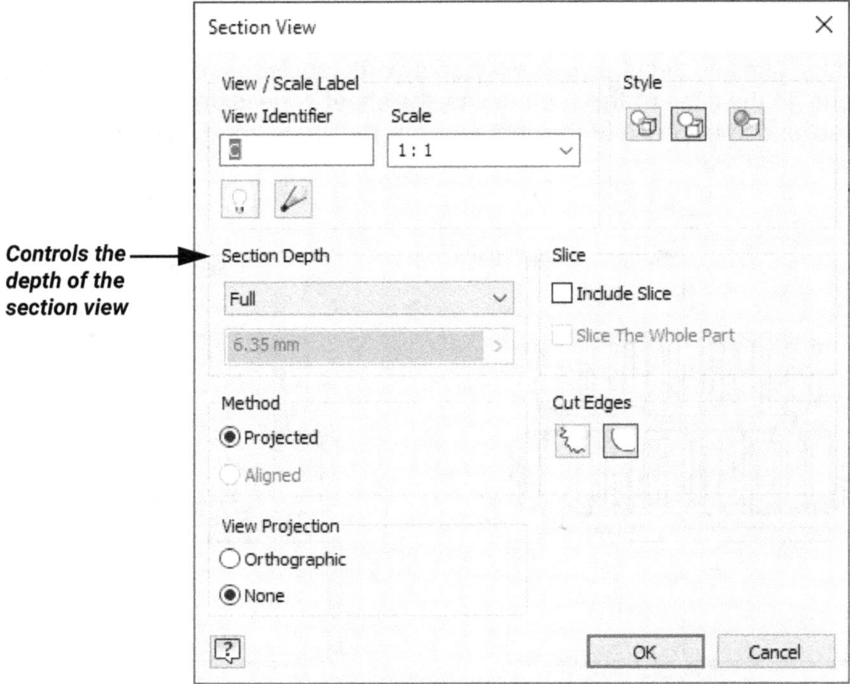

Figure 25–14

5. Set the options in the dialog box, as required.
   - In the *View/Scale Label* area, enter a name for the view, select/enter its scale value, and control its label visibility ( ) and label text ( ).
   - Set the display setting for the view in the *Style* area.
   - Select the section depth (**Full** or **Distance**) of the view in the *Section Depth* area.
   - (Optional) Set whether to **Include Slice** and **Slice The Whole Part** (part drawing) or **Slice All Parts** (assembly drawing).
   - In the *Method* area, define the method of projecting the section view. **Projected** is the default if a single line entity represents the section line. If multiple section lines are sketched, you can select between **Projected** or **Aligned**.
   - Define how the break lines for partially sectioned components will display using the options in the *Cut Edges* area. The options enable you to select a smooth ( ) or jagged ( ) break. The default option is smooth.
   - In the *View Projection* area, select whether the new view remains aligned with the parent view (**Orthographic**) or breaks the default alignment (**None**).

6. Select the placement location of the view using the left mouse button. A section view is automatically aligned with the parent view by default. To break the alignment, press and hold <Ctrl> when dragging and left-click to locate the section view or right-click and clear the **Align View** option.

- A sketch that is associated with a view, can be used as the section line for a section view. To use a sketch as the section line, the sketch must already exist and be associated with the parent view. Once created, right-click the sketch in the Model browser and select **Create Section View**. The *Section View* dialog box opens to define the view.

  Note: *To edit a sketched line, select it, right-click and select* ***Edit****. Any section view that is based on the sketch is updated with the changes.*

- To change the section properties, right-click on the view and select **Edit Section Properties**.
- To change the hatch patterns on section views, right-click on the pattern and select **Edit**. The default pattern is set in the Drafting Standards. Hatch patterns can also be assigned to material styles in the *Style and Standard Editor*.
- By default, when you add the section line for a section view, it is simply placed based on the sketch location. Once you have placed the section view, you can edit its location to fully locate it using standard dimension and constraint techniques. Hover the cursor over the section line, right-click, and select **Edit**. The *Sketch* tab becomes the active tab. In the Constrain panel, click (Dimension) and dimension the section line to locate it. Alternatively, you can use constraint options. Once constrained, click **Finish Sketch**.

  Note: *The sheet zone in the section view label will vary depending on where you placed the section view on the sheet.*

25.7 Detail Views

Detail views typically enlarge an area of a parent view to display the information more clearly, as shown in Figure 25–15. Both the resulting detail circle and detail view will display with labels that describe the detail number and sheet zone. In the case of the detail circle, the sheet zone identifies where the detail view is located, and in the case of the detail view, the sheet zone identifies the zone of the detail circle.

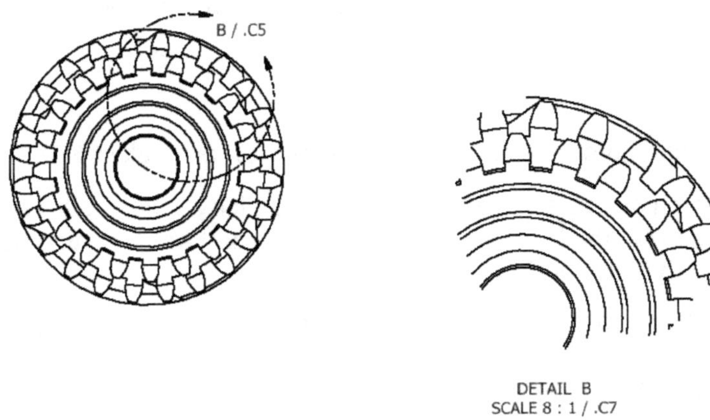

Figure 25–15

How To: Create a Detail View

1. In the *Create* panel, click (Detail). Alternatively, you can also right-click on the parent view and select **Create View>Detail View**.

2. Select the view that the detail view is going to reference. The *Detail View* dialog box opens, as shown in Figure 25–16. Alternatively, select the base view, right-click and select **Detail View**.

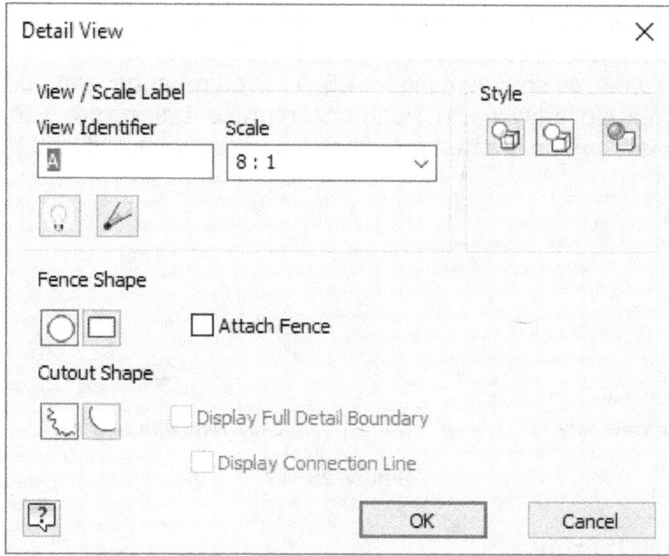

Figure 25–16

3. Set the options in the dialog box, as required. In detail views, you can have a circular or rectangular fence shape. You also can have jagged or smooth cutout lines. Additionally you can change the view style and customize the view identifier.
4. Select a point on the view from which the detail is taken to specify the center point of the fence.
5. Move the cursor away from the center point. A circle displays on the screen. Move the cursor to determine the size of the area that should be included in the detail view, and select a point.
6. Select the placement location of the view using the left mouse button.

- After a detail view is placed, you can edit the Fence Shape and Cutout Shape by right-clicking on the detail view circle and selecting **Edit Detail Properties**.
- To attach a detail view's fence to geometry in the parent view, select the center green dot on the detail view's fence, right-click, and select **Attach**. This prevents the fence from shifting during model changes.

  Note: *The sheet zone in the detail view label will vary depending on where you placed the detail view on the sheet.*

25.8 Overlay Views

You can document assembly motion or component visibility using overlay views. These views use positional representations, or model states to display an assembly in multiple positions or visibilities in a single view, as shown in Figure 25–17. You must have at least two positional representations to create overlay views. Positional representations are discussed as advanced topics. The overlay view can be created for unbroken base, projected, and auxiliary views.

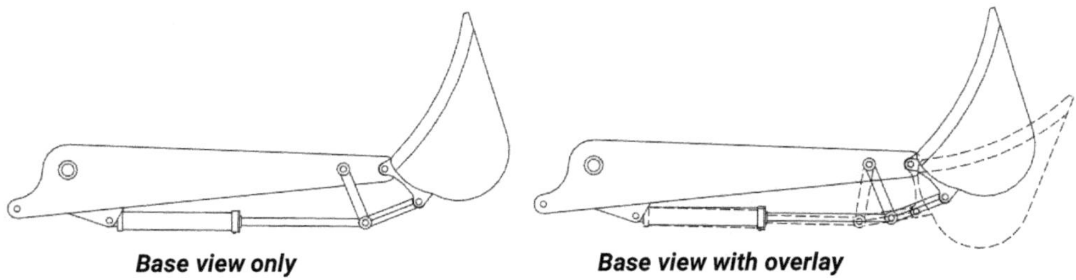

Figure 25–17

How To: Create an Overlay

1. Create a base view.
2. In the *Create* panel, click (Overlay) and select the view. Alternatively, you can right-click on the parent view and select **Create View>Overlay View**. The *Overlay View* dialog box opens, as shown in Figure 25–18.

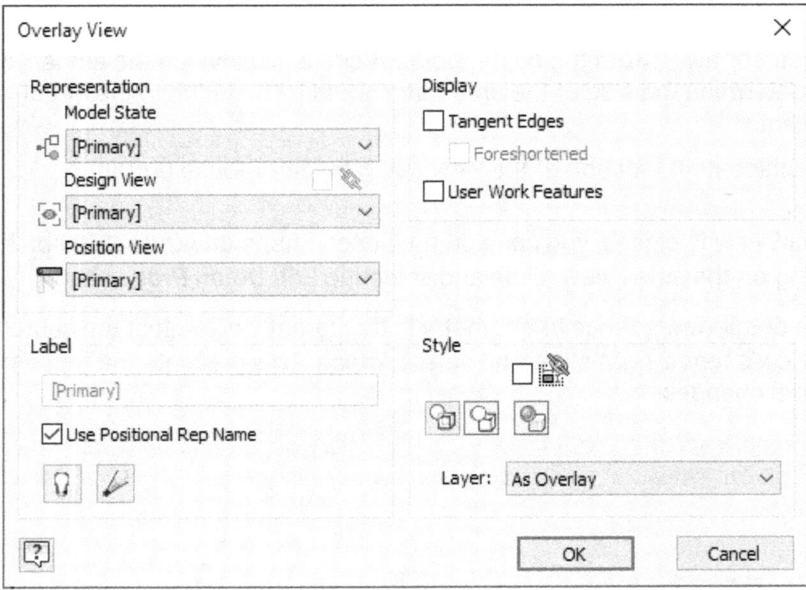

Figure 25–18

3. Select the positional representation, model state, or design view to use.
4. Configure any other options, as required.
5. Click **OK**.

25.9 Draft Views

Draft views enable you to create independent sketches that can provide additional information, as shown in Figure 25–19. The draft view can contain information on the drawing model, be unique, or can also be used to add AutoCAD .DWG data into a drawing.

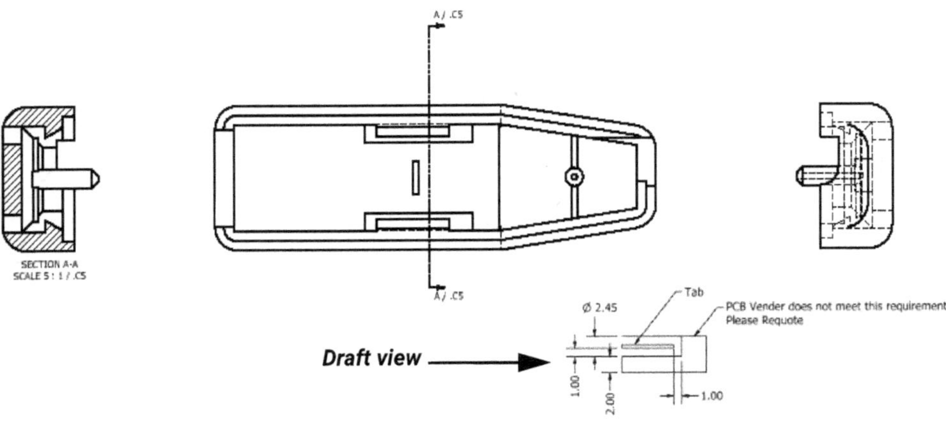

Figure 25–19

How To: Create a Draft View

1. In the *Create* panel, click (Draft). The *Draft View* dialog box opens, as shown in Figure 25–20.

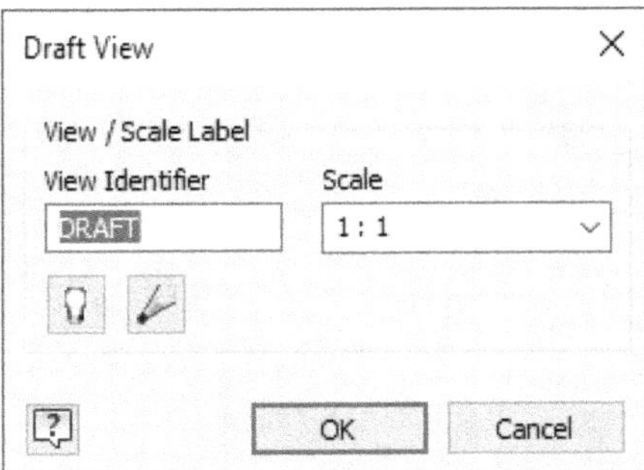

Figure 25–20

2. Set the options as required to define the view. Click **OK**. The *Sketch* tab becomes active.
3. Use the standard sketching tools to create the entities that are to be represented in the Draft view. To import AutoCAD .DWG data, use (ACAD) in the *Insert* panel or copy and paste from an AutoCAD drawing file.
4. In the *Exit* panel, click **Finish Sketch** to complete the view.

25.10 Break Views

A break view displays portions of the drawing model with material removed. You can change any view to a break view, as shown in Figure 25–21.

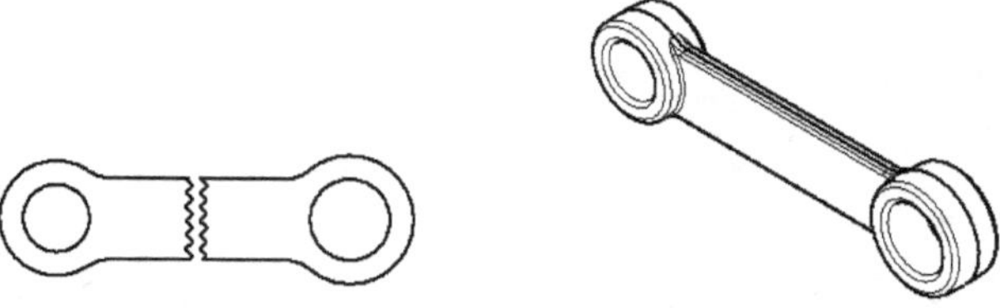

Figure 25–21

How To: Create a Break View

1. In the *Modify* panel, click (Break). Alternatively, you can right-click on the parent view and select **Create View>Break**.
2. Select the view to be broken. The *Break* dialog box opens, as shown in Figure 25–22.

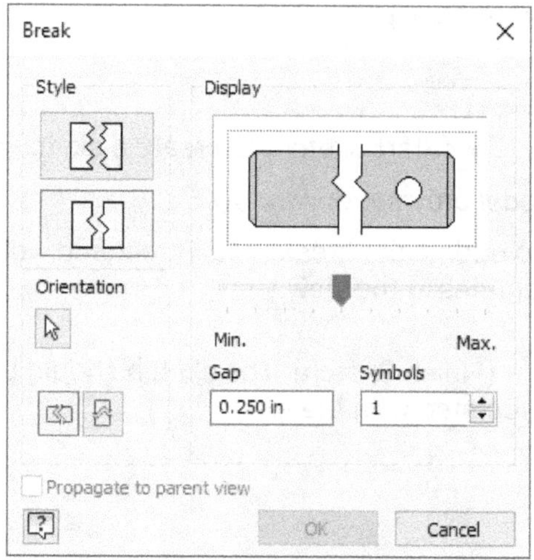

Figure 25–22

3. Set the options as required. You can control the location and size of the breaks and appearance of the break lines. A view can have multiple breaks.
4. Select a point on the view where you want the break to begin, and select a point on the view where you want the break to end. The Break view is automatically created.

   Note: *To control the location of the break view, you can add dimensions to it. Edit the sketch under the Break view listed in the Model browser to add dimensions to the break lines. Alternatively, you can start a break view and select an existing sketch with two dimensioned parallel lines (horizontal or vertical) to create a break view.*

25.11 Break Out Views

A break out view is a view of the drawing model with a portion of the components removed. This type of view is used to expose areas hidden by assembly components and is created from an existing drawing view. An example is shown in Figure 25–23.

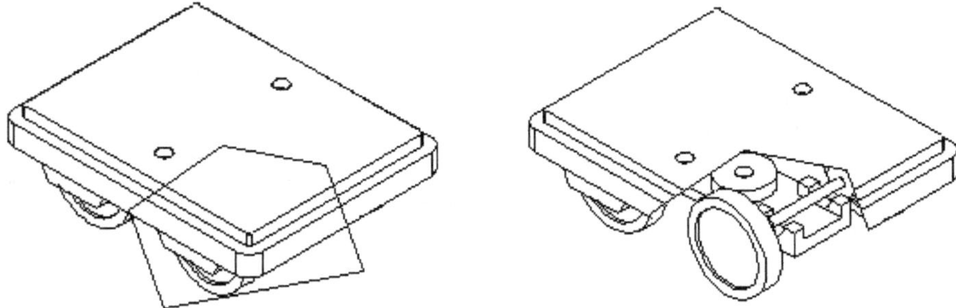

Figure 25–23

A break out view requires a sketch to define the break. The sketch must be associated with the drawing view and be a closed loop.

How To: Create a Break Out View

1. Create a view.
2. In the *Sketch* panel, click (Start Sketch) to create a sketch associated with the view.
3. Select the view in the Model browser or window.
4. Sketch a closed profile to outline the break area. If required, you can dimension and constrain the sketch to entities in the view.
5. In the *Exit* panel, click (Finish Sketch). The sketch should be listed within the view. If not, the sketch is not associated with the view.

6. In the *Modify* panel, click (Break Out) and select the view. Alternatively, you can right-click on the view and select **Create View>Break Out**. The *Break Out* dialog box opens, as shown in Figure 25–24.

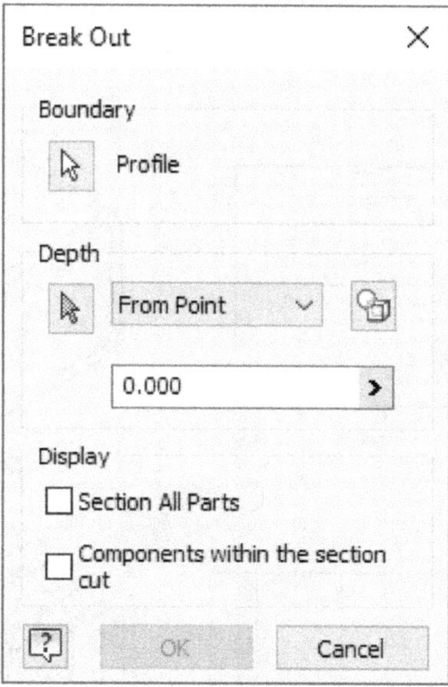

Figure 25–24

7. If multiple closed profile sketches are associated with the view, click (Profile) and select the required profile you sketched. If only a single sketch is associated with the selected view, the profile sketch will be automatically selected.
8. Select the depth type (**From Point**, **To Sketch**, **To Hole**, **Through Part**) and the required references.
9. Set the *Display* options, as required. The **Section All Parts** option enables you to cut all parts within the boundary. If you want to show components that are inside the cut volume, select **Components within the section cut**.

Note: *The (Use Hidden Lines) option is only active if the selected view being broken out was originally created with hidden lines removed.*

10. Click **OK**.

25.12 Slice Views

A slice view enables you to display slices of the model with zero-depth sections. An open sketch is used to create the slices in the model. The views at the top of Figure 25–25 show the target view and the associated sketch that was created on a planar part view. The views at the bottom of Figure 25–25 show the final slice view created on a 3D isometric view.

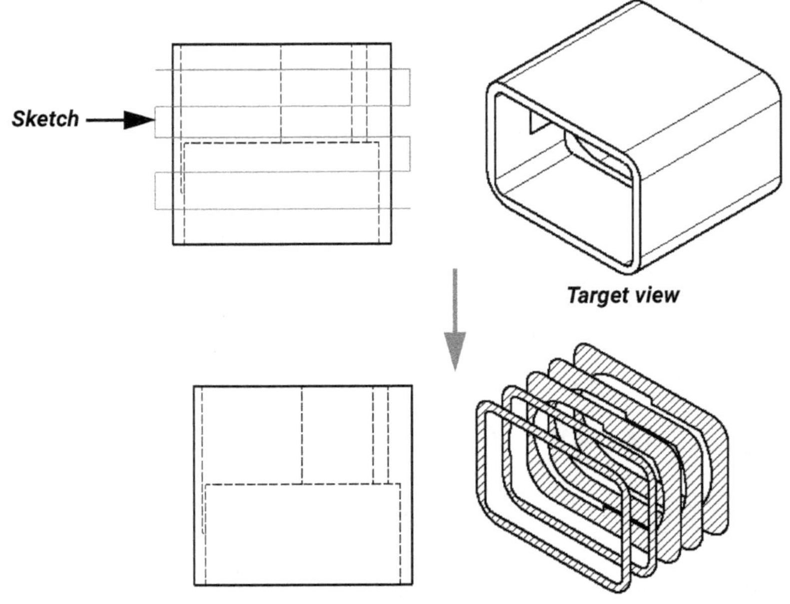

Figure 25–25

How To: Create a Slice View

1. Create the required base and projected planar views and an isometric view. The isometric view is used as the target view that is going to be sliced. The base or projected planar views provide the view to sketch the slice lines.
2. Create an associated sketch on the base or projected view defining the slicing that is to be displayed in the target view. The sketch must be an open section to be defined as a slice line, must be unconsumed, and cannot be created in a Draft view.

   Note: *To create an associated sketch, select the view before selecting* ***Start Sketch****.*

3. In the *Modify* panel, click (Slice).
4. Select the target view to be sliced. The target view does not have to be an isometric view. However, multiple slices are not visible if it is a planar view.
5. Select the associated sketch to define the slice view.

6. For an assembly drawing, enable **Slice All Parts** to slice all intersecting components. Otherwise, leave this option cleared.
7. Click **OK**.
8. (Optional) To manually select assembly components to display as sliced in the target view (i.e., participate), expand the assembly node for the target view, right-click on a component name, and select **Section Participation>Slice**.

25.13 Crop Views

Existing drawing views can be cropped/clipped to help focus on important areas of a view, as shown in Figure 25–26. Cropping is permitted on most existing views. However, it is not available for broken or overlay views, or previously cropped views. Although you cannot create an additional crop on a previously cropped view, you can create a broken view, detail view, or slice on a cropped view.

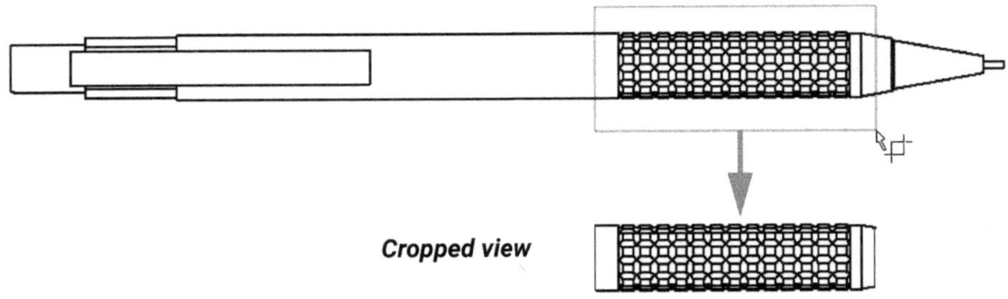

Figure 25–26

How To: Crop a View

1. Create a view.
2. Select the view in the Model browser or graphics window.
3. In the *Modify* panel, click (Crop) or right-click and select **Crop**.
4. (Optional) By default, the cropped area is rectangular and crop cut lines display where the cut intersects model geometry. To change the crop settings, right-click and select **Crop Settings** before sketching the area. Define the options using the *Crop Settings* dialog box, as in Figure 25–27. Alternatively, you can right-click and select **Circular** to change the boundary type instead of opening the *Crop Settings* dialog box.

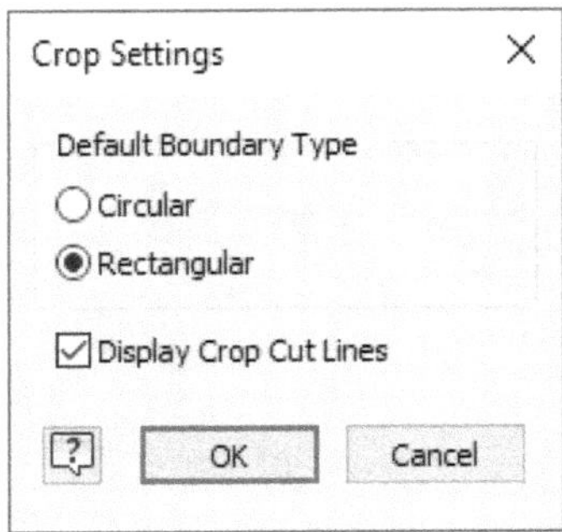

Figure 25–27

5. Sketch a bounding box around the area of the selected view that is to be cropped. You can also select an existing sketch as the crop boundary.

- Model dimensions that have been added to a view that is being cropped remain displayed. Existing drawing dimensions also remain and reference points are added to the view. It is recommended that you crop views before annotating your drawing. Drawing dimensions can be added after cropping and can reference the cut lines of the crop boundary, if required.
- To customize how the edges of a cropped view are displayed, use the **View Annotation** node in the *Style and Standard Editor* dialog box. By default, the edges are set to appear straight along the cut line, as shown previously in Figure 25–26; however, you can also set the detail view *Type* to **Zigzag**, as shown Figure 25–28.

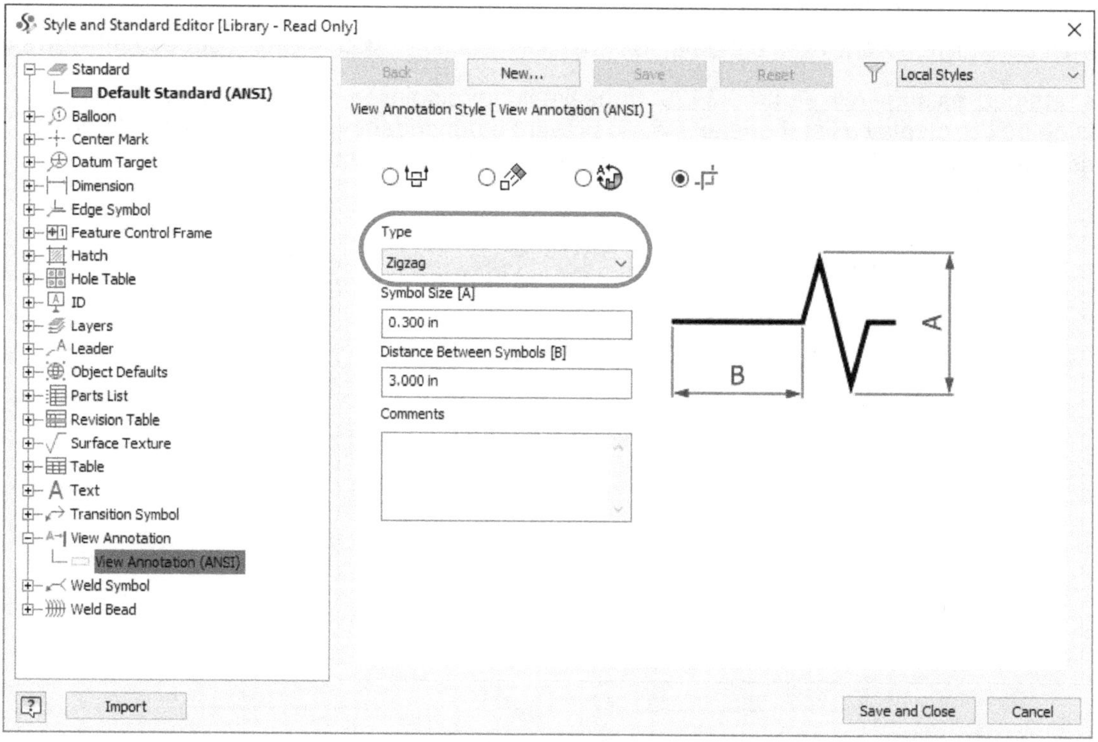

Style and Standard Editor [Library - Read Only]
Standard
Default Standard (ANSI)
Balloon
Center Mark
Datum Target
Dimension
Edge Symbol
Feature Control Frame
Hatch
Hole Table
ID
Layers
Leader
Object Defaults
Parts List
Revision Table
Surface Texture
Table
Text
Transition Symbol
View Annotation
View Annotation (ANSI)
Weld Symbol
Weld Bead
Back
New...
Save
Reset
Local Styles
View Annotation Style [View Annotation (ANSI)]
Type
Zigzag
Symbol Size [A]
0.300 in
Distance Between Symbols [B]
3.000 in
Comments
A
B
Import
Save and Close
Cancel

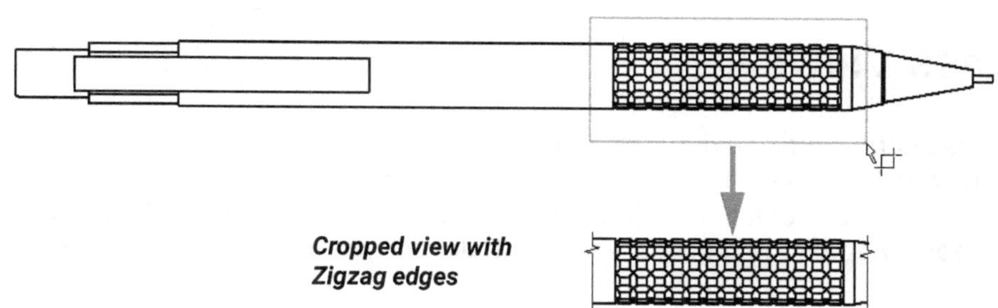

Figure 25–28

25.14 Manipulating Views

Once views have been added to a drawing, changes might be required. Some common changes that can be made to drawing views include the following:

Delete Views

Views can be deleted from a drawing using any of the following methods:

- Right-click on the view in the graphics window or the view name in the Model browser and select **Delete**.
- Select the view and press <Delete>.

When deleting a parent view, a dialog box opens that enables you to select dependent views to be retained, as shown in Figure 25–29. If the list is not displayed by default, click >> in the dialog box to display a list if one exists. To prevent a dependent view from being deleted, click **Yes** in the *Delete* column for the view to toggle it to **No**. Any retained children remain associative with the source model.

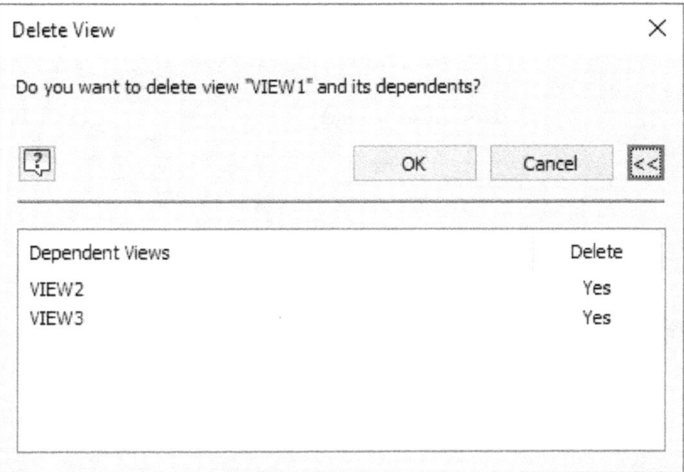

Figure 25–29

Suppress Views

Views can be suppressed in a drawing. When a view is suppressed, it is not visible on the drawing sheet and is grayed out in the Model browser. This is similar to suppressing features. To suppress a view, select it in the Model browser or on the drawing sheet, right-click, and select **Suppress**. Repeat the procedure in the Model browser to unsuppress a view.

Move Views

To move a view, select its border and drag it to the new location on the drawing. All dependent views move relative to their parents.

View Orientation

View orientation for a base view can be modified in the *Drawing View* dialog box. Select the view to reorient, right-click and select **Edit View**. Use the ViewCube to reorient the model. Click **OK** to update the view. Any dependent views also inherit the new orientation.

Transparent Components

In an assembly model drawing view you can set individual components to be transparent in a precise view (not raster). Setting as transparent keeps the component visible in the view but prevents it from hiding the geometry of other components in the same view. To make a component transparent, right-click on the part in the Model browser or in the graphics window and select **Transparent**.

View Alignment

Dependent views (projected views, auxiliary views, etc.) are aligned to parent views and update position if the parent view is moved. You can also explicitly remove or add view alignment as follows:

- To remove an alignment, in the Model browser or in the drawing sheet, right-click the dependent view and select **Alignment>Break** or click (Break Alignment) in the *Modify* panel. Once the view alignment is broken, a section or view line is added to the parent view to identify its origin. The dependent view remains dependent on the parent view although it is broken.
- To add an alignment, in the Model browser, right-click on the view and select **Alignment>Vertical / Horizontal / In Position**.
    - (Vertical), (Horizontal), and (In Position) can also be selected in the *Modify* panel.
    - The **Vertical/Horizontal** options line up the vertical/horizontal centerline of the view with the centerline of the other view. **In Position** maintains the position of the view horizontally and vertically, relative to the base view.

The available alignment options in the *Modify* panel are shown in Figure 25–30.

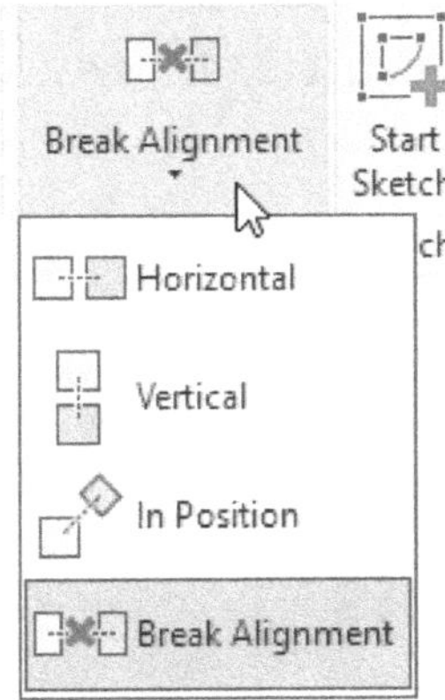

Figure 25–30

Change View Scale

To modify a view scale, right-click on the view and select **Edit View**. The *Drawing View* dialog box opens. Enter a new scale in the *Scale* field or drag the corners of the view outline and click **OK**. Changing this value affects the scale of all child views, except independently scaled views.

To independently change the view scale on a child view (i.e., Projected view), clear (Scale from base) in the *Drawing View* dialog box to enter an independent scale value for the child view.

Editing View Labels

You can add extra lines of text in a view label and control the formatting. Hover the cursor over a label (an **A** displays near the cursor), right-click, and select **Edit View Label**. The *Format Text* dialog box opens, as shown in Figure 25–31.

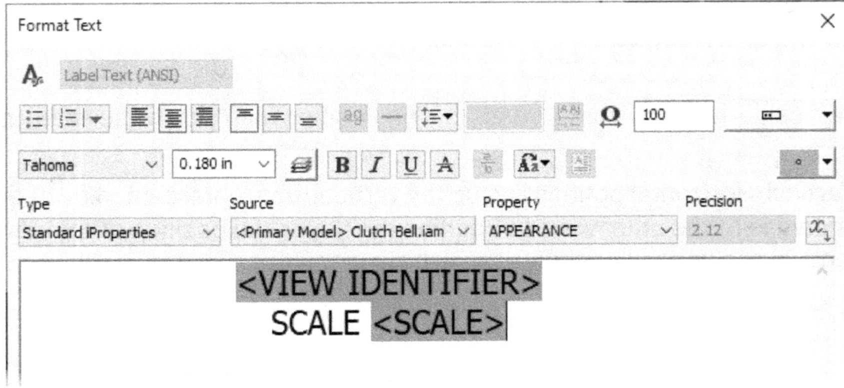

Figure 25–31

- The label information is represented by brackets in the edit area. The top brackets represent the title, and the bottom brackets represent the scale. You cannot change the text inside the brackets, but you can add text before, between, or after them. You can also change the format of the text inside the brackets.
- The dialog box offers standard options for text formatting, such as font, height, justification, etc. To change the font or style of existing text, highlight the text to be changed in the edit box and apply the changes.
- Move a label by dragging it. It remains connected to the view even after it has been moved.
- To return a moved view label to its original location when the view was placed, right-click on the view label and select **Restore View Label**.

Replace Models

When a base drawing view is added to a drawing, you must select a drawing model to reference. Dependent views are created referencing this base view. Once a reference model is selected for use in the drawing, it is possible to replace it with another model. The replacing model is then reflected in all existing views. Replacement models must be the same file format as the original model. For example, you cannot replace a part file with an assembly file.

How To: Replace an Existing Drawing Model

1. In the *Manage* tab>*Modify* panel, click (Replace Model Reference). The *Replace Model Reference* dialog box opens as shown in Figure 25–32.

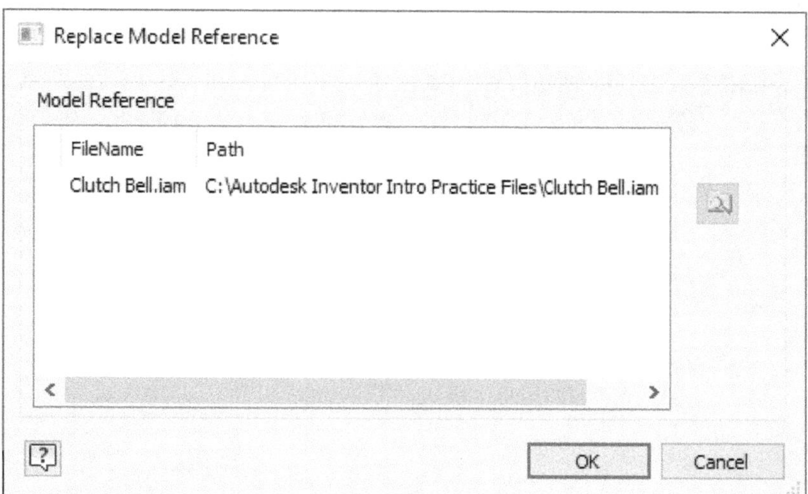

Figure 25–32

2. Select the drawing model to be replaced.

3. Click and browse and select a new model.
4. Click **Yes** and **OK** to confirm replacement.

View Properties

You can change the line weight, line type, or color of an object in a view. Select the item, right-click, and select **Properties** to open the *Edge Properties* dialog box, shown in Figure 25–33.

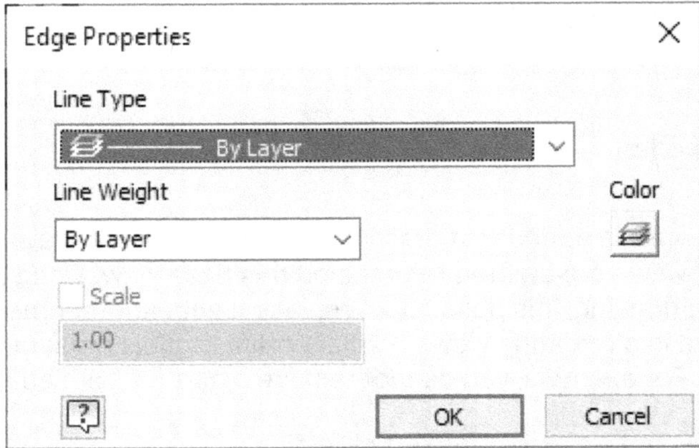

Figure 25–33

The **By Layer** setting for *Line Type* and *Line Weight* means that the property is determined by the layer on which the line is located. The settings for the layers can be modified in the *Style and Standard Editor*.

> **Note:** *Consider using the Selection filter to select all of the lines of a part or assembly instead of simply selecting individual lines. As an alternative to using the filter options in the Quick Access Toolbar, you can also display the list of filter options, press <Shift> and right-click.*

Create a Drawing I

Practice Objectives

- Create a new drawing based on a drawing template.
- Add base, projected, section, detail, and break out views to create a drawing.
- Edit a drawing view to change the location, display style, and scale.

In this practice, you will create the drawing shown in Figure 25–34. You will start a new drawing, add all the required views, and manipulate them as required.

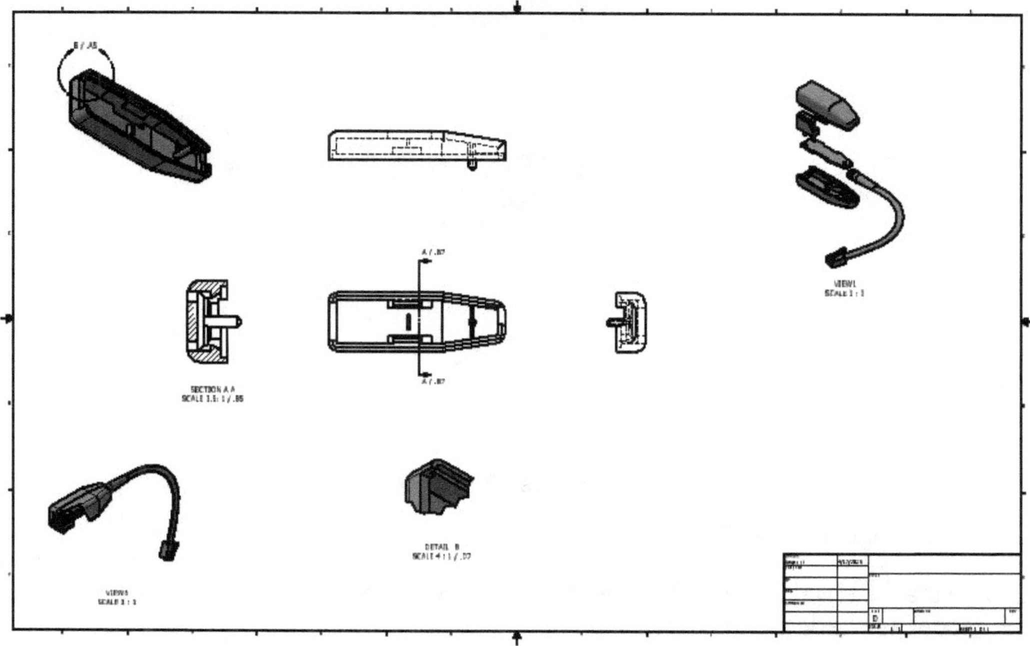

Figure 25–34

Task 1: Create a drawing and add a base view to the drawing.

1. Start a new drawing using the *Create New File* dialog box and select the **ANSI (mm).dwg** metric template. Select the empty sheet format (labeled **Use Template**) at the top of the right-hand column of the dialog box to provide an empty drawing sheet. Click **Create**.

   Note: *If you are unsure about which default template is assigned, select* ***New*** *to manually select the Template, instead of clicking* ***Drawing****.*

2. In the *Create* panel, click (Base). The *Drawing View* dialog box opens.
3. Click and open **socket_drawing_presentation.ipn**.
4. If you cannot see the preview of the drawing view that is being placed, relocate the *Drawing View* dialog box.
5. Click on the ViewCube to orient the model to its default orientation, as shown in Figure 25–35. Note that in the *Presentation* area of the *Drawing View* dialog box the **Explosion1** view is selected by default. This is because this is the only snapshot view that exists in the presentation file.

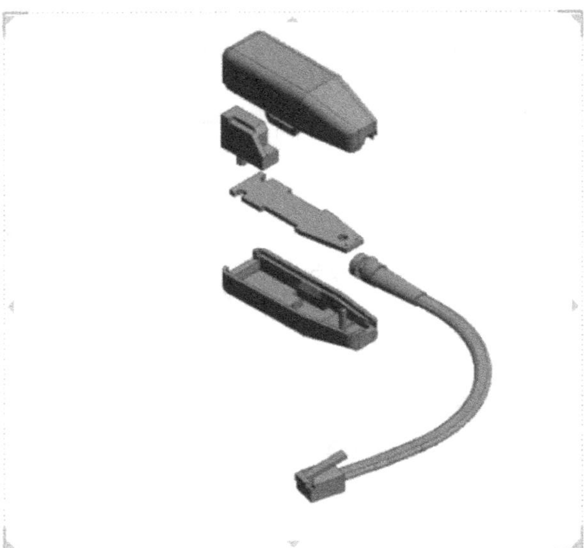

Figure 25–35

6. Click (Toggle Label Visibility) in the *Label* area to toggle on label visibility.
7. Ensure that (Hidden Line Removed) and (Shaded) are set in the *Style* area to display the model as shaded with hidden lines removed.

   Note: *Shaded views use the lighting style that was set for the model.*

8. Click and hold the cursor inside of the drawing view's frame and drag it to the top-right corner of the drawing sheet.
9. Right-click and select **OK (Enter)** or click **OK** in the *Drawing View* dialog box. The view is added and its label is displayed.

Task 2: Add another base view.

1. In the *Create* panel, click (Base). The *Drawing View* dialog box opens.

2. Click [icon] and select and open **encbase.ipt** to add a part model to the drawing.
3. By default, the ViewCube is set to the model's front view. Keep this orientation.
4. Click and hold the cursor inside of the drawing view's frame. Drag and drop it in the middle of the drawing sheet to place it, as shown in Figure 25–36.
5. Enter **2.5:1** in the *Scale* field.
6. Hover the cursor above the base view. A preview of the projected view's display area appears at the crosshairs. Select a point to place the projected view.

   Note: *Alternatively, if you had completed placement of the Base view, you can create projected views by clicking [icon] (Projected) in the Create panel, selecting the base reference view, and placing the new projected views.*

7. Continue moving the crosshairs to the new location (bottom-left corner of the base view). Select the location for the isometric view.
8. Right-click and select **OK (Enter)** to create the views that were placed.
9. If dimensions display, toggle them off by selecting the view in the Model browser, and right-clicking and selecting **Annotation Visibility>Model Dimensions**.
10. Move the new views as required so that the drawing displays as shown in Figure 25–36.

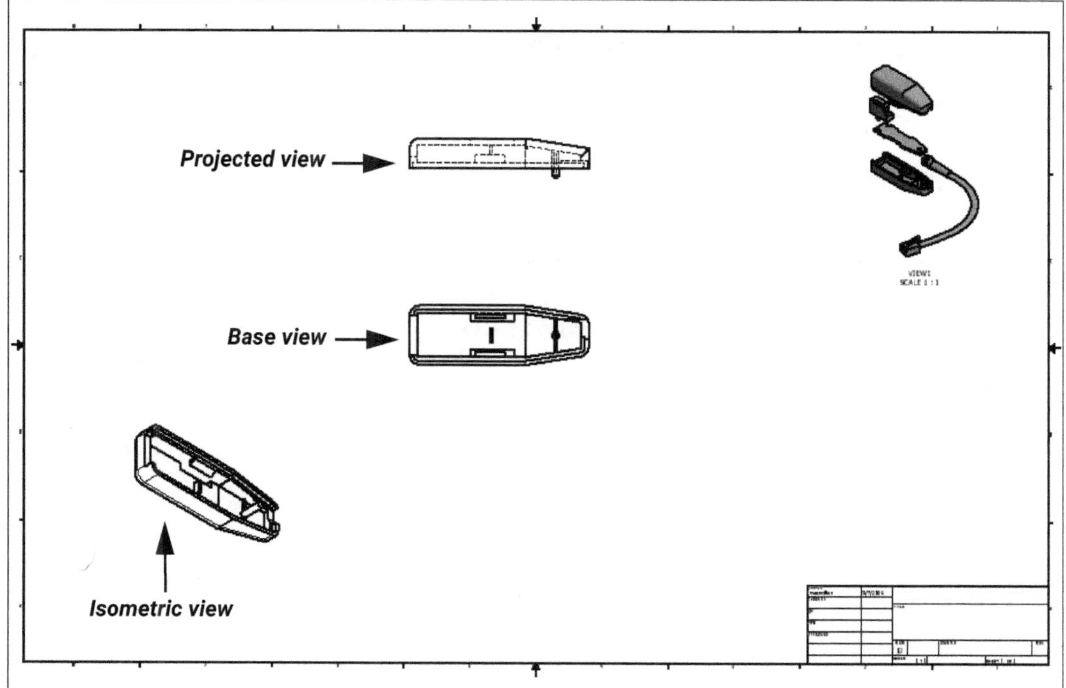

Figure 25–36

Task 3: Edit the isometric view.

1. Right-click on the isometric view of the part file shown previously in Figure 25–36 and select **Edit View**. The *Drawing View* dialog box opens.
2. Click (Shaded) in the *Style* area to set the view to shaded and then click **OK**.
3. Move the isometric view to the location shown in Figure 25–37. To move the view, select it so that view's outline displays around it, select the outline, and drag it.

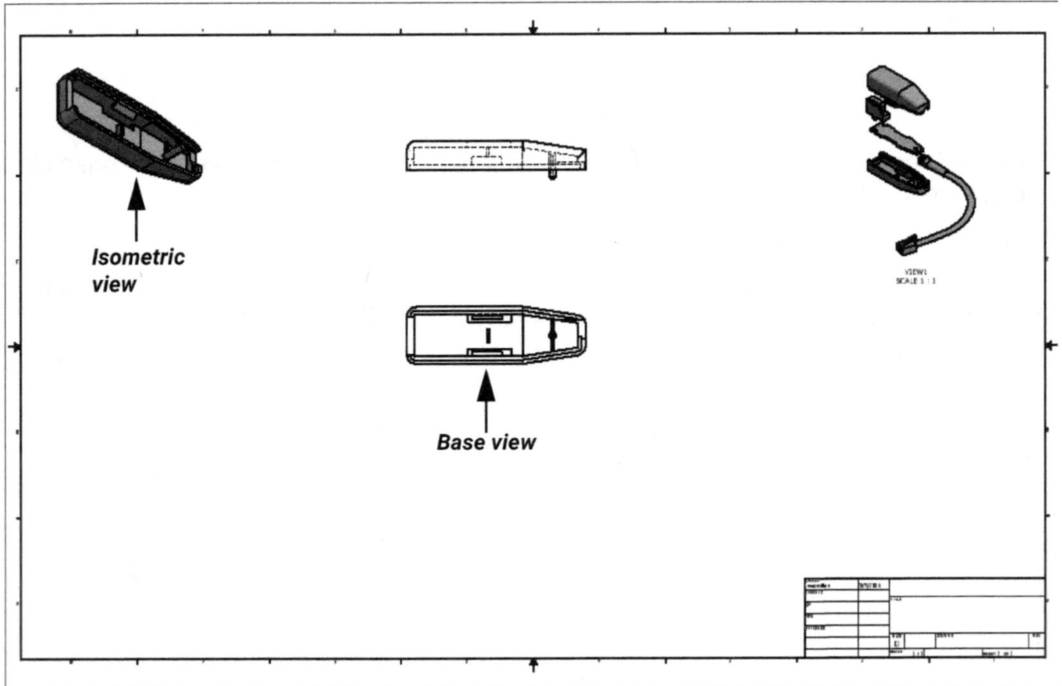

Figure 25–37

Task 4: Add a section view.

1. Select the base view, right-click, and select **Section View**. Alternatively, you can create section views by clicking (Section) in the *Create* panel.
2. Select points on the base view to draw the section line shown in Figure 25–38.

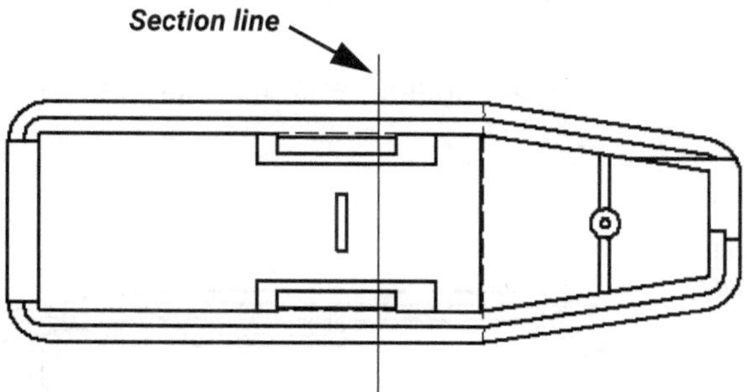

Figure 25–38

3. Right-click and select **Continue**. The *Section View* dialog box opens and a preview of the section view appears on the drawing sheet.
4. Enter **3.5:1** in the *Scale* field.
5. Ensure that is set to display the label.
6. Select the location shown in Figure 25–39 to place the section view. The default section depth option is **Full**.

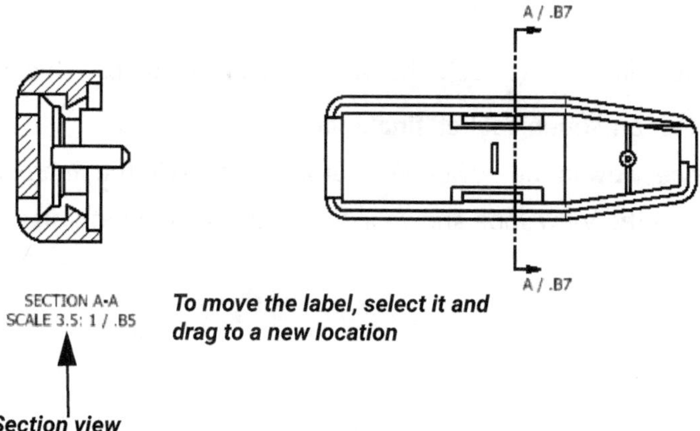

Figure 25–39

Note: *The sheet zone included in the labels will vary from the image depending on where you placed the section view on the sheet.*

7. If dimensions display, toggle them off by selecting the view in the Model browser, and right-clicking and selecting **Annotation Visibility>Model Dimensions**.

   Note: *To toggle off the addition of model dimensions on view creation, select the Tools tab and click (Application Options) in the Options panel. Select the Drawing tab and clear the* ***Retrieve all model dimensions on view placement*** *option.*

8. Hover the cursor over the section line, right-click, and select **Edit**. The *Sketch* tab becomes the active tab.
9. In the *Constrain* panel, click (Dimension) and dimension the section line as shown in Figure 25–40.

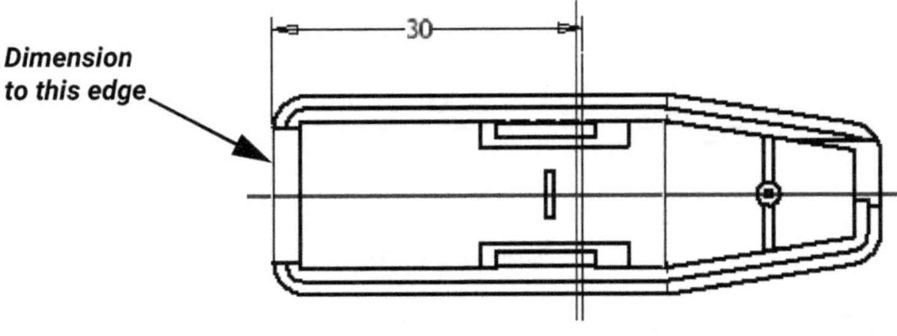

Figure 25–40

10. In the *Exit* panel, click (Finish Sketch). The section line is now parametrically placed and cannot be moved in error. To move the line, right-click and select **Edit** and change the dimension value.

Task 5: Add a base view of another assembly.

1. In the *Create* panel, click (Base). The *Drawing View* dialog box opens.
2. Click and select and open **socket_final.iam**.
3. Select **Interference_view** in the *Design View* drop-down list in the *Representation* area.
4. Select the corner of the ViewCube shown in Figure 25–41 to customize the view's orientation.

Figure 25–41

5. Click (Hidden Line Removed) and (Shaded) in the *Style* area, enter **1:1** in the *Scale* field, and select to display the label.
6. Place the view as shown in Figure 25–42.
7. Right-click and select **OK (Enter)**.

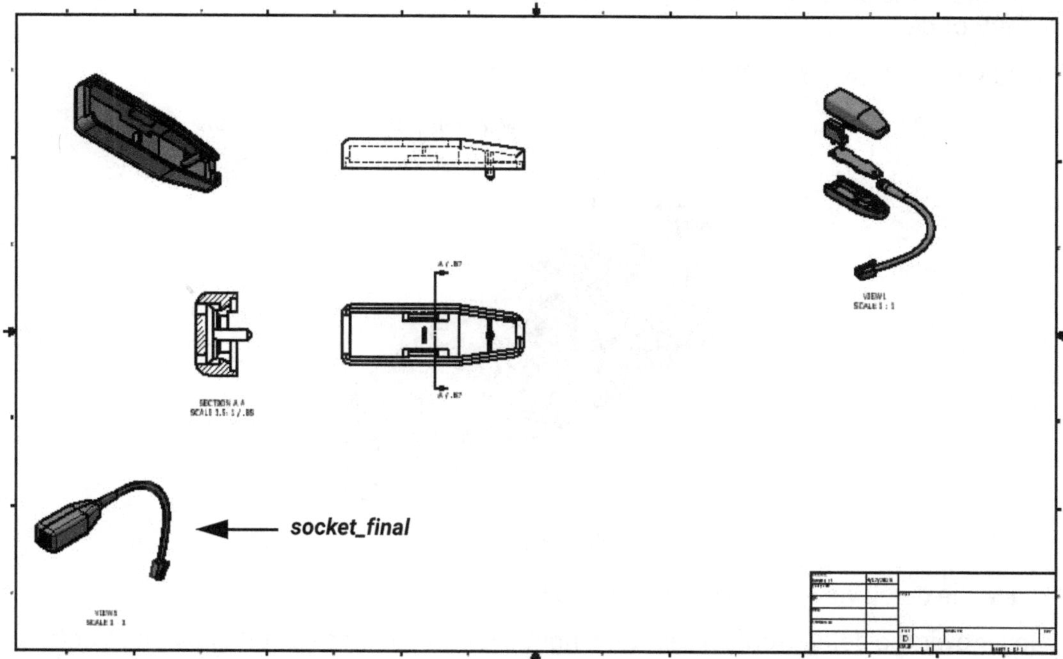

Figure 25–42

Task 6: Add a detail view to the drawing.

1. In the *Create* panel, click (Detail) and then select the isometric part view in the top-left corner of the window as the reference view. The *Detail View* dialog box opens.
2. Display the view as **Hidden Line Removed** ( ) and **Shaded** ( ). Accept the remaining defaults in the *Detail View* dialog box and select the point shown in Figure 25–43 for the center of detail.
3. Drag the cursor away from the point and click to create a circle.

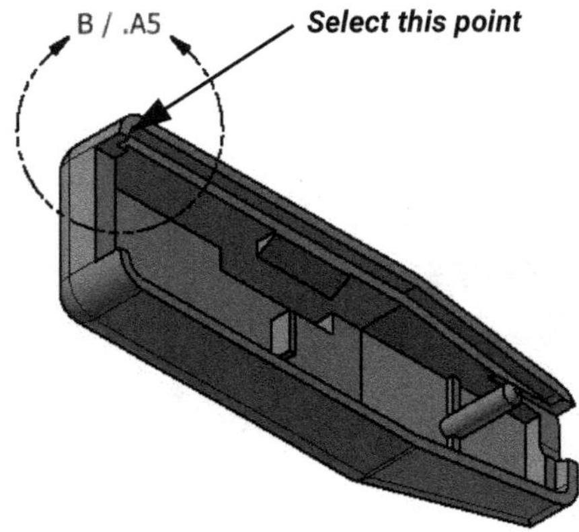

Figure 25–43

4. Place the detail view, as shown in Figure 25–44.
5. Hover over the detail view's fence, then right-click on the green dot that displays at the center and select **Attach**. Select a vertex in the same area where the fence was created. This attaches the fence to the geometry of the view, regardless of any changes that are made to the view.

6. Add another projected view, as shown in Figure 25–44.

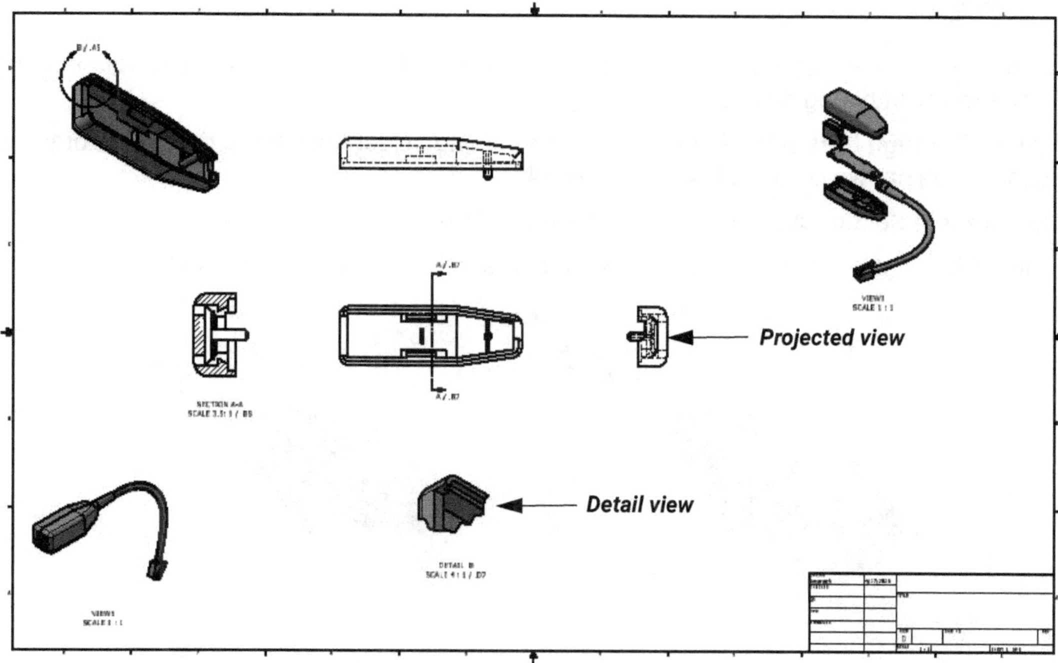

Figure 25–44

Task 7: Add a break out view to the drawing.

1. A break out view requires a sketch that is associated with the drawing view to define the break. To create a sketch associated with the drawing view, select the bottom left view on the drawing sheet and in the *Sketch* panel, click (Start Sketch).
2. Sketch the closed profile shown in Figure 25–45.

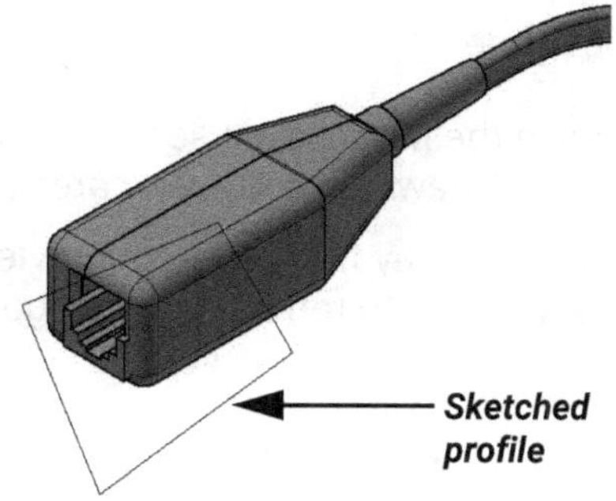

Figure 25–45

3. In the *Exit* panel, click (Finish Sketch). The sketch is now listed under the view name in the Model browser.
4. In the *Place Views* tab>*Modify* panel, click (Break Out) and select the bottom left view. The *Break Out* dialog box opens.
5. Select **Through Part** in the *Depth* drop-down list and select the **enctop** part in the drawing window, as shown on the left in Figure 25–46.
6. Ensure that **Section All Parts** is selected in the *Display* area.
7. Click **OK** to cut away that part. The view displays as shown on the right in Figure 25–46.

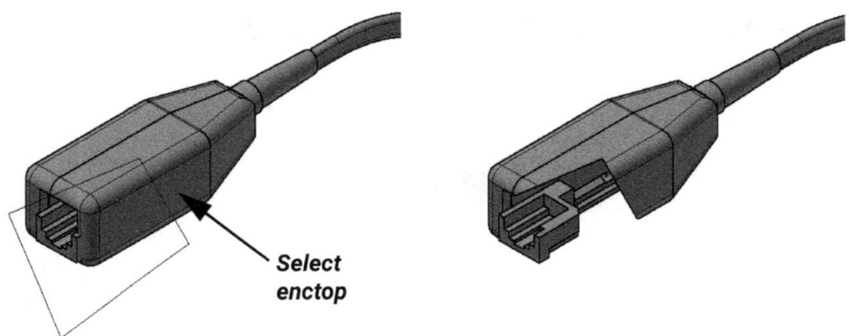

Figure 25–46

Task 8: Convert all of the views to raster views.

1. Right-click in the graphics window, away from an existing view, and select **Make All Views Raster**. If prompted, click **OK** to update the components used by the drawing. All of the views display with green corners and their view icons in the Model browser are changed to include a slash (e.g.,). This indicates that the views do not update if changes are made.

   Note: *The purpose of a raster view is to help improve drawing view calculation times when working on complex drawing models. This is done by temporarily breaking the associativity with the drawing model.*

2. Right-click on any of the views in the Model browser and select **Make View Precise**. This enables you to make any selected view in the drawing precise.
3. Right-click in the graphics window, away from an existing view, and select **Make All Views Precise**. All of the views are generated to reflect any changes to the model.

4. Save the drawing as **socket_drawing_presentation.dwg**. The drawing displays as shown in Figure 25–47.

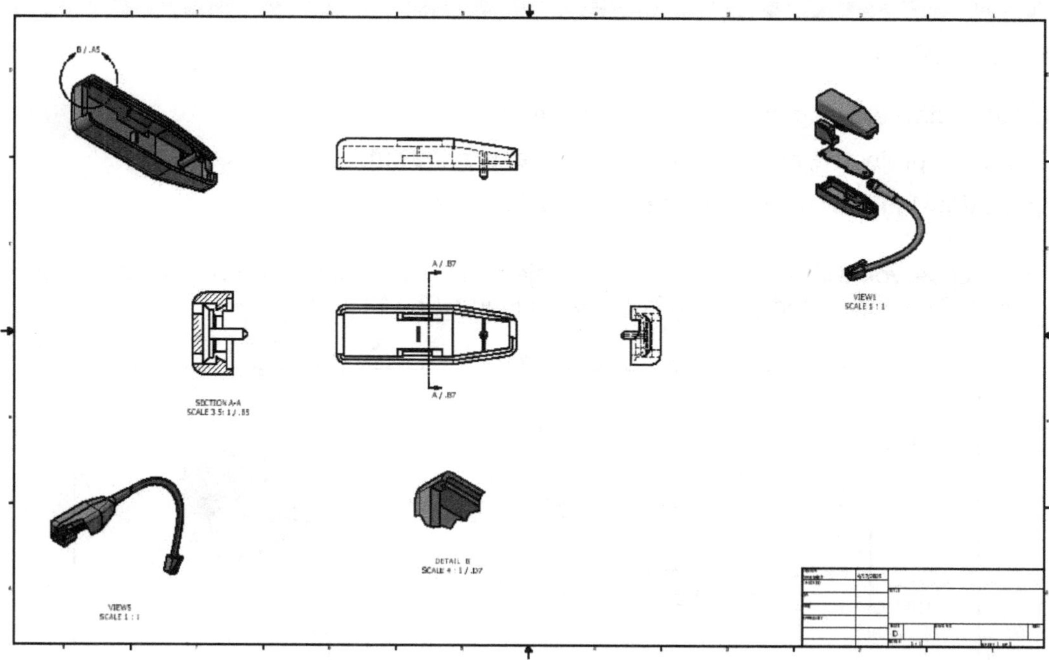

Figure 25–47

End of practice

Practice 25b
Create a Drawing II

Practice Objectives

- Create a new drawing based on a drawing template.
- Add base, projected, and section views to create a drawing.
- Edit a drawing view to change its display style and scale.

In this practice, you will create a base view, projected views, and section views. You will also edit a view. The completed drawing is shown in Figure 25–48.

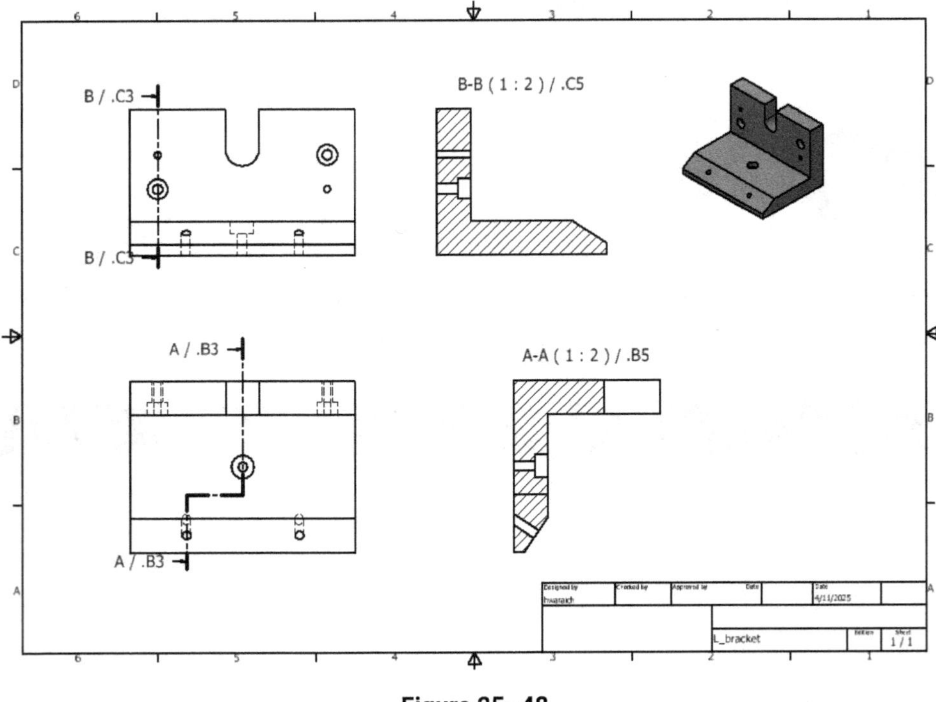

Figure 25–48

Task 1: Create a drawing and create base and projected views.

1. Start a new drawing file using the **ISO.dwg** metric template and the empty sheet format.
2. In the *Create* panel, click (Base).
3. Click and open **L_bracket.ipt**.
4. Set the *Scale* to **1:2** and the set the orientation of the view to **Top** using the ViewCube.

5. Move the view, as shown in Figure 25–49.
6. Hover the cursor above the base view. A preview of the projected view displays. Select a point to place the projected view.
7. Create a second projected view in the top-right corner of the drawing, as shown in Figure 25–49.
8. Right-click and select **OK (Enter)** to create the views that were placed.

Note: Alternatively, you can create projected views by clicking (Projected) in the Create panel, selecting the base reference view, and placing the new projected views.

9. If dimensions display, toggle them off by selecting the view in the Model browser, right-clicking, and selecting **Annotation Visibility>Model Dimensions**. The drawing displays as shown in Figure 25–49.

*Note: To toggle off the addition of model dimensions on view creation, select the Tools tab and click (Application Options) in the Options panel. Select the Drawing tab and clear the **Retrieve all model dimensions on view placement** option.*

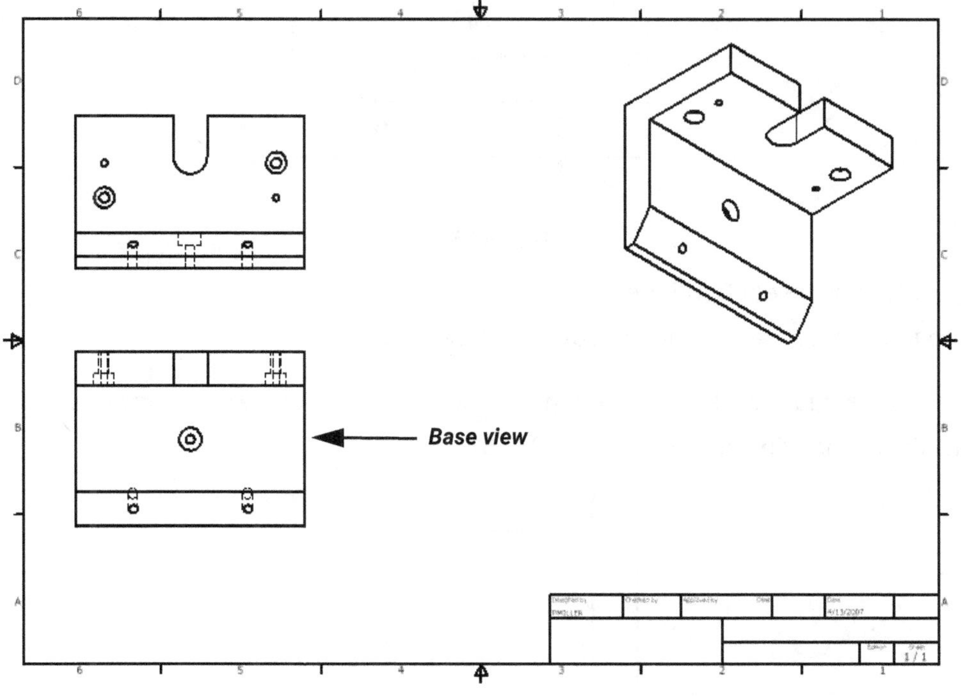

Figure 25–49

Task 2: Edit the isometric view.

1. Right-click on the isometric view (VIEW3) in the Model browser and select **Edit View**.
2. In the *Drawing View* dialog box, set the *Scale* to **1:4**. In the *Style* area, click [icon] and [icon] to set the view as shaded with hidden lines displayed. Click **OK**.

Task 3: Create section views.

1. In the *Create* panel, click [icon] (Section) and select **VIEW1** as the reference view.
2. Draw the section line shown in Figure 25–50. To align to the center of the holes, hover the cursor over a hole and move the cursor. Select the required point with the dashed line displayed.

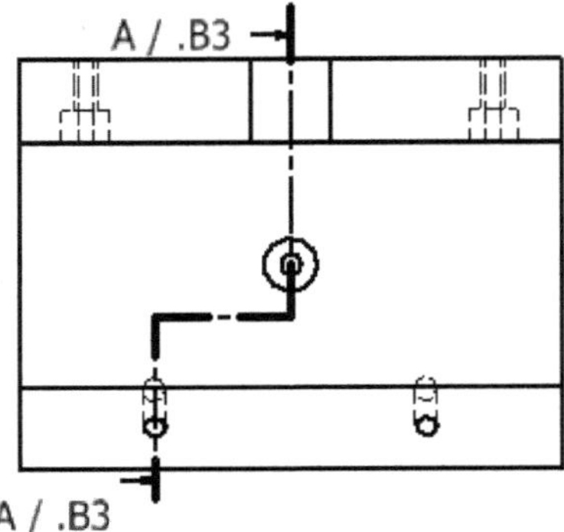

Figure 25–50

3. Right-click and select **Continue**.
4. Place the section view to the right of the reference view.
5. In the *Create* panel, click [icon] (Section) and select **VIEW2** as the reference view.
6. Draw the section line shown in Figure 25–51.

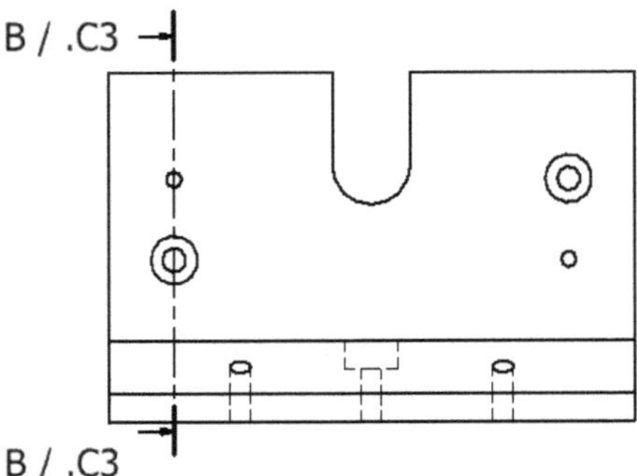

Figure 25–51

7. Right-click and select **Continue**.
8. Place the view to the right of the reference view.
9. The drawing displays as shown in Figure 25–52.

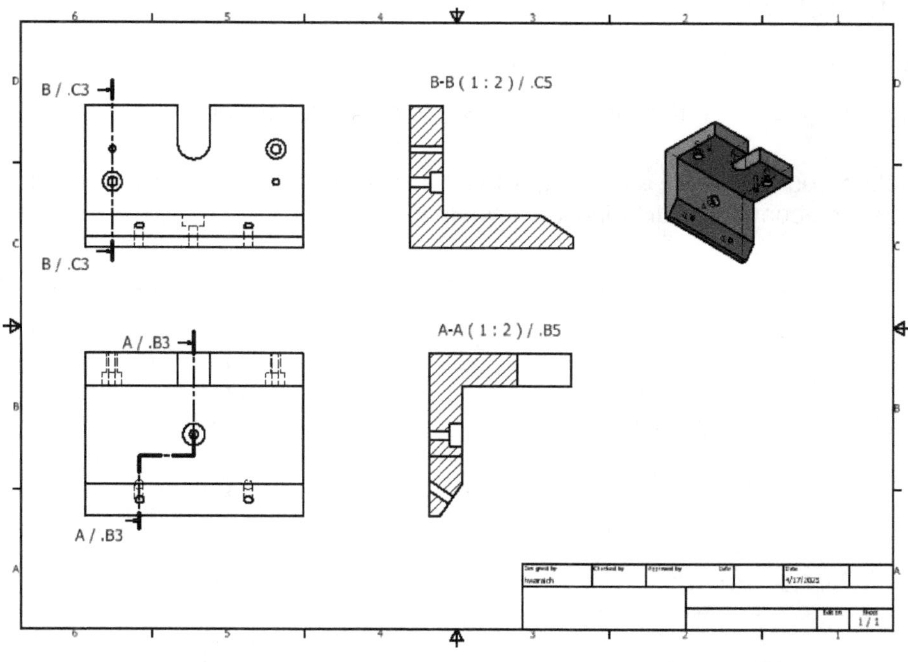

Figure 25–52

Task 4: Modify the orientation of the isometric view.

1. Double-click on the isometric view and use the ViewCube to reorient the view to the orientation shown in Figure 25–53.

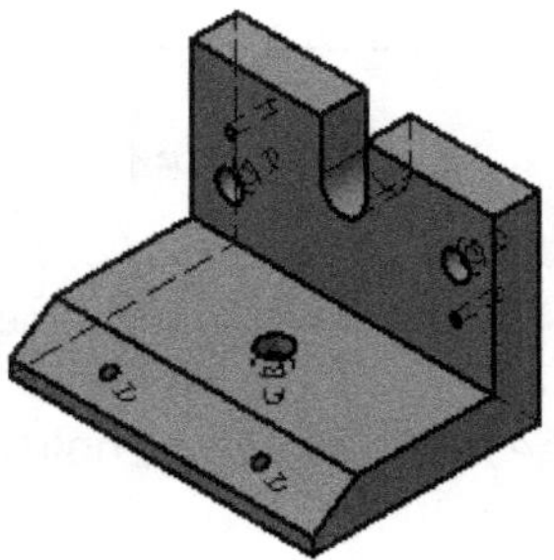

Figure 25–53

2. Save the file as **L_bracket.dwg**.

End of practice

Practice 25c
Create a Drawing III

Practice Objectives

- Create a new drawing based on a drawing template.
- Add base, projected, section, and detail views to create a drawing.

In this practice, you will create a drawing with a base view, projected views, a section view, and a detail view. The completed drawing is shown in Figure 25–54.

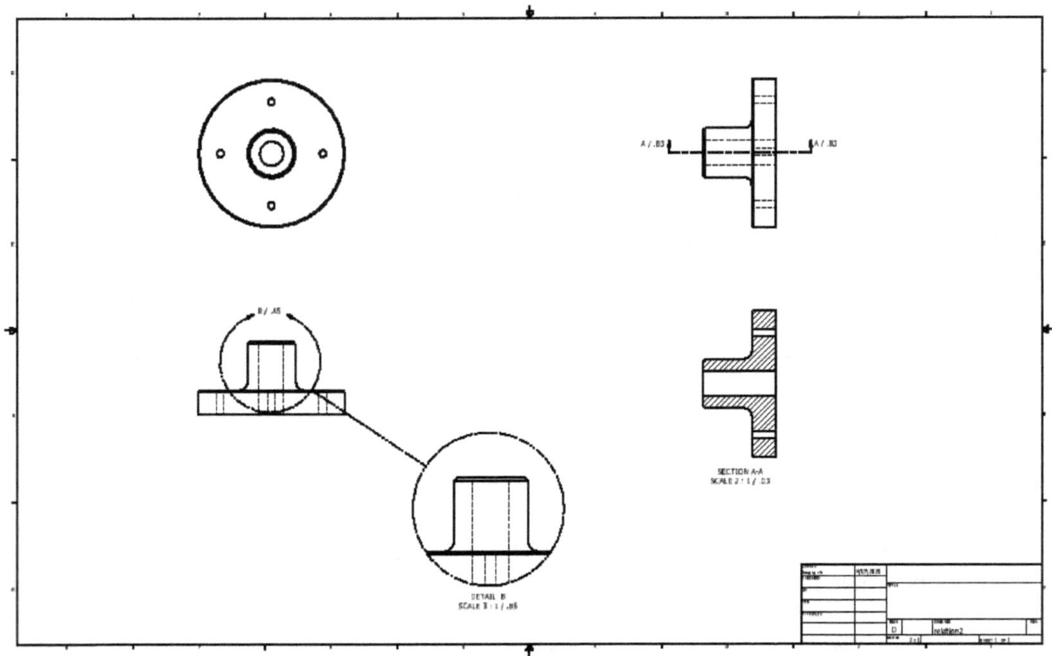

Figure 25–54

Task 1: Create a drawing and create base and projected views.

1. Start a new drawing file using the **ANSI (in).dwg** English template and the empty sheet format.
2. Create a base view of **relation.ipt**. Move the view to the upper-left corner of the drawing, as shown in Figure 25–55.
3. As an alternative to entering a scale value in the *Drawing View* dialog box, drag a corner of the view. Drag until the scale is 2:1.

4. Create the projected views shown in Figure 25–55.
5. Right-click in the graphics window and select **OK (Enter)**.

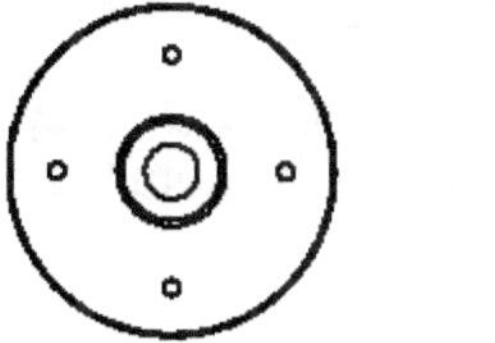
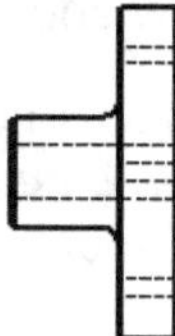
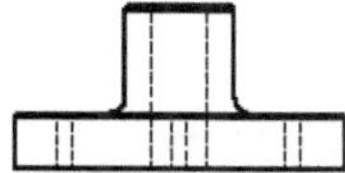

Figure 25–55

Note: *If dimensions display, toggle them off by selecting the view in the Model browser, and right-clicking and selecting **Annotation Visibility>Model Dimensions**. Alternatively, you can select the Tools tab and click (Application Options) in the Options panel. Select the Drawing tab and clear the **Retrieve all model dimensions on view placement** option.*

Task 2: Create a section view.

1. Create the section view shown in Figure 25–56. Use extension lines to ensure that the section line cuts through the center of the part.

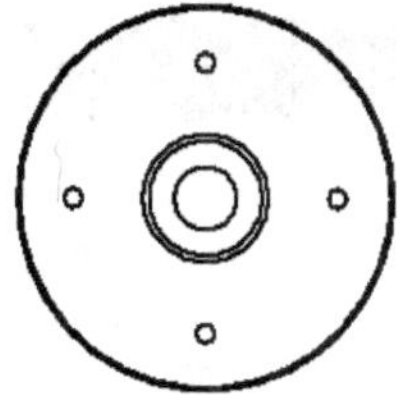
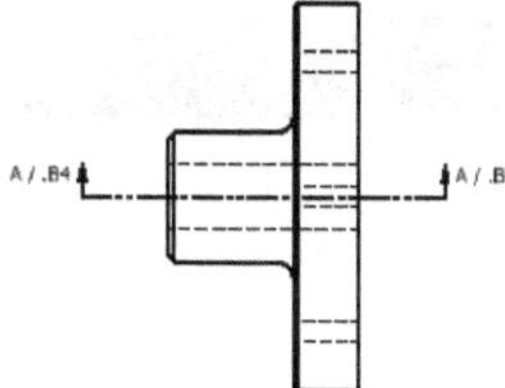

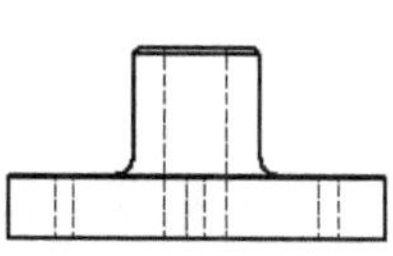
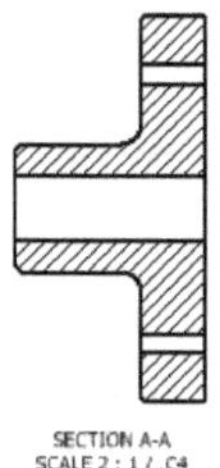

Figure 25–56

Task 3: Create a detail view.

1. Create a detail view and select the bottom projected view as the reference view. Click (Set cut edges as smooth) as the *Cutout Shape*. Select **Display Full Detail Boundary** and **Display Connection Line**. Set the *Scale* at 3:1, create the detail circle, and place the detail view as shown in Figure 25–57.

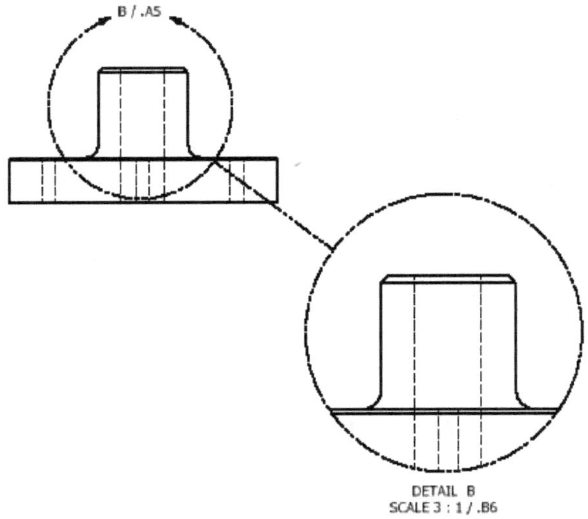

Figure 25–57

2. Save the file as **relation.dwg.**

End of practice

Chapter Review Questions

1. Which of the following view types must be the first view in a drawing?
   a. Projection
   b. Base
   c. Auxiliary
   d. Detail

2. If you have already placed a front view of a part in a drawing, which tool most easily creates a side view aligned with the front view, as shown in Figure 25–58?

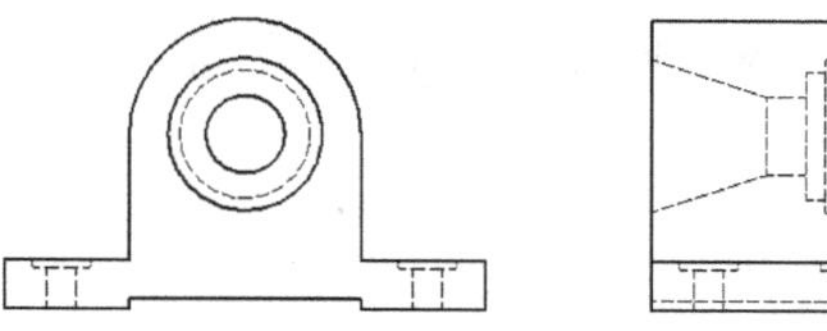

Figure 25–58

   a. Projected View
   b. Base View
   c. Draft View
   d. Aligned View

3. Which command can create the foreshortening effect in the views shown in Figure 25–59?

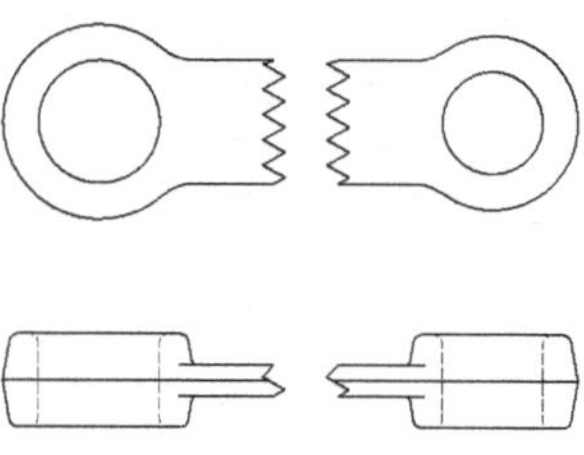

Figure 25–59

   a. Break View
   b. Crop View
   c. Auxiliary View
   d. Break Out View

4. Which view types enable you to create an independent 3D view? (Select all that apply.)
   a. Projection
   b. Base
   c. Auxiliary
   d. Detailed

5. You can break the alignment dependency between a parent and a child view.
   a. True
   b. False

6. If you change a part or assembly file, drawing views that show it update automatically by default.
   a. True
   b. False

7. When inserting a base view into a drawing file, what is required to display a view name, similar to that shown in Figure 25–60?

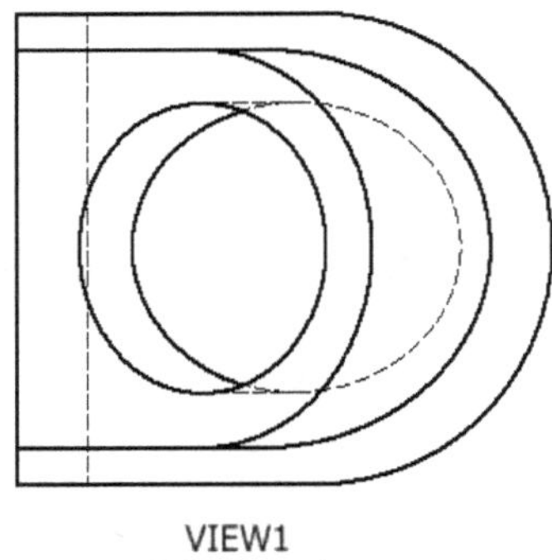

Figure 25–60

   a. Enable/Disable feature preview.
   b. Toggle the label Visibility.
   c. Ensure that you have edited the view label.
   d. Ensure that the Scales are on.

8. Which type of file is required to be created when you want to show an exploded view of an assembly in a drawing file, as shown in Figure 25–61?

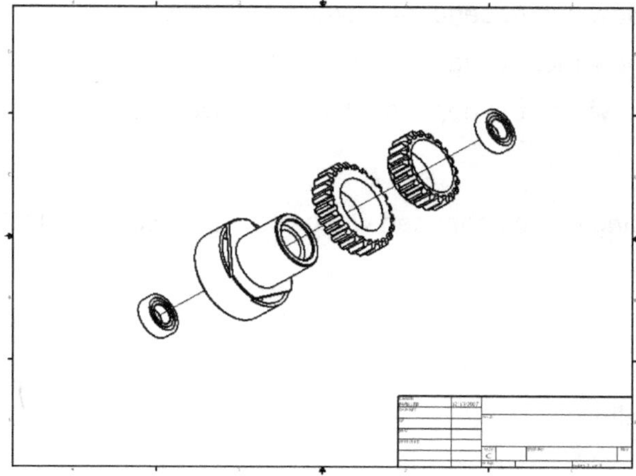

Figure 25–61

   a. Project
   b. Part
   c. Presentation
   d. Assembly

9. When you delete a view what happens to the dependent views?
   a. They are automatically deleted.
   b. The dependent views are suppressed.
   c. You cannot delete a view that has dependent views.
   d. You are prompted to delete its dependent views.

10. A shaded base view exists in a drawing. This base view is automatically displayed as shaded and it cannot be modified to remove the shaded display.
   a. True
   b. False

11. How can you move a base view and its dependent views?

a. Move one of the dependent views and the base view moves with it.

b. Move the base view and dependent views individually.

c. Move the base view then realign the dependent views.

d. Move the base view and the dependent views move with it.

12. Which of the following can be changed when you edit a view? (Select all that apply.)

a. View Scale

b. Line type

c. View Label

d. Hidden line visibility

13. You can change the scale of the projected views independent of the parent view scale.

a. True

b. False

Command Summary

Button	Command	Location
	Auxiliary (view)	• **Ribbon:** *Place Views* tab>*Create* panel • **Context Menu:** In the graphics window with a view selected • **Context Menu:** In Model browser with a view selected>Create View
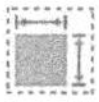	**Base (view)**	• **Ribbon:** *Place Views* tab>*Create* panel • **Context Menu:** In the graphics window with a view selected • **Context Menu:** In Model browser with a view selected>Create View
	Break (view)	• **Ribbon:** *Place Views* tab>*Modify* panel • **Context Menu:** In Model browser with a view selected> Create View
	Break Alignment	• **Ribbon:** *Place Views* tab>*Modify* panel • **Context Menu:** In Model browser with a view selected>Alignment
	**Break Out (view)**	• **Ribbon:** *Place Views* tab>Modify panel • **Context Menu:** In Model browser with a view selected>Create View
	Crop (view)	• **Ribbon:** *Place Views* tab>*Modify* panel • **Context Menu:** In the graphics window with a view selected • **Context Menu:** In Model browser with a view selected>Create View
N/A	**Delete (view)**	• **Context Menu:** In the graphics window with a view selected • **Context Menu:** In Model browser with a view selected • (*select view in the graphics window and press <Delete>*)
	**Detail (view)**	• **Ribbon:** *Place Views* tab>*Create* panel • **Context Menu:** In the graphics window with a view selected • **Context Menu:** In Model browser with a view selected>Create View
	**Draft (view)**	• **Ribbon:** *Place Views* tab>*Create* panel
N/A	**Edit Sheet**	• **Context Menu:** In Model browser with a sheet selected

Button	Command	Location
N/A	**Edit View**	• **Context Menu:** In the graphics window with a view selected • **Context Menu:** In Model browser with a view selected
N/A	**Edit View Label**	• **Context Menu:** In graphics window with a view label selected • Double-click on the view label
	Horizontal (alignment)	• **Ribbon:** *Place Views* tab>*Modify* panel • **Context Menu:** In Model browser with a view selected>Alignment
	In Position (alignment)	• **Ribbon:** *Place Views* tab>*Modify* panel • **Context Menu:** In Model browser with a view selected>Alignment
N/A	**Make All Views Raster / Make All Views Precise**	• **Context Menu:** In the graphics window
N/A	**Make View Raster / Make View Precise**	• **Context Menu:** In the graphics window with a view selected • **Context Menu:** In Model browser with a view selected
	Overlay (view)	• **Ribbon:** *Place Views* tab>*Create* panel • **Context Menu:** In Model browser with a view selected>Create View
	Projected (view)	• **Ribbon:** *Place Views* tab>*Create* panel • **Context Menu:** In the graphics window with a view selected • **Context Menu:** In Model browser with a view selected>Create View
N/A	**Properties**	• **Context Menu:** In Model browser with a sheet selected
	Replace Model Reference	• **Ribbon:** *Manage* tab>*Modify* panel
	Section (view)	• **Ribbon:** *Place Views* tab>*Create* panel • **Context Menu:** In the graphics window with a view selected • **Context Menu:** In Model browser with a view selected>*Create* View
	Slice (view)	• **Ribbon:** *Place Views* tab>*Modify* panel • **Context Menu:** In Model browser with a view selected>Create View

Button	Command	Location
N/A	**Suppress (view)**	• **Context Menu:** In the graphics window with a view selected • **Context Menu:** In Model browser with a view selected
	Vertical (alignment)	• **Ribbon:** *Place Views* tab>*Modify* panel • **Context Menu:** In Model browser with a view selected>Alignment

Chapter 26

Detailing Drawings

Adding details to your drawings enables you to communicate additional information to other designers working on a project. You can also apply styles and standards to control the appearance of your model.

Learning Objectives

- Show model dimensions and create dimensions to detail a drawing view.
- Edit the values, locations, and styles of dimensions in a drawing view.
- Work with multiple sheet drawings to manipulate their sheet display, sheet numbers, and the views on each sheet.
- Add a parts list to a drawing and edit it to customize values and column display.
- Create and edit balloons that identify the components in a drawing's parts list.
- Review and edit the style options to customize the display of annotations in a drawing.
- Assign and edit hatch patterns.

26.1 Adding Dimensions to Drawing Views

When you create a view, you have the option to display dimensions that are used to create the 3D model. These dimensions are called model dimensions. You can also add drawing dimensions directly in the drawing.

Model Dimensions

There are two ways to add model dimensions in a drawing. You can display all available model dimensions in a new view while creating the view, or display selected dimensions on existing views. It is important to note that model dimensions can only be displayed in one view at a time.

- **Method 1:** To display model dimensions in a view while it is being created, in the *Drawing View* dialog box, in the *Recovery Options* tab, select **All Model Dimensions**, as shown in Figure 26–1.

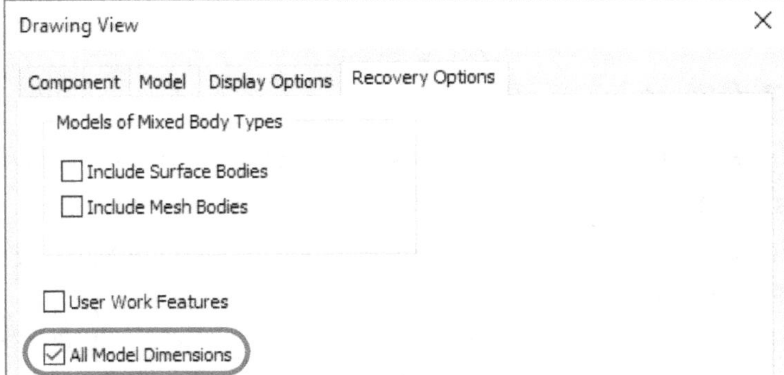

Figure 26–1

When the view is placed, the dimensions used to create the model are displayed in the view, as shown in Figure 26–2. This method may provide too many unnecessary dimensions.

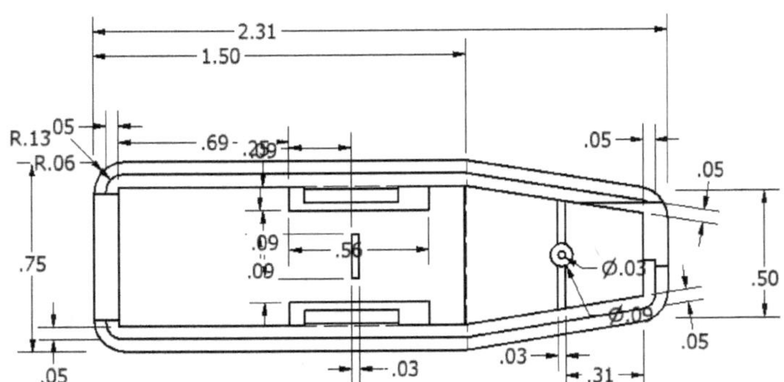

Figure 26–2

- **Method 2:** Dimensions can be selectively displayed once the view is created using the **Retrieve Model Annotations** option.

How To: Display Model Dimensions

1. Activate **Retrieve Model Annotations** using one of the following methods:
   - In the *Annotate* tab>*Retrieve* panel, click (Retrieve Model Annotations).
   - Right-click on the drawing sheet and click **Retrieve Model Annotations**.

   The *Retrieve Model Annotation* dialog box opens, as shown in Figure 26–3. Orthographic and Isometric appear in the title of the dialog box depending on the view selected.

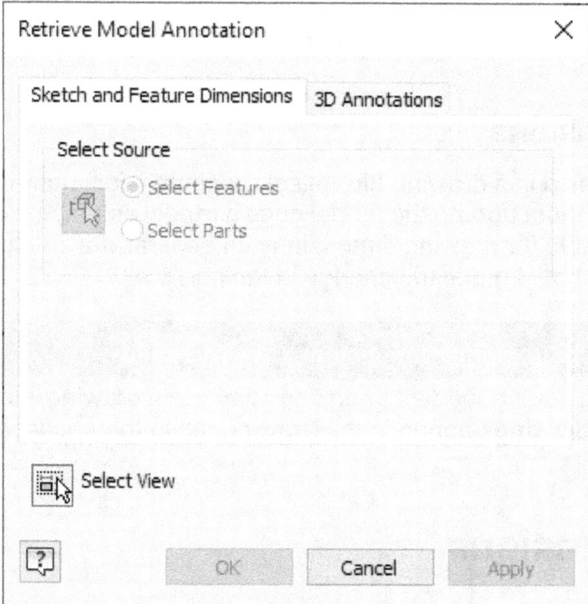

Figure 26–3

2. On the *Sketch and Feature Dimensions* tab, ensure that (Select View) is active and select the view to which you want to retrieve the dimensions. All dimensions are previewed in that view.
3. Select dimensions to keep them in the view. You can select using any of the following techniques:
   - Select individual dimensions to keep them.
   - Drag a boundary box to keep multiple dimensions.
4. To retrieve dimensions on specific parts or features, select **Select Features** or **Select Parts** in the *Select Source* area, and then select the parts or features. The dimensions on the selected items become available.
5. Click **OK** to add the dimensions to the drawing view.

Figure 26–4 shows a model with feature dimensions added to the view.

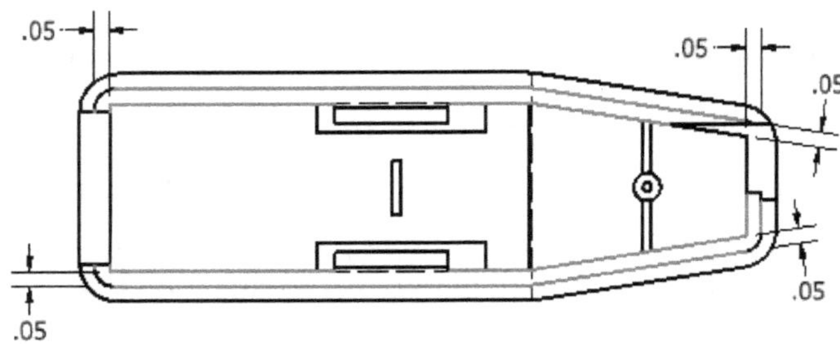

Figure 26–4

Edit Model Dimensions

To edit a model dimension in a drawing file, select the dimension, right-click, and select **Edit Model Dimension**. You must update the model once a model dimension is changed. **Edit Model Dimension** is not available for drawing dimensions. In general, if a change is major or affects multiple features, you should make the change in the part file.

 **Hint: Controlling Where Model Dimensions Can Be Edited**

To prevent users from editing model dimensions while in a drawing, clear the **Enable part modification from in drawings** option in the Drawing tab in the *Application Options* dialog box.

Drawing Dimensions

In addition to model dimensions, you can also create dimensions directly on a drawing. Drawing dimensions are dependent on the part geometry and their value cannot be changed. However, if the part size changes, the drawing dimension updates automatically. Drawing dimensions can be placed on any view type (e.g., Base, Projected, or Isometric).

The **Dimension** option in the drawing environment provides additional dimensioning flexibility than in the Sketch environment. For example, when a radius is selected for a drawing dimension, you can right-click and assign **Angle**, **Chord Length**, and **Arc Length** dimensions. These options are not available when dimensioning a sketch.

To add dimensions to your drawing, select the *Annotate* tab and use any of the Dimension creation types (General Dimension, Baseline, Ordinate, and Chain) shown in Figure 26–5. The General dimension type is also located on the marking menu.

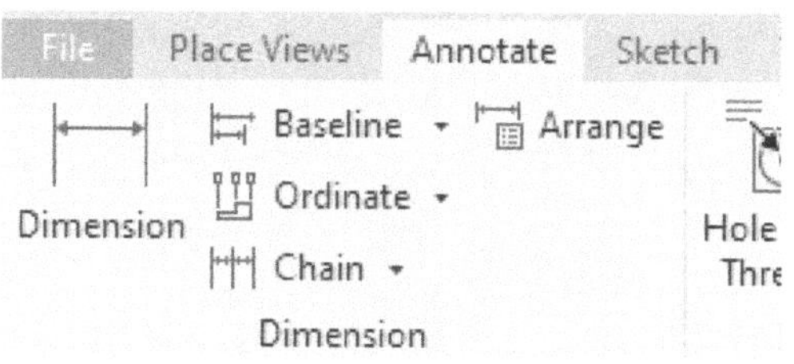

Figure 26–5

 **Hint: Measurements in a Drawing**

The **Measure** command can be used in the Drawing environment to measure entities in the same way as they are measured in part and assembly models. These measurements are temporary and do not create dimensions.

General Dimensions

A general dimension ( ) adds dimensions the same way model dimensions are added in the part file. The type of dimension placed (linear, diameter, angular, etc.) depends on the entity or entities selected.

- When a general dimension is placed, the *Edit Dimension* dialog box opens by default, enabling you to immediately modify the dimension.
    - You can modify the position of the text in relation to the text box, the display of the dimension value, add and edit text and symbols to go with the dimension, modify the tolerance format, or modify inspection dimensions.
    - To disable this dialog box from opening when a dimension is placed, clear the **Edit dimension when created** option and click **OK**.
- In addition to the standard entities and vertices that can be selected as references for dimensions, a virtual intersection of two lines can also be used. Select a line, right-click, and select **Intersection**. Then select a second line for the second dimension reference before placing the dimension as you would normally.
- When placing a Radial dimension, you can move it in 15-degree increments by holding <Ctrl> while dragging.

- When placing a general linear or diameter dimension, you can right-click and select from a list of types to customize the dimension type being placed or its orientation. Examples of the options are shown in Figure 26–6. Before locating the dimension, right-click and select a type in the *Dimension Type* list.

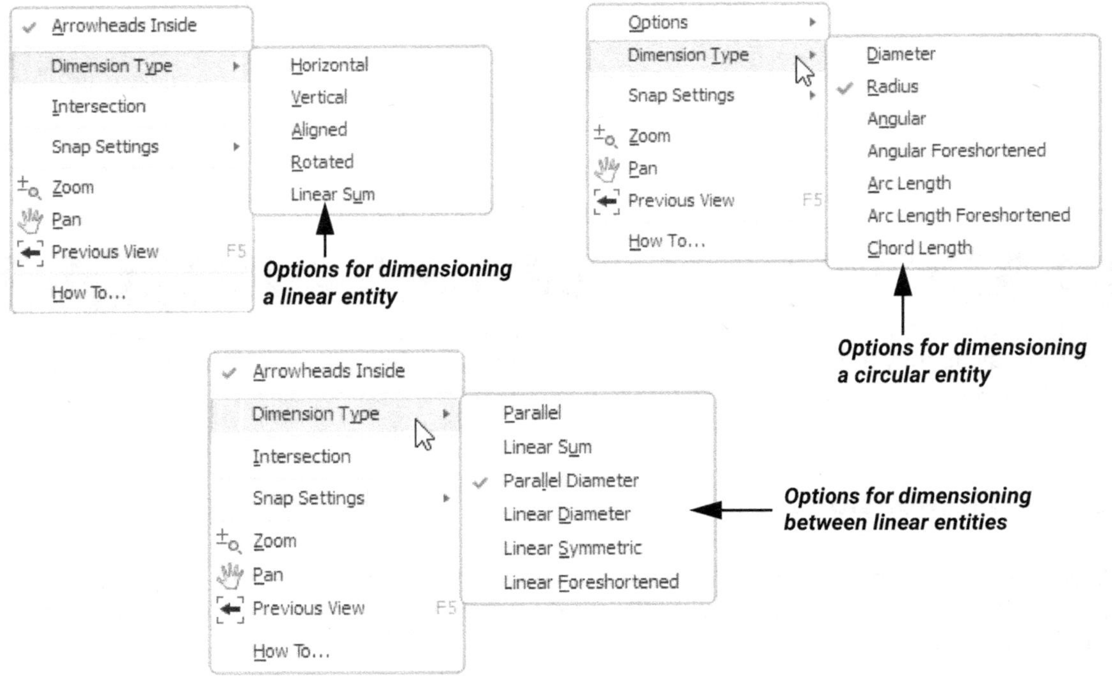

Figure 26–6

Foreshortened General Dimensions

Foreshortened dimensions are used for linear, angular, and arc length dimension types for referencing objects (e.g., work geometry) that are outside a drawing view. A foreshortened dimension displays even if the visibility of the referenced object is cleared in the view. Figure 26–7 shows two foreshortened dimensions. On the left, the arrow to the 2nd reference is shown and on the right, it is not shown.

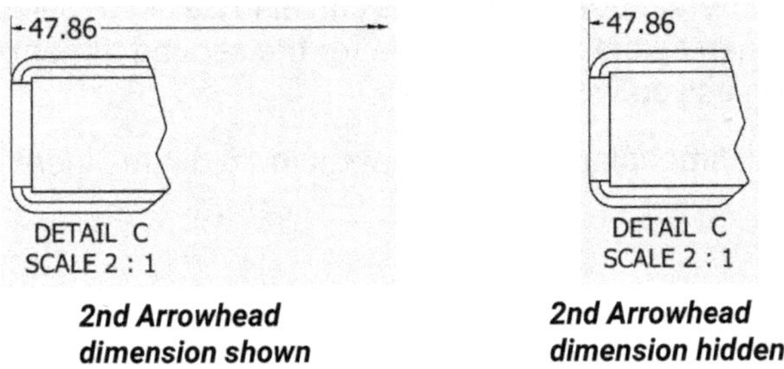

Figure 26–7

How To: Create a Foreshortened General Dimension

1. In the *Dimension* panel, click (General Dimension).
2. Select the entities to be dimensioned. The first entity selected should be the reference that is going to remain or is visible in the drawing view. Select the included reference geometry as the second reference.

   ***Note:** To select the second reference you must ensure that it is included in the view. In the case of work geometry, locate the geometry in the view, right-click and select **Include**.*

3. Before locating the dimension, right-click, expand **Dimension Type**, and select from the available foreshortened options (e.g., **Linear Foreshortened**, **Angular Foreshortened**, or **Arc Length Foreshortened**).
4. Select the placement location for the foreshortened dimension.
5. (Optional) To clear the display of the second arrowhead, right-click on the dimension and select **Options>Hide 2nd Arrowhead**.

Hint: Adding Text to Foreshortened Dimensions

Additional text can be added to a dimension value to further explain the intent of the dimension, as shown in Figure 26–8. To add text, double-click on the dimension value and enter text in the *Edit Dimension* dialog box. Ensure that the text is added before or after the **<<>>** symbols. These symbols represent the dimension value.

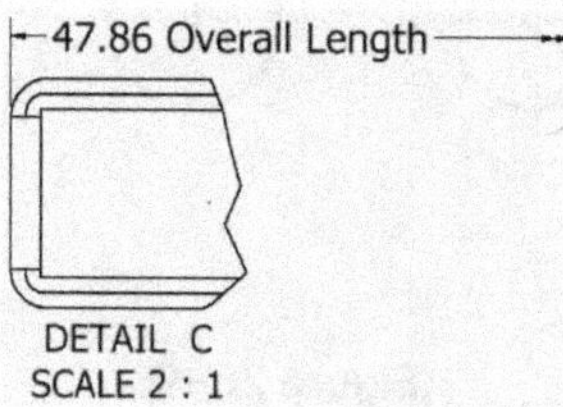

Figure 26–8

Linear and Angular Sum Dimensions

To dimension equally spaced features in a drawing, you can add linear (as shown on the left in Figure 26–9) and angular (as shown on the right) sum dimensions.

How To: Create a Linear or Angular Sum Dimension

1. Create a general dimension between the first two features. This represents the spacing value between all of the equally spaced features.
2. Create a second general dimension between the first and last feature. Do not fully locate the dimension.
3. Right-click on the previewed dimension value and select **Dimension Type>Linear Sum** or **Angular Sum**.
4. Select the first general dimension (spacing value), then place the new dimension.

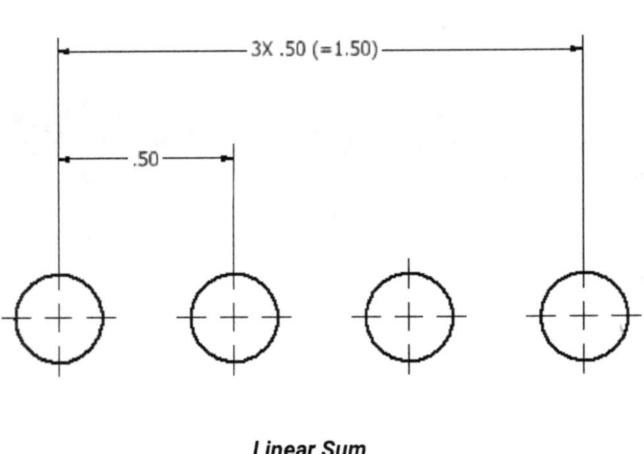

Linear Sum

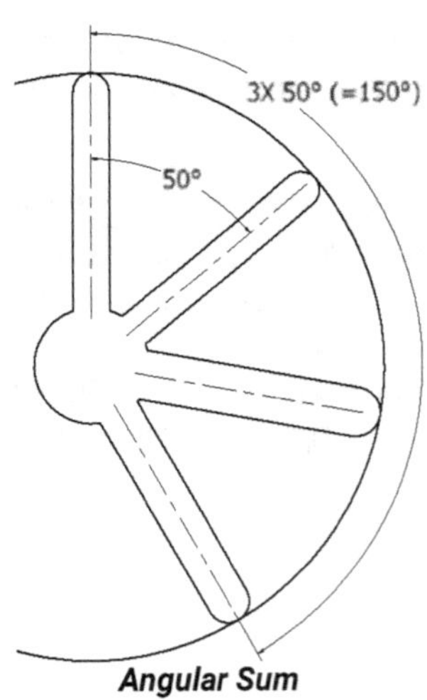

Angular Sum

Figure 26–9

Isometric General Dimensions

You can place general dimensions on a view that is placed in an isometric orientation, as shown in Figure 26–10. Press <Spacebar> while placing dimensions to toggle between alternate dimension orientations, if available.

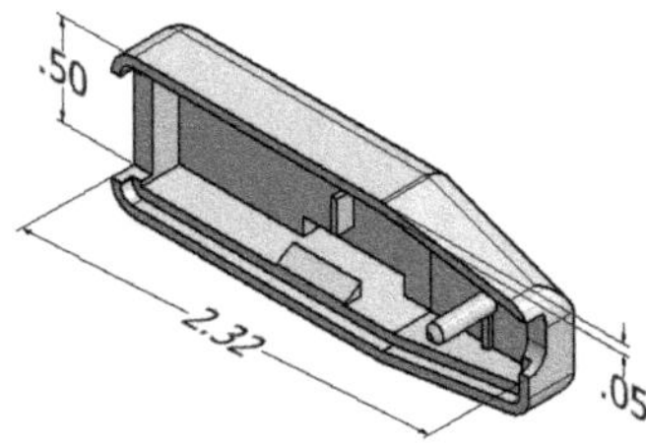

Figure 26–10

Baseline Dimensions

A baseline dimension enables you to create dimensions that share a common extension line. Baseline dimensions are shown in Figure 26–11.

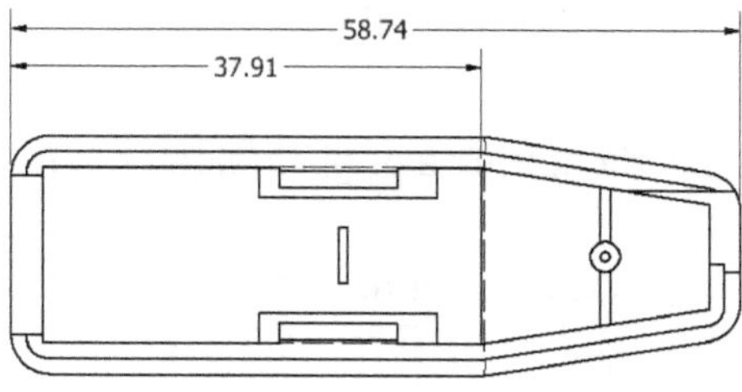

Figure 26–11

How To: Create a Baseline Dimension

1. In the *Dimension* panel, click (Baseline). To create a set of baseline dimensions that act as one unit, consider using (Baseline Set).
2. Select the entities to be dimensioned. The first entity selected is used as the default origin from which all other dimensions are dimensioned. You can also drag a window to select multiple edges for dimensioning.
3. Right-click in the graphics window and select **Continue**.
4. Move the cursor and left-click to place the dimensions.
5. With the command still active, select additional entities to add more baseline dimensions. The baseline dimensions are created.

***Note:** If required, you can change the origin point/entity that is used prior to placing the dimensions. This is done by right-clicking the entity you want to assign as the new origin, and selecting **Make Origin**.*

Ordinate Dimensions

An ordinate dimension enables you to create individual ordinate reference dimensions. Ordinate dimensions are shown in Figure 26–12.

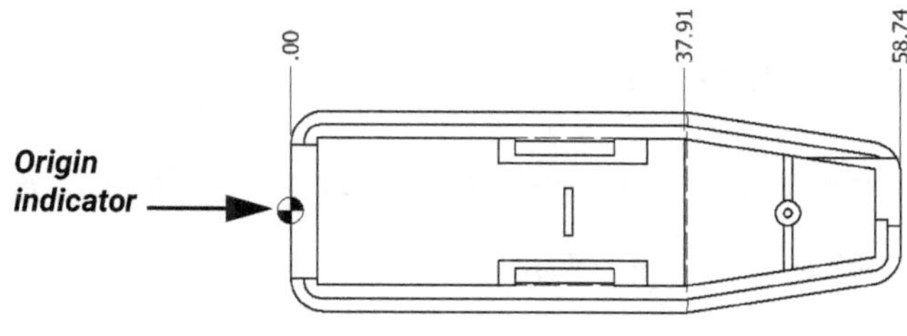

Figure 26–12

How To: Create Ordinate Dimensions

1. In the *Dimension* panel, click (Ordinate). To create a set of ordinate dimensions that act as one unit, consider using (Ordinate Set).
2. Select the view to dimension.
3. Select a point for the origin indicator. The origin indicator is the location from which the dimensions are referenced.
4. Select the entities to which you want to dimension. You can also drag a window to select multiple edges to dimension.
5. Right-click in the graphics window and select **Continue**.
6. Move the cursor and left-click to place the dimensions.
7. Select additional entities to add more baseline dimensions, if required.
8. Once you are finished selecting additional references, right-click in the graphics window and select **OK**. The ordinate dimensions are created.

- If you delete an origin indicator in a view, you will be prompted that all annotations that reference the indicator will also be deleted. Click **OK** or **Cancel** as required.
- To hide an origin indicator, select the indicator, right-click, and select **Hide Origin Indicator**.

Chain Dimensions

A chain dimension enables you to create multiple dimensions that are chained to one another, as shown in Figure 26–13.

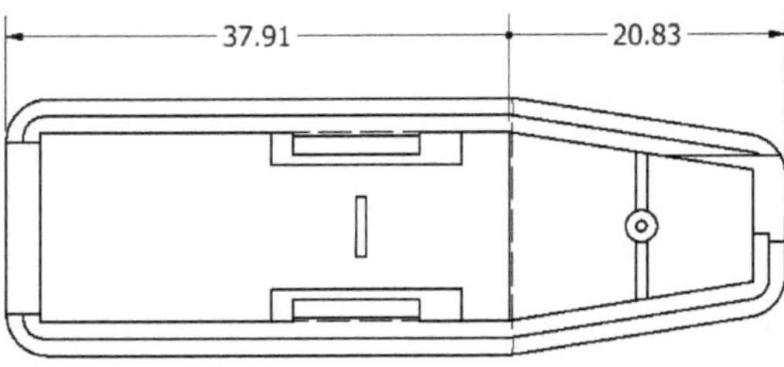

Figure 26–13

How To: Create a Chain Dimension

1. In the *Dimension* panel, click (Chain). To create a set of chain dimensions that act as one unit, consider using (Chain Set).

2. Select the entities to be dimensioned. The first entity selected is used as the default origin from which all other dimensions are dimensioned. You can also drag a window to select multiple edges for dimensioning.
3. Right-click in the graphics window and select **Continue**.
4. Move the cursor and click to place the dimensions.
5. Select additional entities to add more chain dimensions, if required.

Editing Drawing Dimensions

Some common editing options are available in the shortcut menu that can be used when editing drawing dimensions. They vary depending on which dimension is selected. The options are as follows:

Delete	Deletes the dimension from the drawing.
Move Dimension	Enables you to select another view, and have the dimension switch to that view. If no valid reference points exist in the selected view, a message displays indicating this, and the operation is canceled.
Arrange Dimensions	Enables you to arrange groups of selected dimensions so that they lie along one axis or multiple axes. The dimensions can be selected in one or multiple views. This command is also available in the *Annotate* tab in the *Dimension* panel.
Copy Properties	Enables you to copy dimension properties, including style, layer, text, precision, and tolerance between dimensions.
Hide Extension Line	Enables you to clear the display of an extension line in the drawing. Right-click on the extension line that is to be removed to select the option. Right-click on the dimension and click **Show all Extension Lines** to return them to the display.
Edit 1st/2nd Arrowheads	Enables you to change the display style of either the first or second arrowhead associated with the dimension.
Options	The options available vary depending on the type of dimension selected. For example, for General dimensions you can customize the arrow heads and leaders.
Precision	Sets the precision for the dimension.
Edit	Opens the *Edit Dimension* dialog box, in which you can modify the position of the text in relation to the text box, the display of the dimension value, add and edit text and symbols to go with the dimension, modify the tolerance format, and modify inspection dimensions.
Edit Model Dimension	Opens the *Edit Dimension* toolbar that enables you to enter a new dimension for the model. Changes made here will reflect in the model geometry.
Text	Opens the *Format Text* dialog box.

Edit Dimension Dialog Box

When editing a model or drawing dimensions using the **Edit** option, the *Edit Dimension* dialog box is available, as shown in Figure 26–14. Unlike a general dimension, the *Edit Dimension* dialog box does not display when a Baseline, Ordinate, or Chain dimension is placed.

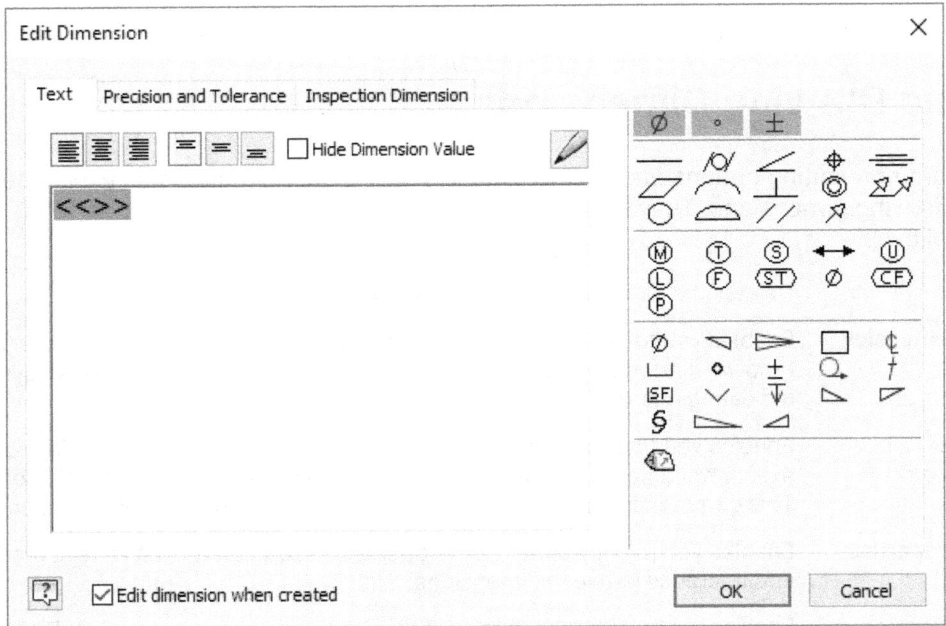

Figure 26–14

- The *Text* tab enables you add text before and after the dimension value (**<<>>**), change its position or justification, and specify text properties ( ). Additionally, symbols can be embedded by selecting them and adding them to the text line.
- The *Precision and Tolerance* tab enables you to override dimension values, set a tolerance method, and define the precision setting for the dimension. Settings specified in the Precision and Tolerance tab for a selected dimension overrides any settings made to the active dimension style.
- The *Inspection Dimension* tab enables you to set the selected dimension as an inspection dimension, and customize how it displays.

Hint: Dimension Selection and Filters

To select dimensions for editing, you can do any one of the following:

- Select individual dimensions in the drawing.
- Hold <Ctrl> to add multiple dimensions to the selection set.
- Drag a selection box around the required dimensions.
- Use any of the four selection filter options in the *Selection Filter* drop-down list in the Quick Access Toolbar, as shown in Figure 26–15.

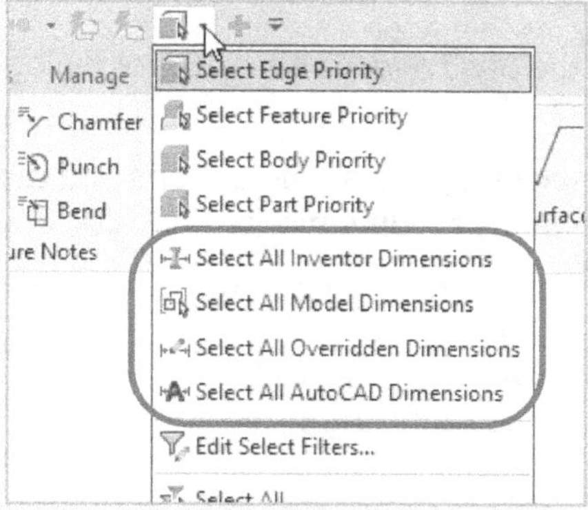

Figure 26–15

Dimension Styles

You can control the appearance of dimensions by applying or changing dimension styles. The software comes installed with a number of predefined styles for each of the major drafting standards such as ANSI, ISO, JIS, etc. The styles available in a new drawing are determined by the active standard in the template that was used to create the drawing file.

- To set the style for a dimension before you place it, start the dimension command, and select the dimension style in the *Format* panel, as shown in Figure 26–16.

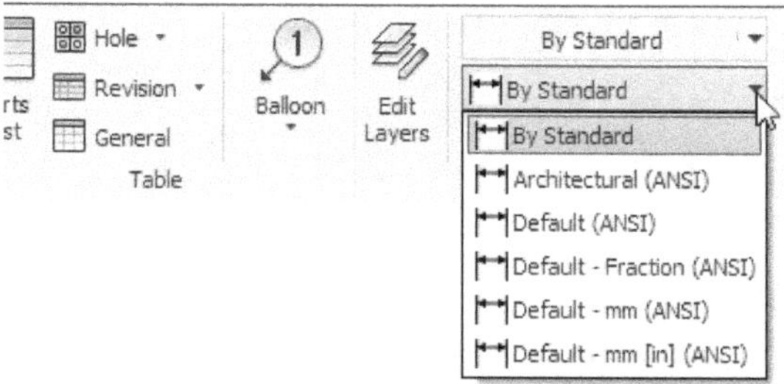

Figure 26–16

- To change the style of an existing dimension, select the dimension first and then select the style in the drop-down list.

  ***Note:** To retain the last used dimension style so that it is automatically used as the style for future dimensions, set the **Default Object Style** option to **Last Used** in the Drawing tab in the Application Options dialog box.*

A dimension style controls the attributes of dimensions, such as units, precision, text size, font, default orientations, etc. You can create your own dimension styles or change existing dimension styles.

- To display dimension styles, select the *Manage* tab and in the *Styles and Standards* panel, click (Styles Editor). In the *Style and Standard Editor* dialog box, expand the *Dimension* area to view the list of styles.
- To edit a dimension style, select it and use the options and tabs in the right-hand pane (shown in Figure 26–17) to make modifications.

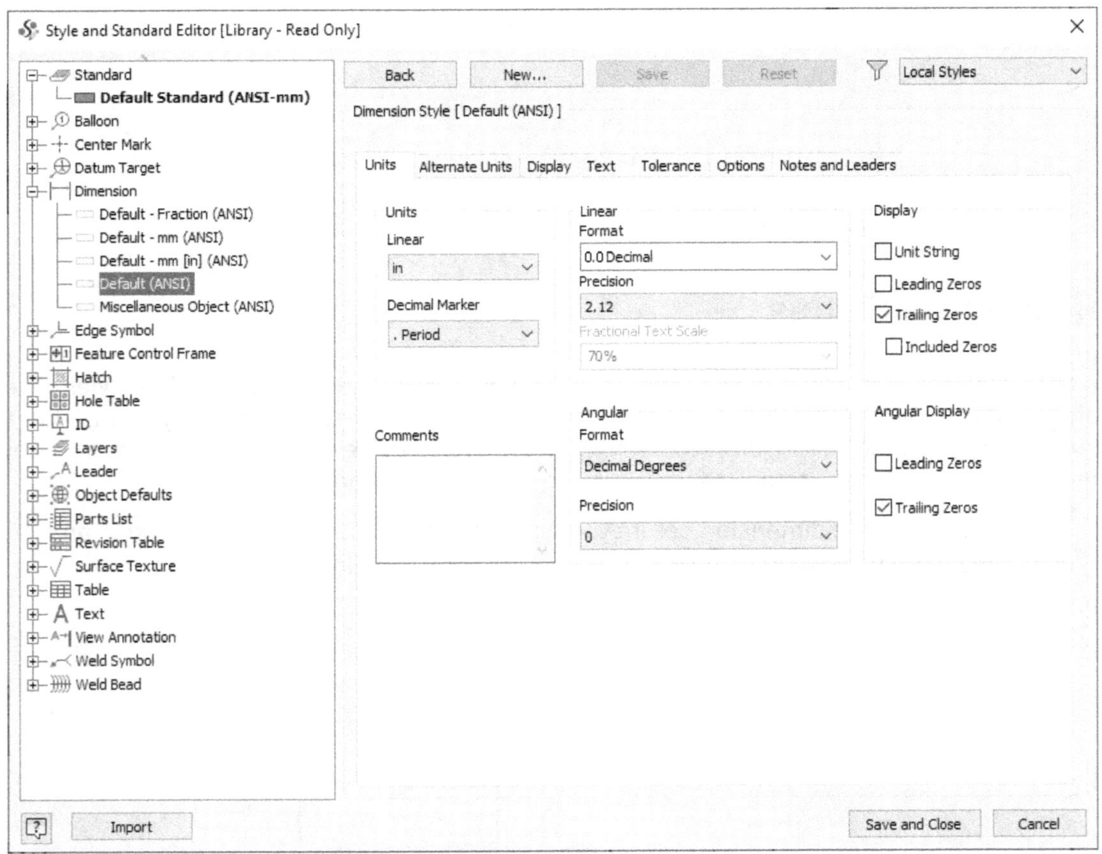

Figure 26–17

26.2 Drawing Sheets

All drawings can contain an unlimited number of sheets and each sheet can contain a variety of views, annotations, tables, etc. Once multiple sheets have been added to a drawing you can use the Model browser to navigate between them, delete them, or move views between them.

Use any of the following procedures to work with drawing sheets:

- To add a new sheet to a drawing using the same sheet format as the active sheet, right-click in the graphics window and select **New Sheet**. Alternatively, in the *Place Views* tab> *Sheets* panel, click (New Sheet). You can also right-click on the drawing name in the Model browser and select **New Sheet**.
- Sheets can be copied within a drawing or between drawings.
- To add a new sheet to a drawing that uses an alternate sheet format, expand the **Drawing Resources>Sheet Formats** nodes, select the required sheet format, right-click, and select **New Sheet**, as shown in Figure 26–18.

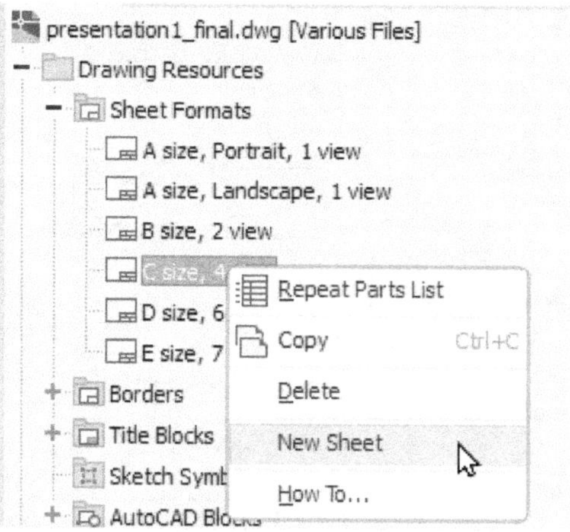

Figure 26–18

- To switch between sheets in a drawing, double-click on the sheet name in the Model browser. The Model browser shown in Figure 26–19 shows that **Sheet:2** is the active sheet.

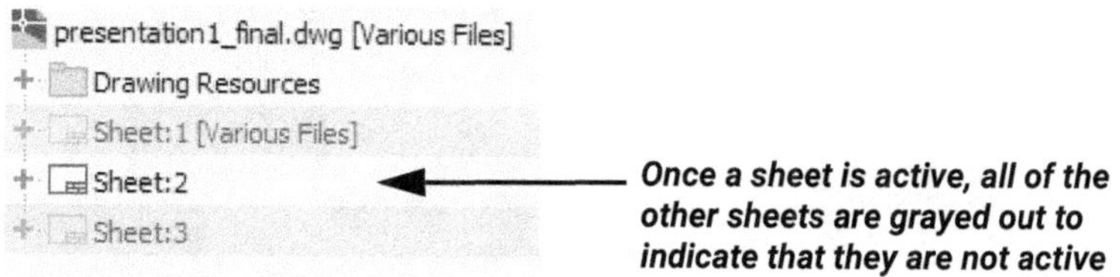

Figure 26–19

- Views can be duplicated on a sheet by selecting them and using the right-click **Copy** and **Paste** commands.
- Views can be copied between sheets by selecting them in the source view, right-clicking, and selecting **Copy**. Activate the new sheet, right-click, and select **Paste**.
- To move a view between sheets, select it in the Model browser and drag it to the new sheet.
- To delete a sheet, right-click on the sheet name in the Model browser and select **Delete**. The *Delete Sheet* dialog box opens. Click **OK** to delete the selected sheet. Click >> to expand the dialog box to refine which sheets to delete.
- To make changes to a sheet, right-click on the sheet name in the Model browser and select **Edit Sheet**. Using the *Edit Sheet* dialog box (shown in Figure 26–20), you can make changes to the sheet's size, name, and orientation, and set exclude options for count and printing.

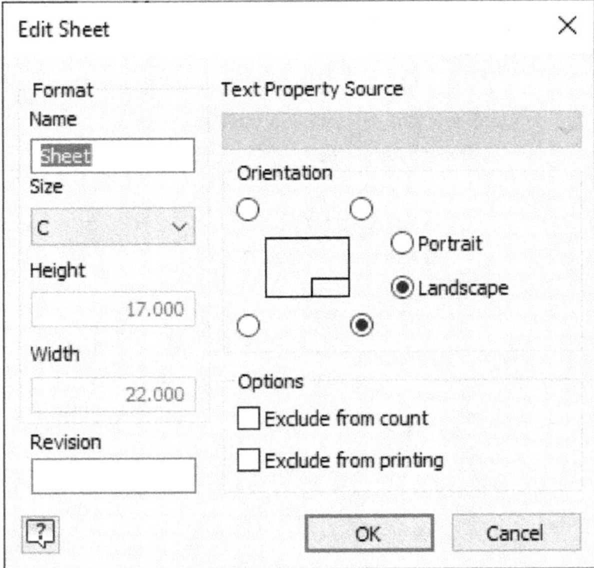

Figure 26–20

- You can replace the existing title block and drawing border on a sheet by deleting the current border and/or title block and assigning a new one from the *Drawing Resources* node, as shown on the left and right in Figure 26–21, respectively.

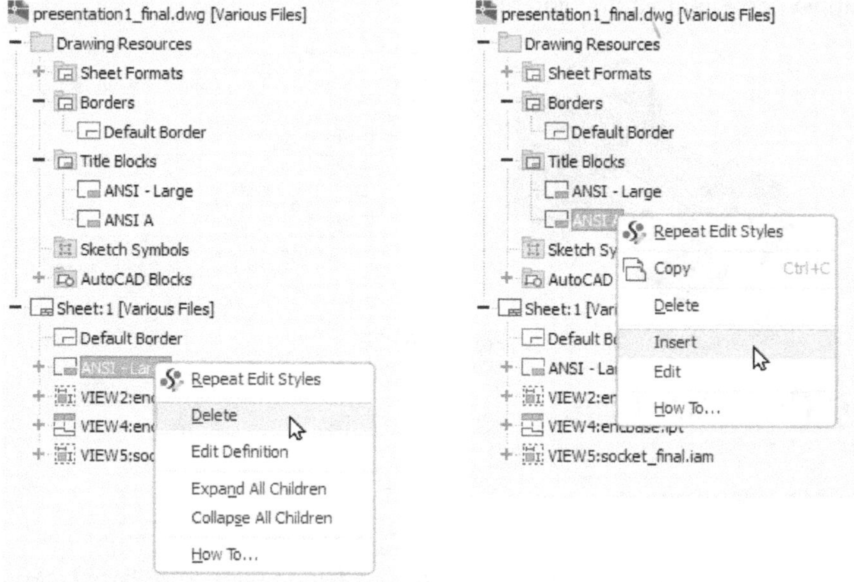

Figure 26–21

Hint: Changing Sheet Colors

The background color of a sheet can be changed at the document level using the *Document Settings* dialog box. To change the color, complete the following:

1. Select the *Tools* tab>*Options* panel and click (Document Settings).
2. In the *Document Settings* dialog box, select the *Sheet* tab.
3. In the *Colors* area, select the color swatch for the **Sheet**.
4. In the *Color* dialog box, select a new color and click **OK**.
5. Close the *Document Settings* dialog box.

Hint: Creating Drawing Sheet Formats

Once the layout of a drawing sheet has been defined (views, tables, parts list, etc.), it can be saved as a sheet format in the existing drawing by right-clicking on the sheet name in the Model browser and selecting **Create Sheet Format**. Once saved, it is listed in the **Sheet Formats** node in the **Drawing Resources**. This format can be used in the future to create additional sheets in the drawing by right-clicking its name in the **Drawing Resources** node and clicking **New Sheet**. To include any custom sheet formats in a drawing template, you must edit the template or create a new template with the new sheet format included.

26.3 Parts List

A parts list is a list of the components in an assembly, as shown in Figure 26–22. You can add a single or multiple parts list to a drawing file.

Parts List			
ITEM	QTY	PART NUMBER	DESCRIPTION
1	1	Base_Vise	
2	1	Sliding_Jaw	
3	1	Collar	
4	2	Jaw_Plate	
5	2	Set_Screw	
6	2	Slide_Key	
7	1	Special_Key	
8	4	ANSI B18.6.3 - 1/4-20 x 3/4	Countersunk Flat Head Screw
9	1	Screw_Sub	

Figure 26–22

Creating the Parts List

How To: Create a Parts List

1. Select the *Annotate* tab>*Table* panel, and click (Parts List). The *Parts List* dialog box opens, as shown in Figure 26–23.

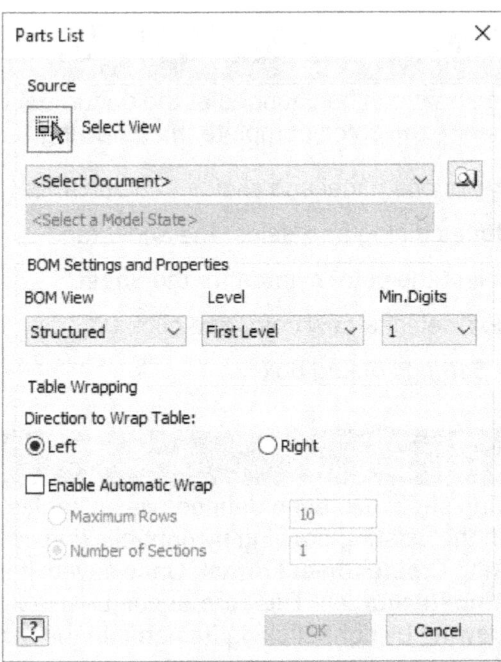

Figure 26–23

2. To identify the assembly from which to generate the parts list, click (Select View) and select a view in the drawing.
   - To add the parts list without creating a drawing view, in the *Source* area browse to and select an assembly to reference.
   - If a Model State exists in the reference assembly, it can be selected for use in the parts list by selecting its name in the *Source* area.
3. Define the remaining options in the *Parts List* dialog box. The options are as follows:

BOM View	Enables you to determine what is shown in the bill of materials, such as whether or not subassemblies are included. • The **Parts Only** BOM View option provides a row in the BOM for each component in the assembly, regardless of whether or not it is in a subassembly. Subassembly components are not provided with a row in this view. • The **Structured** BOM View option provides a row in the BOM for the top-level components (**First Level**) or the top level and all sub-levels (**All Levels**). 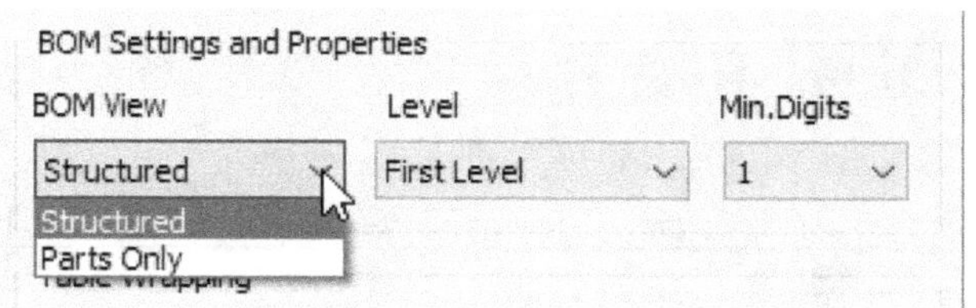
Level	This option (in Structured) controls whether first level children or all children are listed in the parts list.
Min. Digits	This option (in Structured and Parts Only) controls the minimum number of digits in the item number.
Numbering	This option (in Parts Only) selects from numeric or alphanumeric schemes.
Delimiter	This option (in Structured (Legacy)) is a character that marks the beginning or end of data.
Inheritance	This option (in Structured (Legacy)) enables parts at subassembly levels to update with changes made to the item or to the value of the parent assembly. (For example, if the assembly item value changes from 1 to A, the subassembly parts change from 1.1, 1.2, to A.1, A.2).
Table Wrapping	These options enable you to wrap the parts list rows and control the direction to wrap.

4. Once all of the options have been selected, click **OK** and select a point to place the parts list in the drawing.

Once the parts list is placed, consider using the following:

- Selecting a component row in a parts list table will highlight the component in the graphics window. Press and hold <Ctrl> to select multiple rows and highlight all selected components in the graphics window.
- Selecting a component row that has multiple occurrences will highlight all of the components in the graphics window.
- Double-clicking a row in a parts list opens the row's component model.
- Double-clicking when the parts list is fully highlighted in red opens the parts list for editing.

Editing the Parts List

To edit the parts list, select the list, right-click and select **Edit Parts List**. The *Parts List* dialog box opens, as shown in Figure 26–24.

ITEM	QTY	PART NUMBER	DESCRIPTION
1	1	Base_Vise	
2	1	Sliding_Jaw	
3	1	Collar	
4	2	Jaw_Plate	
5	2	Set_Screw	
6	2	Slide_Key	
7	1	Special_Key	
8	4	ANSI B18.6.3 - 1/4-20 x 3/4	Countersunk Flat Head Screw
9	1	Screw_Sub	

Figure 26–24

***Note:** A file can be opened directly from the Parts List dialog box or the Parts List table by right-clicking the model name and selecting **Open**.*

The tools at the top of the *Parts List* dialog box enables you to customize the parts list. The available customizations include the following:

- To change the columns displayed in the parts list, click (Column Chooser) and use the *Parts List Column Chooser* dialog box to add and remove columns from the list.
- Custom instance properties are not automatically available. You must click **New Property** in the *Parts List Column Chooser* dialog box to create the property. Once created, it is automatically assigned to the parts list.
- To group rows, click (Group Settings) and use the *Group Settings* dialog box to assign the keys that define groupings. You can define up to three keys to specify groupings.
- To filter items from display in the parts list, click (Filter Settings). Use the *Filter Settings* dialog box to define the filter items. You can assign one or more filters. Once a filter has been assigned, the Parts List node in the Model browser changes from to to easily identify that there has been filtering set in the parts list. These icons also appear in the header of the *Parts List* dialog box depending on whether there was filtering set or not.
- To specify a sort order, click (Sort). The *Sort Parts List* dialog box enables you to specify the column name that is going to be used for initial sorting. Additionally, you can specify a second or third column by which to sort as well. Expand the dialog box to set whether the sort is done numerically or by string.

  Note: *By default, a sort must be re-executed if parts are added or removed from the list. To automatically sort when a change in parts is made, select* ***Auto Sort on Update****.*

- To export the parts list, click (Export) and select the file format to export to. Available types include .XLS, .TXT, .CSV, etc.
- To customize the layout of the parts list table, click (Table Layout) to open the *Parts List Table Layout* dialog box to set how the parts list text will display and will wrap.
- If the assembly contains iParts or iAssemblies, click (Member Selection) to select the members to include in the parts list.

Hint: Displaying Subassembly Components

To show all components of a subassembly in the parts list, verify that the assembly BOM's *View Property* is set to **All Levels** (right-click on the *Structured* tab heading in the BOM and select **View Properties**). This enables you to click the + sign in the drawing's parts list to list the sub-components.

Additional customization of the parts list can be done with direct manipulation of the rows and columns in the list.

- To make changes to editable items in the list (e.g., item numbers or descriptions) click in the cell and enter a new value. Edited cells display in bolded blue. Items displayed in red cannot be edited.
  - To return an override to the BOM value, right-click on the cell and clear the **Static Value** option so that it is no longer enabled.
  - To save item numbers changes to the assembly BOM, click (Save Item Overrides to BOM) or right-click an individual overridden value and select **Save Item Overrides to BOM**.
- To create an additional row to represent a part, right-click and select **Insert Custom Part**. A custom part can be used to represent a part that is referenced in the assembly but not modeled. It can also be used as a placeholder for a removed part.
- To make a row invisible, select the row, right-click and clear the **Visible** option. Invisible rows are shaded gray in the dialog box, and are not displayed in the drawing.
- Columns can be dragged to adjust their width. Headings automatically wrap and can be resized to fit the largest word.
- To force a column break in the list, select a row in the *Parts List* dialog box, right-click and select **Wrap Table at Row**. An unwrapped and wrapped table is shown in Figure 26–25.

Unwrapped table

PARTS LIST		
ITEM	QTY	PART NUMBER
1	1	Base_Vise
2	1	Sliding_Jaw
3	1	Collar
4	2	Jaw_Plate
5	2	Set_Screw
6	2	Slide_Key
7	1	Special_Key
8	4	ANSI B18.6.3 - 1/4-20 x 3/4
9	1	Screw_Sub

Break row (row 6)

Wrapped table

PARTS LIST			PARTS LIST		
ITEM	QTY	PART NUMBER	ITEM	QTY	PART NUMBER
6	2	Slide_Key	1	1	Base_Vise
7	1	Special_Key	2	1	Sliding_Jaw
8	4	ANSI B18.6.3 - 1/4-20 x 3/4	3	1	Collar
9	1	Screw_Sub	4	2	Jaw_Plate
			5	2	Set_Screw

Figure 26–25

- A parts list table can be split multiple times and the split tables moved freely on the sheet or dragged between sheets in the Model browser.
  - To split a table into multiple individual tables, right-click on a row in the parts list table (not on a row in the *Parts List* dialog box that is used for editing) and select **Table>Split Table**.
  - Once split, the **Parts List** node in the Model browser is subdivided to represent the parent table and split tables.
  - To unsplit a table, select anywhere in the table and select **Table>Un-split Table**. An original parts list table and split table are shown in Figure 26–26.

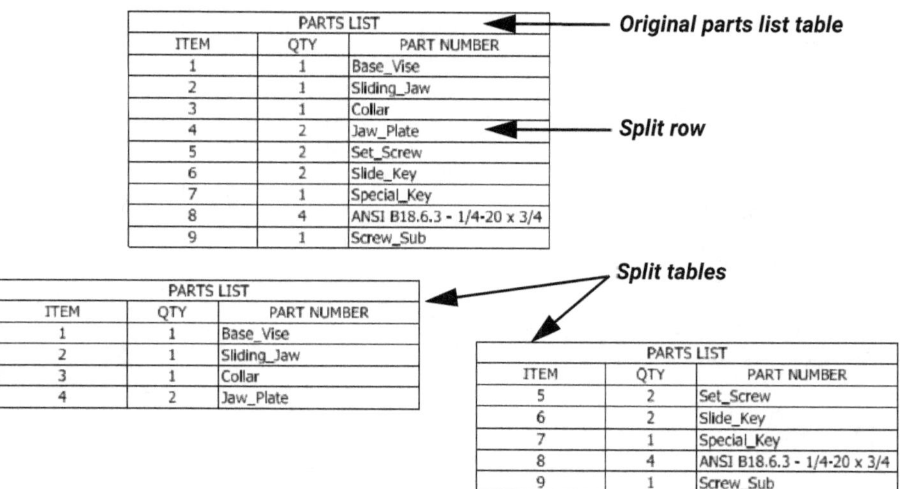

PARTS LIST		
ITEM	QTY	PART NUMBER
1	1	Base_Vise
2	1	Sliding_Jaw
3	1	Collar
4	2	Jaw_Plate
5	2	Set_Screw
6	2	Slide_Key
7	1	Special_Key
8	4	ANSI B18.6.3 - 1/4-20 x 3/4
9	1	Screw_Sub

PARTS LIST		
ITEM	QTY	PART NUMBER
1	1	Base_Vise
2	1	Sliding_Jaw
3	1	Collar
4	2	Jaw_Plate

PARTS LIST		
ITEM	QTY	PART NUMBER
5	2	Set_Screw
6	2	Slide_Key
7	1	Special_Key
8	4	ANSI B18.6.3 - 1/4-20 x 3/4
9	1	Screw_Sub

Figure 26–26

- To format individual columns, right-click on the column and select the required option, as shown in Figure 26–27. The **Format Column** option enables you to change the column heading, justification, units formatting, and substitute values from another column. The **Column Width** option enables you to enter an exact width for the column.

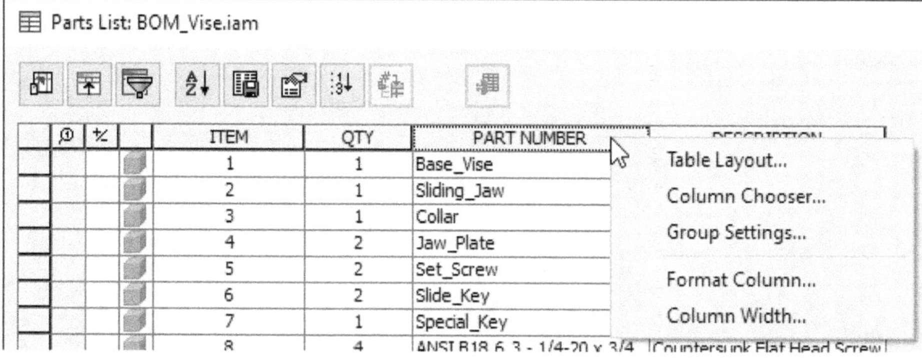

Figure 26–27

Hint: Parts Lists for Design Views

For parts list tables, you can control how the parts list is filtered if you are creating a parts list for a design view. To enable the Autodesk Inventor software to take into account the design view settings, you must edit the parts list table and in the Filter settings ( ), set the filter to **Assembly View Representation**, select the view name, and then enable the **Limit QTY to visible components only** option, as shown in Figure 26–28.

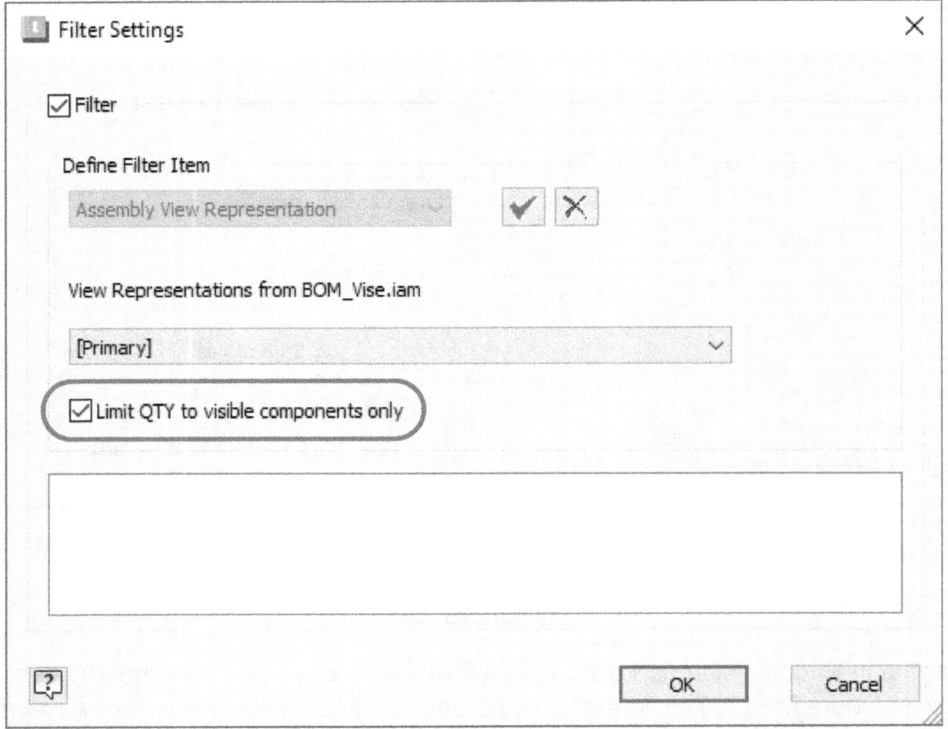

Figure 26–28

26.4 Drawing Balloons

Balloons are used to identify the components in the parts list with their associated geometry in a drawing view. This is done using item numbers. You can place balloons either individually on parts or globally on all parts in a view, as shown in Figure 26–29. Balloons are associated with the view to which they are attached. If you move the view, the balloons also move.

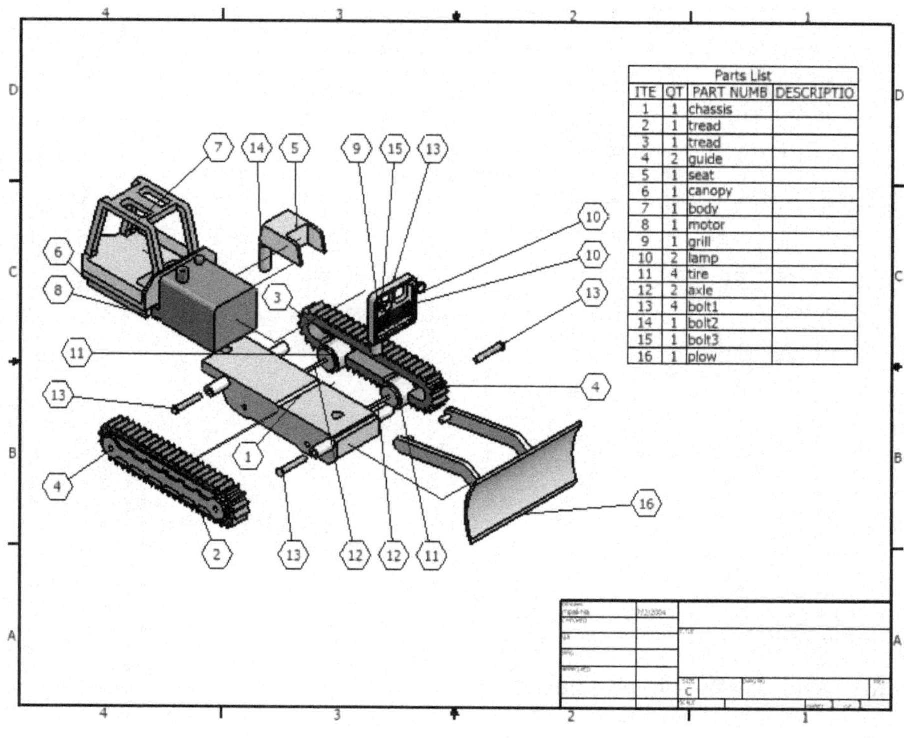

Figure 26–29

How To: Place Individual Balloons

1. Select the *Annotate* tab>*Table* panel, click (Balloon).
2. Select the part.
3. Click to select vertices for the leader. Drag to position the leader. To enable 15-degree snapping when placing the balloon, hold <Ctrl> while dragging.
4. Right-click after the final location for the balloon has been set, and select **Continue** to add a balloon for another part.
5. Right-click and select **Cancel [Esc]** to finish creating the balloons.

How To: Globally Place Balloons

1. Select the *Annotate* tab>*Table* panel, expand **Balloon** and click (Auto Balloon). The *Auto Balloon* dialog box opens, as shown in Figure 26–30.

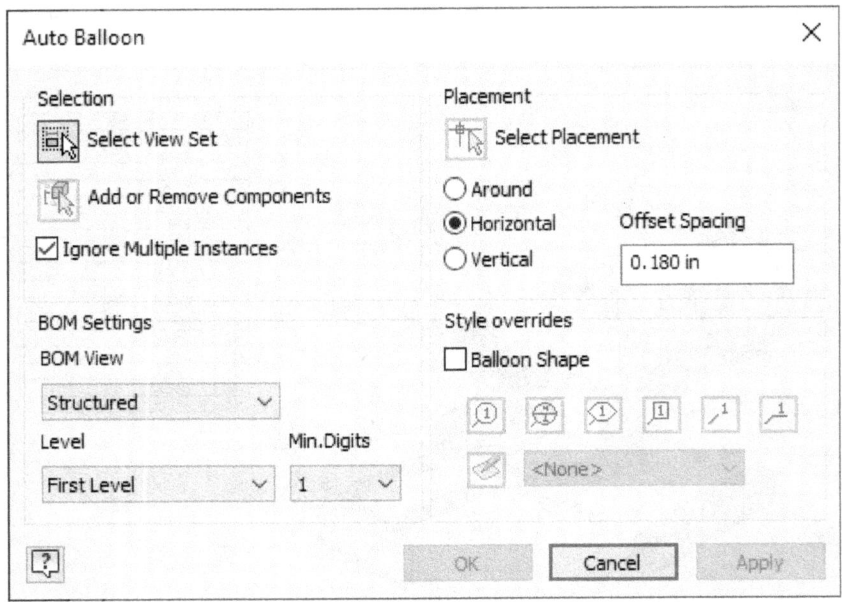

Figure 26–30

2. Select the drawing view.
3. Select the parts to which to add balloons.
4. Click to place balloons and select the **Around**, **Horizontal**, or **Vertical** option to place balloons around, in a horizontal row, or in a vertical column of the view, respectively.
5. Enter a value in the *Offset Spacing* field to fix the spacing between balloons.
6. If required, select **Balloon Shape** to override the balloon default shape.
7. Click in the drawing to place the balloons.
8. Click **OK** to place the balloons and complete the operation.

Manipulating Balloons

Once a balloon has been placed, you can manipulate it in the following ways:

- Move balloons and the ends of the balloon segments by dragging them.
- Align multiple balloons by selecting them by holding <Ctrl> or window selecting, right-clicking, and selecting an **Align** option in the context menu. The alignment options can be horizontally or vertically with one another, horizontally or vertically with an offset, or aligned based on a reference edge.
- Create additional segments by right-clicking on the balloon and selecting **Add Vertex/ Leader**. Select the location on the existing leader to place the new vertex and then drag it.
- Add another balloon and label to an existing balloon by right-clicking on the balloon and selecting **Attach Balloon**. An example is shown in Figure 26–31. To sort the attached balloons from smallest to largest or from A to Z, right-click on the stack and select **Sort Balloons**.
- To delete a balloon, right-click on the balloon and select **Delete**. Alternatively, select the balloon and press <Delete>. To delete a balloon from a multi-item balloon, right-click on the balloon that you want to remove and select **Remove Balloon**.
- To open a component identified with a balloon, right-click on the balloon and select **Open**.
- To change a balloon arrowhead, right-click on the balloon and select **Edit Arrowhead**. Change the arrowhead in the *Change Arrowhead* dialog box, as shown in Figure 26–31.

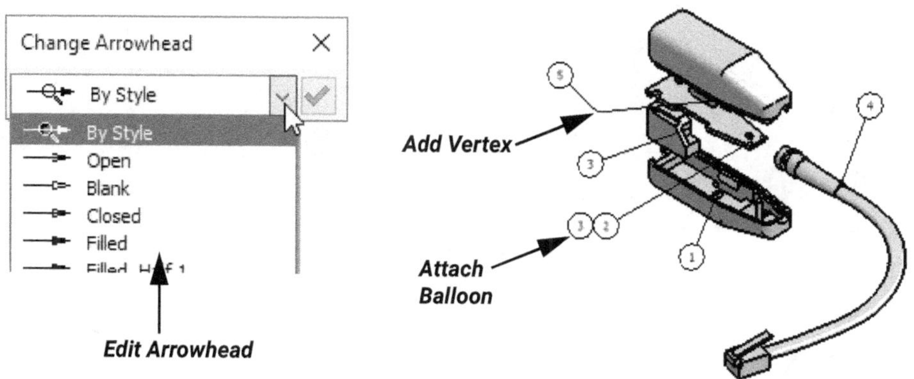

Figure 26–31

- To edit a balloon, right-click on the balloon and select **Edit Balloon**. The *Edit Balloon* dialog box opens. Use this dialog box to change the balloon type, the symbol used (standard or custom), and the value of the balloon. Alternatively, you can double-click on the balloon or on its leader to edit the balloon.

Note: *Balloon styles can be specified in the Style and Standard Editor dialog box.*

- To edit the iProperties of a component in the parts list, right-click on the component in the list and select **iProperties**.
- Instance property values can be displayed in a balloon by editing the balloon style (right-click on the balloon and click **Edit Balloon Style**). In the *Property Display* area, use (Column Chooser) to create and assign the instance property as a new property. Once created, edit the order of the properties to have the instance property displayed first if using the Circular - 1 Entry *Shape* option or first or second if using the Circular - 2 Entries *Shape* option. You can set up a custom balloon style for use with instance properties and assign it for use as needed.

  Note: *Once a parts list is placed on a sheet, you can hover over the rows to highlight the balloon and component in the view. Alternatively, you can hover over a component in the view to locate its row in the parts list.*

26.5 Styles and Standards

The *Style and Standard Editor* controls the appearance of part edges, centerlines, dimension components, layers, part lists, balloons, and other annotations in a drawing. The software is installed with a default standard, and several other drafting standards are included (e.g., ANSI, ISO, and JIS). You can also create your own standards, as required.

- A central library is used to store information pertaining to styles and standards. A file can reference one or more styles from this library. If a change is made to a style in the library, it is reflected in all files that reference that style. The central library is located in the following location: *C:\Users\Public\Public Documents\Autodesk\Inventor 20XX\Design Data*.
- Unique styles and standards can be created and stored with the drawing file. These can include new styles or modifications to existing library styles.

To open the *Style and Standard Editor*, select the *Manage* tab>*Styles and Standards* panel and click (Styles Editor). The *Style and Standard Editor* dialog box opens, as shown in Figure 26–32.

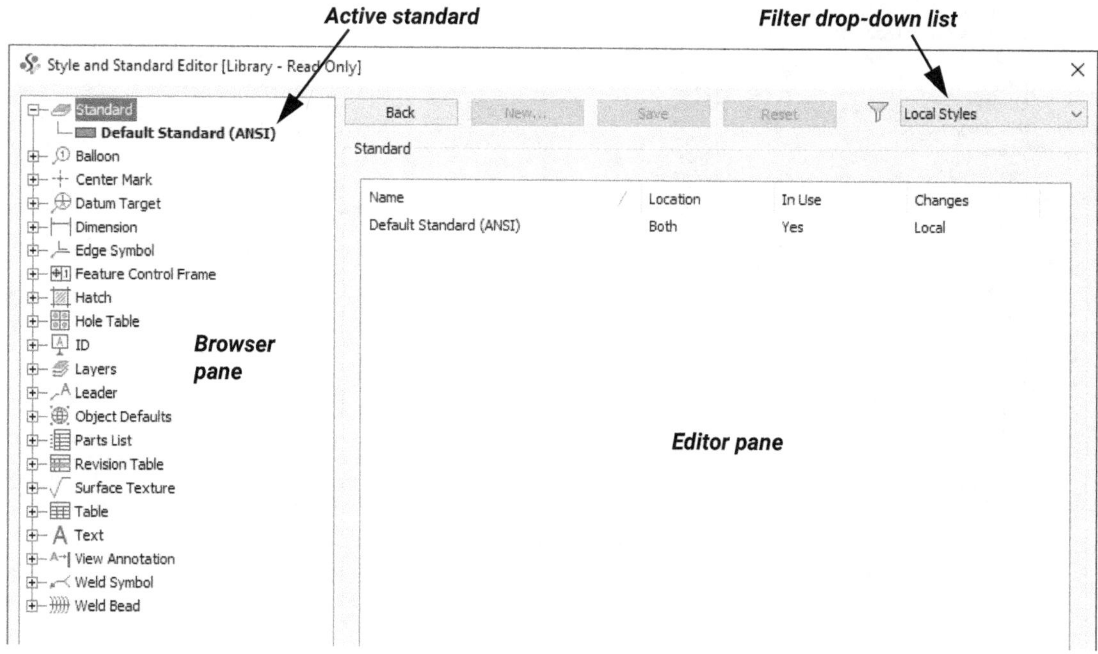

Figure 26–32

Hint: Displaying All Styles

By default, only styles and standards used in the active document are listed, as indicated by the **Local Styles** option in the *Filter* drop-down list. To display all of the available styles and standards, select **All Styles** in the *Filter* drop-down list.

Standards

Standards are comprised of all of the styles assigned for the various annotation types (e.g., dimensions, balloons, hatching, parts list, etc.). They also control the appearance of such drawing items as part edges, line weights, and projection type (first angle or third angle). The active standard is identified in bold in the dialog box. Select the standard to review the settings in the right-hand pane, as shown in Figure 26–33.

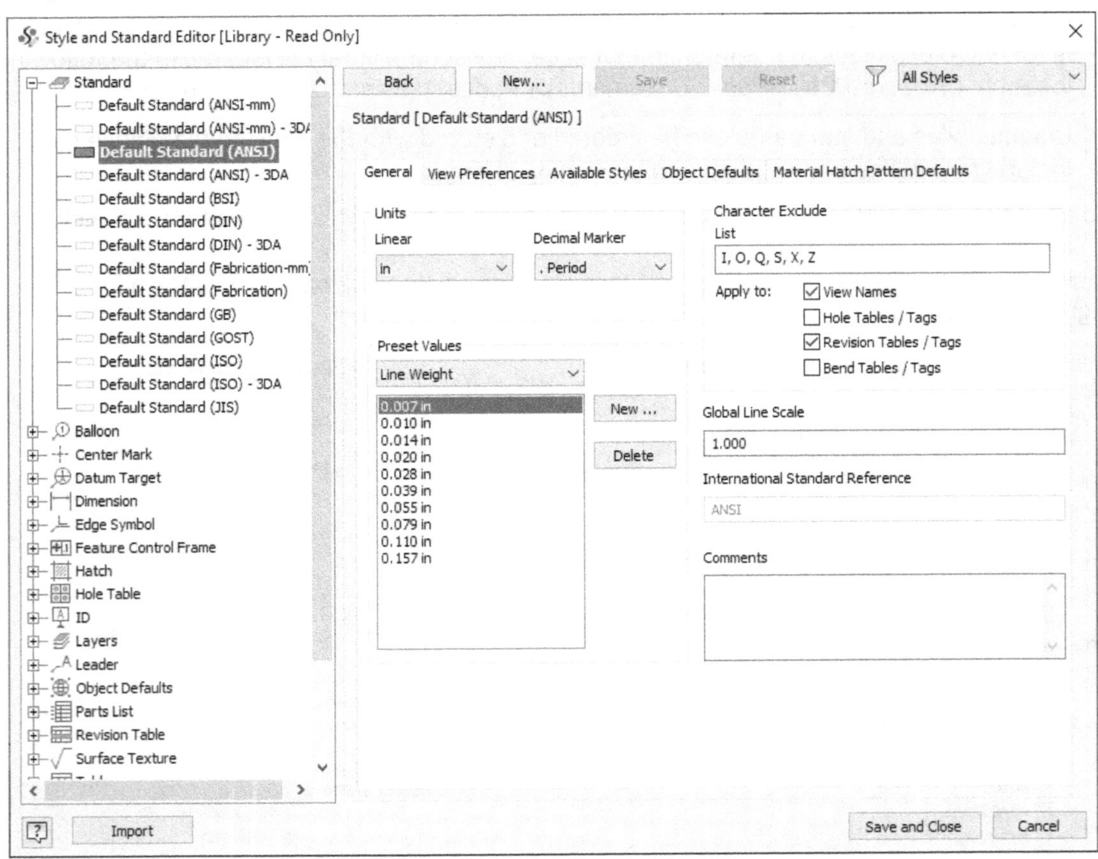

Figure 26–33

The active standard for a new drawing is based on the template file that is selected to create the drawing file. However, you can double-click on a different standard to activate it. The tabs that are available for the selected standard enable you to customize drawing annotation. If multiple standards are used, consider creating a different template for each standard you use.The following two tabs specifically enable you to set further styles for annotation categories and objects:

- The *Available Styles* tab for a Standard controls the style being used for each of the drawing annotation categories.
- The *Object Defaults* tab controls the default layer and style for specific drawing objects.

Styles

Multiple styles can exist in each of the style type categories. To display a category's available styles, select it in the browser pane. For example, Figure 26–34 shows the styles available for the **Dimension** style type category.

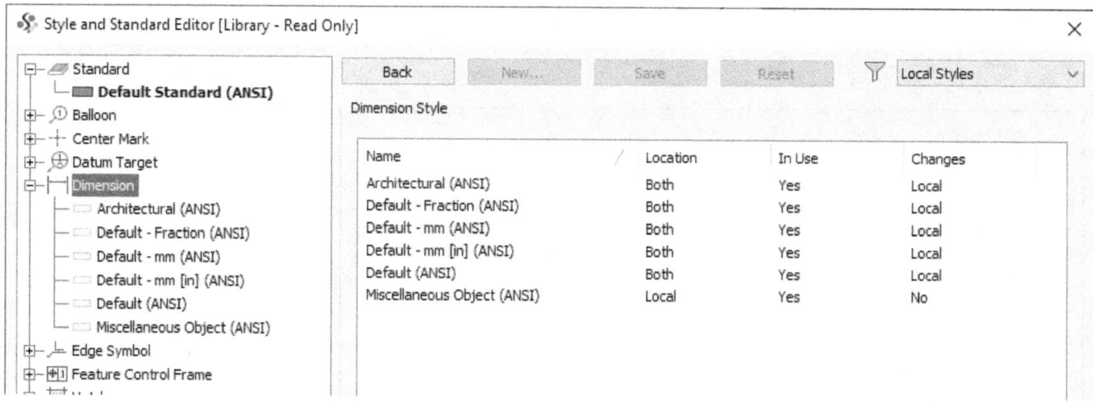

Figure 26–34

- The *Name* column lists the names of the available styles.
- The *Location* indicates whether the style is located in the **Library**, **Local** to the file, or **Both**.
- The *In Use* column indicates whether the style is used in the active standard.
- The *Changes* column indicates whether the changes that have been made are in the **Library**, the **Local** file or **Both**, or if **No** changes have been made.

To edit a style, select it in the browser pane and edit the options as required. For example, Figure 26–35 shows the options that can be edited to modify the Default (ANSI) Dimension style type.

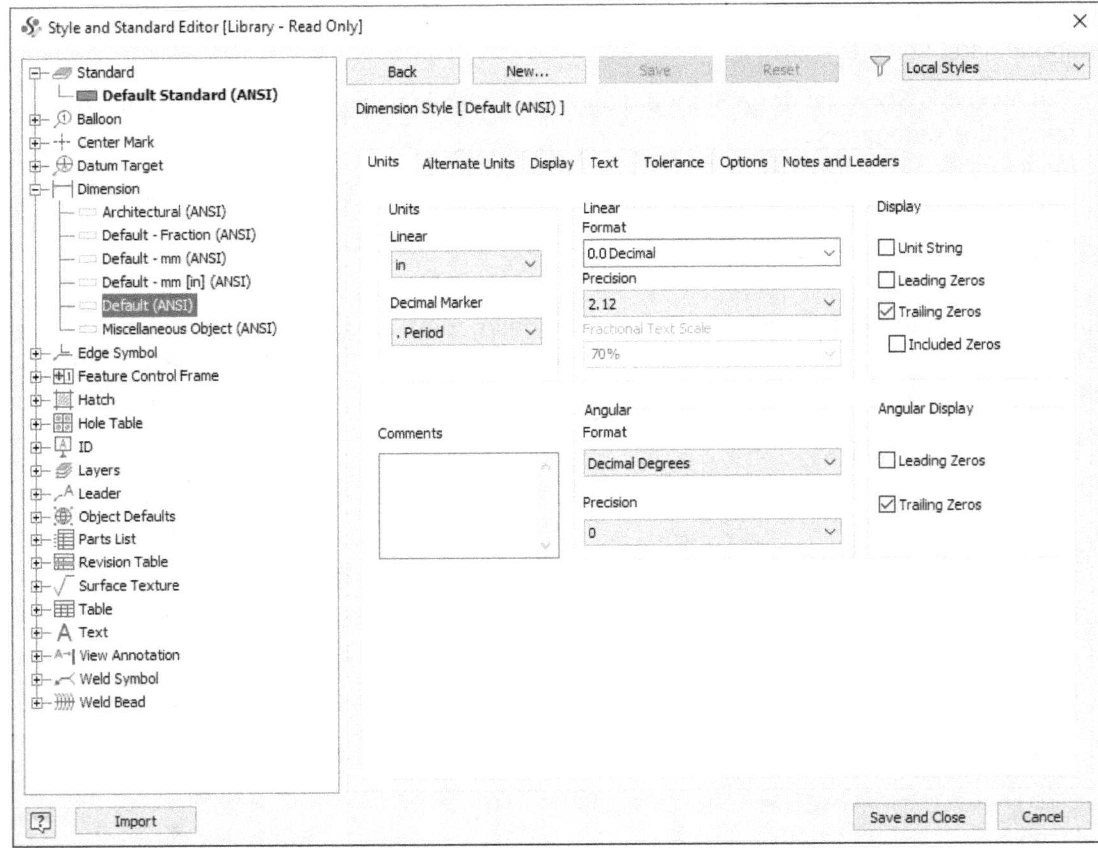

Figure 26–35

- When changes are made and saved for a style, they are saved to the active file.
- To save the changes to the style library, right-click on the style and select **Save to Style Library**. You need to have the correct permissions to save to the style library (controlled in the project file).
- To replace local changes by overwriting with the settings from the original style library, right-click on the style and select **Update Style**.
- To create a new style, select a style and click **New** in the browser pane. The selected style becomes the basis for the new style.

  Note: *To share a style library, copy the styles to a common network location and map the Design Data in the project file. You can also set the Application Options to identify the network location in which the style library is stored.*

26.6 Drawing View Hatching

The default hatch pattern is set in the **Hatch** style type category in the *Style and Standard Editor*, as shown in Figure 26–36.

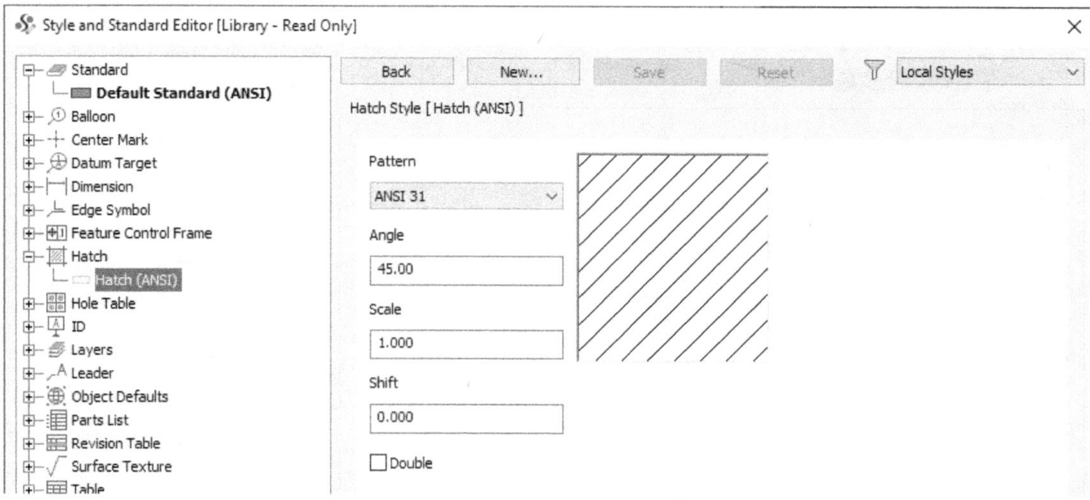

Figure 26–36

- Hatch patterns can be assigned from the internal style library or from an external *.PAT file. To load or assign additional patterns, select **Other** in the *Pattern* drop-down list to open the *Select Hatch Pattern* dialog box, as shown in Figure 26–37.

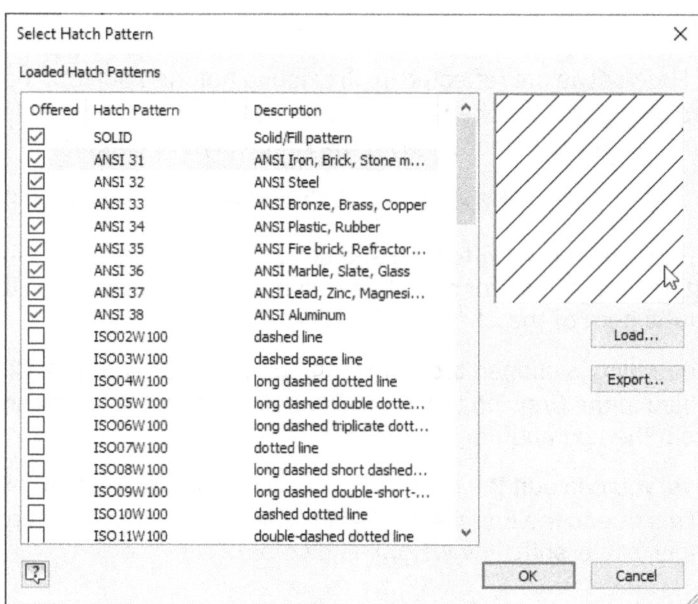

Figure 26–37

- Hatch patterns can be individually assigned to material types. In the default drawing standard, select the *Material Hatch Pattern Defaults* tab, select (From Style Library), and assign the hatching for each material, as shown in Figure 26–38.

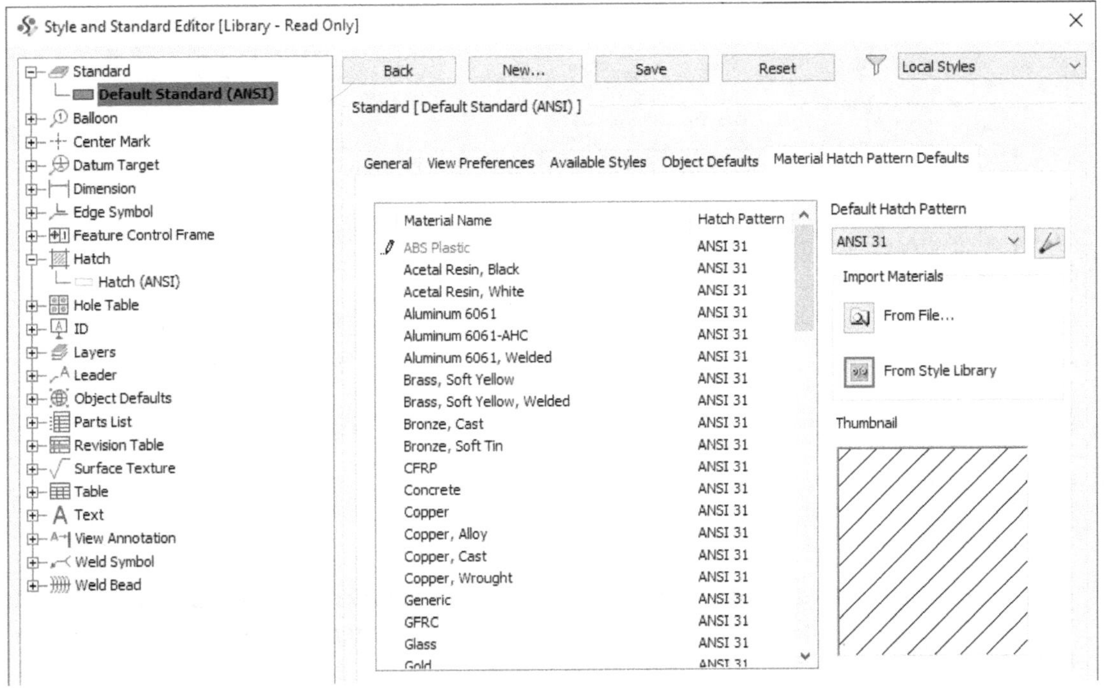

Figure 26–38

- Changes to the Hatch style are reflected in all existing hatched objects that use it. Any hatch overrides done directly on a hatched section in the drawing are independent of the Hatch style. Hatch overrides remain unchanged if the Hatch style is changed.
- Hatch patterns (or fill) can be assigned to a closed sketched section in a drawing by clicking (Hatch/Fill Region) on the *Sketch* tab and selecting a closed area in the sketch. The default Hatch style that is used for sketches is specified for the **Sketch Hatch** object type in the **Object Defaults** item of the *Style and Standard Editor*.
- To ensure that hatching is clipped around overlapping text, ensure that **Cross Hatch Clipping** is enabled in the *Drawing* tab in the *Document Settings*. To change the clipped border size, select the text and drag.
- For section views, you can edit the hatching by right-clicking on the hatching in the view and selecting **Edit**. This opens the *Edit Hatch Pattern* dialog box, where you can change the pattern type, angle, scale, shift, line weight, and color.

Practice 26a
Detail a Drawing I

Practice Objectives

- Change the sheet color of the active drawing.
- Retrieve and create the dimensions in the drawing.
- Add a new drawing sheet in a drawing.
- Move a drawing view between drawing sheets.
- Create a parts list table in a drawing.
- Add balloons to a drawing view to identify the components listed in a parts list table.

In this practice, you will open an existing drawing, modify it, and add the dimensions shown in Figure 26–39.

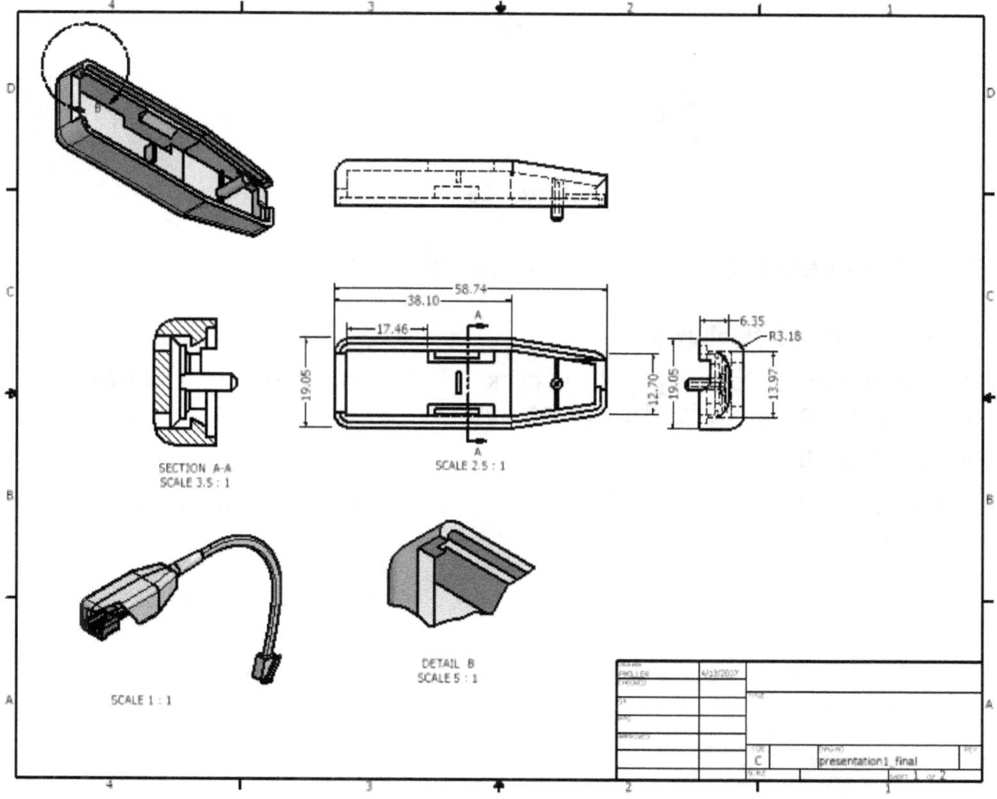

Figure 26–39

On a second drawing sheet, you will move a view from a previous sheet, create a parts list for the model, and add balloons to the drawing view, as shown in Figure 26–40.

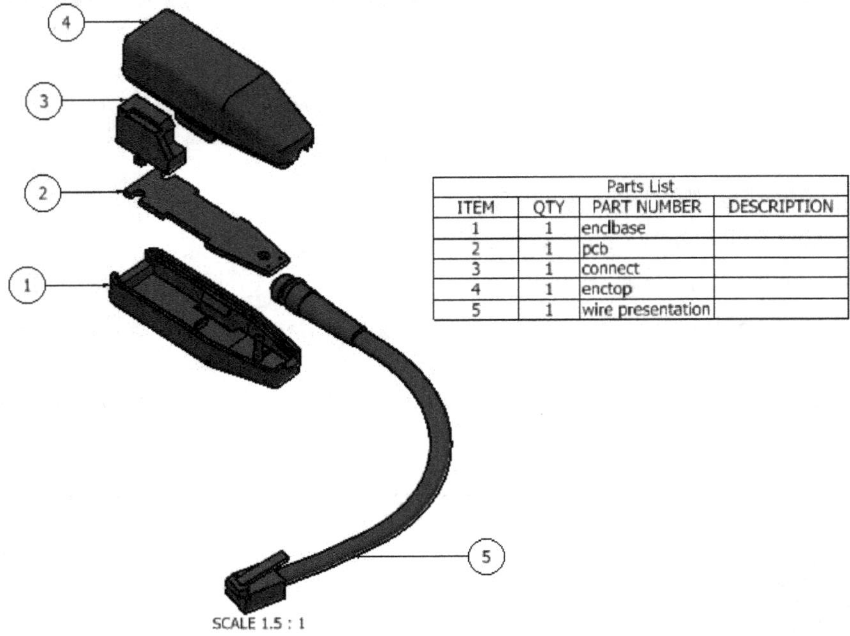

Parts List			
ITEM	QTY	PART NUMBER	DESCRIPTION
1	1	enclbase	
2	1	pcb	
3	1	connect	
4	1	enctop	
5	1	wire presentation	

Figure 26–40

Task 1: Open a drawing file and modify the sheet color.

1. Open **presentation1_final.dwg**.
2. Select the *Tools* tab>*Options* panel and click (Document Settings). The *Document Settings* dialog box opens for the current drawing.
3. Select the *Sheet* tab.
4. Select the colored box in front of **Sheet** in the *Colors* area. Select the white cell in the *Basic colors* area.

5. Click **OK** in the *Color* and *Document Settings* dialog boxes. This enables you to change the sheet color, in this case to white. The drawing displays as shown in Figure 26–41.

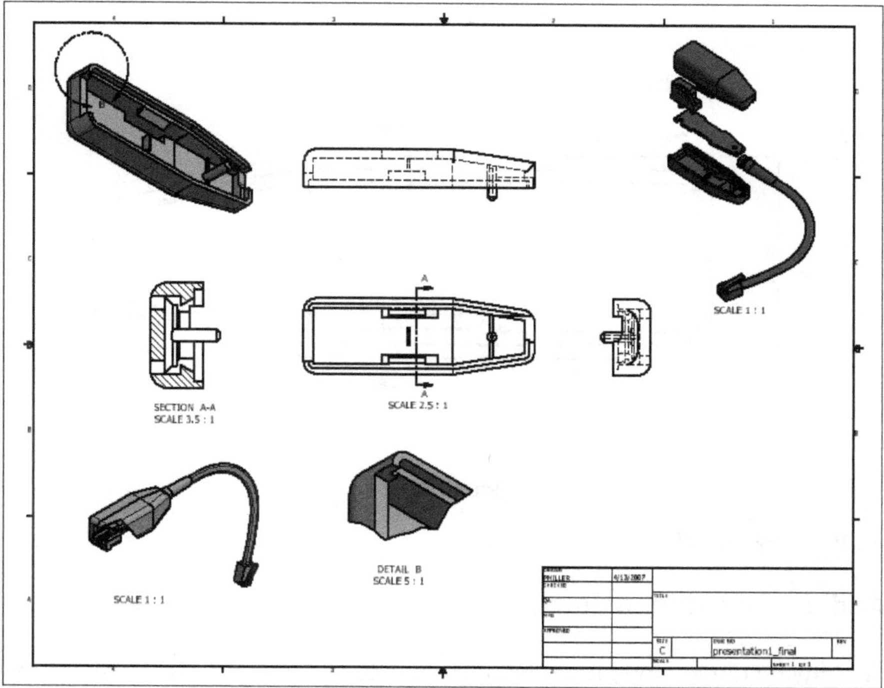

Figure 26–41

Note: To display an assembly in an exploded state, the assembly must be inserted into a presentation file, an exploded snapshot view created, and the presentation file then inserted into a drawing so that the snapshot can be used.

Task 2: Retrieve model dimensions.

1. Right-click in the graphics window and select **Retrieve Model Annotations**. The *Retrieve Model Annotation* dialog box opens. Alternately, you can retrieve dimensions by selecting the *Annotate* tab>*Retrieve* panel and clicking (Retrieve Model Annotations).
2. Ensure that the *Sketch and Feature Dimensions* tab is active.
3. Select the base view in the center of the drawing as the view to retrieve dimensions into. All dimensions are displayed.

4. Ensure that the **Select Features** option is active in the *Select Source* area and select the dimensions to keep, as shown in Figure 26–42.

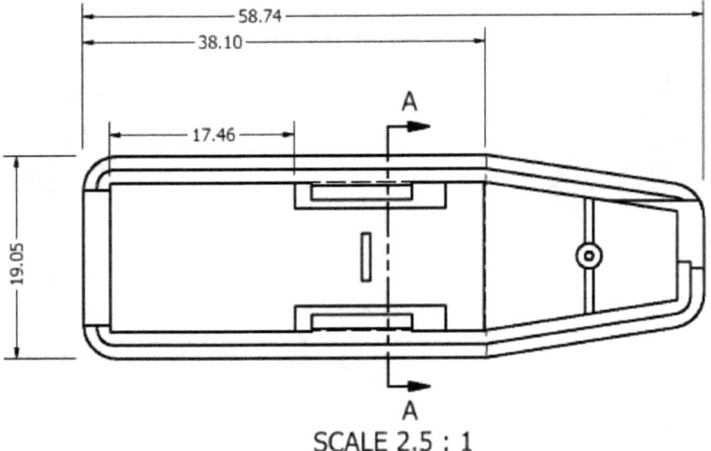

Figure 26–42

5. Click **OK** to apply and close the dialog box.

Task 3: Add drawing dimensions.

You can use drawing dimensions to add dimensions to your drawing that are not model dimensions. Drawing dimensions can be placed as you would place model dimensions in a part file, but the dimensions are dependent on the part geometry, and you cannot change their value. If the part changes, the drawing dimensions update automatically.

1. Select the *Annotate* tab.
2. In the *Dimension* panel, click (Dimension).
3. Add the **12.7** dimension shown in Figure 26–43 to the middle base view. This dimension references points that are at the virtual intersections of lines in a drawing view. To place the dimension, select the top slanted edge first, right-click, select **Intersection**, and select a vertical line (not a point) on the right edge. The first reference point for the dimension is now assigned. Select the bottom slanted edge, right-click, select **Intersection**. Select the right vertical edge again to define the second reference point. Use the left mouse button to place the dimension.

4. The *Edit Dimension* dialog box opens, enabling you to immediately edit the dimension (not the value). Click **OK** to close the dialog box without making changes to the dimension. The (Dimension) option remains active.

   Note: *To disable the Edit Dimension dialog box from displaying when a dimension is placed, clear the* ***Edit dimension when created*** *option at the bottom of the dialog box. To open this dialog box to edit dimensions, select a dimension value and it becomes available. You can enable the option again if you want the Edit Dimension dialog box to open by default on dimension placement.*

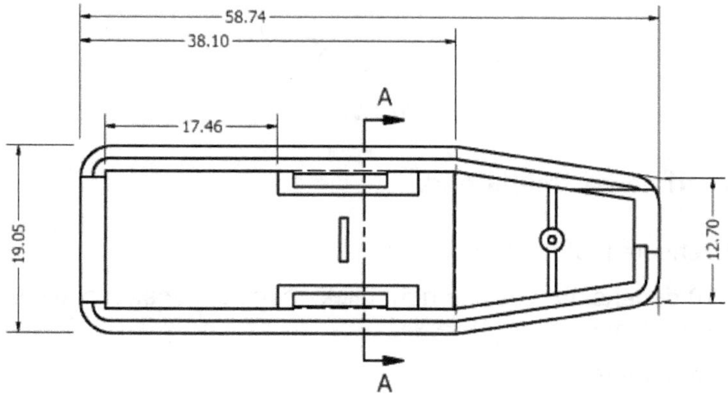

Figure 26–43

5. Add the **6.35** dimension shown in Figure 26–44 to the middle right view. To create this dimension, select and dimension the horizontal linear edge. Selecting the end points of the entity is also possible. However, it is sometimes difficult to ensure that you are selecting the correct end point. Zooming into a view can help ensure that the correct end points are selected.

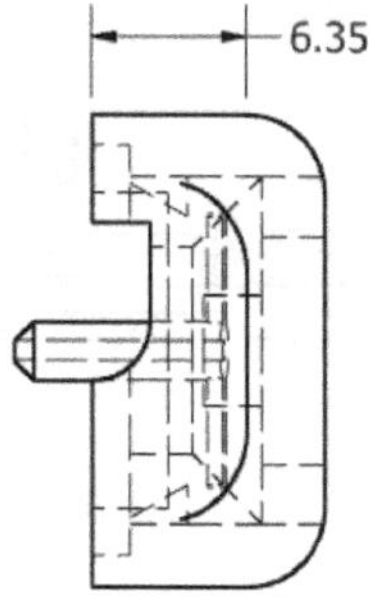

Figure 26–44

6. Click **OK** to close the dialog box without making changes to the dimension.

7. Add the remaining three dimensions shown in Figure 26–45. If your dimensions display differently to those shown, you might have selected points as references instead of edges.

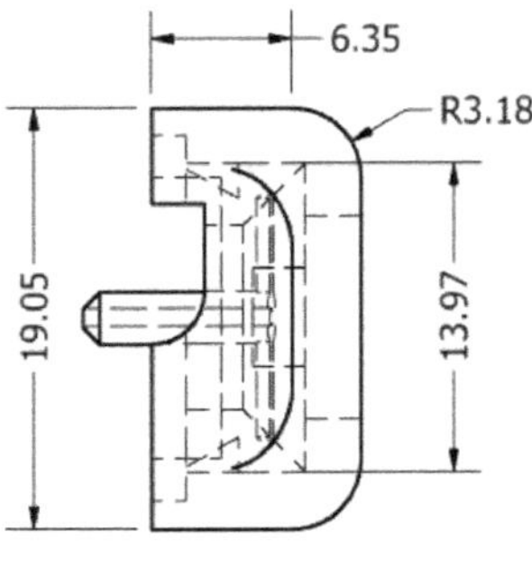

Figure 26–45

Task 4: Create ordinate dimensions.

1. Press <Esc> to ensure that the **Dimension** option is disabled.
2. Delete the **38.10** dimension. You can right-click on the dimension and select **Delete**, or select the dimension and press <Delete>.
3. Delete the **58.74** dimension.
4. In the *Dimension* panel, click (Ordinate).
5. Select the base view, as shown in Figure 26–46.
6. Select the location for the origin, as shown in Figure 26–46.

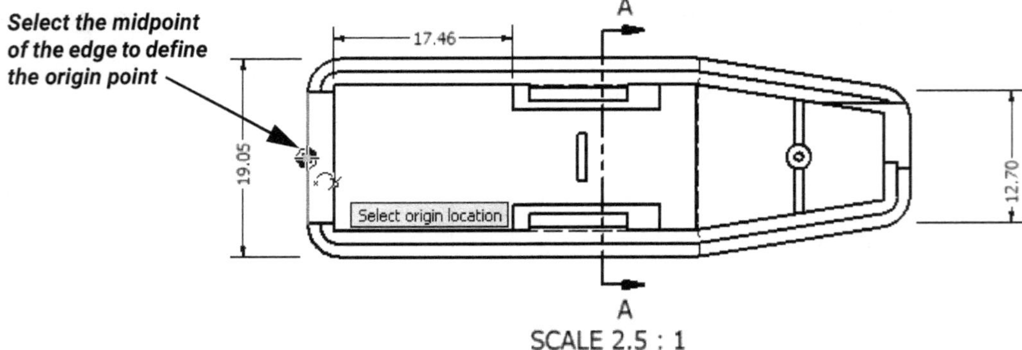

Figure 26–46

7. Select the three edges shown in Figure 26–47 for the dimension references.

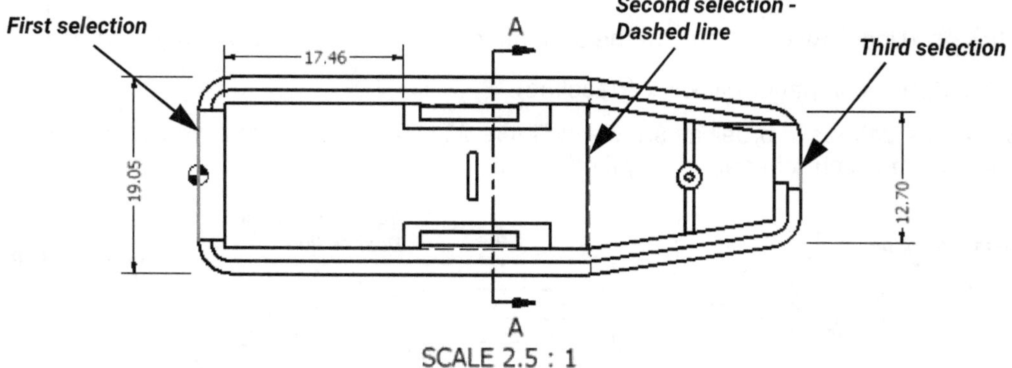

Figure 26–47

8. Right-click and select **Continue**.
9. Click a location above the view to place the dimensions.

   Note: *Depending on where you place the cursor, both horizontal and vertical ordinate dimensions are previewed.*

10. Right-click and select **OK**. The ordinate dimensions display as shown in Figure 26–48. You may need to move them once placed.

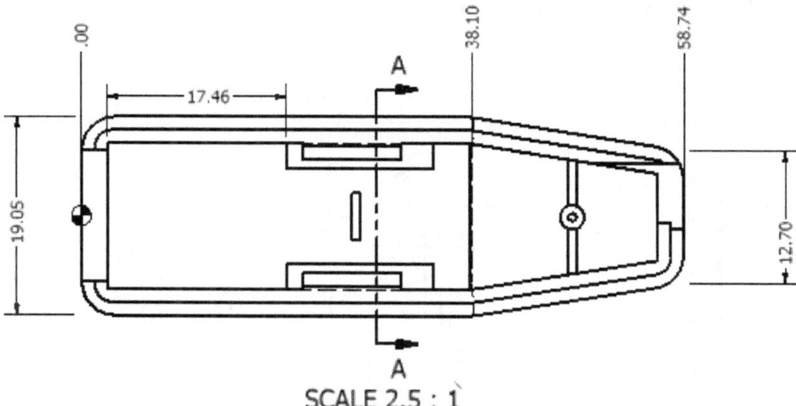

Figure 26–48

Task 5: Create baseline dimensions.

1. Click (Undo) twice to remove the ordinate dimensions and the origin indicator.
2. In the *Dimension* panel, click (Baseline).
3. Select the entities in order, as shown in Figure 26–49. The first entity you select will be the origin from which other entities will reference.

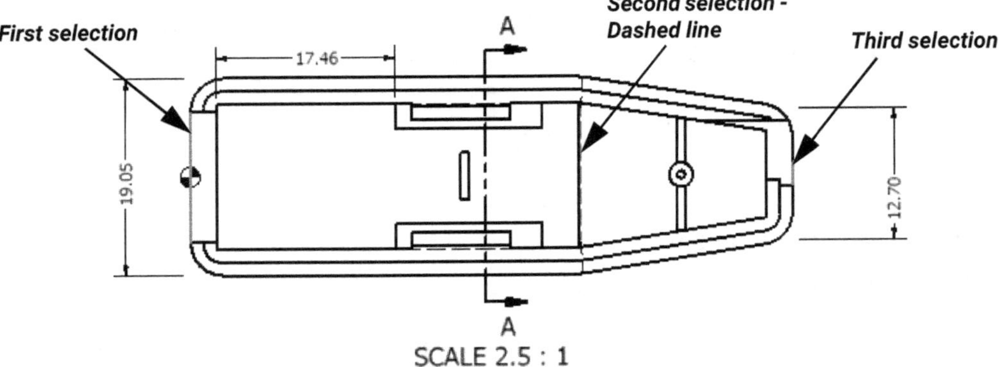

Figure 26–49

4. Right-click and select **Continue**.
5. Select a location above the view to place the dimensions.The baseline dimensions display as shown in Figure 26–50.

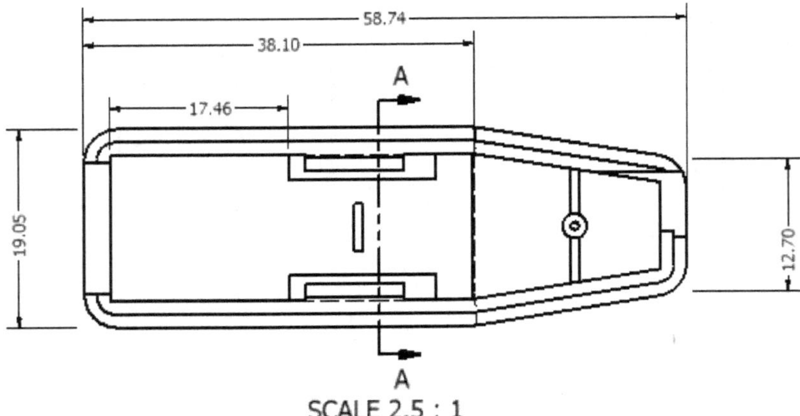

Figure 26–50

Task 6: Create chain dimensions.

1. Click (Undo) to remove the baseline dimensions.
2. In the *Dimension* panel, click (Chain).
3. Select the entities in the order shown in Figure 26–51. The first entity you select will be the origin from which other entities will reference.

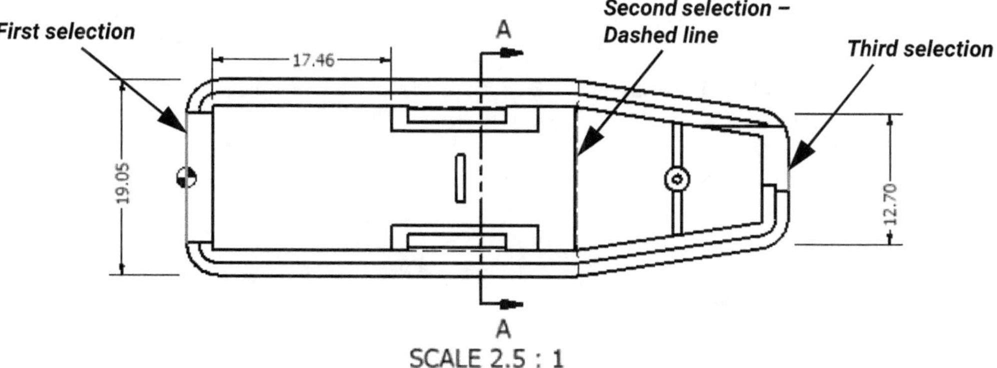

Figure 26–51

4. Right-click and select **Continue**.
5. Select a location above the view to place the dimensions. The chain dimensions display as shown in Figure 26–52.

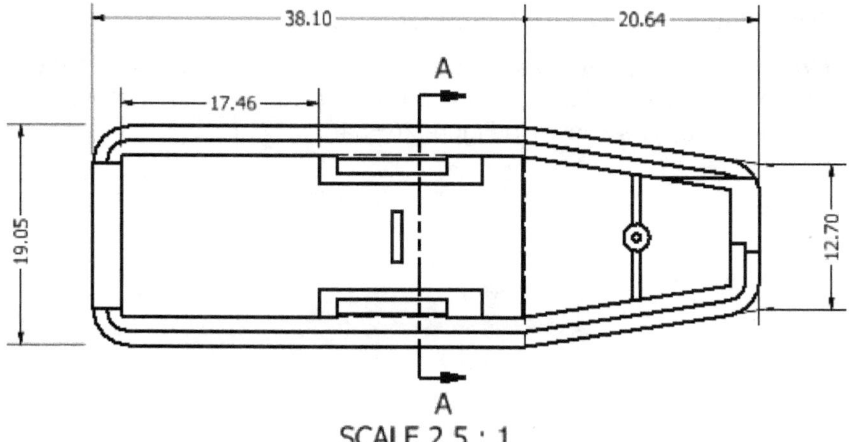

Figure 26–52

Task 7: Create a new drawing sheet.

In this task, you will create a new sheet, move the exploded view to the sheet, and add a parts list and balloons.

1. Right-click anywhere in the graphics window and select **New Sheet**. A new drawing sheet (Sheet:2) becomes active. The drawing sheet is created using the same sheet format as the active sheet. All elements of Sheet:1 become inactive (gray), as shown in Figure 26–53.

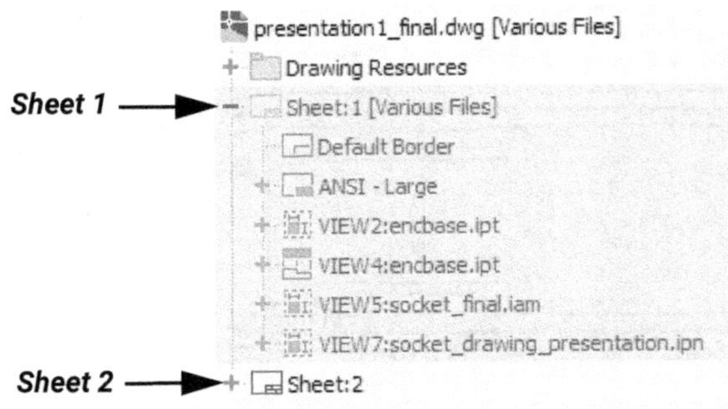

Figure 26–53

__Note:__ Alternatively, you can add a sheet by selecting the Place Views tab>Sheets panel and clicking (New Sheet). To add a sheet with an alternate format, expand the Drawing Resources>Sheet Formats nodes, select the required sheet format, right-click, and select __New Sheet__.

2. Double-click on **Sheet:1** in the Model browser to activate it
3. Select **VIEW7:socket_drawing_presentation.ipn** in the Model browser, hold the left mouse button, and drag the view to **Sheet:2** in the Model browser. The view moves to **Sheet:2**. The Model browser displays as shown in Figure 26–54.

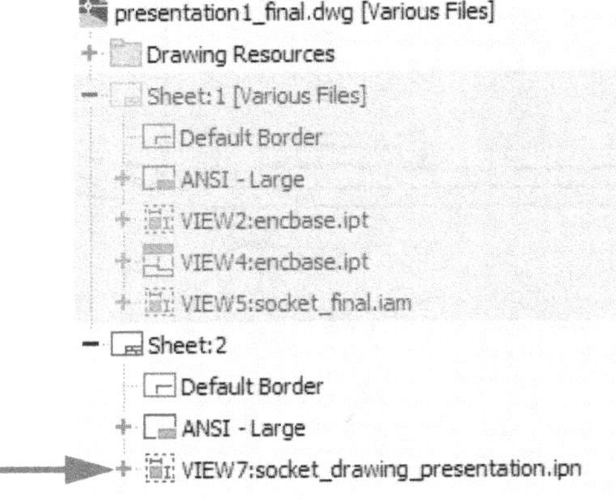

Figure 26–54

4. Once the view is moved, **Sheet:2** becomes active. Move the view to the center of the sheet.
5. Edit the view and change its view scale to **1.5: 1**.

Task 8: Create a parts list.

1. Select the *Annotate* tab, if it is not already active. In the *Table* panel, click (Parts List) to create a parts list for the model.
2. Click (Select View), if not selected, and select the drawing view in **Sheet:2**.
3. Maintain all of the default settings in the *Parts List* dialog box. Click **OK** and place the list, as shown in Figure 26–55. Update the view, if prompted.

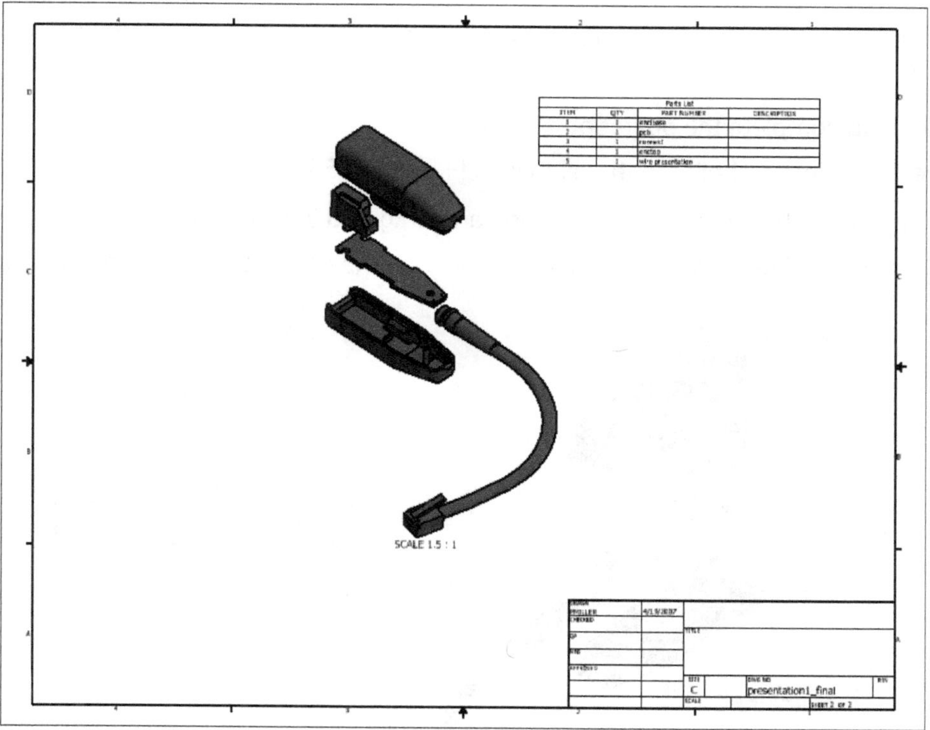

Figure 26–55

4. Select the parts list, right-click, and select **Edit Parts List Style**. The *Style and Standard Editor* dialog box opens. Note the style and standard options.
5. Click to the right side of the *Title* drop-down list.
6. Set the *Text Height* to **5.00mm**.
7. Click **Save and Close** to close the dialog box and save the changes. The *Style and Standard Editor* dialog box has many options to customize the parts list display.

Task 9: Add balloons.

1. In the *Table* panel, expand **Balloon** and click (Auto Balloon). The *Auto Balloon* dialog box opens.
2. In the graphics window, select the drawing view in **Sheet:2**.
3. Select all of the parts in the view.
4. Select **Around** in the *Placement* area in the dialog box so that balloons are placed around the view.
5. Click (Select Placement) in the *Placement* area, and select the location on the view to place balloons.

   Note: *If required, you can select* ***Balloon Shape*** *to override the balloon default shape in the Style overrides area in the dialog box.*

6. Click **OK** to complete the operation.
7. Move the balloons similar to that shown in Figure 26–56.
   - To move the balloons, select a balloon and drag it to a new location.
   - To move the leader, select the balloon and drag the end of the leader to a new location.

Parts List			
ITEM	QTY	PART NUMBER	DESCRIPTION
1	1	endbase	
2	1	pcb	
3	1	connect	
4	1	enctop	
5	1	wire presentation	

Figure 26–56

Task 10: Change the title block and drawing border.

Replace the existing title block and border in the drawing.

1. Click (Zoom All) in the Navigation Bar to refit the drawing to the full screen, if not already done.
2. In the Model browser, expand **Sheet:2**, if required. Right-click on **ANSI-Large** and select **Delete**. The title block disappears.
3. In the Model browser, expand **Drawing Resources** and expand **Title Blocks**. Right-click on **ANSI A** and select **Insert**. A smaller title block containing the same Properties information is inserted in the lower-right corner.
4. Zoom to examine the border. Note that each edge is divided into areas and that each area is labeled with numbers across the top and bottom, and letters on both sides.
5. Right-click on **Default Border** under **Sheet:2** in the Model browser and select **Delete**. The border disappears.
6. Expand **Drawing Resources** and expand **Borders** in the Model browser. Right-click on **Default Border** and select **Insert Drawing Border**. The *Default Drawing Border Parameters* dialog box opens, as shown in Figure 26–57.

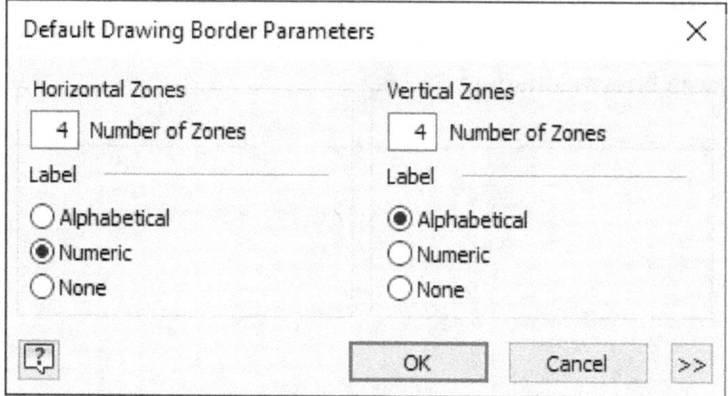

Figure 26–57

7. Set *Horizontal Zones* to **6** and label them alphabetically.
8. Set *Vertical Zones* to **4** and label them numerically.
9. Click **OK** to place the border. Note that the new border is now divided as you specified.
10. Save the drawing and save all of the files that require saving.
11. Close the window.

End of practice

Practice 26b
Detail a Drawing II

Practice Objectives

- Create a parts list and customize the information displayed in the columns.
- Map material styles to hatch patterns such that the hatching pattern varies for different materials.
- Modify the cut inheritance for a projected view.
- Duplicate a parts list between sheets.
- Add dimension to an isometric assembly view.

In this practice, you will map hatch patterns to material styles and create a section view using those styles. Next, you will modify the cut inheritance properties of a view, copy and paste a parts list from one sheet to another, and create dimensions on an isometric view.

Task 1: Open a drawing file.

1. Open **Clutch Bell.dwg**.
2. (Optional) Change the sheet color to white, as described in the previous exercise. The drawing displays as shown in Figure 26–58.

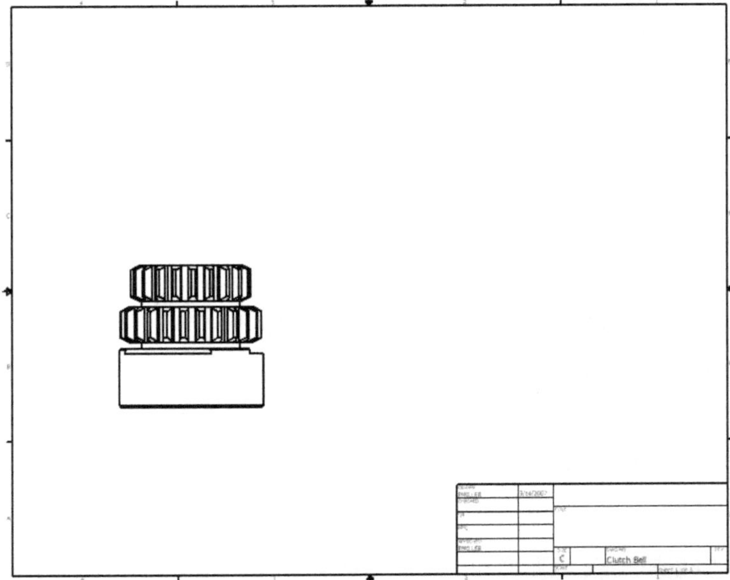

Figure 26–58

Task 2: Create a parts list.

1. Select the *Annotate* tab>*Table* panel and click (Parts List).
2. Select the view and click **OK**.
3. Place the parts list as shown in Figure 26–59.

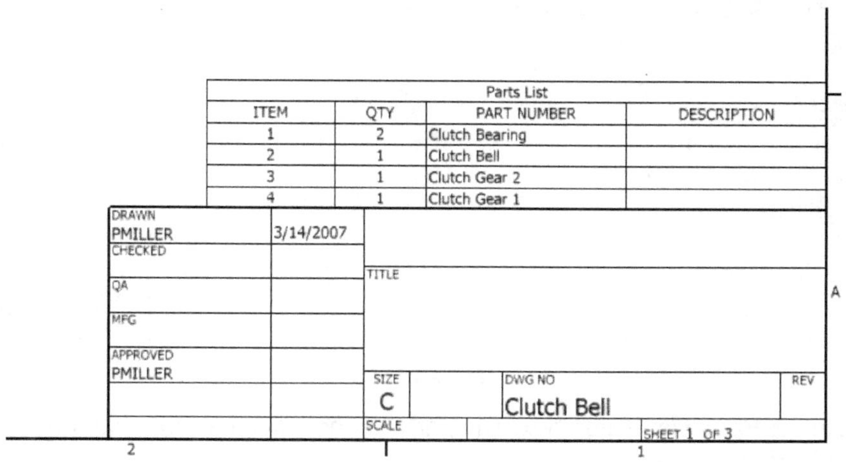

Figure 26–59

Task 3: Add a material column to the parts list.

1. Right-click on the parts list and select **Edit Parts List**. The *Parts List* dialog box opens.
2. Click (Column Chooser). The *Parts List Column Chooser* dialog box opens.
3. Select **DESCRIPTION** on the right side and click **Remove**.

4. Select **MATERIAL** on the left side and click **Add**. The *Parts List Column Chooser* dialog box updates as shown in Figure 26–60. Click **OK**.

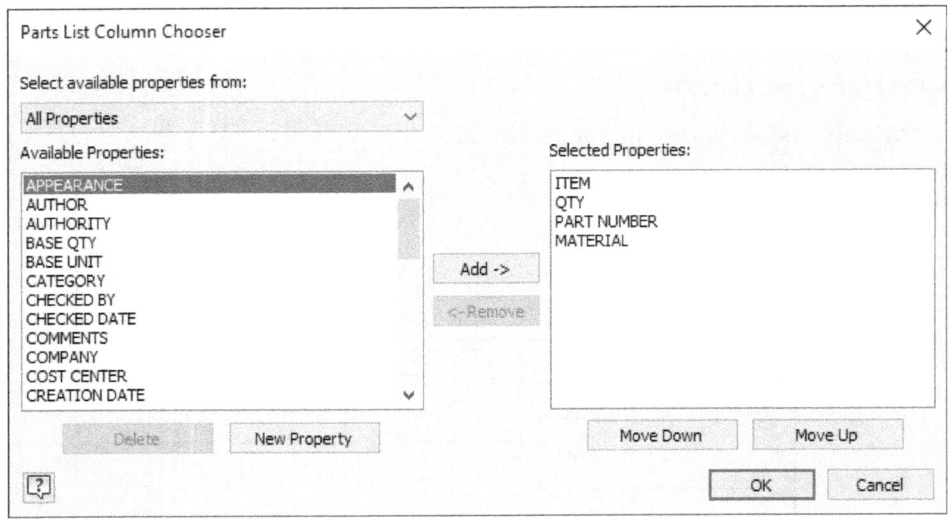

Figure 26–60

5. Click **OK** in the *Parts List* dialog box. The parts list now displays the material for each part, as shown in Figure 26–61.

Parts List			
ITEM	QTY	PART NUMBER	MATERIAL
1	2	Clutch Bearing	Bronze, Cast
2	1	Clutch Bell	Steel
3	1	Clutch Gear 2	Generic
4	1	Clutch Gear 1	Copper, Cast

Figure 26–61

Task 4: Map material styles to hatch patterns.

1. Each part in the table is assigned a material. Zoom all to display the entire drawing.
2. Select the *Manage* tab. In the *Styles and Standards* panel, click (Styles Editor).
3. In the *Style and Standard Editor*, expand **Standard** if it is not already expanded. Select **Default Standard (ANSI)**.
4. Select the *Material Hatch Pattern Defaults* tab. Note that it is empty. You need to map the material styles to hatch patterns.
5. Click (From Style Library) in the *Import Materials* area. This imports all of the material styles from the style library. You will only map the materials used in the assembly.

6. Locate **Bronze, Cast** in the *Material Name* column. Select **ANSI 31** in the *Bronze, Cast* row and select **ANSI 32** in the drop-down list.
7. Change **ANSI 31** for *Copper, Cast* to **ANSI 33** in the drop-down list.
8. Change **ANSI 31** for *Steel* to **ANSI 34** in the drop-down list.
9. Click **Save and Close** to save the changes to the standard and close the *Style and Standard Editor*. This only saves the changes for the active .DWG file.

Task 5: Create a section view and customize its inheritance.

1. Select the *Place Views* tab and create a section view through the middle of the assembly, as shown in Figure 26–62. Note that each part receives a different hatch pattern as assigned in the standard.

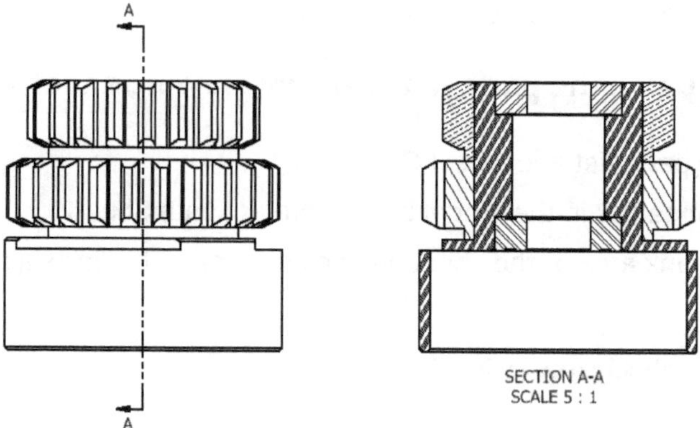

Figure 26–62

2. Create the isometric view projected from the section view, as shown in Figure 26–63.

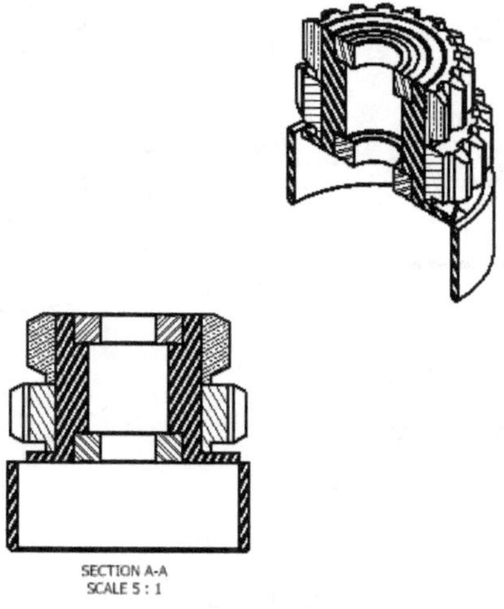

Figure 26–63

3. Right-click on the isometric view and select **Edit View**.
4. In the *Drawing View* dialog box, select the *Display Options* tab.
5. Clear the **Section** option in the *Cut Inheritance* area.
6. Click **OK**. Note that the cut is removed from the isometric view.
7. Right-click on the isometric view and select **Edit View**.
8. In the *Drawing View* dialog box, select the *Display Options* tab.
9. Select **Section** to add the cut back to the isometric view.
10. Click **OK**. Note that the cut is added to the isometric view and hatching should be displayed. If hatching is not displayed, edit the view again and on the *Display Options* tab select **Hatching**.
11. In the Model browser, right-click on the section view and select **Suppress** to suppress the section view. Note that the isometric view remains.

Task 6: Copy and paste the parts list to a new drawing sheet.

1. Right-click on the parts list and select **Copy**.
2. Double-click on **Sheet2:2** in the Model browser to activate **Sheet2**.
3. Right-click on a blank area of the sheet and select **Paste**. The parts list is copied onto **Sheet2**.

Task 7: Dimension the isometric view.

1. Create an isometric view projected from the base view on **Sheet2**, as shown in Figure 26–64.

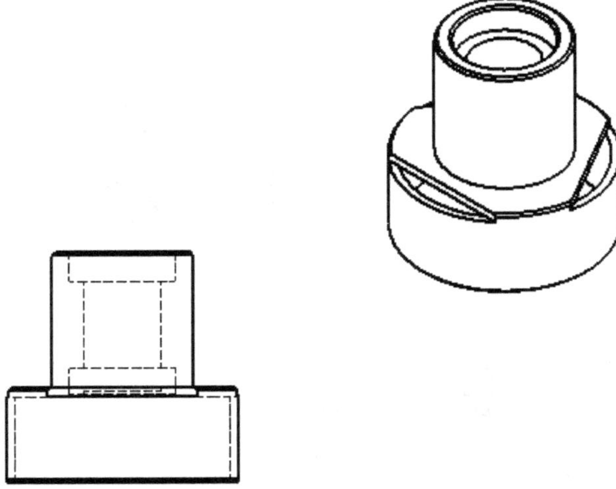

Figure 26–64

2. Select the *Annotate* tab>*Dimension* panel, click (Dimension), and add the dimensions shown in Figure 26–65. You can press <Spacebar> while placing dimensions to toggle the dimension orientation if different dimension placements are available.

   Note: *To create the .10 dimension, select the circular edge, then select the linear edge, and finally select the snap point on the circular edge prior to placing the dimension.*

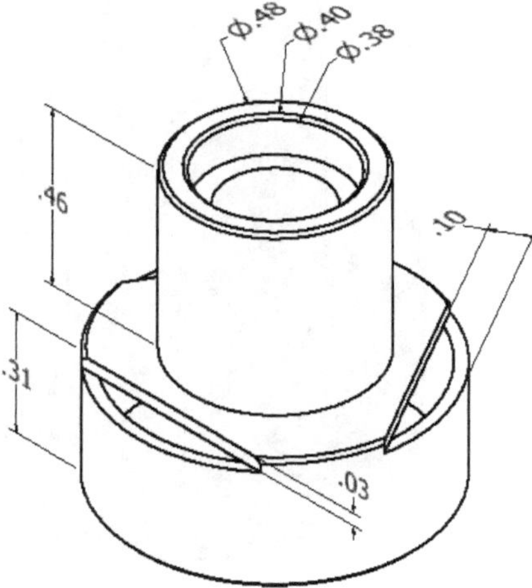

Figure 26–65

3. Right-click on the isometric view and select **Edit View**.
4. In the *Drawing View* dialog box, change the view display to **Hidden Line** () and **Shaded** ().
5. Click **OK**.
6. Delete the model dimensions.
7. Right-click in the graphics window and select **Retrieve Model Annotations**. The *Retrieve Model Annotation* dialog box opens. The options in the marking menu are context sensitive. If the **Retrieve Model Annotations** option is not available in the marking menu, verify that the view is not active or hold <Ctrl> if a view is active.

   Note: *Alternatively, you can retrieve dimensions by selecting the Annotate tab>Dimension panel and clicking (Retrieve).*

8. Select the isometric view. All of the model dimensions for the base view display.
9. Select all of the dimensions by drawing a bounding box around the view.

10. Click **OK** to apply and close the dialog box. The isometric view displays as shown in Figure 26–66. The dimensions can be moved as required to clean up the view.

    Note: *Depending on how the dimensions are placed, it might be more efficient to create the dimensions you require for an isometric view.*

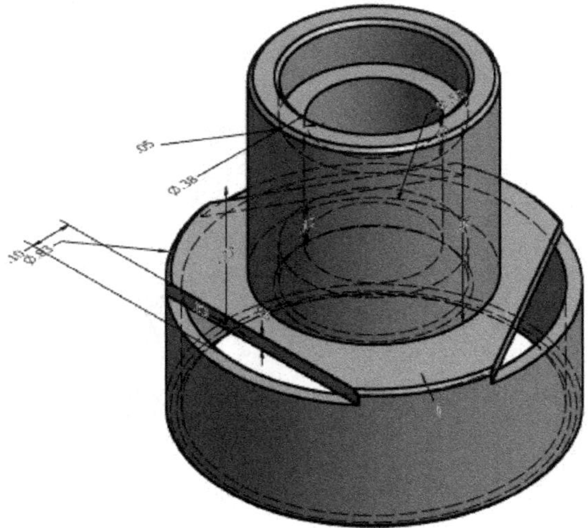

Figure 26–66

11. Save and close the drawing.

End of practice

Practice 26c
(Optional) Create a Drawing

Practice Objectives

- Create a new drawing using a default template.
- Create drawing views of a part model.
- Add dimensions to a drawing view.

1. Create a new drawing file named **Project_I**, using the **ANSI (in).dwg** template. Create drawing views of the part file **valvebody.ipt** and add dimensions. The completed drawing displays as shown in Figure 26–67. Save the drawing file.

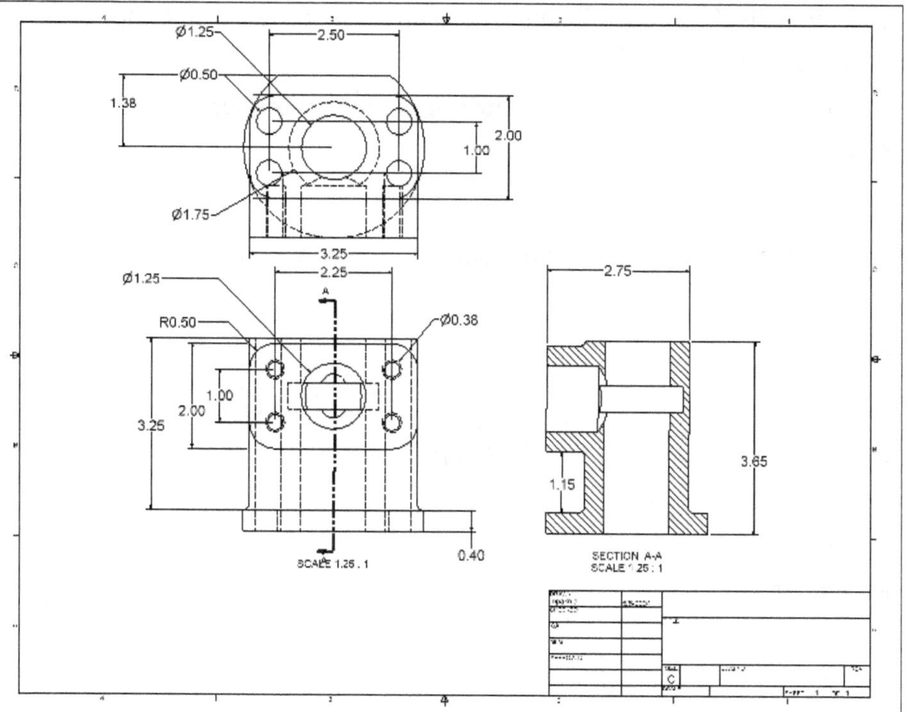

Figure 26–67

- To change the dimension text height, open the *Style and Standard Editor* dialog box and in the **Text** category edit the **Note Text (ANSI)** standard that is being used for the dimension size.

End of practice

Chapter Review Questions

1. Which describes the difference between Model dimensions and Drawing dimensions?
   a. Model dimensions can be edited to change the part, while Drawing dimensions are descriptive only and cannot be edited directly.
   b. There is no difference, except whether you are viewing the dimensions in the model or in the drawing.
   c. Model dimensions only display in part files, while Drawing dimensions display in drawing views.
   d. Model dimensions cannot be deleted, but Drawing dimensions can be deleted.

2. How would you display model dimensions in an existing view where they are not showing?
   a. Use **General Dimension**.
   b. Right-click on the view and select **Retrieve Model Annotations**.
   c. Update the view.

3. You can display the same model dimension in multiple views at the same time.
   a. True
   b. False

4. How many sheets can you add to a drawing?
   a. Two
   b. Odd number
   c. Even number
   d. No limit

5. Only a single sheet can be deleted at one time.
   a. True
   b. False

6. Which of the following best describes the **Ordinate Set** command, as shown in Figure 26–68?

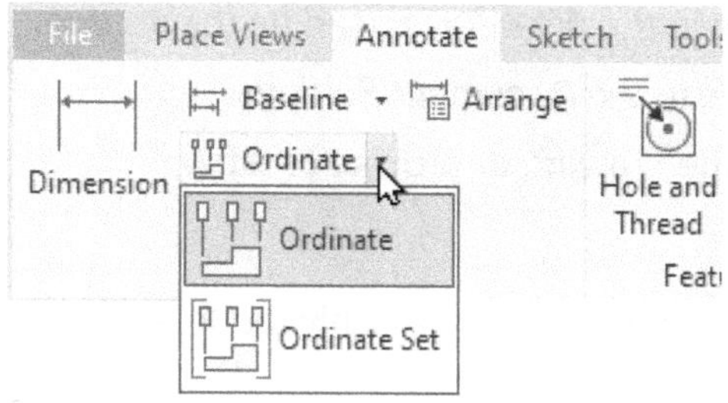

Figure 26–68

a. It sets the 0,0 point to be used with ordinate dimensions.

b. It creates a group of dimensions that act as one unit.

c. It sets the format to be used for ordinate dimensions.

d. It creates the dimensions automatically without picking points.

7. How would you change a single dimension to a different dimension style, as shown in Figure 26–69?

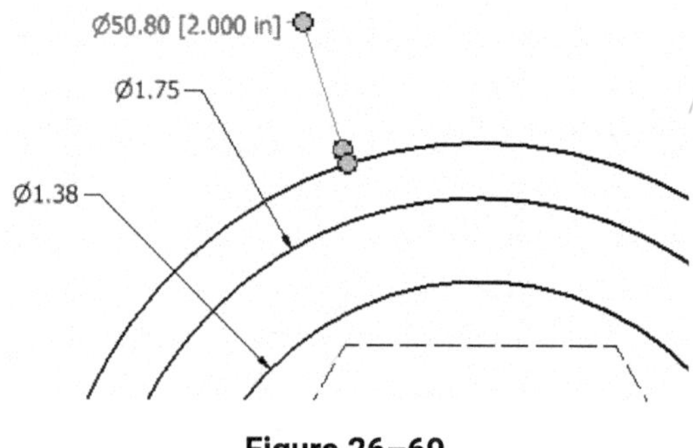

Figure 26–69

a. Edit the text to change the dimension.

b. Delete the dimension and reapply using a different style.

c. Select the dimension and choose a different style from the toolbar list.

8. When creating a parts list, how do you set the assembly that is used as the source?
   a. You set the source file in the *Style and Standard Editor* dialog box.
   b. The first view created in the drawing is used as the source.
   c. You set the source file in the *Document Settings*.
   d. You select a view in the drawing or browse to a file.

9. When creating a parts list, you can display only top-level components.
   a. True
   b. False

10. Which of the following statements is true regarding balloons in a drawing view?
    a. Balloons identifying item numbers in a parts list must be individually placed on each component in the assembly view.
    b. When using **Auto Balloon**, you can use the **Around**, **Horizontal**, or **Vertical** sub-options to align balloons around the view.
    c. Offset spacing enables you to position balloons at a fixed distance from the model.
    d. The shape of all balloons driven by the parts list is circular.

11. What controls the appearance of drawing annotations, such as centerlines, default text style, or parts lists?
    a. Document Settings
    b. Styles Editor
    c. Sheet Formats
    d. Application Options

12. What is the process to edit the hatching for a component in a section view, as shown in Figure 26–70?

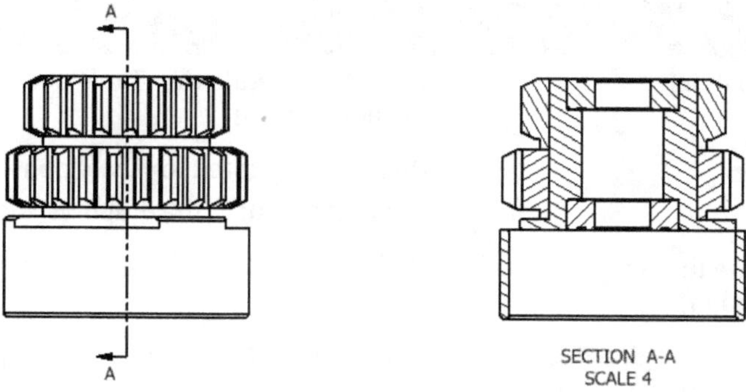

Figure 26–70

a. In the *Tools* tab, select **Document Settings** and select the *Drawing* tab.

b. Right-click on the hatch and select **Edit** to open the *Edit Hatch Pattern* dialog box.

c. In the *Tools* tab, select **Application Options**, and select the *Drawing* tab.

d. Delete the section view and create a new one.

Command Summary

Button	Command	Location
	Auto Balloon	• **Ribbon:** *Annotate* tab>*Table* panel> expand Balloon
	Balloon	• **Ribbon:** *Annotate* tab>*Table* panel • **Context Menu:** In the graphics window
	Baseline (drawing dimension)	• **Ribbon:** *Annotate* tab>*Dimension* panel
	Baseline Set (drawing dimension)	• **Ribbon:** *Annotate* tab>*Dimension* panel
	Chain (drawing dimension)	• **Ribbon:** *Annotate* tab>*Dimension* panel
	Chain Set (drawing dimension)	• **Ribbon:** *Annotate* tab>Dimension panel
	Dimension (drawing dimension)	• **Ribbon:** *Annotate* tab>Dimension panel • **Context Menu:** In the graphics window
N/A	**Edit Model Dimension**	• **Context Menu:** In the graphics window with a dimension selected
	New Sheet	• **Ribbon:** *Place Views* tab>Sheets panel • **Context Menu:** In the graphics window • **Context Menu:** In Model browser with the drawing name selected
	Ordinate (drawing dimension)	• **Ribbon:** *Annotate* tab>Dimension panel
	Ordinate Set (drawing dimension)	• **Ribbon:** *Annotate* tab>Dimension panel
	Parts List	• **Ribbon:** *Annotate* tab>Table panel
	Retrieve Model Annotations	• **Ribbon:** *Annotate* tab>Retrieve panel • **Context Menu:** In the graphics window with a view selected • **Context Menu:** In Model browser with a view selected
	Styles Editor	• **Ribbon:** *Annotate* tab>Styles and Standards panel

Chapter

27

Drawing Annotations

Drawings communicate design information. In most cases, drawings, dimensions, and parts lists are not enough and drawing annotations are required to identify additional information.

Learning Objectives

- Add leader and non-leader text to a drawing to communicate information about the drawing.
- Add various symbol types to a drawing to identify important drawing information.
- Create and edit a hole or thread note in a drawing view.
- Create and edit a chamfer note in a drawing view.
- Add center marks, centered patterns, centerlines, and bisector lines to drawing views.
- Create hole tables based on selected features, feature types, and views.
- Add and edit revision tables, tags, and clouds in a drawing to track model changes.

27.1 Drawing Text

Text is used to communicate information that cannot be communicated through views or dimensions. You can create text with or without a leader.

How To: Create Text with a Leader

1. In the *Annotate* tab>*Text* panel, click (Leader Text).
2. Select a location to point the leader. Select another location to create the line. Each click creates an *elbow* in the leader line.
3. Select a location to place the text, right-click, and select **Continue**. The *Format Text* dialog box opens.
4. In the *Format Text* dialog box (shown in Figure 27–1), enter the required text and modify the text options, as required:
   - Use the editing tools available in the dialog box to customize the look of the text.
   - To add a symbol, place the cursor and select a symbol from the Ø drop-down list.
5. Text is previewed on the drawing sheet as you enter information in the dialog box.

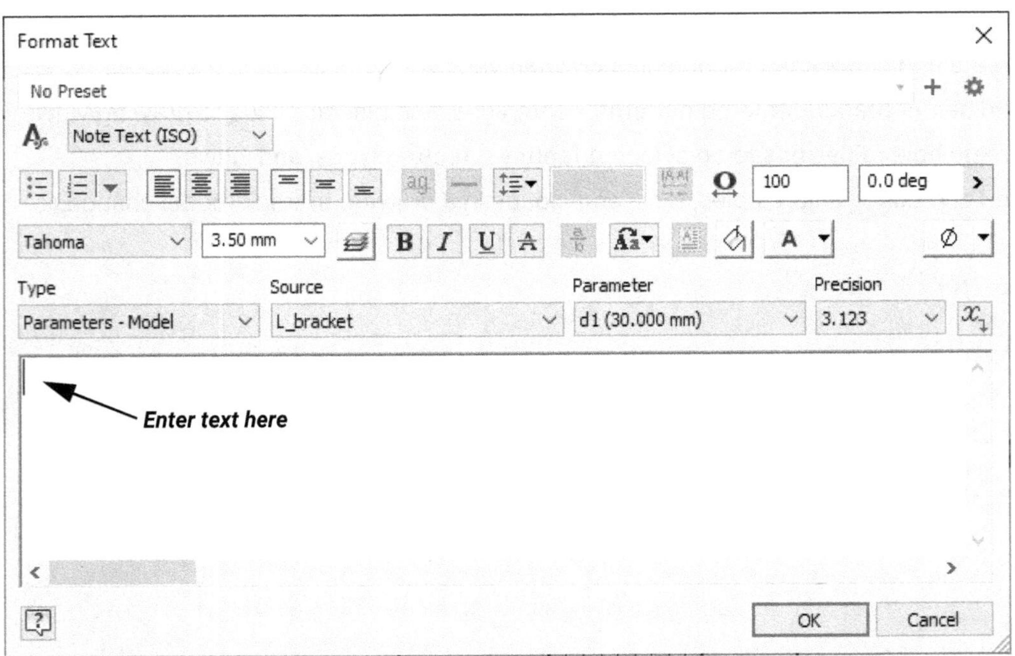

Figure 27–1

6. Click **OK** to complete the text

   ***Note:** Any leader or dimension lines that intersect with a text box are clipped.*

 **Hint: Creating Single-Segment Leaser Notes**

To create note text immediately after placing the first segment, right-click during note creation and select **Single-Segment Leader**. With this option enabled you are not required to right-click and select **Continue**. The *Format Text* dialog box will immediately open to create the note. Once enabled it remains active until it is disabled.

To create text without a leader, click A (Text) in the *Text* panel and select a location on the drawing. As with text created with a leader, the *Format Text* dialog box opens, in which you can enter the text.

Text Presets

The *Format Text* dialog box enables you to create and save unique and commonly used text settings as presets that can be easily accessed to conveniently avoid having to redefine the same text settings.

- By default, the preset list at the top of the dialog box indicates that **No Preset** is active. This means that all of the current settings in the *Format Text* dialog box are the default values.
- To create a custom preset, set the formatting options in the *Format Text* dialog box and click + (Create new preset) adjacent to the preset list, as shown in Figure 27–2. The preset is created with a system-defined name, and you can immediately enter a new descriptive name.

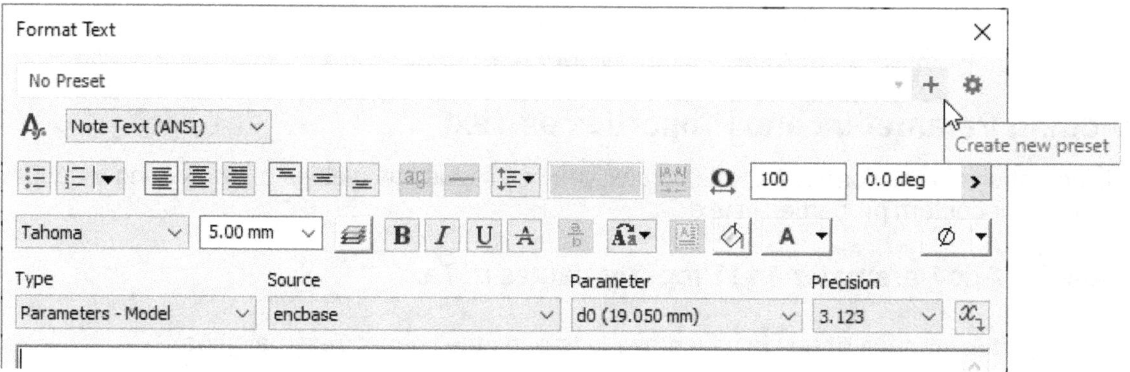

Figure 27–2

- To use a saved preset, simply select it from the drop-down list once the **Text** option has been activated.
- Use the (Preset Settings) option adjacent to the preset list to set the additional options. This enables you to customize the sort order for the preset list and define whether new text uses **No Preset**, the **Last Used** preset, or a saved preset.

Note: *The presets created and saved for Text are different than those used for Leader Text.*

Modifying Text

You can modify the following text properties:

- Edit existing text by double-clicking on it in the drawing. Use the *Format Text* dialog box to modify the text and formatting.
- Move text that has leaders by selecting the text, pressing and holding the left mouse button on any of the green dots, and dragging the mouse to the required location. To move text without leaders, the dots display around the text.
- To rotate text without a leader, select the text and drag the blue dot associated with the text.
- For text without a leader, you can adjust the size of the text box by dragging the green dots in the required direction.
- To align multiple text boxes with leaders or without leaders, select them, right-click, and select **Align**. Define how to align the selected text boxes using the options in the *Align Text* dialog box, as shown in Figure 27–3.

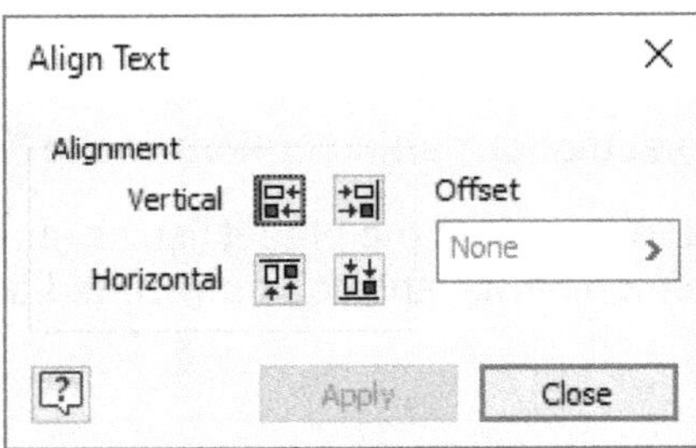

Figure 27–3

Adding Parameters and Properties as Text

Using options in the *Format Text* dialog box, you can include the values of an existing model, drawing, or custom properties in text.

How To: Add Parameter and Property Values in Text

1. Begin the creation of text in your drawing to open the *Format Text* dialog box.
2. In the *Type* drop-down list, select the type of parameter value that will be used in the text. The available list is shown in Figure 27–4.
3. In the *Source* drop-down list, select the model that will be used as the source file. For drawings with a single reference model, only one component is going to be listed. For assembly drawings, you can select from any of the components in the assembly.
4. In the *Parameter* drop-down list, select the parameter that is to be added. The list of parameters displayed is dependent on the type selected for the selected source component.
5. In the *Precision* drop-down list, define the precision format for numerical parameters.

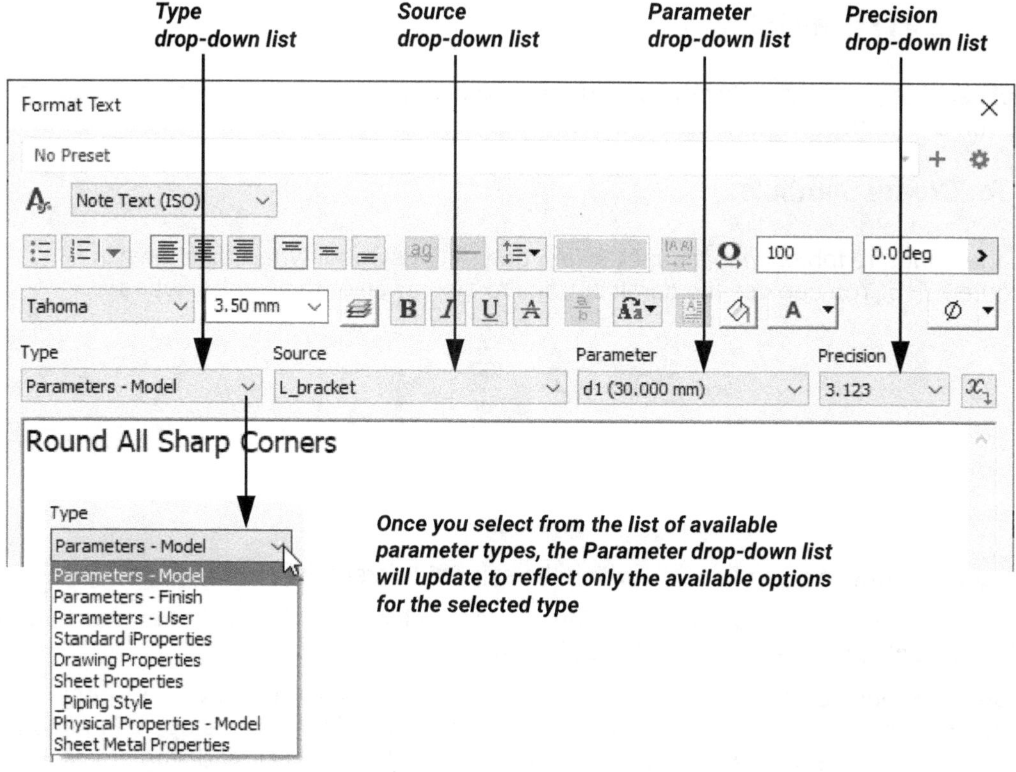

Figure 27–4

6. Click (Add Parameter) to include the selected parameter in the text area at the bottom of the *Format Text* dialog box. Parameter values are highlighted in gray and cannot be edited, but you can add text around the value or delete it.
7. Click **OK** to complete the text and add it to the drawing.

Hint: Using Instance and Parts List Properties in Text

Consider the following:

- Instance properties can only be used in text if the **Leader Text** option is used and the leader location is attached to an assembly component. Once the leader reference point is selected, the **Custom iProperties** option appears in the *Type* drop-down list and the instance property can be selected and inserted into the text.
- Parts list properties can be used in assembly drawings. In the *Type* drop-down list, select **Parts List Properties**. Select the (Select Parts List Item) option, then select the row in the parts list that will be used to populate the property's value and click **OK**. In the *Property* drop-down list, select the property that is to be used in the text. Click (Add Parameter) to include the selected parameter in the text area at the bottom of the *Format Text* dialog box.

27.2 Symbols

Symbols enable you to identify critical surfaces, explain how they relate to one another, and set inspection or manufacturing criteria.

How To: Create Symbols

1. In the *Annotate* tab>*Symbols* panel, select one of the symbol types, as shown in Figure 27–5. You can use the scroll buttons to display all of the symbol types.

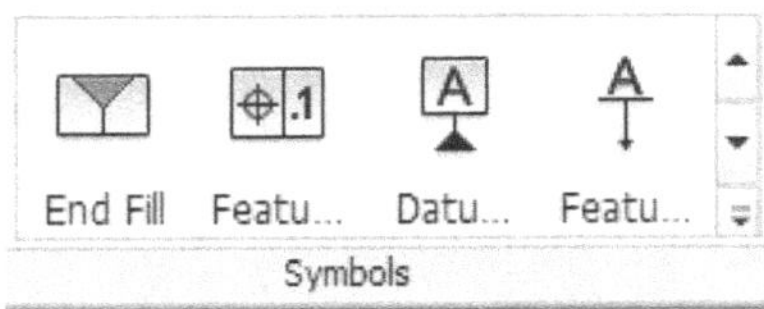

Figure 27–5

2. Select an entity (e.g., an edge) to which the symbol references.
3. To add the symbol with a leader, continue making selections with the left mouse button after the entity has been selected to define the leader location.
4. Right-click, and select **Continue.** The dialog box associated with the symbol opens. Depending on the type of symbol being created, different dialog boxes open. Figure 27–6 shows the *Surface Texture*, *Feature Control Frame*, and *Datum Target* dialog boxes.

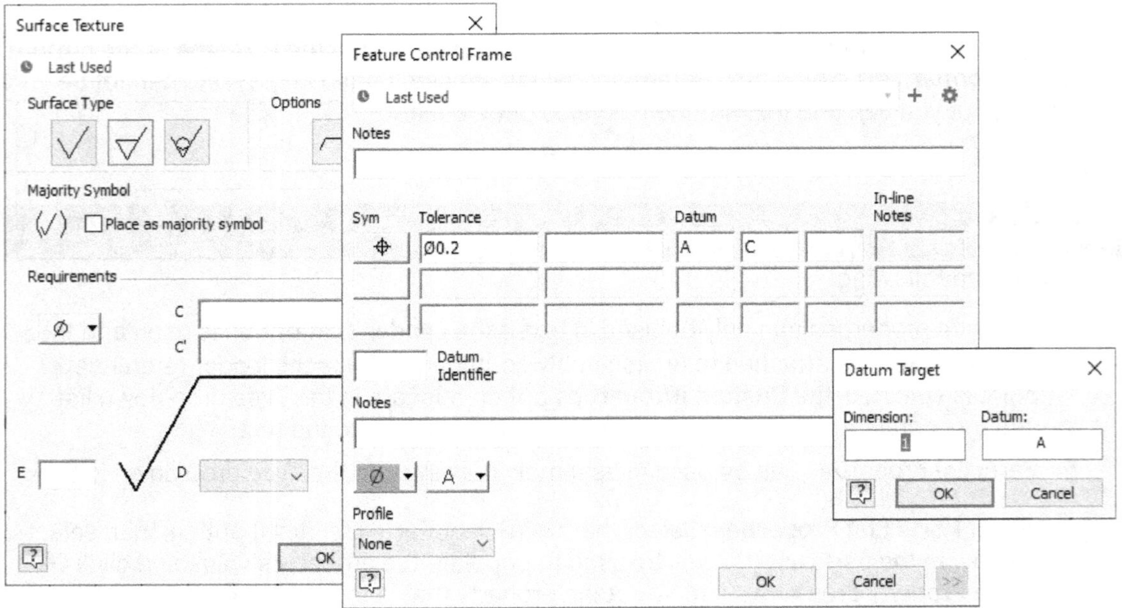

Figure 27–6

5. Regardless of the type of symbol, define the required symbol parameters in their respective dialog boxes.
6. Click **OK** in the dialog box to complete the symbol. The symbol displays based on the selected references.
7. (Optional) Continue to add symbols of the same type.
8. Right-click and select **Cancel [ESC]** or press <Esc> to cancel the operation.

Hint: Custom Symbols

Custom symbols can be created and shared in a read/write library for quick access by an entire team. Creating custom symbols is discussed in the *Autodesk Inventor: Advanced Part Modeling* guide.

27.3 Hole and Thread Notes

You can add hole notes in a drawing view to holes, slots, extruded cuts (other than mid-plane extrusions), iFeatures, patterned holes, center marks, or sheet metal flat patterns.Thread notes can be added in a drawing view to features that were created with a thread feature. Changes made to the hole or thread in the model update in the hole drawing note.

Creating a Hole or Thread Note

How To: Create a Hole or Thread Note

1. In the *Annotate* tab>*Feature Notes* panel, click (Hole and Thread).
2. Select the required hole, slot or thread in the drawing view.
3. Position the note with the cursor and click the left mouse button to place it. To enable 15-degree snapping when placing the note, hold <Ctrl> while dragging.
4. Complete the creation of the note by right-clicking and selecting **OK**.

   Note: *The default settings for how hole notes display are set in the Styles Editor.*

Notes can include generic text and symbols, if necessary.

How To: Add Text or Symbols to an Existing Hole/Thread Note

1. Right-click on the hole/thread note and select **Text**. The *Format Text* dialog box opens.
2. Enter text before and after the <<>> symbols, as required. The symbols are placeholders for the hole/thread note. You cannot enter additional data between the symbols.
3. To add a symbol to the note, expand the Ø flyout to display the symbol palette. Place the cursor at the required location and select a symbol in the drop-down list.
4. To change text properties, highlight the text to change, and select the required properties.
5. Click **OK** to update the hole note.

Editing a Hole Note

How To: Modify a Hole Note

1. Right-click on a hole note and select **Edit Hole Note** or double-click on the note. The *Edit Hole Note* dialog box opens, as shown at the top of Figure 27–7. If your note is for a slot feature, right-click on the slot note and select **Edit Slot Note**. The options on the *Edit Slot* dialog box are shown at the bottom of Figure 27–7.

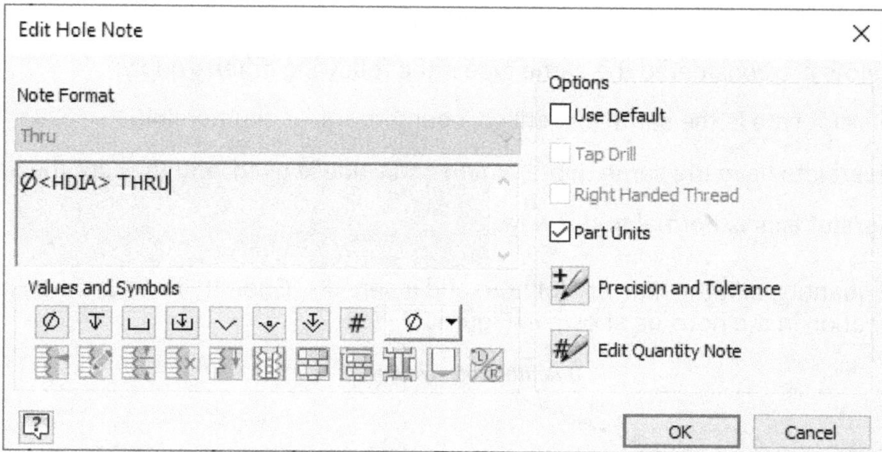

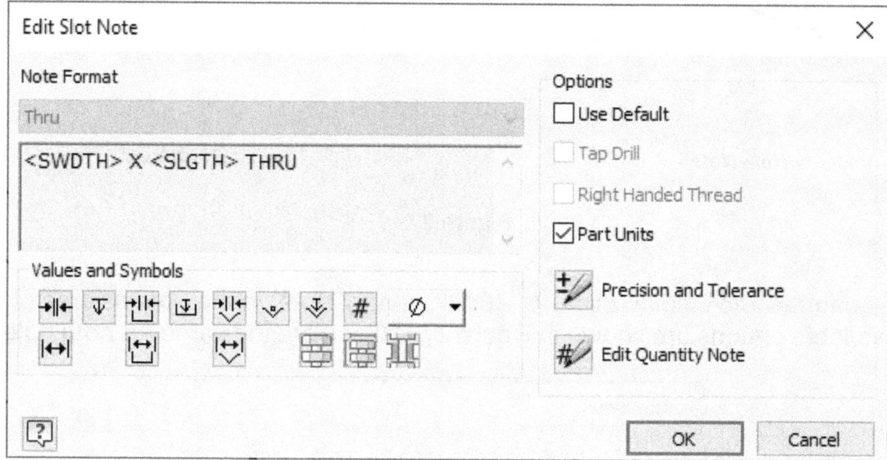

Figure 27–7

2. Clear the **Use Default** option, if required, to enable editing. The option in the *Note Format* drop-down list cannot be modified, but the hole note itself can be modified using the options, icons, and changing the text.
3. Click **OK** to update the hole note.

Note: *To edit a thread note, double-click it and use the standard Format Text dialog box.*

Hole Quantity in Notes

In a hole or slot note, you can add the quantity of holes/slots of the same type, as shown in Figure 27–8.

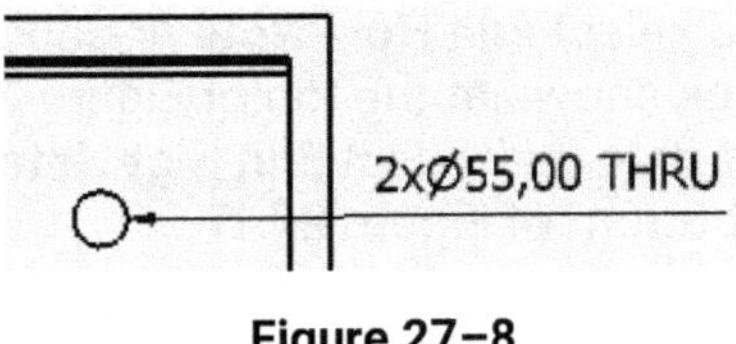

Figure 27–8

Holes and slots are considered the same type if the following criteria apply:

- The hole/slot type is the same (i.e. drilled, counterbore, or countersink).
- The holes/slots have the same depth option and value is used, and they are the same size.
- The hole/slot axis is normal to the view.

To add the quantity, edit the hole or slot note and insert (Quantity Note Symbol) in the required location in the note, as shown in Figure 27–9.

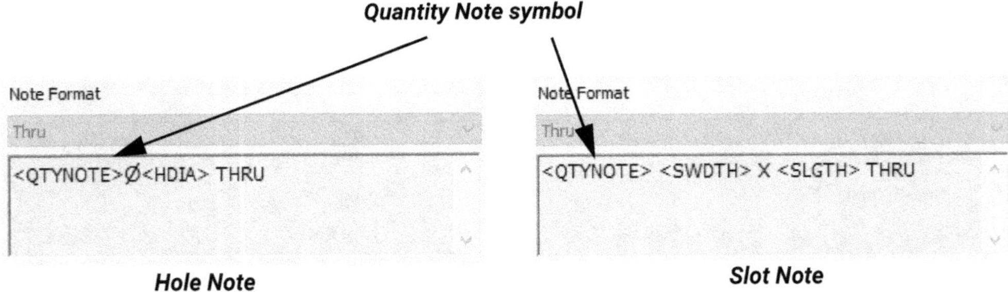

Figure 27–9

To edit the quantity note display, click (Edit Quantity Note) in the *Options* area of the dialog box. The available options are shown in Figure 27–10 and are the same for both hole and slots.

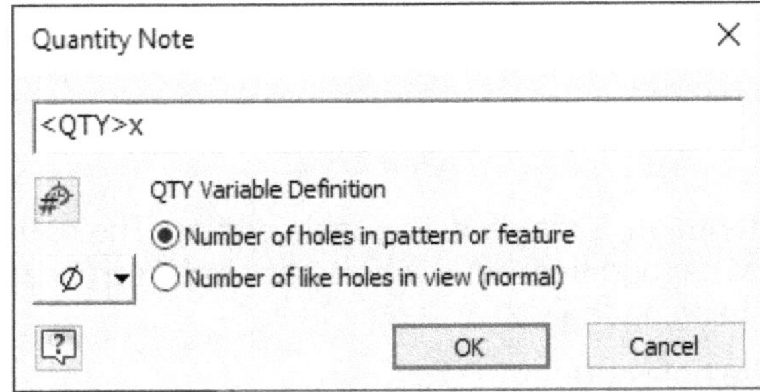

Figure 27–10

Hiding Note Values

You can hide note values. However, any text or symbols added to a note remain visible on the drawing.

To hide note values, right-click on the note and select **Hide Value**. The note value is hidden and any custom text is shown as <Text>. Toggle the option again to display the value.

27.4 Chamfer Notes

Creating Chamfer Notes

You can add chamfer notes in a drawing view to a linear model edge or sketch line. Note that the reference edge used in a chamfer calculation must be a linear model edge, or a sketch line that has common end points or intersects with the chamfer.

How To: Create a Chamfer Note

1. In the *Annotate* tab>*Feature Notes* panel, click (Chamfer).
2. Select the required linear model edge or sketch line in the view.
3. Select a reference line in the drawing view to calculate the dimension.
4. Position the note with the cursor and click the left mouse button to place it.
5. Complete the creation of the note by right-clicking and selecting **OK**.

   Note: *The default settings for how chamfer notes display are set in the Styles Editor.*

Editing Chamfer Notes

How To: Modify a Chamfer Note

1. Right-click on a chamfer note and select **Edit Chamfer Note**. The *Edit Chamfer Note* dialog box opens, as shown in Figure 27–11.

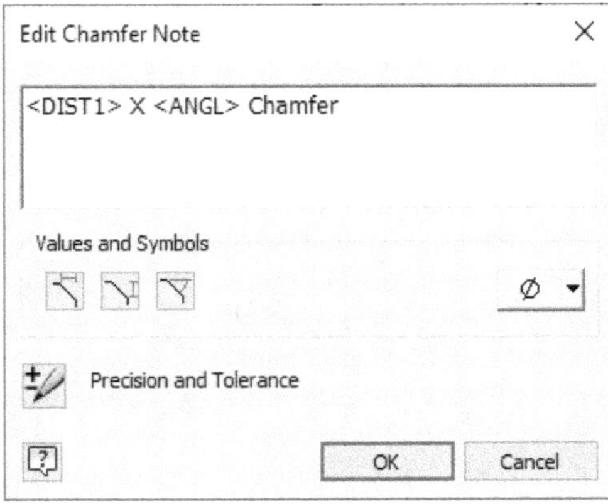

Figure 27–11

2. Enter the required text or edit/remove existing text.

3. You can also add parameters by selecting the required options in the *Values and Symbols* area. Three different parameters are available:

    - **(Distance 1):** Horizontal distance between selected edge and reference line.
    - **(Distance 2):** Vertical distance between selected edge and reference line.
    - **(Angle):** Angle between selected edge and reference line.

4. To add a symbol to the note, expand ⌀ to display the symbol palette. Place the cursor in the required location and select a symbol in the drop-down list.
5. Click (Precision and Tolerance) to modify settings.
6. Click **OK** to close the dialog box and complete the change.

27.5 Center Marks and Centerlines

The **Center Mark**, **Centerline**, **Centerline Bisector**, and **Centered Pattern** options in the *Annotate* tab>*Symbols* panel enable you to manually add these annotation features to your drawing views.

Center Marks

You can add center marks to circular, arc, or ellipse shaped geometry on features or parts in a in a drawing view, similar to that shown in Figure 27–12.

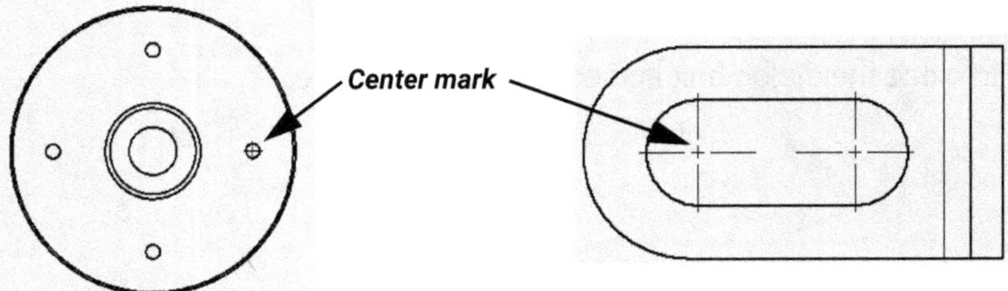

Figure 27–12

How To: Create the Center Mark

1. In the *Annotate* tab>*Symbols* panel, click (Center Mark).
2. Select a feature to which to add the center mark.
3. Complete the creation of the center marks by right-clicking and selecting **OK**.

Centerlines

You can add centerlines between two selected locations in a drawing view, similar to that shown in Figure 27–13.

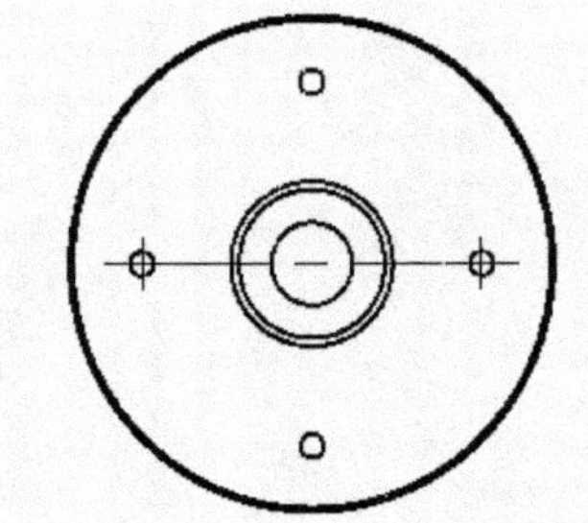

Figure 27–13

How To: Create the Centerline

1. In the *Annotate* tab>*Symbols* panel, click (Centerline).
2. Select an entitiy (location) in the drawing view to start a centerline.
3. Select a second location to define a linear centerline. Continue to select additional entities to further define the centerline(s).
    - Selecting three locations defines an arc-shaped centerline.
    - Selecting four or more locations creates linear centerlines between each location.
4. Complete the creation of the centerlines by right-clicking and selecting **Create**.

As an alternative to individually selecting features to add centerlines and center marks, click (Automated Centerline) in the *Symbols* panel and select a view. The *Automated Centerlines* dialog box enables you to determine which types of features to apply centerlines and center marks to in a view, as well as to define thresholds for radius and arc angle values. Alternatively, you can also access the Automated Centerlines option by right-clicking on a view and selecting **Automated Centerlines**.

Centerline Bisector

You can add centerlines between two selected linear edges in a drawing view, similar to that shown in Figure 27–14.

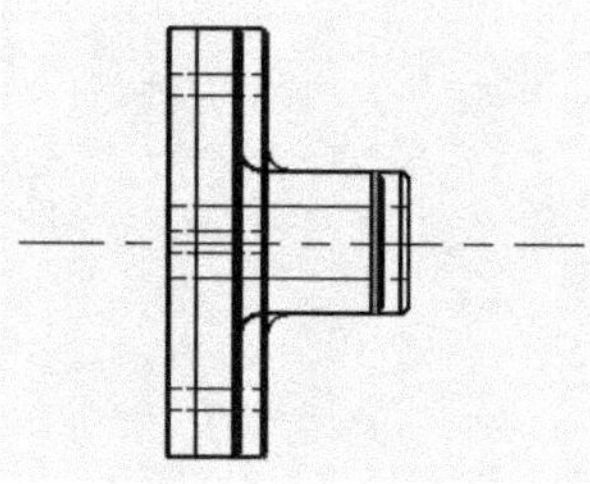

Figure 27–14

How To: Create the Centerline Bisector

1. In the *Annotate* tab>*Symbols* panel, click (Centerline Bisector).
2. Select two lines to add the centerline bisector between them. The centerline is immediately added to the view.
3. To cancel creation of additional centerline bisectors, right-click and select **Cancel [ESC]**, or press <Esc>.

Centered Pattern

You can add center marks on circular feature patterns in a drawing view, similar to that shown in Figure 27–15.

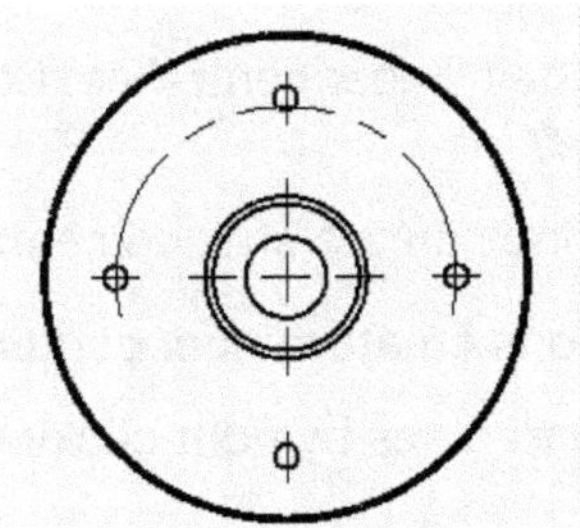

Figure 27–15

How To: Create the Centered Pattern

1. In the *Annotate* tab>*Symbols* panel, click (Centered Pattern).
2. Select a circular feature to locate the center of the pattern.
3. Select all of the required circular features.
4. Complete the creation of the centerlines by right-clicking and selecting **Create**.

27.6 Hole Tables

Using hole tables in a drawing is an effective method of providing information on the holes or slots in a model. A hole table can be created to contain information for all holes/slots, selected holes/slots only, or extruded cuts (except for mid-plane extrusions) in a selected drawing view.

How To: Create a Hole Table

1. In the *Annotate* tab>*Table* panel, select one of three hole table creation methods shown in Figure 27–16. The hole selection method defines how the holes or slots are identified for inclusion in the table.

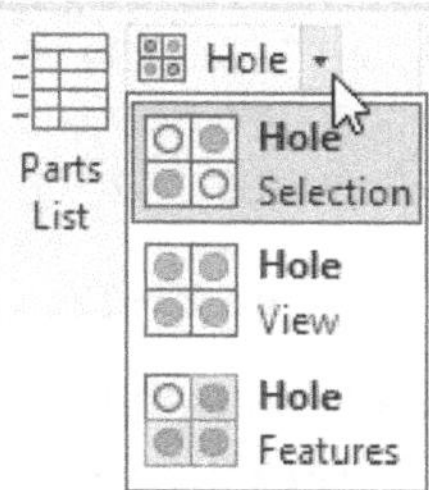

Figure 27–16

Method	Description
(Hole Selection)	Each hole/slot included in the hole table is selected individually.
(Hole View)	All holes/slots of any type in a selected view are included in the hole table.
(Hole Features)	All identical holes/slots of a selected type are automatically included.

2. Select the drawing view that includes the holes or slots, which are required in the table.
3. Define a location to use as the origin for the hole table by selecting a point on the view from which all hole or slot locations are measured. The origin used for a hole table is also used for ordinate dimensions and vice-versa.
   - The origin indicator displays with . Only one origin can exist per view.
   - To hide the origin indicator, right-click on it and select **Hide Origin Indicator**.
   - To move the origin indicator relative to its current location, right-click on it and select **Edit**. Enter dimension values for the X- or Y-direction (relative to the original location).

4. If you selected either **Hole Selection** or **Hole Features**, select the holes or slots required for the hole table.
   - If you used the **Hole View** selection method, you can skip this step because all of the holes and slots in the selected view are automatically added to the hole table. If both exist, they are both included in the table together.
5. Once you have finished selecting the holes, right-click anywhere in the drawing and select **Create**.
6. Place the hole table by clicking to place it. The hole table displays similar to that shown in Figure 27–17 for holes.

Hole Table			
HOLE	XDIM	YDIM	DESCRIPTION
A1	150,00	400,00	Ø50,00 -5,00 DEEP
B1	590,00	300,00	Ø70,00 -5,00 DEEP
B2	690,00	300,00	Ø70,00 -5,00 DEEP

Figure 27–17

Tags (e.g., A1 and B1) are assigned to each hole and slot identified in the hole table and each is automatically labeled with the tag in the drawing view. Holes or slots of the same type contain the same letter. For example, holes B1 and B2 are of the same type.

> ***Note:** By default, the Hole Table includes slots. To disable their inclusion in hole tables, on the Manage tab>Styles and Standards panel, click **Styles Editor**. For the Hole Table style type, select **Hole Table** and in the Options tab, clear **Slot** from the Included Features area.*

Editing Hole Tables or Tags

Consider the following when editing a hole table or tag:

- To edit the text format for an individual tag, right-click on the tag and select **Edit Tag**. Use the standard *Format Text* dialog box to edit the tag.
- To hide a tag in the drawing view, right-click on the tag name and select **Hide Tag**. To show hidden tags in a view, right-click on **Hole Table** in the Model browser and select **Visibility>Show All Tags**.
- The table can be modified by right-clicking on the table and selecting **Edit Hole Table**. You can use the options in the *Formatting* and *Options* tabs as required to customize the look of the table. The **Edit Hole Table Style** option enables you to open the *Style and Standard Editor* to create a style to be used when creating all your company tables.

- You can make additional modifications to the table and its contents using the shortcut menu, as shown in Figure 27–18.

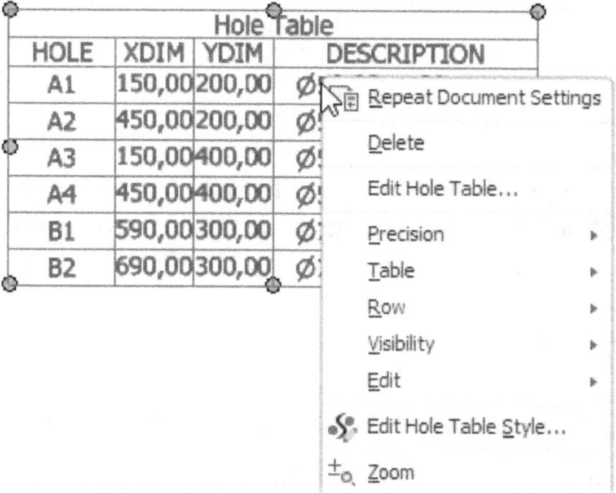

Figure 27–18

Hint: Splitting Hole Tables

To split a table into multiple individual tables, right-click on a row in the table and select **Table>Split Table**. A table can be split multiple times to create individual tables. Once split, the **Hole Table** node in the Model browser is subdivided to represent the parent table and split tables. Select a portion of the table and freely move it on the sheet or use the Model browser to select a portion of the split table and drag it to another sheet.

To unsplit a table, select anywhere in the table and select **Table>Un-split Table**. All portions of the table (even those on other sheets) are returned to the parent table.

27.7 Revision Tables, Tags, and Clouds

Revision tables, tags, and clouds help track and distinguish the various changes in the model between revisions.

Revision Tables

Revision tables provide a single location that can list all of the changes made to a drawing. They can have custom defined columns that provide the information that you need (i.e., date, description, revision, etc.).

How To: Create a Revision Table

1. Select the *Annotate* tab>*Revision* panel and click (Revision).
2. Define the options in the *Revision Table* dialog box:
   - Use the *Table Scope* area to define whether the table is for the entire drawing or for the active sheet.
   - Use the *Revision Index* area to define if indexing is done alphabetically or numerically.
   - Use the **Update Property on Revision Number Edit** option to ensure that the active row is connected with the revision number property in drawing iProperties.
3. Click **OK** to close the *Revision Table* dialog box.
4. Move the cursor and click to place the table. A table displays similar to that shown in Figure 27–19.

REVISION HISTORY				
ZONE	REV	DESCRIPTION	DATE	APPROVED
	1		3/11/2023	

Figure 27–19

Note: The same revision table can be displayed on multiple sheets within the same drawing so that the model's revision history is available on all the sheets. This can be done using ***Copy*** *and* ***Paste****.*

Once a revision table has been created, it can be modified to customize its display in the drawing.

How To: Edit the Revision Table

1. Right-click on an existing revision table and select **Edit**. The *Revision Table: Drawing Scope* dialog box opens, similar to that shown in Figure 27–20.

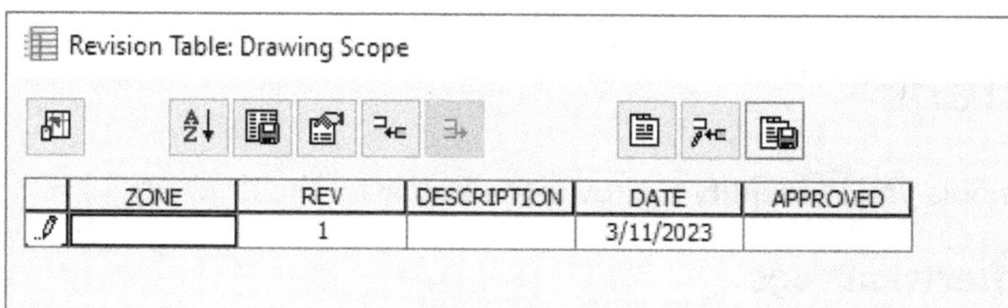

Figure 27–20

2. Click (Table Layout) to open the *Revision Table Layout* dialog box. The options in this dialog box enable you to customize the look of the table. The options include the following:
   - Changing the Title row title.
   - Locating the title row heading at the top or bottom of the table, or not including it at all.
   - Controlling the list of table entries in ascending or descending order.
   - Controlling the format of the text in the table.
   - Controlling the table wrapping for the table.
3. Click (Column Choose) to add and move columns in the table, as required. Revision tables can include any iProperties.
4. Right-click on the revision table and select **Rotate** to rotate the table in 90-degree increments. You can rotate **clock-wise** (**CW**) or **counter clock-wise** (**CCW**).
5. Right-click on the revision table and select **Add Revision Row** to add a revision to the table. The new row automatically increments the revision number.
6. Click (Add Revision Rows) in the *Revision Table* dialog box to add a blank row to the table.
7. Place the cursor between two rows or columns and drag to adjust the height and width. When editing the layout of the table you can also customize the Heading Gap and Row Gap for the cells in the table.
8. Double-click the field to modify. The *Revision Table* dialog box opens to enable you to edit the text.

Hint: Revision Table Styles and Standards

The default table that is added to a drawing is controlled by the default *Style and Standard* entry. You can edit this standard by selecting the revision table so that it is highlighted, right-clicking and selecting **Edit Revision Table Style**. The customization options are the same as the *Revision Table Layout* dialog box, and are stored as a style that can be used for future tables.

Revision Tags

Revision tags enable you to identify the revision directly on the drawing.

How To: Add Revision Tags

1. In the *Annotate* tab>*Revision* panel, click (Revision Tag).
2. Select the entity or location to which the revision tag refers.
3. Click to place the revision tag or select again to place an elbow on the tag. Once placed, right-click and select **Continue**. You can continue to place tags or right-click and select **Cancel [ESC]**.
4. To set the revision level of a placed tag, right-click, select **Tag** and select the revision level.

To change the symbol shape or change the format, right-click and select **Edit Revision Tag** or double-click on the tag to open the *Edit Revision Tag* dialog box

Revision Clouds

Revision clouds can be attached to a selected view or added to a sheet to identify an area where a change was or is being made, or to better identify an area that needs attention in the model. Once created, it is added to the drawing as a sketch that can be modified like any other sketch using the options on the *Sketch* tab.

How To: Create a Revision Cloud

1. Select the *Annotate* tab>*Revision* panel and click (Revision Cloud).
2. Select a view in the drawing or a location on the drawing sheet.
3. Select a starting location with the left mouse button to begin the cloud and continue to place points (clockwise) to define the shape of the cloud. The cloud will always be closed and each selection helps define the shape of the cloud.
4. Once you have placed the last point, right-click and select **Create**.

Revision clouds that are associated with a view will move with the view if it is moved and will be listed in the view node in the Model browser. A revision cloud on a sheet acts independently and is listed as a node at the top-level of the sheet in the Model browser. To modify a revision cloud, select it to activate it and use any of the options in the right-click menu, as shown in Figure 27–21. Alternatively, you can right-click on the **Revision Cloud** node in the Model browser to access the same options.

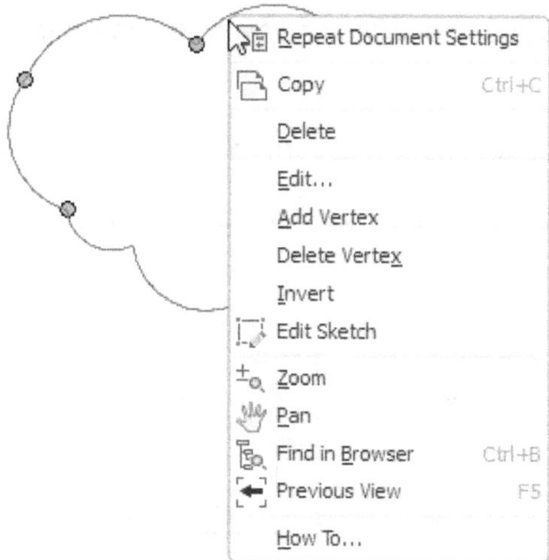

Figure 27–21

- For clouds that are placed on a sheet (independent of views) you can use the **Copy** and **Paste** options to copy a cloud.
- Use the **Delete** option to remove a cloud from the drawing. Alternatively, you can select the cloud and press <Delete>.
- Use the **Edit** option to access the *Revision Cloud* dialog box to modify the min./max. arc radius values or the arc direction. Once values are set, you can enable the **Save as the default** option to save the setting so that new clouds are created using the same settings. Additionally, you can enable the **Edit when created** option so that this dialog box is opened automatically when you create any new revision cloud.
- Use the **Add Vertex** and **Delete Vertex** options to add and delete vertices in the cloud, respectively. Once either of these options are activated, the cloud reverts to linear entities and you can select vertices to delete them or select on the linear entities to add new ones.
- Use the **Invert** option to reverse the arcs of a cloud. In drawings, this is sometimes used to help identify changes that are incomplete.
- Use the **Edit Sketch** option to open the Sketch environment and gain access to all the sketching tools available on the *Sketch* tab.

Practice 27a
Add Text and Symbols

Practice Objectives

- Add text to a drawing file to provide additional information.
- Create surface texture, datum identifier, and feature control frame symbols to views in a drawing.

In this practice, you will create the note and symbols shown in Figure 27–22.

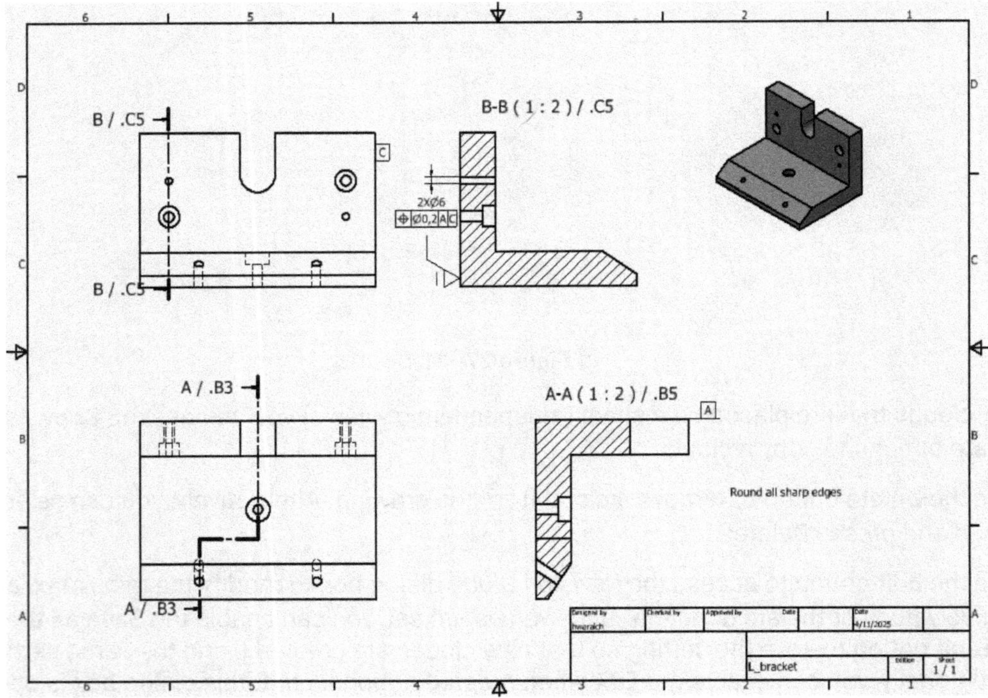

Figure 27–22

Task 1: Open a drawing file.

1. Open the **L_bracket.dwg** that you created previously. If you did not complete it, open **L_bracket_final.dwg** instead. The drawing displays as shown in Figure 27–23.

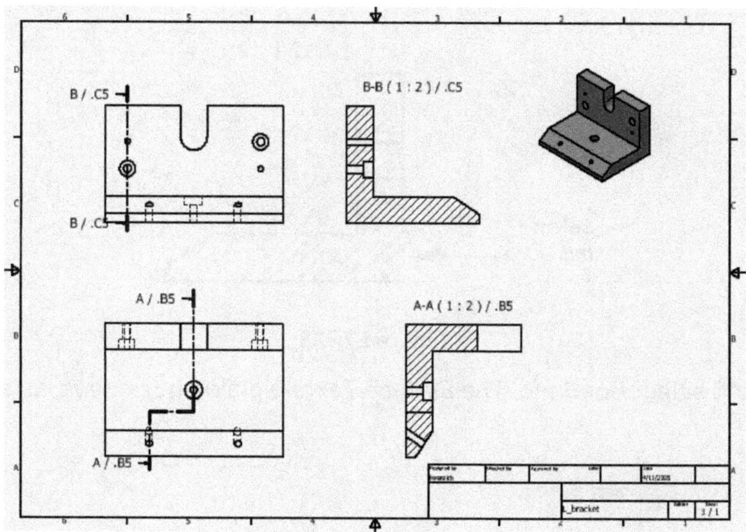

Figure 27–23

Task 2: Add text.

1. In the *Annotate* tab>*Text* panel, click A (Text).
2. Select in the open area on the right side of the drawing to place the text. The *Format Text* dialog box opens.
3. Enter **Round all sharp edges** in the *Text* field and click **OK**. The text displays as shown in Figure 27–24.

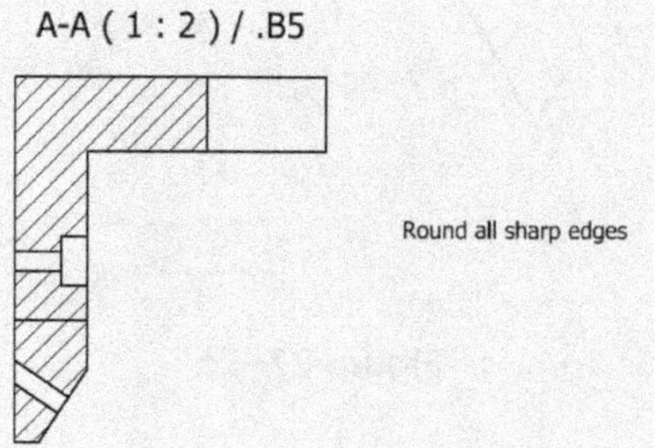

Figure 27–24

4. Select and move the text, if required.

Task 3: Add surface texture symbols.

1. In the *Symbols* panel, click √ (Surface).
2. Select the edge in section B, as shown in Figure 27–25.

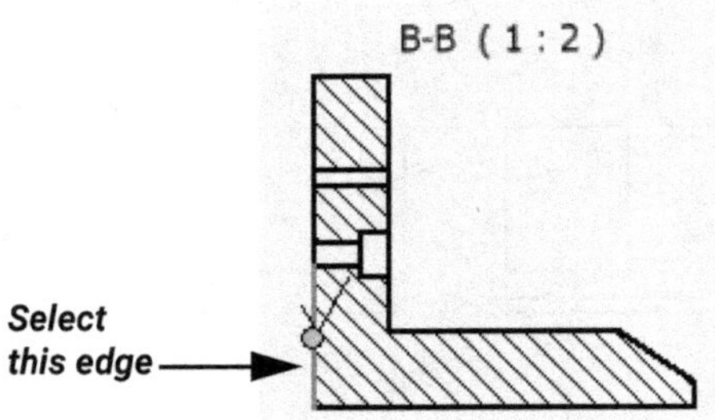

Figure 27–25

3. Right-click and select **Continue**. The *Surface Texture* dialog box opens, as shown in Figure 27–26.

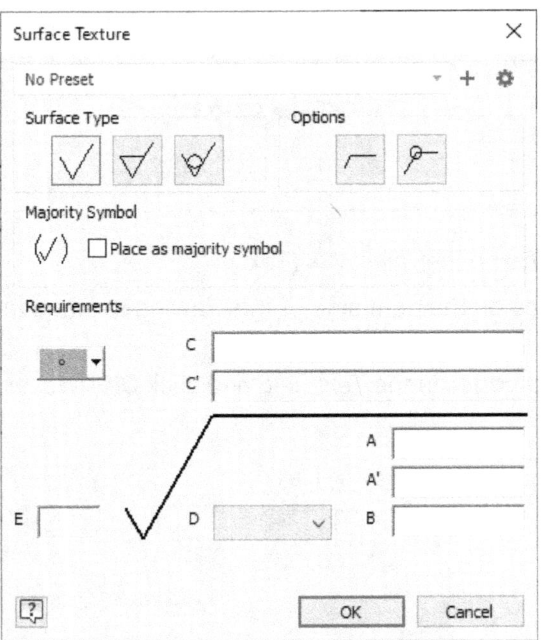

Figure 27–26

4. Click (Removal of material required) in the *Surface Type* area.
5. Values can be entered in the fields, as required, to define the symbol. Click **OK** without assigning specific values.

6. Press <Esc> to end the command.
7. The surface texture symbol displays. If the surface texture symbol is not oriented correctly, select it and drag the green dot to the required location. It will toggle through the available placement options as you drag. Release when the preview is as shown in Figure 27–27 to place it.

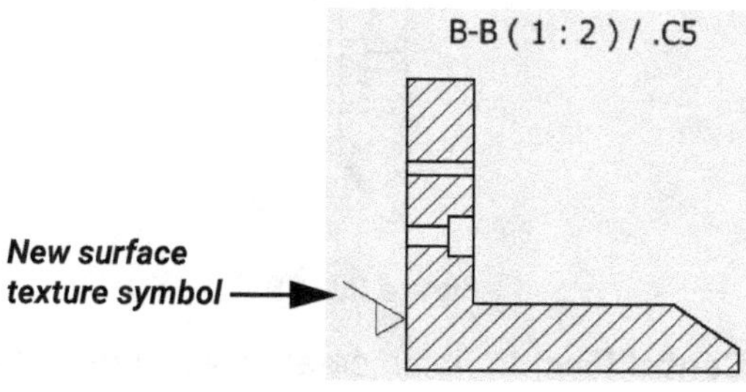

Figure 27–27

Task 4: Add datum identifier symbols.

1. Scroll down in the *Symbols* panel and click (Datum Identifier Symbol).
2. Select the edge in section A, as shown in Figure 27–28.

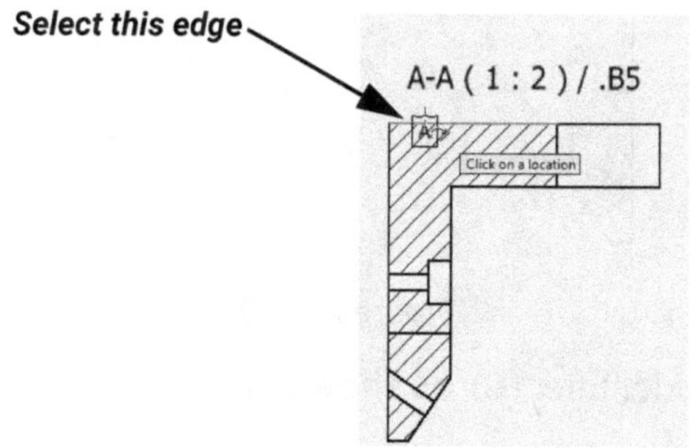

Figure 27–28

3. Right-click and select **Continue**. The *Format Text* dialog box opens. The letter **A** is entered automatically. Accept this default.

4. Click **OK**. The datum identifier is added, as shown in Figure 27–29.

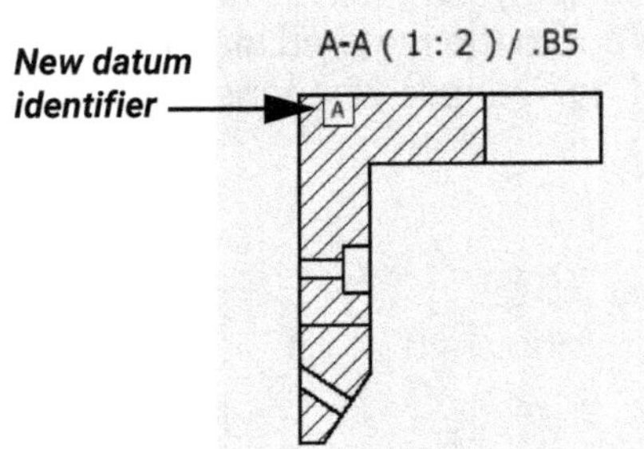

Figure 27–29

5. Right-click and select **Cancel [Esc]** to finish creating additional datum identifiers.
6. Move the datum identifier by selecting it. A green-colored dot will display, indicating that the symbol has been selected.
7. Drag the green circle to position the symbol as shown in Figure 27–30.

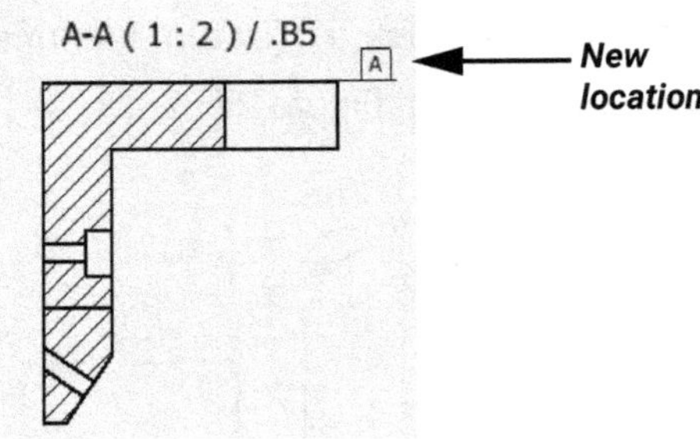

Figure 27–30

8. Create a second datum identifier (C), as shown in Figure 27–31.

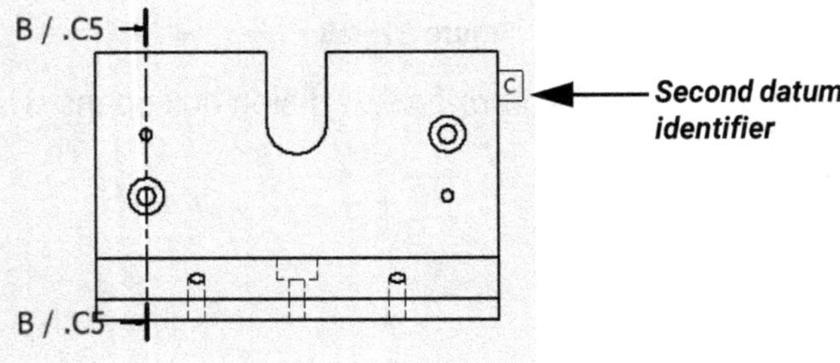

Figure 27–31

Task 5: Add a feature control frame.

1. Start the creation of a General Dimension and select the dimension style **Default-Method 2b** in the *Style* drop-down list, as shown in Figure 27–32.

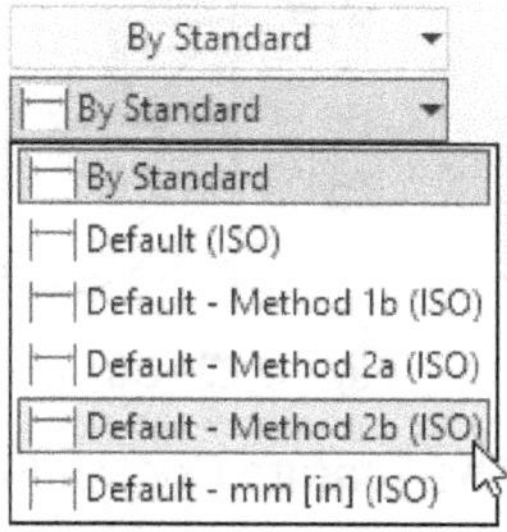

Figure 27–32

2. Add the dimension shown in Figure 27–33.

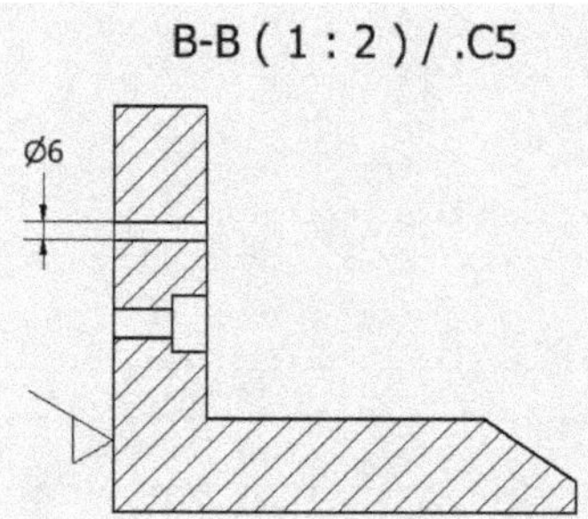

Figure 27–33

3. Edit the dimension to indicate two holes, as shown in Figure 27–34. You must edit the text for the dimension (before the **<<>>** symbols). You can add the diameter symbol, if it does not automatically appear.

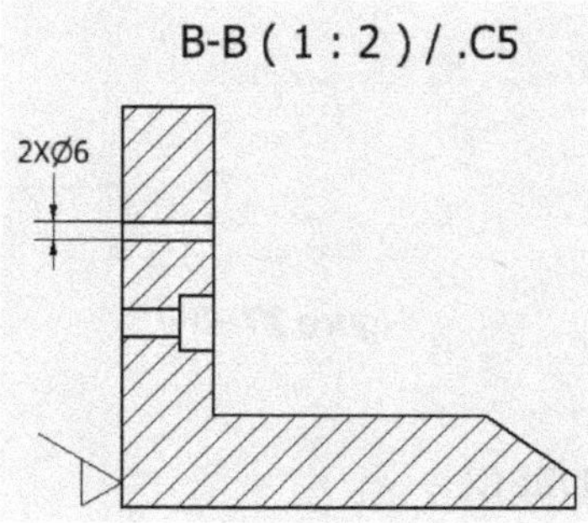

Figure 27–34

4. Scroll down in the *Symbols* panel and click (Feature Control Frame).

5. Select the dimension in section B, as shown in Figure 27–35.

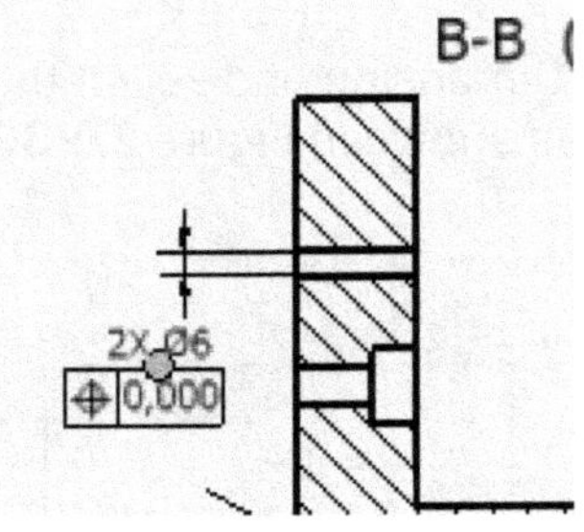

Figure 27–35

6. Right-click and select **Continue**. The *Feature Control Frame* dialog box opens.
7. Place the cursor at the beginning of the *Tolerance* field.
8. Click to expand the symbols list and select Ø to insert the diameter symbol, if not already assigned. Fill in the rest of the dialog box with the values shown in Figure 27–36.

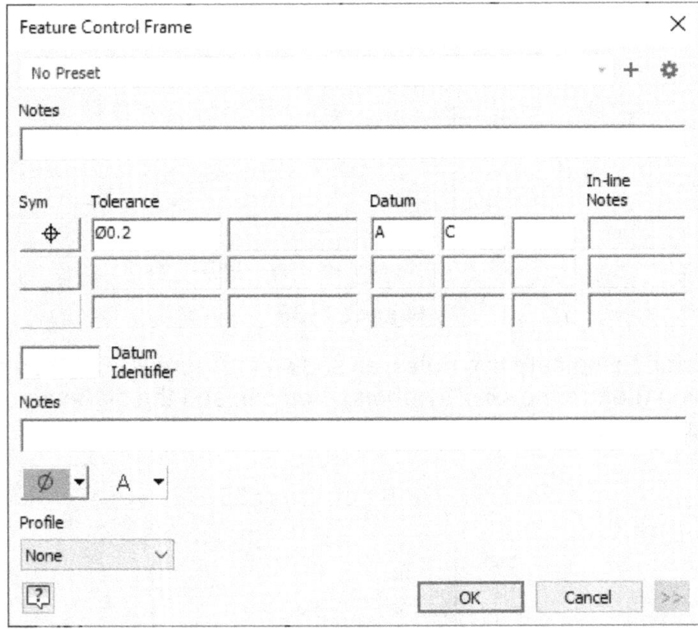

Figure 27–36

9. Click **OK**.
10. Right-click and select **Cancel [ESC]**.

11. Move the dimension and symbol as required. The feature control frame should display similar to that shown in Figure 27–37.

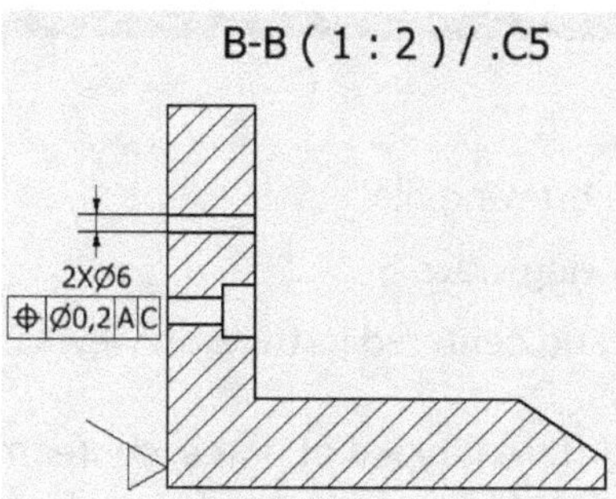

Figure 27–37

12. Save and close the drawing.

End of practice

Practice 27b
Add Notes, Center Marks, and Centerlines

Practice Objectives

- Add and edit a hole note in a drawing file.
- Add a chamfer note to a drawing view.
- Create a centerline bisector and centered pattern on views in a drawing.

In this practice, you will create different types of notes, center marks, and centerlines. The completed drawing is shown in Figure 27–38.

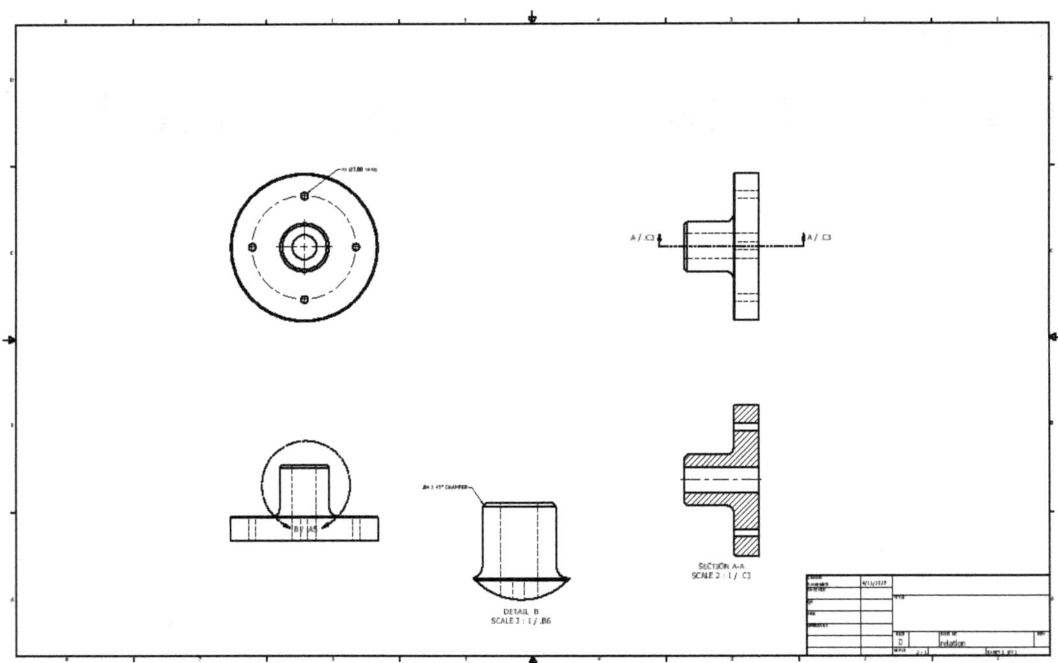

Figure 27–38

Task 1: Open a drawing file.

1. Open the **relation.dwg** that you created previously. The drawing displays as shown in Figure 27–39. If you did not complete it, open **relation_final.dwg** instead.

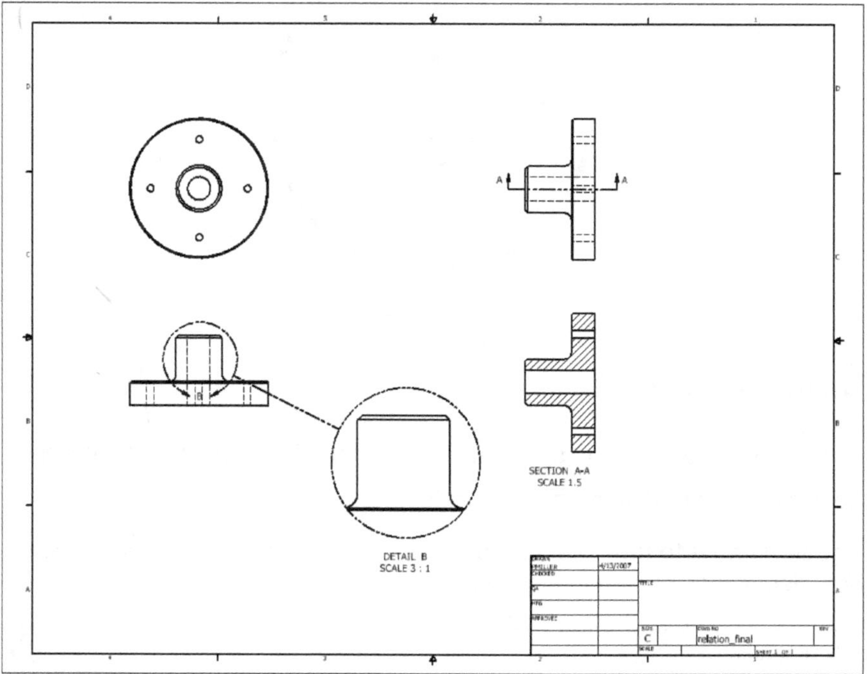

Figure 27–39

Task 2: Add a hole note.

1. In the *Annotate* tab>*Feature Notes* panel, click (Hole and Thread).
2. Select the hole in the drawing view shown in Figure 27–40.

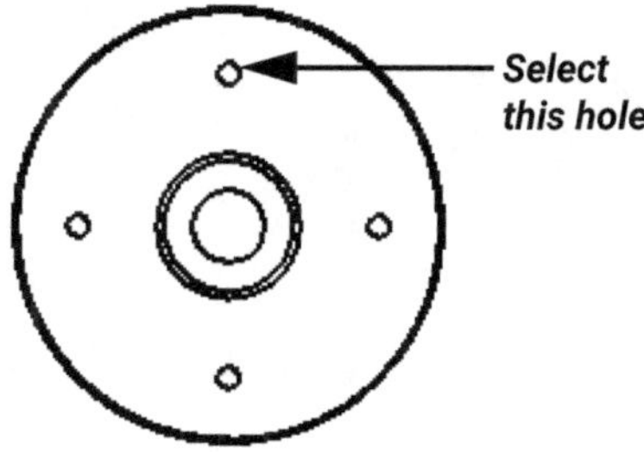

Figure 27–40

3. Position the note with the cursor and click the left mouse button to place it.

4. Complete the creation of the note by right-clicking and selecting **OK**. The hole note is added to the drawing, as shown in Figure 27–41.

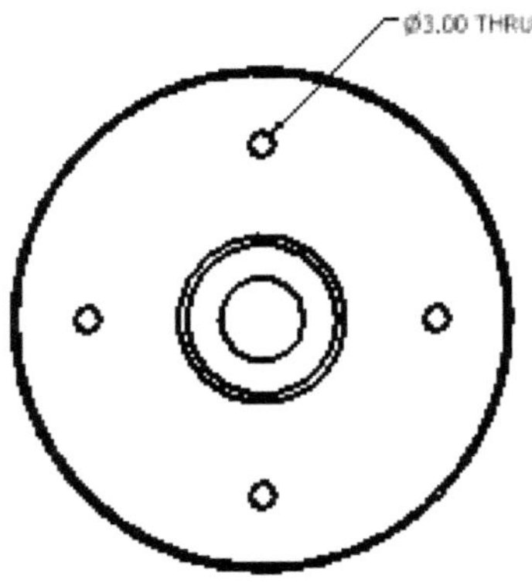

Figure 27–41

Task 3: Edit the hole note.

1. Right-click on the hole note and select **Edit Hole Note**. The *Edit Hole Note* dialog box opens.
2. Place the cursor at the beginning of the hole note.
3. Add the quantity note to the hole note by clicking # in the *Values and Symbols* area. The dialog box displays as shown in Figure 27–42.

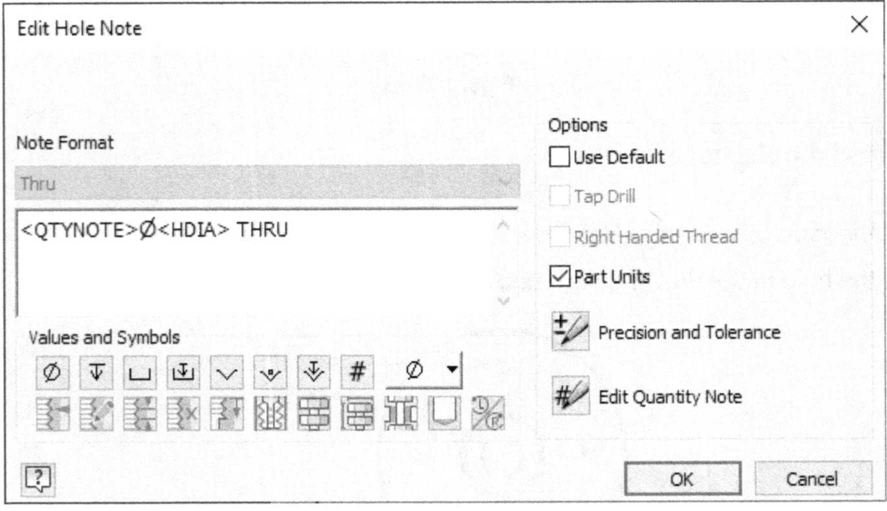

Figure 27–42

4. Click **OK**. The revised note displays as shown in Figure 27–43.

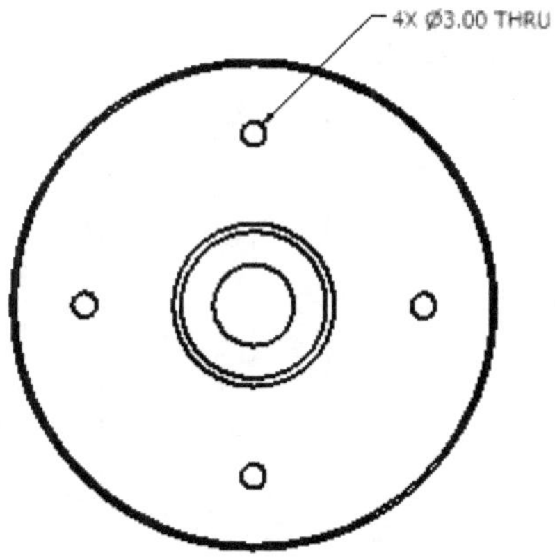

Figure 27–43

Task 4: Add a chamfer note.

1. Right-click on the detailed view and select **Edit Detail Properties**.
2. Clear the **Display Full Detail Boundary** option and click **OK**.
3. In the *Feature Notes* panel, click (Chamfer).
4. Select the two edges of the detailed view, as shown in Figure 27–44. Review the prompts in the Status Bar to verify the order of selection.

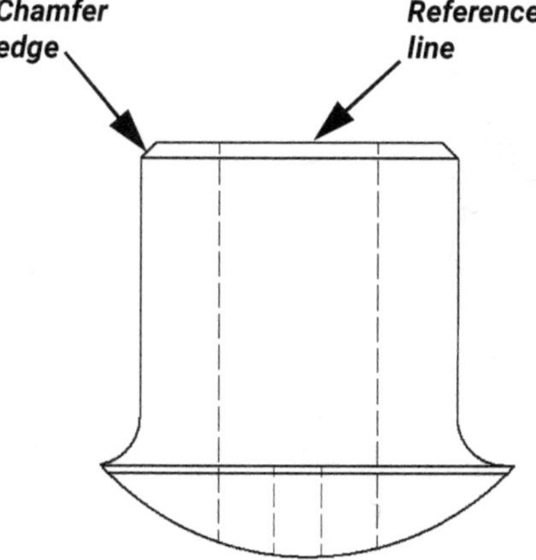

Figure 27–44

5. Position the note with the cursor and click the left mouse button to place it, as shown in Figure 27–45.

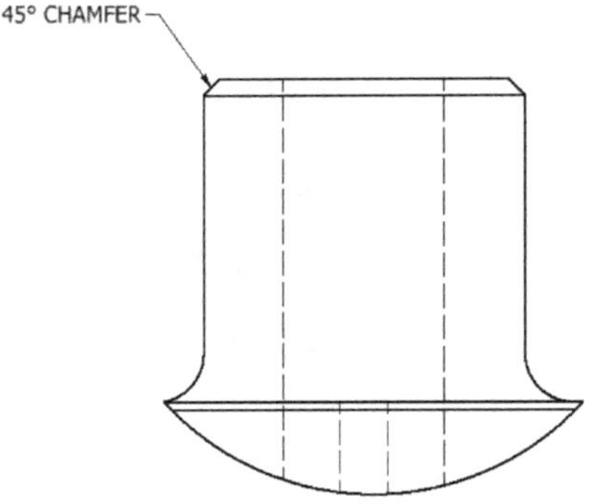

Figure 27–45

6. Complete the creation of the note by right-clicking and selecting **OK**.

Task 5: Add a centerline bisector.

1. In the *Symbols* panel, click (Centerline Bisector).
2. Select the two lines shown on the left in Figure 27–46 to add a centerline bisector to the section view.
3. Complete the creation of the centerline bisector by right-clicking and selecting **Cancel [ESC]**. The centerline bisector is added to the drawing view, as shown on the right in Figure 27–46.

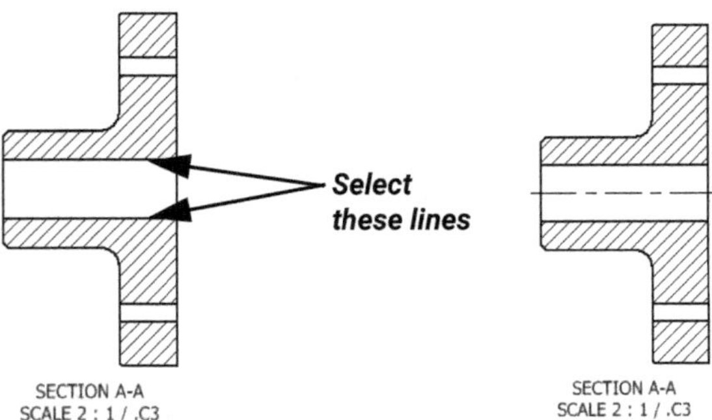

Figure 27–46

Task 6: Add a centered pattern.

1. In the *Symbols* panel, click (Centered Pattern).
2. Select the circular edge of the center circle to locate the center of the pattern, as shown in Figure 27–47. Any of the circular edges at the center of the circle can be selected.

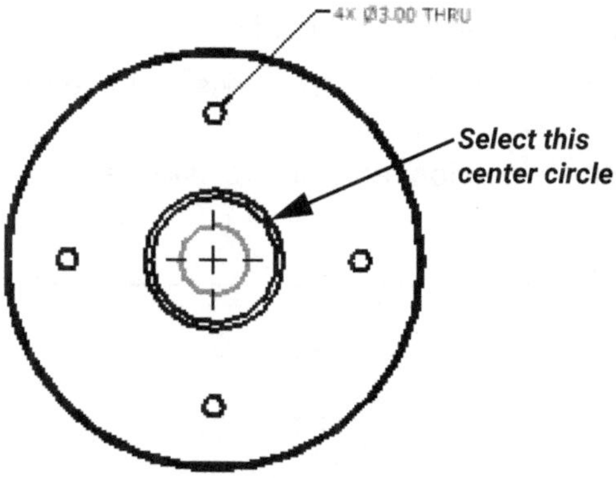

Figure 27–47

3. Select the four hole features shown on the left in Figure 27–48 in the order specified. You must select the first hole a second time. Alternatively, you can select the holes in a counter-clockwise order.
4. Complete the creation by right-clicking and selecting **Create**. The centered pattern is now added to the drawing view, as shown on the right in Figure 27–48.

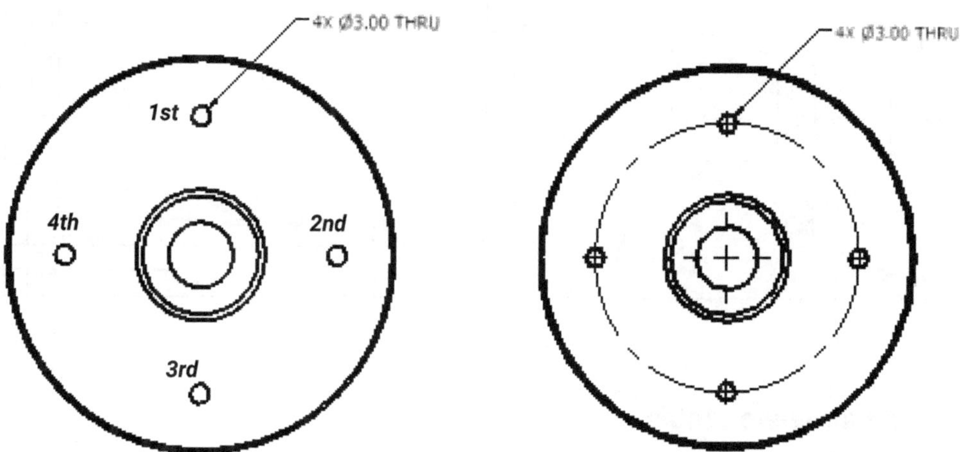

Figure 27–48

5. Save and close the drawing.

End of practice

Practice 27c
Add a Revision Table and Tags

Practice Objectives

- Add a revision table to a drawing file.
- Add revision tags to dimensions in a drawing file to indicate modifications made to the file.
- Edit the number of rows and properties of the Revision table to create a required table.

In this practice, you will create a revision table and revision tags. The completed drawing is shown in Figure 27–49.

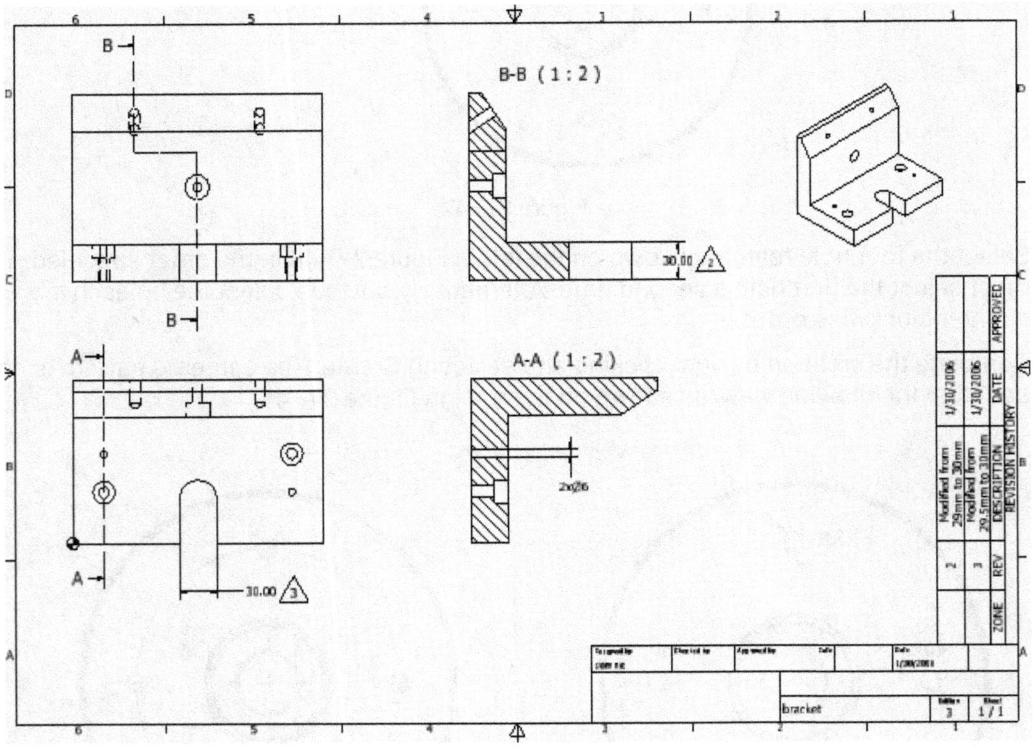

Figure 27–49

Task 1: Add a revision table.

1. Open **bracket_Rev Table.dwg**.
2. In the *Annotate* tab>*Revision* panel, click (Revision Table).

   Note: *The Revision Table dialog box provides you with options to create the table for the entire drawing or for the active sheet.*

3. Accept the default values in the *Revision Table* dialog box and click **OK**. A border displays that moves with the cursor.
4. Move the cursor to the bottom right side of the drawing, just above the title block. The revision table snaps to the title block and border. Click to place the revision table, as shown in Figure 27–50.

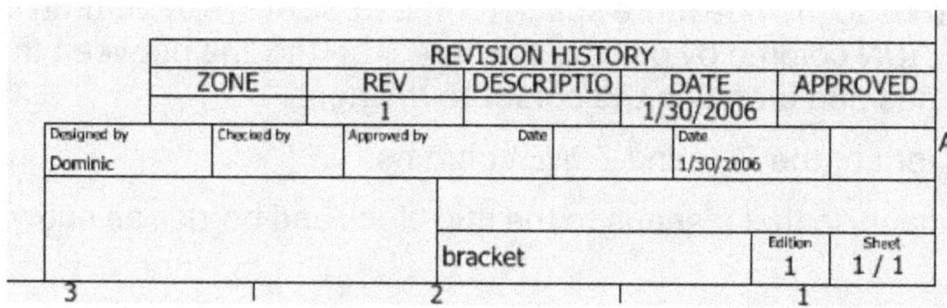

Figure 27–50

5. Right-click on the *Revision History* title in the table and select **Edit Revision Table Style**. The *Style and Standard Editor* dialog box opens. You can customize text styles, line format, gap for rows, position of the title, and whether the title displays. You can also use the *Revision Tags* tab to customize tags.
6. Select the *Heading* drop-down list and click to place the title of the revision table at the bottom. Click **Save and Close**. The revision table displays as shown in Figure 27–51.

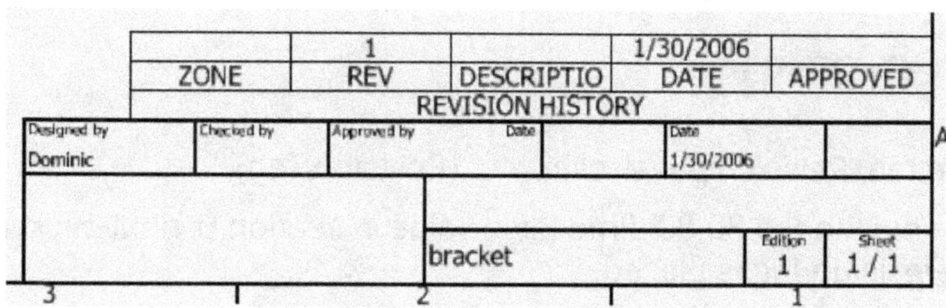

Figure 27–51

7. Add a new row by right-clicking on any of the text in the table and selecting **Add Revision Row**. The *Revision Table: Drawing Scope* dialog box opens. Verify that the new row has been added and click **OK**. A revision row is added, as shown in Figure 27–52.

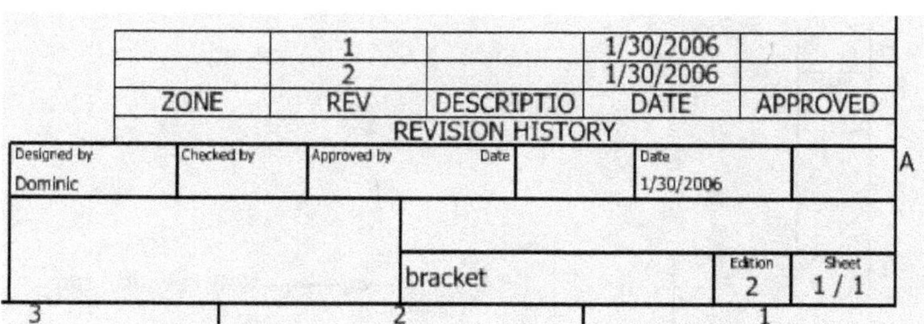

Figure 27–52

8. Delete the row that was just created in the table by selecting a value in the first row, such as 1, right-clicking and selecting **Delete Row**. The row is removed. You cannot delete the default row in the table.
9. Drag the entire table away from the title block and border by selecting on any text in the table and dragging the table.
10. Adjust the columns to provide more space for the *DESCRIPTION* column. Increase the width of the *DESCRIPTION* column by placing the cursor on the line between the *DESCRIPTION* and *DATE* columns and dragging the cursor to the right.
11. Decrease the width of the *REV* and *ZONE* columns.
12. Move the table back so that it snaps to the title block and border, as shown in Figure 27–53.

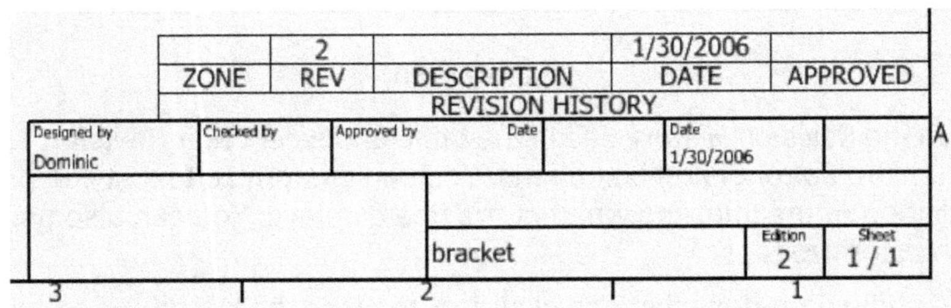

Figure 27–53

Task 2: Add a revision tag.

1. In the *Annotate* tab>*Revision* panel, click (Revision Tag).
2. Select the area next to the 30.00 dimension value in section B, right-click, and select **Continue**. The revision tag is placed.
3. Press <Esc> to cancel creating another revision tag.
4. Move the revision tag as shown in Figure 27–54.

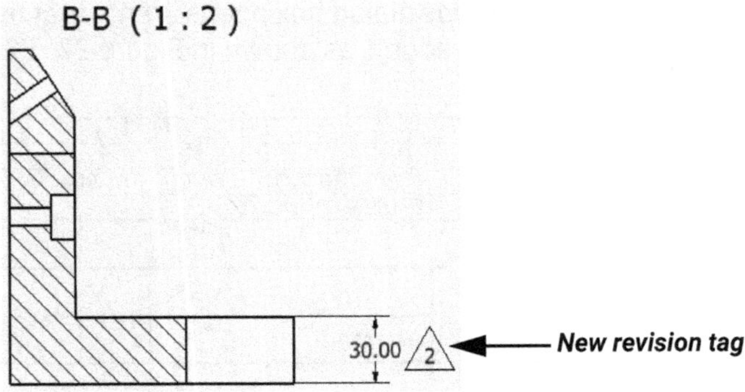

Figure 27–54

5. Right-click on the table and select **Edit**. The *Revision Table: Drawing Scope* dialog box opens.
6. Enter the text **Modified from 29mm to 30mm** in the *DESCRIPTION* column. Edit the date field to show today's date.
7. Click **OK**. The table displays as shown in Figure 27–55.

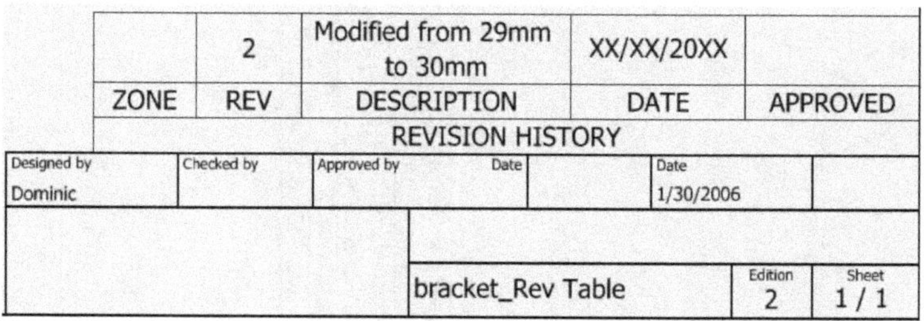

Figure 27–55

Task 3: Add a row to the revision table.

1. Select any text in the revision table, right-click and select **Add Revision Row**. The *Revision Table: Drawing Scope* dialog box opens.
2. A new revision row is added with an incremental revision value. Modify the *DESCRIPTION* column in this new row of the table to **Modified from 29.5mm to 30mm** and edit the date field to show today's date. Close the dialog box.
3. Add the revision tag to the 30.00mm dimension located in the other view, as shown Figure 27–56. The revision tag number is incremented when a new revision row is added in the revision table.

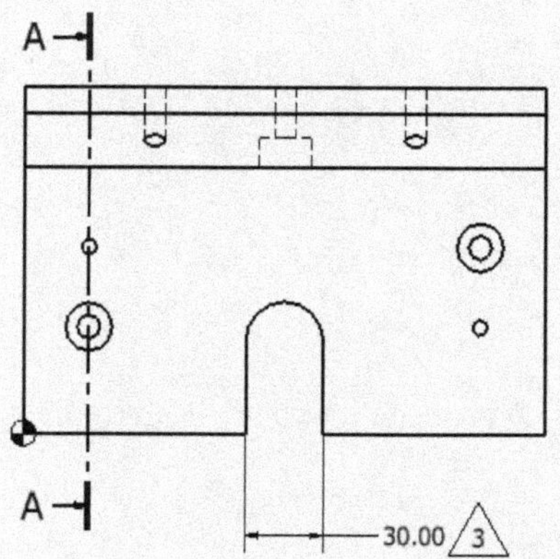

Figure 27–56

4. Right-click on the table, select **Rotate>Rotate 90 CCW**, and position the table along the right edge, as shown in Figure 27–57.

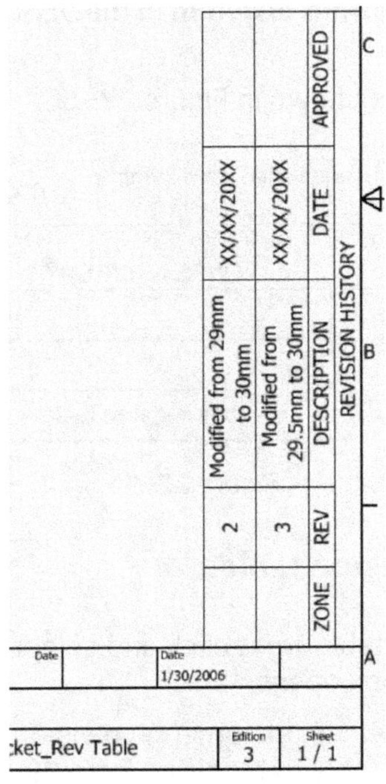

Figure 27–57

5. Save and close the drawing.

End of practice

Practice 27d
Add Hole Tables

Practice Objective

- Create hole tables based on selected features, feature types, and views.

In this practice, you will create three hole tables using three different methods. The completed drawing is shown in Figure 27–58.

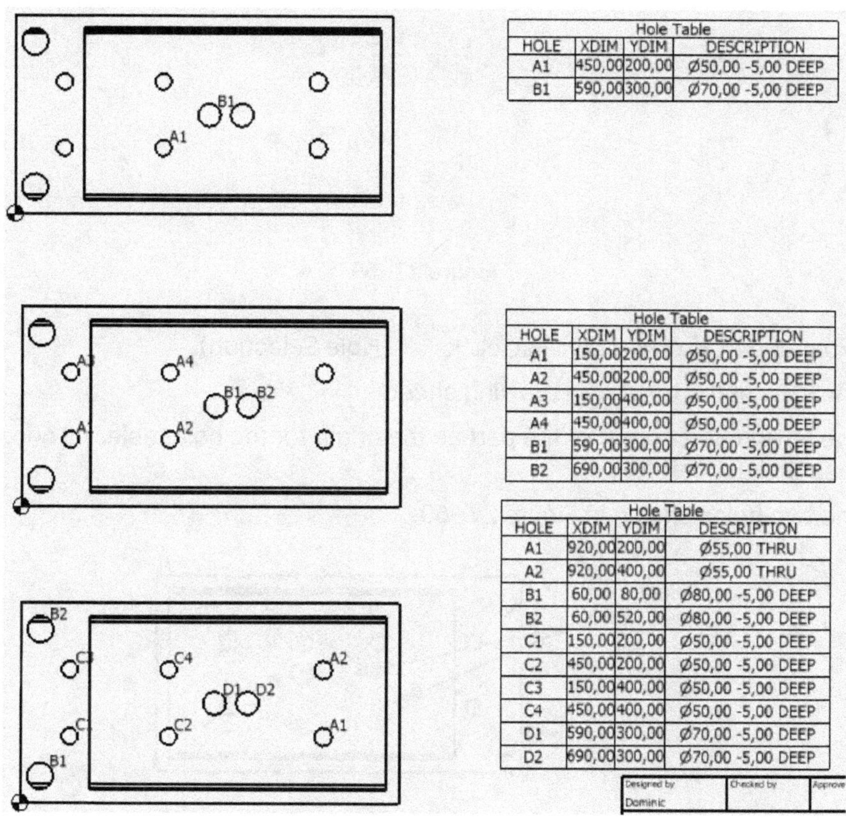

Hole Table			
HOLE	XDIM	YDIM	DESCRIPTION
A1	450,00	200,00	Ø50,00 -5,00 DEEP
B1	590,00	300,00	Ø70,00 -5,00 DEEP

Hole Table			
HOLE	XDIM	YDIM	DESCRIPTION
A1	150,00	200,00	Ø50,00 -5,00 DEEP
A2	450,00	200,00	Ø50,00 -5,00 DEEP
A3	150,00	400,00	Ø50,00 -5,00 DEEP
A4	450,00	400,00	Ø50,00 -5,00 DEEP
B1	590,00	300,00	Ø70,00 -5,00 DEEP
B2	690,00	300,00	Ø70,00 -5,00 DEEP

Hole Table			
HOLE	XDIM	YDIM	DESCRIPTION
A1	920,00	200,00	Ø55,00 THRU
A2	920,00	400,00	Ø55,00 THRU
B1	60,00	80,00	Ø80,00 -5,00 DEEP
B2	60,00	520,00	Ø80,00 -5,00 DEEP
C1	150,00	200,00	Ø50,00 -5,00 DEEP
C2	450,00	200,00	Ø50,00 -5,00 DEEP
C3	150,00	400,00	Ø50,00 -5,00 DEEP
C4	450,00	400,00	Ø50,00 -5,00 DEEP
D1	590,00	300,00	Ø70,00 -5,00 DEEP
D2	690,00	300,00	Ø70,00 -5,00 DEEP

Figure 27–58

Task 1: Add a hole table by selecting each hole.

1. Open **hole_chart.dwg**. There are three identical views.
2. In the *Annotate* tab>*Table* panel, expand the *Hole* drop-down list, as shown in Figure 27–59. The expanded list displays three hole options.

   Note: *Once selected, each option displays on the ribbon in the same way; you can identify the option by its icon or by hovering the cursor over the command and reviewing its tooltip.*

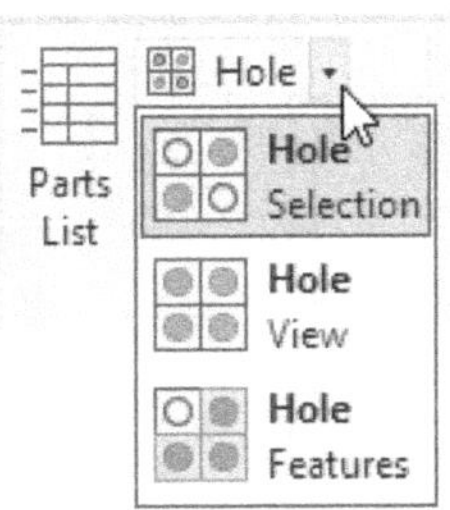

Figure 27–59

3. In the expanded *Hole* drop-down list, click (Hole Selection).
4. Select the view at the top of the drawing sheet.
5. Select the bottom-left corner of the part as the origin for the hole table. All coordinates will use this as their 0,0 reference.
6. Select the two holes shown in Figure 27–60.

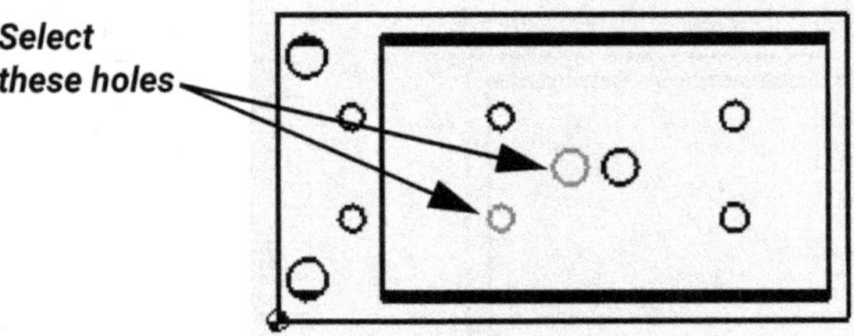

Figure 27–60

7. Right-click and select **Create**. A box opens that now follows the cursor.

8. Place the hole table in the top right area of the drawing by selecting the left mouse button. The hole table displays and is automatically populated with the hole information for the two holes that were selected, as shown in Figure 27–61.

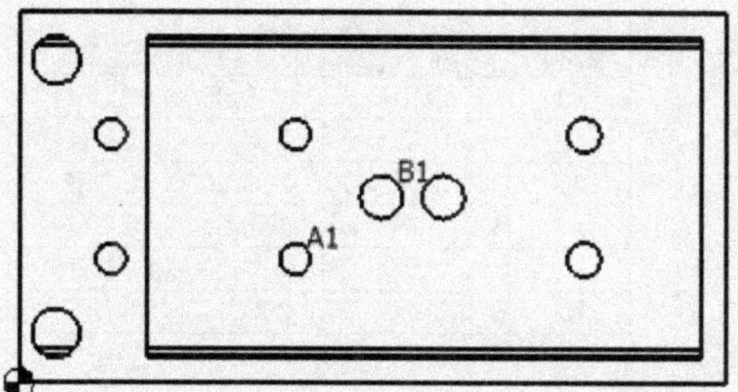

Hole Table			
HOLE	XDIM	YDIM	DESCRIPTION
A1	450,00	200,00	Ø50,00 -5,00 DEEP
B1	590,00	300,00	Ø70,00 -5,00 DEEP

Figure 27–61

Task 2: Add a hole table by selecting feature types.

1. In the expanded *Hole* drop-down list, click (Hole Features).
2. Select the middle view on the drawing sheet.
3. Select the bottom-left corner of the part as the origin.
4. Select the two holes shown in Figure 27–62.

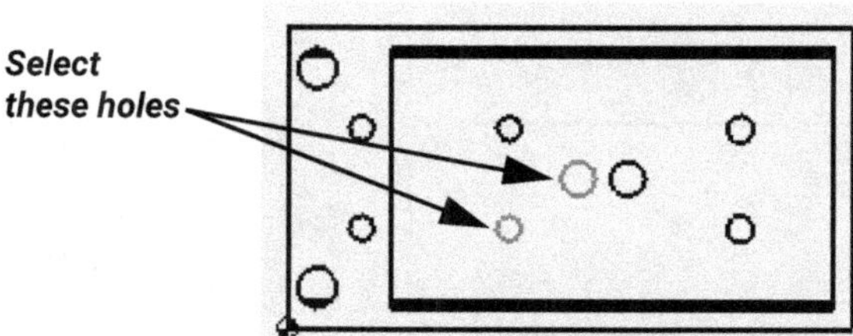

Figure 27–62

5. Right-click and select **Create**.

6. Place the hole table in the middle right area of the drawing. The hole table displays and is automatically populated with the information for the two holes and any hole that is similar to those selected, as shown in Figure 27–63.

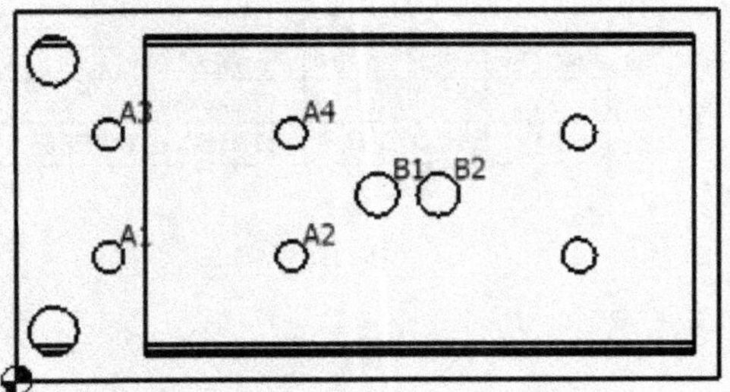

Hole Table			
HOLE	XDIM	YDIM	DESCRIPTION
A1	150,00	200,00	Ø50,00 -5,00 DEEP
A2	450,00	200,00	Ø50,00 -5,00 DEEP
A3	150,00	400,00	Ø50,00 -5,00 DEEP
A4	450,00	400,00	Ø50,00 -5,00 DEEP
B1	590,00	300,00	Ø70,00 -5,00 DEEP
B2	690,00	300,00	Ø70,00 -5,00 DEEP

Figure 27–63

Task 3: Add a hole table by selecting a view.

1. In the expanded *Hole* drop-down list, click (Hole View).
2. Select the bottom view of the drawing sheet.
3. Select the bottom-left corner of the part as the origin.
4. Place the hole table in the bottom-right area of the drawing. The hole table displays and is automatically populated with all of the hole information for the selected view, as shown in Figure 27–64.

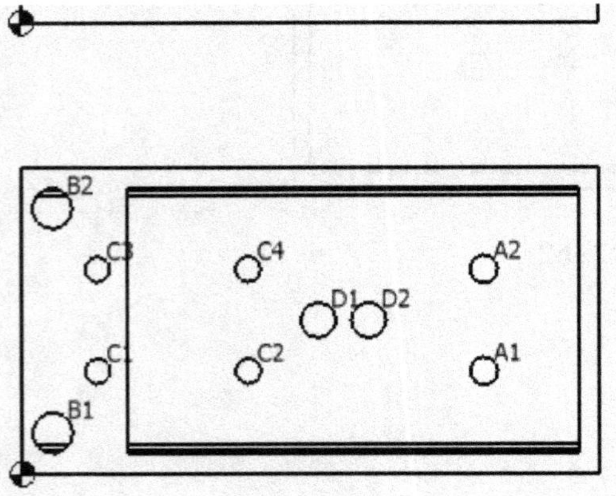

Hole Table			
HOLE	XDIM	YDIM	DESCRIPTION
A1	920,00	200,00	Ø55,00 THRU
A2	920,00	400,00	Ø55,00 THRU
B1	60,00	80,00	Ø80,00 -5,00 DEEP
B2	60,00	520,00	Ø80,00 -5,00 DEEP
C1	150,00	200,00	Ø50,00 -5,00 DEEP
C2	450,00	200,00	Ø50,00 -5,00 DEEP
C3	150,00	400,00	Ø50,00 -5,00 DEEP
C4	450,00	400,00	Ø50,00 -5,00 DEEP
D1	590,00	300,00	Ø70,00 -5,00 DEEP
D2	690,00	300,00	Ø70,00 -5,00 DEEP

Designed by Dominic | Checked by | Appro

Figure 27–64

5. Save and close the drawing.

End of practice

Chapter Review Questions

1. You can only create text with a leader.
   a. True
   b. False

2. Which of the following are valid symbols that can be created in a drawing? (Select all that apply.)
   a.
   b.
   c.
   d. A

3. To which of the following features can you add a hole note in a drawing view? (Select all that apply.)
   a. Holes
   b. Extruded circular cuts
   c. Extruded circular solids
   d. Chamfer

4. Which chamfer note option displays the horizontal distance between a selected edge and a reference line?
   a. (Distance 1)
   b. (Angle)
   c. (Distance 2)

5. Which command is used to automatically place center marks on all holes in a view, as shown in Figure 27–65?

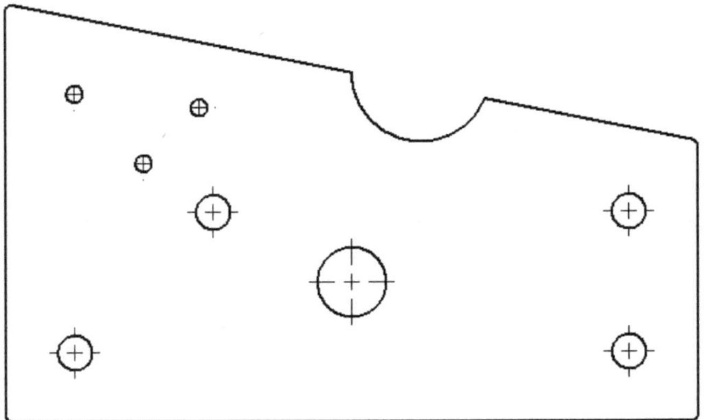

Figure 27–65

a. Centerline

b. Center Mark

c. Automated Centerlines

6. Fill in the Hole Table type, **Selection**, **View**, or **Features**, with the best description of how it can be used to create a table.

a. Using the ______ type, all identical holes of all selected types are automatically included.

b. Using the ______ type, all holes included in the hole table are selected individually.

c. Using the ______ type, all holes of any type in a selected view are included in the hole table.

7. Which of the following drawing annotation types is used to help track and distinguish the various changes in the model between revisions?

a. Parts list

b. Revision table

c. Hole table created using Hole View

d. Balloons

Command Summary

Button	Command	Location
	Center Mark	• **Ribbon:** *Annotate* tab>*Symbols* panel • **Context Menu**: In the graphics window
	Centered Pattern	• **Ribbon:** *Annotate* tab>*Symbols* panel
	Centerline	• **Ribbon:** *Annotate* tab>*Symbols* panel
	Centerline Bisector	• **Ribbon:** *Annotate* tab>*Symbols* panel
	Chamfer (note)	• **Ribbon:** *Annotate* tab>*Feature Notes* panel
	Hole and Thread (note)	• **Ribbon:** *Annotate* tab>*Feature Notes* panel • **Context Menu**: In the graphics window
	Hole Features (table)	• **Ribbon:** *Annotate* tab>*Table* panel
	Hole Selection (table)	• **Ribbon:** *Annotate* tab>*Table* panel
	Hole View (table)	• **Ribbon:** *Annotate* tab>*Table* panel
	Leader Text	• **Ribbon:** *Annotate* tab>*Text* panel • **Context Menu**: In the graphics window
	Revision (table)	• **Ribbon:** *Annotate* tab>*Table* panel
	Revision Tag	• **Ribbon:** *Annotate* tab>*Table* panel
A	**Text**	• **Ribbon:** *Annotate* tab>*Text* panel
N/A	**Various Symbol Types**	• **Ribbon:** *Annotate* tab>*Symbols* panel

Chapter 28

Customizing Autodesk Inventor

Customizing the software enables you to change the system's default appearance and options to tailor to specific needs or preferences. You can customize settings to affect the entire company or changes can be user-specific.

Learning Objectives

- Use the *Application Options* to globally customize the modeling environment.
- Use the *Document Settings* to customize the active part, assembly, or drawing file.
- Edit iProperty information for parts, assemblies, and drawing files.
- Change the part units in your model.
- Customize the ribbon appearance.
- Add a *User Commands* panel with commands to any of the tabs on the ribbon.
- Assign command aliases using keyboard keys for commonly used commands.
- Customize the marking menu that displays when accessing commands in the shortcut menu.

28.1 Application Options

The *Application Options* dialog box settings control the software's behavior and configuration.

In the *Tools* tab>*Options* panel, click (Application Options) to open the dialog box. Alternatively, you can click **Options** in the **File** menu to open it.

General Tab

The *General* tab sets operation behaviors, such as startup, tooltips, selection, etc., as shown in Figure 28–1.

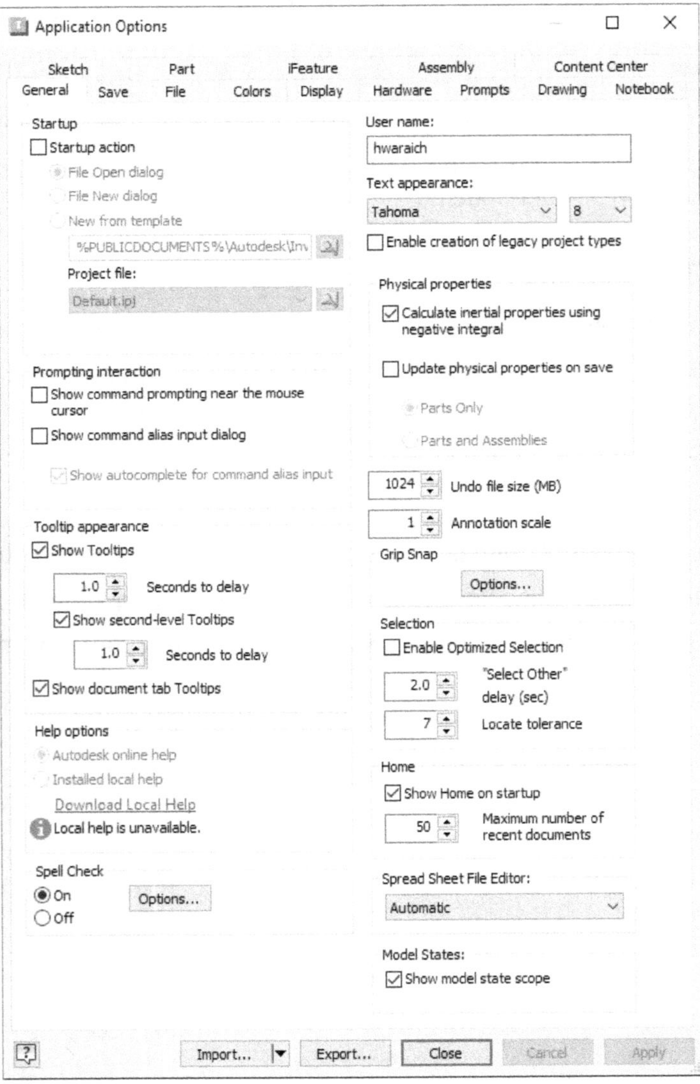

Figure 28–1

Save Tab

The *Save* tab can be used to set the default save behavior when assembly components or library files are saved, as shown in Figure 28–2.

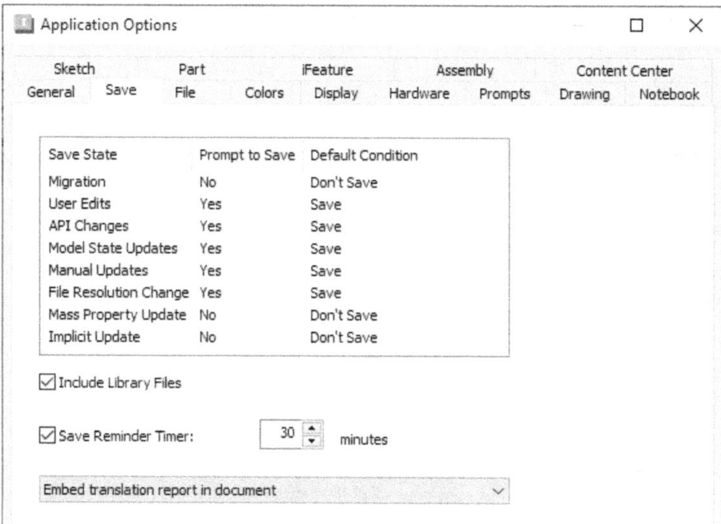

Figure 28–2

File Tab

The *File* tab controls the default locations of the files used by the software. To change a file location, click next to the appropriate field. It also controls the default options and settings to accelerate file opening times for assemblies, and set the default templates.

Colors Tab

The *Colors* tab controls the colors used in the graphics window and the presence of reflections and textures, assigns a color scheme for objects in the graphics window or drawing files, or assigns a background color (color, gradient, or background image). The *Colors* tab also enables you to control the color theme of the user interface (UI) for software (Light or Dark) and the in-canvas color theme for the graphics window.

Display Tab

The *Display* tab controls the appearance of active and inactive components and a model's display quality. In addition, it controls the 3D Navigation controls and behavior for the software. Options on this tab also enable you to customize the middle mouse button behavior.

Hardware Tab

The *Hardware* tab enables you to customize settings for graphical appearance and system performance.

Prompts Tab

The *Prompts* tab enables you to select the prompts that display while working. To do so, select a prompt and right-click in their *Response* or *Prompt* columns.

> **Note:** *A convenient keyword search field is available at the top of the tab to locate specific prompts in the list.*

Drawing Tab

The *Drawing* tab (shown in Figure 28–3) sets options for the behavior of drawings.

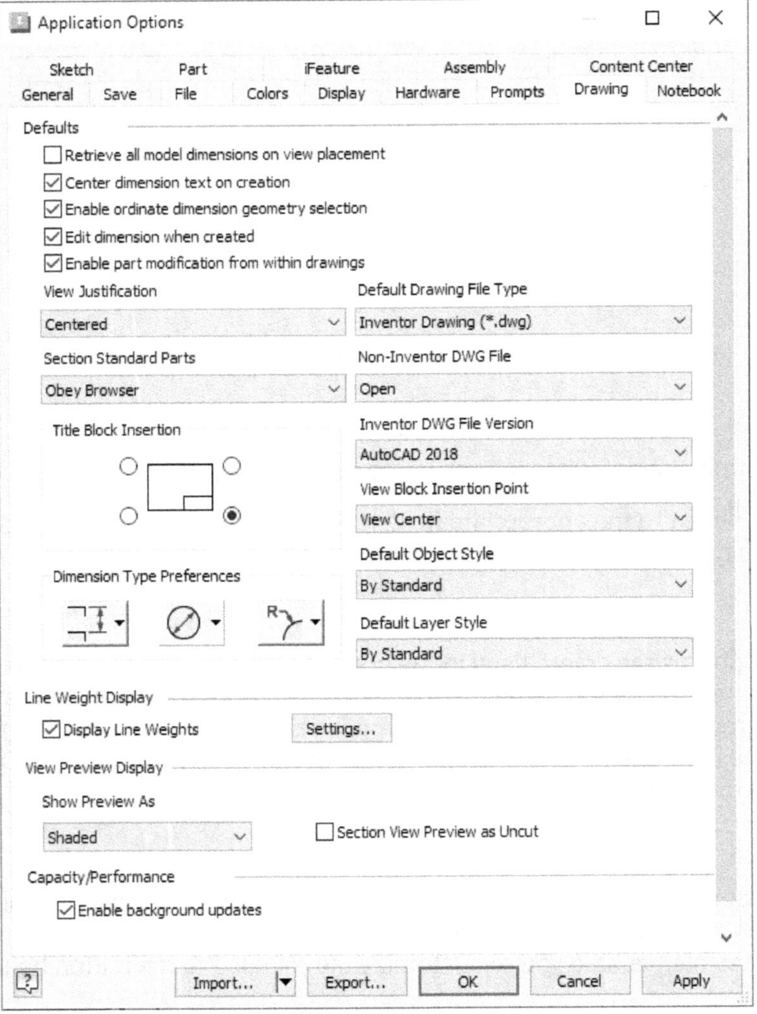

Figure 28–3

> **Note:** *The* **Enable part modification from in drawings** *enables you to allow model dimension changes at the drawing level, or not.*

Sketch Tab

The *Sketch* tab (shown in Figure 28–4) controls the sketch settings.

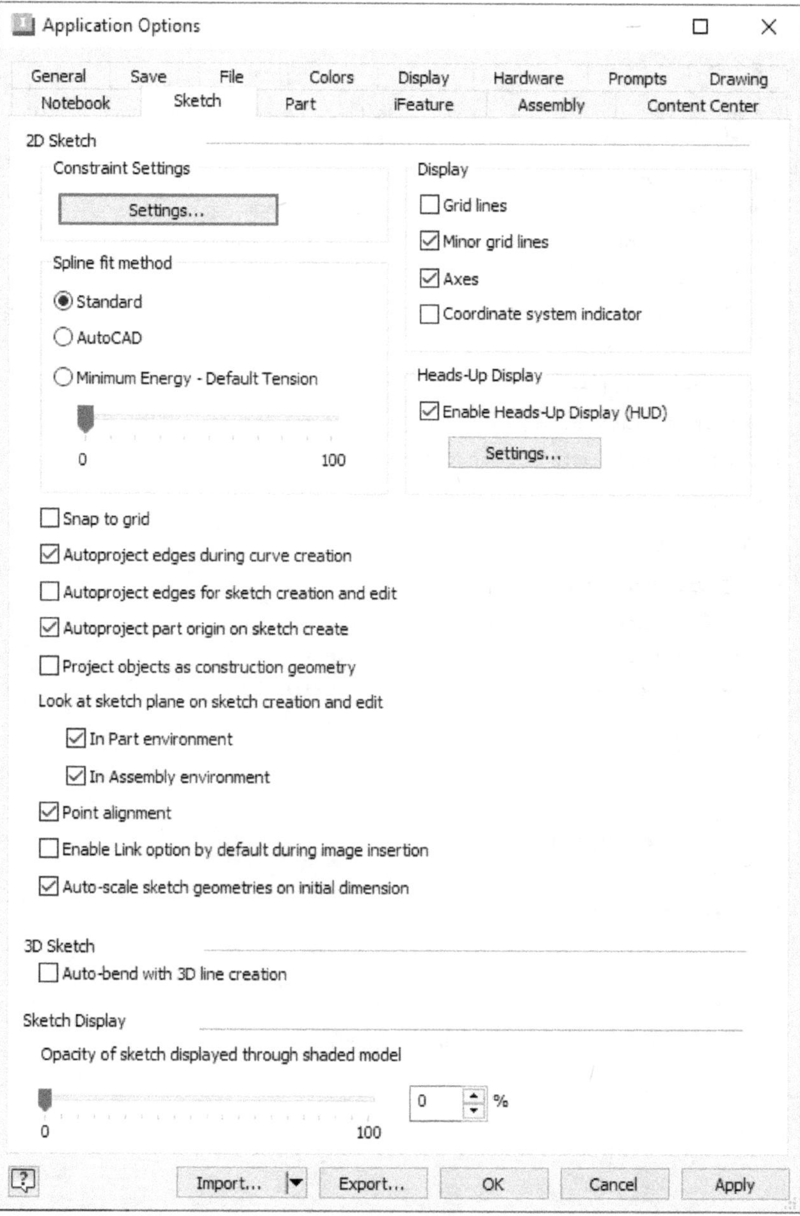

Figure 28–4

Part Tab

The *Part* tab (shown in Figure 28–5) controls the defaults for creating new parts, along with some constraint settings.

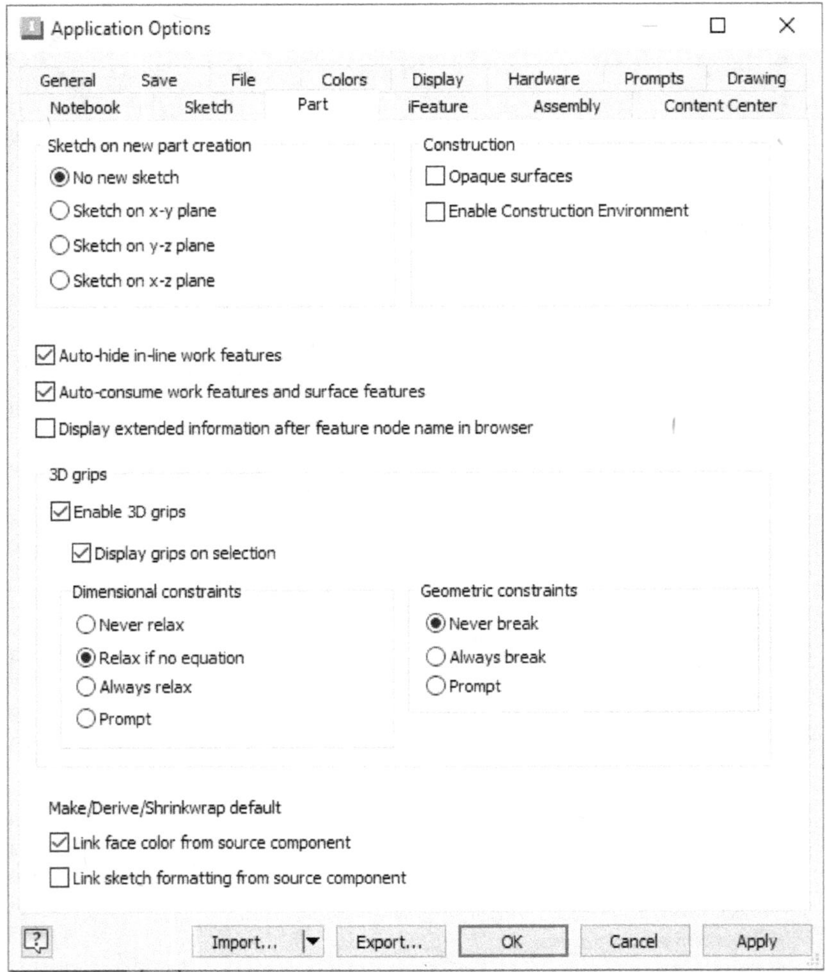

Figure 28–5

Assembly Tab

The *Assembly* tab (shown in Figure 28–6) controls the defaults for working with assemblies.

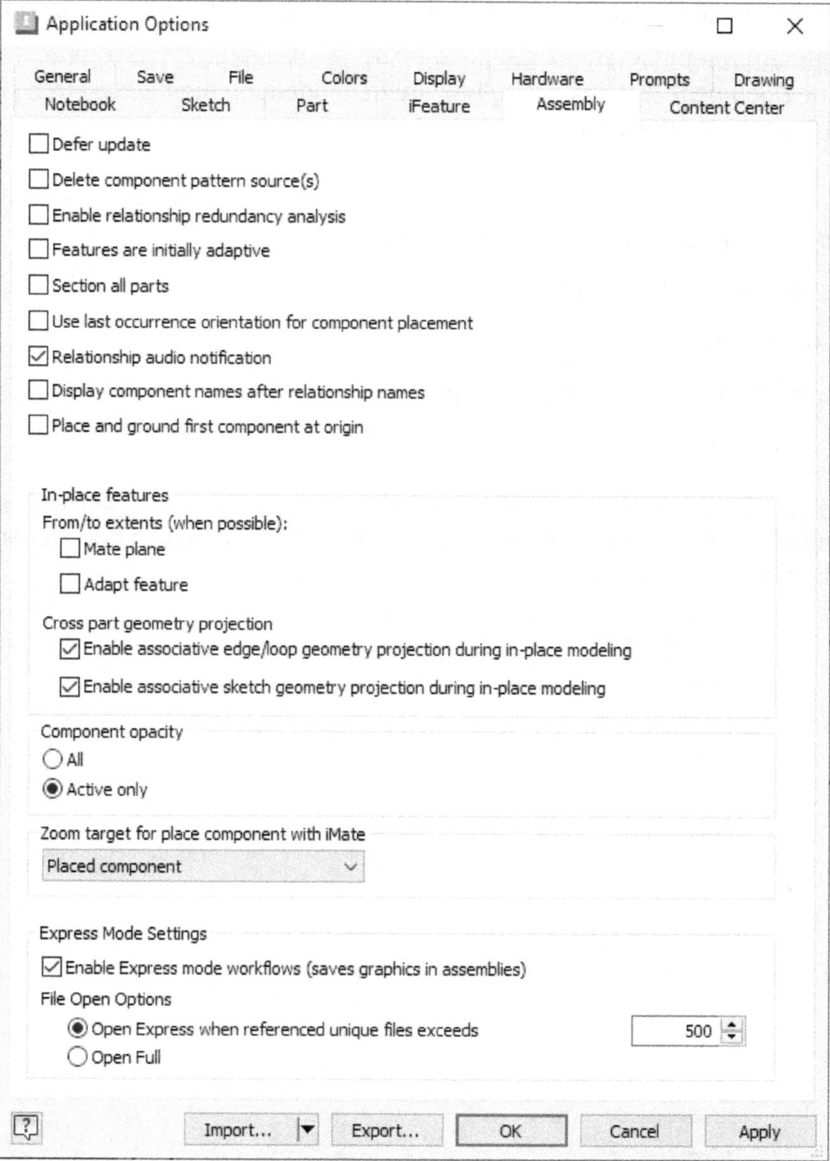

Figure 28–6

28.2 Document Settings

To control the current file settings (e.g., grid or units) you use the *Document Settings*. Settings made here only apply to the current file. Select the *Tools* tab>*Options* panel, and click (Document Settings) to open the *Document Settings* dialog box. The options that are available in the *Document Settings* dialog box are dependent on the file type that was active when the dialog box was opened.

Standard Tab

The *Standard* tab enables you to set the following:

- Lighting style and display appearance
- Material for the model
- Active standard for annotations in a drawing

Units Tab

The *Units* tab (shown in Figure 28–7) displays the default unit system, precision values, and display settings for model dimensions and parameters. The *Units* tab is not available in a drawing. In an assembly, the Units tab is the same as in a part.

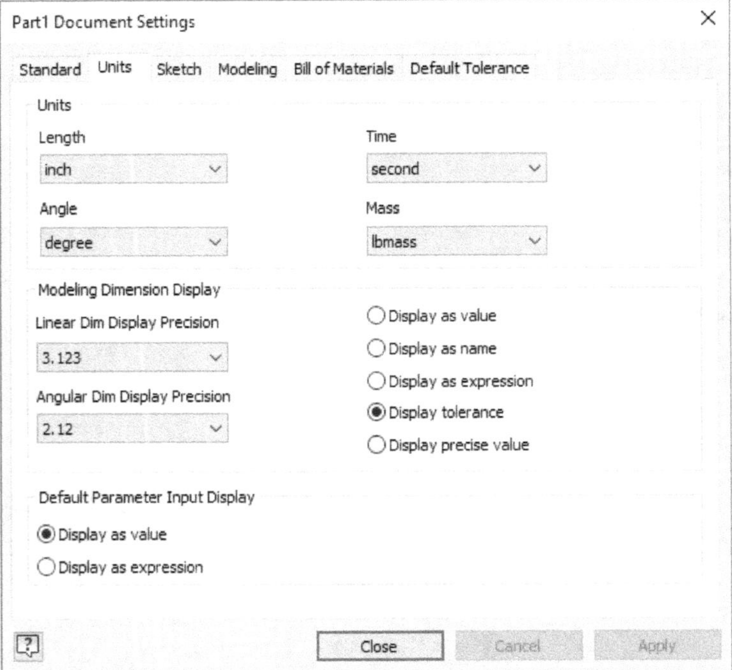

Figure 28–7

Sketch Tab

To set the sketch grid settings, select the *Sketch* tab, as shown in Figure 28–8. You can also set the radius for corner bends placed on 3D lines as you sketch them, as well as line weight display. In an assembly, the *Sketch* tab has the same options as a part, except for the *3D Sketch* area. In a drawing, the *Sketch* tab only contains *Snap Spacing* and *Grid Display* areas.

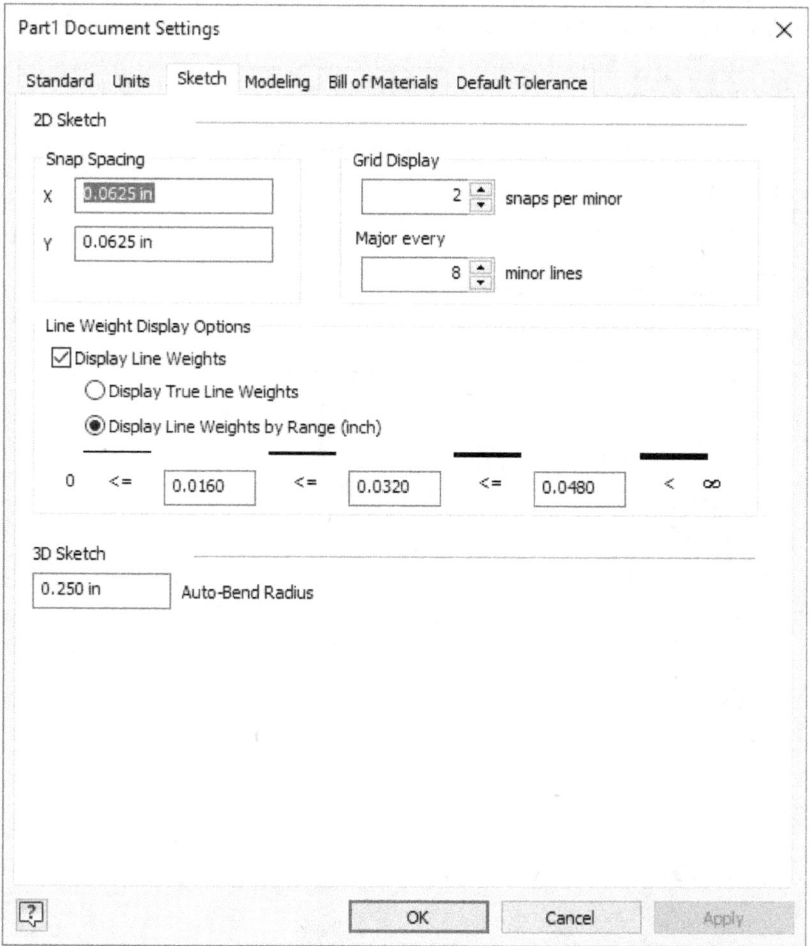

Figure 28–8

Modeling Tab

The *Modeling* tab (shown in Figure 28–9) controls whether adaptivity is available in an assembly, 3D snap spacing when you sketch in 3D in an active part, sectioning through a part, and tapped hole diameter, initial view extents. In addition, you can define naming prefixes and defaults. In an assembly, the *Modeling* tab has a reduced set of options that pertain to the assembly environment, and it also contains some additional options for Interactive Contact. The *Modeling* tab is not available in a drawing.

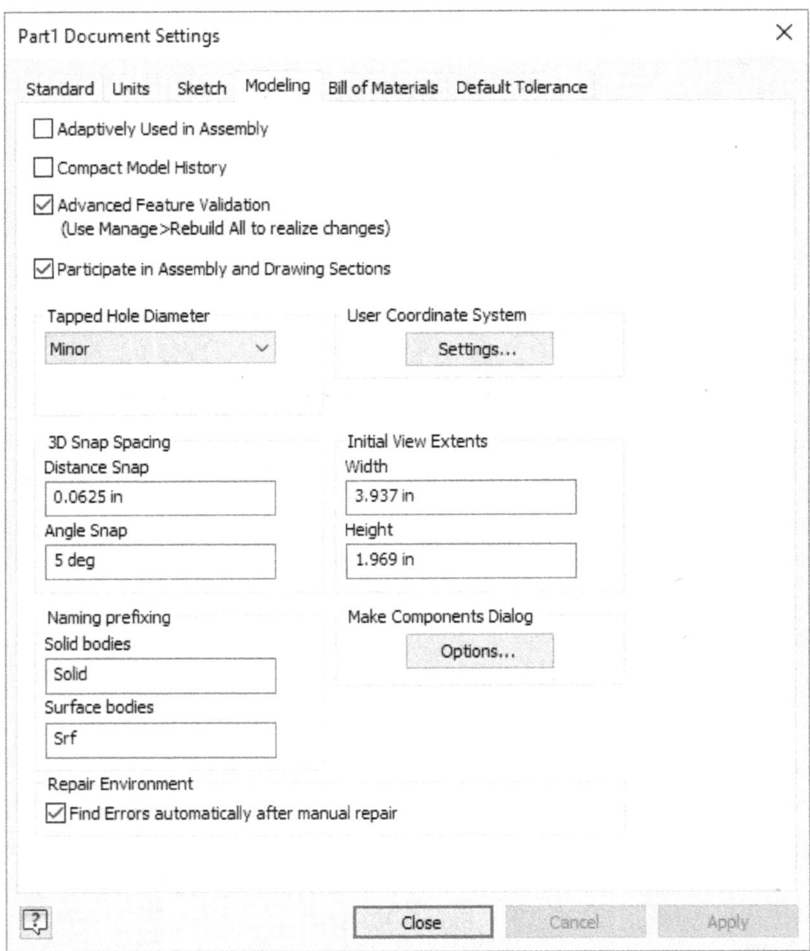

Figure 28–9

Bill of Materials Tab

The *Bill of Materials* tab (shown in Figure 28–10) controls the bill of materials settings, such as BOM structure and unit quantity. In an assembly, the *Bill of Materials* tab is the same as in a part. The *Bill of Materials* tab is not available in a drawing.

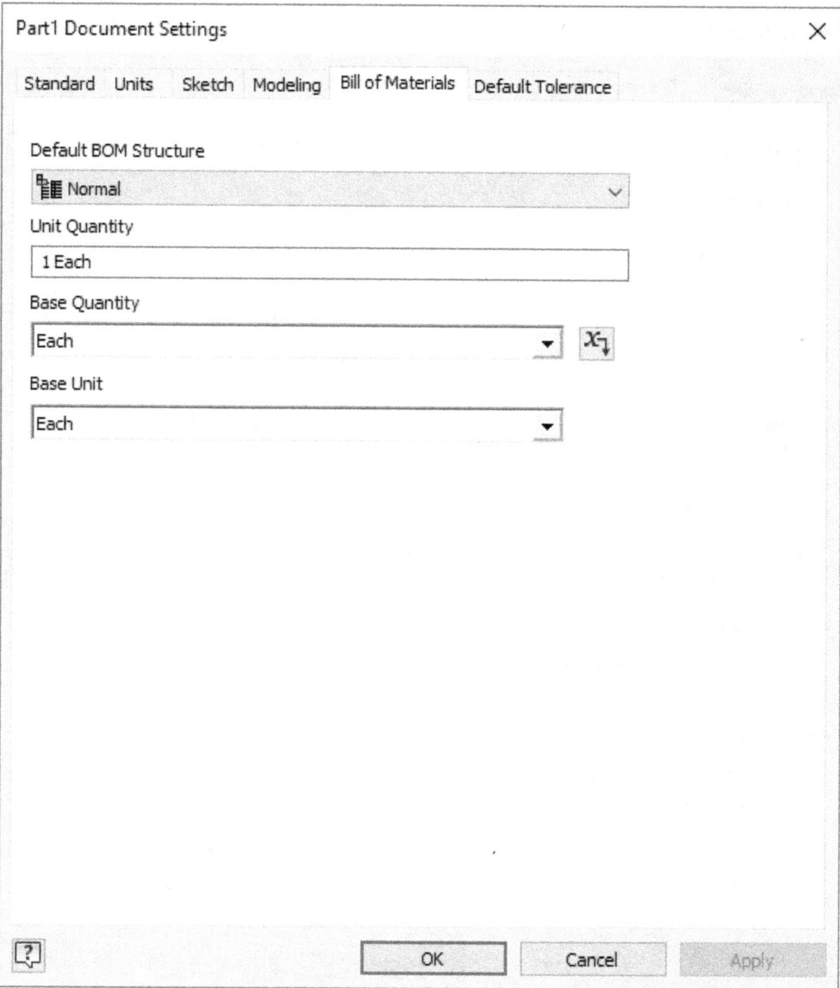

Figure 28–10

Default Tolerance Tab

The *Default Tolerance* tab controls the linear and angular part dimension tolerances and precision levels. The *Default Tolerance* tab is not available in a drawing or in an assembly.

Drawing Tab

The *Drawing* tab (shown in Figure 28–11) controls settings such as deferring updates to drawings, dimension updates, cross hatch clipping, automated centerlines, and shaded view settings. This tab is only available in a drawing.

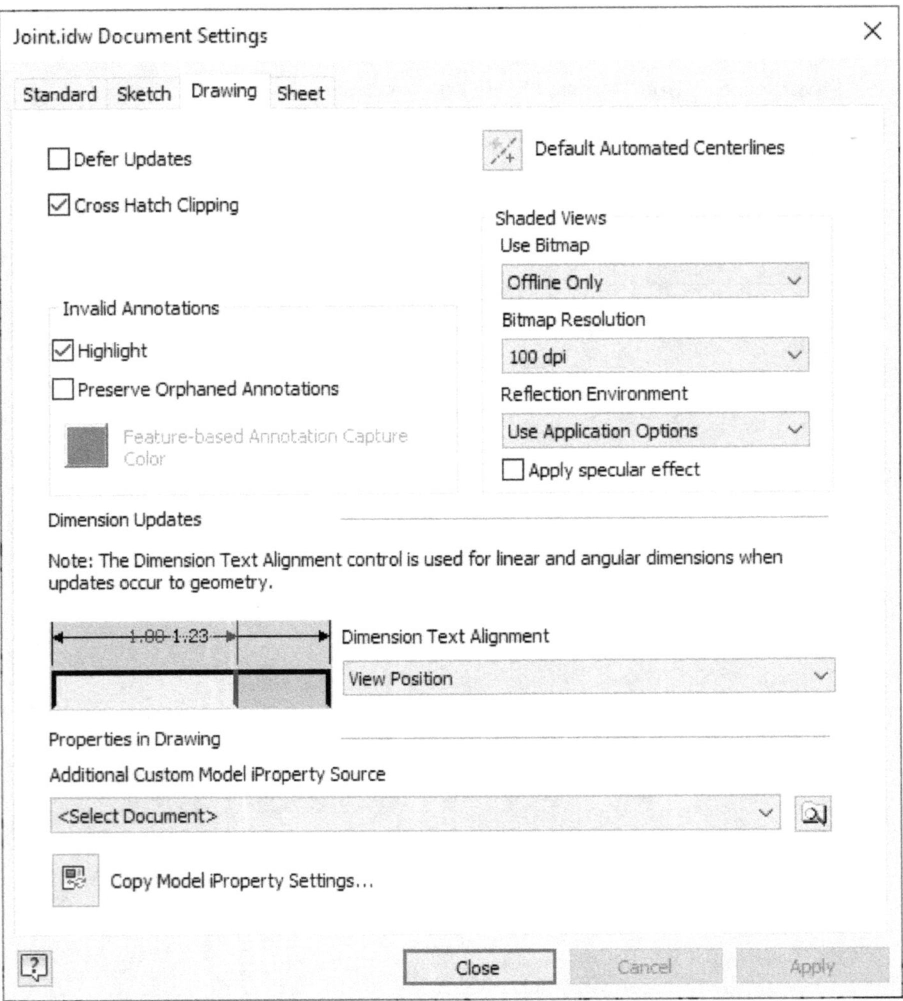

Figure 28–11

Sheet Tab

The *Sheet* tab controls colors in a drawing and the default name for each sheet (default is Sheet). This tab is only available in a drawing.

28.3 File Properties

You can store non-graphical information in a file using the *iProperties* dialog box. To open the *iProperties* dialog box, right-click on the filename at the top of the Model browser and select **iProperties**. Alternatively, in the **File** menu, select **iProperties** to open the it. The *iProperties* dialog box for the current file opens, similar to that shown in Figure 28–12. Information from this dialog box is automatically entered in the drawing title block of your model.

Figure 28–12

The tabs on the *iProperties* dialog box are as follows:

Tabs	Description
General tab	Displays basic file information, such as file format, location, and size. This information is read-only.
Summary tab	Enables you to enter information in several categories. The information can be used in a title block, or for sorting and searching for files. • In the *Author* field, the username for the user logged onto the computer is automatically entered when the file is created. You can change the name by typing over it. • The **Save Preview Picture** option at the bottom of the dialog box is grayed out and is no longer used.
Project tab	Enables you to enter information for tracking the design. • **Location:** Entered automatically when you assign the filename. It contains the path where the file is located. • **File Subtype:** Entered automatically and describes the type of file, such as **Modeling**, **Assembly**, or **Drawing**. • If you do not enter a *Part Number*, the name of the file is automatically entered in that field. • The *Designer* field populates with the username for the user logged onto the computer when the file is created. You can change the name by typing over it. • The *Creation Date* field populates with the date on which the file was created. You can change the date by selecting the calendar on the right and selecting a new date.
Status tab	Enables you to track the status of the file.
Custom tab	Enables you to define your own properties. The properties display in the lower area of the dialog box. • You can set the type to **Text**, **Date**, **Number**, or **Yes/No**. • Custom properties can be used to search/sort files and create reports.
Save tab	Enables you to create a thumbnail image of the file that displays in the *File Open* dialog box and to determine which image is used.
Physical tab	Enables you to display the physical properties of the part or assembly. It is not available in presentation or drawing files. In a part file, you can change the material of the part to change the properties.

Some information in the *iProperties* dialog box can also be accessed from outside of the Autodesk Inventor software. Right-click on the name of the file in a File Explorer window and select **Properties** to open the *Properties* dialog box for that file.

28.4 Changing Part Units

To change the part units of a model, you need to convert the existing units to the new system of units. Select the *Tools* tab>*Options* panel, click (Document Settings), and select the *Units* tab. The *Document Settings* dialog box displays as shown in Figure 28–13.

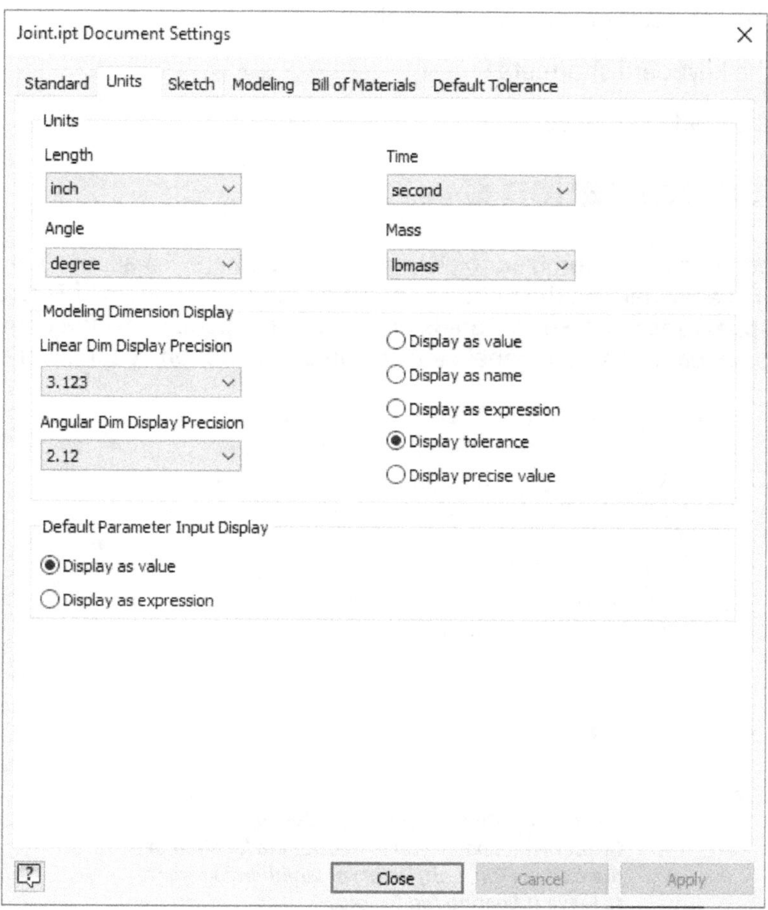

Figure 28–13

Select new units in the *Units* area and select the required **Modeling Dimension Display** options. Click **Apply** to apply the new units and click **OK** to close the dialog box.

> ***Note:*** *The* ***Display As...*** *options determine how you want to display dimensions and parameters in your model.*

Note that this controls the display units. The system remembers the original value of a dimension. If you switch from inch to millimeter, all dimensions display in millimeters. If you edit a dimension that was input in inches, the original value displays in the *Edit Dimension* dialog box.

28.5 Inventor User Interface Customization

How you access commands can be customized to help you work more efficiently. The Inventor UI can be customized in the following ways:

- Customize the display of the ribbon commands.
- Add commands to custom panels on the ribbon.
- Customize the keyboard shortcuts.
- Customize the marking menus.

Ribbon Customization

The default ribbon can be customized to change how it appears. To access the customization options, right-click anywhere on the ribbon to access the menus shown in Figure 28–14. The options **Show Appearance** and **Show Panels** enable you to specify how the commands on the tabs and panels appear and which panels are shown on the ribbon, respectively.

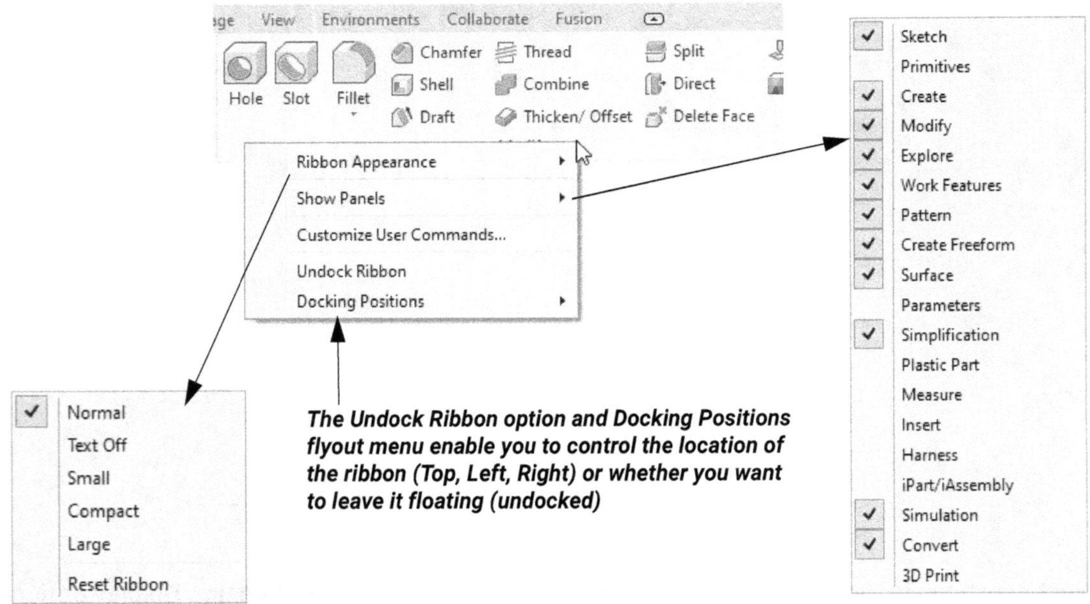

Figure 28–14

Custom Panels on the Ribbon

A *User Commands* panel can be added to any of the tabs on the ribbon. This enables you to add specific commands to the ribbon for easy access. To create a *User Commands* panel, use the *Customize* dialog box. This is accessed in the *Tools* tab>*Options* panel by clicking (Customize). You can customize the panels on the *Ribbon* tab (shown in Figure 28–15).

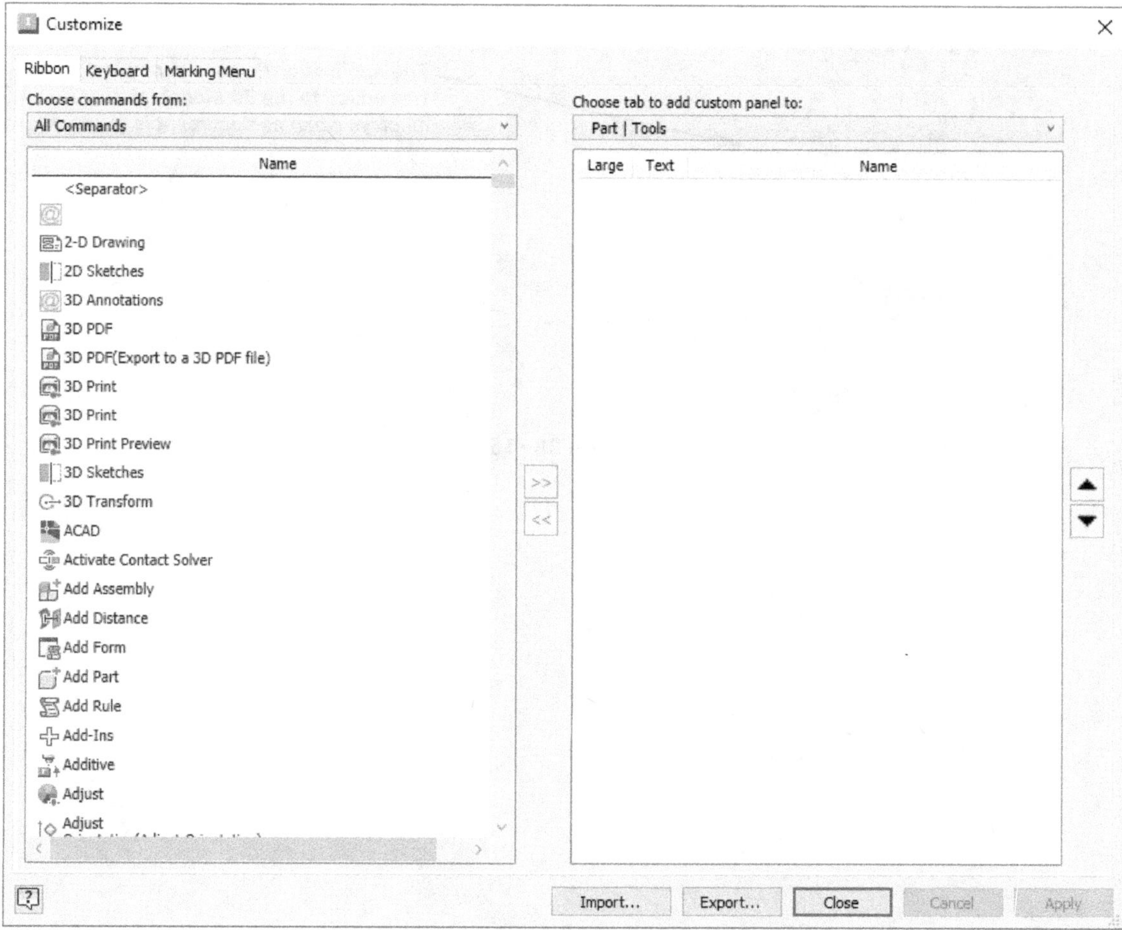

Figure 28–15

To add a *User Commands* panel, in the *Choose tab to add custom panel to*: drop-down list, select the tab to which you want to add the panel. In the left column, select the command to be added and click >> to add the command. The command that was added to the *Part | 3D Model* tab is shown at the top in Figure 28–16. You can also customize whether the command is shown as **Large** and/or with **Text**. The resulting panel on the *3D Model* tab is shown at the bottom in Figure 28–16, where the **Application Options** command was added. Multiple commands can be added to each *User Commands* panel.

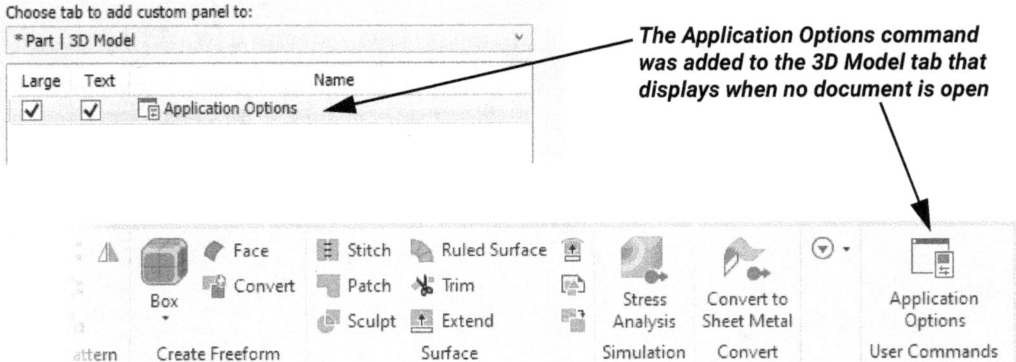

Figure 28–16

Keyboard Shortcuts

You can expand the functionality of keyboard shortcuts by assigning command aliases in the *Customize* dialog box. This is accessed in the *Tools* tab>*Options* panel by clicking (Customize) and selecting the *Keyboard* tab in the dialog box. The *Customize* dialog box is shown in Figure 28–17.

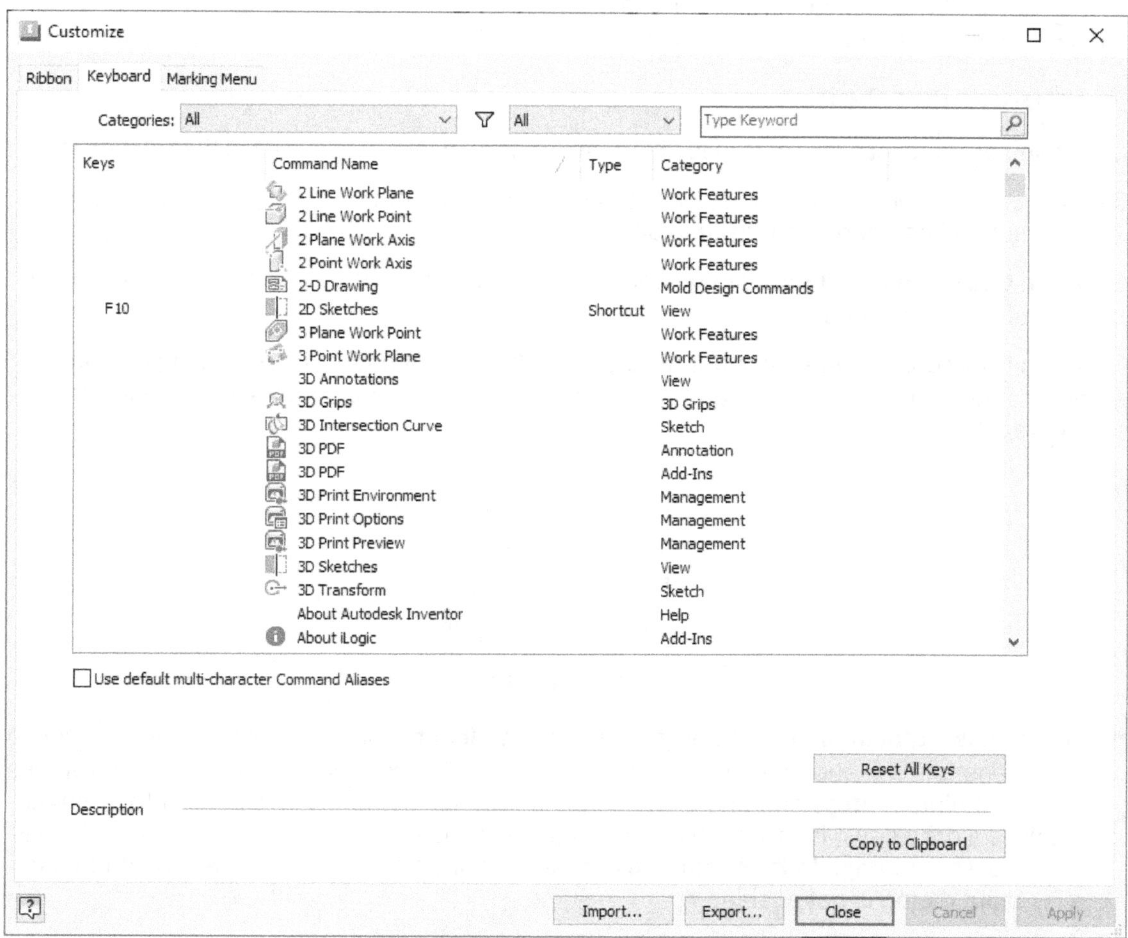

Figure 28–17

Command aliases are alphanumeric key sequences, where shortcuts are keys or key combinations. Both quickly start commands versus selecting options. The following keyboard sequences can be used:

- A single or sequence of keys with letters (A-Z) and numbers (0-9).
- A punctuation key (e.g., ` - = [ ] \ ; ' , . /).
- A miscellaneous keyboard key (e.g., Home, End, or Page Up).

- A combination of <Shift> and numeric (0-9), punctuation, or the miscellaneous keyboard keys mentioned above.
- Any combination of <Shift>, <Ctrl>, and <Alt> with alphanumeric characters. It is not recommended that you use <Alt> without a modifier.

Once assigned, you might have multiple commands starting with the same alpha character. In that case, a list of options displays in the Status Bar and you can use the up and down keyboard arrows to scroll through them. There are many predefined aliases and keyboard shortcuts that can be loaded using **Import**. You can also create your own and save them using **Export**.

Prompting Interaction

Command prompts can be controlled using the *Prompting interaction* area in the *General* tab, in the *Application Options* dialog box (*Tools* tab>*Options* panel, click (Application Options)). The *Prompting interaction* options include:

- When **Show command prompting near the mouse cursor** is on, command prompts display as tooltips at the cursor.
- When **Show command alias input dialog** is on, the *Command Alias Input* dialog box opens next to the cursor when you start typing the first character of a command, as shown in Figure 28–18.

Figure 28–18

- When **Show autocomplete for alias command alias input** is on, the *Autocomplete List* dialog box opens for ambiguous or incomplete commands. For example, if you have **Center** as the alias for **Point**, **Center Point** and **CIRCLE** as the alias for **Center Point Circle**, autocomplete displays a drop-down list for both commands when you enter **C**, as shown in Figure 28–19. The **Show autocomplete for command alias input** option has no effect if **Show command alias input dialog** is not enabled.

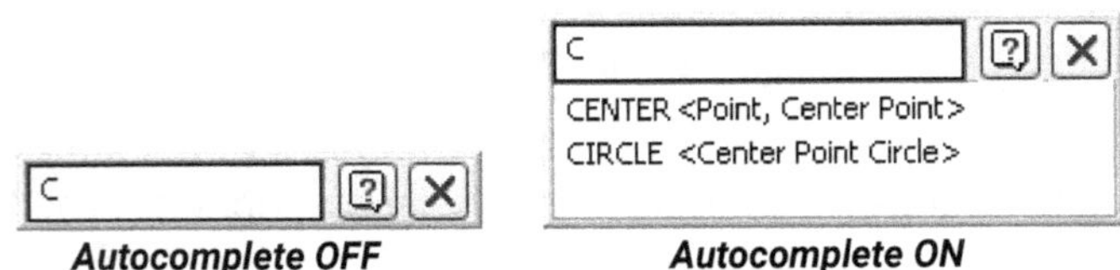

Figure 28–19

Marking Menu Customization

The marking menu can be customized for each environment (e.g., Part, Assembly, Drawing). To customize the marking menu, you use the *Customize* dialog box (in the *Tools* tab>*Options* panel, click (Customize) and select the *Marking Menu* tab), as shown in Figure 28–20.

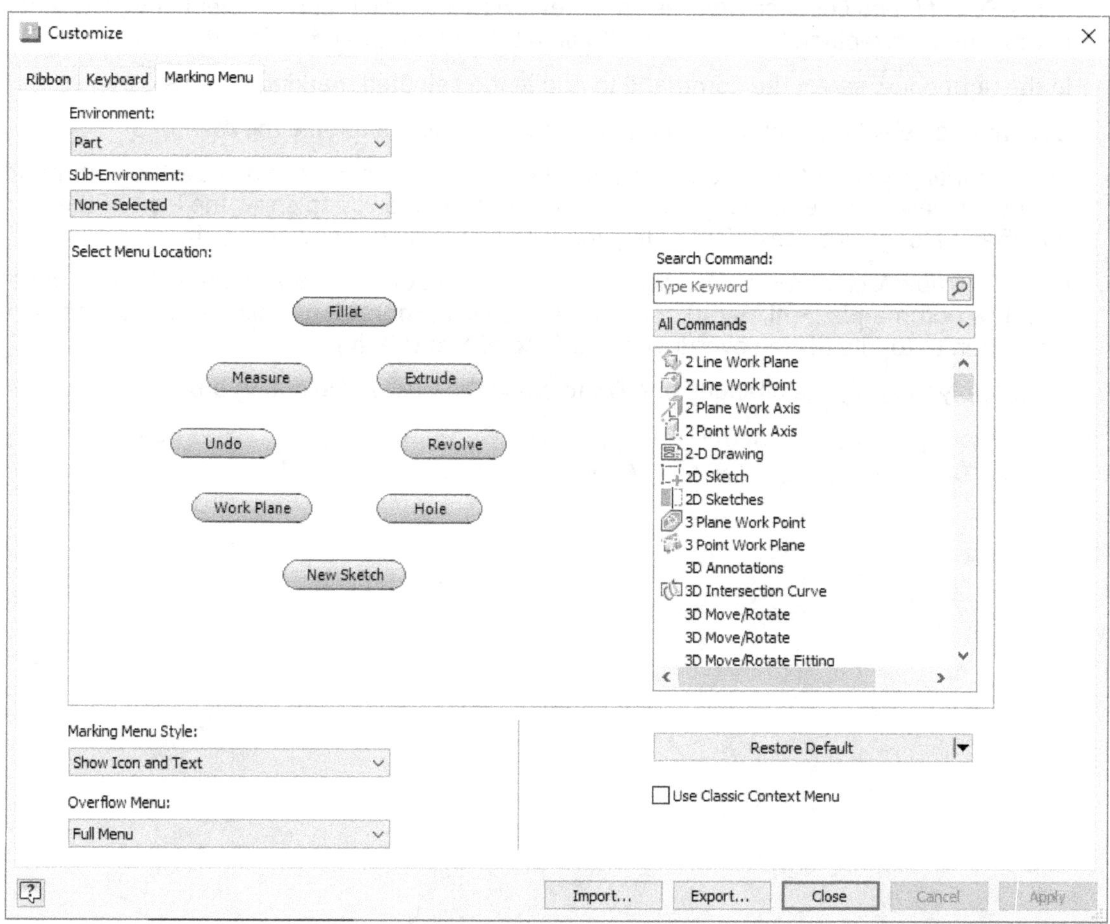

Figure 28–20

How To: Customize the Marking Menu

1. Select the required environment and sub-environment from their respective drop-down lists. If no sub-environment is required, select **None Selected** in the *Sub-Environment* drop-down list or you can select **Ctrl + Right Click Menu** to add a custom shortcut menu.
2. In the *Select Menu Location* area, use the previewed marking menu to select any of its slots. For example, to replace the Line slot with an alternate command, select it.
3. In the right pane, select the command to add in the selected marking menu slot.
4. Continue to select slots and commands, as required, to customize the menu.
5. In the *Marking Menu Style* drop-down list, select an option to determine how the command will be displayed in the marking menu. The options enable you to show the icon of the command along with a text descriptor, show an icon only, or show text only.
6. In the *Overflow Menu* drop-down list, select an option to determine whether a detailed list of overflow commands (**Full Menu**) or if a shortened list (**Short Menu**) displays. You also have the option to toggle off the overflow menu (**Radial Menu Only**).
7. Click **Apply** to apply the changes and **OK** to close the *Customize* dialog box.

   Note: *To restore all of the marking menu commands to their defaults, select* ***Restore Default****. Select* ***Use Classic Context Menu*** *to disable the marking menu.*

Practice 28a
Customize File Properties

Practice Objectives

- Set an application option so that dimensions are brought into a drawing when views are placed.
- Set drawing properties using the *iProperties* dialog box to ensure that the drawing titleblock updates as required.

In this practice, you will customize the properties of a file and ensure that they update in the drawing's title block.

Task 1: Open a part file and set the drawing options.

1. Open **2sides.ipt**.
2. Select the *Tools* tab>*Options* panel and click (Application Options). The *Application Options* dialog box opens.
3. Select the *Drawing* tab and ensure that **Retrieve all model dimensions on view placement** is selected.
4. Click **Apply** and click **Close** to close the dialog box.

Task 2: Create a new drawing file.

1. Create a new drawing file using the **2sides.ipt** model. Use the **ANSI (mm).dwg** template and create the drawing views shown in Figure 28–21. Note that the dimensions for the base view are automatically displayed when the view is placed. You might need to move them so that they display as shown in Figure 28–21.

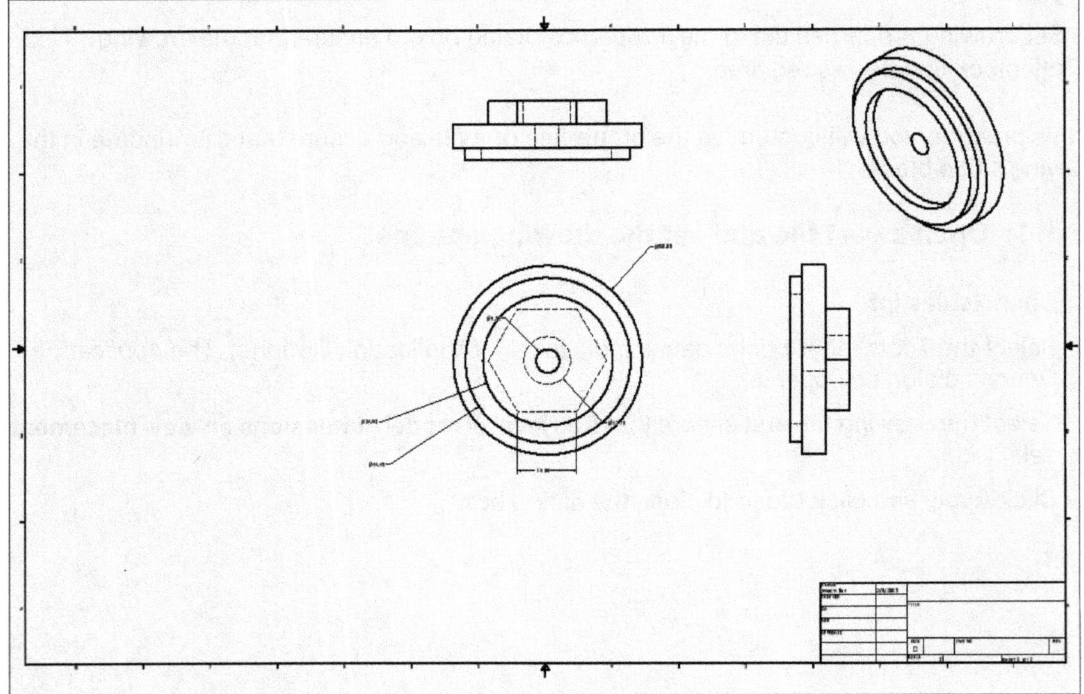

Figure 28–21

Task 3: Set the drawing properties.

1. Zoom to examine the information in the drawing title block.
2. Right-click on **2sides** at the top of the Model browser and select **iProperties**. Alternatively, you can expand the **File** menu and select **iProperties** to open the *iProperties* dialog box.
3. Select the *Summary* tab and set the following information in the respective fields.
    - *Title*: **Disk Drawing**
    - *Author*: **Your Name**
    - *Manager*: **Your Manager**
    - *Company*: **Your Company**

4. Select the *Project* tab and set the following information:
    - *Part Number*: **365-584**
    - *Revision Number*: **1**
    - *Designer*: **Your Name**
    - *Engineer*: **Your Engineer**
5. The *Creation Date* field must display today's date. If not, click to open a calender. Select today's date as the creation date.
6. Click **Apply** to update the iProperties.
7. Select the *Status* tab and set the following information.
    - *Design State:* **Released**
    - *Checked By:* **Engineer**
    - *Eng. Approved By:* **Primary Engineer**
    - *Mfg. Approved By:* **Manager**
    - Select the boxes next to the dates and verify that the date is correct.
8. Select the *Custom* tab. Set the *Name* to **Date Completed**, set the *Type* to **Date**, and place a check in the box next to today's date in the *Value* field.
9. Click **Add** to add that property to the list. The information is listed in the lower half of the dialog box.
10. Click **Apply** to apply the changes and click **Close** to close the dialog box. The drawing title block displays as shown in Figure 28–22.

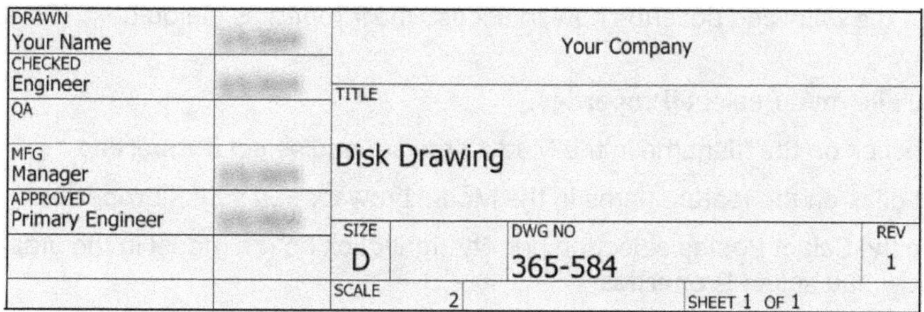

Figure 28–22

11. Save the drawing file and enter **DWGProperties** as the name.
12. Close all of the windows.

End of practice

Chapter Review Questions

1. Which of the following statements is true about the *Application Options* or *Document Settings* dialog box?
   a. The options set in the *Document Settings* dialog box only apply to the current file.
   b. The color scheme for the software is applied only to the current file using the *Document Settings* dialog box.
   c. The *Document Settings* dialog box is only accessible when working in a drawing file.
   d. Any *Application Options* settings are maintained for the entire session that the Autodesk Inventor software is open. The option must be reset in any future sessions, even if using the same model file.

2. Which of the following best describes how to change the part units?
   a. In the *Tools* tab>*Options* panel, select **Document Settings** and use the options in the *Units* tab.
   b. In the *Tools* tab>*Options* panel, select **Application Options** and use the options in the *Display* tab.
   c. In the *Tools* tab>*Measure* panel, select **Distance** and set the units in the *Measure* dialog box.
   d. Model units cannot be changed once the template is selected.

3. Which of the following describe how to access the *iProperties* dialog box? (Select all that apply.)
   a. In the **File** menu, select **iProperties**.
   b. Right-click on the filename in the Model browser and select **iProperties**.
   c. Right-click on the feature name in the Model browser and select **Properties**.
   d. Using the Select Bodies selection priority, right-click on the model in the graphics window and select **Properties**.

4. Using the *Customize* dialog box, which interface components can be customized to control the commands that are displayed? (Select all that apply.)
   a. Ribbon tabs
   b. Ribbon panels
   c. Marking menu

5. What can you control by right-clicking on the ribbon and selecting **Ribbon Appearance**, as shown in Figure 28–23?

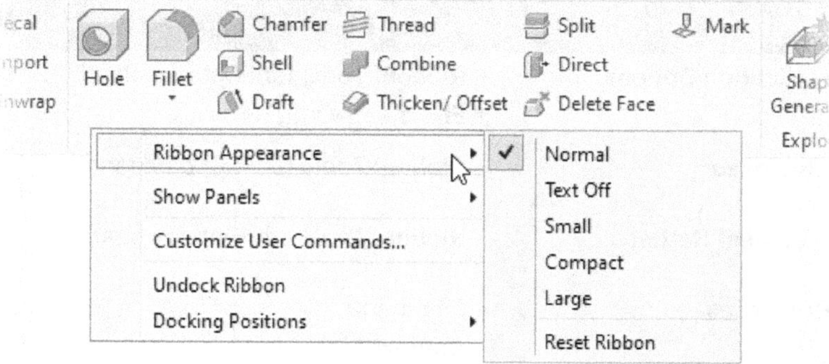

Figure 28–23

a. Text descriptions next to buttons in the panel.
b. Menus at the top of the interface.
c. Command prompts at the cursor.
d. Pop-up tooltips for commands.

6. Which tabs in the *iProperties* dialog box (shown in Figure 28–24) are used to add non-geometrical information to the model? (Select all that apply.)

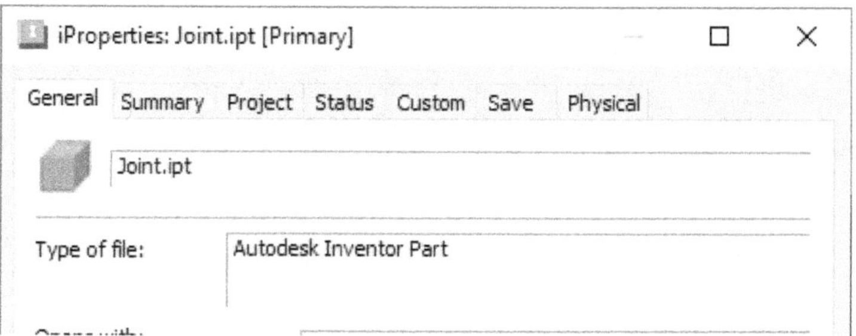

Figure 28–24

a. Summary
b. Project
c. Status
d. Custom
e. Save
f. Physical

Command Summary

Button	Command	Location
	Application Options	• **Ribbon:** *Tools* tab>*Options* panel • **File** menu>Options
	Customize	• **Ribbon:** *Tools* tab>*Options* panel
	Document Settings	• **Ribbon:** *Tools* tab>*Options* panel
N/A	**iProperties**	• **File** menu • **Context Menu**: In Model browser with model name selected • **File Explorer**: Right-click on the model name and select **iProperties**

Appendix

D

Effective Modeling Final Review

Before creating any model (part or assembly), you should consider its design intent. Planning ahead helps you select the most appropriate options to maximize design flexibility.

Learning Objectives

- Understand the key modeling questions that should be considered before creating a new model.
- Understand the techniques that help you build parametric, feature-based solid models so that their behavior is flexible and predictable.

D.1 Tips for Capturing Design Intent in Your Models

A designer strives to create models with the following criteria:

- Communicates design intent.
- Can be manufactured to meet design goals.
- Is flexible to future design changes with minimal effort.
- Can be used to generate design documentation (drawings).

Considerations for Getting Started

Considering *what if* scenarios that might be introduced into the model in the future helps to create a robust model that requires minimal effort when the time comes for modifications.

Part Design Considerations

- What is the best selection for the base feature?
- Which feature relationships are required and which should be avoided?
- Which dimensions are required to drive the design?
- Which dimensions on the part might change?
- How should the part react to dimension changes?
- Which dimensions are required in the drawing?
- Should equations be added to capture design intent?
- What feature order best captures the design intent?

Assembly Design Considerations

- What is the best selection for the base component?
- Which assembly constraints capture the design intent?
- Which feature relationships are required and which should be avoided?
- Should subassembly components be incorporated?
- Should assembly equations be added?
- What component order best captures the design intent?

Modeling Strategies

The key to building robust, parametric, feature-based solid models is to construct them so that their behavior is flexible and predictable. The result of constructing them this way is known as the *design intent*.

Design intent can be captured in a variety of ways. When creating models, pay special attention to the features used, how they are created (pick and place or sketched), and the dimensioning scheme. The feature relationships established during feature creation and the explicit relations set after feature creation are also important for incorporating design intent.

Many companies have their own design requirements or *best practice* recommendations. The following sub-sections discuss some common recommendations:

Features

Features add or remove material from the model. Consider the following when adding features to a model:

- Select a stable base feature that does not require many changes. It is used as a parent for additional features.
- Use feature forms (extrude, sweep, etc.), feature types (pick and place or sketched), feature attributes, and equations to capture design intent.
- Select references that correctly reflect the design intent. Any reference that is selected while creating a new feature, establishes a dependency between the new feature and the reference. This is true when defining the sketching plane, sketching references, and dimensioning references.
- Use the sketching tools that best capture the design intent.
- Use depth options (**Distance A**, **Through All/Full**, **To Next**, **To**, **Between**, **From**) to capture the design intent.
- Create features in the order that best captures the design intent.
- Change feature names to easily identify them in the Model browser.

Dimensioning Scheme

This method of capturing design intent is used to determine the feature's dimensioning scheme. A part with a hole is shown in Figure D–1. When the base feature increases in length, the design intent of the hole determines how it behaves. If the hole is dimensioned to the end of the base feature, the hole moves when the length of the base feature increases, but remains 3.00 from the end. If the hole is dimensioned to the face, it remains 6.00 from that face.

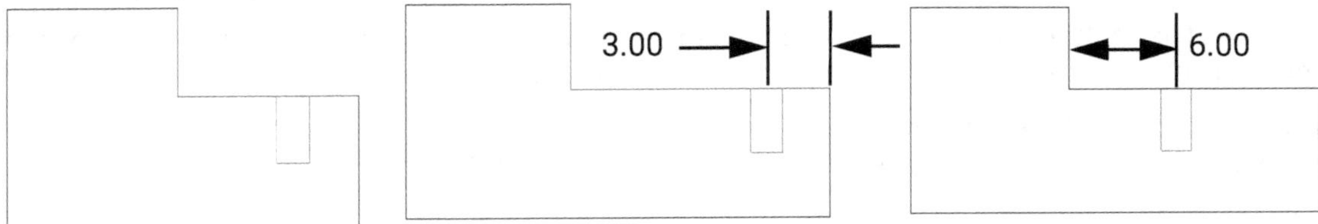

Figure D–1

Depth Options

This method of capturing design intent is to determine the type of depth required for your feature. A part with a hole is shown in Figure D–2. The design intent is for the hole to pass through the entire model. When the depth of the base feature changes from 5.00 to 6.00, the resulting geometry displays differently, depending on the depth option set for the hole. If the hole is given a blind depth value of 5.00, it no longer passes though the entire part. Therefore, the hole depth must also be changed to maintain the design intent. A better solution is to set the depth option for the hole to **Through All**. As a result, the hole always passes through the part, regardless of the height of the base feature.

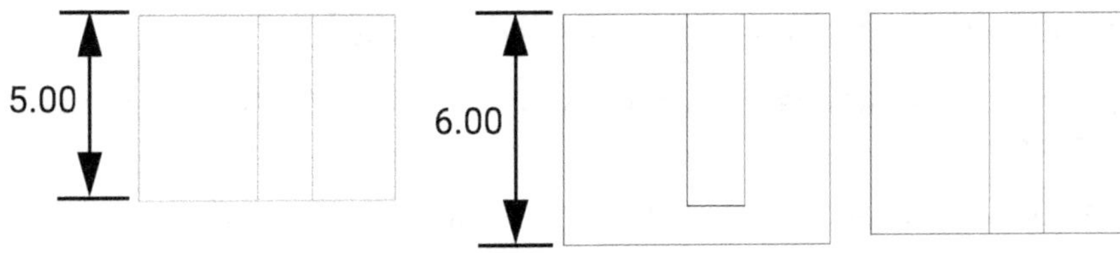

Figure D–2

Symmetrical Geometry

This method of capturing design intent is to create symmetrical geometry. The design intent for the part shown in Figure D–3 is to have the extruded cut remain at the center of the part. Constraining the cut from either end of the base feature does not capture the design intent. Constructing the base feature and cut relative to the center of the part is preferable, or you can use relations.

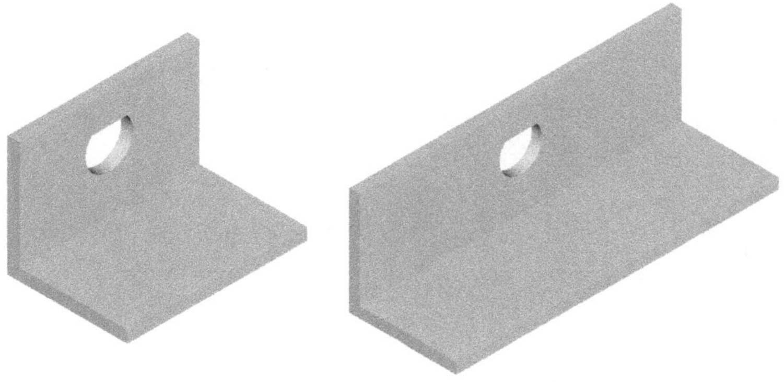

Figure D–3

Face Drafts and Fillets

Review company standards when considering whether to add face drafts. Some companies prefer not to add face drafts, while other companies insist on it. Some considerations include the following:

- Does adding face drafts increase model accuracy or is it going to adversely affect drawing creation?
- If face drafts are not added to the model, how are you going to communicate this requirement to the manufacturer?
- Does the model need to undergo interference or analysis testing? If so, consider adding the face draft to ensure accurate results.

Fillets generally represent the finishing stages of the design. Similar to face drafts, always consider company standards when deciding whether to add fillets. Some considerations include the following:

- Is the model going to be used for FEA analysis? If so, fillets are sometimes removed before the analysis and are therefore not required.
- The manufacturing department might remove fillets that are created at the end of the process (depending on the type of fillets that make up the model). In this situation, you might want to add all of the fillets and only suppress the ones that you do not need for generating the NC toolpaths.
- Variable and G2 fillets are difficult to manufacture. Consider the necessity of this feature as you are creating your model.

Always consider the order in which features are manufactured. The order of fillet and face draft creation can affect the resulting geometry and should be added as late as possible in the feature order. For example, face draft geometry should be added to the model before fillets. Also consider the order in which fillets are added to the model and how the order affects the geometry and each other.

You can suppress the display of the face drafts and fillets. They remain suppressed until you un-suppress them. In the Model browser, suppressed features are grayed out.

Appendix

E

Additional Practices II

This appendix provides additional practices that can be used to review some of the functionality that was previously covered.

Practice E1
Assembling with Joints

Practice Objectives

- Use the **Joint** command to fully connect components in an assembly.
- Apply limits to a joint to define a specified range of motion.
- Drag components to verify the movement in the assembly.
- Copy and paste components to efficiently duplicate components in an assembly.

In this practice, you will create a new assembly and assemble the components as shown in Figure E–1. To assemble the components you will use the **Joint** command, which will connect components relative to one another so that the assembly can easily be tested for movement.

Figure E–1

Task 1: Create a new assembly and assemble the first component.

1. Create a new assembly file using the **Standard (in).iam** template file.
2. In the *Component* panel, click (Place).
3. Navigate to the *Engine* folder in the practice files folder. Select **RBlock.ipt** in the *Place Component* dialog box and click **Open**. The component is added to the assembly.
4. If the component displays in a 2D orientation, return the model to its default Home view using the ViewCube.
5. Right-click on the model and select **Rotate X 90**. Right-click and select **Rotate X 90** again to rotate the component a total of 180 degrees about the X-axis.

6. Right-click on the model and select **Place Grounded at Origin** to ground the component. The model displays as shown in Figure E–2.

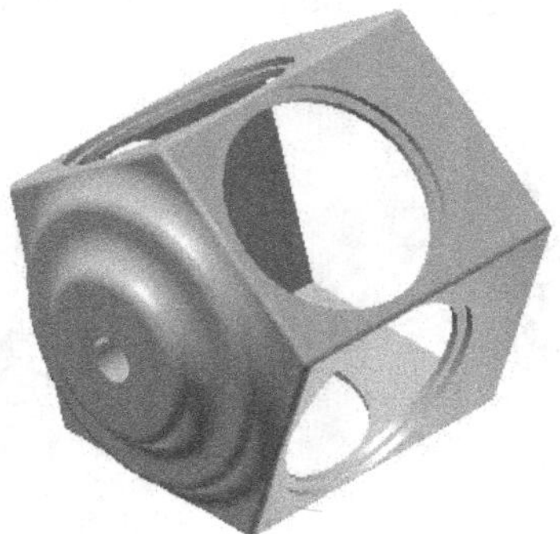

Figure E–2

7. Right-click and select **OK** to assemble a single instance of the component into the assembly.
8. Review the Model browser and note the pushpin ( ) and [•] symbols next to the **RBlock**, as shown in Figure E–3. These indicate the component is grounded and fully constrained, respectively. Hover the cursor over the **RBlock.ipt** component in the graphics window. The cursor symbol also indicates that it is grounded.

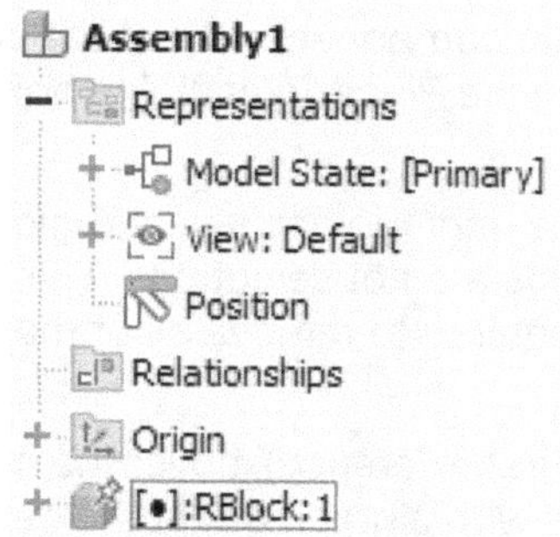

Figure E–3

Task 2: Assemble the Rcylinder component.

1. In the *Component* panel, click (Place).
2. Select **Rcylinder.ipt** in the *Place Component* dialog box and click **Open**. The component is added to the assembly.
3. Right-click on the model and select **Rotate X 90**. Right-click and select **Rotate X 90** again to rotate the component into a more convenient orientation for constraining.

4. Use the left mouse button to place the component next to the **RBlock** component, as shown in Figure E–4. Right-click and select **OK** to assemble a single instance. Note that the component is listed with the [▫] icon in the Model browser, indicating that it is currently under-constrained.

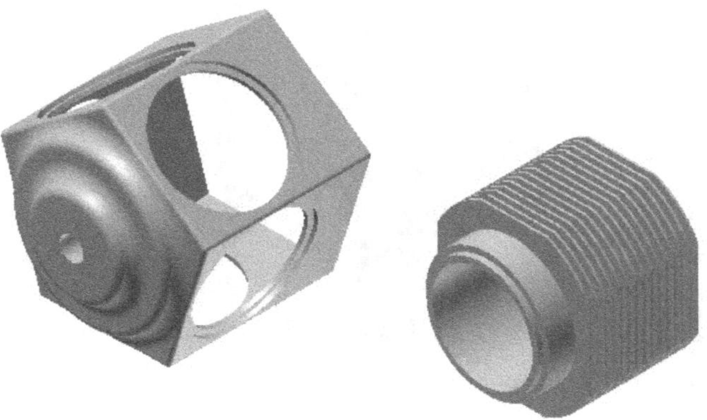

Figure E–4

5. In the *Assemble* tab>*Relationships* panel, click (Joint). The *Place Joint* dialog box and mini-toolbar open.
6. In the mini-toolbar, click (...) to toggle off the display of the *Place Joint* dialog box. You will use the mini-toolbar to constrain components. All of the commands are also available in the *Place Joint* dialog box. Once the *Place Joint* dialog box is toggled off, it must be enabled again to open it.
7. In the *Type* drop-down list in the mini-toolbar, select **Rigid**. Note that the *Connect* fields remain active and the *Align* fields are not selectable. This indicates that to use the Rigid joint only two references are required to remove all of the degrees of freedom from the component.
8. On the **Rcylinder** component (first reference), hover the cursor over the edge shown in Figure E–5. It will display in red with a green dot at the center of the edge. Use the left mouse button to select the reference.
9. On the **RBlock** component (second reference), hover over the edge shown in Figure E–5. It will display in red with a green dot at the center of the edge. Use the left mouse button to select the reference.

   Note: *Figure E–5 shows the reference on* ***Rcylinder*** *already selected and the reference on* ***RBlock*** *highlighted. The images displaying the reference selection in this practice will be shown in this way for the remainder of the practice.*

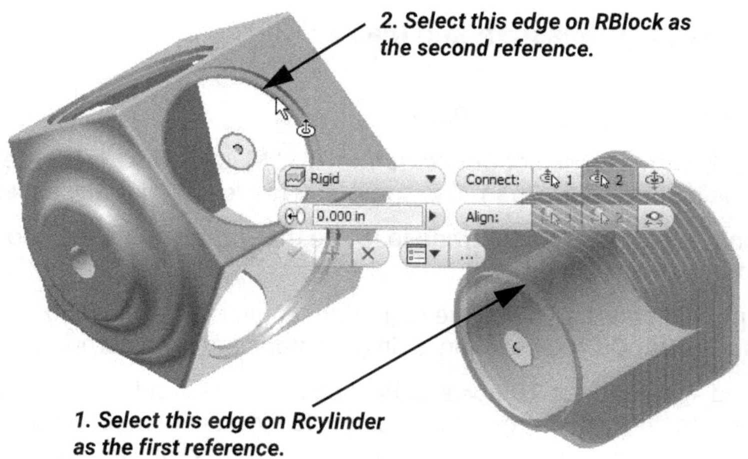

Figure E–5

The **Rcylinder** component (reference 1) moves into position and displays animated movement indicating its allowable degrees of freedom. In this case it is a rigid constraint and because no movement is permitted, the animated movement is very small.

Note that you did not have to activate any of the fields in the mini-toolbar. The first reference field is immediately active and the second is activated once the first reference has been selected. Selecting the reference fields in the *Connect* field is only required when redefining a reference.

10. The components assemble in the wrong orientation. In the *Connect* area in the mini-toolbar, click (Flip Component) to flip the component.
11. Click in the mini-toolbar to complete the joint. The assembly displays as shown in Figure E–6.

Figure E–6

12. Expand the **Relationships** node and note that the Rigid joint has been added. A **Rigid** node is also listed in the node for the two components.

Task 3: Assemble the Crankshaft and Master Rod components in the assembly.

1. In the *Component* panel, click (Place).
2. Press and hold <Ctrl> and select **Crankshaft.ipt** and **Master Rod1.ipt** in the *Place Component* dialog box. Click **Open**. The components are added to the assembly.
3. Right-click and select **Rotate X 90** twice to rotate the two components into a more convenient orientation.
4. Use the left mouse button to place the components next to the existing components. Right-click and select **OK** to assemble a single instance of both components.
5. Press and hold <Ctrl>, select **RBlock** and **Rcylinder** in the Model browser, right-click and select **Visibility** to clear them from the display. Clearing the components from the display enables you to focus on the required components and prevents you from selecting inappropriate references when constraining.
6. Hold the left mouse button on the **Master Rod1** component and move it as shown in Figure E–7. Move the **Crankshaft** component in a similar way, if required.

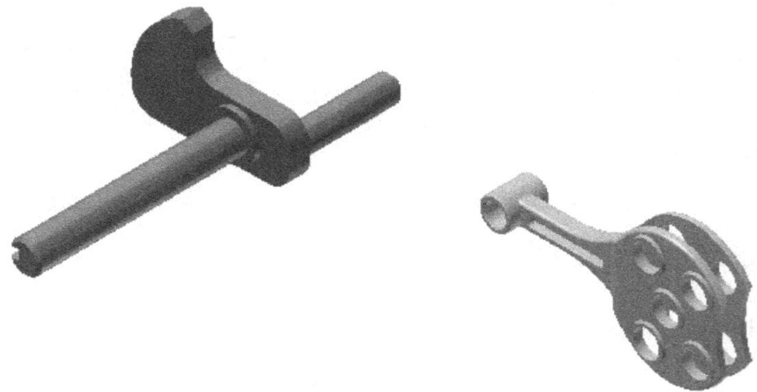

Figure E–7

7. In the *Assemble* tab>*Relationships* panel, click (Joint).
8. In the *Type* drop-down list in the mini-toolbar, select **Rotational**.
9. On the **Master Rod1** component (first reference), hover the cursor over the edge shown in Figure E–8. It will display in red with a green dot at the center of the edge. Use the left mouse button to select the reference.

10. On the **Crankshaft** component (second reference), hover the cursor over the center of the cylindrical surface. The surface highlights in red with a green dot at the center of the cylinder. Continue hovering over different locations on the surface until the model displays as shown in Figure E–8. Use the left mouse button to select the reference.

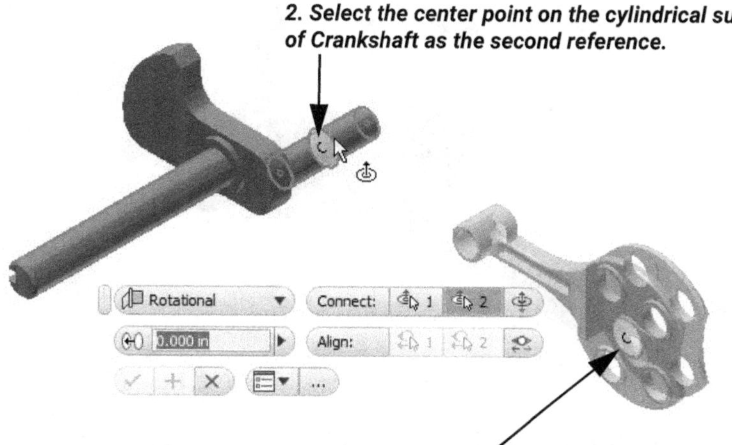

Figure E–8

11. Enter an *Offset* value of **-1.1 in**.

12. Click ✓ in the mini-toolbar to complete the joint. The components display as shown in Figure E–9. (Note: The orientation of Master Rod1 may vary.)

Figure E–9

13. Expand the **Relationships** and **Components** nodes and note that the Rotational joint has been added.

14. Select the **Master Rod1** component and try to drag it to determine its rotational degree of freedom. Both components move together because neither of them are grounded.

15. By temporarily grounding the **Crankshaft** component you can test the joint movement. Select the **Crankshaft** component in the graphics window or in the Model browser, right-click and select **Grounded** to ground the component.

16. Select the **Master Rod1** component and drag it to determine its rotational degree of freedom. Rotate the component as shown in Figure E–10.

Figure E–10

Task 4: Assemble the Piston Head Pin and Piston Head components in the assembly.

1. Place an instance of the **Piston head pin.ipt** and **Piston head.ipt** components in the assembly.
2. Rotate, move, and place the components in a similar orientation to that shown in Figure E–11.

Figure E–11

3. In the *Assemble* tab>*Relationships* panel, click (Joint).

4. In the *Type* drop-down list in the mini-toolbar, select **Rigid**.
5. On the **Piston head pin** component (first reference), hover the cursor over the midpoint shown in Figure E–12. It will display in red with a green dot at the center of the edge. Use the left mouse button to select the reference.
6. On the **Piston head** component (second reference), hover the cursor over the edge shown in Figure E–12. Note that this point is not being recognized. Right-click in the graphics window and select **Between Two Faces**. Select the two planar faces in the middle of the component to enable the midpoint to be used as a placement reference. It will display in red with a green dot at the center of the edge. Use the left mouse button to select the reference.

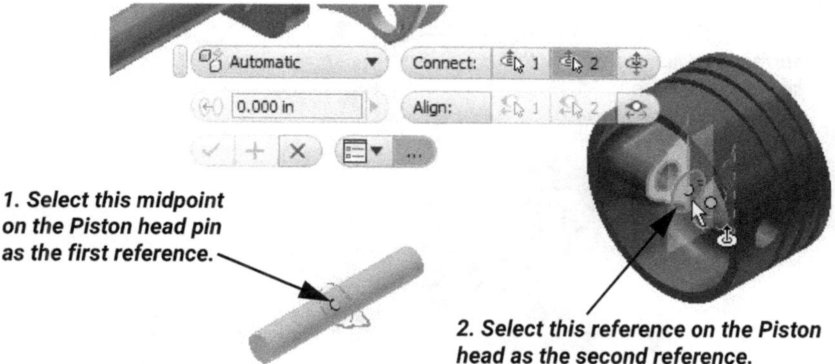

Figure E–12

7. Click ✓ in the mini-toolbar to complete the joint. The components display as shown in Figure E–13.

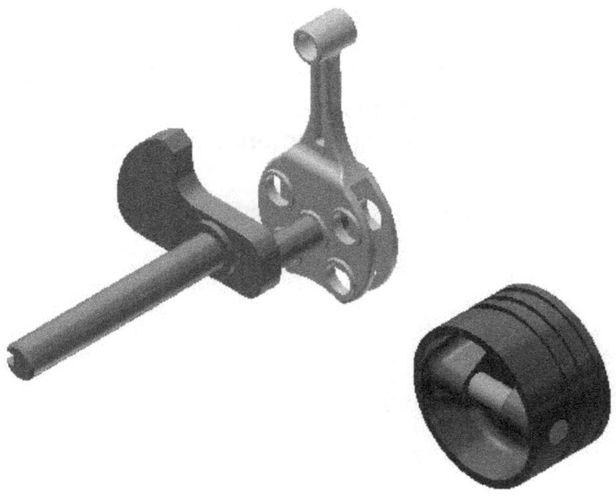

Figure E–13

8. In the *Assemble* tab>*Relationships* panel, click (Joint).
9. In the *Type* drop-down list in the mini-toolbar, select **Rotational**.
10. On the **Piston head pin** component (first reference), hover the cursor over its cylindrical surface. When the green dot displays at the center of the surface at its midpoint (as shown in Figure E–14), click the left mouse button.
11. On the **Master Rod1** component (second reference), hover the cylinder over its cylindrical surface. When the green dot displays at the center of the surface at its midpoint (as shown in Figure E–14), click the left mouse button.

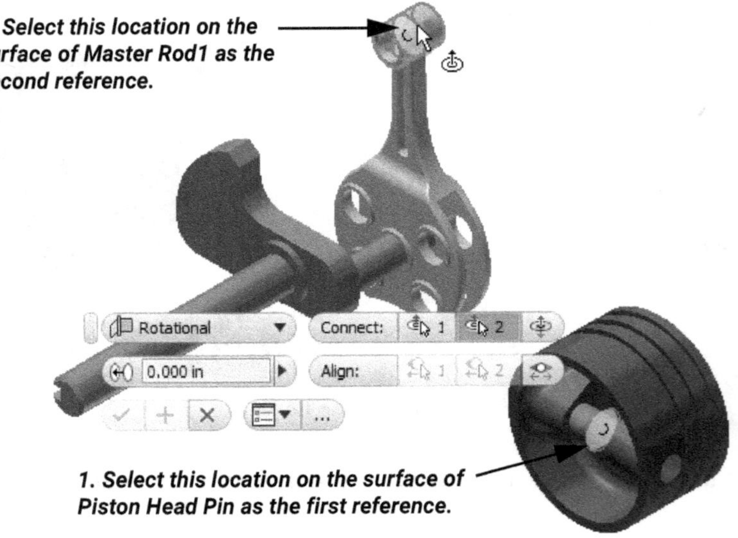

Figure E–14

Note how the preview for the Rotational joint only moves the **Piston head pin** component. The preview does not take into account any secondary constraints. Once completed, the relationship between the **Piston head** and **Piston head pin** will be maintained.

12. Click in the mini-toolbar to complete the joint. Note how both the **Piston head pin** and **Piston head** move into position.

13. Select the **Piston head** component and drag it to verify its rotational degree of freedom. The components should display similar to those shown in Figure E–15.

Figure E–15

14. Select the **RBlock** and **Rcylinder** components in the Model browser, right-click, and select **Visibility**.
15. Select the **Crankshaft** component in the Model browser or the graphics window, right-click and clear the **Grounded** option so that additional joints can be added to join the components to the housing. The components display as shown in Figure E–16. With the **Crankshaft** ungrounded it can be constrained with respect to the other components.

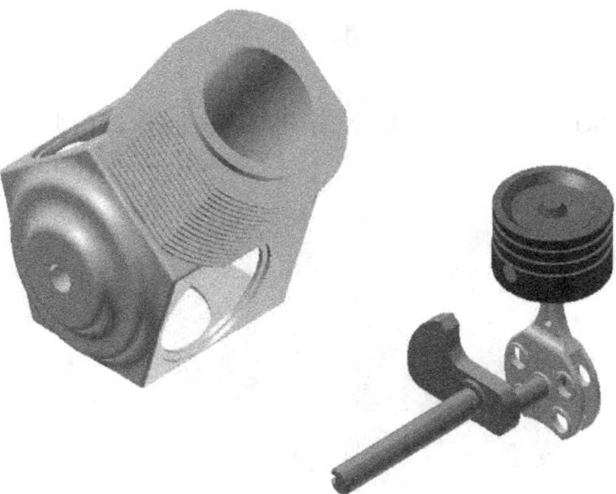

Figure E–16

Task 5: Constrain the piston components in the housing.

1. In the *Assemble* tab>*Relationships* panel, click (Joint).
2. In the *Type* drop-down list in the mini-toolbar, select **Cylindrical**.

3. On the **Piston head** component (first reference), hover the cursor over the edge as shown in Figure E–17. It will display in red with a green dot at the center of the edge. Use the left mouse button to select the reference.
4. On the **Rcylinder** component (second reference), hover the cursor over the edge shown in Figure E–17. It will display in red with a green dot at the center of the edge. Use the left mouse button to select the reference.

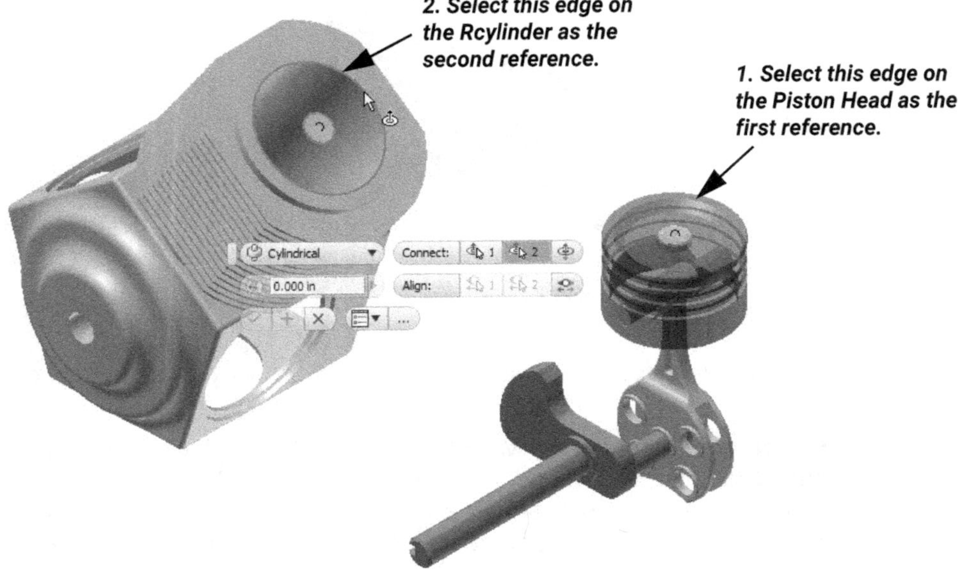

Figure E–17

5. Click ✓ in the mini-toolbar to complete the joint. The assembly displays as shown in Figure E–18.

Figure E–18

6. Select the **Piston head** component and drag it to verify its cylindrical degree of freedom.
7. In the *Assemble* tab>*Relationships* panel, click (Joint).
8. In the *Type* drop-down list in the mini-toolbar, select **Cylindrical**.
9. On the **Crankshaft** component (first reference), hover the cursor over the edge shown in Figure E–19. It will display in red with a green dot at the center of the edge. Use the left mouse button to select the reference.
10. On the **RBlock** component (second reference), hover the cursor over the edge shown in Figure E–19. It will display in red with a green dot at the center of the edge. Use the left mouse button to select the reference.

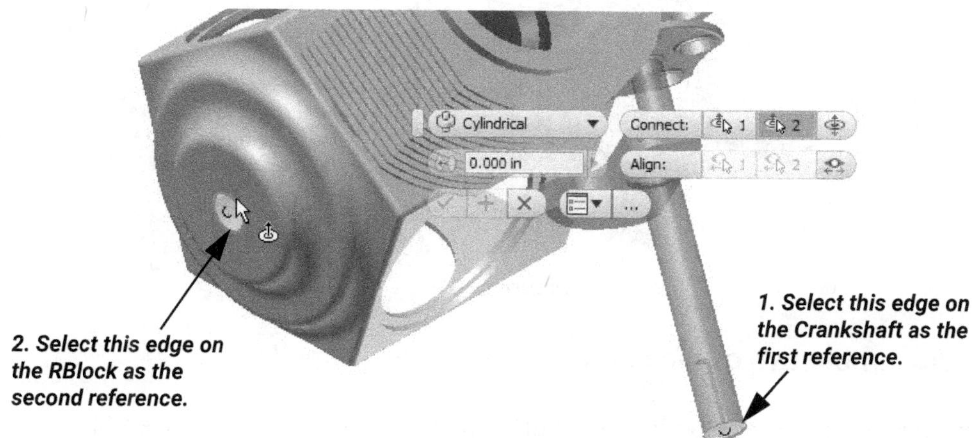

Figure E–19

11. Click in the mini-toolbar to complete the joint. The assembly displays as shown in Figure E–20. Note how both cylindrical joints are used together to correctly position the components.

Figure E–20

12. Rotate the assembly (similar to that shown in Figure E–21), until the **Master Rod1** component displays. Select it and drag it to verify that the assembly movement permits the rotation of the crankshaft while the **Piston head** component maintains its alignment in the **Rcylinder** component.

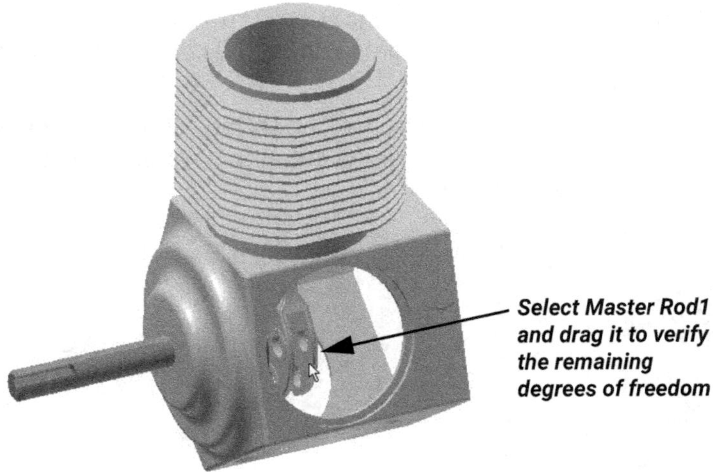

Figure E–21

Task 6: Assemble two of the components for the propeller.

1. Place an instance of the **Hub.ipt** and **Shuttle.ipt** components into the assembly.
2. Rotate, move, and place the components in a similar orientation to that shown in Figure E–22.

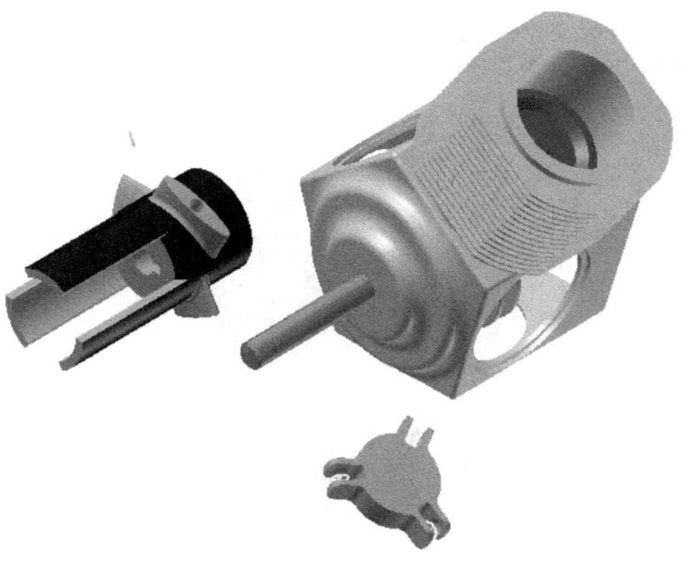

Figure E–22

3. Initiate the creation of a **Rigid** joint connection.
4. On the **Hub** component (first reference), hover the cursor over the face shown in Figure E–23. It will display in red with a green dot at the center of the edge. Use the left mouse button to select the reference.
5. On the **Crankshaft** component (second reference), hover the cursor over the face shown in Figure E–23. It will display in red with a green dot at the center of the edge. Use the left mouse button to select the reference.

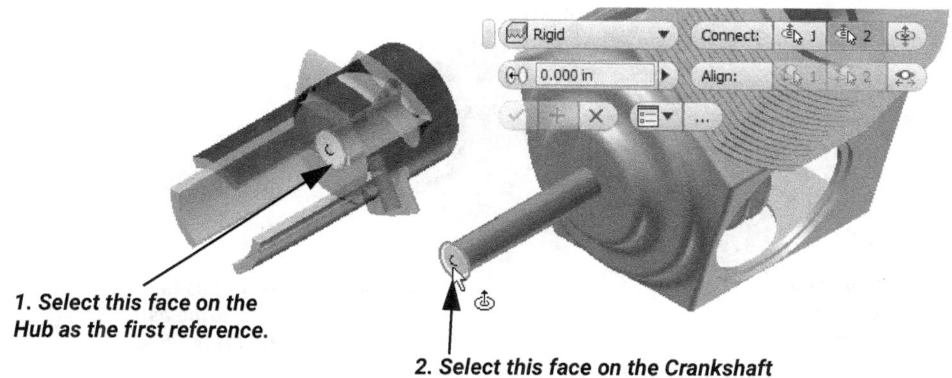

Figure E–23

6. Complete the joint. The components display as shown in Figure E–24.

Figure E–24

7. Drag the **Hub** and note how it moves the shaft and the piston components.

8. Initiate the creation of a **Cylindrical** joint connection.
9. On the **Shuttle** component (first reference), hover the cursor over the face shown in Figure E–25. It will display in red with a green dot at the center of the edge. Use the left mouse button to select the reference.
10. On the **Hub** component (second reference), hover the cursor over the face shown in Figure E–25. It will display in red with a green dot at the center of the edge. Use the left mouse button to select the reference.

Figure E–25

11. Complete the joint. The components display as shown in Figure E–26.

Figure E–26

12. Drag the **Hub** and the **Shuttle** and note how they move. Note that the **Shuttle** component can still rotate and can clash with the **Hub** component.
13. In the *Assemble* tab>*Relationships* panel, click (Constrain). Constraints can be used to remove any unwanted degrees of freedom that result from a joint connection. In this case you will remove the rotational degree of freedom in the **Shuttle** component.

14. Click (Angle) as the constraint type in the *Place Constraint* dialog box. Click (Directed Angle) in the *Solution* area.
15. Expand the **Hub** component in the Model browser and select **Work Plane1**.
16. Expand the **Shuttle** component and its **Origin** node in the Model browser and select the **YZ Plane**.
17. Enter **180** as the *Angle* value to rotate the **Shuttle**, as required.
18. Click **OK** to complete the constraint definition. Drag the Shuttle and note that only one translational degree of freedom remains.
19. The **Shuttle** has a limit to its range of motion in the **Hub**. Right-click on the **Cylindrical** connection in the **Shuttle** node of the Model browser. Select **Edit**.
20. Click on the mini-toolbar to open the *Edit Joint* dialog box.
21. Select the *Limits* tab. Limits can only be set in the dialog box, these controls are not available in the mini-toolbar.
22. In the *Linear* area, select **Start** and enter **1.9 in**. Select **End** and enter **4.3**, as shown in Figure E–27. This sets a limit on the range of movement from the surface that was selected as the reference on the **Hub** component. Depending on your reference selection you might need to enter negative values.

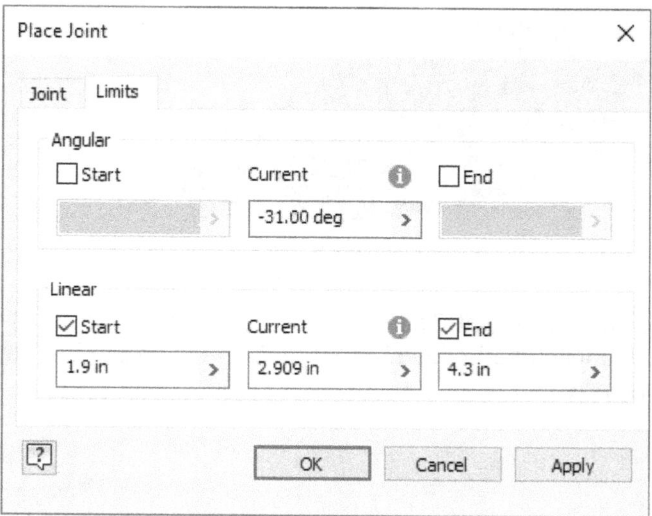

Figure E–27

***Note:** The Current value in the Edit Joint dialog box might vary. It reports the current position of the component.*

23. Complete the edit and drag the **Hub** and the **Shuttle** and note how they move. Note that the **Shuttle** component can no longer rotate and has a defined limit to its translational movement.

Task 7: Assemble the final components for the propeller.

1. Place an instance of the **Pro_blade.ipt** and **Prop_Conrod.ipt** components into the assembly.
2. Rotate, move, and place the components in a similar orientation to that shown in Figure E–28.

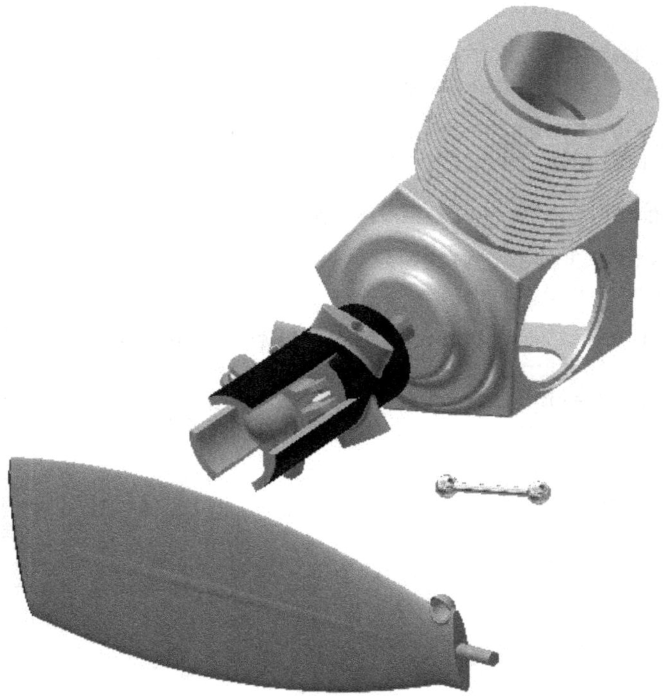

Figure E–28

3. Begin the creation of a new joint. The *Place Joint* dialog was previously opened and remains displayed until closed. Close the *Place Joint* dialog box so that only the mini-toolbar is displayed.

4. Add a **Rotational** joint and select the references shown in Figure E–29 to join the **Pro_blade** and **Hub** components. Flip the component as required if they are not oriented correctly.

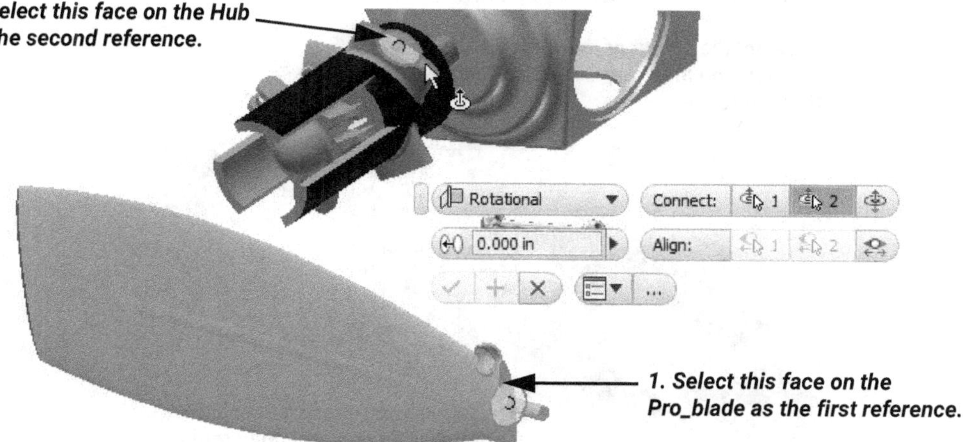

Figure E–29

5. Complete the joint connection.
6. Add a **Ball** joint and select the references shown in Figure E–30 to join the **Pro_blade** and **Prop_Conrod** components. When selecting the reference for a Ball joint, the reference should highlight at the center of the circular feature that is being used as the reference.

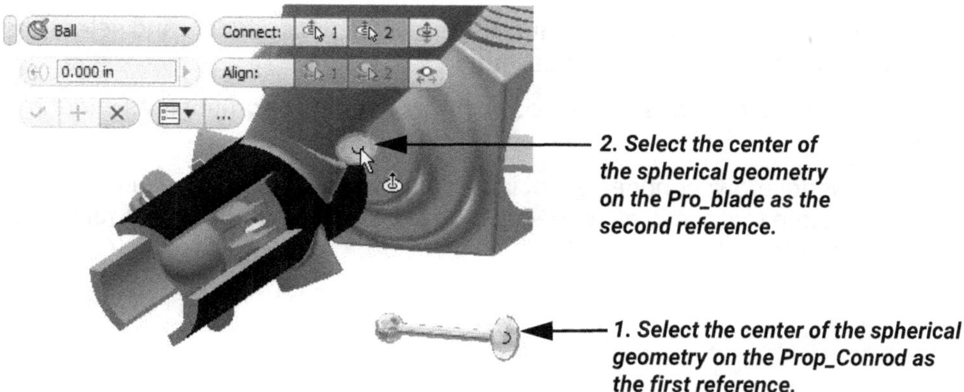

Figure E–30

7. Drag the **Prop_Conrod** to a more convenient location so that there is no interference between the two components. Note that all the other components will also move. You can temporarily ground components to reorient the components, if required.

8. Add another **Ball** joint and select the references shown in Figure E–31 to join the **Shuttle** and **Prop_Conrod** components. The reference that is to be selected on the Shuttle is the center of a sketch that was created to define the center of the joint.

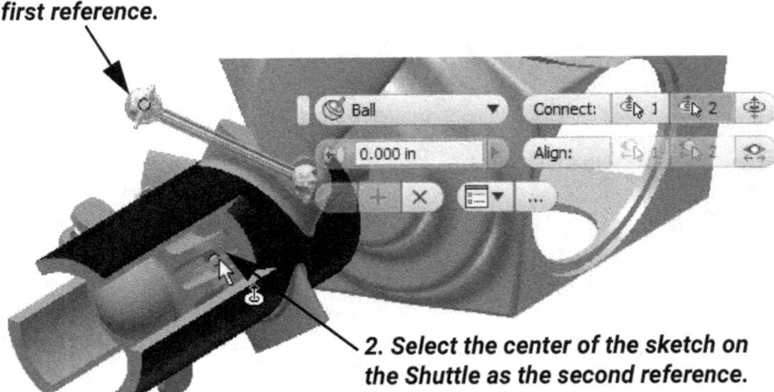

Figure E–31

9. Drag the **Shuttle** and note how the movement is now a little more limited based on the connections that have been defined.
10. Select the **Pro_blade** and the **Prop_Conrod** components in the Model browser, right-click and select **Copy**.
11. Press <Esc> to clear the selection, right-click on the graphics window and select **Paste**. The two components are pasted into the assembly.
12. Right-click and select **Paste** again to copy another set of the components into the assembly.
13. Expand the Model browser nodes associated with the copied **Pro_blade** and **Prop_Conrod** components. Note that the joint connections that placed the components relative to one another are maintained.

14. Add the required additional joint connections to constrain the components as shown in Figure E–32.

Figure E–32

15. Drag the components in the assembly to verify movement.
16. Save the assembly as **Radial Engine.iam**.

    Note: *A completed model called* ***Radial Engine Final.iam*** *has been provided in the practice files folder for your review.*

Task 8: (Optional) Assemble the remaining housings and piston components.

1. Place and use joint connections to complete the Radial Engine assembly, as shown in Figure E–33.

Figure E–33

Consider the following design tips:

- The rod that is used to connect the **Piston head.ipt** to the **Master Rod1.ipt** components is called **Connector Arm.ipt** and is available in the practice files folder.
- You can use the **Copy** and **Paste** functionality to duplicate components that are used multiple times (e.g., **Rcylinder**, **Piston head**, and **Piston head pin**). Doing so copies any joints that already exist between the copied components so that they do not have to be established again.
- When constraining the **Connector Arm** component to the **Master Rod1** component, consider temporarily grounding the **Master Rod1** component to prevent movement. This helps to ensure that the components are not flipped into positions that cannot be easily undone when a connection is made.

2. Save the assembly and close the files. A completed model called **Radial Engine Final2.iam** has been provided in the practice files folder for your review.

End of practice

Practice E2
Turntable Assembly

Practice Objectives

- Create a new assembly file using a standard template.
- Assemble parts with one another to create a required assembly.
- Use the **Drive** command to simulate the required range of motion for an assembly.
- Use the **Contact Solver** command to simulate the required range of motion for an assembly.
- Combine the use of the **Drive** and **Contact Solver** commands to simulate the required range of motion for an assembly.

In this practice, you will use the **Drive** and **Contact Solver** commands to control the range of motion for a turntable assembly.

Task 1: Create a new assembly and add components.

1. Create a new assembly file using the **Standard (in).iam** template file.
2. Add **SRbase** to the assembly. Since this is the first component in the assembly, rotate it, as required, and use the **Place Grounded at Origin** command to ground it. Once placed, the component should be oriented as shown in Figure E–34 when in its default Home view.

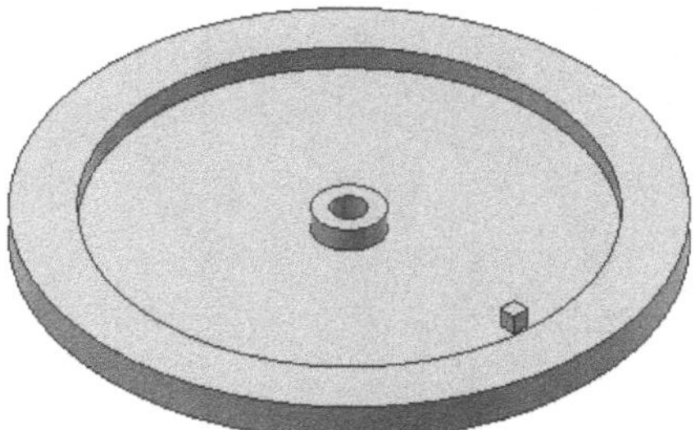

Figure E–34

Task 2: Constrain the SRturntable component.

1. Add **SRturntable** to the assembly. Note the tab in the **SRbase** component and the slot in the **SRturnable** component. The tab and slot features were included to limit the motion of the assembly.

2. Add an Insert constraint between the two components, as shown in Figure E–35.

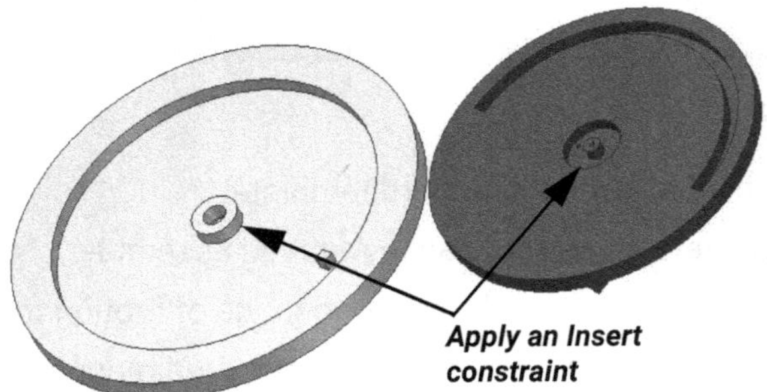

Figure E–35

3. Change the view display to **Wireframe**. This is being done for better clarity when selecting references. This is not a requirement.
4. Rotate the **SRturntable** component. Note that it can turn 360 degrees, but this is not the design intent. The range of motion should be limited by the tab and the slot, as shown in Figure E–36.

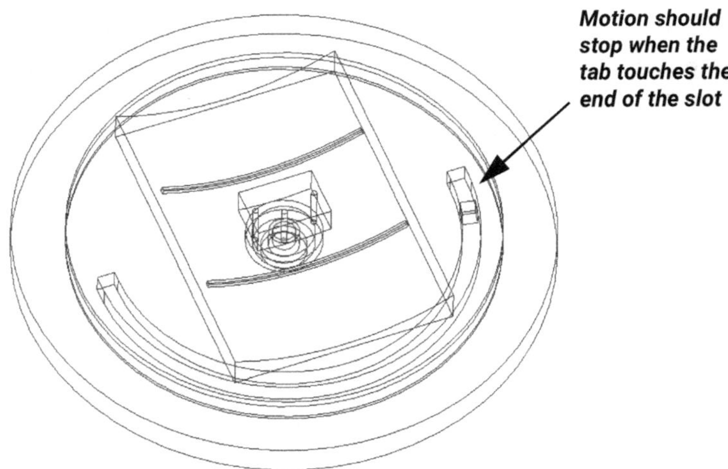

Figure E–36

Task 3: Drive a constraint.

To limit the motion of the **SRturntable** component, you will add an Angle constraint. You will then use the **Drive** command to drive the Angle constraint 180 degrees and observe the motion. In the next task, you will suppress the Angle constraint and use the **Contact Solver** command to limit the range of motion.

1. Create a 0 degree Angle constraint between the XZ Planes in the **SRbase** and the **SRturntable** components.

2. Expand the **SRbase** node in the Model browser to display the constraints.
3. Right-click on the Angle constraint and select **Drive**.
4. Enter **0.00 deg** in the *Start* field and **180 deg** in the *End* field. Depending on the constraint references, you might need to enter **-180 deg** in the *End* field instead.
5. Click in the *Drive* dialog box to view the motion. Click to reverse the motion.
6. Click in the *Drive* dialog box.
7. Enable **Collision Detection** and change the *End* value to **200 deg** (or **-200 deg**), as shown in Figure E–37.

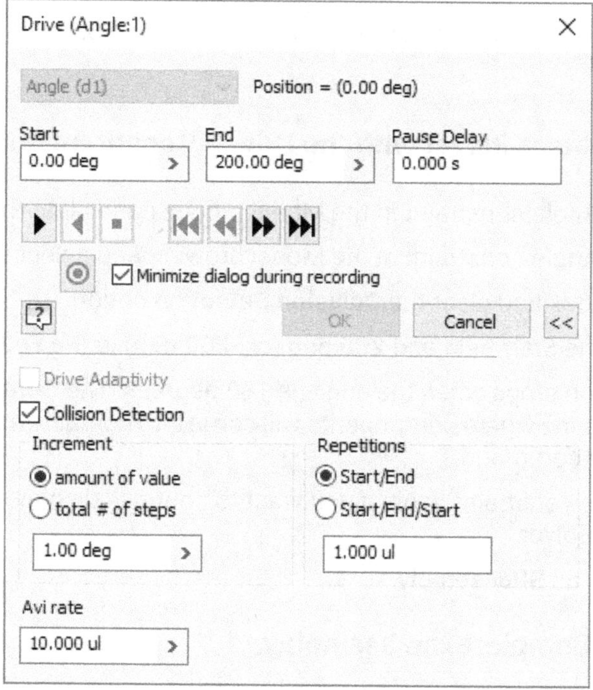

Figure E–37

8. Click . A dialog box opens indicating that collision is detected. If components do not collide, verify the Insert constraint references.
9. Click **OK**.
10. Click **Cancel** to close the *Drive* dialog box.

Task 4: Use the Contact Solver.

In this task, you will use the Contact Solver to simulate the range of motion required.

1. In the Model browser, right-click on the **Angle** constraint and select **Suppress**.
2. Select the *Inspect* tab>*Interference* panel and click (Activate Contact Solver).
3. While holding <Ctrl>, select the **SRbase** and the **SRturntable** components in the Model browser, right-click and select **Contact Set**.
4. Rotate the **SRturnable** component. Note that the rotation stops once it is in contact with the **SRbase** component.

   Note: *If any interference exists between components in the Contact Set, you will not be able to drag the components.*

Task 5: Use the Contact Solver with the Driven Constraint command.

1. Right-click on the **Angle** constraint in the Model browser and clear the **Suppress** option.
2. Right-click on the **Angle** constraint in the Model browser and select **Drive**.
3. Expand the dialog box and clear the **Collision Detection** option.
4. Enter **0.00 deg** in the *Start* field and **200 deg** (or **-200 deg**) in the *End* field, and click .

   Note that the motion stops when the angle is 180 degrees. The **Contact Solver** can also be used to help determine where components will come into contact with each other when you are using the **Drive** command.
5. Suppress the Angle constraint again if you want to continue displaying the range of motion using the Contact Solver.
6. Save the assembly as **SRassembly**.

Task 6: (Optional) Complete the assembly.

1. Assemble **SRrocker**, **SRlocator**, **SRwasher**, and three instances of **SRscrew** to the assembly.

   Note: *To add components at the same time, use <Shift> to select components. If using this technique to populate the first and all subsequent components, ensure that the correct component is grounded.*

Apply constraints to the remaining components and display the degrees of freedom to verify that they are fully constrained. Each screw and washer should have one rotational degree of freedom when you finish. The assembly displays as shown in Figure E–38.

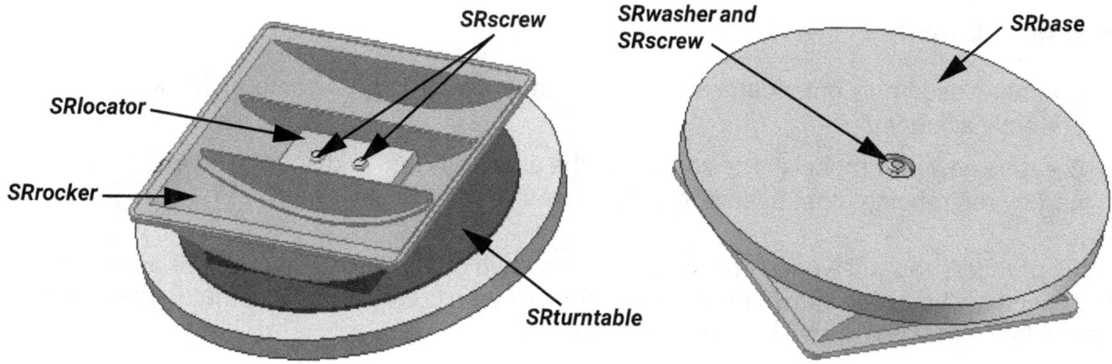

Figure E–38

2. Constrain the **SRturntable** and **SRrocker**:
   - Apply a Mate constraint between Work Axis1 of **SRrocker** and Work Axis2 of **SRturntable**. These axes represent the centerlines of the round portions of each of these components.
   - Apply a Mate constraint between Work Plane3 of **SRrocker** and Work Plane2 of **SRturntable**. This locates the components along the axis. However, the SRrocker can still rotate.
   - Add **SRrocker** to the contact set to find the range of motion.
3. Use Insert constraints to constrain the two holes in **SRlocator** and **SRturntable**.
4. Use an Insert constraint between **SRscrew:1** and **SRlocator**. Repeat the process for **SRscrew:2**.
5. Apply an Insert constraint between **SRbase** and **SRwasher**.
6. Apply an Insert constraint between **SRscrew:3** and **SRwasher**.
7. Save the assembly. A completed model, **SRassembly_final.iam**, has been provided. Enable **Activate Contact Solver** in the *Inspect* tab to use the Contact Solver.

End of practice

Practice E3
Assembly Parts and Features

Practice Objectives

- Create an assembly hole feature and ensure that the participant components are correctly assigned.
- Create a new part model in the context of the assembly and add solid geometry to the part by referencing other assembly components.

In this practice, you will work with the assembly shown on the left in Figure E–39 and create four assembly holes, as shown on the right. You will then create new parts that fit inside these holes while remaining in the Assembly environment.

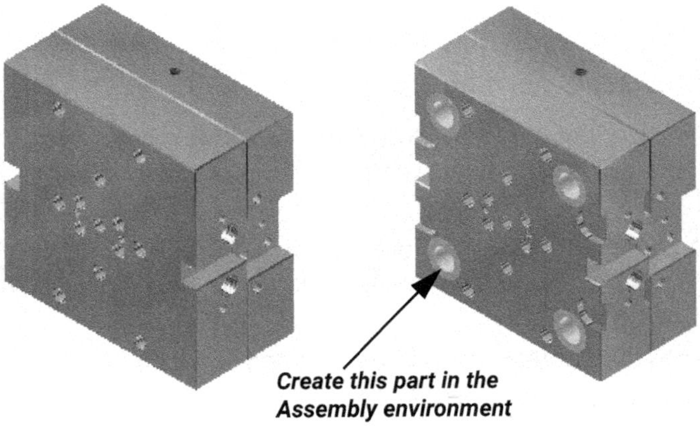

Figure E–39

Task 1: Create the assembly holes.

In this task, you will create four assembly holes based on sketched points. Creating the holes in this way enables you to create all of the holes at once.

1. Open **Final Mold Assy.iam** from the practice files *Mold Assembly* folder.
2. Toggle off the display of all of the assembly components, except the **topplate2 Assy** and the **Middleplate Assy** subassemblies. To clear a component from the display, select it, right-click, and clear the **Visibility** option. Alternatively, you can select the components that you want to keep, right-click and select **Isolate**.

3. In the *3D Model* tab>*Sketch* panel, click (Start 2D Sketch) and place the sketch for the holes on the large face shown in Figure E–40. Note that the image is shown in the Wireframe display style for clarity in the image.
4. Sketch a point on the face, and then dimension and pattern it, as shown in Figure E–40. Modify the dimensions as shown, if required.

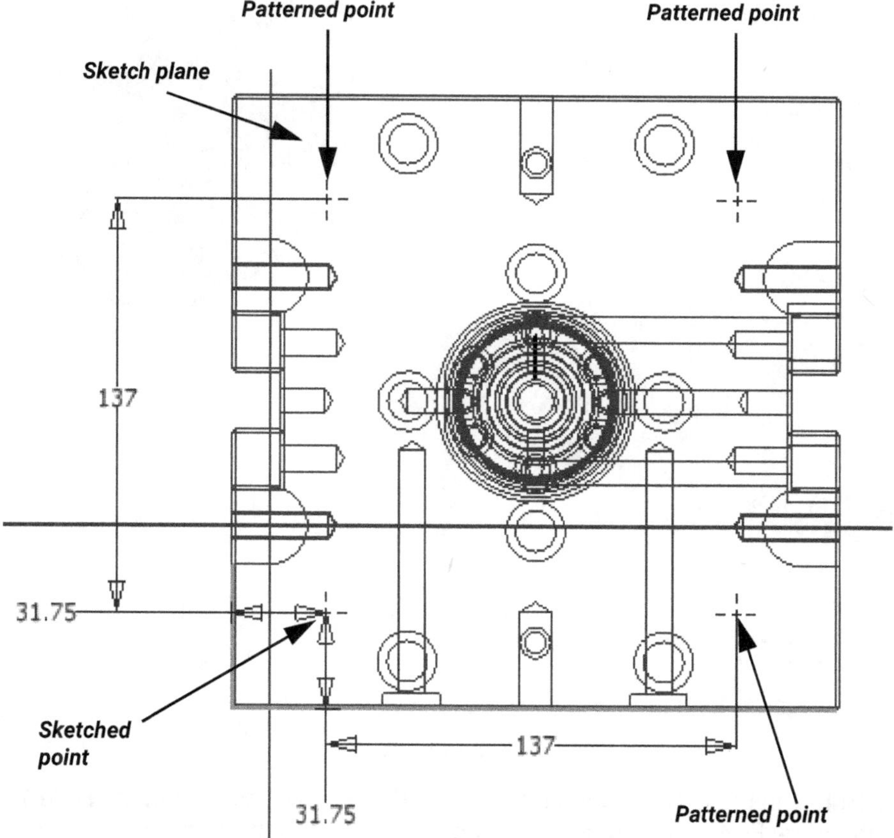

Figure E–40

5. In the *Exit* panel, click (Finish Sketch).

6. In the *3D Model* tab>*Modify Assembly* panel, click (Hole). Create four counterbore assembly holes as shown in Figure E–41. The holes are by default added to the sketched points from the sketch.

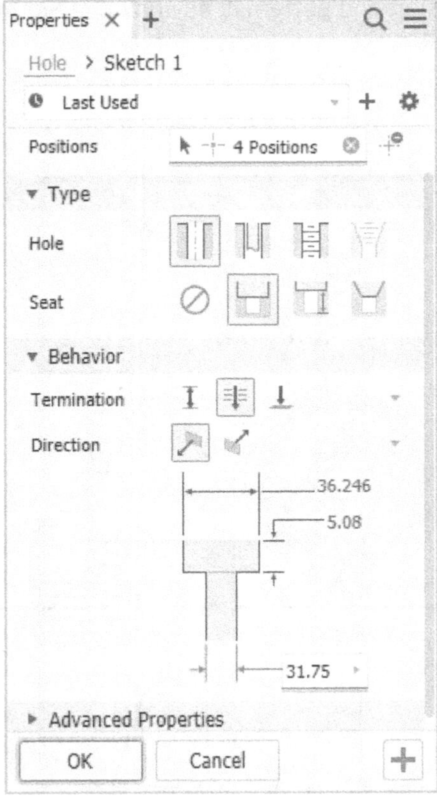

Figure E–41

7. Expand **Hole 1** in the Model browser to display the two participants in the **Hole 1** feature, as shown in Figure E–42. This means that the hole is cutting through both of these components. These components were selected by default. You can manually add or remove components, if required.

Note: To add a participant component so that it is intersected by the hole, right-click on the hole in the Model browser, select ***Add Participant****, and select a component.*

Figure E–42

Task 2: Create an assembly part.

1. Select the *Assemble* tab>*Component* panel, click (Create). The *Create In-Place Component* dialog box opens.
2. Enter **bush_part** in the *New Component Name* field.
3. Browse to and select the metric standard part template, **Standard (mm).ipt**.
4. Clear the Constrain sketch plane to selected face or plane option and accept the defaults in other fields.
5. Click **OK** to create the part.
6. Select the counterbore face of one of the holes shown in Figure E–43 as the sketch plane. All of the assembly components are grayed out in the Model browser, except **bush_part**. This means that only **bush_part** is active and you can add features to it.

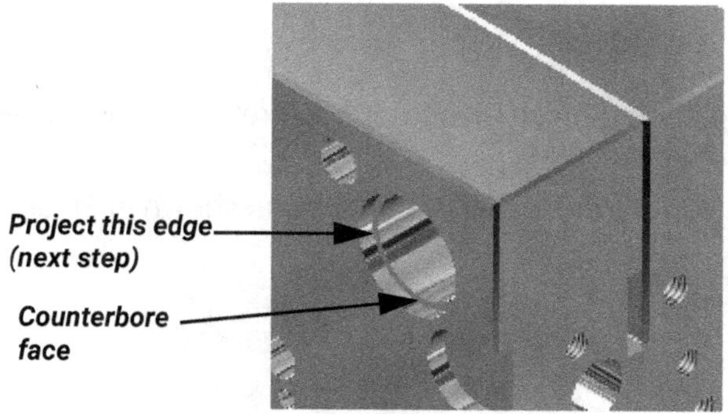

Figure E–43

7. In the *3D Model* tab>*Sketch* panel, click (Start 2D Sketch). Select the XY Plane in the new **bush_part** component as the sketch plane.

8. In the Sketch environment, project the edge of the 31.75mm diameter circle shown previously in Figure E–43, and sketch the concentric circle, as shown in Figure E–44.

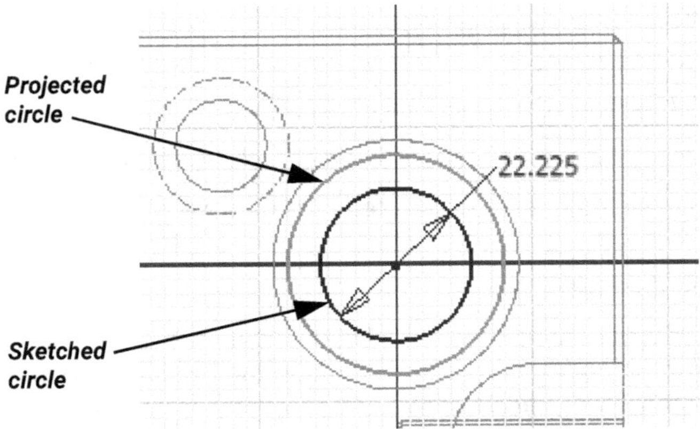

Figure E–44

9. In the *Exit* panel, click (Finish Sketch). Do not return to the **top-level** assembly or you will have to reactivate **bush_part**.
10. Extrude the sketch **47.625mm** inside of the hole, as shown in Figure E–45.

Figure E–45

Note: *To disable the automatic assigning of adaptivity during reference selection, consider pressing and holding <Ctrl> (e.g., when selecting a face to extrude).*

11. Create another extruded feature for **bush_part**. Select the front face of the protrusion that you just created as the sketch plane. This reduces the number of references to other parts in the assembly. Project the geometry as required to obtain the sketch shown in Figure E–46. (**Hint:** You will need to work in the part.) Extend the extrusion to the top face of the **topplate2 Assy** subassembly. The completed **bush_part** is shown in Figure E–46.

    Note the adaptive icons in front of **bush_part** and its features and sketches. The adaptive icon indicates that the feature contains references to other components in the assembly and requires these references to generate its geometry.

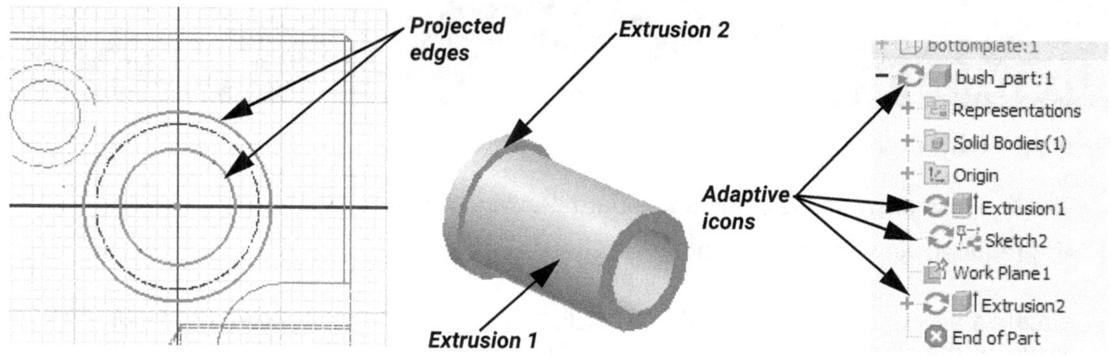

Figure E–46

12. Activate the top-level assembly and open **bush_part** in its own window.
13. Display the dimensions for **Extrusion1**. The only dimensions that can be modified are its depth (currently 47.625) and the inside diameter (currently 22.25), as shown in Figure E–47. These are not dimensions that are driven by other references in the assembly and that is why you can still modify them. The outside diameters on the two extrusions are examples of dimensions that are being driven by references in other components of the assembly, as the design intent for the model requires.

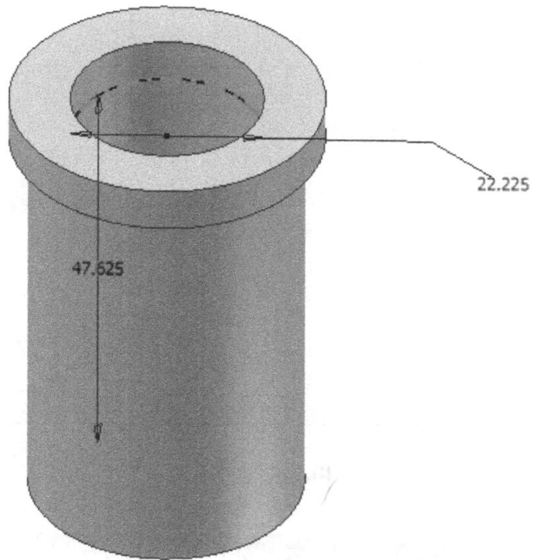

Figure E–47

14. Save **bush_part** and close the window.
15. Save the assembly and close the window.

End of practice

Practice E4
Drawing Creation I

Practice Objectives

- Create a new drawing file using a standard drawing template.
- Add required views to a drawing file.

1. Create a new drawing file named **Project_II**, based on the **Standard.dwg** template. Add views of the part file **bevelwasher.ipt** (as shown in Figure E–48), using base views, projected views, auxiliary views, and section views.

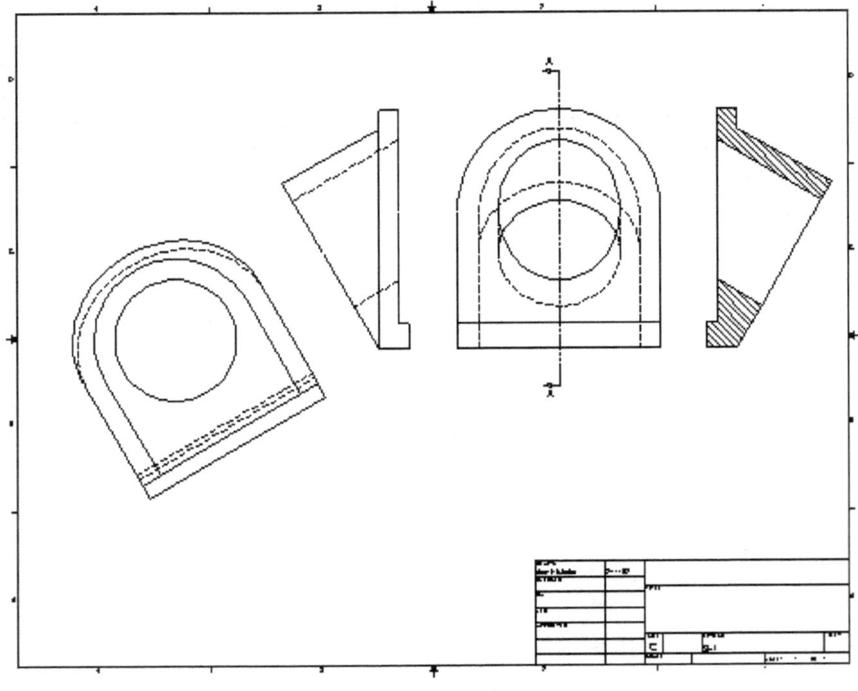

Figure E–48

End of practice

Practice E5
Drawing Creation II

Practice Objectives

- Create a new drawing file using a standard drawing template.
- Add required views to a drawing file.
- Create a new presentation file using a standard presentation template.
- Add manual tweaks and trail line to the presentation to explode the components.

1. Create a new drawing file named **Project_III**, based on the **Standard.dwg** template. Add views of the following four parts, as shown in Figure E–49. Show projected views (top and side) for the parts. Include labels and scale as appropriate. Save the drawing file.
    - **latchbase.ipt**
    - **handle.ipt**
    - **tongue.ipt**
    - **latchpin.ipt**

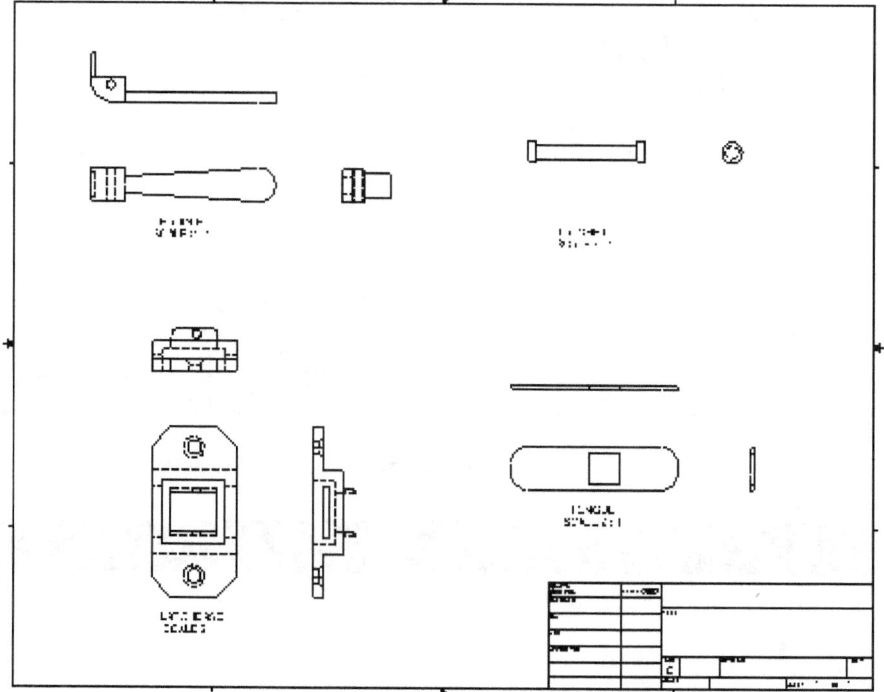

Figure E–49

2. Create a new assembly file named **Latch** using the **Standard.iam** template. Assemble and constrain the following components, similar to that shown in Figure E–50.
   - **latchbase.ipt**
   - **handle.ipt**
   - **tongue.ipt**
   - **latchpin.ipt**
3. Create a new presentation file named **Latch Presentation**, using the **Standard.ipn** template. In the presentation, create a view of the assembly **Latch.iam** to display the components exploded, as shown in Figure E–50. Save the file.

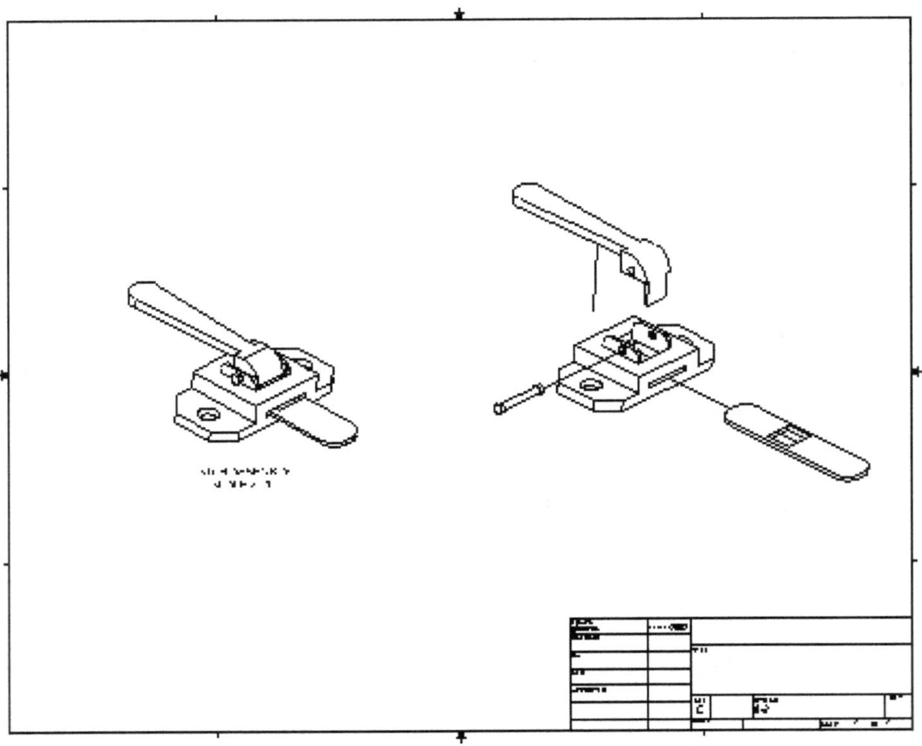

Figure E–50

End of practice

Practice E6
Drawing Creation III

Practice Objectives

- Generate a bill of materials and change the BOM structure for assembly components.
- Create virtual components to represent purchased components in the assembly.
- Create a parameter to represent the base quantity of virtual components.

In this practice, you will create virtual components and generate a BOM using general instructions. The final drawing is shown in Figure E–51.

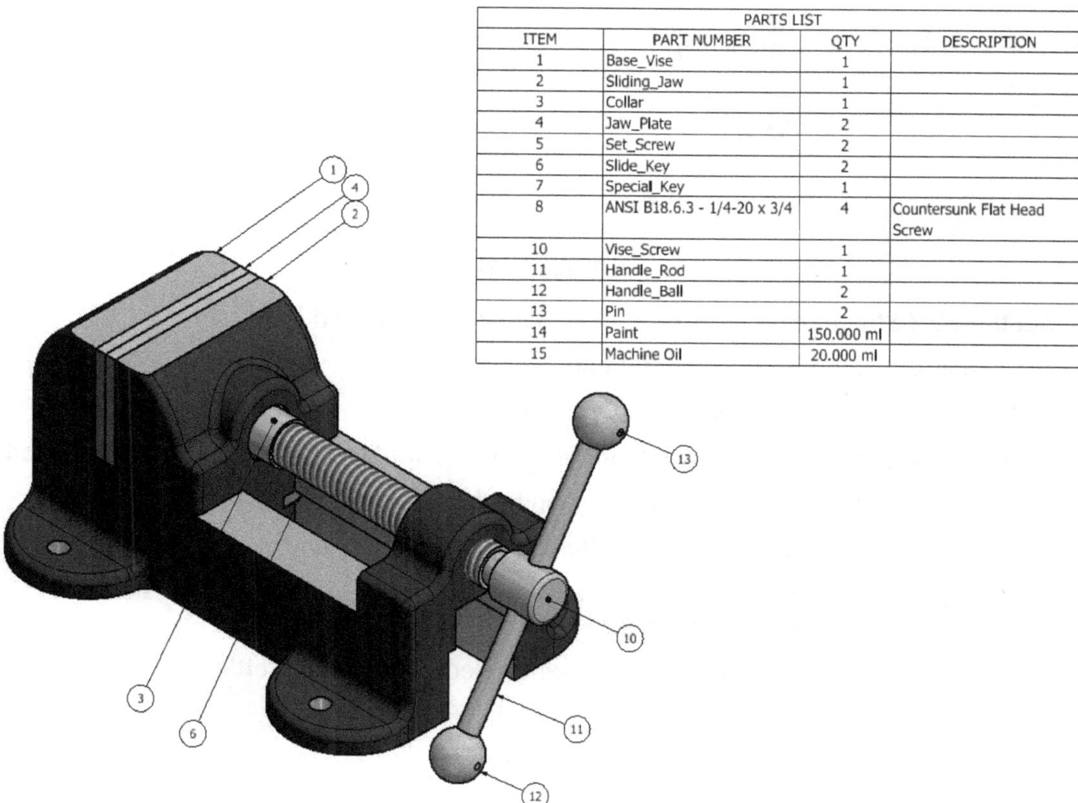

PARTS LIST			
ITEM	PART NUMBER	QTY	DESCRIPTION
1	Base_Vise	1	
2	Sliding_Jaw	1	
3	Collar	1	
4	Jaw_Plate	2	
5	Set_Screw	2	
6	Slide_Key	2	
7	Special_Key	1	
8	ANSI B18.6.3 - 1/4-20 x 3/4	4	Countersunk Flat Head Screw
10	Vise_Screw	1	
11	Handle_Rod	1	
12	Handle_Ball	2	
13	Pin	2	
14	Paint	150.000 ml	
15	Machine Oil	20.000 ml	

Figure E–51

1. Open **BOM_Vise.iam** from the practice files *BOM_II* folder.
2. In the *Assemble* tab>*Manage* panel, click (Bill of Materials) to open the *Bill of Materials* dialog box, as shown in Figure E–52.

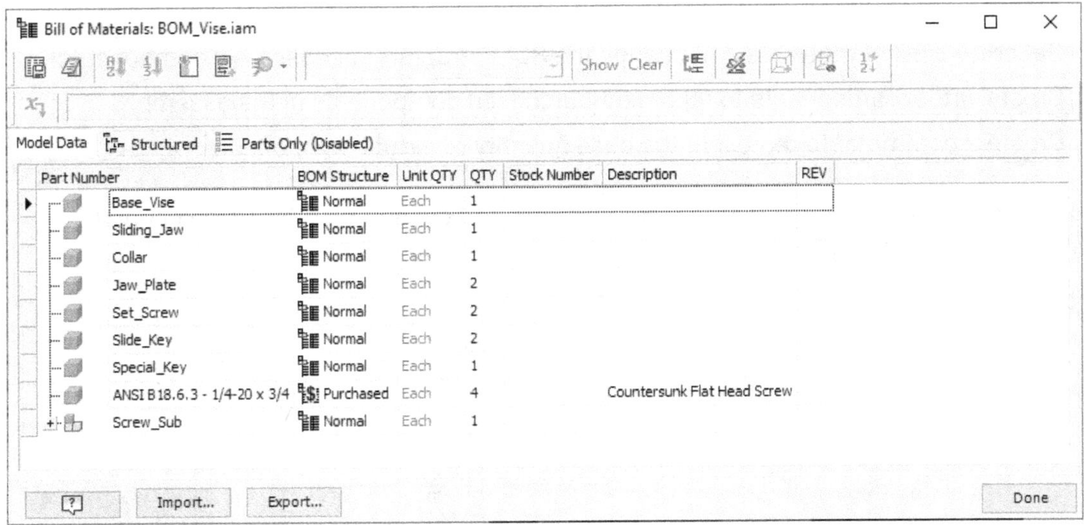

Part Number	BOM Structure	Unit QTY	QTY	Stock Number	Description	REV
Base_Vise	Normal	Each	1			
Sliding_Jaw	Normal	Each	1			
Collar	Normal	Each	1			
Jaw_Plate	Normal	Each	2			
Set_Screw	Normal	Each	2			
Slide_Key	Normal	Each	2			
Special_Key	Normal	Each	1			
ANSI B18.6.3 - 1/4-20 x 3/4	Purchased	Each	4		Countersunk Flat Head Screw	
Screw_Sub	Normal	Each	1			

Figure E–52

3. Set the *BOM Structure* property of the **Set_Screw** to **Purchased**.
4. Set **Screw_Sub** subassembly to **Phantom**.
5. Click **Done** to close the *Bill of Materials* dialog box.
6. Create a virtual component called **Paint** and set its *BOM Structure* property to **Purchased**.
7. Right-click on **Paint** in the Model browser and select **iProperties**.
8. In the *Project* tab, ensure that the *Part Number* is set to **Paint** and close the dialog box.
9. Create a parameter called **Base_Qty** and set the *units* to **ml**. You will need to enter the value as **1.0ml**, once the units have been set.
10. Right-click on **Paint** in the Model browser and select **Component Settings**.

11. Set the *Base Quantity* to the **Base_Qty** parameter, as shown in Figure E–53, and click **OK** to close the dialog box.

Figure E–53

12. Create another virtual component called **Machine Oil**. Set the *BOM Structure* property to **Purchased** and change the base quantity to **Base_Qty** in the component settings, as you did for the **Paint** component. Ensure that **Machine Oil** is set as the *Part Number* for the component in its *iProperties* dialog box.
13. Return to the *Bill of Materials* dialog box and change the quantities of the **Paint** and **Machine Oil** components to **150ml** and **20ml** respectively.
14. Save the assembly and close the file.
15. If time permits, create a new drawing of the assembly and create a structured parts list with balloons.

End of practice

Index

A

Adding Parameters as Text **27-4**
Alternate Solution **5-5**
Animations **20-5**
Annotation
  Center Mark **27-14**
  Centered Pattern **27-16**
  Centerline **27-15**
  Centerline Bisector **27-15**
  Chamfer Note **27-12**
  Hole Table **27-17**
  Hole/Thread Note **27-8**
  Revision Cloud **27-22**
  Revision Tags **27-22**
  Symbols **27-6**
  Tables **27-20**
  Text **27-2**
Appearance **19-14**
Application Options **4-13, 28-2**
Arc **3-3**
Assemble
  Assembly Browser **16-24**
  Autodrop **16-23**
  Bill of Materials **23-4**
  Components **16-2, 17-2**
    Copy **21-5**
    Create **22-2**
    Degree of Freedom Analysis **16-6**
    Degrees of Freedom **16-6**
    Enable **18-7**
    Interference **21-14**
    Isolate **18-7**
    Mirror **21-3**
    Move **18-2**
    Pattern **21-6**
    Place **16-3**
    Place and Insert **16-18**
    Place Grounded at Origin **16-3**
    Replace **21-2**
    Restructure **21-7**
    Rotate **18-3**
    Transparent **18-8**
    Visible **18-6**
  Constraint
    Angle **16-8**
    Assemble Mini-Toolbar **16-20**
    Drive Constraint **21-10**
    Edit **16-13**
    Insert **16-9**
    Mate **16-7**
    References **16-11**
    Suppress **18-5**
    Symmetry **16-10**
    Tangent **16-8**
    UCS **16-10**
  Contact Solver **21-12**
  Content Center **16-22**
  Explode **20-2**
  Failure **21-17**
  Joint **17-2**
    Automatic **17-3**
    Ball **17-4, 17-10**
    Cylindrical **17-4, 17-9**
    Editing **17-13**
    Limits **17-11**
    Planar **17-4**
    References **17-4**
    Rigid **17-4, 17-8**
    Rotational **17-4, 17-8**
    Slider **17-4, 17-9**
  Methods **16-2, 16-20, 17-2**
  Presentations **20-2**
  Resolve Link **24-10**
  Save Files **16-27**
  Section View **18-9**
  Selection Options **18-16**
  Storyboards **20-18**
  Update **18-4**
  Virtual Component **22-2, 23-2**
Assembly Features **22-5**
Assembly Modeling **1-7**
Associative Design **1-7**
AutoCAD
  Insert Data **5-14**
Autodesk Assistant **1-21**
Automatic Dimensions **2-14**
Auxiliary Views **25-12**
Axis **2-5, 7-6**

B

Ball Joint **17-10**
Balloons **26-25**
Base View **25-4**
Baseline Dimension **26-9**

Bill of Materials
BOM Structure Types **23-8**
Generate **23-4**
Instance Properties **23-19**
Parts List **23-16**
Virtual Components **23-2**
BOM Settings for Suppressed Components **23-11**
Boss **9-26**
Box **B-2**
Break Link **5-9**
Break Out View **25-22**
Bridge Curve **3-3**
Broken View **25-21**

C

Camera View **18-15**
Center Mark **27-14**
Centerline **27-15**
Centerline Bisector **27-15**
Chain Dimensions **26-10**
Chamfer
Feature **6-2**
Notes **27-12**
Sketch **3-5**
Circle **2-10, 3-3**
Component
Interference **21-14**
Replace **21-2**
Restructure **21-7**
Constraints
Assembly
Angle **16-8**
Drive **21-10**
Insert **16-9**
Mate **16-7**
References **16-11**
Suppress **18-5**
Symmetry **16-10**
Tangent **16-8**
UCS **16-10**
Inferred Constraint Reference **2-15**
Joint *(see Joint)*
Show **2-15, 3-12**
Sketch **2-15, 3-12**
Coincident **3-15**
Collinear **3-15**
Concentric **3-16**
Constraint Settings **3-19**
Delete **3-22**
Equal **3-16**
Fix **3-17**
Horizontal and Vertical **3-17**
Inference **3-20**
Over Constrained **3-19**
Parallel and Perpendicular **3-13**
Reference **3-18**
Relax Mode **3-22**
Smooth (G2) **3-14**
Symmetric **3-18**
Tangent **3-14**
Suppress **18-5**
Construction Entities **3-8**
Contact Solver **21-12**
Content Center **16-22**
Copy
Components **21-5**
Entities **4-2**
Crop View **25-26**
Cut **5-3**
Cylinder **B-2**
Cylindrical Joint **17-9**

D

Dark User Interface **28-3**
Degree of Freedom Analysis **16-6**
Degrees of Freedom **3-12, 16-6**
Delete
Constraints **3-22**
Dimensions **2-14**
Features **15-10**
Parameter **8-12**
Patterns **14-27**
Demote **21-8**
Depth/Direction **2-19, 5-4**
Design Doctor **11-6**
Design Views **10-9, 18-12**
Detail Views **25-16**
Dimensions **A-7**
Delete **2-14**
Display **8-2**
Drawing
Baseline **26-9**
Chain **26-10**
Edit **26-4, 26-11**
Foreshortened **26-6**
General **26-5**
Isometric **26-8**
Model **26-2**
Ordinate **26-9**
Styles **26-13**
Modify **2-13**
Show **2-24**
Sketch **2-12, 3-24**
Angular **3-25**
Arc Length **3-27**
Automatic **2-14**
Center Dimensions **3-24**
Diameter **3-25**
Driven **2-14**
Linear **2-12**

Linear Diameter **2-12**
Over Dimensioned Entities **3-28**
Radius **3-25**
Revolved **3-26**
Tangent **3-26**
Direction **2-20**
Document Settings **4-14, 28-8**
Draft
Face **9-2**
Fixed Edge **9-3**
Fixed Plane **9-4**
Parting Line **9-4**
View **25-20**
Drawing **1-7**
Annotation
Balloons **26-25**
Center Mark **27-14**
Centered Pattern **27-16**
Centerline **27-15**
Centerline Bisector **27-15**
Chamfer Note **27-12**
Dimensions **26-2**
Hole Table **27-17**
Hole/Thread Note **27-8**
Revision Table **27-20**
Symbols **27-6**
Tags **27-22**
Text **27-2**
Creating Drawings **25-2**
Hatching **26-33**
Parts List **26-18**
Sheet Formats **25-2, 26-17**
Sheets **26-15**
Style and Standard Editor **26-13, 26-29, 26-33**
Symbols **27-6**
Transparent Component **25-29**
View Orientation **25-29**
Views *(see Views)*
Drawing Resources Folder **25-3**
Driven Dimensions **2-14**
DWG **1-3, 5-14**
Dynamic Input **5-11**

E

Edit
Feature **2-25**
Redefine **2-26**
Sketch
Entities **2-25, A-5**
Plane **2-26**
Ellipse **3-3**
Enabling Components **18-7**
Environments **1-2**
Equation Curve **3-3**
Equations **8-2, 15-9**
Explode **20-2**
Extend **3-10**
Extrude **2-17, 5-2**
Extrude Between Plane **2-19, 5-5**

F

Failure
Assembly **21-17**
Design Doctor **11-6**
Resolving Assembly Failures **24-10**
Sketch **11-2**
Feature Based Modeling **1-4**
File Types **1-2**
Fillet Workflow **6-8, 6-15, 6-20, 6-23**
Fillets
Constant **6-8**
Full Round **6-23**
Sketch Entity **3-5**
Variable **6-15**
Finish Features **22-7**
Folders **21-9**
Foreshortened Dimensions **26-7**
Full Navigation Wheel **1-28**
Functions **8-7**

G

General Dimension **2-12**
Graphics Window **1-14**
Grid Lines **2-9**

H

Hatching **25-15, 26-33**
Help **1-20**
Hole Notes **27-8**
Hole Table **27-17**
Holes
Create **6-25**
Threads **6-46**
Home Page **1-8**

I

Import/Export Parameters in XML **8-13**
Insert ACAD File **5-14**
Insert Features **10-3**
Instance Properties **23-19**
Interface **1-12**
Application Options **28-2**
Autodesk Assistant **1-21**
Customization **28-16**
Document Settings **28-8**
Feature Dialog Box **1-18**
Help **1-20**
Marking Menu **28-21**
Mini-Toolbar **1-18**
Model Browser **15-8, 16-24, 21-9**
Properties Panel **1-18**

Interference **21-14**
Intersect **5-3**
iProperties **28-13**
Isolating Components **18-7**
Isometric Dimensions **26-8**

J

Join **5-3**
Joint **17-2**
  Automatic **17-3**
  Ball **17-4, 17-10**
  Cylindrical **17-4, 17-9**
  Editing **17-13**
  Limits **17-11**
  Planar **17-4, 17-10**
  References **17-4**
  Rigid **17-4, 17-8**
  Rotational **17-4, 17-8**
  Slider **17-4, 17-9**

L

Line **2-10, 3-4, 3-5**
Line Close **2-11**
Loft **2-17**
  Center Line Loft **13-2**
  Conditions **13-6**
  Rail Loft **13-2**
  Transitions **13-11**
Look At **1-27**

M

Marking Menu **1-17, 28-21**
Materials
  Appearance **19-14**
  Assigning **19-12**
Measure
  Add to Accumulate **19-8**
  Angle **19-6**
  Between Components **19-5**
  Context Sensitive **19-10**
  Cylindrical Faces **19-7**
  Distance **19-3**
  Entities **19-3**
  Planar Faces **19-7**
  Region Properties **19-11**
  Restart **19-8**
  Using Values **19-10**
Middle Mouse Button Behavior **28-3**
Mini-Toolbar **1-18**
Mirror **3-11, 21-3**
  Components **21-3**
  Features **14-25**
  Sketch Entities **3-11**
  Solids **14-25**
Model Browser **1-15, 16-24**
  Folders **21-9**
  Representations **18-13**
Model Dimensions **26-2**
Model Parameters **8-9**
Move
  Components **18-2**
  Entities **4-2**
Move EOP Marker **10-3**
Move EOP to End **10-3**

N

Navigation Wheel **1-28**
New
  Base Feature **2-6**
  Sketch **2-6**
  Solid **5-4**

O

Operators **8-7**
Orbit tool **1-25**
Ordinate Dimension **26-9**
Orientation
  Drawing Views **25-7, 25-29**
Origin Features
  Axes **2-5, 7-6**
  Planes **2-5, 7-2**
  Points **2-5, 7-9**
  Visibility **2-5**
Overlay Views **25-18**

P

Pan **1-24**
Panels **1-13**
Parameters
  Delete **8-12**
  Dialog Box **8-9**
  Drawing Text **27-4**
  Filtering **8-12**
  Immediate Update **8-13**
  Key **8-12**
  Make Multi-Value **8-11**
  Model Parameters **8-9**
  Numeric **8-10**
  Purge Unused **8-12**
  Text **8-10**
  True/False **8-10**
  User Parameters **8-10**
Parametric **1-6**
Participant Parts **22-5**
Parts List **23-18, 26-18**
Paste **4-4**
Patterns
  Circular Feature **14-13**
  Components **21-6**
  Delete **14-27**

Edit **14-27**
Rectangular Feature **14-2**
Sketch
Circular **4-9**
Rectangular **4-5**
Sketch Driven Features **14-21**
Suppress **14-27**
Planar Joint **17-10**
Planes **2-5, 7-2**
Point Snaps **3-7**
Points **2-5, 7-9**
Polygon **3-4**
Precise Input **5-12**
Presentations **20-2**
Publish **20-23**
Snapshot Views **20-18**
Storyboard Animations **20-5**
Primitives **B-2**
Project
Cut Edges **5-9**
DWG Geometry **5-14**
Geometry **2-8, 5-2, 5-9**
Project Files **24-2**
Projected View **25-9**
Promote **21-8**
Properties
File iProperties **28-13**
Instance **23-19**
Properties Panel **1-18**
Publish Presentations **20-23**

Q

Quick Access Toolbar **1-15**

R

Raster Views **25-11**
Recent Documents **1-9**
Rectangle **2-10, 3-3**
Redefine **2-26, 15-10**
Refit **1-27**
Relax Mode **3-22**
Reorder Features **10-2**
Replace
Components **21-2**
Drawing Models **25-31**
Resolve Link **24-10**
Restructure **21-7**
Retrieve Model Dimensions **26-3**
Revision Cloud **27-22**
Revision Table **27-20**
Revision Tags **27-22**
Revolve **2-11, 2-17, 5-2**
Rib **9-21**
Ribbon **1-13**
Rigid Joint **17-8**
Rotate **1-25**
Components **18-3**
Entities **4-2**
Rotational Joint **17-8**

S

Scale
Drawing View **25-30**
Entities **4-2**
Section View Projection **25-14**
Section Views
Assemblies **18-9**
Drawings **25-13**
Parts **10-6**
Select All Invisible Components **18-17**
Select All Suppressed Components **18-17**
Selection
Hidden Features **1-34, 2-51**
Selection Filter **1-34, 18-16**
Sketched Entities **1-32**
Tangent Entities **1-33**
Share Sketch **5-10**
Sheet Format **25-2**
Sheets **26-15**
Shell **9-15**
Show All Constraints **3-12**
Show Dimensions **2-24**
Show Input **2-25**
Sketch
Constraints *(see Constraints)*
Creation **2-9**
Dimensions *(see Dimensions)*
Edit **2-25**
Entities
Arc **3-3**
Bridge Curve **3-3**
Chamfers **3-5**
Circle **2-10**
Construction **3-8**
Copy **4-2**
Copy and Paste **4-4**
Degrees of Freedom **3-12**
Ellipse **3-3**
Equation Curve **3-3**
Extend **3-10**
Fillets **3-5**
Line **2-10, 3-4, 3-5**
Line Close **2-10**
Mirror **3-11**
Move **4-2**
Over Dimensioned **3-28**
Polygon **3-4**
Rectangle **2-10, 3-3**
Relax Mode **3-22**
Rotate **4-2**

Scale **4-2**
Slot **2-11, 3-4**
Split **4-4**
Stretch **4-2**
Tangent Arc **3-4**
Tangent Line **3-5**
Trim **3-9**
Grid and Axis **2-9**
Patterns **4-5, 4-9**
Point Snaps **3-7**
Preferences **4-13, 4-14**
Revolved Sections **2-11**
Share Sketch **5-10**
Show Sketch Plane **2-25**
Visibility **2-24**
Sketch Plane **2-7**
Slice Graphics **5-2**
Slice Views **25-24**
Slider Joint **17-9**
Slot
Create Feature **6-37**
Sketch Entity **2-11, 3-3**
Snapshot Views **20-18**
Sphere **B-2**
Spline **3-2**
Split
Entities **4-4**
Face **9-11**
Solid **9-11**
Status Bar **1-16**
Storyboards **20-5**
Stretch Entities **4-2**
Style and Standard Editor **26-13, 26-29, 26-33**
Suppress
Constraints **18-5**
Features **10-4**
Views **25-28**
Sweep **2-17, 12-2**
Symbols **27-6**

T

Table
Revision Table **27-20**
Tabs **1-13**
Tags **27-22**
Taper **5-7**
Template **2-2**
Templates **2-2, 25-2**
Text **27-2**
Threads **6-46**
Tool Palette **19-2, 19-18**
Tooltips **1-20**
Torus **B-2**
Trails **20-12**
Transparency **25-29**
Transparent Components **18-8**
Trim **3-9**
Tweaks **20-7, 20-13**

U

Units **8-7, 28-8, 28-15**
Update Assembly **18-4**
User Parameters **8-10**

V

ViewCube **1-27**
Views
Adding Dimensions **26-2**
Alignment **25-29**
Annotations *(see Drawing Annotation)*
Auxiliary **25-12**
Balloons **26-25**
Base **25-4**
Break **25-21**
Break Out **25-22**
Crop **25-26**
Delete **25-28**
Design Views **10-9, 18-12**
Detailed **25-16**
Draft **25-20**
Hatching **26-33**
Labels **25-30**
Move **25-29**
Orientation **25-7, 25-29**
Overlay **25-18**
Projected **25-9**
Properties **25-32**
Raster Views **25-11**
Replace Models **25-31**
Scale **25-30**
Section Views **10-6, 18-9, 25-13**
Sheets **26-15**
Slice **25-24**
Snapshots from Presentations **20-21**
Suppress **25-28**
Transparent Components **25-29**
Virtual Component **22-2, 23-2**
Visibility **2-24**
Components **18-6**
Sketch **2-24**

W

Work Features
Axis **7-6**
Planes **7-2**
Points **7-9**

Z

Zoom **1-26**

www.ingramcontent.com/pod-product-compliance
Lightning Source LLC
LaVergne TN
LVHW081312110826
845149LV00006B/1493

* 9 7 8 1 9 6 7 6 2 5 6 6 6 *